Leasing and Asset Finance

FOURTH EDITION

The Comprehensive Guide for Practitioners

Knowledge is of two kinds. We know a subject ourselves,
or we know where we can find information upon it.

Dr Samuel Johnson, 1709–1784

Vivek Menon
21-9-2004.

Leasing and Asset Finance

FOURTH EDITION

The Comprehensive Guide for Practitioners

Edited by
Chris Boobyer

EUROMONEY BOOKS

Published by

Euromoney Books, Nestor House, Playhouse Yard, London EC4V 5EX, United Kingdom

Tel: +44 (0) 20 7779 8999 or USA +1 800 437 9997

Fax: +44 (0) 20 7779 8300

www.euromoneybooks.com

E-mail:hotline@euromoneyplc.com

ISBN 1 85564 985 3

Printed in England by The Cromwell Press, Trowbridge, Wiltshire.

Contents

Appendix A: International and national leasing associations 428

Appendix B: International Accounting Standard IAS 17 440

Appendix C: Unidroit convention on international financial leasing 455

Glossary 464

List of exhibits and annexes

Chapter 19   The European Union

Chapter 20   International perspectives

Author biographies

Marc Baert graduated from the Leuven School of Law in Belgium and was a barrister at the Brussels Bar between 1969 and 1972. He was appointed as sales and marketing director for International Factors in 1972, where he remained for 12 years, before becoming the secretary general of Leaseurope and Eurofinas in 1985.

Chris Boobyer is finance director for the Asset Finance, Sales Financing and Venture Finance businesses within Barclays Business Banking and head of its Acquisitions and Mergers team. In addition to his finance duties he has responsibility for Barclays' leasing operations in France, Germany and Italy, and the specialist structured asset finance team based in London. He is a board member of the FLA, chairman of the Asset Finance Division and the Tax Review Group. A graduate in social sciences, politics and economics, he lectures on industry training courses and is a regular chairman and speaker at conferences on leasing, accounting and taxation.

Colin Dowsett joined KPMG in 1990 after qualifying as an accountant at a small firm. Currently he works as a senior manager in KPMG's Leasing and Asset Finance unit and has specialised particularly in the motor finance industry. Colin has advised on a wide range of accounting and evaluation matters and has dealt with big-ticket, cross-border transactions; contract hire; and valuations of leasing portfolios. He has written for a number of leasing periodicals and the *World Leasing Yearbook*.

Michael J. Fleming graduated from Drake University, Des Moines, Iowa with a Master's degree with honours. His career, prior to becoming president of the Equipment Leasing Association of America in 1979, included periods as a teacher, lobbyist and political organiser. He is past chancellor of the Exchequer Club of Washington and has served as a director of the American Society of Association Executives and is a member of the US Chamber of Commerce Committee of 100.

Bruce Gaitskell is director and co-founder of Capital Consultants (UK) Limited and currently specialises in securitisation and corporate finance. He has been a major force in the European securitisation market over the past 15 years, completing Europe's first rated securitisation in 1987 for National Home Loans. He has also completed a number of groundbreaking transactions for CIBC, including Europe's first CP funded securitisation. In 1991 he became executive director and head of European securitisation at UBS Limited where he was responsible for both the autoloan securitisation by Nissan UK and Europe's first securitisation of vehicle leases (Truck Funding for DAF (UK)). He then became head of securitisation for Daiwa Europe Limited, Sakura Finance International and National Australia Bank. A graduate of the University of Wales (Economics & Materials Science, University College,

Swansea), he is a regular, worldwide speaker and teacher of securitisation seminars and courses. In addition he is a contributing author to two securitisation textbooks.

Sam Geneen has been managing director at Five Arrows Leasing Group Limited (FALG), a subsidiary of the Rothschilds banking group, since its inception in 1988. Prior to joining FALG he spent six years as managing director at United Financial Services Limited, a subsidiary of United Leasing plc. A graduate of the University of Strathclyde in Economics, he trained as an accountant, working for Levi Strauss & Co, and he is a Fellow of the Chartered Association of Certified Accountants. A director of the Finance & Leasing Association and chairman of the Asset Finance Division, he is a regular contributor to industry training courses and specialises in operating leasing.

Philip Griffin completed his formal education at the Australian National University where he earned a Bachelor of Economics and Bachelor of Laws degrees with First Class Honours and was awarded with the University Medal. After practicing at a specialist Sydney law firm, Philip joined the Sydney office of Allco Finance Limited in 1989 and was made a director in 1991. He is now managing director of Allco's London office. In the course of his career Philip has structured, placed and closed a wide variety of cross-border leases for primarily blue-chip and sovereign lessor and lessee clients, gaining experience in most cross-border jurisdictions, including Australia, Austria, Canada, Denmark, Germany, Hong Kong, Ireland, Japan, Sweden, the United Kingdom and the United States.

Martin Hall was appointed director general of the UK Finance & Leasing Association in 1995 having previously been head of public policy and external relations at the London Stock Exchange. After graduating from Merton College, Oxford, he joined the diplomatic service prior to transferring to the UK Treasury in 1976. After serving as press secretary to the Chancellor of the Exchequer, he headed the banking division from 1984 to 1987.

Simon A. D. Hall was educated at Ampleforth College and St Catharine's College, Cambridge. After law school he joined Freshfields in 1977. In 1983 he was seconded to the Wall Street firm of Cravath, Swaine & Moore and joined the Freshfields New York office in 1984. He returned to the London office in September 1985 as a partner and is now co-head of Freshfields Bruckhaus Deringer's finance practice. He is a co-author of *Aircraft Finance* which is now in its third edition, published by Euromoney Books in 1997.

Ron Hardaker is federal director of the Australian Equipment Lessors Association (AELA) the national industry association and lobby group representing equipment lessors and financiers. He has held this position since AELA's inception in 1986. He is also executive director of the Australian Finance Conference (AFC), which he joined in 1973. His responsibilities at both organisations encompass economic, taxation, industrial relations, public affairs, legislative and other regulatory matters.

Professor Chris Higson is a professor in Accounting at London Business School, where he was formerly Chair of the Accounting Group and director of the School's Financial Seminar for Senior Managers. He studied Philosophy and Economics at University College London and received his doctorate in Financial Economics from London Business School. Previously a chartered accountant with Deloitte and Touche, he is an international authority on company valuation and financial performance measurement, and on mergers and acquisitions. He is the author of *Business Finance* (Butterworths), now in its second edition, and has advised many leading financial institutions, industrial companies and governments in the UK and overseas.

Dorothy Livingston joined Herbert Smith in 1972 having gained a Master's degree from Oxford, and became a partner in 1980. She is a specialist in EU and UK competition and regulatory law with a background in financial law, including leasing finance. Dorothy is chairman of the City of London Law Society Banking Law Sub-Committee, a member of its EU and Competition Law Sub-Committee and a member of the newly established Bank of England Committee on Financial Markets Law, headed by Lord Browne-Wilkinson. She also sits on the Advisory Board of the Centre for European Law at King's College, London. Her publications include *Competition Law and Practice* (Sweet & Maxwell, 1995), *Cross Border Payment Systems* (European Cash Management, 1993) and the *Competition Act 1998: A Practical Guide* (Sweet & Maxwell, 2001).

Vic Lock is the founder and editor of the equipment and asset finance news monthly LEASING*Life*. He has a long and distinguished career in financial journalism and was responsible for the World Leasing Convention from 1984 to 1992, and was editor of *Asset Finance & Leasing Digest* following its acquisition by Euromoney between 1986 and 1992. He later became head of Euromoney's Asset Finance & Leasing Division, and during this time he originated a number of conferences and training events, including the Aircraft Finance School and the International Rail Finance Conference. After travelling extensively in his roles as a journalist and conference arranger, he left the company in September 1992 to further develop his interest in water sports in general and dingy sailing in particular. He launched LEASING*Life* in October 1993.

Philip Marwood has been a tax partner of KPMG and its predecessors since 1989. He is head of Leasing Services for KPMG LLP in the United Kingdom, and chairman of KPMG's International Leasing Tax Group. He specialises in advising financial clients, particularly those involved in asset finance and leasing and other clients seeking finance for major assets. He has been responsible for advising a number of multinational groups on the structuring and financing of their asset-finance arms and has advised on many cross-border leasing transactions. He has advised clients on acquisitions and disposals of asset-finance subsidiaries. He has lectured and written on asset-finance taxation on many occasions and has regularly advised the Finance & Leasing Association on representations to the government, for example, most recently on the asset finance aspects of the substantial shareholdings and the intangibles legislation.

David Maxwell joined KPMG in 1976 after completing an engineering apprenticeship at the British Aircraft Corporation (now BAE Systems). He is currently director of lease accounting and evaluation at KPMG. He has been involved in leasing and asset finance throughout his career in the firm, primarily advising on accounting and evaluation issues. This has covered the entire range of asset-finance activities from big-ticket leasing to contract hire, including structuring large cross-border leases and the valuation of leasing portfolios and leasing companies in connection with their acquisition or disposal. He is the author of KPMG's leasing software, Classic, which is used by all major UK leasing companies. He writes for a number of leasing periodicals, speaks regularly at leasing conferences, lectures on industry courses and serves the Finance & Leasing Association on various working parties and committees.

Katsuhiko Otaki has recently joined ChuoAoyama Audit Corporation. Previously he was director and general manager of the International Planning Department for IBJ Leasing Co Ltd and the chairman of the Japan Leasing Association International Committee. He joined IBJ in 1967 having graduated from Hitotsubashi University, Tokyo, with a Bachelor of Commerce and gained an MBA from Harvard Business School in 1971. Katsuhiko was president and CEO of IBJ Canada between 1993 and 1997.

Stephen Potts is a manager in the PricewaterhouseCoopers credit risk management solutions group in London. Stephen has seven years' financial services experience, in both retail lending and corporate banking. Before joining the firm, he spent three years in various management roles at the Royal Bank of Scotland. He now specialises in credit and operational risk, and most recently played a key role in the development of PWC's Basle solutions for clients in the United Kingdom and overseas.

Malcolm Rogers is director of Training at Standard & Poor's. Previously he was the head of Retail Credit & Fraud for HBOS plc (the merged Halifax and Bank of Scotland Group), and before that head of Wholesale Credit for Halifax plc. He entered banking after leaving Clare College, Cambridge, in 1980 and in his career to date has also held a number of senior credit management positions in the leasing and banking operations of both Lloyds Bank and TSB Group. He first specialised in leasing risk management in 1989 and lectures regularly on risk topics.

Nicholas Sanderson is a solicitor and a partner in the Banking Group at DLA specialising in asset finance, including the financing of equipment. He spent five years in the Inland Revenue Solicitor's Office and three years with Slaughter and May's corporate tax group. His current practice includes very little tax-based leasing and a great deal of financing of equipment, motor and consumer finance companies, often through capital markets-related structures.

Richard Smith heads the PricewaterhouseCoopers credit risk management solutions group in London. He has over twenty years of banking experience and, until 1995, held a number of management positions with Barclays Bank. He has led a number of projects to implement new risk management approaches and redesign the risk and business processes of some of the world's leading financial institutions. He is currently leading a number of Basle initiatives to develop solutions to help clients tackle the challenges presented by the new accord.

Sally Williams is director of group risk management at Aviva. She spent 15 years at PricewaterhouseCoopers, where she specialised in advising financial services clients on operational risk, particularly in respect of governance and regulatory risk management issues. During her time at PricewaterhouseCoopers, she spent two years on secondment to the Bank of England's supervision and surveillance team. Here she was responsible for assessing the adequacy of the higher-level controls at a wide range of banks. More recently at PricewaterhouseCoopers she led the development of new operational risk services for financial services clients, particularly in respect of the Basle guidelines.

Foreword

Chris Boobyer is passionate about everything to do with asset finance. In this book he has assembled a number of leading authorities from around the world to comment on the factors and policies that drive this industry.

If your contribution to the national or global economy is through asset finance, then this book is likely to give you additional insight to help you stay ahead of the game.

Digby Jones
Director General, CBI
London

Preface

Since the last edition of *Leasing and Asset Finance* was published in 1997, there have been a number of momentous changes that have reshaped the social, economic and political world in which we live. I doubt that anyone could say that his or her professional life has not changed in some material way or that the business challenges that we face every day are getting easier! My objective for this textbook is to explain current trends, techniques and market development opportunities, and to map the future direction of existing markets in a comprehensive and practical way. The principal focus is on the small and medium ticket sectors, but more than a passing interest is paid to the big ticket sector, particularly in relation to cross-border leasing.

In reflecting on what this new edition should address and how it should be shaped, I read some of Tom Clark's words in the very first edition of *Leasing Finance* published in 1985. He wrote of leasing's long history, the evidence that before 2000 BC, the Sumerians used a form of leasing of agricultural equipment. Also, that the first regulations to distinguish between finance and leasing were drawn up in Roman times by Justinian and appear in *Book III of the Institutes*. So, there really is nothing new in the world; global and national regulators may simply be recycling old ideas held in their files since time immemorial!

As this book is published, the leasing industry is facing a number of global and local challenges. At the time of writing, the global leasing industry is awaiting new regulatory and policy frameworks in the shape of the Basle capital adequacy regime and international accounting standards (IAS). The long heralded revisions to IAS 17 seek to change the reporting of lease transactions by both lessees and lessors, particularly in relation to what is currently accepted as off-balance sheet financing. Although this is beginning to take a recognisable shape, its implementation seems to be slipping back towards 2006/7. New proposals on capital adequacy under Basle II, expected to be implemented in 2006, are already shaping the attitude of many lenders and causing great concern to asset financiers who, despite extensive evidence of their ability to manage loss rates as a result of default, may be affected by higher than necessary capital ratios.

The UK government published a consultation document on the Reform of Corporation Tax in August 2002 which looked to be a thorough set of root and branch reforms. In the April budget, it was announced that a further consultation document would be issued in the summer of 2003. There are a number of different opinions on its potential implementation timetable. Some commentators believe that once all of the comments have been distilled the proposals will quickly be implemented in accordance with a prepared plan. Others, myself included, believe that the amount of opposition and new data that emerged during the consultation process will cause some deep reflection and result in a lengthier implementation over a number of years. The sheer complexity and breadth of the proposals, together with their potential conflict with other incoming regulatory changes, such as IAS and Basle II, should be sufficient reasons for a delay in implementing proposals which, whilst apparently overdue, may have already missed their implementation window.

Since all of these initiatives will have an impact on how leasing and asset finance is conducted in the immediate future, there is no room for complacency even in markets that appear to be settled. The spate of corporate scandals in early 2002 will no doubt also have an impact on the leasing industry, despite the fact that the industry may not have been directly involved. The new millennium is thus the start of a new century, not a new industry. Leasing and asset finance is an inherently dynamic industry; it has to be innovative and react quickly to changing circumstances and fortunes.

Leasing and asset finance makes a major contribution to capital investment throughout the world. In established economies, its application is well understood if not always overtly welcomed. In developing economies, it has a real chance of making a material contribution to economic, and subsequently social, welfare. This edition focuses on the basic operation, value and contribution of asset finance in its various forms. Many of the contributors explain the changes that have taken place since the last edition that might affect its performance and return. The threats and opportunities from proposed new regulatory and accounting frameworks are discussed in depth, providing an update on taxation environments in the major markets and some views on alternatives to maximise returns from lease portfolio management and company purchase and sales. In short, a composite guide to the many intricacies, nuances, and in some cases straightforward challenges and opportunities that influence the everyday lives of asset financiers.

The book has a strong global emphasis and in this fourth edition I am delighted to have been joined by many colleagues from the previous edition and to introduce 11 new authors. Each a specialist in their field, they help guide us around the complex and global asset finance industry. The introductory chapters begin with a review of major leasing markets, selected sectors and some industry trends by Vic Lock. In Chapter 2, Chris Higson considers the contribution of asset finance to national economies and questions the value placed upon them by governments and their exchequers. Chapter 3 provides an explanation by Malcolm Rogers of the importance of thorough risk analysis and examines some of the techniques available. The objectives of the Basle Proposals on Capital Adequacy are explained and analysed by Sally Williams, Richard Smith and Stephen Potts in Chapter 4.

The legal, tax and accountancy section begins with a thorough review of documentation, transaction structures and the legal features of cross-border transactions by Simon Hall in Chapters 5, 6 and 7. These are followed by Dorothy Livingston who considers the competition laws in the European Union and the United Kingdom in Chapter 8, and in Chapter 9 she examines State aid and procurement, which have been the subject of much recent discussion in Europe and of great interest to asset financiers. Chapter 10 reveals the latest developments in taxation as explained by Philip Marwood. David Maxwell reassesses the techniques of lease evaluation in Chapter 11 and Colin Dowsett, explains the concepts of lease accounting and capitalisation in Chapters 12 and 13.

We then examine some areas of specific business focus; Nicholas Sanderson reviews the dynamic areas of financing leasing companies and some of the related operational and security issues involved in Chapter 14. He then moves on to discuss the purchase and sale of leasing companies in Chapter 15. Sam Geneen follows in Chapter 16 by explaining the principles, problems and opportunities of operating leasing. In Chapter 17, Philip Griffin takes us around the world explaining and challenging the vagaries and some of the mysteries of cross-border leasing from an intermediary's perspective. In Chapter 18, Bruce Gaitskell reviews the many developments in securitisation and the wide applications for lessors. In Chapter 19, I attempt to provide an explanation of what the European Union is in terms of its construction, powers and future direction as an economic and autonomous semi-state and what this might mean for the development of asset finance in Europe.

The final chapter provides an in-depth look at the leasing industry in Japan and individual reviews by the respective senior lease association officers in the major leasing continents around the world. Their responses to a series of questions provide a comprehensive global picture of the asset finance industry.

I strongly recommend dipping into this textbook starting with topics of personal interest. The introductory chapters set the scene and in these you will find the start of recurring themes throughout the book. Wherever practicable, I have sought to bring a number of cross references to your attention in the relevant chapters. For example, there are a number of complementary and contrasting themes brought out in the chapters by Chris Higson on the value of asset finance and the aspirations of the national leasing associations. He draws some interesting parallels between the United Kingdom and the United States and firmly believes that asset finance 'has a compelling story to tell'. Philip Marwood, Philip Griffin and Katsuhiko Otaki comment on the Japanese leasing industry from their different perspectives – and sometimes agree! There are growing similarities between the Japanese approach to environmental liability for lessors and the developing position of the European Union and there is much comment about the ability of lessors to make an impact in that region.

My thanks go to my colleagues; all have done a remarkable job in writing so comprehensively and to very demanding formats. They have covered their topics well and made my role as editor much easier than I deserved it to be. Together, they form part of the broad church of expertise within this edition and the leasing industry in general. By enthusiastically participating in this enterprise, they have achieved the most demanding and constructive position that any leasing practitioner can achieve – to pass on their knowledge and experience for the benefit and development of others.

So enjoy their work. As seasoned lessors and lessees well know, there are always a huge number of new perspectives on a small number of old, and apparently unchanging, problems and issues. I hope this book will cast light on some of them. The intention is to help give a better understanding of where the industry has been, where it is now and in which direction it appears to be heading. If the vision of the future appears a little vague, then welcome to the real and fascinating world of asset finance. It will always surprise you, but rarely will you be disappointed.

Chris Boobyer
Editor
London, April 2003

Chapter 1

Review of the leasing and asset-finance industry

Vic Lock

Introduction: the evolution and growth of leasing

Leasing remains an enigma to many in both mature and emerging economies. Although the practice dates back over 2000 years, it is a phenomenon that to all intents and purposes arrived in Europe from the United States some 40 years ago. Since then, the leasing industry has grown in importance around the world.

Since its introduction to the United Kingdom in 1960, it has established deep roots and approaching 25 per cent of capital equipment is now financed through leasing arrangements annually. Growth in other parts of Europe has been explosive. From a standing start in 1991, leasing in the Czech Republic financed almost €3 billion (US$3.2 billion) of equipment and real estate investment in 2001, up from around €0.2 billion 10 years earlier.

While the US represents the largest single leasing market in the world, at US$242 billion (€230.5 billion) of new business in 2001 (or 31 per cent of total business investment in equipment), the industry has a wide geographical spread. In Australia, for example, leasing financed A$23 billion (US$13.5 billion) of a total capital expenditure of A$43 billion in 2001 (see Exhibit 1.1).

Exhibit 1.1

Five-year new business trends in Australia, the United States, the five leading European Union leasing nations plus the Czech Republic

Country	2001 (billions)	2000 (billions)	1999 (billions)	1998 (billions)	1997 (billions)
Australia	A$23	A$15.83	A$13.66	A$13.49	A$13.35
US	US$242	US$247	US$234	US$207	US$179
Germany	€46.3	€38.2	€31.1	€27.2	€24.7
UK	€33.4	€33.6	€30.5	€31.0	€29.6
Italy	€32.3	€26.7	€14.1	€11.6	€9.4
France	€26.8	€24.9	€17.9	€15.5	€13.0
Spain	€9.7	€8.5	€6.8	€5.6	€4.2
Czech Republic	€2.9	€2.5	€2.0	€1.9	€1.8

Sources: European Federation of Leasing Company Associations (Leaseurope) and national leasing associations.

Because of the fiscal, regulatory and accounting impact on leasing, it is an industry in constant transition. Whether tax or non tax-based, however, leasing retains a single guiding principle: that ownership of assets resides with lessors which hire them to lessees over defined periods in exchange for regular rental payments.

Later chapters in this book provide much greater detail of the different forms of asset finance and the tax and accounting impact. Suffice to say here that in some countries of the world a pay-out, or finance, lease must include a purchase option exercisable by the lessee at the end of the primary period of the contract; in other countries a purchase option is specifically excluded. The general test is broadly that a purchase option is applicable in jurisdictions where the lessee might wish, ultimately to own the asset and where there are no tax benefits for the lessor. However, in countries where the lessor claims investment tax credits (in the United Kingdom, capital allowances), the inclusion of a purchase option would have adverse tax consequences, but the equipment user can achieve ultimate ownership through a hire-purchase contract.

In both domestic and international cross-border markets, it is the tax impact that has significantly shaped leasing's evolution. Such has been the aggression of some of the world's tax authorities against leasing that some professional advisers have predicted its eventual demise. Certainly a number of cross-border leasing structures – for example the Japanese leverage lease, the US lease-in, lease-out product and Australian cross-border structures – have been neutralised, but the pessimists have yet to be proved accurate soothsayers.

Optimists counter the doom mongers by pointing to the 1984 UK budget that signalled the end of the then 100 per cent first-year capital allowance regime by phasing it down to a 25 per cent writing down allowance by 1986. Some thought this change would herald the end of leasing in the United Kingdom. They could hardly have been more wrong: in 1983, UK lessors wrote €4.8 billion of new business; in 2001 they wrote €33.4 billion. Similarly, the US Internal Revenue Service terminated the investment tax credit and imposed an alternative minimum tax effective from 1 January 1986. At the time, US lessors were writing some US$90 billion of new business annually; in 2001 they closed transactions valued at approaching US$244 billion.

The benefits and limits of leasing

Leasing is thus a fluid and extensively used product. Whatever its form, its relevance transcends tax efficiency. Its universal benefits to lessees include: the preservation of working capital; the mitigation of the risk that equipment becomes obsolescent; often 100 per cent financing; the matching of rental profiles to income streams; and the quiet enjoyment of the equipment leased, providing rentals are paid according to contract.

However, it is perhaps unfortunate that some lease arrangers have pushed their structuring ingenuity to the edge of the envelope in large value transactions. The response of tax authorities was, in some cases, draconian. In the United Kingdom, the two finance acts of 1997, enacted by the former Conservative government and the succeeding Labour administration, sent as large a shock wave through the leasing industry as the budget changes of 1984.

In an attempt to counter perceived tax-abusive leasing structures, the UK Treasury – advised by the Inland Revenue – introduced sweeping legislative changes that fundamentally altered the nature of leasing. (For greater detail, see Chapter 10 and the section on the UK in Chapter 20 of this book; also the two UK finance acts of 1997.) One of the many changes of the first act, made law under the then Conservative administration, was the introduction of the long-life asset regime. This reduced from 25 per cent to 6 per cent the writing down allowances available on assets capable of a useful life of over 25 years 'in the hands of any user'.

While certain assets were granted a time limited exemption from the regulations – notably rail equipment and ships – aircraft and plant used in some utilities sectors were caught by the regime. Such was the lobbying efficacy of, for example, the aviation industry, that the Inland Revenue eventually granted a three-year concession (from 2000) that by and large provided an effective 15 per cent allowance on most large aircraft and 25 per cent on smaller types. Given the changes wrought on the airline industry by the 11 September 2001 attack on the US, it is difficult to believe that the concession will not be extended for qualifying airlines and lessors.

Notwithstanding the aviation compromise (and other understandings that mitigate the impact of the long-life rules in regard to assets such as those used in the water and printing industries), the tax regime continues to discriminate against lease finance. The UK Finance Act 2000, for example, made permanent an enhanced 40 per cent first-year-allowance regime for small- and medium-sized enterprises (SMEs), but continued to exclude specifically the leasing industry from claiming the allowances on behalf of equipment users.

The Inland Revenue believes that the exclusion is necessary to counter tax abusive structures and has, in fact, imposed such an exclusion in most cases where enhanced allowances have been introduced. The result is a complex set of rules (see Exhibit 1.2) that serves to confuse most equipment users, not least SMEs, and, if anything, has reduced allowance claims by those companies that they were introduced to help.

Cynics might say that this was the Inland Revenue's intention, but private and unsolicited comments suggest otherwise. In the words of one Inland Revenue official in 2001: 'We are very concerned that tax payers are not claiming all that they are entitled to'. Contrast this with the views of another official: 'We couldn't possibly allow lessors to claim the enhanced allowances on behalf SMEs, they might abuse the system'.

The thought of big-ticket lease arrangers, who barely stir for transactions of less than €150 million, seriously sharpening their pricing pencils to contrive clever little packages for €80,000 SME deals is at best amusing. The position does, however, serve to illustrate the dichotomy of many tax authorities around the world. On the one hand they must ensure that those eligible for tax allowances receive them; on the other they must preserve revenue for their national exchequers.

The dividing line is a narrow one and often hinges on interpretation. Did, for example, those that drafted the UK Finance Act that introduced capital allowances after World War II intend that only those companies that pay corporation tax should be eligible to claim investment allowances as the Inland Revenue seems to believe? Or did the legislators recognise that after six years of war, any incentive to invest, by any party, was essential for economic and social regeneration?

No matter the jurisdiction, such statutes are ultimately for the courts to decide and for governments, in their wisdom, to amend as they see fit. Outside of the legislative and legal processes, however, over the past 10 years there has been an apparently concerted effort on the part of certain national tax authorities to reduce or eradicate capital allowances in the hands of lessors, especially in cross-border transactions. Conversely, however, many governments continue to recognise the effectiveness of capital allowances and their availability through the leasing industry. A growing feature of equipment finance has been the introduction of selective investment allowances by governments for economic sectors judged to be in need of help.

Exhibit 1.2

Tax allowances available in the United Kingdom for the acquisition of commercial assets

Effective rate (%)	Relevant assets	Allowance	Available to lessor	Available to asset user	Time limit	Comments/ conditions
4, 25, 100	Industrial buildings (25% if in enterprise zone, 100% on initial construction in EZ)	WDA/FYA	Yes	Yes	No	Includes qualifying hotels and sports pavilions. FYAs apply to initial construction.
6	Long-life assets	WDA	Yes	Yes	Rail/ships exempt till 31 Dec 10	Assets with a useful economic life, when new, of 25 years or more. Cars not treated as long-life assets.
6, 15.5, 25	Executive jets, helicopters, turboprops	WDA	Yes	Yes	31 Dec 03	Subject to number of flying hours and turboprop take-off weight levels.
10	Export leasing: plant and equipment	WDA	Yes		13-year maximum lease	Little used allowance. Not economically viable. 6% for long-life assets.
15.5	Large aircraft	WDA	Yes	Yes	31 Dec 03	Allowances subject to certain registration conditions.
25	Plant and equipment exc. long-life assets	WDA	Yes	Yes	No	The general UK writing down allowance.
25	Affordable warmth programme	WDA	Yes	No	31 Dec 07	Covering expenditure on boilers and radiators in one million low-income homes.
25, 10	Qualifying ships (25% on first £40 million value; 10 on next £40 million)	WDA	Yes	No	Ship owner election by 27 Jul 01	Available under tonnage tax regime. Leases subject to restrictions. See REV BN 21.
33.3	Films (feature length)	SLD	Yes	No	31 Jul 02	Film maker must be incorporated in EU, any studio used must be in the United Kingdom.

Exhibit 1.2 *continued*

Tax allowances available in the United Kingdom for the acquisition of commercial assets

Effective rate (%)	Relevant assets	Allowance	Available to lessor	Available to asset user	Time limit	Comments/ conditions
40	Plant and equipment exc. long-life assets, cars, rail or ships	FYA	No	Small/ medium- sized enterprises	No	SMEs must satisfy two of three upper limits: turnover £11.2 million; assets £5.6 million; employees 250.
100	Films (up to £15 million production cost)	FYD	Yes	Yes	1 Jul 02	Subject to place of filming rules and performer nation-ality restrictions.
100	IT/communications equipment/software	FYA	No	Small companies	31 Mar 04	Must satisfy two of three upper limits: turnover £2.8 million, assets £1.4 million; employees 50.
100	Northern Ireland	FYA	No	Small/ medium- sized enterprises	11 May 02	Excludes long-life assets, aircraft, commercial vehicles agriculture/fishing.
100	Demolition and reuse of oil installations	FYA	No	Yes	No	Covers oil rigs, pipelines and other N. Sea oil installations.
100	Low emission cars	FYA	Yes	Yes	31 Feb 08	Cars registered after 17 April 2002 that emit no more than 120gm/km CO_2 or that are electrically propelled.
100	Hydrogen fuel equipment	FYA	Yes	Yes	31 Feb 08	Equipment used in connection with refuelling cars with natural gas or hydrogen.
100	Certain energy-saving and water measurement/ quality-improvement equipment	FYA	Yes	Yes	No	Available on a specified list of energy-saving technologies, reduction of water use/ quality-improvement* plant and equipment.

Note: This list is not intended to be exhaustive. It should be used as a guide only.

WDA: writing down allowance. FYA: first-year allowance. FYD: first-year deduction. SLD: straight-line deduction.

*See the section 'Current issues' for the United Kingdom in Chapter 10.

Source: LEASING*Life*.

In some cases, the selective allowances have applied to whole economies. In France, for example, rules introduced in 1998 regulated the use of leverage leasing but, subject to ministry of finance approval, left the door wide open for transactions that, amongst other things, 'provide significant economic and social benefit to France'. Meanwhile in Ireland a wide variety of social projects, such as student accommodation, car parks, park-and-ride schemes and property built for holiday lets, have been accorded favourable capital allowance treatment.

In a move that took much of the UK leasing industry by surprise, the 17 April 2002 budget opened the enhanced-allowance door to leasing. In a move that clearly demonstrated the selective use of capital allowances, as well as the UK government's green credentials, new rules were introduced for the financing of low-emission cars, refuelling infrastructure and energy saving technologies. Low-emission cars were removed from the United Kingdom's luxury cars rule, which restricts capital allowances, available on a reducing balance basis, to cars valued at no more than £12,000 (US$19,320). The 100 per cent first-year allowances (FYAs) on cars and refuelling equipment are available until 31 March 2008. FYAs applicable to energy saving equipment are available on an open-ended basis and have been extended in an amendment to the Finance Bill 2003 by the addition of lessor entitlement to 100 per cent FYAs for assets to measure/reduce water consumption, and on investment to improve water quality.

The growth of additional services leases

Leasing is not entirely driven by taxation issues, however. It is increasingly about lessors investing in equipment and taking real residual-value (RV) risk under an operating lease. In its simplest form, an operating lease can protect the lessee from equipment obsolescence, provide for upgrades in line with advancing technology and provide for shorter-term asset needs such as in the construction industry. In recent years however, the operating lease product has become increasingly sophisticated. The provision of an asset for, say, a three-year period, has moved on to varying degrees of accompanying services. Arguably the trend towards additional service leases started in the car sector. In contract hire, which has become a fairly generic term, specialist car operating lessors have been providing maintenance, fuel management, insurance, breakdown cover and the like since the early 1990s, often on a fleet basis.

The contract hire, or full-service concept, has gradually migrated to other assets and customer types. It is now not uncommon for operating leases on medical equipment to cover equipment maintenance, or for delivery lorries to be provided with drivers. Rental profiles are also changing. Driven to a large extent in the United Kingdom since 1993 by the government's private finance initiative, rentals in an increasing number of contracts – more typically, but not exclusively, for public-sector lessees – are priced on a usage basis. Examples might include the provision of: turnstiles financed on customer throughput numbers; computer equipment on a cost per keystroke; or medical equipment on a cost per scan.

Whilst the move to the provision of a service as well as an asset might look a logical commercial step, it is not without significant risks to lessors. Although many equipment manufacturers own their own leasing companies, known as captives, the majority of lessors are either bank owned or operate independently from either manufacturers or banks. For either of the latter to make the quantum leap from the provision of an asset to the provision of a raft of associated services requires a major investment in additional resources. Some lessors have addressed this by acquiring companies with the relevant infrastructure and experience, others have formed strategic alliances with service providers.

Whatever the guise they choose, it is likely that a growing number of lessors will become service providers. One obvious reason is the pursuit of enhanced returns; another is price volatility in the used-equipment market.

Calculating residual value

Operating leasing is a risk business. Different jurisdictions have different ways of measuring risk for tax and accounting purposes, but the practical common denominator is the lessor's assessment of the RV of a given asset at the end of the primary period of a lease, and how that value might be achieved to realise, ultimately, a profit from the ownership of the asset. This contrasts with a finance lease under which a lessor would expect to recoup its investment in the asset – its overheads, cost of funds, etc – and take a profit at the end of the primary period.

While operating leasing is not a new concept and has been used in aircraft and car finance, for example, for many years, interest in the product has accelerated over the past five to 10 years. To a certain extent the growth of RV-based leasing products has been driven by increased competition within the finance leasing industry and changes in tax legislation. More importantly, however, operating leasing fulfils commercial demands in both the private and public sectors that are met by no other equipment financing product.

World economic cycles can destroy a lessor's assessment of the resale value of an asset, an assessment which is made three or five years into the future at the very least. While various RV risk mitigation instruments – for example manufacturer buy-backs, residual value insurance and guarantees – can be important elements of an operating lessor's risk containment strategy, the ability to forecast economic cycles, to achieve a balanced portfolio either of asset types or transaction periods and to re-market equipment is critical. A potentially large secondary market for each asset class is also often an important factor.

A quick review of the past 15 years or so illustrates the importance of economic cycles. If a lessor had started writing five-year operating leases in the mid-1980s, it would have faced re-marketing the relevant equipment around the time of the Gulf war and the early 1990s recession. Similarly, to have written new five-year deals in the early 1990s on the assumption of an economic recovery would have left the lessor trying to re-market equipment in the mid 1990s at the height of the Asian economic slump when a vast array of new equipment was being dumped into Western markets at huge discounts.

Currency fluctuations and general improvements in equipment manufacturing processes can also have an adverse impact on a lessor's residual value assumptions. For example, early in 2002 the auctioneer Henry Butcher offered for sale by private treaty a 1999 1,600-tonne hydraulic machine used in the plastics injection-moulding industry. The new machine had cost €1.3 million, yet in 2002 the same machine could be purchased new for €1 million. Clearly, any lessor that had based its RV assumptions on this asset at its 1999 price might wonder where its profit had gone, especially since the machine in question realised only €333,333.

This example illustrates yet one more essential skill required by the operating lessor. In order to be able to assume residual risk, the lessor must have a detailed understanding of likely technological advances in each asset type in which it invests, the commercial nature of the industry in which the asset is to be used and its specific operating environment. A forklift truck used in a food retail warehouse, for example, will be in far better condition after five years use than the same piece of kit used in a builder's yard or an oil refinery.

Although lessors finance a wide range of equipment, in Europe, at least, the financing of motor cars has represented a major portion of the business over the past five years. A plethora of institutions finance motor cars through a variety of instalment payment plans which span hire purchase, finance and operating leasing and contract hire. As governments change taxation policies on, for example, the use of company cars, so the financing products change. In the UK, for example, the growth of personal contract purchase or contract hire schemes introduced in the 1990s accelerated in 2002 with the introduction of an emissions-based tax policy that basically favoured cars of a lower cubic capacity and also diesel-engined models.

It is at the car-finance level that the provision of finance to the business and consumer sectors becomes most closely aligned. Perceived wisdom suggested in the early 1990s that, based on historic databases and the huge size of the secondary market for cars, their RVs were very predictable. The three years to 2002 proved just how dangerous assumptions can be. One of the largest car lessors in the United Kingdom at the time – with a fleet of over 90,000 vehicles – made a provision in its accounts for 2000 of €75 million against future RV losses. Nobody in the industry is under any illusions that this was an isolated case; in fact the problem is more or less uniform. In 2000, members of the British Vehicle Leasing and Rental Association invested in 1.1 million vehicles, the equivalent of 49.4 per cent of the total new vehicle market for the year.

The collapse in RVs was caused by a concerted consumer campaign launched in 1999 against the high price of cars in the United Kingdom compared with most other European countries. That the price differential was largely because of different national car-purchase tax regimes and the high value of sterling was of little interest to consumer groups or the UK Competition Commission. As 1999 gave way to 2000, new car sales dried up in anticipation of lower prices. By early 2001 they were down by around 10 per cent. Used-car values fell in unison with a devastating impact on lessors' RV assumptions.

In 2001 the consumer finance market for new vehicles recovered strongly, although the business market remained depressed. In March 2002, the long-awaited European Union (EU) consultation paper on block exemption was released. Introduced in 1985 and amended 10 years later, block exemption essentially excluded new-car distribution and sales from EU competition laws in an attempt to enhance consumer service and protect manufacturers' brand image. The concession also protected cash outflows from those EU member states that on the one hand did not have an indigenous car manufacturing sector and on the other imposed very high car-purchase taxes. One of the major effects of block exemption has been to give manufacturers total control over their sales channels and thus their pricing policies.

The block exemption rules were changed in September 2002, with a new freer and more flexible regime entering force in October 2003. A central plank of the European Commission's policy is to harmonise car prices across the EU. Although prices in, for example, the United Kingdom remained higher than those in most EU member states in the first half of 2002, price convergence was thought likely to see an increase in new car price rises in some member states and falls in others.

The issue is of critical importance to much of the European leasing community. According to statistics from the Brussels-based umbrella federation Leaseurope, which unites some 25 national leasing associations around Europe, car finance, at €53.4, represented over 25 per cent of the €192.7 billion total for equipment leasing new business in 2001. In some countries the percentage of car finance business is much higher; in Switzerland, for example, it was 65 per cent; in Hungary 62 per cent; and in Ireland 52 per cent. In several other coun-

Exhibit 1.3

Top 12 European car finance markets in 2001, new car-finance business for the preceding five years and the percentage of total new business represented by cars in each country (€ billion)

Country	2001	%	2000	%	1999	%	1998	%	1997	%	1996	%
Germany	19.0	50	16.70	53	15.83	51	13.66	50	13.49	55	13.35	58
United Kingdom	10	30	10.90	28	10.91	36	11.83	38	11.25	38	8.38	35
France	4.4	20	3.50	18	4.18	23	1.64	11	1.43	14	1.90	19
Italy	3.7	19	3.34	20	3.13	22	2.53	22	2.34	25	2.54	29
Switzerland	3.4	65	2.63	61	2.50	68	2.11	72	1.78	77	1.61	69
Sweden	2.9	50	2.51	51	1.09	34	1.02	27	0.88	31	0.76	31
Austria	1.5	48	1.65	50	1.47	51	1.22	49	1.10	50	1.10	53
Czech Republic	1.3	47	1.16	49	1.02	50	0.89	47	0.87	49	0.73	55
Ireland	0.9	52	0.96	52	1.12	52	1.07	52	0.21	–	0.70	32
Portugal	0.75	26	0.86	30	0.75	29	0.56	28	0.33	–	0.36	–
Hungary	1.1	62	0.71	58	0.63	–	0.54	–	0.38	64	0.42	79
Belgium	0.7	24	0.66	24	0.68	27	0.54	24	0.48	24	0.45	25

Sources: Leaseurope and LEASING*Life*.

tries, including Austria, the Czech Republic, Germany and Sweden, it was hovering around 50 per cent (see Exhibit 1.3).

Any changes in car distribution or taxation could thus have a dramatic impact on many leasing companies' businesses. While lessors that provide car finance to consumers, as opposed to fleet services to businesses, are less exposed to movements in RVs, they are nonetheless subject to movements in values, especially when faced with a default by the car user. Lessors have traditionally been very good at managing credit underwriting when dealing with businesses, but as more become exposed to the consumer market, the risks change.

The impact of recent shocks on the leasing industry

Following events of 11 September 2001, lessors of all hues began reassessing their exposures across a huge range of assets. At the obvious level, fewer airline passengers reduced the requirement for aircraft. Less obvious was the impact on sectors such as chauffeur-driven cars and short-term car rental. While the latter showed signs of recovery in the first half of 2002, the chauffeur-driven-car sector remained depressed as, amongst other things, investment banks continued to cull their expenses in an effort to stem losses from the huge decline in mergers and acquisitions and other corporate work.

It was at the aircraft level, however, that the greatest exposure lay. Throughout 2002, credit-rating agencies downgraded securitisation vehicles of a number of aircraft-lease-receivable issues. The agencies' primary concerns were declining lease rentals and the difficulty that the securitisation servicers might have in re-marketing aircraft as they came off-lease. Non-aircraft lessors that relied on securitisation techniques to fund their books were also watching the market nervously. In the United States, for example, the situation exacerbated the challenge as capital for investment in new equipment dried-up.

While events of 11 September 2001 formed one of the largest human tragedies of the past decade, the collapse of Enron, Worldcom, *et al* came as large corporate shocks. US regulators and the accounting standard setters were scurrying around in the early months of 2002 to establish just what had gone wrong. Clearly much of Enron's exposure was hidden through off-balance sheet structures. Leasing can, of course, also be used as an off-balance sheet instrument, but one that is normally covered in the notes to a lessee's accounts. By the close of the year, the business world, in the United States at least, had to contend with new corporate governance rules. New accounting standards on such vehicles as special purpose entities were issued by the Financial Accounting Standards Board in January 2003 following extensive consultation.

Conclusion: the future for transparent asset financing

Lease accounting has been the subject of much debate over the past 20 years (see Chapter 13). The capitalisation of finance leases in the books of the lessee has been commonplace for many years. In 1996, the prospect of operating leases also being capitalised by the equipment user was raised in a discussion paper published by major accounting regulators. More recent proposals, combined with EC and International Accounting Standards Board policy objectives, are likely to see the demise of off-balance sheet leases sometime this decade. The process was already in motion; the Enron debacle merely gave more urgency to the regulators' intentions.

Nonetheless, as the dust settled on Enron's collapse, so the benefits and potential of leasing as a transparent equipment financing instrument were once again being recognised. In reality, neither the tax nor the off-balance sheet issues are of any consequence to the majority of lessees who operate small- and medium-sized businesses around the world. In early 2002, a study by the UK Competition Commission into banking services for the SME sector gave leasing a clean bill of health. The report stated: 'Other lending to SMEs is by providers other than the big four [UK] banks. This competitive environment is especially true of asset finance'.

Whether or not some regulators in some parts of the world dislike leasing, it has stood the test of time and, at times, it has proved to be a much more transparent and flexible means of equipment finance than any other so far devised. The next 10 years could see further significant reductions – or the gradual demise – of the two historic drivers of finance leasing: corporation tax and, where applicable, capital allowances. Such changes will not sound the death knell of leasing, they will merely mark further stages in its evolution.

Chapter 2

The economic role of asset finance[1]

Professor Chris Higson

Introduction

The main focus of this chapter is the lease financing of equipment and property. However, it also covers secured lending against inventories and against receivables as factoring or invoice discounting. The first part reviews some theory and economic evidence to understand why asset financing exists as a class of financing contracts in the capital market. The second part examines the role of asset financing in the evolving network economy.

There are compelling arguments for asset financing based on its economic efficiency. The evidence for the role of asset financing in promoting economic efficiency is as strong as for any aspect of capital market efficiency. This economic logic drives the development and marketing of new products, but it should also inform the public face of the industry. When the industry is arguing its case with governments and regulators, the asset-finance industry has sometimes found itself on the back foot. Examples are the debate with tax authorities on the tax treatment of leasing and the debate with accounting standard setters on the capitalisation of operating leases.

The asset financing industry's public stance should be built around a clear understanding of the capital market function of asset financing. Its role in financing small- and medium-sized businesses (SMEs) has been voiced energetically, but this is part of a wider argument for using asset financing whenever firms face capital market impediments. As for tax, efficient resource allocation requires that firms that are otherwise similar should face the same after-tax cost of investment. Leasing is an effective mechanism for redistributing taxable capacity to achieve this, and both consumers and suppliers of asset financing should reasonably expect to face a level playing field in this respect.

Contractual relationships that involve asset financing seem likely to grow in importance in the outsourced, network economy. We are witnessing continuing economic restructuring, triggered by deregulation and developments in information technology, that have radically changed the cost structure of business. Non-recourse asset financing will have a central role in this process, permitting firms to focus their use of capital and shift the ownership of assets that are not strategic to people that can more efficiently own and manage them.

Both from an economic perspective and from the perspective of customers, equipment leasing, property leasing and receivables financing are viable substitute methods of financing. The task of thinking broadly about the future dynamics of the asset financing industry, and of advancing a coherent economic rationale for asset financing, means taking a holistic view of the business. Though some firms are now doing this, historically the different segments of the industry have remained largely separate and this shows up in the data. In researching the

11

background to this chapter, I have been struck by how hard it still is to get a complete picture of the extent to which corporate balance sheets, and the main asset classes within them, are asset financed. Equipment leasing organisations, such as the UK Finance & Leasing Association (FLA) and the US Equipment Leasing Association (ELA), provide good quality data on the penetration of equipment leasing. However, equivalent data on property leasing and on the financing of current assets are either fragmented or non existent. The production, on a continuing basis, of data that is both comprehensive and customer focused is an important challenge for the broad asset-financing industry.

The role of asset financing in capital markets

There are compelling arguments for asset financing based on economic efficiency. We know this because asset financing is an area of capital market activity where economic theory – that is, theory that models rational cost minimising behaviour – successfully explains what happens in practice. The theory-based predictions about which firms will lease, and which assets will be leased, are borne out in reality. So smaller firms, and firms that face capital market impediments and therefore a higher cost of capital, are more likely to lease. Firms that do not expect to possess the tax capacity to make full use of available investment tax allowances are likely to lease. And firms tend to lease re-deployable, non-specific assets, rather than unique or specific assets.

How asset financing reduces the cost of capital

Asset financing can reduce the contracting costs that arise in financing firms, particularly agency costs and transaction costs. In showing how asset financing contributes to economic efficiency by reducing costs, economic theory can make clear predictions about what type of asset will be asset financed.

Economists argue that a valuable function of asset financing lies in its ability to resolve potential agency costs.[2] Investors may have difficulty in monitoring and controlling the use to which their money is put since investment in other assets may be substituted for planned investment, or the money may not be spent on assets at all, resulting in under investment. Since asset financing is secured finance, leasing resolves this potential problem. Leasing or secured debt allows the firm to segregate its cash flow. Because leasing is essentially the provision of finance that is specific to a particular asset, these under investment and asset substitution problems can be avoided.[3]

Smith and Wakeman (1985) note other efficiencies in leasing that are likely to differentially impact smaller firms. They note that leasing may lower the costs in bankruptcy, since leased assets are easier to repossess. They also argue that by increasing the amount of debt-like finance available to firms, correspondingly less equity is required. This is particularly valuable to the principal of a smaller enterprise, since it relaxes the constraint to achieve an optimal portfolio diversification and so reduces the cost of capital.

Furthermore, Sharpe and Nguyen (1995) provide, in an important paper, strong arguments why, at least in a US legal setting, operating leasing (considered true leasing in the United States) is even more effective than secured debt in alleviating financial contracting costs. Their argument is that after filing for bankruptcy, the lessee can assume or reject a true lease. If the lease is assumed, the lessor continues to receive full compensation after bankruptcy while the claims of other creditors, including secured creditors, are accrued. In other words, operating lease rentals rank alongside employee and management costs as administrative expenses which must be paid immediately. This puts operating leases at the top of the pecking-order of external financial claims.

The link between asset type and leasing

Theory shows that the more specialised an asset is, the more likely it is to be owned rather than leased. Smith and Wakeman (1985), and Williamson (1998), argue that firms are unlikely to lease assets that are highly specific to the organisation because this would create agency problems between the lessor and the lessee. So leasing is more likely to occur if its assets are non specialised. And if a firm is going to lease, it is more likely to lease its generic assets. Similarly, the more sensitive an asset's value is to use and maintenance, the more likely it is to be owned so that the incentives to maintain it are maximised (Alchian and Demsetz, 1972).

Arguments based on transaction costs also successfully explain the relation between the nature of assets and the use of lease finance. Williamson (1988) argues that as the costs of both debt and equity finance increase, the costs of debt financing rise more rapidly than the cost of equity as 'asset specificity' increases, that is, where the firm is using assets with fewer alternative uses. This is because a rule-governed debt-financing regime will force liquidation or otherwise cause the firm to compromise value enhancing decisions that a more adaptable regime such as equity could implement.

Especially where the lessor has expertise in the relevant asset markets, leasing may offer lower costs in the event of bankruptcy (Mukherjee, 1991). The more frequently an asset needs to be transacted, the greater the cumulative savings associated with the lessor's asset-market expertise will be. So assets that are not expected to be used for their whole life are likely to be leased.

Evidence on the relationship between the use of asset financing and the size and financial condition of the firm

Theory predicts that smaller firms, and firms that are financially distressed and are already highly geared, are more likely to lease. Sharpe and Nguyen (1995) find strong evidence that US firms that are likely to face higher financial costs are more likely to lease. They also find that small firms are more likely to use operating leases, which they explain both in terms of the higher financing costs faced by small firms, but also in terms of other size related factors.[4] They find positive, but weaker, evidence that financially constrained firms finance a greater share of their on-balance sheet assets using capital leases. In the United Kingdom, Lasfer and Levis (1997) also report a strong relation between leasing and size. For the largest 10 per cent of firms, leasing and hire purchase accounts for less than 7 per cent of debt, whereas amongst firms with assets of less than £1 million, almost 55 per cent used leasing during the period 1988 to 1995.

The differential impact on large and small firms is very important when considering the economics of asset financing. However, studies that use published accounting data may only have a limited ability to observe this since they tend to focus on publicly-quoted firms and larger private firms that are frequently the subsidiaries of foreign multinationals. Although there is an enormous range of firm size within the quoted population, the smaller quoted firms may not reliably represent the population of the smallest enterprises in the economy.

The best source of data on the impact of asset financing on the very smallest enterprises in the economy is the biennial survey of Profitability and Finance in UK SMEs by Andy Cosh and Alan Hughes (Cosh and Hughes, 2000). The work is invaluable because it surveys three SME size classes: the micro firm, the small firm and the medium-sized firm. The medium group probably corresponds to the smaller end of the quoted population. The survey confirms the predicted importance of asset financing amongst small and very small firms. It shows that 84.2 per cent of the overall sample approached their bank for finance during the study period. But the next most important source of finance, approached by around half of the sample, was leasing and hire purchase. The reported approach rates are: micro, 34.5 per cent; small, 53.7 per cent; and medium, 47.9 per cent.

Cosh and Hughes also collect failure rates, which is the proportion of approaches rejected by financiers. These figures are important because they provides a direct test of the hypothesis that asset financing provides access to firms with capital market impediments. Hire purchase and leasing show far and away the lowest failure rate of any of the financing sources surveyed by Cosh and Hughes. Overall 9.8 per cent of approaches to banks were rejected, compared to 3.0 per cent of hire purchase and leasing approaches. Factoring, which emerges as one of the least popular sources of finance for SMEs (10.6 per cent of all approaches), also displays one of the highest failure rates at 18.9 per cent.

Evidence on the relationship between asset financing and asset type

Economic theory also predicts that firms will lease re-deployable and non-specific assets, assets intended to be used for less than their full life and assets with relatively low maintenance costs. Because firms do not disclose the type of assets that they are leasing in sufficient detail, this cannot be tested directly. However, since asset specificity is likely to differ from industry to industry, this would also predict different levels of leasing activity in different sectors. There is plenty of evidence for different levels of leasing activity in different sectors, for example by Finuncane (1988) and Krishnan and Moyer (1994) in the United States. In the United Kingdom, Lasfer and Levis (1997) report that the incidence of leasing is higher in engineering, pharmaceuticals, support services, transport, water and, paper and packaging.

Property leasing

Rodney *et al* (2001) used lease disclosures in company accounts to report specifically on the changing nature of property leasing in the United Kingdom. They find a marked shift from freehold ownership of property to capital-leased property in the 1990s. By 1999, roughly 40 per cent of on-balance sheet property was held under capital leases as against 28 per cent in the early years of the decade (it is unclear whether these figures are gross or net of revaluations). As predicted, companies using leases were much more likely to be younger and fast growing, while companies using ownership were more likely to be large and mature. The incidence of operating leasing of property was also size related, being significantly higher amongst larger companies (76 per cent of FTSE 100 companies used operating leases compared to 50 per cent of small companies).

The authors also surveyed senior corporate management. In shifting to leasing, managers were looking primarily for flexibility and for the provision of a high-quality service. Again, consistent with the theory that asset specificity deters leasing, the most likely property to be leased was headquarters and administration accommodation, while the least likely was research facilities, laboratories and manufacturing property.

Both casual observation and empirical studies suggest that property is more likely to be operating leased than other assets. Agency theory would predict this. But the prevalence of operating leasing of property also reflects the fact that property tends to have a long economic life; even a lengthy property lease may cover the smaller part of the life of an asset, and fall well below the SSAP 21 threshold for operating leasing.[5] Also, the upward rent review characteristic of many property leases is *prima facie* evidence that the lessee is buying a service and that ownership remains with the lessor.

The role of asset financing in tax arbitrage

The role of leasing in tax arbitrage is well-known and early research into leasing focused almost entirely on the tax motives for leasing.[6] However, what needs constant re-emphasis is that tax arbitrage is also an economic efficiency argument for leasing. The argument runs broadly as follows: the (lessee) firm that pays little or no corporation tax may be unable to enjoy the available tax capital allowances associated with capital investment. Leasing can restore the investment incentives provided by the tax system by transferring the investment tax allowance to a firm, the lessor, that has sufficient taxable capacity to enjoy it. The lessor then returns the tax allowance to the lessee through a suitably reduced lease schedule, restoring the incentive structure intended by the tax system.[7] On the assumption that the capital allowance system is intended to have investment incentive consequences, governments should therefore be expected to encourage, rather than discourage, tax arbitrage of this sort.

Well-conducted studies such as Graham *et al* (1996), which control for other factors, have shown that firms with less taxable capacity are more likely to use lease finance. Using measures such as reported-tax-loss carry-forwards and recoverable ACT to signal lack of tax capacity, Lasfer and Levis (1997) argue that leasing is tax driven for large firms, but that for the SME and unquoted sectors, leasing is driven by growth and access to finance. They say: 'The results suggest that the decision to lease by large firms is tax driven and that leasing contributes to these firms' profitability'.

Limitations of existing data on asset financing

Data on asset financing derived from company accounts have provided the basis for most economic analysis because, being at the company level, it can be directly related to other economic descriptors of the firm. Since company accounts are produced annually, they appear to offer a valuable resource for continuous monitoring of trends in asset financing. In fact, researchers have not used them in this way and published studies have tended to be one-off projects. Continuous research may only be feasible if the relevant data are stored in machine-readable databases.

Furthermore, accounts data have significant limitations that stem from the limited detail firms are required to provide on finance leases and from the non-capitalisation of operating leases. Because only finance leases and hire-purchase agreements in the United Kingdom, and capital leases in the United States, are recognised in the balance sheet, research that sources accounts data from databases tends to exclude operating leases.[8] Also, while balance sheets show the stock of asset financing, databases typically do not report a separate cash flow or profit and loss (ie flow) figure. Finally, balance sheets report a separate asset figure for property leases, but all other types of leased asset are aggregated (some database services do not even report the split between property and other leased assets), and Generally Accepted Accounting Principles (GAAP) requires no disaggregation of the lease liability by type of underlying asset.

Hitherto, operating-lease rentals have been footnote disclosures in UK company accounts and these disclosures are not collected in machine-readable databases. Consequently research into operating leasing at the company level requires expensive hand collection of data and studies that do this have been infrequent and done on a one-off basis.[9] Failure to study operating leasing means ignoring an increasingly important method of asset financing and, since property appears to be predominantly operating leased, it means significantly understating property in company accounts. Since operating-lease rentals are flows, researchers must capitalise them to get a stock figure. However, GAAP requires only a limited disclosure with respect to operating leases. Lease rentals for property are separately disclosed, but are not disclosed separately for other asset classes and, outside the United States, future rentals commitments need be reported only one year ahead. As a result, researchers have been forced to use a more or less arbitrary capitalisation rule to estimate the stock of operating-leased assets (Imhoff, Lipe and Wright, 1991 in the US; see also Beattie, Edwards and Goodacre, 1998).

Resource systems in the network economy

A different economic motive for asset financing to those discussed so far is the desire to outsource assets that may be more competently managed by others and which are not strategic resources of the business. This will increase the demand for true leasing and non-recourse financing of existing and new asset classes.

Outsourcing is not new. For instance, companies frequently leased their fleet when they did not wish to maintain in-house the necessary skills in fleet management, insurance and repair, and access to second-hand vehicle markets. What appears to be changing is the growing willingness and energy with which firms are applying this logic to reconfiguring their resource systems, and the use of networks, rather than ownership-like contracts, to provide resources.

Airlines have long mixed outright ownership with capital leasing and operating leasing of planes. In addition, firms like British Airways (BA) now operate a number of routes through franchised affiliates. These operators fly planes that bear the BA livery but, as independent airlines, their assets do not appear in the BA balance sheet. Planes are clearly core assets to airlines, unlike executive car fleets in most cases. Nonetheless, planes are not a strategic resource for an airline; airlines all use much the same planes and planes are in competitive supply. A list of the resources that confer competitive advantage on airlines would include control of sites and slots, reputation for safety and service quality, membership of strategic alliances, code-sharing arrangements and reservation systems. None of these appear in the balance sheet.

In the new economic order sketched by writers such as Hegel and Singer (1999), firms are moving away from growth-restricting vertical integration in favour of specialisation along resource lines. Hegel and Singer see firms re-engineering and reconfiguring into three types of business: product development; infrastructure and logistics; and customer-facing. Each of Hegel and Singer's business types has a quite different tangible/intangible asset profile. Whereas infrastructure businesses may be conventionally capital-intensive, the key asset for the product development business is likely to be intellectual property, while for the customer-facing business it is brand equity. Crucially, the span of resource control increasingly extends beyond conventional ownership to include extended supply and complementary networks.

Ford was a frequently used example of this process (for example, Lev, 2001). Lev argues that the potential for manufacturing economies of scale is now largely exhausted and that excellence in manufacturing has been widely mimicked. So manufacturing production has become commoditised. Increasingly, a firm like Ford would look to innovation and to the development of brand equity to build competitive advantage. In consequence, Ford saw little purpose in owning manufacturing assets and was busy 'deverticalising', pushing manufacturing, and the ownership of manufacturing assets, out to third parties. Intensive use of IT permits Ford to manage these network relationships tightly and efficiently.

These changes are having a significant effect on the return on capital profile of firms, an increasing number of which do not have a return on capital that can sensibly be measured because they do not directly use capital. The key strategic resources or intangible assets do not figure in the balance sheet, while tangible assets that are needed may be held off-balance sheet, or held in some other company within a network or alliance.

Take Dell Computer, which can be classed as an old or a new economy stock according to taste. Since 1997, Michael Dell has radically re-engineered the business model, and thus the balance sheet, of Dell. Energetic use of internet selling and IT to manage a network of suppliers gave Dell negligible inventory and negative net trade credit. Fixed assets are largely operating leased. Dell's other creditors are more than sufficient to finance the small amount of on-balance-sheet operating assets, so Dell's net operating assets became negative. In consequence, an operating margin of 10 per cent to 12 per cent combined with an infinite asset turn, gives a reported return on capital at Dell which is infinite.

The response of analysts (and of accounting standard setters) might be to capitalise the operating leases, and perhaps the relatively small amount that Dell has spent on R&D, and this would doubtless yield a finite return on capital. But these adjustments essentially miss the point. Capital is not the scarce resource at Dell, nor is it the appropriate measure of Dell's performance. The shifts described above will lead to greater variance in return across sectors and shifts in habitual patterns of return generation as firms re-engineer.

Implications for the asset financing industry

For the asset-finance industry, the above arguments seem likely to generate an increased demand for non-recourse financing. Companies which are on this path and are energetically shrinking their inhouse-owned resource systems and their balance sheets are likely to be open to innovative financing contracts for hitherto hard-to-finance assets.

This type of re-engineering is clearly the most advanced in the property sector, where it is being energetically pursued. As noted earlier, a very large proportion of property is already operating leased. An excellent example of the potential of such financing to transform economic performance is the hotel sector. The hotels and lodging sector, where incumbents struggled to return at or above the cost of capital, was traditionally an unpromising sector. The profitability of major hotel groups such as Four Seasons and Marriott has been transformed by judiciously migrating the business model away from ownership towards management and service provision. In this case, the strategic partner has commonly been a Real Estate Investment Trust (REIT).

17

Another factor that will tend to push people towards operating leasing is the growth of a contractual culture. For example, bus operators may find themselves receiving a franchise for only five years, whereas before deregulation they may have held the franchise for a lengthy or unspecified period, or may even have believed they owned the rights.

We have frequently come across the view that institutional impediments in Europe could slow the growth in operating leasing relative to the United States. This view could be paraphrased as follows. 'One reason that the US is well ahead of, say, the UK in the implementation of operating leasing is the historically smaller influence of big banks in the leasing industry. There are two very different cultures to be found in the leasing industry: big banks have a dominantly credit view of the world, they do not know how to trade assets and are reluctant to take asset risk. Banks are used to full security and are reluctant to accept the idea of lending their balance sheets. Asset management companies have asset savvy and take a portfolio view of risk. The US growth in manufacturing leasing is a result of the relative importance of leasing subsidiaries of manufacturing companies. While there is an old-fashioned view prevalent in the United Kingdom, US banks have been more inclined to buy into asset management companies.'

Although leasing, particularly property leasing, has received the most attention in the context of outsourcing, most asset classes are likely to be affected. Take the example of factoring. Factoring enables firms to outsource their credit management functions and perhaps improve their quality in the process. Credit functions include the approval and validation of credit applications, where the factor will not only bring economies of scale, but may bring objectivity since the factor's credit decisions will not be coloured by the need to make a sale. The factor will have good access to commercial credit databases and may be able to employ more-highly-trained credit analysts. The factor may employ more sophisticated accounting and data analysis systems. The factor's scale advantages will be greatest when managing transactions that may be relatively infrequent for the client, for instance, export invoices. As factors extend and enrich their product offering, some are expanding into the adjacent areas of asset-based finance for stocks and equipment.

The speed and extent of this re-engineering, and the implications for asset financing, are hard to quantify. It is at this point that the real limitations of publicly available aggregate data are most keenly felt. We need more data. The equipment lease associations produce regular series on the penetration of equipment leasing. For instance, in the United Kingdom FLA data show that historically up to 30 per cent of UK equipment investment, measured as gross fixed capital formation (GFCF), has been asset financed. There was a sharp upturn in asset financing in 1996 when the leased proportion reached 31.8 per cent. However, this proportion then fell sharply to just over 25 per cent by 2000. Although GFCF has a continuing upward trend, the value of UK domestic leases written stayed roughly constant from 1996 to 2000.

Although we would believe property leasing to have the highest penetration, aggregate data are not easily available on this. We rely on studies like that of Rodney et al (2001), mentioned above, which find that the number of UK firms reporting operating leasing increased dramatically from 27 per cent in 1990 to 68 per cent in 1998.

In the United Kingdom, according to the Factors & Discounters Association (FDA), domestic invoice discounting grew by approaching 20 per cent per annum over the years 1997 to 2001 and had grown by over 30 per cent per annum over the previous three years. However, the degree of penetration that this represents is unreported. Manufacturing still accounts for a disproportionate part of UK factoring activity, though its take-up by services is growing. According to the FDA, in 1990 46 per cent of companies using factoring were in manufacturing and 18 per cent in services; by 2000 these figures were 37 per cent and 29 per cent respectively. International comparisons are dangerous for factoring because of definitional differences. However, while rather less than 10 per cent of UK SMEs used factoring, in France the figure appears to be over 30 per cent.

Conclusion

I have argued that the asset-financing industry has a compelling story to tell. Theory shows how asset financing can reduce financing costs. This is particularly true for firms that face capital market impediments, smaller firms and firms that would otherwise face high financing costs. Economics also helps us understand what sort of assets will be financed in this way: assets that are not specific to the firm, are less subject to wear and tear, and assets not used for their whole life. Tax also provides a strong economic efficiency argument for leasing. If a firm pays little or no corporation tax, it may be unable to enjoy the available tax allowances associated with capital investment. Leasing can restore the incentives to invest that are provided by the tax system by transferring the investment tax allowance to a lessor which has sufficient taxable capacity to enjoy the incentives.

In the network economy, or the 'new economy' as it is sometimes known, it increasingly seems that firms are re-engineering their businesses and their balance sheets. The effect is to outsource assets that others may have greater competency in managing and to focus the use of capital on assets that are strategic to the firm, which are frequently intangible. This should further increase the demand for certain types of asset financing.

So this is an environment that offers rich, and probably growing, opportunities for asset financing. Frequently, this will be non-recourse and to take advantage of these opportunities requires a financing culture that is comfortable with asset risk and understands asset markets. The main aim of this chapter has been to lay out a clear vision of the economic role of asset financing. Finally, the asset-financing industry should be taking a customer-oriented, rather than a producer-oriented view of the market and its evolution. This needs to be a holistic view, because from the point of view of the customer, equipment leasing, property leasing, receivables financing and other forms of asset financing are all pretty much substitutes for one another.

References

J Ang and P Peterson, 1984, 'The Leasing Puzzle', *Journal of Finance*, Vol 39.

M Barclay and C Smith, 1995, 'The Priority Structure of Corporate Leasing', *Journal of Finance*, Vol 50 (July), pages 899–917.

V Beattie, K Edwards and A Goodacre, 1998, 'The Impact of Constructive Operating Lease Capitalisation on Key Accounting Ratios', *Accounting and Business Research*, Vol 28, 4, pages 233–254.

V Beattie, A Goodacre and S Thomson, 1988, 'Operating Leases and the Assessment of Lease-Debt Substitutability', *University of Stirling, discussion paper* 98/03.

S Fazzari, G Hubbard and B Petersen, 1988, 'Financing Constraints and Corporate Investment', *Brookings Papers on Economic Activity*, 1, pages 141–195.

D Flath, 1980, 'The Economics of Short-term Leasing', *Economic Inquiry*, Vol 18, pages 243–255.

Harris, Milton and Raviv, 1991, 'The Theory of Capital Structure', *Journal of Finance*, Vol 46, pages 297–356.

G Hamel and J Sampler, 1998, 'The E-Corporation: More Than Just Web-based', *Fortune magazine*, (July).

J Hegel and M Singer, 1999, *Net Worth*, Harvard Business School Press.

E Imhoff, R Lipe and D Wright, 1991, 'Operating Leases: Impact of Constructive Capitalization', *Accounting Horizons*, Vol 5, 1, pages 51–63.

V Krishnan and R Moyer, 1994, 'Bankruptcy Costs and The Financial Leasing Decision', *Financial Management*, Vol 23, pages 31–42.

B Lev, 2001, *Intangibles: Management, Measurement and Reporting*, Brookings Institution.

G Loveday, 1995, 'Leasing Up', in *Financial Reporting 1994–95: A Survey of UK Reporting Practice,* D Tonkin and L Skerratt (editors). Milton Keynes: Institute of Chartered Accountants in England and Wales, pages 15–28.

Miller, Merton and Upton, 1976, 'Leasing, Buying, and the Cost of Capital Services', *Journal of Finance*, Vol 31, pages 761–786.

E Morgan, J Lowe and C Tomkins, 1980, 'The UK Financial Leasing Industry – A Structural Analysis', *Journal of Industrial Economics*, Vol 28, (June).

S Myers, 1977, 'Determinants of Corporate Borrowing', *Journal of Financial Economics*, Vol 5, pages 147–175.

S Myers and N Majluf, 1984, 'Corporate Financing Decision When Firms Have Investment Information That Investors Do Not', *Journal of Financial Economics*, Vol 13, pages 187–220.

S Sharpe and H Nguyen, 1995, 'Capital Market Imperfection and the Incentive to Lease', *Journal of Financial Economics*, Vol 39, pages 271–294.

C Smith and L Wakeman, 1985, 'Determinants of Corporate Leasing Policy', *Journal of Finance*, Vol 40, pages 895–908.

C Smith and L Wakeman, 1985, 'Large Shareholders and Corporate Control', *Journal of Finance*, Vol 45, pages 895–908.

C Smith and J Warner, 1979, 'Bankruptcy, Secure Debt, and Optimal Capital Structure: Comment', *Journal of Finance*, Vol 34, pages 247–251.

R Stulz and H Johnson, 1985, 'An Analysis of Secured Debt', *Journal of Financial Economics*, Vol 14, pages 501–521.

A Sweigh, 1993, 'Why the Equipment Lessor Will Usually Fare Well in the Bankruptcy of the Equipment Lessee', Presented in Conference on New Opportunities in Lease Finance (Institute for International Research, New York).

O Williamson, 1988, 'Corporate Finance and Corporate Governance', *Journal of Finance*, Vol 43 (July), pages 567–591.

[1] This article is based on research funded by the UK Finance & Leasing Association. I am grateful to the FLA both for funding this research and for facilitating many useful discussions with its staff and members on these issues.

[2] The phrase 'agency cost' is used here to describe the costs that arise because there is a separation between the people who own the firm and the people who manage it. Investors suffer a loss of value to the extent that managers choose policies that might not be chosen by investors. Although investors can reduce this loss by monitoring and 'bonding' managers, that is, making sure that the interests of investors and managers are aligned, these activities are themselves costly. Agency costs are the sum of these various costs: monitoring and bonding costs and any residual loss of value. Harris and Raviv (1992), and Fazzarri, Hubbard and Petersen (1988) provide a good review of the impact on company financing of capital market imperfections and of conflicts between managers and investors.

[3] See Myers (1977), Smith and Warner (1979), Myers and Majluf (1984), Stulz and Johnson (1985), Smith and Wakeman (1985) for the development of the key arguments.

[4] In the United States, Barclay and Smith (1995) also report that large firms relied less on leasing than smaller firms.

[5] Indeed, this was anticipated in SSAP 21 itself when it was published.

[6] For example, Miller and Upton (1976); Myers, Dill and Bautista (1976); for a review see Higson (1990).

[7] In the United Kingdom, operating and finance leasing offer tax arbitrage, as does operating leasing in the United States. By contrast in the United Kingdom, hire-purchase contracts (and in the United States capital leases) leave the investment tax allowance with the lessee.

[8] Lasfer and Levis examine the use of leasing over the period 1982 to 1995 amongst UK firms that have accounting data collected in electronic form. They are only able to comment on finance leasing and hire purchase and exclude operating leases.

[9] The leading example of this in the United Kingdom is the work done by Beattie, Edwards and Goodacre at the University of Stirling.

Chapter 3

Risk underwriting

Malcolm Rogers

Introduction

Risk underwriting is the process by which the various risks faced by a lessor are assessed in order to make a decision on whether to provide the requested leasing facility. These risks are not limited to those relating to the lessee's creditworthiness. This chapter looks at the following: the need for risk underwriting; the key elements of assessment of the potential lessee; the other risks that have to be considered in entering into a lease; the typical frauds perpetrated on lessors and preventative measures; the relevance and nature of ongoing monitoring of existing lessees; and the future form of risk underwriting.

The need for risk underwriting

If a lessee defaults on a £1 million lease with a 1 per cent margin and there is no recovery of the outstanding debt, a capital loss of £1 million occurs. This is the equivalent to the annual profit from 100 similar deals as well as the earnings that would have otherwise been achieved on the lost £1 million of capital. On the default of a lease of similar size with a 5 per cent margin, the capital loss is the same, but is equivalent to the annual profit of only 20 similar deals. Thus a higher margin is justified on deals more likely to default.

Although the pricing of a lease is usually undertaken by marketing personnel remote from the risk assessment process, the pricing should reflect the likelihood of default of that lease. There is a right price for every lease, but it is essential that an appropriate assessment is made of risk to find that price. A lessor concentrating on return and ignoring risk is likely to fail through bad debts. One that has an over-cautious approach to risk is likely to fail through lack of new business.

As a general rule, the higher the risk, the higher the return appropriate to justify writing that lease. However, since the capital advanced to a lessee might equally well be placed in a risk-free investment (for example gilts), a reward in excess of that risk-free return is necessary to justify entering into a leasing transaction.

A facility for a major bluechip public company will probably be low risk and that, together with the competitive pressure for the same business, will, in a perfect market, result in a low level of return for a lessor providing a lease to that company (see position A in Exhibit 3.1). A facility for a new company engaged in a speculative venture will be high risk and an appropriately high return will be necessary to justify the higher likelihood of default (see position B).

Exhibit 3.1

The risk/return model

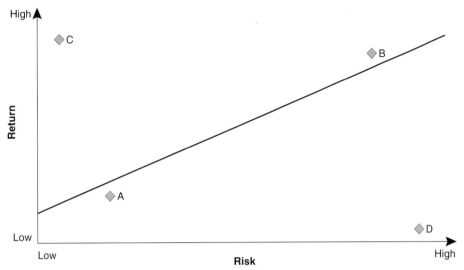

The ideal position for lessors is position C, where risk is low and return is high. Some of the highly-structured lease transactions in the market are attempts to achieve such a position. All lessors should be seeking to avoid low-return, high-risk business (position D). Yet market pressures can, particularly in times where there is little bad debt and low demand for leasing, steer margins towards that unsatisfactory position.

Each facility does not have to have a perfect balance of risk and return, but a lease portfolio as a whole should provide a balance, with individual facilities mapped in a cluster around the upward sloping line in Exhibit 3.1.

Measuring return in numerical terms is easy, whether it be in terms of margin, return on capital or another parameter. The measurement of risk in similar quantitative terms is, however, more difficult. In recent years the concept of expected loss has become established as a potential means of measuring risk in the banking sector and its use has become widespread in the leasing industry. The principle of expected loss is that it is possible to predict with reasonable accuracy the likelihood of a lease defaulting in the future (ie, the probability of default) and the proportion of outstanding debt that will be lost in the event of that default (ie, the loss given default) from historical data on a large portfolio of similar leases. By multiplying these two outputs together an expected loss for a similar lease can be produced and used as a quantitative measure of the risk in entering into that lease. It must be recognised, however, that such an approach requires historical experience of a large portfolio of similar leases and assumes that past experience is a reasonable guide to future lessee performance. This can potentially be a risky assumption.

Some lessors build quantitative measures of believed risk in a transaction into a pricing model to generate an estimated risk-adjusted return on capital (RAROC), particularly at the large-ticket end of the market. This allows potential leases to be compared on a consistent basis and, where there is insufficient capacity to enter into all potential transactions, a decision using RAROC can ensure that only the potentially most remunerative leases net of risk are written.

Risk underwriting is therefore essential to the business of leasing and asset finance. In considering a new lease proposal the risk assessment process can be viewed as consisting of two elements: first lessee assessment and secondly facility assessment. The deliberate order of these two elements is significant. If the lessee is of poor quality there is a strong argument for not providing the facility at all, irrespective of the apparent quality of the lease and its likely return.

Lessee assessment

Introduction

Credit risks are considered at the initial stage of the risk assessment process. The question of whether a prospective lessee can and will meet the lease rentals is critical to underwriting decisions.

The focus of much lessee analysis in the past has often been the lessee's financial statements. However, there is far more to lessee assessment than looking at historic accounting information and attempting to make projections from these in order to forecast potential lessees' ability to meet future rentals. Financial analysis does of course have a role, but it must be as part of a broader assessment of the lessee consisting of business analysis, management analysis and financial analysis.

These categories of analysis are similar to the three Cs – Character, Capability and Capital – often used by lenders as a framework for assessing a borrower, but these categories better illustrate the far-reaching analysis that must be undertaken.

The aspects included in these individual elements of lessee assessment are considered further below. It is important to note that there is a strong interrelationship between them, as illustrated in Exhibit 3.2. A lessee with a good business position and a strong financial condition can still fail through bad management.

Exhibit 3.2

The three aspects of lessee assessment

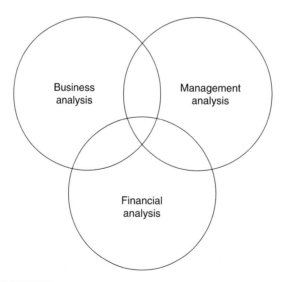

Business analysis

In order to understand a lessee, it is necessary to understand its business. Analysis of this can use a variety of frameworks, but for the analyst to make a reasonable assessment of a potential lessee's future prospects the areas that need to be considered must include:

- history (eg, time in business, past record etc);
- industry (eg, life cycle stage, external influences);
- products (eg, life cycle stage, diversity, substitutes);
- market position (eg, share, reputation, strategy);
- competitors (eg, number, market share, strategy);
- suppliers (eg, number, negotiating power); and
- customers (eg, number, negotiating power).

Assessment of a potential lessee's future business success, and therefore its ability to meet rentals as they fall due, is at least in part conjecture. However, such guesswork is likely to be more accurate where there is a full understanding of the lessee's business environment.

Management analysis

A company is normally only as good as its management. Experience in the late 1980s and early 1990s was that many companies collapsed not because their underlying business was unsound or their financial position poor, but because management wasted opportunities, failed in its responsibilities or even abused its position of trust.

Various checklists have been drawn up by accountants, analysts and others detailing the common features of corporate failures. Among the more obvious features, such as loss of market, these lists regularly include a number of elements relating to management, for example: a combined chairman and chief executive position; an egocentric top manager who regards the company as his own and not the shareholders'; and the lack of a competent finance director. This is not to say that companies with management illustrating these characteristics are certain to fail but that the likelihood of failure is higher. One of the key predictive tools in lessee assessment therefore is an analysis of management since it may take a small amount of bad management to destroy what is otherwise a healthy company. Critical elements of management that need to be considered are:

- the number of executive directors and their age, qualifications, personality and experience;
- the number of non-executive directors and their age, experience and role;
- the frequency and cause of management changes;
- the nature and effectiveness of management information systems;
- the past record in managing the business (measured by both financial and non- financial criteria); and
- the future strategic plans, including nature and planned funding of expansion plans.

Financial analysis

'Audited accounts are like a fine perfume – to be sniffed but not swallowed.'
Abraham Belloff

25

A review of a potential lessee's published financial information has some value in the assessment process, but the limitations of such information must be recognised. Audited accounts are out of date by the time they are produced and in the case of the balance sheet provide only a snap shot of the company's financial position at a particular point in the past. The scope for creative accounting has been reduced in recent years by the revision of some accounting standards, but there remains a need for analysts to understand fully the impact on audited figures of the particular accounting policies used by the potential lessee. This is particularly so where the accounts are drawn up using overseas accounting standards with which the analyst may be less familiar. It must also be remembered that past performance is no guide to the future, and it is usually a worthless exercise to try to project with certainty a lessee's future financial position by extrapolating forward much more than a year or so the past trends in its audited accounts.

As with any financial analysis, it is totally inappropriate to look at one year's figures in isolation. It is essential to look at trends over a number of years and also to compare the potential lessee's figures with its peer group. The best means of making comparisons, both over time and against peers, is to use accounting ratios that translate the actual numbers into a common accounting language (eg, interest cover, profit margin and gearing) to allow proper comparisons to be made. Most lessors have their own version of financial spreadsheets that calculate such ratios and a summary of some of the most commonly used ratios is to be found in the appendix to this chapter. It is important to note that discrepancies or unsatisfactory trends should be the cause for further investigation rather than the reason for outright rejection of a particular lessee. There may well be a good reason for a discrepancy or trend ascertainable from the notes in the audited accounts. This is just one of the reasons why it is necessary to look at the audited accounts in their entirety rather than just the financial statements.

It must be remembered that audited accounts are drawn up by accountants using information provided by the potential lessee, only a sample of which is tested for accuracy. If the audited accounts prove to be incorrect in their content there is no right of recourse for the lessor against the auditors, who are usually only liable for the accuracy of the figures to the party being audited and not to third parties such as lessors.

Potential lessees sometimes provide management figures which are more up-to-date than their audited accounts and these can be of value to the financial analysis provided their limitations are recognised. In particular, such figures have not been audited and may be subject to amendment in due course. Perhaps even greater caution should be exercised in looking at projected financial information provided by a potential lessee. There is an element of guesswork in all projections. The analyst needs to know the assumptions underlying the projections, and should test and assess their reasonableness. Short-term projections are likely to be more accurate than those for longer periods, but all projections need to be treated with care and must not on their own be regarded as evidence of ability to meet future rentals or obligations. Sensitivity analyses can, however, be valuable in testing the lessee's future viability.

Notwithstanding these various caveats, there is considerable value in financial analysis as part of the overall lessee assessment process. Areas of particular value to this part of the assessment process include:

- *profitability*, including sales growth, profit margin trends, debt-servicing capability and dividend policy;

- *balance sheet structure*, including total net assets, liquidity, gearing, debt type and term, reserve movements and off-balance sheet liabilities (identifiable in the notes to the accounts); and
- *cash flow*, including operating cash flow, financing cash flow, investment cash flow and funding cash flow.

Of these, cash flow is often the least analysed. Cash is critical to the ongoing survival of a potential lessee since it is used to meet the lessee's debts, including lease rentals, as they fall due. Ultimately, it is lack of cash that results in lessee insolvency, but it is a symptom rather than a cause of lessee difficulty. Investigation of apparent cash shortages or outflows is valuable in leading the analyst to problems elsewhere in a potential lessee's financial position.

Credit enhancement

Having assessed the ability of a potential lessee to meet rentals as they fall due, a view may be reached that it is likely, but not sufficiently certain, that the rentals will be met throughout the lease term. To overcome this uncertainty, it may be necessary to require some form of credit enhancement. However, this should only be regarded as a means of turning a borderline decision into a definite, positive one. Credit enhancement means exactly what it says; it should not be the reason for entering into a lease with what otherwise would be an unsatisfactory lessee.

Credit enhancement is usually achieved by taking additional security and this can take a variety of forms. The most common form is a guarantee, for example from directors of a small company or an inter-company guarantee to support a weak potential lessee which is part of a large financially sound group. In some cases these guarantees may themselves be supported by additional security such as charges over properties or other assets. The key point to remember, as with all forms of collateral, is that the easiest part is taking the security, the hardest part is realising it. Whilst it is outside the scope of this book to consider the various types of security available and the methods of perfecting and realising such collateral, it is relevant to note that any lessee assessment must also include detailed assessment of the offered security. In the case of guarantees this should be a full analysis of the guarantor's business, management and financial strength to at least the same standard as that performed for the lessee.

Other forms of security offered by potential lessees may include bank guarantees, bank letters of credit or even cash collateral. These particular forms of security can have an additional benefit to the lessee since a lower margin on the lease facility may be agreed by the lessor than would otherwise have been made available. This is because bank owned lessors may be subject to capital adequacy requirements laid down by some central banks in accordance with international banking agreements. A risk-asset weighting is applied to each lease exposure: 1.0 for a corporate risk, 0.2 for an Organisation for Economic Cooperation and Development (OECD) bank-guaranteed risk and 0.0 for a cash-secured or sovereign risk. With return on regulatory capital being a key performance criteria for many banking groups, the lower risk weighting applied to bank- or cash-secured transactions may persuade the lessor to offer a lower margin on the transaction whilst enabling it to achieve an enhanced return on its capital. However, the lessee may incur additional costs in arranging such security (eg, a fee will normally be paid to the provider of a bank guarantee) and this may partially offset the benefit to the lessee from the reduced margin.

This regulatory capital arbitrage has been particularly common in large-ticket transactions, but the planned amendment of the existing capital adequacy rules (laid down in the 1988 Basle Accord) is likely to impact upon this form of credit enhancement. At the time of writing, the new Basle Accord is unlikely to be in place until at least 2006 and it may be 2007 before it is fully effective. Although the final details of the new Accord have yet to be announced (and are expected to be published in 2003), those elements that are known will reduce the risk-asset weighting for good quality corporates and increase the weighting for OECD banks rated single A and lower, thus removing some or all of the benefit previously achievable from regulatory capital arbitrage.

An alternative means of overcoming the marginal nature of some potential lessees for the term of the proposed lease is to include financial covenants or credit rating triggers in the documentation. The principle of these is that they provide a means for the ongoing monitoring of the lessee's creditworthiness using objective criteria which, if breached, enable the lessor to take specific actions to protect properly its position. This may include the right to call for additional security or, in extreme cases, for the lease to be prematurely terminated. There are specific limitations in the use of such covenants or rating trigger clauses in that by the time the lessor is aware of the breach, the lessee may not be in a position to meet the termination sum, but at least the inclusion of such clauses provides the lessor with early notice of potential difficulties.

Credit scoring

In the small- and middle-ticket markets, traditional lessee assessment by experienced underwriters has to a large extent been replaced by automated lessee assessment using credit scoring. Although this brings the benefits of low cost, objectivity and consistency of decision making, it is only appropriate for assessing lessees for which there is a large, comparable population of similar lessees.

Credit scoring uses statistical models to predict the likelihood of future repayment based on the lessor's own previous experience. A scoring model consists of a scorecard and a set of statistical tools for interpreting scores in terms of risk. The scorecard collates certain items of information (or characteristics) about a potential lessee obtained both from the lessee itself and from external sources (such as a credit reference bureau). Each element has a statistically derived score (or weighting) and the scorecard calculates an overall score for the potential lessee. This score is used to predict the likely risk of nonrepayment in the future and is compared against a cut off, at or above which the potential lessee is accepted.

Whilst this description of credit scoring sounds very different from the lessee assessment process discussed above, it is in fact merely an automation of that process. The scorecard characteristics are those pieces of information which indicate the likelihood of the lessee meeting the lease rentals in full. Typical characteristics relate to information such as time in business (an element of business analysis) and size of turnover (part of financial analysis). For smaller businesses, and particularly for start-ups, information about the managers is also used to calculate the lessee score, such as whether they are on the electoral roll at their claimed home address and whether there is negative credit information recorded against them at a credit bureau (management analysis).

Credit scoring has proved its effectiveness, with the bad debt performance of a scored portfolio typically being lower than that of a similar portfolio assessed using traditional manual underwriting. This is attributable to its objectivity, but it does, however, lack the ability to underwrite lessees with unusual circumstances which a scorecard does not assess, for example a start-up run by a person who has long years of relevant experience but who lacks sufficient equity to invest in their new business. It is, therefore, important for a lessor using credit scoring to have a manual underwriting team to review applications which have unusual circumstances or are marginal.

Information

Lessee assessment is, therefore, a thorough analysis of the proposed counterparty(ies), and of any envisaged credit enhancement package, involving the collection and synthesis of a considerable quantity of information and data.

Useful sources of information include:

- the potential lessee;
- competitors of the potential lessee;
- credit-reference agencies;
- press articles;
- trade journals;
- brokers' reports;
- company searches;
- annual report and accounts (for at least the last three years); and
- the internet.

There is now a danger of information overload, particularly as a result of the development of the internet. Today there is far more information available to underwriters, not only on potential lessees, but also upon their market competitors etc than there was 10 years ago. Such information should make an underwriting decision a sounder one, because it is better informed. However, there is a danger that too much information can lead to failure to identify key negative information which would otherwise have resulted in the appropriate decision to decline an application.

The internet has a benefit, however, in its ability to provide information across national borders. The 1990s was a period of globalisation, with international borders losing relevance in many types of business. There remain some national rules that affect the provision of cross-border financial services, but the internet nevertheless allows a lessor in one country to obtain information quickly and cheaply on, for example, a potential lessee's operations in another country or on its parent.

Running counter to this greater availability of information has been an increase in data protection and human rights legislation in some countries. Such legislation, whilst sound in its principles of seeking to control the inappropriate use of information about individuals and businesses, can be a potential threat to sound risk underwriting if it also prevents appropriate use of such information.

Summary

In undertaking the assessment of a potential lessee there is a need to know the customer; to understand its present and future business direction, its management's abilities and strategy, and its financial strength. Once satisfied from this assessment that the potential lessee is in a sound condition it is possible to move on to the facility assessment.

Facility assessment

Introduction

Having assessed the creditworthiness of the lessee, the other risks which the lessor may face in entering into the proposed lease still need to be assessed. Many of these risks are common to any lease facility, but there are some which will be specific to particular lease structures.

Ownership risks

As the legal owner of the leased asset, there are certain risks that can arise for the lessor:

Ineffective title

In entering into a lease, a lessor believes it has good title to the leased assets and indeed usually needs to have such title if tax allowances are to be obtained. However, a lessor cannot get better title than that of the supplier of a particular asset. For example, if a supplier has delivered equipment to a lessee before paying the original manufacturer and then goes into receivership, the manufacturer may be able to repossess the asset notwithstanding that the lessor has already paid the supplier. This position could escalate if the lessor has given the lessee the right to quiet possession, in which case the lessee may have a right of action against the lessor if the manufacturer attempts any action to repossess the leased asset.

It is crucial for a lessor to be satisfied that it has effective title and it may well be appropriate to undertake investigation of the supplier, particularly when new or unknown, and to ensure that any previous owner has also transferred good title. Other circumstances where the lessor may find difficulty in proving title include where equipment is fixed to a building (for example a lift). In these circumstances, it is vital that a waiver of title, generally known as a landlord's waiver, is obtained from the landlord or any debenture holders.

Supplier non-performance

A lessor will normally seek to avoid any implied warranties regarding merchantability or fitness for purpose of the leased equipment, and to establish clearly that the equipment was selected by the lessee. This is intended to remove the lessor from any obligation in the event that there has been misrepresentation of the capabilities of the equipment by the supplier, or if the equipment fails to perform to the expected or agreed standard. The lessor will also wish to remove itself from any difficulties or defects under any of the guarantee or maintenance obligations of the supplier. It is, however, quite normal for the lessee to receive the benefits of any manufacturer's warranties made to the lessor as owner of the asset.

This protection against various types of supplier non-performance is normally achieved through appropriate clauses in the lease documentation. This does not always, however, prevent a lessee from being unwilling to pay rentals as they fall due on unsatisfactory equipment in the event of a supplier failing to meet its obligations. This can lead to the lessor being drawn into bitter disputes which may present expensive and time-consuming customer management opportunities!

A lessor must therefore assess the level of supplier risk in any particular transaction and it may be appropriate to investigate the strength of the supplier to be satisfied that the likelihood of their non performance is remote.

Asset loss

In the event that the leased asset is lost, stolen or destroyed, the lessor will need to ensure that the outstanding sum due under the lease is repaid. This will normally be achieved by including in the documentation a specific requirement for the lessee to take out appropriate insurance. The extent to which the lessor vets such insurance on inception of the lease, and on a regular basis thereafter, will vary with the amount at risk and the perceived standing of the lessee. It may be considered appropriate for the lessor to be named as joint insured or at least to have its interest noted on the policy. Where a lessee seeks to self-insure part or all of the risk, or there is a large excess on the policy, the lessor must give serious consideration to the level of additional financial risk being borne by the lessee and therefore by the lessor.

Some lessors take out their own insurance to cover all their leased assets as an additional protection against the risk of loss of assets.

Third-party liability

As owner of the asset, a lessor can in theory find itself facing claims from third parties in the event of the asset causing damage or injury (eg, a worker injured by a piece of leased machinery). It is normal for the lessor to protect itself from such claims through specific lease documentation including indemnification by the lessee and by requiring the lessee to take out adequate third-party liability insurance cover. The lessor must consider any levels of excess on such policies and, of course, the extent of any self-insurance. In most circumstances the lessor will wish to be named as joint insured on the lessee's insurance policy.

The risks faced by lessors under third-party liability claims are real and could be substantial depending on the circumstances, for example, if a leased aircraft crashes in the middle of a major US city or a lathe operator is maimed or killed by faulty machinery. The lessor must review and be satisfied with the level of insurance cover obtained by the lessor and in addition may consider it appropriate to arrange its own contingent third-party insurance in respect of assets such as aircraft and ships. Such insurance protects the lessor in the event that the lessee's insurance proves to be insufficient to meet all claims or proves to be invalid in some way.

The deep pocket syndrome is a risk for every lessor almost irrespective of the type of asset being financed. The lessor or affiliated bank or group may in most cases be financially stronger than the lessee and will be a natural target for carefully aimed claims from injured parties. Whilst distancing itself as far as possible from any third-party claims, the lessor may nevertheless find itself involved in lengthy legal defences. In the event that it pays any third-party damages, it will have the right to recover the amount involved from the lessee through indemnities in the lease documentation. This of course relies upon the lessee being able to meet any such claims upon it.

Environmental liabilities

The risk of lessors being found liable for damage to the environment caused by leased assets has come into sharper focus in recent years. Many countries have introduced legislation intended to make the polluter pay for the damage caused. For the lessor this can have a direct and an indirect impact. As owner of the equipment the lessor could be required by regulatory authorities to meet the clean-up costs. The lessee would undoubtedly be called upon to reimburse the lessor via its indemnity in the lease documentation. Alternatively, the lessee might be required to meet any clean-up costs. In either case, the amount could be substantial and the capability of the lessee to meet such costs must be considered. The risks for the lessor in these circumstances are similar to those stated in the insurance section above. The likelihood of a particular leased asset leading to environmental liabilities for the lessee or lessor must be incorporated into the risk appraisal process in the appropriate circumstances. By way of example, a leased oil tanker or chemicals plant would have far greater environmental risks and potential clean-up costs than office furniture.

The whole area of environmental liabilities, regulation and monitoring, and the respective obligations that could fall on manufacturers, owners and operators, is still developing. For example, new European Union directives came into force in early 2002 on the disposal of refrigerators and freezers and waste electrical and electronic equipment. Whether an asset is provided on a finance lease or an operating lease, there is always the potential for it to be returned to the lessor at the end of the lease term. In the case of the directive on waste electrical and electronic equipment, it is stated that the manufacturer is ultimately responsible for the cost of such disposal, but the lessor will, as part of its risk assessment, need to consider whether the manufacturer is likely to be around to meet that obligation at the end of the lease, failing which it might have to meet that cost itself.

Lessors should continue to monitor developments on environmental matters very closely. The position in Japan, mentioned in Chapter 20, is perhaps an indication of policy direction in this area.

Reputational risk

Within its assessment of environmental risk, a lessor should give consideration to any reputational issues that may arise if its ownership was to become public knowledge. For example, a lessor might not welcome the negative publicity surrounding its ownership of equipment used for armament manufacture or experimentation on animals. Some lessors have lists of specific assets that they are simply not prepared to lease, but for every proposed lease facility the nature of the equipment and the potential for a negative reputational risk issue to arise should be considered.

Another form of reputational risk that a lessor should consider is whether it wishes to be involved in a proposed transaction which appears to have an unnecessarily complex structure and could have negative publicity implications were the lessee to collapse. Whilst there can be many legitimate reasons for such structures, and the use of offshore special purpose vehicles is common in the big-ticket sector, the collapse of Enron in 2002 has caused some lessors to question whether they wish to be involved in such structures where they do not understand the full circumstances underpinning their use or application. As a minimum, many lessors are asking for much more information about the need for, and nature of, such structures.

Contingent risks

These are additional and often unquantifiable risks associated with the provision of a lease facility. They may not be apparent at the time of the initial risk assessment, but nevertheless need to be considered.

Funding risks

A lease may be provided on a variable- or fixed-rate basis. When it is on a fixed-rate basis, the most conservative arrangement is to have fixed funding that exactly matches the profile of the lease. This may be possible on big-ticket leases, but on a portfolio of small-ticket transactions, the achievement of perfectly matched funding presents great difficulties and can generate significant costs.

Borrowing at variable rates whilst providing leases at fixed rates (ie, borrowing short to lend long) is the least conservative form of funding and can lead to losses for a lessor when funding costs rise during the lease term. However, having a perfectly matched fixed-rate book also has risks. If a lessee default leads to early lease termination, and it is not possible to find a profitable alternative use for the funding as a result of interest-rate movements since the lease's inception, breakage costs on the interest-rate swap can be penal. Interest rates may have moved in a beneficial direction for the lessor, providing an additional and unexpected benefit, but a lessor needs to consider whether interest-rate speculation is part of its core business.

Lessors generally expect any fixed-funding break costs to be met by the lessee and the lease documentation will state this to be the case, with the lessee equally being entitled to any break benefits. If the costs arise, however, because the lessee has defaulted through insolvency, the lessee may be unable to meet the lease termination sum irrespective of any funding break costs. As the quantum of this contingent risk cannot be assessed at the lease inception, because the future level of interest rates cannot be accurately predicted, lessors use various formulae to estimate the possible risk if interest rates were to move in the wrong direction. The ability of the lessee to meet the assessed funding contingent risk is then incorporated into the risk underwriting process.

Other causes of funding mismatches can include equipment upgrades, refinancings and agreed early terminations. A lessor therefore has to establish a maturity profile of its assets which is going to be no more than a best estimate of its funding requirements and accept that there is always going to be a funding mismatch risk. The level of such risk that the lessor is prepared to accept on its portfolio forms a key part of its operational strategy.

In addition to funding mismatch risks, there are also potential difficulties with variable-rate leases if subsequent higher money costs incurred by the lessor, and reflected in higher rentals, cannot be met by the lessee. This is also an unquantifiable risk, but one that needs careful consideration in the risk appraisal process. A view may be taken that the lessee can meet the initial rentals, but could it continue to do so if interest rates doubled? The provision of a fixed-rate lease is an obvious way of removing this risk but, as discussed above, it can introduce equally concerning risks.

A further funding risk, but this time focusing on the lessor, is whether the lessor is able to access the necessary funding required to finance a lease throughout its entire term. This liquidity risk obviously increases in proportion to the length of the proposed lease and the financial stability of the lessor. Even where the lessor is able to continue to raise the necessary funding, the cost of money may rise, reducing the profitability of the underlying lease if the additional financial costs cannot be passed on. Some lessees therefore have an equal interest in the strength of the lessor as the lessor has in the lessee.

Tax risks

When evaluating a lease, lessors make assumptions about prevailing tax rates and the value of capital allowances. Subsequent changes in these key factors of tax-based leasing may affect the profitability of the lease unless the rentals paid by the lessee are capable of variation to preserve the lessor's after-tax margin.

Some lessors enter into leases in which they agree to bear the costs of any tax changes, particularly where they operate in a high-tax-rate regime and believe rates will fall. In such situations, unchanged rentals will bring additional profit to a lessor. In big-ticket deals a tax rate rise in the initial period enhances the value of the capital allowances (until they are exhausted), which will offset the rise in tax payable on the rental income and can bring enhanced profitability during this period.

Most leases, however, fully incorporate variable rentals for the lessee, but this assumes that the variable rental amount can be met by the lessee. A prudent lessor will carry out a sensitivity analysis to establish the level of possible increased risk on the lessee.

Beyond a change of tax rate or level of capital allowance, there is also the risk of a significant change in the tax regime, such as the removal of capital allowances for certain types of assets or a transfer of entitlement to such allowances from the lessor to the lessee. Most big-ticket lease documentation incorporates clauses to allow the lease to be terminated in such circumstances, but once again an assumption is made that the lessee is in a position to meet the necessary termination sum. This is another factor for consideration in the underwriting process.

One tax risk for which the lessee is not normally responsible is the lack of sufficient taxable profits against which the lessor can set off the capital allowances that arise from ownership of the leased equipment. It is the lessor's responsibility to monitor its level of tax capacity and ensure that it does not become overcommitted. This, however, is not an exact science, as evidenced by the loss of tax capacity and subsequent withdrawal from the market of many very experienced UK bank-owned leasing companies in the early 1990s.

Political risk

An area of contingent risk which has become more pertinent in recent years is that arising from political actions. As governments focus more on competitive tendering and the outsourcing of services previously provided by the public sector, there are implications for lessors that have provided lease facilities to public sector entities on the basis that they constituted sovereign risk. A transfer of the lessee from the public sector to the private sector by way of statute (statutory novation) or other means may lead to a change in the perceived standing of the lessee. In these circumstances it is often not possible for the lessor to adjust the lease pricing to reflect the increased risk. This has an additional impact on the lessor's return where the underlying risk-asset weighting changes from 0.0 for a sovereign risk to 1.0 for a corporate risk. This additional area of risk has to be considered therefore as part of the underwriting process.

This issue of political risk has become particularly relevant in the United Kingdom with the government's placing of Railtrack, the privatised company responsible for the UK rail infrastructure, in administration in 2001. This created a lack of confidence in the government's commitment to the Public Private Partnership (PPP), with significant potential implications for the future funding of PPP projects. Whilst documentation can be produced which appears to protect lessors against government intervention, subsequent parliamentary legislation can negate that protection. It is therefore important for the risk assessment of such transactions to include a review of the political risk and what, if any, protection is available.

Residual risk

In the case of an operating lease rather than a finance lease, the lessor is likely to be as reliant upon the future value of the leased asset for its profit as the lessee's ability to pay the lease rentals. Indeed, if a lessor significantly overestimates a future value in setting the level of operating lease rentals, it may lose an element of its initial capital expenditure. Those lessors who provide operating leases therefore have a significant additional area of risk to appraise as part of the facility assessment.

Operating leasing is covered in detail in Chapter 16 in this book, but, as part of an introduction to the topic under the heading of risk underwriting, the following brief comments are offered.

In assessing a prudent residual value, the lessor must obtain detailed information on the particular asset to be leased. In particular used prices, technological developments (which may cause obsolescence) and future expected supply and demand trends should be considered. In many cases, a lessor will use third-party information, such as trade publications and specialist equipment valuers, to assess an appropriate residual value. For some assets, such as cars and aircraft, information is relatively easy to obtain. On other assets, such as a unique high-value production line, predicted future value information may not be available and the lessor is forced to make little more than an educated guess. On such assets, it is sometimes possible to agree with the lessee a sharing of any subsequent realised loss.

Another means of mitigating the asset risk is to arrange for the manufacturer or a third party to agree a price at which the equipment will be purchased from the lessor at a fixed future date, perhaps through a put arrangement. Whilst this removes the residual risk from the lessor, there is a need to consider whether the asset purchaser has a sufficiently strong covenant for what is effectively a lump sum future commitment which may be of considerable size. The appraisal of that third party may need to be as thorough as that for the lessee itself.

Portfolio risk

Beyond the consideration of a proposed lease facility in isolation, there is also a need to consider its impact upon the overall lease portfolio. A diverse portfolio will be spread in a number of ways, including:

- by customer;
- by leased-asset type;
- by lessee industry;
- by facility term; and
- by funding (fixed versus variable).

A portfolio which includes one major lessee or exposure to only one industry is clearly more risky than one which is diverse in its content. A lessor with a total portfolio of, for example, £50 million should, therefore, consider carefully the wisdom of agreeing a new £100 million lease with a new lessee even though the lessee and facility assessments have both reached positive conclusions. Ideally a lessor should have ongoing guidelines on the required diversity of its portfolio for staff marketing lease facilities to potential lessees. It should be for the risk underwriting function, working independently but in harmony with the marketing team, to monitor the spread of the portfolio and recommend changes to such guidance as appropriate.

Dynamic portfolio management is sometimes used to manage existing portfolio risk. Where an institution is uncomfortable with the risk structure of its portfolio, it is possible to transfer existing credit risk out, or new credit risk in, through the use of credit derivatives, securitisation and other techniques. Such portfolio management may become more common as the impact of the new Basle Accord upon regulatory capital requirements for financial institutions is implemented and fully appreciated.

Fraud

Surveys undertaken in the United Kingdom in 1991 and 1996 by the Finance & Leasing Association (FLA) found that most of its members had suffered losses through fraud in the five years before each survey. It was particularly significant that the surveys highlighted a rapid increase in the incidence of fraud when the UK economy was in recession. This suggested that potential lessees struggling to survive were more likely to attempt to defraud lessors and that some existing well-intentioned lessees might sacrifice their honesty to save their businesses.

Fraud is perpetrated by lessees on the vast majority of leasing companies although many lessors are reluctant to admit the level to which they have been affected. Risk underwriting should give due consideration to the possibility of fraud and appropriate enquiries made before lease inception are undoubtedly the best protection.

Types of fraud

The most common forms of fraud committed against leasing companies are listed below.

- *Provision of false information on lessee creditworthiness.* Incorrect financial and other information, together with false references, can be used to induce a lessor to provide a lease, particularly when the sources of independent information on a potential lessee are limited.
- *Non-existent assets.* A lessor may be persuaded by a lessee to provide a facility for an asset that does not and never will exist. This may involve collusion on the part of the lessee with an apparent supplier of the asset, with the benefits of the fraud being shared between them. Methods of undertaking this fraud include the provision of forged documentation such as a supplier's invoice.
- *Inflated pricing of assets.* Again, the supplier may be involved when a lessor is induced to provide a lease for a sum substantially in excess of the value of the underlying leased asset. An invoice from the supplier showing an inflated price can be used and the benefits again shared between the supplier and the lessee. Alternatively, in a sale and lease-back transaction, the lessee may forge or alter the supplier's invoice to mislead the lessor.
- *Multi-funding of assets.* Obtaining lease finance for the same piece of equipment from more than one lessor is a particularly common fraud. Such multi-funding is not necessarily limited to just two or three lessors and examples of more than ten lessors each believing they were leasing the same piece of equipment are known. Again the provision of false documentation is a common means of committing such a fraud, with the sale and lease-back of equipment already owned by another lessor also being used. With colour photocopiers and ever-improving information technology, it is becoming easier to mislead lessors into believing that they have taken possession of the original documents of title.

- *Unauthorised disposal of assets.* Perhaps the easiest form of fraud to commit, a lessee may simply sell the leased asset to an unsuspecting third party and retain the cash.

In many cases the fraudulent lessee does not disappear once the fraud has been committed. In order to avoid arousing lessor suspicions the lease rentals have to be met and this usually involves committing further frauds to raise the required cash. Once the initial fraud has been undertaken, the lessee is caught in a spiral of escalating fraud which is only discovered when the lessee is unable to raise new lease funding from which to service existing lease rentals.

Preventative measures

Lessors take various measures to try to reduce fraud, but the amount of due diligence invested, and the effectiveness of such measures, varies widely. The measures below include some of those that can be used.

- *Verification of lessee information.* Checking the information provided by the lessee with objective sources or conducting reality checks against information from similar lessees can be useful. Credit-referencing agencies are of valuable assistance, particularly where their records include details of past frauds which other lenders have reported.
- *Checking the price paid for the leased asset with independent sources.* This avoids paying inflated prices for assets and is a simple and effective fraud-prevention measure. For some lessors it is possible to verify the price by reference to amounts paid for similar assets leased to other lessees in their portfolios.
- *Researching the supplier.* This is a useful measure as a means of preventing non-existent assets or inflated pricing frauds. Thorough research of new or unknown suppliers is important, but can be costly. Building a long-term relationship with suppliers can be valuable to avoid such frauds and also provide useful new business opportunities.
- *Inspecting the leased asset on delivery.* This should avoid the non-existent asset fraud, but its effectiveness depends on the ability of the inspector to recognise the particular asset involved. For specialist equipment, a third party may be required to confirm that the appropriate equipment has been delivered.
- *Auditing the asset throughout the lease term.* This is a good measure to take as a means of preventing unauthorised disposal. Some lessors also view it as a useful protection against multi-funding, but how do they know that their visit to see the asset is not to be repeated by another lessor the following day?
- *Labelling or plating the asset.* Attaching plastic labels or metal plates can be a useful measure against multi-funding, provided all lessors do it. If one lessor does not do so, the work of other lessors may be wasted. Periodic checks to ensure that the labels or plates are still attached are also important.
- *Registering the lessor's title on a central register.* Where available, a register can provide strong protection against multi-funding and unauthorised disposal of leased assets. However, such a register requires that each asset has a unique identifier and as a result the only significant registers helping the leasing industry have tended to be those for vehicles and aircraft etc. As with labelling and plating, the failure of only one lessor to use the register can undermine all the registration efforts made by other lessors.

However, the most effective protection against fraud is to follow the classic banking maxim of knowing your customer. This is consistent with the regulatory obligations upon financial institutions in many countries to prevent money laundering. A key measure in combatting money laundering is obtaining evidence of identification at the outset of the customer relationship and the Guidance Notes for the UK Financial Sector issued by the Joint Money Laundering Steering Group provide valuable assistance to lessors on what constitutes adequate identification. Following these guidelines will help to minimise fraud.

A determined fraudster will find means of circumventing some or even all of the measures listed above, but experience shows that it is those lessors who do not take sufficient steps to minimise the risk who are the most likely targets of successful fraud. There is, of course, no substitute for a thorough investigation of the lessee's standing as part of the full risk underwriting process since any fraud on a lessor is likely to involve the collusion of the lessee. Lessee frauds not involving suppliers are common but supplier frauds without lessee involvement are rare. This level of enquiry should therefore be extended to the leased-asset supplier and any other third parties in the transaction (including any broker) if a lessor has the slightest suspicion about any part of the transaction.

Whilst there is undoubtedly a high embarrassment factor amongst lessors who have suffered fraud where their inhouse routines leave something to be desired, it would benefit all lessors if there was greater openness within the industry on this problem. It may be that the number of successful fraudsters is small but the quantum of lost profit is substantial.

Ongoing monitoring

The reader may be forgiven for thinking that having undertaken a thorough risk underwriting process, the role of the underwriter is complete, particularly as the provision of a lease is a term commitment by a lessor only capable of being broken in the event of a default by the lessee. However, there is a need to continue to monitor the standing of lessees if any potential future loss is to be minimised. Whilst a deterioration in a lessee's covenant may not allow a lessor to terminate a lease and demand early repayment (in the absence of credit-rating triggers or other financial covenants), by being aware of the lessee's deterioration, the lessor will be in a better position to act if a default event does subsequently occur. For example, an asset audit or asset labelling may enable a lessor to act quickly to recover its asset when the default occurs.

Some lessors operate a watch system on potentially troublesome lessees which may involve the lessor in simply locating the documentation and rehearsing default and termination procedures for the transaction internally. In particularly concerning cases, the lessor may provisionally book asset recovery agents and have lessor ownership name plates made so that it is ready to act immediately if the occasion arises.

The levels of monitoring undertaken will depend on the level of perceived risk with the lessee, but forms of monitoring should include those listed below.

- *Periodic meetings with the lessee.* These should be at the lessee's premises, providing an anti-fraud measure as well as being better suited to judge the ongoing performance of the lessee. A walk around an empty factory or full stock room is far more revealing than having the lessee coming to the lessor to provide a briefing on their business.

38

- *Scrutiny of rental arrears.* Regular arrears can trigger concern about shortage of ca
  the lessee. Deteriorating punctuality of rental payments and sudden nonpayment ar
  important clues that further enquiry is justified.
- *Review of audited accounts.* Out of date as they are, audited accounts are an important
  source of information on the lessee's progress.
- *Press comment.* Although such comment is rare for the smallest lessees, regular checks of
  the press, both general and trade, can be of great value in tracking the lessee's own performance and also the state of the industry in which they operate.
- *Sector monitoring.* It was commented earlier that initial lessee assessment should involve
  research of the sector in which the lessee operates. Ongoing monitoring of that sector
  throughout the lease term is valuable in identifying potential problems, often before the
  lessee is aware of them. Published information is one source, but there is also value in talking to the lessee's competitors where possible.

The future of risk underwriting

In the few years since the last edition of this book was published, there have been several significant trends in risk underwriting in leasing. These include:

- increased automation through the use of credit scoring;
- wider lessee information availability through the use of the internet;
- increased cross-border lease underwriting as a result of greater globalisation of the leasing
  industry; and
- greater analysis of residual risk, necessary to support the growth of operating leasing's
  share of the total leasing market.

Risk underwriting has become more challenging, notwithstanding the increased use of
automation. Credit scoring has enabled the specialist skills of the lease underwriter to be
focused on the more interesting lease proposals, for example, in the big-ticket market, or
where the decision is marginal.

The trends above are likely to continue and automation will extend ever further into the
underwriting process. The challenge for experienced underwriters will be to re-focus on those
areas where credit scoring is not effective and on the management of credit scoring itself.

Summary

This chapter illustrates that risk underwriting is essential to the business of leasing and
involves a thorough analysis of both the intended lessee and the proposed facility itself.
Ongoing monitoring of the lessee has value notwithstanding the term nature of a lease commitment; it also has some welcome new business connotations as well. In tackling fraud the
old adage, 'prevention is better than cure', has no better application and is best achieved by
completing a thorough assessment of the lessee before commitment. Other steps may also be
appropriate to reduce the risk of a lessor being exposed to an initially sound lessee that subsequently becomes fraudulent. Complacency is the greatest risk in the risk business; vigilance
and careful thought are the greatest weapons.

By this time readers may well think that the risk underwriter's main role is business prevention: many new business developers certainly believe this. This is not the case. Good risk appraisal processes will help lessors avoid entering into leases where bad debts arise and will identify what would otherwise be a lost opportunity to do good quality business with a lessee that looks unsatisfactory on a more superficial assessment. The best risk underwriters are those who help their marketing colleagues by not just rejecting a lease proposal but explaining why it is unacceptable and what could be done to structure it so that it becomes an acceptable risk.

Managing an ongoing portfolio enables a dynamic risk team to assess the overall balance of the company's business and can help direct the marketing and sales teams towards countercyclical, infill or complementary business sectors to maintain profitable growth. The high demands of current business performance on the entire company means that individual functions, whether they be risk, finance, sales or marketing, need to work together and be focused on the same goal. Each team has its own particular specialism but should not have different goals; their effort is dissipated if they do not focus on the same company objectives and work together towards one definition of success. There is no room for intra-company or inter-function rivalry in today's tough business world. Only cohesion, focus and attention to detail will deliver the main prize of profitable and sustainable growth. The risk team can and must make a valuable contribution towards achievement of this aim.

Annex

Accounting ratios used for financial analysis

The following list is not exhaustive, but provides definitions of some of the most commonly used financial ratios. There are, however, a number of variations on these definitions used by different lessors.

Profitability

Gross profit margin (%)

$$\frac{\text{Gross profit}}{\text{Turnover}} \times \frac{100}{1}$$

Net profit margin (%)

$$\frac{\text{Net profit}}{\text{Turnover}} \times \frac{100}{1}$$

Working capital

Stock turn (days)

$$\frac{\text{Stock}}{\text{Turnover}} \times \frac{365}{1}$$

Debtor turn (days)

$$\frac{\text{Debtors}}{\text{Turnover}} \times \frac{365}{1}$$

Creditor turn (days)

$$\frac{\text{Creditors}}{\text{Turnover}} \times \frac{365}{1}$$

Liquidity

Current ratio

$$\frac{\text{Current assets}}{\text{Current liabilities}}$$

Acid test

$$\frac{\text{Current assets - Stock}}{\text{Current liabilities}}$$

Debt capability

Interest cover

$$\frac{\text{Operating profit}}{\text{Interest paid}}$$

Gross gearing

$$\frac{\text{Debt}}{\text{Net assets}}$$

Net gearing

$$\frac{\text{Debt - Cash}}{\text{Net assets}}$$

Chapter 4

The Basle Proposal on Capital Adequacy: how the Basle requirements for banks will affect asset-finance businesses

Sally Williams, Richard Smith and Stephen Potts

Introduction

At first sight the Basle Capital Accord[1] might not appear to be of great relevance to asset-finance firms since it is primarily aimed at large international banks. However, the indirect impact of this accord could be considerable and this subject warrants significant scrutiny by asset-finance executives. At the moment it is unclear whether asset-finance firms will be net winners or losers following the implementation of the accord and related new European Union (EU) directives. However, between the imminent changes in local regulations and these new proposals, it is certain to be a challenging time.

In the EU, the capital requirements of asset-finance firms – whether they are banks or part of a financial services group subject to regulation – are currently driven by the Own Funds and Solvency Ratio Directives, which are in turn modelled on the standards set by the Basle Committee. The European Commission's decision to amend its capital adequacy framework in line with the proposals in the Basle Capital Accord will mean that all EU credit institutions, including asset-finance firms, will effectively be subject to Basle-like rules. Thus, from 2006, it is anticipated that all EU asset-finance firms, like internationally active banks, will be required to meet the proposed Basle standards. Therefore changes to these directives will apply to even the smallest EU asset-finance firms, including EU-based asset-finance firms that are subsidiaries of US and non-EU financial institutions where these are banks or part of financial services groups.

Background to changes proposed by the Basle Committee

The Basle Committee's proposals constitute a root and branch reform of the 1988 Capital Accord, the main objective being to make regulatory capital more risk sensitive. The January 2001 consultation paper alone ran to more than 500 pages, and numerous supplementary papers have since been added. The Committee has also published an excellent overview of the proposals.[2] However, in order to gain a proper understanding of their far reaching nature, the full document, together with supplementary papers, must be read. This chapter attempts to identify the key implications for asset-finance firms, rather than to attempt to summarise the work of the Committee in a few pages.

Once finalised, the accord will apply to all major banks (and their asset-finance subsidiaries) in the G10 countries and it is likely that regulators in many other territories will adopt it; indeed market forces are likely to ensure that the new requirements become *de facto* required practice. As noted above, the impact in the EU will be more widely felt as the European Commission has stated its intention to apply the accord to all credit institutions (authorised under the banking directives) as well as investment businesses (authorised under the Investment Services Directive).

The current intention is to finalise the accord in 2003 and to pass the related EU directives in time to allow parallel running of the old and new accords to start in 2006. This may seem a long way off, but there is significant work to be done to ensure that firms are in a position to meet these deadlines. As a result, large international banks all over the world and EU based credit and investment businesses are busy establishing Basle projects to ensure that they adequately interpret and apply the proposed new capital requirements in order to minimise the new regulatory capital that they will need.

The main areas of change

The key differences between the new and the old accord are summarised in Exhibit 4.1.

The proposals on operational risk represent the most innovative change to the original 1988 accord. This is because the Basle Committee has noted the increasing evidence that operational risk is growing. The Committee noted that this is in part due to the factors listed below.

- A greater reliance placed on globally integrated systems and the use of more highly automated technology, where not controlled, has the potential to transform risks arising from manual processing errors into system failure risks.
- The growth of e-commerce, which brings with it potential risks (eg, external fraud and system security issues) that may not yet be fully understood.
- Large-scale mergers, de-mergers and consolidations, which test the viability of new or newly integrated systems and have resulted in a number of significant problems at financial services firms.
- The emergence of banks acting as very large-volume service providers; which creates a greater need for continual maintenance of high-grade internal controls and back-up systems.

Exhibit 4.1

Changes in the new accord

1988 accord	*New accord*
Focuses on a single risk measure to quantify capital adequacy	More emphasis on firms' internal methodologies, supervisory reviews and market discipline (ie, disclosure)
One size fits all	Flexibility, menu of approaches, capital incentives for good risk management
Broad brush approach with no explicit charge for operational risk	Increased risk sensitivity and the introduction of an explicit charge for operational risk

- The increase in the use of risk mitigation techniques, for example, collateral, credit derivatives and asset securitisations, which optimise exposure to market risk and credit risk, but may in turn produce other forms of risk.
- The growing use of outsourcing arrangements and the participation in third-party run clearing systems, which can mitigate some risk, but can also present significant other risks to financial services firms.

The 1988 Basle accord implicitly covered these and other operational risks in the capital buffer for credit risk. However the proposals for the revised accord will take explicit account of operational risk, especially in the context of a greatly amended and refined approach to credit risk.

Overview of the new requirements

As noted above, the Basle Committee's primary objective is to make regulatory capital more risk sensitive. The current proposals intend to achieve this by, amongst other things:

- introducing a menu of increasingly sophisticated approaches for calculating minimum capital requirements;
- increasing board-level and senior management focus on risk management;
- embedding sound risk management principles into credit and operational processes;
- raising the standards for credit and operational risk reporting;

Exhibit 4.2

Basle's three pillar model

Pillar I	*Minimum capital requirements for all risks* Capital is calculated based on the firm's selected measurement approach.
Pillar II	*Supervisory review* Supervisory evaluation of how well firms are assessing their capital needs relative to their risks. This includes the need to demonstrate to supervisors that the firm has a governance structure, infrastructure and processes to manage the risks inherent in the business. It also includes the collection of data on loss experiences to meet regulatory requirements. In respect of operational risk in particular, this process will be used to establish whether firms have met the qualifying criteria to progress to the more sophisticated approaches. In addition, supervisors will assess how well the supervisory model used to calculate the minimum capital requirements under Pillar 1 actually reflects the risk profile of the firm. These processes may result in additional capital charges for firms where risk management is considered to be inadequate, or where the capital buffer calculated under Pillar 1 is for any reason considered to be inadequate.
Pillar III	*Disclosure* Disclosure requirements include the capital charge, as well as the governance, control structures and processes.

- increasing the emphasis on firms' own economic capital calculations; and
- raising the requirements of internal audits.

Both the Basle and the related EU proposals plan to achieve this by introducing the three pillar model illustrated in Exhibit 4.2.

These proposals introduce significant changes both to credit and operational risk capital charges, which are addressed separately below.

Pillar I: credit risk

The new accord proposes fundamental changes to the identification, management and control of credit risks across those institutions affected. Under the Pillar 1 proposals, asset-finance firms will have three different approaches to credit risk to select from.

As Exhibit 4.3 indicates, these approaches are progressively more sophisticated, rewarding the application of the more sophisticated approaches with lower capital charges.

The standardised approach

The standardised approach is essentially an update of the existing 1988 accord. Under this approach, asset-finance firms will use some standard risk weightings for particular exposures, for example facilities secured by residential lending. They are also free to use ratings ascribed to counterparties by external rating agencies to assign risk weightings to other exposures. There are, however, significant drawbacks to this approach for larger firms. Capital requirements will not be as sensitively aligned to actual risk as measured in the internal ratings based (IRB) approaches. For larger firms, this will result in a higher capital requirement than for those firms using the more sophisticated IRB approaches. In addition, as Basle requires the approach selected to be publicly disclosed, analysts and investors may well view large firms that remain at the most basic level of credit risk management unfavourably.

Exhibit 4.3

Three approaches to credit risk

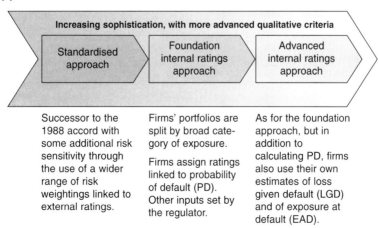

Standardised approach	Foundation internal ratings approach	Advanced internal ratings approach
Successor to the 1988 accord with some additional risk sensitivity through the use of a wider range of risk weightings linked to external ratings.	Firms' portfolios are split by broad category of exposure. Firms assign ratings linked to probability of default (PD). Other inputs set by the regulator.	As for the foundation approach, but in addition to calculating PD, firms also use their own estimates of loss given default (LGD) and of exposure at default (EAD).

Internal ratings based approach

There are two internal ratings based approaches, the foundation and advanced levels, which introduce the most significant element of change to credit capital requirements. For the first time, banks and asset-finance firms using both IRB approaches will be able to use probability of default (PD) information generated by their internal models when calculating their capital requirement. At the foundation level, the additional inputs to the capital charge are: the loss given default (LGD), which accounts for collateral held against facilities, and the exposure at default (EAD), which measures the likely defaulting exposure on undrawn facilities. Both are based on formulae supplied by the regulator. These three components of expected loss (EL), PD, LGD and EAD, are then multiplied to give a risk weighting to the exposure which, at a portfolio level, provides the input into capital requirements.

Asset finance firms that select the advanced IRB approach are instead able to use LGD and EAD based on internal models.

Clearly there are significant benefits in adopting the IRB approaches. First, these approaches are likely to result in a lower capital requirement. Secondly, the implementation of the IRB requirements should generally enhance firms' risk management practices. The downside is that achieving compliance with the IRB approaches is likely to result in significant expense as illustrated in the explanations of PD, LGD and EAD below.

Key credit issues

Probability of default

Robust data histories to validate forward-looking estimates are fundamental to the calculation of PD. The Basle proposals require at least five years of historic default data to calibrate internal models used to generate PD. Many firms have historically not collected this data in the robust format that the accord requires. Changes to internal rating models and risk rating methodologies often mean that firms have incomplete or poor quality data on which to calibrate their PD estimates. At the most basic level, definitions of default often vary between business lines and include subjective criteria which mean that the data collected does not mirror the actual default experience. Models used to generate PD must also be calibrated to relevant data sets and this may not be practicable on some portfolios with very low default experience.

Loss given default

Firms that select the advanced approach are required to calculate their own LGD estimates based on historical experience. The Basle proposals are very prescriptive in this area and stress that the data used must include the true losses associated with a default. This means that not only principal and interest, but also recovery costs, discount effects, funding and other costs must be included. In addition, firms must have an LGD grading system and assign exposures to one of these grades. Many firms face an enormous task in collating this data from their systems, if it is even available at all. Better collateral management, enabling this loss data to be collected in a robust format in the future, is undoubtedly closely correlated with this exercise.

Exposure at default

To calculate accurately EAD, firms must be able to calibrate internal risk-rating models to historical experience. In common with PD and LGD, many firms do not have the data in the format required; many may not have the information at all. To collate the required data, systems need to record facility limits and balances at the time of default and this will present a challenge to firms that have historically not stored this information on defaulted counterparties.

Other requirements

In addition to the requirements for calculating expected losses, there are a number of other areas that firms need to address to ensure compliance with the new accord. For example, management of collateral will need to be enhanced in many firms to enable robust data extraction to identify clustering and correlations, and to ensure the enforceability of collateral in the event of default. Governance frameworks need to be addressed, particularly the structure for reviewing risk rating systems. Management reporting at many levels, including to board and senior management, is a key area of concern in the new accord; the frequency, quality and depth of reporting will need to be reconsidered in many institutions.

How asset finance specifically is affected

The key concern for asset financiers is perhaps collateral management. With the exception of commercial and residential real estate and financial collateral, which is recognised as collateral in all approaches, the benefits of full recognition of a wide range of physical collateral to reduce the estimated loss given default are currently only available to those firms that adopt the advanced approach. However, in November 2001, the Basle Committee published a consultation paper proposing that an even wider range of physical collateral could be recognised to reduce loss given default estimates by 5 per cent to 45 per cent for facilities fully secured by physical collateral. Asset-finance firms could argue that this revision is not enough as loss experience on many asset classes is historically very low. This is an important lobbying issue for asset-finance companies before the accord is finalised. At present, it appears that the proposals are focusing on collateral taken against vanilla corporate lending and not on asset-finance facilities where collateral recognition, evaluation and management is highly developed.

The treatment of small- to medium-sized enterprises (SMEs), and in particular the definition of such enterprises, is an issue that has yet to be fully covered by the new proposals and is still subject to debate between national regulators at the time of writing. Classifying some of these exposures as corporate, whereas in reality they are more akin to retail exposure, would have a serious impact, particularly under the standardised approach. Pricing would almost certainly increase and, in extreme cases, firms may wish to reduce their exposure to the SME sector. There is already some evidence of this approach in Germany where there is an apparent difference in the attitudes of banks and asset-finance companies when it comes to financing SMEs. Asset-finance companies are keen to exploit this difference.

In addition to the above issues, firms must also address the calibration of models that are used to grade asset-finance exposures. The reality of asset finance is that there is often insufficient historic default data to calibrate accurately risk rating models in order to generate an appropriate PD.

Future developments

It is clear that the credit risk proposals, as they stand, will have a significant impact on firms' resources, systems development, and on their fundamental strategies and business objectives. For asset-finance firms in particular, the proposals are currently unclear and perhaps do not adequately account for the unique structure of many asset-finance transactions. The recognition of collateral and historical default experience do not yet appear to have been fully addressed by the existing proposals. The ongoing dialogue between the Basle Committee, national supervisors and asset-finance representatives globally should focus on revisions to the final accord that reflect these concerns.

Pillar I: operational risk

Background

If these proposals on operational risk are fully implemented, all EU incorporated asset-finance firms and non-EU asset-finance firms that are part of internationally active banks will be required to allocate regulatory capital against operational risk.

Before we can consider the nature of the proposed capital requirements for operational risk, it is first necessary to explore what operational risk actually encompasses and how it can be managed. The Basle Committee's definition of operational risk is: 'the risk of loss resulting from inadequate or failed internal processes, people and systems or from external events'. Historically, financial services firms have tended to be acutely aware of the need to manage financial risks such as credit and market risk. Whilst managing operational risks has historically had a lower profile, there have been numerous large and well-publicised operational losses in recent years that have significantly affected financial services firms, hence the increasing focus on operational risk.

The first step for asset-finance firms is therefore to consider how the Basle definition of operational risk can be applied to their businesses. Once this has been determined, firms need to develop operational risk management strategies that reflect their strategic objectives, risk appetite and nature of the operational risks to which they are exposed. Operational risk policies to support these strategies need to be documented. For asset-finance firms, these will typically include policies focusing on the internal controls in respect of transaction processing, documentation risk, third-party risks and related insurance, tax and environmental risks. The details of these policies should take account of the specific nature of the assets which individual firms specialise in financing. For example, the emphasis on environmental risk management policies will be far greater for a firm that specialises in financing assets for commercial oil and gas exploration than it will be for an asset-finance firm specialising in leasing televisions and audio equipment.

In addition, firms should also produce policies in the following broader risk areas:

- product development;
- compliance and regulation;
- information technology;
- change management;
- human resources;
- business continuity planning;
- internal audit;
- legal; and
- outsourcing.

Organisations then need to implement procedures to ensure adherence to these policies. They must also assess and report on operational risk levels within business areas on a regular basis.

The different Pillar I operational risk approaches

Once the definition of operational risk and how it is managed have been explored, the focus needs to be on the requirements of the accord. The proposals include three potential measurement approaches for calculating the capital necessary for operational risk as illustrated in Exhibit 4.4.

As is the case for credit risk, these approaches are progressively more sophisticated, rewarding the application of the more sophisticated approaches with lower capital charges.

Basic indicator approach

The Basic indicator approach is the least sophisticated of the three approaches and has no qualifying criteria (although all firms will have to be able to meet the standards set out in a recent Basle paper on Sound Practices for the Management and Supervision of Operational Risk – see below). Whilst in theory the basic indicator approach is open to all asset-finance firms, those firms that are part of large international banking groups are likely to be expected by their regulators to reach at least the standardised approach. Furthermore, there is a significant downside to this approach since it will almost certainly result in the highest capital charges and the possibility of additional charges under Pillar II.

Standardised approach

The key qualifying criteria for the standardised approach include the need for:

- board and senior management oversight of risk management;
- independent operational risk management and control processes;
- identification of operational risk across the firm and regular reporting of risk data to senior management;

Exhibit 4.4

Three approaches to operational risk

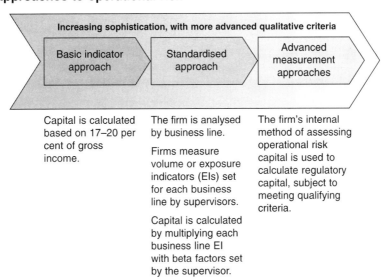

- income streams to be mapped to the standardised business lines;
- defined operational risk appetites;
- adequate supporting data for capital charge calculations; and
- internal audit reviews of risk processes.

These criteria for the standardised approach will represent a significant change for many asset-finance firms. There are undoubtedly many firms that have yet to establish an independent risk function. Of those firms that have passed this hurdle, most recognise that they have significant work to do before they are able to comply with the rest of the standardised criteria. This might include, for example, completing a comprehensive risk assessment exercise and incorporating risk responsibilities within the firm's objectives and job descriptions.

Advanced measurement approaches

The criteria for the advanced measurement approaches (AMA) are even more extensive. These include satisfying the supervisory authority on the following issues:

- the conceptual soundness and integrity of the implementation of risk management systems;
- that risk management systems are closely integrated into the day-to-day risk management processes and can capture low-frequency high-impact operational risk events;
- the sufficiency of staff resources to apply the AMA both in major business lines and in the control and audit areas;
- the use of rigorous analysis of internal and external data in the AMA with a minimum of three years of data history;
- the regular use of scenario analysis; and
- compliance with further qualitative and quantitative standards where firms use internal measurement methodologies.

While a few of the largest banks are undoubtedly targeting attainment of the AMA, they will need to apply significant resources in order to achieve this objective. Given these criteria, one would expect that most asset-finance firms are likely to be targeting the standardised approach unless they are part of a larger group that has a change management and implementation programme in place for the advanced measurement approach.

Pillar I operational risk capital implications for asset-finance firms

As mentioned above, the accord will result in an explicit capital charge for operational risk for the first time. At the simplest, basic indicator level, this charge is calculated as 15 per cent of gross income. Not surprisingly financial institutions have been heavily involved in lobbying against these new capital requirements and a number of concessions have already been made. In particular, until September 2001, the proposal was to allocate 30 per cent of gross income to regulatory capital and in July 2002 a floor limiting the possible available capital reduction under the AMA was removed. Thus it is unlikely that there will be any further significant easing of the calibration of the capital charge.

For firms that progress to the standardised approach and can satisfy their regulator that they have met the related qualifying criteria, the capital charge is arrived at individually for each business line.[3] The capital calculation is similar to that at the basic indicator level using gross income as the exposure indicator. However, based on the information contained in the Bank for International Settlements (BIS) working paper on operational risk,[4] the multiplier, or beta factor, set by the regulator is likely to vary from between 11 per cent to 21 per cent of gross income, depending on the business line.

Firms that qualify for the AMA need to select from a menu of alternative quantification techniques. The key distinguishing feature of these approaches is the greater use of internal data on operational risk losses in addition to some external data. As with the standardised approach, there are also demanding qualitative criteria for firms' operational risk management practices and these must be satisfied before supervisors will allow firms to progress to the AMA.

Pillar II: what the supervisory review entails for asset-finance firms

Under the second pillar of the new accord, supervisors should ensure that each firm has sound internal processes in place to assess the adequacy of its capital based on a thorough evaluation of its risks. Pillar II is regarded as an integral component of the new accord and directly compliments the Pillar I operational risk capital charge. In particular, Pillar II stresses the importance of firms' management developing internal capital assessment processes and setting targets for capital commensurate with their particular risk profile and control environment.

Through Pillar II, supervisors will be responsible for evaluating how well firms are assessing their capital adequacy needs relative to their risks. This includes evaluating whether or not they are appropriately addressing the relationship between the different types of risks. In doing so, supervisors would draw on, among other considerations, their knowledge of best practice across institutions and the minimum criteria attached to approaches to regulatory capital assessment. The key principles against which supervisors will assess firms are set out in the BIS Sound Practices Paper[5] and are summarised below:

Developing an appropriate risk management environment.

Principle 1	Board responsibility for risk strategy and operational risk framework.
Principle 2	Senior management responsibility for implementing risk strategy and developing policies, processes and procedures for managing operational risk.
Principle 3	Appropriate operational risk information and reporting flows to enable senior management monitoring and board oversight.

Risk management – measurement, monitoring and control.

Principle 4	Identification of inherent risks in current and new products, activities, processes and systems.
Principle 5	Establishing processes for measuring operational risk.
Principle 6	Systems for monitoring operational risk exposures and loss events by business line.
Principle 7	Policies, processes and procedures to control or mitigate operational risk.

Role of supervisors.

Principle 8   Supervisory requirements for firms to have an effective system to identify, measure, monitor and control operational risks.

Principle 9   Independent supervisory evaluation of firms' strategies, policies, procedures and practices related to operational risks.

Role of disclosure.

Principle 10   Requirements for public disclosure to allow market participants to assess their operational risk exposures and the quality of operational risk management.

If as part of this supervisory review process firms are able to demonstrate to their supervisors their increased sophistication and precision in management of operational risk, then they should be able to move into one of the more advanced approaches for operational risk. Conversely, in cases where supervisors determine that a firm's operational risk management is either inadequate or ineffective for that firm's specific risk profile, supervisors are likely to require improvements, together with an interim additional capital buffer for operational risk.

It should be noted that supervisory review is an area where local regulators will have considerable discretion, unlike Pillars I and III. Therefore, it is quite possible that different regulators will take different approaches. The issues are also likely to be different for those countries applying Pillar II for the first time than for those who will be modifying a well-established approach to risk based supervision, such as the United Kingdom.

Pillar III: the disclosure implications

The Pillar III disclosure requirements are underpinned by a requirement for boards to develop and implement a disclosure policy covering, amongst other things, information on compliance with the Basle guidelines. This includes the approaches adopted for calculating credit and operational risk capital charges.

It is as yet unclear how much, if at all, these disclosures may influence customers and suppliers of asset-finance firms. Nevertheless, where the asset-finance firm is part of a larger group, more emphasis is likely to be attached to the nature of these disclosures and there may be an expectation that some of the more sophisticated approaches will be applied in order to manage the expectations of customers and investors.

What asset-finance businesses should be doing now

While the implementation of the accord is not now likely until 31 December 2006, systems and process changes will need to be made much sooner. Importantly, the work needed to make these changes will need to be established from 2002 onwards. In addition, operational risk loss data should be available for a period of three years upon implementation day if a sufficient track record is to be available to justify the use of the more sophisticated capital methodologies for operational risk. Similarly, on the credit risk side, retail asset-finance firms will need to have two years worth of historical loss data. They will need to plan the gathering of this loss data by 2004 at the latest. Worse still, asset-finance firms serving corporate clients will need to have been gathering this loss data for seven years! Hence those that do not have this data available from 1999 onwards will not be eligible for the IRB approaches for credit.

Firms should therefore develop an action plan designed to address all of the qualification criteria for their intended Pillar I approaches as well as the key areas of the Pillar II supervisory review.

Some key questions for senior management to address are stated below.

Pillar I
- How much more capital will the business need and how much is this reduced if the more sophisticated approaches are applied?
- How will data availability issues be addressed, particularly in respect of operational and credit loss data?
- Does the firm have the ability to manage appropriately the more detailed requirements in terms of process, data and systems?
- Can the firm refine its credit grading systems to meet the new requirements?
- Is there a sufficient audit trail to stand up to regulatory scrutiny?

Pillar II
- Does the firm have a strategic capital planning and management framework that allows it to relate its level of capitalisation taking into account its risk profile? Is the firm able to demonstrate and explain this, or its economic capital process where this is in place, to the regulator?
- Does the firm have an appropriate organisational structure for risk management which meets the requirements of the Sound Practices Paper?
- Has the firm established an adequate risk management framework, including policies and procedures, governance, and roles and responsibilities?
- Is there a process in place to set economic capital requirements?

Pillar III
- Is the firm able to meet the disclosure requirements set out and is it confident that it could meet the verification requirements that will be applied?

The most pressing question for the boards of asset-finance firms is whether these requirements will significantly affect their overall competitive position after taking into account both the cost of the increased capital and improved systems and processes. Firms will need to assess whether the current range of activities will still be viable in their current form given the new levels of regulatory capital and current pricing levels.

Actions that need to be taken

In the banking sector, leading firms have already selected their Pillar I approach for each of credit and operational risk, completed a gap analysis against the key Basle criteria and commenced implementation plans to ensure compliance by 2006. Those asset-finance firms that are part of large groups that are already undertaking such programs are lucky since they need only ensure that they are fully involved in this programme. Other asset-finance firms not part of a group-wide Basle program will need to implement a structured Basle II compliance programme with well defined plans, dedicated resources and budgets. This should include the items listed below.

Initial appraisal against Basle criteria to:

- identify major gaps and problem areas; and
- select the target level of compliance for operational and credit risk.

Key implementation steps will vary from firm to firm but will normally include:

- defining a development strategy to drive strategic and operational benefits as well as compliance;
- establishing a Basle II development programme, with clearly defined milestones and responsibilities, lobbying activities, dedicated resources and budgets;
- assessing the required system and infrastructure development;
- evaluating component solutions and determining short-term data collection requirements; and
- rolling out the programme of activities required to achieve compliance and realise the strategic and operational benefits.

Careful planning is inevitably required to ensure that these and any other issues identified are either factored into existing systems or risk projects, or addressed by establishing new projects. The overall program management of these Basle related projects will inevitably be a key area for management attention. It is therefore critical to gain strong support and sponsorship of the programme by the board and senior management.

Conclusion

The financial services industry as a whole has already acknowledged that the existing 1988 accord is out of date and that it does not reflect the improvements made in risk management over the past 14 years. At face value, the Basle proposals to address these shortcomings are sensible and provide a strong framework for aligning economic and regulatory capital. Nevertheless, the proposals will present significant difficulties for most firms, not only in meeting the requirements for calculating expected loss components, but also in wider areas such as data and collateral management.

---

[1] The Basle Proposal on Capital Adequacy, published 16 January 2001, is available from www.bis.org.

[2] The overview of the new capital accord available from www.bis.org.

[3] These business lines are: corporate banking; trading and sales; retail banking; commercial banking; payment and settlement; agency services and custody; asset management; and retail brokerage.

[4] Basle Committee on Banking Supervision, Working Paper on the *Regulatory Treatment of Operational Risk*, published September 2001.

[5] Basle Committee on Banking Supervision, Sound Practices Paper for the Management and Supervision of Operational Risk, published December 2001.

Chapter 5

Documentation

Simon Hall

Introduction

This chapter examines general documentation issues that arise in leasing transactions. Although the structure of leasing contracts has always been fluid and reactive to changes in the legislative background, there are a few common approaches that are used to approach certain basic types of leasing transactions. Documentation lies at the heart of each transaction; however, considerable attention must always be paid to jurisdictional differences in legislation, taxation and accounting, especially in cross-border transactions. National differences can and will affect both the substance and later interpretation of transactions and their documentation.

Although the approach varies depending on the country or countries involved, the following key aspects are usually covered by leasing documentation: the purchase of an asset; the structure of the lease; security documents; the participation agreement; lease provisions; an introduction to the agreement; the definitions; the conditions precedent; the hiring of the asset; rent; indemnification; disclaimer of warranties; protection of title; maintenance obligations; insurance; representations and warranties; other covenants; events of default; remedies; conditions of voluntary termination; and other miscellaneous provisions.

Although the underlying legal framework of the jurisdictions involved in a transaction have a strong bearing on the way the above issues are structured, there are equally many areas where skilful negotiation and due diligence play an important part in providing additional comfort and security for the parties involved.

Confusion of terminology

Leasing is a word that describes a number of different legal relationships and can have a very different meaning in various jurisdictions. However, generically it covers any kind of contract where possession of an asset is transferred to another party to use in the transferee's business, in circumstances where the transferor retains an interest in the asset.

Using English legal terminology, the following distinctions can broadly be drawn between the different types of agreement.

- *A lease* is a contract of hire or bailment where the lessee has the right to use the asset leased in consideration of payment or other compensation being made to the lessor. Leases can be divided into two main categories: finance leases and operating leases. The division between finance leases and operating leases is made by market practice, but does not conform, necessarily, to accounting or tax distinctions.

- *A hire-purchase agreement* is a contract that contains an option on the part of the lessee to purchase the asset. Traditionally the option can only be exercised on payment of a specified amount, which is usually nominal. A hire-purchase arrangement where the option price is other than nominal has become known in some circles as a lease purchase; however, there is no distinction from an English legal point of view if the agreement contains an option.
- *A conditional sale agreement* is an agreement for the sale of an asset under which the purchase price, or part of it, is payable in instalments. Title to the asset remains with the seller, notwithstanding the transfer of possession, until certain conditions have been satisfied, including the payment of all instalments of the purchase price. The distinction from a hire-purchase agreement is that title passes automatically on fulfilment of the condition(s).
- *A credit sale agreement* is an agreement where title in the asset passes immediately, but where the purchase price is left outstanding as a loan and is repayable over time with interest.

International leasing can involve any one of these forms of agreement, although the precise legal effect has to be determined by reference to applicable local law in the respective jurisdictions, notwithstanding any choice of law provision in the lease itself. In each of the above instances, the lessee of the asset wishes to fund the acquisition of that asset, obtaining the use of it over a period approximating to much of the asset's anticipated useful life, while the lender of the funds retains an interest in the asset.

More importantly, in sophisticated tax jurisdictions leasing is a device that merits special tax treatment whereby depreciation benefits are conferred upon either the legal or economic owner, depending upon the jurisdiction.

Economic ownership is generally regarded as residing with the lessee in circumstances where the lessee is responsible for the operation, maintenance and all outgoings attributable to the asset and its use, and where the lessee has the right to and the risk in the residual in the asset through purchase or lease renewal options. In some jurisdictions, the retention of title by a lessor in circumstances where economic ownership resides with the lessee is regarded as merely conferring upon the lessor a security interest in that asset.

Lack of uniformity of structures

Because of the different considerations that apply to leasing transactions, whether tax, legal, commercial, registration or otherwise, it is unlikely that any leasing transaction in one jurisdiction is going to be structured in exactly the same way as in another jurisdiction. Therefore different documentation is required to suit the circumstances. Although there have been efforts to standardise certain documents, these are unlikely to have much effect on most leasing transactions at present because of the number of variable factors involved.

The structure of the transaction will affect its complexity. If the type of lease aimed at is an operating lease where the lessor retains certain obligations, then the document will necessarily be structured in a different way. If the lease is not really a lease, but a credit sale with security being taken on the equipment, then clearly that would also affect the structure of the documents. A single investor lease, as opposed to a lease with third-party debt (for example, a leveraged lease such as a Japanese operating lease), is going to require considerably less complex documentation with a corresponding reduction in transaction costs.

Types of agreement

It is not possible to analyse all the different documents involved in leasing arrangements around the world, but a brief general outline of the key parts of a leasing transaction and what documentation may be generated may be helpful.

Purchase of asset

The lessor will acquire the asset from either the lessee, a manufacturer or a supplier. If, as is often the case, the lessee has an existing purchase agreement with the manufacturer or supplier, some form of novation agreement or assignment will be needed whereby the right to take title and the obligation to pay are transferred by the prospective lessee to the lessor. This route avoids questions which may arise regarding sale and lease-backs, such as whether or not the transaction is in reality a loan rather than a lease.

Where the asset is being purchased from the lessee, which would be the case when title had already passed, the sale document might be relatively simple, perhaps with the original purchase agreement with the manufacturer or supplier attached as an exhibit, or at least referred to. Where the lessee has not yet placed the order, the lessee could be appointed the agent of the lessor to purchase the asset on its behalf. Such an arrangement depends on a degree of trust being placed in the lessee since rules relating to ostensible authority might enable the lessee to exceed its express authority and commit the lessor to a greater sum.

In a secondary transaction or refinancing, the asset may be sold subject to and with the benefit of a lease attached, which would necessitate the novation or assignment of the lease to the new owner.

On small-ticket transactions, there may well be nothing more than a purchase order and invoice. In such circumstances, the invoice should be addressed to the lessor to provide evidence of the purchase by the lessor. In some jurisdictions, notwithstanding what purchase documentation is used, a bill of sale might also be taken as evidence of the sale although this can sometimes have adverse documentary tax or stamp duty consequences.

Lease

The typical provisions of a lease are discussed in greater detail in the next section of this chapter. It is not unusual in some complex leasing transactions to find that a series of leases are necessary, for example when the credit support of an intermediate lessor is needed. Such a structure leads to increased complexity of documentation, the major factor being the extent to which obligations should be imposed on the intermediate lessor. Should the immediate lessor be required to assume obligations on a primary basis, or just on a reasonable endeavours procurement basis, recognising that it will not have possession of the asset? Another question is whether an act or breach of the sub-lease should trigger a default or termination right under the head lease. The credit analysis of the transaction should determine the degree to which the intermediate lessor should incur legal liability for breaches of the underlying lease obligations. An assignment of the sub-lease could also be taken to provide direct access to the head lessor against the ultimate lessee.

Security documents

If third-party debt is being provided, there will be loan documentation in addition to the lease. There will also probably be a mortgage and an assignment or some form of security document giving the lenders a security interest in the lessor's interest in the asset and the lease (this may be included in the loan agreement). Some lessors may require separate additional security in the form of security interests on other tangible property or receivables of the lessee.

Where credit support is required, this may be given either in the form of a back-to-back lease, such as the head lease and sub-lease structure discussed above, or a guarantee, or a standby letter of credit. Alternatively, the manufacturer or supplier may provide some credit support in the form of a buy-back or recourse agreement.

Although it can hardly be called a security document, in the absence of a guarantee, a comfort letter may be sought from the parent company of the lessee acknowledging the transaction, providing for maintenance of its shareholding and perhaps also some comfort about maintaining the subsidiary's ability to perform its obligations under the lease. From a legal perspective – which is not the only relevant criterion – a comfort letter is really only of value if it creates legal liability for financial support of the lessee.

Participation agreement

In a multi-party transaction, it is often convenient to have a single document in which each party can give representations, warranties and covenants to all parties The common conditions precedent can be specified and the whole transaction pulled together. This is typical in US leveraged leases, project related leases and securitisation and will generally be helpful where there are more than two parties involved in a complex transaction, subject to any tax sensitivities on presentational issues.

Typical lease provisions

Whatever the governing law and whatever the tax position, most leases will contain certain common provisions. This section focuses particularly on the provisions of a typical equipment finance lease, although such provisions will be found in substantially similar form in a conditional sale, credit sale or hire-purchase agreement. Leases of specialised equipment, such as aircraft and satellites, will include other provisions tailor made for the asset in question.

Recitals or introduction to agreement

After the naming of the document, the first thing that appears will be an identification of the parties. Practice differs as to whether or not the place of incorporation should be included and whether the address of the registered or principal office should be specified at this point. In international agreements, it is good practice to specify the place of incorporation. The address for communications will usually be specified in the back of the document in a notice provision and the place for service of process will also be identified if different from the address for notices, so it is unnecessary to repeat it here.

Having identified the agreement and parties, it is then usual to introduce the agreement by reciting the history of the transaction in a brief outline. This is helpful to subsequent readers of the document to put it in its proper context, although, at least under English law, it is a rule of construction that the recitals will be resorted to only to assist in construction of a contract where the contract is itself ambiguous. For this reason alone, substantive provisions, including definitions to be used elsewhere in the document, should not be included in the recitals.

Definitions

It is essential to understand the defined terms that are being used in the document when reading a lease agreement of any description. To assist in reading a document, it is helpful to have all the definitions located in one place and, sensibly, this should be at the front of the document. It is preferable to avoid including too much in the definitions by, for example, introducing substantive provisions beyond the mere description of a meaning. Each time a defined term is used in the body of a document, it should be considered whether or not it is appropriate. Mistakes can easily be made by altering defined terms late on in negotiations when that term appears in a large number of places in a document.

In some very complex leases it has become common practice to have a separate appendix of definitions, which then serves as a set of common definitions for each of the main operative documents, whether it be the participation agreement, the lease, the indenture, the support agreement or, if applicable, the site lease. This approach is helpful, although it means that the definitions have to be considered all the more carefully and drafted neutrally in order to adapt to each document. It is certainly a more readily understood approach than that adopted more commonly in leveraged lease documentation where the participation agreement, indenture and lease incorporate definitions from the others by reference.

Further interpretation provisions that need to be stipulated include:

- headings of sections which are inserted for convenience only and do not affect construction;
- the singular includes the plural and vice versa when the context requires;
- all references to agreements are to those agreements as amended or supplemented from time to time (although this requires careful amendment of documents or provisions which are incorporated by reference into other documents since the impact of such an amendment may not always be fully considered in the context of the other document); and
- references to statutes etc are deemed to be to those statutes as amended, re-enacted or supplemented from time to time (although statutory provisions that have been incorporated by reference or referred to and which are not intended to change in the context of the document, will have to be specifically excluded).

Conditions precedent

There will generally be a list of conditions precedent that have to be satisfied before the lessor's obligations arise. These may not be contained in the lease but in an ancillary document such as a participation agreement in the US style, or an agreement to acquire and lease, or the related loan if applicable. In a sale and lease-back context, they may be found in both the sale agreement and the lease. The content of the conditions precedent is very much a subjective matter for each transaction, but will probably include:

- execution and delivery of all documentation in the form agreed or with such changes as may be approved;
- the availability of funds where the lessor is being funded by outside sources;
- the acquisition of title by the lessor, free and clear of any liens or encumbrances;
- the accuracy of the representations and warranties given by the lessee and, if appropriate, any other parties;
- that no event of default or event which, with the giving of notice, lapse of time or relevant determination, would constitute such an event of default shall have occurred;
- that all necessary governmental, regulatory or other consents, approvals and authorisations shall have been obtained;
- that all necessary registrations or filings shall have been effected;
- that insurance cover in the form required by the terms of the lease shall have been effected;
- that all taxes, fees and duties payable in connection with the execution, delivery, registration and filing of the documentation shall have been paid in full;
- that all required opinions shall have been delivered in acceptable form; and
- that there has been no material adverse change in the financial condition of the lessee since the date of the last published audited accounts.

Other conditions precedent will be dictated by the nature of the asset and by the degree of commercial risk being assumed by the lessor. Often a finance lessor will not accept that the transaction can commence unless and until the asset is in operation. For example, in a satellite lease there might be a requirement that the satellite be in its geostationary orbit and the transponders meet the relevant performance specifications; with an electricity generating unit there would be an additional condition precedent to the effect that the unit is synchronised with the rest of the electricity supply grid system and is operational; with an aircraft it will be expected to have passed the acceptance test procedures specified.

The lease or hiring of the asset

The first provision of the lease document should be the letting or hiring of the asset to the user. This provision will specify that the asset is being leased for the applicable term. The asset that is being leased has to be defined and it is essential from a lessor's point of view that the description is adequate to identify the asset precisely so that delay is not experienced in any recovery situation. This is particularly important where a number of different lessors have leased to the same lessee discrete sections of the same asset, for example in the context of a chemical plant built in stages.

The term also needs to be similarly defined. For tax or commercial reasons, the period during which a lease is paid out may be shorter than the useful life of the asset. In such circumstances, a lessee may seek a renewal option to extend the term of the lease. Tax considerations may also prohibit giving a lessee a purchase option, and in such circumstances a renewal option may be the only way to enable the lessee to enjoy the residual value of the asset over the rest of its useful life.

Rent

From a lessor's perspective this is the most important and fundamental provision which, failing all else, should be precise and correct. A fixed rent can be documented easily by describing the number of instalments payable and the amount of each instalment as a factor, for example, per US$1,000 of asset cost. A level repayment basis may not suit a user's cash flow, or the asset may be of a type where revenue is generated on a seasonal or cyclical basis, in which case the rentals will not be in equal instalments, but staggered to suit that cash flow. A stepped rental flow which increases over time may be used to reflect a plant coming on stream to full production, or to optimise the tax structure. The different structures of rentals are infinite and can have a significant impact on the economics of the transaction from the perspective of both the lessor and the lessee, particularly as a result of the respective tax treatments.

Depending on the requirements of the parties, and to some extent the term of the lease and the currency in which it is being funded, the rentals might not be fixed but be on a floating basis tied to a variable interest rate such as Libor. In addition, the lease may grant to the lessee, or more unusually, the lessor, the right to fix the rate from time to time. Alternatively, this might be automatic when the reference rate rises or falls to a certain level. Such a provision, sometimes known as a droplock, might apply to all or part of the rentals.

Although agreed rental factors and stipulated loss and termination values will be included in the documents, if there are a number of variable factors still open at the time the lease or participation agreement is signed, some mechanism for adjustment to the rental and values to reflect the variations has to be built in. For example, on a project financing the final cost may still be open and retentions may not be released for years. The purchase price may be payable in a different currency to that of the lease obligation. Transaction costs may be added in. The extent of availability of investment tax or energy credits may be determinable only after the event. In all these circumstances, the lease will provide for the rent, stipulated loss and termination values to be adjusted by the lessor upon the finalisation of such variables (or perhaps periodically), but using the same methods and non-variable assumptions as were used in calculating the original rental and values.

A lessee might seek to have the right to contest any adjustment, but most lessors will, at best, permit a certificate to be provided by their external auditors to the effect that the calculations are correct and that the same methods and assumptions have been used as were used for the original figures. There is no standard approach as to who bears the cost of the certificate, but a compromise sometimes reached is that the cost of the auditors' certification has to be borne by the lessee unless the lessor's figures were wrong by more than some *de minimis* factor.

Unless the rentals were calculated by looking ahead at a calendar and factoring in those days which are not business days, a normal rent calculation will assume that payments are to be received on the specified dates. It is necessary to provide that if a payment falls on a day which is not a business day, it will either be paid on the preceding day or succeeding day which is a business day. It is a matter of negotiation as to which it is, although, if the rentals are calculated on a floating-rate basis tied, for example, to Libor, the market convention will be followed. The lessor will want to ensure that the payment convention matches its own actual or notional funding position, whether the rentals are calculated on a fixed- or floating-rate basis.

In circumstances where the lease permits a renewal term after the initial full pay-out period, unless tax considerations dictate otherwise, generally the rental for the secondary period can be nominal. From the lessor's perspective, it will need to be set at a level sufficient to cover administrative costs and this would include a contribution to the premium for any residual liability insurance policy that the lessor may carry in respect of the asset. With a long secondary period, an indexation factor may be applied. From the lessee's perspective, in a finance lease, there is no justification for the rental being anything other than nominal since the lessor has recovered his initial outlay together with the agreed return. Tax considerations may have some bearing on the result (see Chapter 10).

Next is the hell or high water provision, so called because it requires payments to be made come hell or high water, or net lease provision. In a typical US leveraged lease this provision can run to several pages whereas in an English law lease it will be covered in a paragraph. However, the thrust of the provisions is the same: whether the asset be defective; title to the asset not reside in the lessor; the asset be confiscated or appropriated; the asset cease to function or not be fit for the purpose for which it was acquired; any change occur in the status of the lessor or lessee; any illegality, invalidity or other constraint on the enforceability of the document; or any other reason whatsoever; the rent must be paid in the amounts and on the dates agreed. This provision should also provide that even if there is another claim that the lessee might have against the lessor as a result of other dealings or even under the lease in question, the lessee is not entitled to deduct, set off or counterclaim any amount against the rent.

Despite their draconian terms, these provisions are unlikely to be fully enforceable in all the circumstances they purport to cover. For example, it is arguable under English law that rent is not payable in circumstances where the asset which is leased has ceased to exist. A court is also unlikely to look kindly upon a lessor which has defaulted in its obligations and which is trying to enforce the rental obligation of a lessee because of the provisions of this section. In addition, if the agreement becomes invalid or illegal, this provision may not be enforceable, notwithstanding the presence in the agreement of a severability clause (see the section 'Miscellaneous provisions' at the end of this chapter).

A further incentive to the lessee to make payments on the due date will be contained in the default interest provision. Any payment, whether of rent or otherwise, will bear interest at a default rate higher than the implicit lease rate for the period during which the payment is overdue. A lessee should try to ensure that default interest on unscheduled amounts, such as indemnity payments, should not begin to run until such time as a demand has been made for payment. Some jurisdictions may prohibit the recovery of interest on interest or have usury limitations (eg, New York) which will affect the enforceability of such a provision. Rules against penalties may also be applicable (see the section 'Remedies' below).

Indemnification

Consistent with the approach that the rentals should be received on the dates and in the amounts specified, the lessor should be protected from any other liability arising out of, or in connection with, the asset during the term of the lease. This is covered both by insurance, which is discussed in the section 'Insurance' below, and by the indemnification provisions. In a finance lease, the lessor's approach is that it should be in no different position than a lender under an ordinary loan financing. In other words, it should not incur any additional liability by virtue of ownership of the equipment.

As a matter of law, different jurisdictions impose strict liability on owners in certain circumstances. For example, the UK Civil Aviation Act 1982, section 76(2) imposes strict liability upon an owner of an aircraft, although under section 76(4), that reference to the owner is replaced by an operator to which the aircraft has been demised, hired or let out for a period in excess of 14 days (note that such terms may not include a conditional sale agreement). The law of negligence also imposes strict liability in certain circumstances. Because the lessor will generally be financially more sound than a lessee, particularly in circumstances where there has been a catastrophe with the asset, it is possible that the lessor will be sued by a person who has suffered damage as a result of the catastrophe. Renewed focus by lessors on strict liability arose following the 11 September 2001 terrorist atrocity, as a result of which the availability of public-liability war risks insurance cover was severely curtailed (see the section 'Insurance' below).

It is not just physical damage or personal injury for which there is potential liability. Potential claims could be made in respect to infringement of copyright, patent, trademark or other intellectual property rights, conversion, passing off or claims for business interruption and other consequential damage. That is why, generally, indemnities will be phrased extremely widely and cover 'any and all liabilities, obligations, losses, damages, penalties, claims, suits, costs, expenses, fees and disbursements... of whatever kind and nature which in any way relate to or arise out of the manufacture, design, financing, construction, purchase, acceptance, rejection, ownership, acquisition, delivery, non-delivery, lease, sublease, preparation, installation, storage, maintenance, repair, transportation, transfer of title, abandonment, possession, rental, use, operation, condition, sale, return, import, export or other disposition of all or any part of...' the asset.

The liability assumed by the lessee under this section is therefore considerable, but its protection should be in the form of liability insurance or indemnities from a supplier or manufacturer. If an indemnity payment ever becomes payable, the lessor needs to be protected on an after-tax basis; if the indemnity payment is taxed as its income, it will not recover the full loss suffered unless any payment out on its part is equally deductible in the same tax period.

In mitigation of the potential liability, it is reasonable for the lessee to ask for the right to control or at least participate in any contest of liability on the part of the lessor. One fear on the part of lessees is that since lessors have an indemnity for any liability they may not be as diligent in contesting or defending any claim which alleges the lessor has liability. Some lessors are more sensitive than others about giving up contest rights. Not only do they regard any suggestion that they would not be as diligent as the lessee as an indication of a lack of trust in the relationship, but also they would have concern that the litigation could be conducted in a manner which is prejudicial to their reputation or, indeed, increases their financial exposure. A lessor which is part of a bank or regulated financial institution is likely to be particularly concerned about being involved in litigation outside its control.

However, there are clearly different interests. The lessee needs to protect the financial exposure it has under the terms of the indemnity, whereas the lessor might have wider business interests which would inhibit it in pursuing or defending a claim with all the unpleasantness that can become associated with litigation. If the lessor as the indemnitee is willing to pass over the rights to contest any claim, then it should be entitled to receive security for its costs including, perhaps, the cost of any counsel it elects to appoint to look after its interests. This latter request may be rejected by the lessee since it potentially doubles the cost of any litigation. If a lessor does give up contest rights to the lessee, it should always reserve the right to deny these rights to the lessee in circumstances where the lessee is otherwise in default, or where it forgoes its right to be indemnified, just in case other business considerations at the time would make it more prudent not to engage in any sort of litigation.

The general indemnity can also cover general tax liability on the transaction, or there may also be a general tax indemnity. This could be expected to cover such matters as operational, stamp or documentary taxes, transfer or sales taxes, property taxes, value added tax and so on. In a tax-based transaction there would also be a specific tax indemnity. Tax indemnities vary from jurisdiction to jurisdiction in scope and the allocation of risk (see Chapter 10 and Chapter 17). Contest rights could be expected to be given to a lessee with regard to these aspects as well, although a lessor will be even more inclined to retain some or full control, because it will be its own tax accounts that are the subject of any challenge.

With any indemnity, the lessee should be entitled to restrict its liability to those situations where the loss arises for a reason other than the wilful default or the gross negligence of the lessor. If the lessor interferes with the lessee's possession when it is not entitled to, clearly it should be liable for the consequences of its action. Similarly, the lessor should be liable if it exercises its rights of inspection of the asset and the asset is damaged during the course of that inspection. If it is negligent in the way it files its tax returns or accounts for the transaction, it should suffer the consequences without being indemnified by the lessee. If its taxable income position is such that it cannot use the depreciation allowances or interest deductions fully as anticipated at the outset of the transaction, that again is a cost which a lessor should bear. These exclusions are, however, always a matter for negotiation and will reflect the respective bargaining positions of the parties.

Disclaimer of warranties

Another way in which lessors seek to insulate themselves from liability for the asset is by disclaiming any warranty with respect to merchantability, fitness for purpose or compliance with specification or description. From a lessor's point of view, unless the manufacturer of the asset is actually the lessor, its involvement in the transaction is purely financial: since it has not taken part in the selection or design of the equipment it should have no liability for the asset. Even as a lessor under a true lease, as opposed to a vendor under a conditional sale, it will have potential liability in certain jurisdictions as a supplier of the asset (for example, in the United Kingdom under the amended Sale of Goods Act 1979, the Supply of Goods and Services Act 1982 or, in some circumstances under the Consumer Protection Act 1987, and in the United States under Article 2 of the Uniform Commercial Code).

A lessor should also be able to support its argument for not having any liability by virtue of the fact that, more often than not, the lessee will have inspected the asset and may, as part of the lease documentation, have been required to sign some form of certification of acceptance. Under such a certificate, the lessee would confirm that, as far as the lessor is concerned, it had accepted the asset, without qualification, as being entirely satisfactory.

Having achieved the measure of protection sought by the lessor, it is important for the lessee still to be in a position where it can enforce the warranties against the manufacturer or intermediate supplier. The only sure way to achieve this result is for the manufacturer to give direct warranties to the lessee and to give the lessee a right to claim under those warranties directly, at least until an event of default has occurred (compare the provisions of Article 10 of Unidroit's uniform rules on leasing contracts – see Chapter 7).

To protect themselves in the circumstances of a default, lessors will wish to maximise the return from the asset and therefore have the right to recover any moneys due from a manufacturer for defective parts, or the right to enforce the warranties to make the asset more saleable. It is not unusual for a lessor to require that all the manufacturer's warranties are assigned to the lessor on the sale of the equipment; the lessor will in turn pass these down through the lease to the lessee with a retraction provided in the document in circumstances where there is a default. The trouble with such arrangements is that a manufacturer might be able to argue successfully that because the beneficiary of the manufacturer's indemnity (the lessor) is in turn indemnified by the lessee, the lessor has suffered no loss and therefore there is nothing for which the manufacturer need indemnify the lessor. It is sometimes unclear whether the method by which the warranties are passed down to the lessee constitutes an assignment or something else, such as an agency. In some jurisdictions, including England, if the assignment is not an absolute assignment, of which notice to the obligor has been given, the lessee may not be able to sue in its own name and will have to join the lessor as an additional party to the litigation. This works against the basic intention, which is to ensure that the lessee is able to enforce the warranties directly so that its business can effectively be conducted as though it owned the asset outright.

An alternative would be for the lessee to keep the warranties and provide for an automatic assignment in the event of a default. The disadvantage of such a springing assignment is that its enforceability is uncertain in a bankruptcy or liquidation.

Protection of title

As already mentioned, one of the significant advantages of leasing transactions is that title resides with the lessor either all the time or until the conditions to purchase, or to the exercise of the option to purchase, are fulfilled. As part of a lessor's overall appraisal of a transaction, its security in ownership of the equipment is a significant factor which becomes more significant the less creditworthy the lessee. It is vital, therefore, to acquire clean title to the asset in the first place. The safest way to ensure that title has been effectively passed to the lessor, free and clear of liens and encumbrances, is to take title direct from the manufacturer either by a bilateral purchase contract or a novation of the purchase contract.

Assignments by the lessee to the lessor of its right to take title are acceptable if the vendor consents or otherwise has notice. If not, the lessor could take title subject to the intervening rights of third parties without notice of the assignment. However, such assignments might also give rise to stamp or other transfer taxes. In a sale and leaseback, the lessor is exposed to whatever interests may have attached to the asset while it was in the hands of the lessee. At the very least, some evidence should be provided that the lessee has paid the manufacturer in full to avoid problems arising out of retention of title provisions.

Most jurisdictions recognise a lessor's title and its right to retain such title subject to certain procedural exceptions such as the right to distrain where an asset is in the reputed ownership of a lessee. Once title has been obtained, it needs to be retained. Therefore a lease agreement can be expected to provide certain covenants directed towards the protection of the lessor's title to the asset. Clearly such covenants are only as good as the company behind the obligation. Certain precautions can, however, be taken in advance of delivery of the asset. For example, it can be required that nameplates specifying the lessor as owner and noting the holders of any security interests be affixed to the asset in conspicuous places in a form which is legible, thereby putting third parties on notice and reducing the risk of conversion.

Labelling becomes more difficult if, for example, the asset being leased is a discrete part of a chemical plant. One option is to paint the section which is owned by a particular lessor a different colour or ensure that each item is given a separate serial number. The lessee can also be expected to covenant that it will protect the title of the lessor and refute any claims by third parties. The lessee may be required to covenant that it will not hold itself out as owner of the equipment and, where it is available, will be required to ensure that the lessor is registered as the owner of the equipment and such registration is maintained (for example, in the aircraft registries of title for signatory states to the Convention on the International Recognition of Rights in Aircraft, Geneva 1948).

Another facet of the protection of the lessor's title built into the document is the restriction on what the lessee can do with the asset. The lessee might be required to covenant that it shall not, without the consent of the lessor, sublease the asset or otherwise part with possession of it. However certain assets demand more flexible covenants. For example, aircraft operators commonly have pooling arrangements whereby significant parts of aircraft such as the engines can be pooled with those of other carriers who are then entitled to use those parts. That is why it is not unusual to find that an aircraft has another lessor's or user's engines on it. Fleet operators like to preserve the right to swap engines with the engines of their other aircraft. Normally the lease provides that title to the engine remains, wherever situated, with the lessor unless and until a substitute is provided to which the lessor obtains title (see the section 'Maintenance obligations' below). Where the asset is moveable, the lease may also seek to restrict the area of operation, to ensure that it does not go into areas of high political risk or areas where the legal environment is such that recovery of the equipment is extremely difficult or impossible.

There will be a restriction upon the lessee creating liens upon the asset other than certain permitted liens. In a number of jurisdictions a lien-holder, such as a repairer, can acquire the right to sell an asset as a result of it acquiring possession of the asset after having a repair bill unpaid. The restriction on the creation of liens should extend to statutory liens whether for taxes or, for example, unpaid landing charges at airports. Permitted liens excluded from the restriction might include:

- mechanics' and repairers' liens which arise in the ordinary course of business and which do not secure overdue amounts;
- tax liens contested in good faith and for which adequate reserves have been provided as long as such contest proceedings do not involve the risk of forfeiture or sale of the asset;
- judgment liens for which a stay of execution has been obtained and for which adequate reserves have been provided, as long as such proceedings do not involve the risk of forfeiture or sale of the asset; or
- liens created by the lessor or any party to the transaction other than the lessee. The lessee would also be prohibited from creating any charges or encumbrances upon its own interest in the asset to avoid any interference with the lessor's powers of disposition in the event of a default.

Where the lessor's interest constitutes a security interest and that security interest is registrable, registration will take place on delivery and the lessee will be required to maintain such registration and perhaps give annual or semi-annual certificates of compliance. In the United States, where there is doubt as to whether the lease would constitute a true lease or a secured financing under the definition in section 1-201 (37) of the Uniform Commercial Code, a protective filing is still carried out, although it is provided that the filing itself is not determinative of the characterisation.

Whatever the document says, certain jurisdictions have consumer protection legislation that can extend to wholly non-consumer transactions and which can enable a lessee, as ostensible owner, to have the right to pass good title to a third party acting in good faith without notice of the lessee's deficiencies in title (for example, in the United Kingdom under sections 24 and 25 of the Sale of Goods Act 1979).

Special considerations apply to assets that are of such a nature that they become affixed to land, buildings or other chattels. In many common law jurisdictions, by operation of law, title to an asset which becomes affixed to land can pass to the owner of land. Arguably similar principles apply to chattels. Whatever the proper law of the various contracts, this question would be determined by the *lex situs,* that is the law of the place where the asset is located. Relevant principles include the degree and purpose of annexation and the degree of damage to the land or buildings on the asset's removal. If the asset is simply bolted to the floor, it is less likely to be held to be part of the land than where the asset is partially buried in concrete.

Some jurisdictions recognise contractual elections to the effect that something is to constitute or remain personal property. One protection that can be built into the document is a provision to the effect that the lessee must obtain waivers or non-interference undertakings from any owner or mortgagee of land, buildings or chattels with which the asset might merge or to which the asset might become affixed. In practice these may prove difficult to obtain in a timely fashion, if at all.

The agreement should also provide that during the term of the lease, the lessor is entitled to inspect the equipment periodically, not just to check that it is there, but also to investigate its state and condition.

Maintenance obligations

Even though the lessee is the user of the asset and is therefore primarily concerned with its state and condition, a lessor is also interested in seeing that the equipment is maintained. This is either to preserve its residual interest, if the lessor is the party entitled to it, or to preserve its security for the transaction. Maintenance covenants should not impose an obligation upon the lessee in excess of the standards to which an ordinary prudent operator of the asset would adhere. A lessee should not be restricted in its day-to-day business activities by virtue of the level of obligation assumed.

Fair wear and tear should clearly be an exception. However, consumable parts that have a useful life less than the asset will need to be replaced periodically. The usual breakdowns and overhauls that occur or are required during the operation of an asset also need to be attended to. Where the asset is of a type where maintenance agreements are entered into with the manufacturer or supplier, as in the case of a computer, the lessee will have an obligation to maintain such agreements in full force and effect. Aircraft will, in any event, be required by the relevant aviation authority to be maintained in order to preserve their air worthiness certificate from such authority. However, smaller airlines often do not have a maintenance capacity themselves and will have a maintenance agreement with another airline. A lessor may well require an assignment of such a maintenance agreement as security for the obligations of the lessee to maintain, thus enabling the lessor to enforce the maintenance agreement in its own right following a default.

Certain assets, such as aircraft engines, become time expired and need to be overhauled periodically which usually occurs as a matter of routine in an ordinary maintenance programme. The lease should, however, include a covenant to institute and carry out such a maintenance programme in accordance with the recommendations made by the manufacturer and the requirements of the relevant regulatory authority. In the case of ships, lessors require that the specified class certificate is maintained to provide periodic confirmation that the lessee is complying with proper maintenance and overhaul procedures.

As part of the maintenance programme for most assets, parts are likely to be removed from time to time or replaced. That is why leases contain complex replacement provisions, the substance of which is that until a part has been replaced, wherever it is located, it remains in the ownership of the lessor. When it has been replaced by a part which meets certain conditions, including, by way of example, that title to it is free and clear of any lien or encumbrance and resides with the lessee, and that such replacement part has a value and utility at least equal to the part which it replaces, then, upon title to the replacement part vesting in the lessor, title to the removed part can pass to the lessee. The removal and replacement of a part may have significant tax implications which have to be considered particularly in any tax oriented transactions.

Similarly, lessees will wish to retain the right to substitute or upgrade components of the asset to maximise the operating capabilities in the light of technological developments. Again a lessor will permit this where the substitute equipment is such that the lessor obtains title to it unencumbered and the value of the asset following the substitution is no less than it was before the substitution. The requirement that value be maintained cannot necessarily be adhered to in some instances where assets, for example computers, have become cheaper as they become more advanced and efficient. However, if inflation is taken into account, this situation is relatively unlikely with most assets.

The other area that might concern lessees is that the individual components that are being upgraded may be sufficiently severable and expensive enough for separate financing to be desirable, whether by way of lease or otherwise. This is not something that can really be adequately provided for in the document. At most, the lessor can assume an obligation to discuss the situation if it should arise, but the lessee will not want to be constrained by having to finance the addition itself. From the lessor's perspective, if it ever comes to dispose of the asset, it is essential that the asset has all the necessary parts for it to be operated. Sometimes a lease will provide for the lessor to have first call on any financing of the additional part which makes sense from a practical point of view, assuming of course that the terms are acceptable to the lessee and that the lessor is content with the additional credit exposure.

Insurance

Insurance is one means by which lessors can protect themselves against potential third-party liability exposure. Equally, insurance is a way lessees can lay off the risk they assume by virtue of the indemnification provisions (see the section 'Indemnification' above). Another function of insurance is to provide financial compensation in circumstances where the asset becomes damaged or destroyed. The lessor is, in turn, able to look to the insurance proceeds for maintenance of the value of the asset or the recovery of its investment.

The type of insurance carried depends to a large extent upon the nature of the asset and the business of the lessee. A lessor may be prepared to give up a requirement for physical damage insurance if it is totally comfortable with the credit of the lessee. With some assets, for example films, such insurance should be unnecessary in any event because duplicates of the master print are usually retained in more than one location.

The first question that needs to be addressed if insurance is being taken out concerns the amount of cover. It is possible to have insurance on an agreed value basis whereby the insurers become liable to the insured for that value in the event of the destruction of the asset. This agreed value is irrespective of the asset's market or replacement value and thereby avoids the policy being made subject to average. Where the amount is not an agreed value the insurers would be liable only for a proportion of the sum insured if the asset proved to have a higher or lower value at the time of the claim.

The lessor's exposure at any time is generally measured by the stipulated loss value or termination value which a lessee is required to pay upon the occurrence of a total loss. A total loss will be defined in the lease to include an actual, agreed or constructive total loss and any circumstances where the asset becomes irreparably damaged or incapable of use (including by reason of dispossession through requisition for a fixed period of time). From a lessee's perspective, it is important that the occurrences which are included in the definition are also covered by the insurance policy as situations in which the insurers will indemnify.

A common solution to the question of how much the insurance should be for, is for the insurable amount to be specified to be the greater of the stipulated loss value and the market or replacement value. A lessee is entitled to resist an obligation that it insures for anything more than the stipulated loss value, although it might elect to do so as a matter of prudence. Replacement value does not mean replacement as new unless so specified. Rather the replacement cost of an asset of the same type, age and value as the one lost. This goes hand-in-hand with the usual right retained by insurers on a total loss which is to provide a replacement rather than having to pay up the amount for which the asset is insured. This right will usually be specifically removed in the context of a finance lease.

The normal physical damage policy excludes war risks. With assets such as aircraft, it is usual to require that war risk insurance be taken out. The war risk policy excludes hostilities between the United States, the United Kingdom, France, Russia and the People's Republic of China, and also nuclear risk and confiscation by the state of registration. If there is a political risk in the state of registration it is possible, for a price, to obtain the removal of this last exclusion.

Following the terrorist acts on 11 September 2001, war risks cover was withdrawn by the aviation insurance market. Short-term measures were introduced relatively quickly by national governments to provide replacement cover either through direct indemnities, insurance or reinsurance arrangements. At the time of writing, the long-term solution for this situation is still being developed. However, it is interesting to note that at that time lessors were confronted with defaulting lessees that could not comply with the requirements in their leases for insurance. Although anxious, most lessors recognised that to exercise default rights in such circumstances would have been pointless since the market was effectively the same for every lessee. Interestingly the loss of insurance cover by airlines in the less creditworthy jurisdictions was much more of an issue, because their government indemnities were not perceived to be of as much value as cover provided by insurers. The short-term measures inevitably had considerable difficulty in coping with the complexities of some of the financing structures entered into and have had to be amended.

For certain types of assets, particularly aircraft, public liability insurance will invariably be required. Environmental liability may be a special factor to be covered with certain assets located in jurisdictions where environmental protection is a sensitive issue, such as the US and the European Community.

Having established the insurance levels, the next step is to ascertain the insurers. Some lessees are sufficiently strong financially for them to bargain for a self-insurance provision up to certain levels and subject to certain accounting protections. The deductibles or excess carried by a policy should be considered in the overall credit appraisal of the transaction, since they effectively amount to self insurance and will generally apply to each incident unless specific agreement to the contrary is obtained from the insurers. With large multinational corporations, it is not unusual to find that the group has a captive insurance subsidiary. From a legal perspective, insurance with a captive subsidiary can be no better than self-insurance, even if the captive insurer arranges reinsurance contracts. This is because reinsurers normally only accept a liability to reimburse the primary insurer, in this case the captive insurance subsidiary. Depending on the reinsurance arrangements, this can be circumvented by entering into cut-through arrangements such as direct letters of undertaking from the reinsurers and by ensuring that the lessor is named as an additional insured and as the loss payee on the reinsurance agreement.

With certain countries, such as the People's Republic of China, it is mandatory that insurance be placed with the state insurance company, although in some cases an obligation to procure reinsurance with Lloyd's or other acceptable reinsurers is allowed. In other countries, such as the Philippines and Argentina, it is a legal requirement that at least a proportion of the insurance is placed through national insurers for assets located in that country.

It is difficult to stipulate objective criteria to determine the acceptability or otherwise of insurers. This is probably best resolved by parties discussing which insurers the lessee intends to use and the lessor perhaps agreeing a list of insurers that are currently acceptable. More often than not, parties have to resort to agreements such as 'with insurers reasonably acceptable to the lessor', since the acceptability or otherwise of the insurers initially approved may well change during the term of the lease. Reference could also be made to the location of the insurance market where the insurances or reinsurances are placed and a list of acceptable countries agreed.

Another area that needs to be studied carefully is whether the asset is to be insured on a group or fleet policy. This will normally be the case with aircraft operators, fleet vehicle operators and large, geographically diverse corporations. The policy should be checked to ensure that the asset in question is effectively separately insured and that the limits on the policy are not affected by claims relating to other assets covered by that policy. Lessees are often reluctant to interfere with the form of their group policy, but it is always possible to prevail upon the insurers to draw up a suitable endorsement for a particular asset and for the particular additional insured party involved with the transaction, usually at no, or very little, cost.

It is almost always impossible to arrange for the full insurance policy to be available in time for completion of the leasing transaction and often the lessee will not be prepared to disclose the full terms of a fleet policy to a single lessor because of its commercial sensitivity. To provide the necessary comforts to the lessor that the insurance that it requires has been effected, the normal practice is to obtain a written confirmation from the insurance brokers to that effect. The lease will often include as a schedule an insurance certificate setting out the coverage expected by the lessor and the brokers' undertaking should include the insurance certificate in the same terms. The brokers have to be acceptable to the lessor since their confirmation is what the lessor is relying upon. Any failure in the insurance cover which was inaccurately represented in the letter is something for which the lessor would expect to recover damages from the brokers.

The next important question is what the insurance policy should state over and above its standard provisions. Insurance underwriters and brokers have in recent years taken a more active role in regulating what additional terms are added for financiers. In the London aviation market, a standard endorsement form (currently entitled AVN67B) has been developed and, in general, accepted by participants in the aircraft finance and leasing industry. The impetus for this, and its primary benefit, was to avoid lengthy negotiation between insurers and lessors on the exact wording of endorsements. The wording of AVN67B is not necessarily ideal from a lessor's point of view (see below for discussion of difficult points), however most underwriters will now not accept amendments to this wording unless an additional premium is offered.

There is no equivalent to AVN67B in other insurance markets and it is only adopted to a limited extent outside London. Underwriters in all sectors are increasingly reviewing financing endorsements more carefully and rejecting the broad terms previously accepted. For this reason, lessors should ensure that the lessee involves its insurance broker early in negotiations to avoid an *impasse* on insurance terms which may cause a delay in completion.

As far as possible, the lessor should always be named as an additional insured with the lessee. This ensures that the interest of the lessor in the insurance is original and not derivative, with the result that the policy cannot be discharged so far as the lessor's interest is concerned, except by the lessor. Often the lessor will also require an assignment of the insurances to create a security interest over the rights to the insurance proceeds payable to the lessee. If an assignment is taken, notice should be given to the insurers and notice of that assignment endorsed on the policy. Another option is simply to note the interest of the lessor and couple that with a loss payable clause. Although this is the most common approach adopted in small and medium ticket leases, the effect is uncertain and at most probably amounts to a revocable mandate to the insurers to pay proceeds to the lessor.

From a lessor's point of view, a loss payable clause should ideally be endorsed on the policy setting out how the insurance proceeds are to be paid. Under AVN67B, insurers will not include a loss payable clause, but the endorsement accepts that total loss proceeds will be paid as determined under the lease. Insurers will usually accept a loss payable clause attached to a notice of assignment and specifically endorse this on the policy. In the event of a total loss, the proceeds should be paid first to the lessor since it is looking for the recovery of its investment in the transaction out of the proceeds of insurance. As a practical matter it may take some time before a total loss can be agreed with the insurers. Therefore the lease will usually provide that, in the event of the occurrence of an event of loss, the lessee will pay the stipulated loss or termination value after a certain period of time (30 to 60 days). Any insurance proceeds received after payment by the lessee of part or all of the stipulated loss or termination value and all other amounts due will be repaid to the lessee.

In circumstances other than a total loss, the application of the proceeds is a matter for negotiation usually determined by the creditworthiness of the lessee. If the lessee is a sound credit then, except where an event of default has occurred, the lessee may be permitted to be

71

the loss payee on all claims other than a total loss. If the lessee is not so creditworthy, it may only be permitted to be the loss payee on claims below a certain financial limit. It is essential that the loss payable clause follows precisely the provisions of the lease agreement including any changes to the arrangements necessitated by the occurrence of, or notice of the occurrence of, an event of default. The lessee will wish to ensure that the financial limit is set at a level which provides it with sufficient operating flexibility and avoids the necessity for constantly approaching the lessor for reimbursement.

In some cases, lessors will restrict reimbursement unless evidence is provided that the damage has been repaired or the damaged part replaced. Mechanically, this could inhibit a lessee, but it provides control over the application of the proceeds as far as the lessor is concerned. Either the money is available or the value of the asset restored. The lessor will however need to address the insurers' position on this as well. AVN67B deliberately does not accept whatever partial loss provisions are set out in the lease since the insurers will in fact only pay out on such a claim where all parties to the insurances have agreed to the settlement proposed by the insurers. AVN67B refers to the insurers consulting with the lessor and other relevant parties in these circumstances. The usual inclination of the insurers is to pay the repairer for the aircraft to be repaired rather than release funds to a financier.

Another problem to be specifically addressed in the policy is the principle of contribution. The standard insurance policy limits the liability of the insurers to the proportion of the loss or liability which the limit of cover under the policy bears to the total amount of valid and collectable insurances in respect of such loss or liability. Therefore, if additional insurance has been effected by the lessee, despite any covenant to the contrary, the amount of cover available to the lessor under the policy in question would be reduced proportionately. Once again, it may be possible to persuade the insurers to overrule this provision by express endorsement, at least so far as the lessor is concerned.

Even if the lessor has an original, as opposed to derivative, interest in the insurances by being a named joint or additional insured, the lessor may still be prejudiced by breaches of warranty on the part of the lessee. For example, if the proposal form has been inaccurately completed, the insurers could avoid liability. To overcome this, a breach of warranty endorsement or non-vitiation cover may be available whereby the insurers agree that as regards the lessor, but not the lessee, no breach of warranty other than one by the lessor will affect the availability of the insurance to the lessor. There is sometimes resistance to accepting a breach of warranty endorsement on a liability policy, or in a situation where there is a joint policy. However insurers can usually be persuaded to accept, particularly once the lead underwriter has been convinced.

There was much negotiation on this issue in the discussions of AVN67B. The present form provides that the lessor is protected from 'any act or omission (including misrepresentation and non-disclosure) of any other person or party which results in a breach of any term, condition or warranty of the Policy PROVIDED THAT the [Lessor] has not caused, contributed to or knowingly condoned the said act or omission'. This will be satisfactory for most lessors.

There used to be a residual concern for an operating lessor whose engineering staff are closely involved in the airline's maintenance arrangements where there is a minor breach of proper maintenance procedures required under the policy which leads to a casualty. In such a case, the insurers could have argued that the lessor 'knowingly condoned' the breach. AVN67B now confirms that if the lessor is acting in any other capacity, its actions etc, in that other capacity, shall not affect the lessor's protection in this respect.

Another common requirement is that the policy is stated to operate as a separate policy for each of the additional named insureds. This is sometimes called a cross-liability clause. This permits a claim to be made by one of the insureds despite the fact that the other insured could not have made such a claim. For example, where one aircraft owned by the lessee collides with another aircraft operated by the lessee and owned by the lessor. Such a provision should also assist in preventing the insurers avoiding liability for breach of warranty or raising a contributions argument.

To avoid any claim lying against them, lessors should insist on the insurers' right of subrogation against them being waived and because of the unlikelihood of any such claim, insurers will generally agree to do so.

Additional provisions which should be included in the policy and required in the lease are requirements of notice of any alteration to the terms of the policy and notice of cancellation of the policy. This is so that the lessor is effectively given the opportunity to pay any defaulted premiums, if that is the reason for cancellation, or, if necessary, arrange other insurance. This notice is usually between 10 and 30 days (except in the case of war risks insurance which traditionally has a maximum notice period of seven days).

We have already touched on the effects of additional insurance carried by the lessee. Additional insurance which does not cover the same subject matter as the main insurance will usually be acceptable and sometimes a lessor requirement. The lessee may well wish to take out business interruption insurance which, although not a requirement of the lessor, may be prudent business practice. If a lessee is a particularly poor credit risk, or in a non-recourse project financing, a lessor may require business interruption insurance to be effected since the proceeds of that insurance are the only means of maintaining the lessee's cash flow in the event of disabling damage to the asset, thereby enabling the lessee to meet its obligations.

A common provision of liability insurance policies is the exclusion of liability on the part of the insurer for any loss or damage for which the insured becomes liable because of a contractual undertaking without which the insured would not have been liable. The lessor may require that the policy be extended to cover specifically the express indemnity provisions of the lease agreement. However, this only provides a limited benefit since the endorsement is subject to the terms of the policy.

As a precaution, in policing compliance with the document, a broker's certificate should be required annually to confirm that the insurance is in place as specified.

Certain transactions may require special or specific insurance cover to be obtained for particular risks; for example, political risk, satellite launch, design deficiencies and residual value insurances.

Notwithstanding the requirements of the lease relating to insurance and the scope of the cover obtained, many lessors feel that it is still worth effecting a residual liability policy to cover them to the extent that any other insurance effected on their leasing transactions does not, or is not adequate to, cover their total liability.

The definition of event of loss or total loss, which is the term that triggers payment of the stipulated loss or termination value, often contains the concept of requisition or government appropriation. Requisition of title should always be included as an immediate total loss event. Requisition of use however, will usually have some time period attached to it which will be dependent upon the nature of the asset. The theory behind this is that although the lessee should be obliged to continue to pay rent under the terms of the hell or high water provisions discussed earlier (see the section 'Rent' above), it is sensible to unwind the transaction where it is anticipated that the asset will be used by a person other than the lessee for much of its useful life. Therefore, a requisition of use for a period of time, or circumstances where it is anticipated that the use by the other party will continue beyond the end of the primary lease term, will trigger payment of stipulated loss or termination value. The document also needs to deal with what happens to the requisition proceeds. Unless tax considerations dictate otherwise, as they could in a tax-based transaction, or the lessor is to be entitled to any residual value, then all requisition proceeds, whether for title or for use, should be paid to the lessee so long as it has met its financial obligations under the lease and is not otherwise in default. The lessor therefore has obtained the return for which it bargained.

Representations and warranties

Representations and warranties are found in all financing agreements. They have a number of different purposes, but in particular they set out the information provided by the lessee on which basis the lessor is induced to enter into a transaction. Inaccuracy in that information will entitle the lessor to sue for breach of representation and recover damages and may also trigger a default. A second purpose is simply to inform and to uncover potential problems at an early stage. The lessor knows nothing about the asset and its use, and the representations and warranties can describe these aspects in greater detail.

The process of due diligence carried out by a lessee in verifying the contents of the representations and warranties is extremely useful. The scope and detail of the representations and warranties will force it to consider the information that is set forth in such provisions with the proper degree of responsibility. The same benefit can be gained for the lessee in respect of the lessor providing warranties where, for example, in a cross-border transaction a lessor is aware of fiscal developments in its own country which could have an impact on the fiscal advantages offered in the transaction.

Another function of the representations and warranties is the allocation of risk. Where an aspect of the transaction is uncertain and it is determined that the lessee should bear the risk, these aspects can be covered in the representations and warranties. For example, with a large, complicated piece of machinery, it may be impossible to say categorically that it does not infringe any copyright, trademark or other intellectual property right, but clearly the risk of such an infringement should be the lessee's. The lessee will therefore be required to represent and warrant that the equipment does not contravene any such right. Another example of allocating risk through the use of representations and warranties is found in tax indemnification agreements in US leveraged leases.

A frequent extension of the representations and warranties is that the lessee is deemed to represent and warrant that all information provided in any statement or certificate provided in connection with the lease of the asset, whether in writing or otherwise, is true and correct. This is extremely dangerous from a lessee's perspective, unless it can be certain that it knows which information is being addressed. Drafted in its widest form, this could include information given casually over the telephone as well as the formal certificates signed by officers of the company and delivered at closing. All information provided in the lessee's published accounts, including forecasts and opinions, could also be covered. Unless a lessor has relied upon this information in reaching the decision to enter into the transaction, it appears to be overreaching on the part of a lessor or its counsel to cover these aspects in the representation.

It is more sensible to confine the extension to written factual material and to identify express-ly the material referred to.

Although the consequences of breaching representations and warranties differ substan-tially between jurisdictions, representations and warranties generally follow a pattern in addressing, as a minimum, the following issues.

- The due incorporation and valid existence of the lessee and confirmation of the authority of the lessee to own its properties and conduct its business as it is currently being (and sometimes proposed to be) conducted and to enter into and perform the lease agreement and ancillary agreements.
- That the execution, delivery and performance of the lease has received all necessary cor-porate authorisations and will not contravene any applicable law or agreement to which the lessee is a party or by which its assets are bound or affected. The latter part of this rep-resentation and warranty addresses such things as negative pledges in loan agreements and other debt instruments.
- That there will be a representation and warranty to the effect that no consents or registra-tions are required in connection with the execution, delivery and performance of the lease agreement; or, to the extent that such consents or registrations are required, they are iden-tified, expressed to be complete, obtained or made and to be in full force and effect.
- That, as part of the allocation of risk to the lessee, there will be a representation and war-ranty to the effect that the lease and the ancillary documents create legal, valid and bind-ing obligations of the lessee, which will sometimes go on to state that such documents are enforceable against the lessee in accordance with their terms. A lessee should try to resist giving a representation as to enforceability since this is a matter covered in legal opinions received by the lessor, or at least only give it subject to qualification with respect to bankruptcy rules and principles of equity and the other qualifications set out in those legal opinions.
- That the lessee confirms that there is no litigation, arbitration or administrative proceed-ing being contested or conducted which would have an adverse effect (or a material and adverse effect) on the financial condition, business or operations of the lessee; or perhaps, but not always, on the ability of the lessee to perform its obligations under the relevant lease agreement.
- That the financial information provided to the lessor has been prepared on a consistent basis and in accordance with generally accepted accounting principles in the applicable jurisdiction. This section would also contain the representations and warranties relating to full disclosure of any other liabilities.
- There might also be a representation and warranty concerning the absence of taxes or duties upon the lease agreement by virtue of its execution, delivery and performance including the imposition of withholding tax on the rentals.
- There may be a further representation relating to the ranking of the transaction in terms of priority with the lessee's other unsecured indebtedness.
- If it has not been adequately dealt with already in the purchase documents, the lessee may be required to give a title or other warranty relating to the sale arrangements and, if there is a related security interest being granted, as for example in any leveraged lease, the lessee would be expected to give a warranty concerning the registration, priority and perfection of such security interest.

- The lessee would be required to confirm that no event of default as defined, or any event which, with the giving of notice, lapse of time or relevant determination, would constitute such an event of default, has occurred.

There may be other representations and warranties peculiar to the transaction. Representations and warranties are generally a fruitful area for negotiation. A difficult question is whether the representations and warranties should be repeated at intervals, for example, on each rent payment date. Where a period of time has elapsed between signature of the documents and delivery of the asset, the representations and warranties should clearly be repeated on the date of delivery and non-compliance would operate as a block on the inception of the transaction. But it may be inappropriate for some of them to be repeated thereafter by reason of their nature. Where there is a representation and warranty that there is no licence, authorisation or permit required for performance under the lease, the position could well change as the law changes. A lessee, by agreeing to repeat the representation and warranty, will then be bound to repeat something which may turn out to be inaccurate in the light of subsequent circumstances. In any event, if a lessee is required to repeat representations and warranties periodically it should ensure that each representation and warranty given is examined closely to establish whether it is appropriate that it be repeated or whether some dispensation is required for future changes outside its control. Where the circumstances covered by the representation and warranty are also dealt with specifically in the covenants or the events of default, repetition is pointless and should be avoided.

Whether or not representations and warranties are repeated, or are of a continuing nature, it is sensible to have a provision somewhere in the document to the effect that the representations and warranties survive the execution of the agreement to avoid any suggestion that they were only given as an inducement to enter into the agreement in the first place and thereby limit the lessor's remedies for misrepresentation.

Another common area of negotiation is the degree of probability related to projections of whether something affects the business of the lessee or its capability of performing the agreement. A lessor would prefer the wording 'might/could materially and adversely affect its ability' to 'would materially and adversely affect its ability'. If the warranties are by their nature continuing, then 'would' is more appropriate, although ultimately the question will be determined by the respective bargaining strength of the parties.

Lessees are equally entitled to representations and warranties on the part of the lessor as to due incorporation, valid existence, corporate authority, legality, validity and binding effect and non-contravention of other agreements, although they will experience some resistance on the part of lessors in giving these.

Other covenants

In addition to covenants relating to maintenance, insurance and protection of title, a lease will include additional covenants, some of which are an extension of the concepts dealt with in the representations and warranties, whilst others relate to certain financial matters.

For example, the lessee will assume an obligation to obtain all necessary licences, permits and authorisations relating to the use and operation of the asset and perhaps to furnish copies to the lessor in respect of the particular transaction. This obligation extends to all permits, including those applicable to the lessor, if any, as well as those directly applicable to the lessee's own position. Permits that have been obtained frequently need to be renewed periodically.

Similarly, if the asset is of a type that has to be registered in the name of the lessor or the lessee, the lessee will be required to maintain that registration. Where the lease has been structured so that the lessor or a lending institution has a security interest in the asset, the lessee will be required to maintain the registration, perfection and priority of that security interest. In addition to other certificates which the lessee is expected to provide periodically, the lessee could be required to certify annually or semi-annually that these registrations have been maintained and are in full force and effect.

The lessee should also be required to covenant that it will pay all outgoings relating to the asset, whether these be taxes, fees, duties, fuel and lubrication expenses, insurance premiums and any other outgoings whatsoever arising out of or in connection with the use and operation of the asset. This covenant should also extend to the premises where the asset will be customarily kept or used, since a landlord may be entitled under the laws of the jurisdiction where the asset is located to distrain against assets of the lessee located on the premises. Accordingly, the lessee should have an obligation to pay the outgoings in the first instance rather than allow the lessor to incur the liability and seek indemnification from the lessee.

There will also be certain notification requirements. For example, the lease should provide that the lessee notifies the insurers of any loss or damage covered by the policy in accordance with the terms of that policy. There will also be a notification requirement about any circumstances that constitute an event of default or which would or could constitute an event of default with the lapse of time, the relevant notice or determination.

In addition, there will be a covenant to provide financial information in the form of audited accounts, interim financial statements and other information circulated to creditors and shareholders. There might also be a general covenant relating to the provision of information to the lessor concerning the location of the asset from time to time and possibly its use. For example, in the case of an aircraft, technical records have to be maintained to retain the certificate of airworthiness, and information concerning the hours of use are helpful in keeping a lessor informed of the position of the residual value of its asset.

Such a covenant would usually provide that 'such other information as a lessor might [reasonably] require from time to time' has to be provided by the lessee. The obvious information that the lessee will be required to provide is published information, whether in the form of annual reports or other financial statements or circulars to shareholders. However, it is a matter for negotiation as to what other information should be made available and how it should be made available. The burdens of such a general obligation and risk of breach of confidentiality should not be underestimated.

Another usual covenant relates to the return of the asset on the expiration of the lease term. If the lessee does not have a purchase option at the end of the term, or if title is not to pass to it, then, at the end of the term, the lessor will be concerned that the asset be returned, and in a reasonable condition. This obligation applies equally in the event of a return of the asset on the occurrence of an event of default, although it is less likely to be performed in such circumstances. The basic obligation imposed upon the lessee should be to the effect that the asset be returned in the state and condition that it would have been in had the maintenance obligations specified in the lease been complied with. The extent of the technical requirements of the return conditions will depend on the type of lease. An operating lease, where the lessor receives the aircraft or rolling stock back during its useful life, will have detailed technical requirements to ensure that the expected market value of the asset is preserved. In the recent downturn in the aviation market, the focus on return conditions has sharpened. Lessors are being stricter because of the difficulty of re-leasing the aircraft and lessees are finding that gaps in the technical details are being exploited. In addition, the asset will have to be free of any liens or encumbrances whatsoever so that the lessor is able to dispose freely of the asset. Any technical records or service records should be returned with the asset.

Finance lessors, being financial institutions, will in all probability not have anywhere to store the asset at the end of the lease term. Rather than having to go to the expense of shipping the asset to one place, selling it and then shipping it to the buyer's premises, the lessor may require the lessee to undertake to provide free storage and maintenance for, say, a period of up to six months which should give the lessor sufficient time to sell the asset. The lessee may also be required to insure and maintain the asset during that period.

A further provision could require the lessee to redeliver the asset to any place within the same jurisdiction or possibly the same continent at the lessee's expense. In this way the lessor has then been insulated against any incremental costs which might otherwise eat into its return. From the lessee's perspective, it is clear that such costs could mount up and the obligation to store, insure and maintain free of charge, as well as being responsible for delivering costs may have a bearing on the economics of the transaction. If, however, there is justified confidence in the residual market for the asset, then such undertakings may be freely given, although the costs should still be considered carefully.

As an addition to the basic restriction on the creation of liens and security interests (discussed in the above section 'Protection of title'), the lessee will be expected to assume an obligation to the effect that it is obliged to lift any lien, encumbrance or security interest that attaches to or is attached to the asset. Sometimes this may be expanded to constitute effectively a transactional lien-lifting obligation by including liens attaching to the rent, the lease agreement, the interest of the lessor and so on. The definition of permitted liens may need to be expanded if this section is widened in such a way.

Addressing the more specific financial concerns, a lessor will have entered into the transaction on the basis that the financial obligations of the lessee under the lease agreement constitute indebtedness which ranks *pari passu* (equally and rateably) with all the lessee's other unsecured obligations and that the lessee will not incur additional indebtedness which ranks in seniority above the lease obligations. A covenant will, therefore, be included in the lease to the effect that the lessee shall ensure that the lease obligations rank *pari passu* with all its other unsecured obligations other than those which achieve priority in the ordinary course of business or by reason of operation of the general law of the relevant jurisdiction. In addition, it may include a negative pledge to the effect that the lessee will not create or permit to exist over all or any part of its business or assets any security interests, other than those specifically listed or to which the lessor has consented, which will rank in point of priority and security ahead of the lease obligations. A lessee should argue to exclude from the scope of this section any past transactions, any purchase money mortgage or security interest, financial obligations below a certain individual or aggregate limit and property which is purchased already subject to some security interest.

As part of the overall credit appraisal, the lessor will have considered various indicators of the lessee's financial strength and may require these indicators as ongoing financial covenants, particularly if the transaction is, from the lessor's analysis, being done on the strength of the lessee's financial performance rather than on the security of the leased asset.

For example, the lessor may have addressed the net worth of the lessee and wish to see this maintained. The lease would, therefore, include a covenant on the part of the lessee to maintain a certain tangible net worth. The definition of tangible net worth will usually go further than simply defining it by reference to what is understood by generally accepted accounting principles. Since accounting principles may well not be the same in both jurisdictions in an international leasing transaction, the definition will need to be specific. The definition will always be a matter for negotiation but could usually be expected to include the paid-up share capital plus capital and revenue reserves after deducting intangible assets such as goodwill, amounts attributable to minority interests in subsidiaries, amounts representing increases in valuation of assets after a set date, and tax reserves.

As part of the same concept, the lease may well contain a provision restricting the lessee from merging with another corporation or substantially transferring all of its assets to another corporation whether by way of sale, lease or other means, particularly if the lessor is looking primarily at the lessee's balance sheet in entering into the transaction or is dealing with a state-owned company. An absolute restriction, or a restriction subject to the consent of the lessor, will often be regarded as an unwarranted intrusion of the lessor into the general business affairs of the lessee. A more acceptable provision might be to restrict such a merger or disposition except where the surviving entity, which must continue to be liable under the lease, has a net worth at least equal to the requirements specified in the lease. The lessor would usually expect the documentation relating to the assumption of the obligations of the lessee by the successor corporation to be satisfactory to it and also, that at the time the merger or other disposition takes effect, no event of default exists. Even where there is no continuing obligation relating to the maintenance of a particular tangible net worth, a restriction on mergers might still be included to restrict mergers to circumstances where the successor corporation has a net worth of not less than the net worth of the lessee immediately before the merger.

Additional covenants relating to liquidity and creditworthiness, requiring the maintenance of debt-to-net-worth ratios and current assets to current liabilities may also be included. The definition of these terms is a matter of negotiation but might be along the following lines.

- *Debt.* Principal amounts owed on any debt instrument including guarantees and other collateral agreements, finance leases, hire-purchase and conditional sale agreements and all other liabilities including current liabilities.
- *Current assets.* Stock in trade, work in progress, cash, receivables after provision for bad and doubtful debts, readily marketable securities and prepayments.
- *Current liabilities.* Demand loans such as bank overdrafts, any debt maturing within the next 12 months, proposed dividends, current taxation provisions and current creditors.
- *Working capital.* Current assets less current liabilities.

The terms as defined do not necessarily tie in precisely with the presentation of such terms according to general accounting principles. This does not matter provided that the numerical ratio calculated when the transaction is entered into is agreed on the basis of the definitions, thereby setting the target for the future. However, a lessee should try to avoid a result which would necessitate the preparation of an additional set of accounts in order to verify the financial covenants.

The lessor will be expected to covenant that so long as the lessee continues to perform its obligations under the terms of the lease it shall be entitled to the quiet enjoyment, possession and use of the asset. Such a covenant may, in any event, be implied in some jurisdictions. It may also include a covenant to lift liens created by, or arising through, the lessor. The lessor is unlikely to give more than this. If the lessor is a special purpose subsidiary, the lessee may require the lessor's parent to guarantee performance of this obligation. Tax considerations might suggest to a lessee that other covenants from the lessor should be sought.

In a lease where there are a number of different lessors acting jointly or severally there may well be restrictions that a lessee needs to impose upon the respective lessors. For example, because the lessee is taking a real credit risk on the ability of the various lessors to perform, unless an acceptable third party is providing comfort, the lessee may wish to impose restrictions on an individual lessor's ability to dispose of their interest in the asset. When it comes to things like discretionary decisions on the part of the lessors, from the point of view of ease of management, the lessee may seek to impose upon the lessors a deemed consensual vote in accordance with the vote of the lead lessor in respect of the more time critical matters.

Events of default

Whatever covenants are written into a document, whether a lessee complies with them or not, will depend upon its status and to some extent on the degree of sanction imposed by the default provisions and the policing of those default provisions. From a lessor's perspective, the default provisions provide an opportunity to end the relationship with the lessee, preferably before liquidation, thereby enabling it to escape with its investment and a certain amount of its return. It is clearly not intelligent, however, to word the events of default in such a way that every minor transgression is caught, thereby triggering cross default provisions in other documents. In a leveraged lease transaction there are different interests at stake in the default provisions. The owner participants do not want events of default which are too stringent, giving debt participants the opportunity to step in too early and effectively deprive the owner participants of the opportunity to realise the full residual in the asset and their equity return.

One other point worth mentioning is that the use of the defined term 'event of default' should be examined carefully. Often it not only includes the specified events of default, but also incipient defaults, that is, events which, with the giving of notice, lapse of time or the relevant determination will constitute an event of default. If a lessee is able to negotiate grace periods in the specified events of default, it is no good if the defined term includes such incipient events and the defined term is the trigger for payment of the liquidated amount in the form of a stipulated loss or termination value. Use of the incipient concept in the conditions precedent, representations and notification covenant is justifiable, but the logic of using it elsewhere is less compelling.

The fundamental basis of the leasing transaction is that the lessor receives payments on specified dates in specified amounts. The most important event of default is, therefore, the payment default. In terms of the timing of the default, a distinction can be drawn between regular scheduled payments and other payments such as indemnity amounts or reimbursements of other outgoings. For payments other than regular scheduled amounts, it would be iniquitous for the default to be triggered before the date of their demand since, in the absence of such a demand, there is a distinct possibility that the lessee will not know of them. With respect to regular scheduled payments, it is a matter for negotiation as to whether or not any days of grace are given to a lessee. A lessee commonly advances the argument that days of grace are necessary because failure to pay can occur by reason of administrative or technical difficulties. It is a point that can be conceded in negotiation since it provides lessees with some comfort. It is important however, that default interest for late payment runs from the due date or the date of demand, as the case may be, rather than the date that an event of default has occurred. In more complex transactions with a series of leases and subleases, or where lease rentals are being assigned to a lender, the lessee will wish to ensure that negligence or default of any intermediate recipient of the money does not give rise to a default under the lease if it had paid it on the due date. Similarly, a lessor will wish to ensure that it has a grace period under any connected loan agreement at least equal to that under the lease to avoid the loan agreement being put into default before the lease.

In some leases, breach of the insurance covenant may be singled out as a separate event of default, the occurrence of which gives rise to immediate remedies. The importance of this largely depends on the nature of the asset; clearly an uninsured aircraft cannot be permitted at any price because of the liability potential. An uninsured computer, on the other hand, may be permissible for a period of time.

The third event of default, if insurance has been separately dealt with, will be a breach of any other covenant which the lessee has agreed to perform under the lease and, possibly, under any other ancillary document. A lessor will commonly give a longer period of grace for these breaches, but a distinction should be drawn between those breaches which are capable of remedy and those which are not. For example, if the lessee has merged with a corporation and ceased to exist as a separate entity, it is not capable of remedy. The event of default should therefore specify that the period of grace applies only to events which can be remedied, even though it may be imprecise as to which those events are. A lessee will wish the grace period to run from the date it receives notice of such default, rather than the date on which it has knowledge or ought to have had knowledge. The lessor should resist this as it shifts responsibility to the lessor for policing the performance of the lessee and operation of the asset. In addition, the lessee might negotiate to restrict this event of default to material breaches or breaches of material obligations (note the distinction). From a lessor's point of view, either of these concepts raises an area of uncertainty which should be resisted although the lessor is not, in practice, going to be concerned with immaterial breaches. If financial covenants have been included, there is likely to be a separate event of default dealing specifically with these without days of grace.

The next event of default is if any of the representations and warranties prove to be incorrect in any respect. Again, an argument may be advanced by the lessee that this should be restricted to matters which have become materially incorrect. The acceptability of this proposal will be determined by the nature of the representations and warranties. The fact that a corporation does not validly exist; is not in good standing; or that the agreement will constitute a breach of other agreements; or that the agreements are not valid, binding and enforceable, will all be materially incorrect matters. On the other hand, the failure to have obtained an emissions permit from an environmental agency may not be material. If at all possible, the uncertainty introduced by the materiality concept should be avoided. Although a misrepresentation cannot, strictly speaking, be remedied, the circumstances giving rise to it could be rectified, for example by obtaining an emissions permit, and the lessor will sometimes be prepared to concede a period for achieving this.

Sometimes a separate event of default will appear relating to the disposition by the borrower of a substantial part of its business or assets. This will have to be varied to tie up with the merger covenant or the other financial covenants. A lessee should resist the use of the term 'substantial part' because this could cover as little as 5 per cent of its business and the words 'all or substantially all' would be far more acceptable. A lessee should also exclude dispositions in the ordinary course of business to avoid any risk that a substantial sale of stock in trade would be caught. The occurrence of the lessee changing the nature of its business, or suspending a substantial part of its business, might be included either as part of the same event of default or separately. The same arguments would apply to the term 'a substantial part'. The concept of 'threatening to change' or 'threatening to suspend', which could catch matters occurring well in advance of final decisions, is sometimes included. The inclusion of such phrases should be resisted by a lessee.

One of the most useful but contentious events of default is the so-called cross default. In its widest form, it reads something like: 'Any indebtedness, guarantee or similar obligation of the lessee becomes due or capable of being declared due before its stated maturity or is not discharged at maturity or the lessee defaults under or commits a breach of the provisions of any guarantee or other obligation (whether actual or contingent) or any agreement pursuant to which any such indebtedness, guarantee or other obligation was incurred'. The effect of such a provision is that a breach of any other agreement under which the lessee incurs indebtedness, which will include a loan or any form of lease or rental agreement, will constitute an event of default under this agreement, whether or not so called under the other agreement. If a lessee has never given a cross default clause, it should resist it since such a provision has the habit of achieving unfortunate precedent status, either through public knowledge or because of 'most favoured nations clauses' which bring it into play.

The provision can, however, be watered down. From a lessee's perspective it should be confined to borrowed money, including finance leases and guarantees for such obligations. It should not cover general indebtedness such as trade indebtedness. If possible, it should be confined to a situation where acceleration has occurred as opposed to having become capable of being declared. The latter formulation means effectively that the lessor has the benefit of the most stringent default provisions in the lessee's other documents prior to a default being called under the other document. The clause should only apply on a default by the lessee as opposed to early termination or prepayment provisions which are not regarded as defaults; in the wording given above for example, it could pick up an event of total loss or prepayment upon a change in law only affecting a financier. The provision should take into account any applicable grace periods contained in any other documents. In addition, the lessee might argue that it should be limited to amounts above a certain aggregate limit or which are material, thereby leaving the dispute as to what these are to another day. It might also exclude amounts being disputed in good faith where any acceleration has been suspended and for which adequate reserves have been provided. So far as guarantees are concerned, the lessee should argue that the provisions should only refer to amounts which are both due and called, and not simply called, to avoid it including a wrong early call by the beneficiary of a guarantee. The lessor may want to limit this exception so that it only applied where the lessee demonstrated that the guarantor was resisting the claim on reasonable legal grounds, for example, by providing a legal opinion to that effect.

Another common default provision, which may be incorporated in the insolvency default (see below), covers execution, attachment or distress being issued or levied against any of the assets of the lessee. The lessee should insist on a grace period so that frivolous actions and unproven claims are excluded. The lessor will usually accept this provided such action is stayed or effectively provided for within, for instance, 30 days of its occurrence. The provisions may also include threats of such action which should be resisted by a lessee since it could catch groundless threats.

The next event of default would generally deal with insolvency. There might be an express event of default to the effect that the 'lessee becomes insolvent or unable to pay its debts as they fall due' and, in addition, an event which would cover the situation where a trustee, receiver, administrative receiver, administrator, custodian, liquidator or similar officer is appointed for any part of the lessee's property, or the lessee convenes a meeting of its creditors or makes any arrangement or composition with, or any assignment for the benefit of its creditors, or a petition is presented in bankruptcy or for the making of an administration order, or a meeting is convened for the purposes of considering a resolution relating to the presentation of such a petition or other steps are taken for the liquidation or the reorganisation of the lessee in bankruptcy or insolvency proceedings. There should not generally be much negotiation on provisions which address the ultimate stages in the financial demise of a lessee, but a strong lessee (or a lessee covered by a strong guarantor) will argue that incipient insolvency proceedings, such as presentation of a petition or convening of a meeting, should not apply unless initiated by itself or, alternatively, should only apply after a failure to dismiss the petition within a fixed period. It is advisable to extend the provision to cover analogous proceedings under the laws of any other relevant jurisdiction.

In addition to the more specific financial defaults discussed above, a lessor may seek to include a general material adverse change event of default. This provision would give rise to a termination right where the financial condition or business of the lessee has suffered such an adverse change. It is for negotiation as to whether this is an objective test or one determined by the lessor. If financial covenants have been included a lessee should resist the clause.

There may well be other specified events of default depending upon the particular transaction. For example, if the lessee's parent is intimately involved with the management of the company, then a disposition of the parent's shareholding might be included. Another question that can arise is whether or not the non-specific defaults, such as the cross default and insolvency default, should relate to the lessee's subsidiaries and affiliates and their assets. If the corporate entity on which the credit risk is being taken is just the lessee and there is no external support, then the only reason for extending these provisions to include subsidiaries and affiliates is on the basis that a sick subsidiary or affiliate is an indication of a group malaise and that this is sufficient reason for terminating the relationship with the lessee. If the transaction has been guaranteed, then it is usual practice to include references to the guarantor in these default provisions and also to add an express event of default relating to the continued valid existence of the guarantee.

Remedies

Having established what events constitute a default, the consequences of such an event or events need to be determined. An event of default usually entitles the lessor at any time thereafter to serve notice on the lessee that the lease is in default and that the right to lease has been terminated. The calling of a default or otherwise is discretionary to the lessor. A lessee should insist that a default can only be called at a time when it is continuing. Some leases provide that insolvency defaults automatically terminate the lease. This is not necessarily always the desired course of action, but it should be carefully considered by the lessor where insolvency legislation prohibits a lessor taking steps to terminate a lease upon insolvency of the lessee. There can be circumstances where a default should not be called because of the adverse consequences on other documentation to which the lessee is a party. The failure to declare a default may give sufficient breathing space to enable the lessee to negotiate a deal with other creditors, or for the affairs of the lessee to be reorganised. The lessee should ensure that the right of the lessor to exercise the remedies (and to impose stricter restrictions on the lessee by reason of a default having occurred) only exists so long as the default is continuing.

The lease will list a number of remedies which are available to a lessor following declaration of default, but the efficacy of those remedies will depend to a large extent on the jurisdiction in which they are being enforced and the proper law of the contract.

A typical finance lease provides as one of the options to the lessor that, in addition to demanding all other amounts outstanding or claiming damages, it can demand a liquidated sum, which in the case of medium- and big-ticket transactions, will invariably be some form of specified stipulated loss or termination value. Instead of specific values, smaller transactions will use a formula of all future rentals which have not then fallen due discounted to present day values at a fairly severe rate (a 'Rule of 78' calculation, for example).

The liquidated sum is supposed to represent a genuine pre-estimate of the damage that the lessor has suffered by reason of the early termination of the transaction. Included in the figure will be the remaining outstanding principal and some premium to reflect the loss of profit and the tax effects of an immediate receipt of the termination sum. In a tax-based transaction, the values include additions for loss of any tax credits and depreciation benefits. It should not, although it sometimes does, include profit through to the end of the transaction since, in theory at least, the funds received can be redeployed to make a return. From a lessee's point of view, the more frequently the values are stipulated, the more accurate and fair they will be. If there are variable factors at the time the lease is signed, such as an uncertain final expenditure on the acquisition price of the equipment, there will have to be variation provisions in the lease providing for an adjustment to the stipulated loss figures once the variables are known.

An alternative to the stipulated loss values, or to specifying a formula for calculation of the amount due, would be simply to leave the matter to be determined by a court in a claim for damages (as is sometimes the case in operating leases). However, a liquidated sum is attractive because it enables a lessor to specify a precise amount and seek a summary judgment in debt accordingly. It also assists the lessor in establishing that the specified sum is a figure representing the agreed compensation for the lessor's losses in terminating the transaction prematurely.

A common problem with the use of stipulated loss or termination values is the confusion about whether or not they are calculated assuming rent has been paid on the rent payment date for which they are specified. The lawyers and lessor should liaise closely on this to check that the lessor is getting everything it should and that the language of the lease reflects the basis of the calculation. Just as importantly, the lessee should check that it is not being asked to pay too much. (This problem applies equally with regard to the amounts payable on a total loss.)

The lessor becomes entitled to recover possession of the asset as part of the default procedure and at this point the lessee's obligations relating to redelivery, storage etc come into play (see the section 'Other covenants' above). In addition to the right to demand payment of the liquidated sum, the lessor will also reserve, either expressly or impliedly, the right to sell, re-lease, hold and let stand idle or otherwise exploit the asset.

To the extent that the lessor recovers proceeds from the sale, re-lease or other exploitation of the asset, the lessee in a finance lease should be credited with the amount received or, if the lessee has already paid the termination sum, then such amount should be paid to the lessee. In a transaction done on the basis that the lessor is entitled to the residual value, as in a typical US leveraged lease, the lessee would only recover up to the stipulated loss value or other amount paid. Some leases are silent on the issue of what happens to the sale proceeds, however in most common law jurisdictions there is a rule against penalties which apply following a breach of contract. English authorities suggest that it would be penal if a lessor is entitled to recover more than, in effect, principal plus interest and margin through to the date of termination (ignoring tax effects). The onus is on the lessee to demonstrate the penal nature of the payment. This may be difficult if the lessee is of equal bargaining strength and was professionally advised at the time a transaction was negotiated. The argument may, however, be open to the lessee to the effect that the lessor could recover the amounts it lost by exploiting the available market for the asset and that, therefore, the amount of stipulated loss value could not be regarded as a genuine pre-estimate of damages.

There may be other limiting factors on recovery. As already stated, in some jurisdictions interest upon interest may not be recoverable and usury limitations may be applicable (for example, New York). This is particularly relevant where a lease provides for default interest to accrue on the entire amount claimed by the lessor from the date of default to the date of payment.

In some jurisdictions there may well be other statutory remedies available in addition to the stated remedies (for example, in the United States under the Uniform Commercial Code). To a large extent a lessor's choice of remedy will be dictated by the circumstances of the lessee. Special problems can arise in cross-border transactions because of the difficulties of actually recovering possession of the asset. Certain jurisdictions also provide lessees with protection which may interfere with the ability of a lessor to recover what it has bargained for under the terms of the lease or to obtain possession of the equipment (for example, US Chapter 11 protection and administration proceedings under the UK Insolvency Act 1986). A lessor would be well advised in a cross-border lease to seek local counsel's opinion on the procedural constraints of enforcing the standard remedies provisions in the jurisdiction of the lessee and the remedies section should be adapted accordingly.

Voluntary termination

A lessee may wish to introduce a voluntary termination right into the lease for commercial reasons whereby, on giving notice, the lessee is able to terminate the relationship on payment of a specified termination value. There may be tax reasons why this should be resisted but, in their absence, the availability of such a provision is a matter of commercial negotiation. Some lessors will insist on a minimum period before which no notice of termination can be given so that the lessee cannot terminate the transaction to take advantage of lower market financing rates before the lessor has started to earn any real return on the lease. The mechanics will be set out providing for adequate notice to be given, usually with the result that termination is to take effect from the next succeeding rent payment date following the issuance of the notice in order to avoid any broken funding costs. The termination becomes effective upon payment of the termination sum and all other amounts then due. Because such a termination is occurring in circumstances other than a lessee default, arguably the termination values should be lower than the stipulated loss values payable on a default, disregarding any tax consequences. However, this militates against the argument that the stipulated loss values are not penal. Where the lessor is to retain the residual value of the equipment, there should be no element of residual included in the termination values since the lessor is getting the asset back. Where the residual in the equipment is to pass back to the lessee, there should be provision for sale of the equipment and the crediting of any proceeds of sale to the lessee's obligation with any surplus being repaid to the lessee by way of a rebate of rentals and/or sales commission.

Miscellaneous provisions

Often buried at the back of a lease agreement are a number of further provisions which all have considerable legal significance, particularly for the construction of the document.

These may include a provision confirming that the rights of the lessor under the agreement are cumulative and that rights can only be waived or varied expressly in writing. Mere inaction does not waive any right. This is particularly important in the context of events of default, although the lessor would still be well advised to give express notice where it does not act immediately on a default to preserve its position.

What is generally known as a further assurances provision also may be included. The substance of this is that the lessee, and perhaps the lessor, agree to enter into any documents and do whatever is necessary to give effect to the true intent and purpose of the document.

There may be a provision confirming that the lease constitutes the entire agreement between the parties. Any commitment letters or exchange of telexes before execution of the lease are thereby excluded from affecting the interpretation of the document. (This may not be appropriate if the lessee's representations extend to pre-contract materials.) It might also go on to say that no amendment to the agreement can be made other than in writing signed by both parties, or at least by the party against whom the amendment is being put forward. Such a provision is of questionable enforceability, at least under English law, where contracts can be effected or varied by conduct or orally. Such a provision should also ideally state that any amendment should refer specifically to the agreement being amended to encourage specific cross-reference and avoid unintentional amendment.

Another aid to construction is commonly called the severability provision. This purports to sever from the rest of the agreement any provision which becomes invalid, illegal or unenforceable under any law, thereby, it is hoped, preserving the validity and legality of the balance of the document. However, a court is unlikely to enforce the balance of the contract if its performance becomes illegal or would breach exchange control regulations.

The important notice provision will usually be contained in this section. Notice provisions commonly require notice to be in writing in one form or another and usually deem receipt to have occurred, for example, on the second business day after the date of despatch. It is important to remember that such deeming operates both ways. If the lease is structured on the basis that the lessee is required to give the lessor a number of notices which trigger obligations on the part of the lessor, there may be good reason for removing the deeming provision and simply having notices effectively given when actually received or only applying the deeming provision to notices to the lessee. After all, it is usually possible to arrange for hand delivery of important notices such as default notices. Practice varies over the acceptability of notices by facsimile and the legal validity of notices by facsimile depends on local laws. Faxed notices should generally be confirmed by a hard copy sent by post or by hand delivery.

A provision relating to the ability of the lessor to delegate or appoint people to act on its behalf might also be included.

Another substantive provision included in this section or in the payment section relates to the application of moneys. In the absence of an express provision as to how moneys are to be applied, they will often be presumed to have been applied to interest first and then principal. This may well not suit a lessor at the time for accounting or commercial reasons. It is therefore sensible to include an application of moneys provision that entitles the lessor to apply any moneys when received in amounts less than those then due, in such order as it thinks fit. The lessee could argue that they should be applied in the order which most effectively reduces the outstanding debt, but this is a weak argument since the provision only applies when the lessee has not paid all amounts due. The lessee may have better grounds to argue this where, for example, an indemnity payment is disputed and the lessor applies a rental payment to the indemnity payment and then claims rental arrears.

Some lessors include a power of attorney in their favour so that, following an event of default, they do not have to rely on the compliance of the lessee for carrying out any necessary functions such as deregistration or changes in permits. Its effect may be severely curtailed by local bankruptcy rules and may give rise to specific execution or registration requirements. For example, under English law, a lease with such a provision would need to be executed as a deed. Registration to give legal effect to a power of attorney may result in additional fees or stamp duty being paid unnecessarily, in which case the power of attorney could be set out on a separate document. The power of attorney may also be important to enable the lessor to effect an insurance settlement in the name of the lessee, although this needs to take into account the loss payee provisions.

This section will also contain provisions dealing with governing law, submission to jurisdiction, appointments of agents for service of process and agreement as to the manner of service of process.

Conclusion

This chapter highlights the key legal documentation features of leasing transactions. The variety of transaction structures and jurisdictional peculiarities dictate that a range of issues, in addition to those listed above, needs to be considered on a case by case basis and this will affect the provisions of the leasing documentation. For this reason, the documentation involved is likely to vary widely between one transaction and the next.

Despite efforts to standardise certain documents in some areas of leasing, because of the large number of variable factors involved in most transactions, documentation is not likely to become standardised for most leasing transactions for some time to come.

Chapter 6

Transaction structures

Simon Hall

Introduction

This chapter examines some important examples of leasing transactions. These include: Japanese operating leases (JOLs); Japanese operating leases containing purchase options (JALCOs); qualified technological equipment (QTE) leasing transactions; synthetic leases; and enhanced equipment trust certificate (EETC) transactions.

Leasing structures are liable to change since they reflect the current tax environment and commercial legislation of the country or countries in which they operate. For example, cross-border Japanese leveraged leases ceased to be economically viable after changes to the Japanese corporate tax regime in 1998. Meanwhile some new structures have come into the market, while others have been updated. For example, equipment trust certificates (ETCs), first employed in the United States in the 1930s to finance the railroads, are still common in an enhanced form. This structure, like others, has crossed over national borders to form the basis of European enhanced equipment trust certificates (EEETCs).

QTE leasing transactions are another good example of transactions that are relevant across national borders. Although QTE transactions are largely driven by US tax depreciation benefits, end users in leasing structures can claim tax depreciation allowances in other jurisdictions outside the United States. To date, cross-border QTE transactions have been concluded between the United States and France, Germany, the UK and many other European countries.

Since most leasing transactions are structured to maximise the allocation of the available tax allowances, regional differences in taxation, accounting and corporate law play a significant part in determining the respective roles played by all parties in leasing transactions. The following examples give an idea of some of the most important structures used in Europe, Japan and the United States.

Japanese operating leases

When the Japanese Corporation Tax Law was revised in 1998, the cross-border Japanese leveraged lease effectively ceased to exist. Although they are not prohibited, they have become economically unattractive, as depreciation must now be taken on a straight-line rather than a declining balance basis.

However, so long as a JOL satisfies the new tax requirements, depreciation may still be taken on a declining balance basis. The main criterion is the '90 per cent test' under which the aggregate lease rentals during the term must not exceed 90 per cent of the lessor's total cost (including interest and fees) for acquiring the asset.

The tax benefits that Japanese equity investors receive via depreciation allowances will, to some extent, be passed onto the airlines in the form of cheaper rentals. Moreover, for the airlines' accounting purposes, JOLs are off-balance sheet. This can be helpful in enhancing the presentation of the airlines' balance sheets.

Japanese equity investors can claim depreciation allowances for used aircraft over a period equal to the operating lease term plus 20 per cent of the existing age of the aircraft (so for example, for a five-year old aircraft with a four-year lease, the depreciation period would be five years). For new aircraft, the depreciation period is eight years. So the benefits can often be obtained more quickly in the case of a used aircraft.

JOLs effectively fall into the following two main categories:

Traditional Japanese operating leases and Japanese operating leases containing purchase options

Japanese operating leases are effectively viewed by airlines in the same commercial perspective as a traditional operating lease. (For example, an airline might be looking for a method of obtaining relatively short-term use of an aircraft to fit in with its fleet planning and non-core business strategy.) However, due to the inherent tax benefits in a JOL structure, JOL lease rentals tend to be cheaper than the rentals airlines might have to pay to a true operating lessor for a non-JOL operating lease of an equivalent aircraft.

The fundamental differences between a JALCO and a JOL are, first, that JALCOs tend to involve a longer-term lease than JOLs (typically 10 years as against five years) and, secondly, that JALCOs contain purchase options in favour of the airline. Further differences are outlined in Exhibits 6.1 and 6.2.

Once again, due to the inherent tax benefits in a JALCO structure, JALCO lease rentals tend to be cheaper than the rentals airlines might have to pay under a non-tax-leveraged structure for a similar lease of an equivalent aircraft.

In a JOL, the aircraft is generally purchased by the owner from either a third-party lessor subject to, and with the benefit of, an existing operating lease (which is novated to the owner) or from an airline, in a sale and leaseback transaction, with the owner granting an operating lease back to the airline.

A bank loan typically provides approximately 70 per cent to 80 per cent of the owner's acquisition cost of the aircraft, with the remaining amount provided by Japanese equity investors. A bank loan can then be secured by a mortgage over the aircraft and a security assignment of the owner's rights under the operating lease and the account into which the lease rentals flow, or further accounts in which security deposits and maintenance reserves paid by the airline will be lodged.

The loan will amortise to a pre-agreed balloon payment at the expiry of the lease which is to be paid off by the proceeds of sale of the aircraft. To facilitate the sale of the aircraft and help ensure that the sale proceeds will at least satisfy the balloon amount, the owner will generally enter into a residual value guarantee and a re-marketing agreement. Any sale proceeds over and above the balloon amount will be for the account of the Japanese equity investors. It should be noted that in certain transactions, the aircraft may be re-leased and the resulting rental stream used to repay the balloon amount over time.

The equity investors will not receive much, if any, return on their investment during the lease term, although they do get depreciation allowances. This lack of return during the lease

Exhibit 6.1

The basic structure of a typical JOL

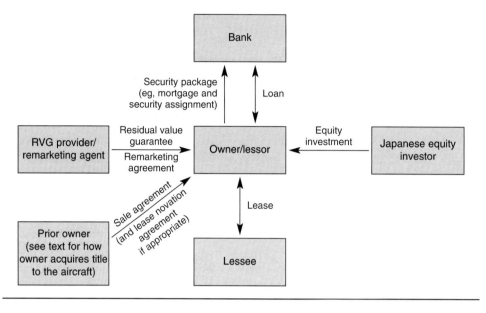

Exhibit 6.2

The basic structure of a typical JALCO

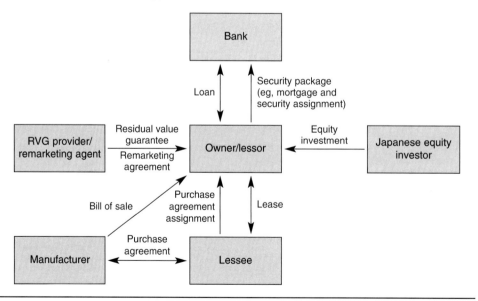

term is important, because the equity investors need to demonstrate that they are taking asset risk on the value of the aircraft in order to qualify for depreciation allowances. The Japanese equity investors will be looking to recoup their investment from the surplus proceeds of sale of the aircraft, or from sharing in the rentals of any future re-leasing of the aircraft on the expiry of the lease term. For this reason the equity investors will carefully negotiate the relevant return conditions.

In a JALCO, an owner will generally purchase a new aircraft from the manufacturer. The owner will then typically enter into a long-term lease (for example, 12 years) with a purchase option granted to the airline (often around year 10).

Once again, a bank loan typically provides 70 per cent to 80 per cent of the acquisition costs of the aircraft, with the remaining amount being provided by Japanese equity investors. The bank loan is secured by a mortgage over the aircraft and a security assignment of the owner's rights under the operating lease and other relevant transaction documents.

Over the course of the transaction, the lease rentals typically pay out the loan. The Japanese equity investors will not receive much, if any, return during the lease term, although they do get depreciation allowances. As in a typical JOL detailed above, this lack of return during the lease term is important, because the equity investors need to demonstrate that they are taking asset risk on the value of the aircraft. If, however, the airline exercises its purchase option, the proceeds will repay the investment of the equity investors. Since it is not certain that the airline will exercise its purchase option, the equity investors might be interested in obtaining residual value guarantees and re-marketing agreements to help protect the asset and the resale value of the aircraft in situations where the owner needs to sell the aircraft in the open market in order to repay the equity investors. Any surplus proceeds from the sale of the aircraft will be for the account of the equity investors. As for JOLs, the Japanese equity investors will carefully negotiate the relevant return conditions.

Qualified technological equipment

Qualified technological equipment leasing transactions are products driven by US tax depreciation benefits and involve a US lessor and US tax considerations. They are often structured so that the US lessor involved in the leasing structure claims tax depreciation in the United States, whilst the end user involved in the leasing structure claims tax depreciation in its own jurisdiction (see Exhibit 6.3 for a typical QTE structure).

To date, cross-border QTE transactions have been concluded between the United States and France, Germany, the United Kingdom and many other European countries.

What constitutes QTE?

'Qualified technological equipment' is defined in section 168 (i) (2) of the US Internal Revenue Code of 1986 as:

• any computer or peripheral equipment; or
• any technology telephone station equipment installed on a customer's premises; and
• any high-technology medical equipment.

'Computer' is defined at section 168 (i) (2) (B) (ii) of the Code as a programmable, electronically activated device which:

• is capable of accepting information, applying prescribed processes to the information and supplying the results of these processes with or without human intervention; or

- consists of a central processing unit containing extensive storage, logic, arithmetic and control capabilities.

'Peripheral equipment' is defined at section 168 (i) (2) (B) (ii) of the Code as any auxiliary machine (whether on-line or off-line) which is designed to be placed under the control of the central processing unit of a computer.

It is under the very broad definition of computer and peripheral equipment that most QTE falls. For example, telephone station equipment generally does not fall within the definition at section 168 (i) (2) (B) (ii) of the Code due to the reference to customer's premises. However telephone station equipment does fall within the definition of computer and is therefore QTE. Telephone switches, although very specific when compared with general purpose computers, do accept and process information and provide output (and possess a central processing unit with storage, logic and arithmetic and control capabilities) and are thus computers for the purposes of the Code. It should be noted that excluded from the definition is equipment used primarily for amusement or entertainment of the user and equipment that is an integral part of other property that is not a computer.

Although QTE leases have traditionally been most actively marketed in the telecommunications sector for digital switching equipment, they have also been used with respect to the following types of equipment:

- postal sorting equipment;
- air-traffic control equipment;
- rail signalling and monitoring equipment;
- flight simulation equipment;
- revenue fare collection equipment;
- satellite components;
- metro and transit ticketing systems;
- power grid control systems;
- set-top boxes;
- hospital scanning equipment;
- automatic train protection (ATP) systems;
- telecommunications equipment;
- digital switch gear (eg, fixed line and cellular switching equipment); and
- aircraft baggage systems.

Depreciation rules relating to QTE

The US tax depreciation rules relating to QTE are an exception to the rules relating to property leased to non-US persons (known as the 'Pickle rules'). The Pickle rules override normal US depreciation rules and provide a special, and unfavourable, depreciation period of 125 per cent of the lease term for property leased to a non-US person. However, if the leased property is QTE, then it is eligible for five year straight-line US tax depreciation.

As Exhibit 6.3 illustrates, the initial step in the transaction is for the lessee to either sell the QTE equipment at fair market value or to lease it to the US lessor. A lease would generally be a lease intended as security (LIS) from the US perspective. These LIS are treated as conditional sales for US commercial law purposes and so create the necessary tax characterisation.

Exhibit 6.3

A typical QTE transaction

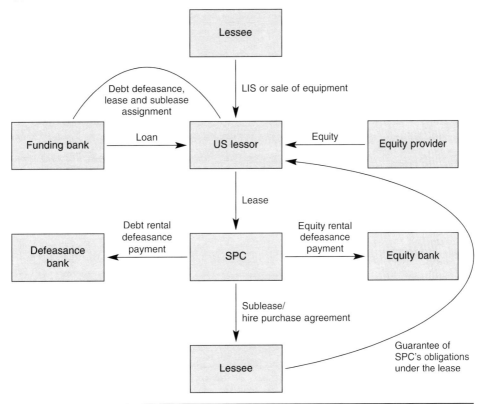

Although such a lease is intended as security, it should not actually create security over the equipment, nor does it need to do so, in the lessee's home jurisdiction. In fact, the LIS creates in favour of the US lessor only an ability to use the equipment (like a conventional lease), the terms of such usage being for the economic and useful life of the equipment. The LIS is not economically that different from an outright sale since the LIS is effectively prepaid.

Below the LIS, there is a lease to the special purpose company (SPC) and thereafter a sublease/hire-purchase agreement from SPC back to lessee who operates the equipment under that agreement.

The LIS and the sublease are effectively prepaid. The lease is paid out over time through a defeasance structure. The day one cash flows are as set out below.

In Exhibit 6.4, 20 per cent of the equipment cost is met by US equity investors and 80 per cent through a bank loan. As a prepayment under the LIS, the US lessor pays 100 per cent of the cost to the lessee. In turn, the lessee prepays the sublease by paying 94 per cent of the equipment cost to the SPC. The SPC places these funds on economic defeasance arrangements, one part to cover the debt element and the other to cover the equity element of its lease payment obligations.

If there is an early termination, an exposure arises on the financing. On the debt side, there is no bank exposure because the loan is effectively repaid through the accelerated debt element termination payment under the lease which is funded with the debt defeasance (that is, the loan

Exhibit 6.4

Cash flows of basic QTE transactions

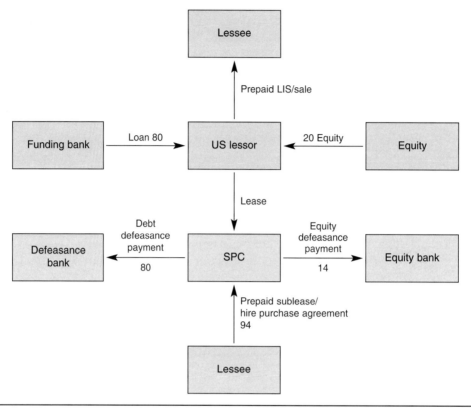

is repaid with the remaining debt deposit held by the defeasance bank). On the equity side, at the time of early termination, the amount held by the equity bank will not have built up to a sufficient amount to pay off the required equity termination sum. The difference between the amount held by the equity bank and the amount required by the US lessor is known as the 'strip'. The US lessor will require cover for that strip which will be drawn by way of guarantees, or letters of credit, from the project banks. Again, on payment of these amounts the leasing structure terminates with title and use of the equipment being free and clear to the lessee.

To assist in the structuring of the transaction from a US tax perspective and to secure its debt, and the debt defeasance, the funding bank will take security from the US lessor over the leasing rights under the LIS, the rights under the lease and the debt defeasance. That security is for the loan amount and so, on application of the deposit held by that defeasance bank, the loan will be discharged and the security, accordingly, released. Note that under any property insurances held by lessee over the equipment, the US lessor would need to be named as loss payee, subject to the usual obligations to account for those funds to lessee.

Synthetic leases

Synthetic leases were originally created in the United States and designed to exploit inconsistencies between US accounting and tax rules. They are also known as off-balance sheet loans, see-through leases and broken leases. Originally they were used in the US real estate market to provide off-balance sheet refinancing for corporate headquarters. Synthetic leases are financing mechanisms that take advantage of a leasehold form to:

- maintain the off-balance sheet treatment of the leasehold form, essentially in order for the lessee to keep the asset and consequential debt related to an acquisition off its balance sheet except as a footnote; and
- allow the lessee to take advantage of significant tax benefits associated with the ownership of the property involved (for example, depreciation allowances relating to the property and interest deductions with respect to the rental payments made by the lessee in respect of the property).

A synthetic lease is effectively a structure that is treated as a lease for accounting purposes, but is treated as a loan for tax purposes. The structure is such that the lessee has the risks and benefits of ownership throughout the lease.

The basic rules applicable to a synthetic lease

The basic accounting rules applicable to synthetic leases are set out in the Financial Accounting Standards Board's (FASB) Statement 13, paragraph L10.103 (equivalent to the International Accounting Standards Rule 17). FASB Statement 13 states that to maintain the off-balance sheet treatment of a synthetic lease, the transaction must not include the following four criteria.

- An automatic transfer of title from lessor to the lessee at the end of the lease.
- A bargain purchase option for the lessee (essentially a below-market price purchase option which makes purchase of the property an economic certainty).
- A lease term that lasts for 75 per cent or more of the estimated economic life of the property.
- At lease commencement, the present value of the minimum lease payments (primarily, these are the minimum rentals plus the lessee's contingent rent obligations as discussed below) discounted at the interest rate implicit in the lease (that is, so as only to capture any repayments of principal amounts rather than interest amounts) meets or exceeds 90 per cent of the fair-market value of the property as at day one of the transaction. Other payments to be taken into account here include any costs of the lessor which are reimbursed by the lessee (for example, lawyers' fees, the costs of re-marketing and/or redelivering the asset). However, costs of maintenance, insurance and taxes are excluded.

The presence of any of the above criteria would lead to the synthetic lease being classified as a finance lease and its off-balance sheet treatment would therefore be lost.

Generally, the parties need to ensure that the lessor is an entity that will not be consolidated with the lessee for accounting purposes, thus leading to the assets of the lessor appearing on the lessee's balance sheet and off-balance sheet treatment thus being lost. A FASB task force has detailed the following three standards that, when they collectively exist in a purported synthetic lease transaction, would lead to such an accounting consolidation.

- Instances where the lessor has not made any substantive 'at risk' investment in the synthetic lease transaction. In response, lessors typically make an at risk equity investment of at least 3 per cent of the purchase price of the asset, which according to FASB guidelines is currently considered sufficient to meet the substantive at risk investment requirement.

- If substantially all of the business or activities of the lessor involve assets or property leased to the lessee. Since lessors in a synthetic lease structure are most often bankruptcy remote special purpose entities (often in the form of trusts) created for the specific transaction, this is usually the case.
- Where the lessee stands to take advantage of all of the residual benefits of the asset or property, while also bearing most of the risk with respect to the same. This is usually the case due to the way synthetic leases are structured.

With synthetic leases, parties will almost always fall foul of the second and/or third condition. Thus, it is crucial for the lessor to satisfy the 3 per cent equity investment FASB guideline (discussed above) if off-balance sheet treatment is to be obtained by the lessee.

The structure of a synthetic lease

Equity investors and lenders

As Exhibit 6.5 illustrates, equity investors will generally fund a lessor with 3 per cent of the day one asset value as an equity investment, whilst the lenders will fund the lessor with the other 97 per cent in the form of secured debt. The debt would be non-recourse to the lessor who would normally be a SPC, with recourse only to the lease rentals and the asset.

Having financed 97 per cent of the asset, the lenders will take a security package that will include a first ranking security over the asset (for example, a mortgage) and assignment of the lease. They will typically have priority and full seniority over the equity investors.

Exhibit 6.5

A typical synthetic lease structure

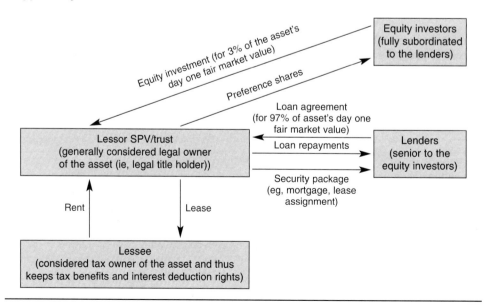

The equity investors may well receive a return during the lease term (for example, through amounts payable under the preference shares they hold in the lessor), but they have no tax depreciation benefits and their 3 per cent equity investment needs to be at risk and unpaid during the lease term. The equity investors have greater exposure to asset risk than the lenders, because they are fully subordinated to the lenders and will only be able to access any amounts payable under the transaction once the lenders have been fully satisfied.

The rentals from the synthetic lease would be used by the lessor, firstly, to pay the interest on the debt and amortise the debt down to a little below the appraised fair market value of the asset as at the end of the lease term and, secondly, perhaps to pay some equity return.

At the end of the lease term, the lessee would have a purchase option at the relevant appraised fair market value of the asset. The proceeds of any such sale of the asset would be used by the lessor to pay off any remaining debt and the equity investment. It should be noted that lenders and equity investors fully expect their funding to be repaid by the lessee exercising its purchase option and thus synthetic leases are structured so that the lessee has an incentive to exercise its purchase option. Typically if there is a sale of the asset to a third party for any reason (for example, the lessee does not exercise its purchase option to buy the asset), then the lessee will have to pay a contingent rent (which is essentially a residual value guarantee) of the difference between the actual sale proceeds and the relevant fair market value of the asset. However, under FASB 13 (discussed above), the contingent rent when added to the rent paid and other payments under the lease and discounted at lease rate cannot exceed 90 per cent of the day one fair market value of the asset, if off-balance sheet treatment is to be obtained by the lessee. Thus FASB Statement 13 effectively caps the contingent rent residual value guarantee payable by the lessee.

Because FASB Statement 13 limits the lessee's potential liability to 90 per cent of the day one fair market value of the property, then, on the assumption that the lenders have funded 97 per cent of the day one fair market value of the asset, the lenders' only true asset risk arises if the value of the asset, at either termination or the end of the lease term, is below 7 per cent of the asset's day-one fair-market value. Similarly, on the assumption that the equity investors have funded 3 per cent of the day one fair market value of the asset, the equity investors' only true asset risk arises if the value of the asset at either termination or the end of the lease term is below 10 per cent of the asset's day one fair market value. This 10 per cent threshold recovery value applicable to equity investors is greater than the 7 per cent threshold recovery value applicable to the lenders because equity investors can only access any contingent rent residual value guarantee to repay their investment once the lenders have been fully repaid their 97 per cent investment.

The lessor

The lessor will probably be the legal title holder in the asset. However, the substance-over-form approach adopted by US law might recognise the lessee (who effectively has the economic burden and benefits of ownership in a synthetic lease transaction) as the true owner of the asset. Thus the US courts might deem that the lessor's title in the asset is limited to a security interest. To protect against this scenario, it would be prudent for the lessor to make any relevant Uniform Commercial Code security filings with respect to the lease. This risk of re-characterisation of the lease as a security document could have significant consequences for the transaction (for example, it will impact on taxation, bankruptcy and contractual analysis) and accordingly should be protected against as far as possible.

The lessee

The lessee, who will be the end user of the property, gains both tax and accounting benefits from a synthetic lease. The accounting benefits for the lessee flow from the fact that the off-balance sheet treatment of synthetic leases means that its accounts would indicate:

- an increase in net income and reported earnings per share;
- a reduction in debt-to-equity ratios;
- an improvement in financial ratios (for example, earnings per share, return on equity, interest coverage ratio); and
- that payments under a synthetic lease are not classified as debt for the purposes of financial covenants in credit agreements.

The tax benefits for the lessee flow from the fact that for tax purposes the synthetic lease is treated as a loan and the lessee as the tax owner of the financed asset. Thus the lessee is entitled to take deductions for depreciation of the financed asset; and is also entitled to take deductions for the interest component of the rent payable under the synthetic lease.

The future of synthetic leasing

There is some general uncertainty about the future for synthetic leases. A recent G4+1 paper stated that: 'The distinction between operating leases and finance leases that is required by present standards is arbitrary and unsatisfactory'. For example this paper considered that: 'The "all or nothing" nature of the approach taken in these standards is arbitrary: for example, if the 90 per cent threshold…is applied literally, a lessee records all or (nearly all) of the asset [on its balance sheet] if 91 per cent of its value is transferred by the lease and none of 89 per cent if its value is transferred. As a result, transactions that are substantially similar are accounted for in very different ways.'

The collapse of Enron has further highlighted this problem and the FASB Emerging Issues Task Force will undoubtedly be looking carefully at off-balance sheet transactions, probably setting the percentage for equity investments at a much higher level than 3 per cent.

European enhanced equipment trust certificates

European enhanced equipment trust certificates (EEETCs) developed from enhanced equipment trust certificate (EETC) transactions, which themselves developed from equipment trust certificate (ETC) transactions (see Exhibit 6.6).

ETCs were first employed in the United States in the 1930s to finance the railroads. The following is a basic summary of an ETC transaction.

- The lessee (in this case a railway operator) typically enters into a conditional sale contract with the manufacturer, pursuant to which the lessee purchases assets (for example, rolling stock) from the manufacturer.
- The lessee then assigns its rights under the conditional sale contract to the trustee (thus enabling the trustee to take title to the assets from the manufacturer).
- The trustee then pays the purchase price to the manufacturer and takes title to the asset. From the trustee's perspective, being the legal owner of the asset is more secure than the

Exhibit 6.6

The structure of an equipment trust certificate

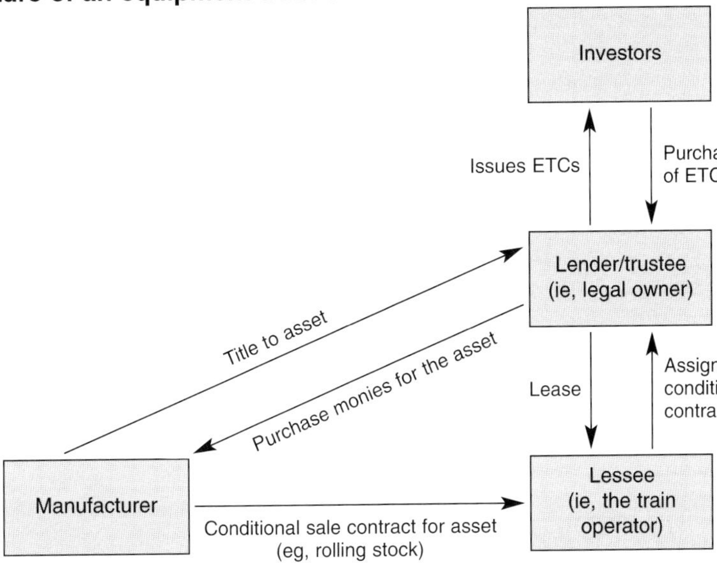

trustee receiving a mortgage over the asset from the lessee. The cost of borrowing will be reduced to reflect this fact.

- The trustee would then lease the asset to the lessee.
- The trustee funds its involvement in the transaction by an issue of certificates (that is, the ETC) to investors.
- The trustee holds title to the assets on trust for the benefit of the investors.
- The lease rental payments are then used by the trustee to repay the ETC.

EETCs are essentially ETC transactions with enhancements, that is, rating or credit enhancing additions or alterations to the ETC structures which effectively give investors who purchased the certificates greater security that they will be repaid. Enhancement matters are discussed below in relation to EEETCs and are equally applicable to EETC. EETCs give the end user a cheaper and more efficient source of financing whilst also permitting them greater balance sheet flexibility. The investor base for EETCs has broadened, partly due to the wide range of differently rated EETCs issued. EETCs have been widely used in the United States, especially to finance aircraft. The United States now boasts a sophisticated EETC investor base which understands and invests in the various classes of notes that are issued in an EETC.

EEETCs are essentially EETCs modified to satisfy the requirements of English law and the rating agencies, and to conform with Eurobond market practices, while still maintaining the economic substance of the EETC transaction. EEETCs are rated transactions. For the EEETC to be viable, the notes issued must receive an appropriate rating. Thus, rating agencies will be heavily involved in stress testing and developing the EEETC transaction structure (see Exhibit 6.7).

The borrower (typically a tax haven SPC, based, for example, in the International Financial Services Centre or IFSC in Dublin) enters into a facility agreement with the issuer (also typically a tax haven SPC, based, for example, in the IFSC in Dublin). Pursuant to this

Exhibit 6.7

The basic structure of a European enhanced equipment trust certificate

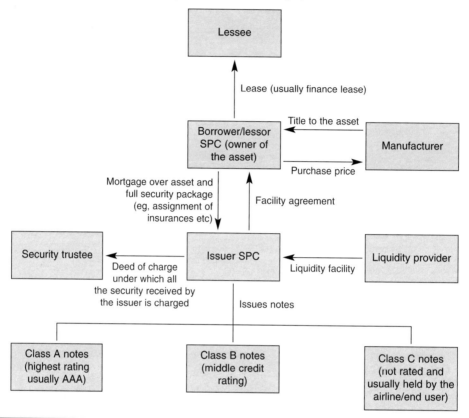

facility agreement, the issuer agrees to make available a euro-denominated fixed-term facility in an amount equal to the purchase price of the asset.

The borrower will draw down amounts under the facility agreement in order to purchase and take title to the asset (usually from the manufacturer). The borrower will then lease the asset to the lessee pursuant to a lease containing customary provisions. The leases are generally long-term finance leases, whose rentals are intended to repay the notes. In some structures, tax leveraged leases are used to further reduce the costs of the funding. Ancillary documents and security agreements typical to the lease of the asset will also be entered into by the relevant parties. For example, in the case of an aircraft, airframe and engine warranty agreements, purchase agreement, assignments etc will be entered into. When the lease term expires, the end user will be able to exercise its rights under either a sales agency agreement to sell the asset to a third party, or a purchase option to buy the asset for an amount not less than the total amount of the outstanding financing under the facility agreement.

At this stage, the outstanding principal amount of the notes is expected to be redeemed. However, the legal maturity date of the notes is set at a later date (for example, four years after the option date) to accommodate any delays effecting the repossession and sale of the asset or aircraft.

The payment of interest on, and repayment of principal of, the notes are limited recourse to the interest and principal payments under the facility agreement which in turn are dependent on and effectively limited in recourse to the payment flows under the lease.

The issuer funds its commitments under the facility agreement by issuing, for example, three classes of euro-denominated amortising Eurobond notes listed on the Luxembourg or London stock exchange. The class A notes are given the highest rating, the class B notes a slightly lower rating, whilst the class C notes are unrated. The proceeds' waterfall provisions ensure that interest and principal payments for the class A notes have priority and are paid out first, followed by the class B notes and the finally the class C notes.

The class B notes are roughly the equivalent of mezzanine debt. The class C notes are roughly equivalent to an equity investment and are often purchased by the end user or lessee in the transaction.

If the liquidity facility has been used, then the liquidity provider becomes senior to the class A notes and will be paid out first in any proceeds waterfall.

The class A notes bear the lowest interest coupon, reflecting the fact that they carry the lowest risk of non payment. The class C notes, which are unsecured, carry the highest interest coupon. The class B notes will bear an interest coupon between the class A and class C notes.

If the issuer has insufficient funds to meet the interest payments on the class A and B notes, then the issuer will be able to draw down the relevant shortfall under the liquidity facility agreement. Such a scenario should only arise when the end user is defaulting on its payments under the lease.

The size of the liquidity facility will be determined by the rating agencies on the basis of the estimated out side (that is, maximum) time which they consider would be required to repossess and dispose of the aircraft after a default.

The borrower will secure its obligations under the facility agreement pursuant to a deed of charge by which it grants to the issuer first fixed security over various contractual rights, any of its bank accounts and a floating charge over the rest of its undertaking. In addition, the borrower will enter into an agreement in favour of the issuer granting an assignment of insurances and requisition proceeds, a mortgage and an assignment of the borrower's rights under the relevant lease.

As security for the issuer's obligations under the notes and the liquidity facility, the issuer will grant in favour of a security trustee a security assignment of all its contractual rights, a charge over all its bank accounts and a floating charge over the rest of its undertaking. If the asset suffers a total loss, the total loss proceeds will be received by the security trustee as loss payee and applied to effect a pro rata redemption of the three classes of notes.

At the heart of the EEETC is the need to ensure that the rated notes receive an appropriate rating in order to maximise their marketability. Rating agencies set about this process by giving the notes a basic rating in accordance with the shadow rating of the airline (since airlines do not have official ratings), on the basis that the repayment of the notes fundamentally depends upon the airline paying rentals under the lease. This basic rating is then upgraded depending upon the enhancements in the transaction structure giving the note holders greater security that they will be repaid. The following are areas which the rating agencies closely consider in evaluating whether to upgrade the basic shadow rating of the airline or end user.

- The quality and type of the asset underlying the EEETC. A new generation of product which is popular and easily resold or released (whilst retaining its resale value) is likely to enhance the rating. This is relevant where the lessee/end user defaults and the asset has to be resold or re-leased to meet note payments.

- The bankruptcy protection available to the owner or chargee of an asset (that is, the ability of the owner or chargee to extract their asset from insolvency proceedings) is an aspect which the rating agencies focus upon very closely. The United States offers section 1110 protection, entitling certain owners or chargees of aircraft to extract their aircraft in bankruptcy proceedings within 60 days of filing an order with the court. This certainty enables the rating agencies to accurately evaluate repossession risks on a bankruptcy. In Europe there is no such certainty as to the insolvency or asset repossession timeframes, thus making it more difficult to obtain the desired rating for transactions where the end user is based in Europe. In this regard, it should be noted that the Cape Town Convention on International Interests in Mobile Equipment (see Chapter 7) hopes to export the idea of section 1110 to all its contracting states. The convention will bring much greater certainty to repossession timeframes in a contracting state and thus facilitate obtaining an appropriate rating.

- The loan-to-value ratio of the notes to the underlying asset. For example, the A notes will be more likely to receive a high rating if their value is low compared with the actual or fair market value of the asset upon which their repayment is secured.

- The use of a servicer to help in the re-marketing of an aircraft in the event of default. It is a moot point exactly what benefits a servicer brings to a typical EEETC structure (which typically consist of long-term finance leases to a single airline or end user) unless there is a default which necessitates a re-marketing of the aircraft. However, this is an area which rating agencies are currently reconsidering.

- The currency risk. As aircraft (especially in the second hand resale or re-leasing market) are priced in US dollars, there can be a problem with a sale or re-leasing at the end of the lease. The currency exchange risk arises from the fact that notes in an EEETC are to be repaid in euros, whilst the proceeds of any sale of the aircraft (and possibly even the rental stream under a re-leasing transaction) to be used to repay the notes might well be denominated in US dollars. The rating agencies will be keen to understand the methods used to minimise this risk (for example, hedging agreements etc).

As of 2002, the only European airline EEETC issues have been the Iberbond 1999 and 2000 issues. The Iberbond issues have typically been euro denominated and relate to the financing of several finance leases of Airbus and Boeing aircraft to a sole end user (Iberia). There have been several EETC issues in the United States for US airlines such as NorthWest, Delta and Continental.

There are other examples of the combination of capital markets funding with aircraft leasing, notably the portfolio aircraft lease securitisations that have been completed. These structures are similar to the EETC/EEETC and their variations have been dictated by the markets accessed and the nature of the portfolio involved.

Chapter 7

Legal features of cross-border transactions

Simon Hall

Introduction: the absence of a uniform body of law

Cross-border leasing transactions involve, by definition, more than one jurisdiction and therefore more than one body of law. Each transaction involves a complex interrelationship between the laws of the jurisdiction of each party to the transaction and of the proper law of the contract. Although considerable attempts have been made at standardising contracts and internationalising contractual relations, the adoption of a standard form can lead to considerable confusion where parties to a contract are based in different jurisdictions. The respective understandings of the standard terms are bound to be different depending on the jurisdiction and this is particularly true when one party operates in a civil law jurisdiction and the other in a common law jurisdiction.

A further disincentive for international standardisation is the fact that some legal differences can work in favour of leasing arrangements. For example, it is precisely the difference in interpretation of what constitutes a lease that has been so successfully exploited in the double-dip transactions completed in Australia, France, Germany, Japan, the United Kingdom and the United States among other countries.

Attempts at standardising international leasing arrangements

Despite the difficulties, numerous attempts at standardisation have been made, particularly on the part of the International Chamber of Commerce, the EU, the United Nations Commission on International Trade Law (UNCITRAL), and the International Institute for the Unification of Private Law (Unidroit) which backed the Convention on International Financial Leasing, adopted in Ottawa in May 1988. Other landmark agreements are the Convention on International Financial Leasing, adopted in Ottawa in May 1988, and the Cape Town Convention, adopted by 53 countries in November 2001.

Uniform Customs and Practice

The Uniform Customs and Practice for Documentary Credits issued by the International Chamber of Commerce (ICC) is probably the best known attempt at internationalisation. The most recent version is set out in the ICC's Publication No. 500, which came into force on 1 January 1994. This lays down the rules governing documentary credit transactions where the bank or other financing institution accepts an obligation to pay against presentation of specified documents. Another example is ISP98, ICC Publication No. 590, promulgated by the ICC on 6 April 1998 to reflect generally accepted practice, custom and usage for standby letters of credit. The International Rules for Interpretation of Trade Terms published by the ICC International Chamber of Commerce, commonly known as the Incoterms, are a further example.

The Uniform Commercial Code (UCC) of the United States is another attempt to break down differences between jurisdictions and it has been adopted in substantially uniform form. The recent substantial revision of Article 9 of the UCC (dealing with security over personal property) has been recently adopted by the states, although in some cases with different effective dates. Meanwhile, the European Union has also made a significant contribution to the harmonisation of various laws throughout its member states by use of directives.

International Sale of Goods Convention

Under the terms of the Uniform Laws on International Sales Act 1967, the United Kingdom has implemented the Uniform Law on the International Sale of Goods adopted at The Hague in 1964 and the Uniform Law on the Formation of Contracts for the International Sale of Goods. The 1967 act provides that these conventions are only applicable if the parties to the contract specifically choose to adopt them.

A further step towards the unification of the law on international sales of goods has been made by the United Nations Convention on Contracts for the International Sale of Goods, Vienna 1980. This convention was the work of the United Nations Commission on International Trade Law (UNCITRAL) and is designed to replace the Uniform Laws adopted at The Hague in 1964 mentioned above. The Vienna Convention only covers contracts for the sale of goods between parties whose places of business are in different states, where the different states are parties to the Vienna Convention and where the proper law of the contract is determined by the rules of private international law to be the law of a contracting state. (A ratifying party can exclude this latter provision which introduces the less than clear rules of private international law.) It does not apply to consumer sales, sales by auction, sales on execution or otherwise by authority of law, sales of stocks, shares, investment securities, negotiable instruments, money, ships, other vessels, hovercraft, aircraft or electricity. The parties are free to exclude or vary its provisions but, unless they are excluded, its provisions will apply. Its scope is concerned only with the formation of the contract and the rights and obligations arising therefrom, as opposed to the substance of the contract. The Vienna Convention is not intended to cover every aspect of a contractual relationship but Article 7(2) provides that matters which are not specifically covered are to be resolved in the first instance by reference to the principles on which the Vienna Convention is based. In the absence of such principles the relevant matters will be resolved by reference to the proper law of the contract. The Vienna Convention came into force on 1 January 1988. By February 2003, 62 countries had ratified and acceded to the Vienna Convention, including the United States. Notable exceptions to the membership of the Vienna Convention include Japan and the United Kingdom. In countries that ratified the Vienna Convention, it takes precedence over the Rome Convention provided circumstances arise that render the Vienna Convention applicable.

The International Financial Leasing Convention

The International Institute for the Unification of Private Law (Unidroit) Convention on International Financial Leasing was adopted at a diplomatic conference in Ottawa in May 1988. By February 2003, 18 countries had signed or acceded to the convention, but only nine had ratified it. The Unidroit Convention goes back to May 1974 when the Unidroit Governing Council recommended the preparation of a preliminary study looking into the desirability of drawing up uniform rules on leasing. Preliminary draft uniform rules were prepared and considered at several symposia before the Unidroit Convention was finalised.

The text of the Unidroit Convention states: (i) that rules of law governing the traditional contract of hire need to be adapted to the distinctive triangular relationship created by the financial leasing transaction (the supplier, the lessor and the lessee); and (ii) the desirability of formulating certain uniform rules relating primarily to the civil and commercial law aspects of international financial leasing. Thus, the Unidroit Convention sets itself two main tasks: first, to remove certain legal impediments to the international financial leasing of equipment while maintaining a fair balance of interests between the different parties to the transaction; and secondly, to make international financial leasing more available.

The scope of the Unidroit Convention is restricted to international financial leasing, and operating leases are intentionally excluded. The broad concern of the Unidroit Convention is to provide for rights between the lessee and the supplier of equipment in order better to protect the lessee. The relationship between lessor and lessee is generally left to be governed by the leasing agreement between the parties; although some rights are granted against the lessor, most of these can be varied or excluded by the lease agreement. The Unidroit Convention does not apply to the leasing of land or consumer transactions which are not generally international in character. It also ignores tax and accounting matters.

Because of the great differences between what constitutes a lease in the various jurisdictions represented, finding an acceptable common definition of the leases to which the Unidroit Convention was to apply proved very difficult. The Unidroit Convention ended up by listing what it regarded as the three main (but not exhaustive) characteristics (Article 1.2). These are:

- the lessee chooses the equipment and supplier;
- the lessor acquires the equipment in connection with a lease agreement which, to the knowledge of the supplier, has been or is to be made between the lessor and lessee; and
- the lease is for a term which takes the period of amortisation of the equipment into account.

Article 1.3 goes on to state that the convention applies whether or not the lessee has, or subsequently acquires, an option to buy the equipment, or hold it on lease for a further period. Although various drafts of the convention have improved the drafting, the terminology remains confusing, and while there is some sympathy for the problems involved in finding common ground, the value of the results are perhaps somewhat questionable.

Although some provisions are mandatory, others may be varied or excluded by the parties. Some of the substantive provisions should be noted. Article 10 states that when the supplier breaches the supply contract, the lessee has a direct right of action against the supplier as if the equipment were supplied directly to it (this provision addresses one area which is inadequately provided for in many leasing transactions – see the section 'Disclaimer of warranties' in Chapter 5). However, Article 10 does not legislate for the division of responsibility for the making of claims against the supplier, or state which claimant has priority for the same loss or damage, for example, following a lessee default.

Article 12 permits a lessee to terminate its lease and to recover any rentals and other sums paid in advance (less a reasonable sum for any benefit the lessee has derived from the equipment) where the equipment is not delivered or is delivered late or fails to conform to the supply agreement. In addition, if the equipment fails to conform to the supply agreement, the lessee is entitled to withhold rentals until the lessor has remedied its failure to tender the equipment in conformity with the supply agreement or the lessee has lost the right to reject the equipment. The appropriateness of Article 12, or the likelihood of its being accepted by lessors, is open to question. A lessor, as simply the financial provider to a transaction, will not normally expect to take responsibility or liability for the matters referred to in this Article.

Article 13 sets out the remedies a lessor may have in the event of a default by the lessee. The definition of default is left for the parties to determine. Where the lessee's default is substantial, then after the lessee has been given a reasonable opportunity of remedying the default, the lessor may terminate the leasing agreement, recover possession of the equipment and recover such damages as will place the lessor in the position in which it would have been in had the lessee performed the leasing agreement in accordance with its terms.

The use of the term 'substantial' is unclear. In addition, there is a rather confusing conflict between the provisions of Articles 13.2 and 13.4 regarding the ability of the lessor to require accelerated payment of the value of future rentals following the termination of the leasing agreement. The parties may not derogate from or vary the effect of certain provisions of Article 13, such as Article 13.3(b) (Limitation on damages) and 13.4 (No rental acceleration). Again the appropriateness of such provisions and their acceptability is in some doubt.

Other articles of the convention are more helpful. Article 7 protects a lessor's title provided it has complied with the public notice laws in the lessee's country, if any. Article 8 protects the lessor from liability in respect of the equipment, save to the extent that the lessee has suffered loss as a result of its reliance on the lessor's skill and judgement and as a result of the lessor's intervention in the selection of the supplier or the specification of the equipment.

Although the convention's attempt at uniformity is commendable, leasing is a type of transaction that involves many different areas of law, each of which is treated differently in different jurisdictions. Therefore it is very difficult to set down minimum criteria which will have a universal application. Furthermore, the interaction of civil and common law jurisdictions, federal and state laws and regulations and international tax law make the application of the convention very difficult. For these reasons, the convention has not been widely adopted to date and looks unlikely to receive general application.

Convention on International Interests in Mobile Equipment

Another example of an attempt at international standardisation is the Cape Town Convention. The remit of Unidroit and the International Civil Aviation Organisation (ICAO) that inspired the Cape Town Convention was simple, but the ramifications were complex: how to avoid legal conflicts between jurisdictions and so have a universal platform for financing high-value mobile equipment (such as aircraft, aircraft engines, rolling stock and satellites). The Cape Town Convention solution was to create a new instrument called an 'international interest' whose characteristics would be set out in the text of the convention. In many ways the Cape Town Convention is an astonishing achievement, because unlike many other international conventions the final text is not a watered down version of the original concept. Some 53 countries adopted the convention texts on 16 November 2001 in Cape Town and are prepared to make changes to domestic laws to reflect the convention. The initial indications suggest that prompt ratification is expected by the home governments. The convention is especially significant since previous attempts at harmonisation of laws have not had a great deal of success, especially where civil and common law approaches to issues diverge significantly (as is definitely the case, for example, with security interests). Although much remains to be done to achieve ratification by contracting states and declarations on certain specific subjects, the work of putting in place the registration system needed for implementation of the new regime is under way and scheduled to be ready by the latter part of 2003.

It should be noted that whilst the convention is generally applicable to various categories of high-value mobile assets (for example, aircraft and space assets), it only comes into force with respect to any one type of mobile asset upon ratification and acceptance of a specific protocol with respect to that asset. The protocol would typically clarify and refine the application of the terms of the Cape Town Convention to the particular type of asset. Currently only the Protocol to the Convention on International Interests in Mobile Equipment on Matters Specific to Aircraft Equipment has been drafted and ratified. (A draft protocol in relation to space assets is in production.)

Moreover, the convention also aims to preserve contractual autonomy; it does not aim to write the contract for parties to the financing of high-value mobile equipment which are likely to be both sophisticated and well advised. The Cape Town Convention provides for an international legal regime for an international interest constituted under or relating to leases, conditional sales and security interests in high-value mobile equipment. It is ambitious since it prescribes rules of enforcement and priority that override relevant national laws. The expectation is that this will be acceptable due to the narrow scope of the Cape Town Convention. A special enforcement and priority rule, which only applies to aircraft and certain other mobile high-value equipment, would not fundamentally undermine a contracting state's laws. The basis of the new law under the Cape Town Convention is the creation and registration of an international interest.

To constitute an international interest, three conditions must be present:

- a security interest, a conditional sale or a lease created under some national law;
- equipment of a type in relation to which a protocol is in force; and
- compliance with the limited formal requirements of the Cape Town Convention.

National law determines the type of security interest and the correct characterisation of the agreement concerned (that is, whether the agreement is a lease, conditional sale or a security agreement). This is important since different rights attach to leases, conditional sales and security agreements. This is primarily because lessors and conditional sellers who are legal owners of the asset need different remedies to chargees who only have a security interest in the asset. For the Cape Town Convention to apply, the obligor, chargor, lessee or conditional buyer must be situated in a contracting state, or the equipment must be connected to a contracting state in a manner specified in the relevant protocol. For airframes, this is straightforward as the convention will apply if the state of registration of the aircraft (to which the airframe relates) is a contracting state. The reason for creating an international interest is that, in addition to any remedies that might be available under the applicable national law, the holder of the international interest is entitled to the remedies described in the Cape Town Convention. Although these may be the same as, or at least similar to, the remedies available under applicable national law, the convention remedies will be available in any contracting state simply by virtue of the convention. This means that there is no need to deal with any of the recognition or conflict of laws issues that would otherwise have been obstacles to enforcement. The remedies granted by the convention are set out separately for a chargee and for a vendor/owner/lessor.

A chargee is entitled to take possession, to sell or lease, and to collect and receive income from use of the equipment. In common law countries, a mortgagee may to some extent exercise self help in the enforcement of its rights. The prevention of abuse by the chargee of its rights under the convention is typically achieved by local law imposing an obligation on the chargee to realise the full value of the equipment, and now by the convention requiring that any remedy is exercised in a commercially reasonable manner. This obligation can be enforced by those having an interest in any surplus proceeds (for example, subsequent mortgagees, guarantors and the mortgagor). Such a degree of freedom in the disposal of someone else's property is not generally permitted in civil law countries. Normally the court arranges disposal of secured property by public auction and then distributes the proceeds. The Cape Town Convention gives the chargee a choice of applying to a court or to exercise self help remedies (although chargees are required to exercise these remedies in a commercially reasonable manner and ensure that interested persons are notified of their proposed action). Chargees can also take title to the asset towards satisfaction of the debt where all interested persons agree or a court allows this. Before permitting this, the parties and/or the court will need to take into account the value of the debt relative to the equipment, and any payment which the chargee may need to pay representing surplus value in the equipment.

Upon a default, a conditional seller or lessor may terminate the agreement and take possession or control of the asset, or apply to a court for an order authorising or directing that to happen.

The role of the local courts in the jurisdiction in which the asset is located may still be very important when repossessing aircraft. Local procedural rules, such as those that relate to the timing and location of judicial sales will still apply. The ability to exercise remedies without applying to court will also depend upon the contracting state where the remedy is to be exercised not having excluded self help in a declaration at the time of signature, ratification, acceptance, approval or accession to the aircraft protocol. The remedies in the convention are not the only ones available to a creditor and others may be agreed so long as they are not inconsistent with the mandatory provisions of the convention (which are designed to protect the interests of the debtor and other interested persons). Interim remedies, that is, the ability to prevent a bad situation deteriorating while the judicial process takes its course, are central to the basic concept of the Cape Town Convention. Rapid access to the asset is the key to being able to treat a financing as asset-based in order to reduce the importance of the airline's credit and credit enhancement methods. The Cape Town Convention provides that a contracting state (that is, the one where the asset is located, where the defendant is located, where the aircraft is registered or whose jurisdiction has been chosen by the parties) shall ensure that orders are available for the preservation, possession, control, custody, immobilisation, sale, lease, management and application of proceeds or income of the aircraft. A contracting state is also obliged to ensure that the interim relief is speedy. The aircraft protocol envisages a maximum time period for obtaining remedies both in relation to court remedies and the associated administrative procedures. The protocol adds as remedies, both at the final and interim stages, the de-registration and export of the aircraft. The obligors' agreement to these remedies may be given at any time, including at the lease's inception.

For each type of equipment to which the Cape Town Convention is applied by a protocol, an international register will be established. There will also be a supervisory authority for registration. Registration is to be asset based so that the register will be searchable by reference to manufacturer's serial numbers. Registration will be available for international interests, prospective international interests (to fix priority before transactions close), assignments of international interests and subordination agreements relating to international interests. In order for the register to be searchable, registration will be effective from the moment when the information has reached the database. The time and date of the registration will also be recorded. The register will be open 24 hours a day with local access facilities available during working hours in the relevant country.

The priority rules are simple and strict. Priority is determined solely by the chronological order of registration. Though priority can be varied by a registered subordination agreement between the relevant parties, it is not affected by any other matters, including notice (actual or constructive) of any other interests. Any other system of priorities, involving, for example, actual knowledge, would not achieve the degree of certainty essential for financiers to have confidence in the registration system.

More problematic is the issue of priority of non-consensual rights and interests. Examples are tax liens, liens for airport and navigation charges and other such rights that arise by law rather than because they have been granted by contract. These have been a problem for financiers because in many jurisdictions they are secret until exercised. The purposes of the Cape Town Convention would be served best by contracting states agreeing that the priority of such rights should depend on registration in the same way as consensual interests. If this is not acceptable, contracting states may make a declaration preserving the super-priority of such rights, notwithstanding that no public notice of them is available.

In order for syndication, debt trades, securitisations and other such transactions to take place without complicating the rights acquired when the international interest was first registered, the Cape Town Convention provides that assignments of international interests are capable of registration. The international register for aircraft will also register sales transactions and the general priority rules established in the convention will apply to registered sales. In circumstances where the first registered sale is from the manufacturer, the register will show a complete chain of title through various owners during the life of an aircraft. In other circumstances the register may not solve all the problems concerning title to used equipment.

It should be noted that the Cape Town Convention and the aircraft protocol apply to aircraft engines, and treat engines as separate assets to the aircraft to which they are attached. Thus, international interests can be registered with respect to engines. Moreover, the protocol states that: 'Ownership or any other right or interest in an aircraft engine shall not be affected by its installation on or removal from an aircraft'. This effectively removes the problem that financiers had with respect to their rights in engines being prejudiced, or extinguished, by accession of the engines to an aircraft not owned by the financier.

Importantly, for rated or capital markets transaction, the aircraft protocol also has an insolvency rule inspired by section 1110 of the US Bankruptcy Code. Contracting states can choose two alternative options, both requiring action to be taken within a time period specified by the relevant contracting state. The alternatives have the effect of requiring that the bankrupt airline's defaults be cured within the time limit, or that the aircraft be handed back to the creditor. Along with the time limit proposed for repossession proceedings outside insolvency, this is crucial to the objective of being able to calculate the cost to a finance provider of an airline's default. A rating agency will have difficulty giving a rating to a transaction where the asset and principal source of revenue may be grounded for an indefinite period while legal proceedings drag on. The aircraft protocol also requires the contracting state in which the aircraft may be situated to co-operate with the jurisdiction where the main insolvency proceedings may be taking place.

Moreover, the aircraft protocol gives legal substance to the practice of obtaining de-registration and export authorisation at the beginning of a transaction. At the moment, such arrangements are entered into more in the hope than the expectation that they will be effective at the time of an airline's default. This provision removes concerns about constructive detention of the aircraft by national registration authorities trying to frustrate a foreign financier's attempts to repossess and re-market the aircraft. The aircraft protocol also provides a legal basis for a waiver of sovereign immunity to be effective as to judgment and enforcement against any body that might have been entitled to such immunity. At the moment, some jurisdictions have clear laws describing the effect of a waiver of immunity, but many do not, and many countries have no clear legal basis for their own governmental bodies to issue waivers.

The provisions of the Cape Town Convention and of the aircraft protocol have been designed with participation of aircraft industry specialists from a number of different countries. These participants have specifically focused on finding solutions to issues that affect financing costs. Independent corroboration of the link between these legal changes and financing costs is provided in the economic impact assessment.

The effect which the Cape Town Convention and the aircraft protocol will have on the legal system of any contracting state is at the same time both profound and very limited. It is profound because it does impose changes on priorities, bankruptcy procedure and judicial procedure. However, it is very limited because currently it only applies to commercial aircraft. While it may be the case that future protocols will introduce the Cape Town Convention principles to other types of high-value mobile equipment, each industry dealing with a type of equipment will have to make its own case to justify making profound changes to the national laws of contracting states. As far as the aircraft industry is concerned (and this is all that potential contracting states are being asked to consider), there is strong evidence of the benefits that will result.

The expectation is that airlines will benefit from a general broadening of the market for aircraft finance to institutions that would not previously have considered taking any asset risks. Airlines may also be able to sublease aircraft to other airlines without themselves taking significant repossession risks in those countries and without infringing subleasing restrictions. The Cape Town Convention is also beneficial for financiers and will have a real impact on the assessment of risks resulting from the international character of transactions and therefore on the pricing of those risks. It should be noted that one independent study estimated that the financial ability to assess such risks more accurately would save airlines as much as US$5 billion in financing costs every year.

Although there is great activity in the area of international standardisation, for the time being, the rules of private international law will continue to be largely responsible for governing the consequences of the contractual relations involved.

Choice of law

Because parties to a cross-border leasing contract are likely to have very different under-standings of the various aspects of the contractual arrangements and their consequences, the law that governs the contract must be established. Even when the governing law of a contract has been established, matters such as formation, misrepresentation, capacity and formal valid-ity may well be governed by the laws of the jurisdictions of the parties, as opposed to the proper law of the contract.

Under English law, in the absence of an express or implied choice of proper law, the proper law of the contract will be that system of law with which the contract has its closest and most real connection. This may not be capable of being readily established in an inter-national contract where, for example, each of the parties is domiciled in a different jurisdic-tion, the equipment is being supplied from a third jurisdiction, and where payments are being made from one jurisdiction and settled in another. Although large numbers of con-tracts are effected without an express choice of law provision, in an international leasing transaction, where a substantial value is attributable to the asset being leased and a financial institution is involved as opposed to simply a supplier, there should invariably be an express choice of law provision.

For the choice of English law to be upheld, the choice must be bona fide and legal although it is not necessary for there to be any direct connection with England. There must, however, be no reason for avoiding the choice on the grounds of public policy. It is general-ly thought that if a choice of English law was made to avoid a mandatory provision of the law of the forum or of the jurisdiction with which the contract is objectively most closely con-nected, then it would not be upheld by the English courts.

New York General Obligations Law

On 19 July 1984, the State of New York adopted a new act amending Article 5 of the exist-ing General Obligations Law to provide for mandatory enforcement of New York governing law provisions in certain contracts. The fundamental provision is that parties to any contract can agree that New York law should govern their rights and duties in whole or in part, 'whether or not such contract, agreement or undertaking bears a reasonable relation to [this] State', provided such contract, agreement or undertaking arises out of a transaction cover-ing in aggregate not less than US$250,000. Certain types of contract are excluded, namely those for labour or personal services and those relating to any transaction for personal, fam-ily or household services. In addition, it is provided that any person can bring an action in the New York courts against a foreign corporation, non-resident or foreign state if the action derives from a contract where a New York choice of law has been made, in whole or in part, provided the contract relates to an obligation arising out of a transaction covering in the aggregate not less than US$1,000,000 and the contract includes a provision whereby such foreign corporation or non-resident agrees to submit to the jurisdiction of the New York courts. The court is prohibited in such circumstances from staying or dismissing any action on the grounds of inconvenient forum. New York law is one of the two bodies of law most frequently selected in international transactions and the act removes any doubts as to whether or not the choice would stand up where there was no obvious relationship of the contract with New York.

The Rome Convention

The Rome Convention of 1980, now adopted by most countries in the European Union, codifies the liberal view of choices of law. Having excluded from its scope certain types of legal questions such as legal capacity, family matters, negotiable instruments, arbitration and jurisdiction agreements, corporate law issues, agency, trusts and procedural matters, the Rome Convention states its principal rule thus: 'A contract shall be governed by the law chosen by the parties'.

The Rome Convention applies to the contractual relations of the parties. It does not displace the rules applying to transfers of title or the creation of security interests, as to which the applicable provisions of the lex situs will need to be observed. Nor does the Rome Convention affect the applicability of any bankruptcy law.

The Rome Convention applies even where a transaction is wholly domestic, (that is, where all parties are in the same country) subject to the continued application of any mandatory rules of that country. As it applies in England, the Rome Convention rule enables contracting parties to choose any EU law. There need be no other EU connection.

In an international transaction, the rule is subject to the following points.

- Effect may be given to mandatory rules of the law of a country with which the transaction has a close connection if under that law those rules are to apply irrespective of the law applicable to the contract, the court having considered the nature, purpose and consequences of those rules. This is perhaps one of the most unsatisfactory parts of the Rome Convention, and leads to uncertainty and a risk of the parties' intentions being overridden. This qualification does not apply to actions brought in the English courts.
- Mandatory rules of the law of the country in whose court the contract is being litigated may override the chosen law if that is the effect of those rules. This would allow an English court to apply its rule that it will not enforce a contract that would be illegal in the place where it is to be performed, notwithstanding the parties' choice of law.
- The Inter-American Convention on the Law Applicable to International Contracts of 1994 is very similar in its terms to the Rome Convention. The courts of contracting states apply the chosen law even if it is not that of a contracting state. It contains similar qualifications of the parties' choice by reference to the mandatory rules of the forum displacing the chosen law and the possible application of the mandatory rules of the country with which the contract has close ties.
- The lessor's choice of law will generally prevail in the event there is any dispute, primarily because the lessor is the one with the most to lose in the transaction. The lessor will, therefore, wish to protect itself to the maximum extent it can. However, there are other factors that will influence the choice. It is clearly desirable to choose the law of a country which will give effect to the intentions of the parties from a commercial perspective, is predictable in its outcome and which is presumed politically stable. However, it should be appreciated that when a law is chosen as the proper law of the contract, as opposed to incorporated in a contract by reference, that law may change from time to time.
- Where a state entity is involved, it may require that the local law governs, at least for those contracts which are of public interest. This is the position in Malaysia. Another consideration may be tax. If certain parties in the transaction are being interposed to take advantage of the tax benefits in their jurisdiction, it may be necessary for the law of that jurisdiction to be the proper law of the contract, or at least of the particular contract which interposes that party, in order to ensure the correct analysis.

Reciprocal enforcement of judgments

Another significant factor which has some bearing on the choice of law is the question of where the contract is most likely to be enforced in the event of a default. Once judgment has been obtained in the forum selected, it will be enforced in the jurisdiction where the asset or lessee is located. To avoid any dispute as to whether the courts of a particular country have jurisdiction, the agreement should contain an express submission to jurisdiction, usually on a non-exclusive basis, so that there is a facility to sue in other courts if need be (subject to any restriction imposed by convention). The choice of forum should follow the choice of governing law to ensure that there is certainty in the application of that law. Just as the law of a contract will have been selected on the basis of the predictability of that law in dealing with the particular business relationship contemplated by the transaction, so the choice of forum will be dictated to some extent by the same predictability in outcome, as well as the sophistication and stature of the courts of the relevant jurisdiction. Consideration should be given to the speed with which suits can be brought in the courts and what possible procedural problems could be raised by a foreign lessee. It is also relevant whether a judgment obtained in the forum selected by the parties will actually be enforced by the jurisdiction in which the lessee and its assets are located.

The position between states in the EC was codified by the EC Convention on Jurisdiction and the Enforcement of Judgments in Civil and Commercial Matters 1968 (the Brussels Convention, see below for further details). This has since been updated by Council Regulation No. 44/2001 of 22 December 2000. Where a treaty or other regulation does not apply and, in the absence of an express submission to jurisdiction by the lessee, the question of whether a court will have jurisdiction will be determined by a number of different factors. In England and the United States, courts have jurisdiction if the lessee appears in the action other than for the purposes of merely contesting jurisdiction. In France and Luxembourg, the nationality of the plaintiff alone is sufficient to give jurisdiction to the courts. In The Netherlands, the Dutch domicile of the plaintiff is sufficient grounds for jurisdiction. Another circumstance in which a court may feel entitled to exercise jurisdiction is where the defendant has some physical presence in that jurisdiction. In England, the presence of a branch office of a foreign corporation, as opposed to a locally operated subsidiary, will entitle English courts to exercise jurisdiction. Under English law, if a foreign entity is conducting business in the jurisdiction (and not simply with the jurisdiction) the courts will have jurisdiction.

The degree of contact required in the United States seems to be less. The New York courts have exercised jurisdiction over the parent company of a subsidiary in New York where that subsidiary, although a separate legal entity, functioned effectively as a department of the parent company. Another basis on which jurisdiction may be available is if the transaction has a connection with the relevant jurisdiction, perhaps because it was concluded there, is governed by the law of that jurisdiction, or the lessee has assets there.

Coupled with the express submission to jurisdiction, and where another rule under a convention or regulation does not apply, there should be an appointment of an agent for service of process. Under English law at least, a submission alone is insufficient to commence proceedings. If no agent has been appointed to accept service of process within the jurisdiction, then permission from the court needs to be obtained to serve the writ abroad. The appointment provision normally includes a requirement that the lessee maintain the appointment and that any appointment remain valid until such time as a substitute has been appointed. The appointee would be expected to provide a letter confirming their acceptance of the appointment and setting out the terms of that appointment.

Part of the selection process of the choice of law and jurisdiction should include consideration of the question of the enforceability of a judgment obtained in the jurisdiction where the lessee or the asset will be located. This is usually a subject for local legal opinion. However, there are certain rules of general applicability and progress has been made through the use of international convention in this area. A judgment obtained in one jurisdiction cannot be enforced directly in another jurisdiction without the sanction of the other jurisdiction through its courts. The important issue is whether that other jurisdiction would seek to have the matter retried *ab initio* or whether the judgment can be enforced either as a debt due or through some registration process under a reciprocal enforcement convention. The United States, England and all Commonwealth countries would generally permit the commencement of a new action by a lessor in their courts if the lessor had not lost the action in the courts of the foreign jurisdiction or if the lessee, as loser of the action, had not already satisfied the judgment in that action.

There are certain rules on the enforcement of foreign judgments which have general applicability in many jurisdictions. In the first place, the original court must have had jurisdiction to try the action. In addition, that jurisdiction must not have been exorbitant in the sense of being exercised simply on the basis of domicile or nationality for example, or some other insubstantial connection. The trial must have been fair and the rules of natural justice followed. Fraud employed in obtaining the judgment would be a bar to its enforcement. The judgment must have been final and conclusive. The fact that an appeal may lie will not prevent enforcement, but will confer upon the courts a discretion to stay enforcement until the appeal has been heard. If the judgment obtained conflicts with public policy in the jurisdiction in which it is being enforced, the courts will decline to enforce it. This public policy exception can be abused and used as a means of retrying a case on its merits.

In order to enforce a foreign judgment in many civil law jurisdictions outside the EU, the enforcing courts will, as a prerequisite, require reciprocity in the sense that the courts in which the judgment was obtained would have enforced a judgment of the enforcing courts in similar circumstances. This is not a requirement under English common law or under New York law. Generally the courts of one country will not enforce claims in respect of taxes, fines, penalties or insolvency proceedings of another. Enforcement of foreign judgments is only generally available for money and not for other remedies such as injunctions and specific performance. These basic rules are expanded and to some extent overridden by statute and reciprocal enforcement conventions (see, for example, the 1968 EC Convention on Jurisdiction and Enforcement of Judgments in Civil and Commercial Matters, also known as the Brussels Convention, and the United States Uniform Foreign Money-Judgments Recognition Act).

The Brussels Convention 1968, which was incorporated into English law by the Civil Jurisdiction and Judgments Act 1982 and came into effect on 1 January 1987, set out a number of principles governing submission to jurisdiction and the mutual enforcement of judgments between the contracting states. This was followed in 1988 by the EC Convention on Jurisdiction and the Enforcement of Judgments in Civil and Commercial Matters (also known as the Lugano Convention). This extends the Brussels Convention to the European Free Trade Association (EFTA) states with the aim of preventing the single European market from becoming insular. The Lugano Convention regulates relations between the EC states and EFTA states, but not between the EC states themselves and was enacted in the United Kingdom by the Civil Jurisdiction and Judgments Act 1991 which came into force on 1 May 1992.

Council Regulation No. 44/2001 of 22 December 2000 has further expanded the earlier conventions with a view to improving the recognition and enforcement of decisions in civil and commercial matters. This regulation became effective 1 March 2002. However, Denmark will continue to be subject to the Brussels Convention; Iceland, Norway, Switzerland and Poland to the Lugano Convention; and the remainder of the EU states will be subject to the application of Regulation No. 44/2001.

These different factors emphasise that there is still a need to take care in the selection of an appropriate jurisdiction. The potential impediments in the legal process to obtaining an enforceable judgment against a lessee must be identified and taken into account in a lessor's overall assessment of the viability and attractiveness of the transaction.

Foreign currency risks

In any cross-border transaction where parties reside in different jurisdictions, a currency exchange risk is usually involved. As far as lessors are concerned, they will account for, and calculate, their return in their home currency. Lessors may be prepared to accept a lease obligation denominated in a foreign currency provided some acceptable form of hedge against the currency risk has been put in place. It is likely that there will always be some residual exchange risk which a lessee will have to take regardless of the completeness or otherwise of the hedge. Clearly parties are free to take a view on how exchange rates are likely to move over the term of the transaction but, from a lessor's point of view, the unpredictability of such movements, and therefore the extent of the corresponding credit exposure, makes it desirable to minimise this risk as far as possible by the use of a hedge.

Forward exchange contracts

There are several ways of hedging a foreign exchange risk. The most usual in a leasing transaction is to use a forward exchange contract whereby foreign currency is sold forward to generate sufficient funds denominated in the currency of the obligation to discharge that obligation as it falls due. Thus in a dollar-denominated lease to a UK-based lessee, the lessee could hedge the exchange risk by selling forward sterling in sufficient amounts to meet the dollar obligation.

It does not always have to be the lessee that takes out the forward exchange contracts. For example, in some of the US/UK double-dip leasing transactions where the head leases were denominated in dollars, the head lessors, which were based in the United Kingdom, entered into forward exchange contracts at closing whereby they sold forward the dollar rentals to generate sufficient sterling to retire the sterling obligation in their books. The cost of the hedge was effectively reflected in the rental rates.

The difficulty with currency hedges of this type is that the market is very thin beyond five to seven years and, as a result, whatever cost advantages are generated by efficient use of tax benefits may in part be removed by the cost of the hedge.

The introduction of foreign exchange contracts into a leasing transaction may also give rise to special tax considerations. For example, in the United Kingdom, if a forward contract is taken out to fix the sterling cost of an asset, this may not simply be reflected in the cost for tax purposes of that asset. Instead, gains and losses may be realised in the forward contract, while the basis for tax purposes of the acquisition cost reflects spot rates when the expenditure is incurred.

Difficulties in hedging currency risk

Hedges become more challenging in the context of a variable rate transaction. Because the obligation is not fixed in amount, any hedge is probably going to be for too much or too little. Notwithstanding this, they are used in variable rate transactions where the tendency is to hedge the principal plus a portion of the interest below which rates are unlikely to fall. This has the merit of considerably, but not entirely, reducing the risk.

Another area that cannot be adequately covered by a currency hedge is the payment of stipulated loss or termination values on early termination. If a lessee is confident of when it will exercise a voluntary termination right, that obligation could be hedged as the stipulated loss or termination value payable on that occurrence will be a set amount (disregarding any variable factors). Obviously, a default termination cannot be hedged since the timing is not known. In practice, a lessor should be aware of the incremental credit exposure on an early termination by reason of the exchange risk. At a minimum, a lessor should seek to cover this by a specific indemnity from the lessee for whatever that is worth.

Alternative methods used to minimise foreign exchange exposure

Subject to tax constraints, a defeasance deposit or time deposit might also be used as another method to minimise the consequences of foreign exchange fluctuations. In some transactions, a lessee may be prepared to place on deposit at the inception of the transaction with the lessor, an associated company of the lessor or a third party, a sum in the denominated currency of the obligation which would then generate sufficient income so that the principal amount and interest would retire the rental obligation. Assuming an effective security interest can be given to the lessor over that deposit, this could also give rise to a significant reduction in the lease rate since the transaction would effectively be cash collateralised.

An alternative might be the purchase and pledge of government backed securities or other bonds with corresponding maturities. In either case, it presupposes that the lessee is prepared to incur a substantial amount of initial expenditure. This type of arrangement was common in Japanese leveraged leases prior to the issue of restrictive guidelines in May 1990 and continues to be used in a number of tax leveraged transactions in other jurisdictions.

Devaluation

Another question which may arise is whether a lessee is obliged to compensate a lessor for a decline in the value of the denominated currency. Under English law, in the absence of a contractual obligation to that effect, there is no obligation to revalorise. Payment by the lessee of the nominal amount of the stated currency is sufficient to discharge its obligation. This approach is followed by most commercial jurisdictions. This question is unlikely to be a problem in practice, except where exchange rates are fluctuating wildly and there is no forward exchange market to reduce the risk. In such circumstances there may be attempts to tie the currency of the obligation to various indices, for example, a basket of other currencies or a commodity.

Having selected the currency of the obligation, the selected currency will be the legal tender of the relevant country for the duration of the agreement. It is perfectly possible for the legal tender of a jurisdiction to be changed. This problem may not just be theoretical in times of dramatic depreciation of one currency against another. In such circumstances the question of what constitutes the legal tender for the purposes of the obligation will be resolved by reference to the laws of the country of the original currency.

Foreign exchange controls

Another currency related matter that requires attention in cross-border transactions is exchange control. Exchange controls are used to control the flow of currency in and out of a jurisdiction. This enables a country to have greater control over its balance of payments and is of particular importance in jurisdictions where hard currency is a scarce commodity. Where such exchange controls are in force, the normal procedure is to obtain consent before the lessee enters into a contract under which it incurs indebtedness denominated in a foreign currency. Such consent will usually be entirely discretionary and, even if given, may not be as complete as a lessor would like since it would not necessarily cover acceleration on default. Obtaining such consent will, where it can be obtained in advance, be expressed as a condition precedent to the inception of the lease agreement. In transactions involving governmental and quasi-governmental entities it is normal practice to seek some comfort from the central bank, or other administering authority of the exchange control regulations, to the effect that sufficient foreign currency will be made available to the lessee to meet its obligations and that the lessee will be permitted to remit that foreign currency to the lessor without restriction. The intention is to create some form of contractual undertaking between the central bank or other authority and the lessor.

International law generally provides that if the governing law of the contract is the law of the lessee's country, effect will be given to the foreign exchange control regulations of that country unless there is some other reason for not recognising that foreign judgment. If, however, the proper law of the contract is a system of law other than that of the lessee's jurisdiction, it will provide that the exchange control regulations of the lessee's jurisdiction be ignored. This could result in the lessee being required to make an illegal payment. The Articles of Agreement of the IMF signed in 1944 at Bretton Woods, which have been subsequently amended, superseded these general rules by providing that: 'Exchange contracts which involve the currency of any member and which are contrary to the exchange control regulations of that member maintained or imposed consistently with this agreement shall be unenforceable in the territories of any member', (Article VIII, 2(b)). Foreign exchange control regulations cannot, in effect, be ignored between members of the IMF under the ordinary rules of private international law. However, two different interpretations of an exchange contract have developed in recent years. The narrow definition, as used in the United Kingdom, New York and Belgium, states that an exchange contract exists where the currency of one country has been exchanged for the currency of another. In Germany, France and Luxembourg, an exchange contract has been deemed to exist where the exchange affected the country's exchange resources, which is a wider approach.

117

Payment in an unspecified currency

The payment section of the lease will provide for an exchange mechanism and indemnity in the event that payments are received in a currency other than that specified for payment (which in a cross-border transaction would generally be US dollars, sterling or some other international currency). Some objectively ascertainable conversion rate will be cited and any deficiency would be the subject of an indemnity.

Judgments for foreign claims may not necessarily operate quite so equitably. It is only since 1975 that, under English law, judgments may be given in a currency other than sterling. Until that date, conversion was made at the rate prevailing on the date of the breach of contract rather than the date of judgment or the date of payment. If a contract provides, expressly or impliedly, for a currency in which damages are to be calculated, or in which the debt is to be paid, judgment should be given in that currency. In the absence of such a provision judgment should be in the currency which most truly expresses the plaintiff's loss. The question is a procedural one for the courts in which the action is brought. In civil law countries, judgments can typically be either in foreign currency or the local currency.

In New York, judgments rendered in a foreign currency, calculated at the date of the breach giving rise to the claim, are converted into a US dollar equivalent of the foreign currency calculated at the rate of exchange prevailing at the date of the judgment. To fully compensate a successful plaintiff, the date of payment is the correct date for conversion and this would normally be provided for in a cross-border lease by the use of the protective language relating to conversion referred to above.

Withholding tax

The fundamental basis of any lease transaction is that the rentals are received on the dates, and in the amounts, specified. There are a number of events that could interfere with this. The most obvious event is the imposition of a withholding tax whereby the lessee is required by its own jurisdiction to deduct tax at source before paying the rentals to the lessor. Although the lessor may be entitled to recover the withheld amounts by claiming them back from the tax authorities in the lessee's jurisdiction, or at least be entitled in its own jurisdiction to a credit for the amount of tax withheld, this could have a serious timing disadvantage for the transaction and the lessor's return could be accordingly reduced. Therefore in the payments section of a cross-border lease will usually be found a grossing-up provision which will provide that, in the event of a withholding, the lessee must gross up its rental so that the net amount received by the lessor is that originally expected and provided for in the agreement. Alternatively, it might be expressed as an indemnity. The lessee will also be required to provide documentary evidence of the tax paid.

This obligation could prove extremely expensive to the lessee and, in the event of an applicable withholding tax at the date the transaction is entered into, will have to be factored into the lessee's appraisal of the economics of the transaction. The lessee should at least ask the lessor to pass back any tax credit realised by the lessor as a result of the deduction of tax. However, the difficult question is how the tax credit is calculated and what benefit should be passed back to the lessee. If the lessor is in a non-paying or partial-tax-paying position it will not necessarily be able to use the credit in the period in which it is received. Equally, the lessor will wish to reserve the right to manage its affairs so it can use tax credits or other deductions in the most efficient way possible. It will be extremely difficult to calculate precisely the amount of the benefit realised by the lessor although it seems equitable that, to the extent a benefit is realised and is capable of calculation, it should be passed back to the lessee which suffered the incremental cost of grossing-up the rental in the first place.

Sovereign immunity

Many leases are written with sovereign entities as lessees and these transactions give rise to additional risks and legal problems. The following risks should be considered.

If the lessee is a sovereign entity or agency of a state, the state could legislate to counter enforcement of the terms of a lease or recovery of property. The likelihood of this occurring depends upon the stature of the country and its government internationally. A change of government could result, for example, in the central bank reneging on its undertakings given with regard to foreign currency availability. Political risk insurance may go some way to alleviate concern on such matters. In recent years, the large burden of debt assumed by certain countries has resulted in their near bankruptcy. There is no international mechanism for dealing with the bankruptcy of a country with the result that the leases could be swept up in any rescheduling of ordinary debt.

Legally, the major additional problem for consideration is sovereign immunity from jurisdiction or enforcement. Historically, 'the courts of a country will not implead a foreign sovereign... whether the proceedings involve process against his person or seek to recover from him specific property or damages' (*The Cristina* [1938] AC 485). This immunity is derived from the rules of public international law which accord foreign states absolute immunity for all activities whether governmental or commercial. However, the doctrine of absolute immunity became anachronistic in the light of the increased involvement of states and state bodies in normal commercial activities. Accordingly, the restrictive theory of sovereign immunity, which confers immunity on states only for public and governmental acts, developed during the course of the twentieth century. This restrictive theory was enacted by the United States in the Foreign Sovereign Immunities Act 1976 and by the United Kingdom in the State Immunity Act 1978.

To have the full benefits of the UK State Immunity Act 1978, the lease agreement should contain an appointment of an agent for service of process within England, together with a consent to the giving of any relief in connection with proceedings on the agreement, a general consent to the issue of any process and the manner of service of process, and a submission to the jurisdiction of the English courts. If such a submission is included, technically, no express waiver of immunity is necessary but would generally be included to avoid any doubt.

Under the United States Foreign Sovereign Immunities Act 1976, the relevant provision should include a waiver of immunity from jurisdiction, an express submission to the jurisdiction of specified United States courts, an agreed procedure for service of process, an express waiver of immunity from attachment prior to judgment, an express waiver of immunity from attachment in aid of execution and from execution, and, though strictly speaking not necessary, a waiver of objection to venue.

In order to lend substance to the waiver provisions where a sovereign entity is involved, the lease agreement can be expected to include a warranty to the effect that the actions involved in the transaction represent private and commercial acts rather than governmental or public acts.

Arbitration provisions

Because of the apparent jurisdictional problems that might arise in the event of a dispute in cross-border transactions, arbitration provisions have been seen as a possible solution. Arbitration is often preferred by commercial people to litigation. The procedure is private, flexible and potentially less costly and time consuming than litigation. Some lawyers, on the other hand, prefer litigation since they feel that the decision is more predictable and less likely to be a compromise.

Arbitration can be expensive. Arbitration provisions may provide for three arbitrators, or two arbitrators and an umpire, each of which will expect significant fees, unlike the judges. Arbitrators will generally have other active professional interests which mean their availability will be limited and this can prolong the arbitration proceedings and therefore increase the costs. The procedural rules of arbitration tribunals are less rigid than court procedures which, while enabling disputes to be dealt with expeditiously, may result in considerable delay if one of the parties is not willing to co-operate.

As a method of resolution, arbitration is well suited to certain types of disputes. In particular, disputes of a technical nature, such as the scope of work in a construction contract. Despite the popularity of arbitration, particularly with sovereign entities where arbitration provisions are politically more acceptable than submission to another state's jurisdiction, the use of arbitration provisions in leasing transactions should not be entertained lightly because it is unlikely that any dispute in such a transaction would be simply of a technical nature.

Challenge to arbitration awards is generally limited by national arbitration laws to setting aside on limited grounds such as excess of jurisdiction or lack of due process (breach of natural justice). Appeals on the merits are not commonly found. In England, appeals are limited to points of law and have become effectively optional since the Arbitration Act 1979. It is often the case with institutional arbitrations that the rules themselves exclude all rights of appeal which would otherwise be available under national law.

As to the rules of procedure to govern the arbitration, it is necessary to decide whether to submit to arbitration under the auspices of an arbitration institution or to provide for ad hoc arbitration. Most international commercial arbitrations are conducted in accordance with the rules of an arbitration institution to which the parties have referred the dispute. The best known and most commonly used arbitration institutions are the Court of Arbitration of the International Chamber of Commerce based in Paris, the American Arbitration Association based in New York and the London Court of International Arbitration. These institutions provide arbitration rules, administer the arbitration and ensure that it proceeds expeditiously and effectively to an enforceable award.

Alternatively, it is possible to refer the dispute to an ad hoc arbitration involving no administering institution, for which the parties draft the rules under which the arbitration is to proceed or adopt a set of rules for use by the arbitrators, such as the UNCITRAL Arbitration Rules.

A further alternative is the International Centre for Settlement of Investment Disputes set up under the auspices of the World Bank in Washington. It was established to resolve disputes arising out of investments made in a contracting state by a national of another contracting state where the parties have agreed to submit the dispute to the centre for resolution.

For an institutional arbitration, the institution's rules will provide the procedure by which the arbitrator or arbitrators are to be appointed. It often takes the form of each party nominating one arbitrator with the institution to appoint the third who will act as chairman or umpire. In ad hoc arbitrations, it is for the parties to agree the method by which the arbitrator or arbitrators will be appointed and it might be that each of the parties nominates one arbitrator and the two arbitrators nominate a third to act as chairman or umpire. Alternatively, the parties could suggest a list of potential arbitrators and, to the extent names coincide, those persons would be selected in the stated order of priority. Another possibility is for a particular institution to make the necessary appointment such as the President of The Law Society of England and Wales or the President of the Institute of Chartered Accountants in England and Wales.

The forum selected for the arbitration should be one in which the parties and their counsel are prepared to arbitrate having regard to local procedural requirements. In the absence of an express provision to the contrary, the law of the forum selected for the arbitration will, almost invariably, prescribe that its procedural law govern the arbitration. When a forum is selected, its laws should be studied because it may classify as procedural matters which the governing law may otherwise regard as substantive, such as the right to interest on the amount of the award. Another issue is whether the local jurisdiction imposes a tax on the arbitral award, as for example in certain Swiss cantons. The language in which the arbitration is to be conducted should be specified.

Once the award has been obtained there follows the question of its enforcement. The New York Convention on the Recognition and Enforcement of Foreign Arbitral Awards 1958, has been ratified by over 100 countries including Austria, Finland, Japan, Mexico, Nigeria, Norway, the Philippines, Poland, Sweden, Switzerland, the Commonwealth of Independent States, the United States, the United Kingdom and other EU countries. The convention provides that parties shall be referred to arbitration where they commence court proceedings in breach of a written arbitration agreement. The convention also provides for the enforcement in one convention state of arbitral awards made in the territory of another state which is a party to the convention. Enforcement can only be refused on limited grounds, such as the incapacity of the parties, lack of due process, excess of jurisdiction or if the award is contrary to public policy. The acceptance of the New York Convention means that in those states which have ratified it, enforcement of arbitration awards is often easier than enforcing foreign judgments.

In conclusion, an arbitration provision should only be agreed after considering whether the transaction is of a nature for which arbitration is the most suitable means of resolution of any disputes. Arbitration may not be as quick to implement as judicial proceedings when a lessor is seeking summary judgment for rental arrears. However the possibility of enforcement of a foreign arbitral award under the New York Convention may be preferable to avoid reliance on local courts whose interpretation of a foreign law contract could be unpredictable. If such a provision is desired, then careful consideration needs to be given to the selection of the forum, the procedural rules to be followed (ad hoc or institutional) and the choice of law.

Conclusion

Complexity and jurisdictional uncertainties add significant costs to cross-border leasing transactions. Further industry consultation is important if attempts at reducing the legal uncertainties of cross-border litigation and enforcement through international standardisation are to be successful. International arbitration is a possible alternative to national courts, particularly in disputes of a technical nature. More than 100 countries have ratified the relevant convention recognising the enforcement of foreign arbitral awards. However, the drawbacks of arbitration include potentially higher costs and the possibility of delays.

Although national accounting, tax and legal differences can work in favour of leasing transactions, for example, in double-dip transactions where both lessors and lessees claim tax depreciation in their own jurisdictions, the potential for economic savings as a result of international standardisation is great. Conventions such as the Cape Town Convention signed in late 2001 will further reduce some of the legal uncertainties, and therefore costs, associated with cross-border transactions.

Chapter 8

Competition law in the European Union and the United Kingdom

Dorothy Livingston

THE BASIC RULES

Introduction

This chapter examines European Community (EC) legislation against anti-competitive practices and relevant legislation in other countries, notably the United Kingdom. The introduction of the Competition Act 1998 brought UK competition law into line with EC competition
law. Most other European countries also have competition laws based on EC law. Several
countries have additional laws including criminal laws and, where applicable, these are also
dealt with in this chapter. This chapter also deals briefly with EC and UK legislation relating
to the control of mergers and joint ventures between businesses for competition reasons.

Article 81 of the EC Treaty (previously Article 85) is the principal instrument for control
of anti-competitive agreements which affect trade between EU Member States. Aimed at
agreements and concerted practices in restraint of trade, Article 81 is directly applicable in
the United Kingdom and can be applied concurrently with national law.[1] In the case of conflict, Article 81 will prevail. A similar provision in the European Economic Area Agreement
means that the rules laid down in Article 81 apply in all western European countries with the
exception of Switzerland.[2]

Article 81 of the EC Treaty now has a UK equivalent in Chapter I of the Competition Act
1998 (the 'Chapter I prohibition') which deals with anti-competitive agreements that affect
trade within the United Kingdom. An agreement is capable of infringing both Article 81 and
the Chapter I prohibition.

Article 81 and the Chapter I prohibition may affect agreements which members of the
leasing industry enter into amongst themselves. They may also affect arrangements by lessees
that are relevant to particular leasing transactions, particularly big-ticket deals.

Article 82 of the EC Treaty provides EC law with an instrument to ensure that powerful
businesses do not use their market power to partition the Common Market and inhibit trade
between Member States. It is mirrored in the United Kingdom by Chapter II of the
Competition Act 1998 (the Chapter II prohibition), which serves the same purpose in respect
of the UK domestic market.

Article 82 and the Chapter II prohibition are far less likely to affect leasing transactions
than Article 81 and the Chapter I prohibition. There may be cases where a lessee is dominant
in its own market place where the leased equipment will be used. It is unlikely that a single
lessor will be dominant in the supply of leasing finance or that a single lessee will be domi-

nant in the acquisition of leasing finance, at least for the purposes of Article 82, and probably for the purposes of the Chapter II prohibition as well. There is some risk of joint dominance in circumstances where a small number of major lessors in a single Member State are able to control the market. Allegations of abuse of a dominant position in breach of Article 82 are made against financial institutions from time to time but have not so far been sustained. However, there is no guarantee that this will remain the case.

Contractual provisions that infringe Article 81 and/or the Chapter I prohibition are void. Where offending agreements have been operated by the parties and have not been notified to the European Commission, or the Office of Fair Trading (OFT) in the United Kingdom, or where there is a breach of Article 82 or the Chapter II prohibition, heavy fines may be imposed of up to 10 per cent of group turnover. The European Commission and the OFT each have extensive powers to seek out evidence, including dawn raids at the premises of companies suspected of infringement. They may also impose interim and permanent orders which restrict the behaviour of infringing businesses. There are, however, some key differences between the system of penalties under the EC and the UK legislation which are discussed in more detail below. Criminal sanctions on individuals are to be introduced shortly for participation in price fixing and other hardcore cartels in the United Kingdom.

Other areas of competition law relevant to the leasing finance industry are the EC and UK merger regulations, the monopolies provisions of the UK Fair Trading Act (FTA) 1973 and the common law doctrine of unlawful restraint of trade. Joint ventures may be assessed under Article 81 and the Chapter I prohibition, or the EC or UK merger regulations, depending on the nature of the joint venture itself.

Article 81 and the United Kingdom's Chapter I prohibition

Prohibition of restrictive agreements

Article 81(1) prohibits as incompatible with the Common Market (an open and functional market comprising all the Member States of the European Union) all agreements between undertakings, decisions by associations of undertakings and concerted practices which may affect trade between Member States and which have as their object or effect prevention, restriction or distortion of competition within the Common Market'. Chapter I prohibits 'agreements between undertakings, decisions by associations of undertakings or concerted practices, which may affect trade within the United Kingdom and have as their object or effect the prevention, restriction or distortion of competition within the United Kingdom'.

Both Article 81(1) and Chapter I give identical non-exhaustive lists of agreements, decisions or practices which are likely to prevent, restrict or distort competition: 'In particular those which:

(a) directly or indirectly fix purchase or selling prices or any other trading conditions;
(b) limit or control production, markets, technical development, or investment;
(c) share markets or sources of supply;
(d) apply dissimilar conditions to equivalent transactions with other trading parties, thereby placing them at a competitive disadvantage; or
(e) make the conclusion of contracts subject to acceptance by the other parties of supplementary obligations which, by their nature or according to commercial usage, have no connection with the subject of such contracts'.

Article 81 and Chapter I are concerned with the restrictive effect of agreements. Any type of agreement may be covered, from formal legally binding agreements to any sort of arrangement between two or more parties, be it a gentlemen's agreement, a side letter to a main agreement, a practice, decision or recommendation of members of a trade association, rules of a trade association or provisions of the articles of association of a company. Concerted practices with anti-competitive objects or effects are also caught by Article 81 and Chapter I.

Provisions in breach of Article 81 and the Chapter I prohibition

Article 81(2) declares that all agreements and decisions prohibited by Article 81(1) are automatically void. Case law has established that only the offending provisions are void. It is a matter for national law whether the rest of the agreement can be enforced. There are several instances of the English Courts enforcing obligations to pay money or to deal with property interests in agreements affected by Article 81.[3] The same should apply to any clause which breaches the Chapter I prohibition.[4]

Exemptions from Article 81 and the Chapter I prohibition

Article 81(3) provides that certain agreements, decisions or concerted practices may be exempted from the application of Article 81(1). The European Commission, as the body primarily responsible for applying Article 81, currently has sole jurisdiction in granting such exemptions. Sections 3, 4 and 50 of the Competition Act 1998 make equivalent provisions for the OFT or a utility regulator with concurrent jurisdiction to declare that an agreement is excluded from the application of the Chapter I prohibition. There are plans, due to take effect in 2004, to give national authorities, such as the OFT, and national courts power to apply Article 81(3) directly, in which case they will apply Article 81 in preference to the Chapter I prohibition when both apply.

Key terms in Article 81 and the Chapter I prohibition

Undertakings. Article 81(1) and the Chapter I prohibition are concerned with the behaviour of 'undertakings'. This is a flexible term used to describe a business or group of related businesses whether incorporated or not. The central characteristic of an undertaking is that it constitutes a single economic unit operating in a business context. The approach taken by the European and UK authorities is to look at the realities of economic control and decision making power and to ignore formal distinctions, such as separate legal personality. Wholly owned subsidiaries will generally be regarded as a single economic unit with their parent, but much will also depend on the facts of each case. Lessor companies that are part of a large banking group are likely to be regarded as part of a larger undertaking comprising the whole of that group. Where leasing is part of the activities of the financial services arm of a conglomerate group, there is a reasonable prospect that the financial services activities, including leasing, may be regarded as a separate undertaking from, for example, the manufacturing activities of that group.

Partnerships, co-operatives, representative bodies, non-profit-making bodies, individuals carrying on a business, and State entities may be undertakings for the purposes of Article 81 and the Chapter I prohibition.

Agreements, decisions and concerted practices. Any type of agreement may be covered by Article 81 or the Chapter I prohibition, from formal legally binding agreements to informal understandings amounting to no more than a mutual, or even a one-sided, expectation in a commercial context. Decisions and recommendations of trade associations or other business interest groupings are also covered. Most importantly, Article 81 and the Chapter I prohibition also cover concerted practices with anti-competitive objects or effects. The court has defined a concerted practice as 'a form of co-ordination between undertakings which, without having reached the stage where an agreement properly so-called has been completed, knowingly substitutes practical co-operation between them for the risks of competition'.[5] However, the mere fact of parallel behaviour is not enough to show a concerted practice, since this may be based on normal market responses to competition.

Effect on trade

Effect on trade between Member States

For Article 81 to apply, there has to be an appreciable effect on trade between Member States. The effect on trade can be actual or potential, direct or indirect, and can occur even though the agreement in question concerns undertakings within one Member State or even undertakings outside the EU. The European Court of Justice (ECJ) has established the principle that an effect on inter-state trade will be found where it was possible to foresee (with sufficient probability) that an agreement might have an influence on the pattern of trade between Member States.[6] In order to limit the all-embracing nature of Article 81, the concept of the need for an 'appreciable' effect on trade has been developed. Factors such as the size of the business, market share, position and size of the parties in the market, the nature of the market, and the potential effect of a network of similar agreements, are taken into account when assessing applicability. There may be barriers, such as differences in the tax system, that make it difficult for lessors from another Member State to offer their services in the United Kingdom. Any additional barriers raised by a contract may still infringe Article 81.

Effect on trade within the United Kingdom

Since the Chapter I prohibition is concerned with domestic competition issues, only those agreements which 'may affect trade within the United Kingdom' are caught. Where an agreement affects trade within the United Kingdom as well as trade between Member States, both Article 81 and the Chapter I prohibition may apply, which raises the possibility of being fined twice for the same infringement.[7] As with Article 81, the effect on trade must be appreciable and the same factors are taken into consideration as for Article 81.

The object or effect of preventing, restricting or distorting competition

Article 81 and the Chapter I prohibition are not concerned with the form of agreements. 'Object or effect' extends their scope to cover any agreement which has either the purpose or result of preventing, restricting or distorting competition. Article 81(1) and the Chapter I prohibition apply where the parties had a clear intention to restrict competition, however ineffective the result in practice; they also apply where the parties had an entirely different aim, but achieved this effect incidentally. In most cases, intention and effect run hand in hand, but this is not always so.

Practices typically prohibited by Article 81(1) and the Chapter I prohibition

There are no hard and fast rules, but certain agreements will normally be prohibited and not exempted under Article 81(3) or section 3 or 4 of the Competition Act 1998 (see the section 'Exemptions from Article 81 and the Chapter I prohibition' above). Agreements between parties at the same level of trade (often called cartels) which fix prices, share markets, rig competition bidding processes, limit production, impose sales quotas, or impose export bans or import bans would almost certainly be prohibited without qualifying for an exemption under Article 81(3) or section 3 or 4. Trade associations have often experienced cartel behaviour by their members. Other types of agreements will normally qualify for exemption. Joint ventures and a whole range of commercial agreements which may have anti-competitive effects, but are generally economically beneficial, should qualify for exemption, possibly with some changes to their original terms.

Exempted and excluded agreements

Article 81(3) individual exemptions

Article 81(3) provides a system to protect certain agreements from the prohibition in Article 81(1). These are agreements that may affect trade between Member States and limit competition, but which have advantages in terms of economic or technical progress, providing benefits that are shared by consumers. An exemption should be given where these benefits outweigh the restrictive effects of the agreement, provided there are no unnecessary restrictions and there is no risk that competition will be eliminated. The European Commission currently has sole jurisdiction in granting exemptions under Article 81(3). An individual exemption may be sought by application to the European Commission as explained below in the section 'Application for exemption or negative clearance from Article 81'.

Article 81(3) block exemptions

There are also important regulations under Article 81(3) that exempt certain categories of agreement. This system of block exemptions operates to exempt various common categories of agreement which have anti-competitive features but carry benefits that allow the vast majority of such agreements to satisfy the criteria for exemption under Article 81(3).

There is a block exemption regulation[8] for vertical agreements between parties trading in goods or services at different levels of the supply chain, under which all vertical agreements are exempt, so long as the parties are not competitors or potential competitors, their market shares does not exceed 30 per cent and the agreement does not contain certain blacklisted restrictions. These include resale price maintenance and absolute prohibitions on the export of goods to other Member States.

There are two block exemptions dealing with beneficial horizontal agreements such as research and development agreements[9] and specialisation agreements[10] between businesses at the same level of trade. These will replace existing horizontal block exemptions from 1 July 2002. There are plans to replace the technology transfer block exemption, covering patents and know-how, with a broadly based exemption for all types of intellectual property licences, subject to market share limits.

There are also block exemption regulations for some particular industries, including motor vehicle distribution agreements, certain co-operative agreements between insurers, freight liner conferences and some types of agreement between airlines. If an agreement benefits from a block exemption it will also be exempt from any infringement of the Chapter I prohibition.

Exemptions from the Chapter I prohibition

In similar wording to that contained in Article 81(3), the Competition Act provides that exemptions are available for agreements that may affect trade within the United Kingdom and limit competition, but which have advantages in terms of economic or technical progress, giving benefits that are shared by consumers. If an agreement benefits from an individual or block exemption by virtue of Article 81(3), or would do so if it affected trade between Member States, it will also be exempt from the Chapter I prohibition. Individual exemptions can be sought by applying to the OFT. There is the possibility of Chapter I specific block exemptions, although at present only one exists on ticketing agreements for bus and train services.

Practices falling outside Article 81(1)

Even though Article 81(1) and the Chapter I prohibition seem to be all-encompassing, legal advisers use case law to distinguish agreements that may infringe Article 81 and the Chapter I prohibition from others.

Agreements that are usually regarded as falling outside the scope of Article 81(1) include those among members of trade associations to collect statistical information published in a form in which individual businesses cannot be identified, certain non-compete clauses of limited duration and scope, certain types of agency agreements and some sub-contracting agreements.

The European Commission has also published an updated notice on agreements of minor importance which indicates that agreements are likely to be outside Article 81(1) where the goods or services which are the subject of the agreement do not represent more than 15 per cent of the total market in the case of vertical agreements and 10 per cent of the total market in the case of horizontal agreements (that is, those between actual or potential competitors).[11]

Practices falling outside the Chapter I prohibition

Agreements which fall outside the scope of Article 81 because of their nature will also fall outside the scope of the Chapter I prohibition. Any agreement by parties whose combined market share does not exceed 25 per cent will not generally be considered by the OFT to infringe the prohibition. However, the parties' market share will not prevent infringement if their agreement imposes extremely anti-competitive (hardcore) restrictions, such as fixing of prices or division of markets.

In a significant divergence from Article 81, the Chapter I prohibition does not apply to any vertical agreements or to land agreements.[12] Vertical agreements are those in which the parties to the agreement are at different levels of the supply chain. Notwithstanding the exclusion, if an agreement contains a hardcore provision such as price fixing or market sharing, it will be prohibited. Several vertical agreements excluded from the Chapter I prohibition will nevertheless breach Article 81 if they have a European dimension. The exclusion for land agreements is aimed at restrictive covenants in commercial leases.

Resale price maintenance

A resale price term is likely to be contained in, or constitute, a vertical agreement. Notwithstanding the general exclusion of vertical agreements from the scope of the Chapter I prohibition, such a term will be an infringement as it is a form of price fixing. It will also be an infringement of Article 81, and in the case of a dominant supplier, Article 82 and the Chapter II prohibition.

If an agreement for the sale of goods (which includes hire purchase agreements and conditional sales) by a supplier to a dealer, or relating to such a sale, contains any term or condition which purports to establish a minimum price for the resale of goods in the United Kingdom, the resale price condition, and potentially the entire contract, is void. There is no prohibition against the stipulation of a maximum price unless, on the facts, it is found that the maximum price operates as a minimum. A supplier, however, may recommend prices considered appropriate for the resale of the goods supplied, so long as they are genuine recommendations and not disguised attempts to impose prices.

Application for exemption or negative clearance from Article 81

The European Commission is overwhelmed with individual applications for exemption or a 'negative clearance' that Article 81 does not apply. Formal exemptions are given only in cases regarded as important to European competition policy or, in a few cases, to end litigation. Most cases are dealt with by 'comfort letters', which are not legally binding. As a result, in the case of litigation (for example, in the UK courts), parties may encounter considerable delay and difficulties in enforcing provisions affected by Article 81 even where these are undoubtedly suitable for exemption.

Agreements which may infringe Article 81(1) and do not benefit from a block exemption may be submitted to the European Commission accompanied by Form A/B.[13] This process involves submitting substantial corporate and market information about the parties as well as arguments on the application of Article 81(1) and 81(3). The same form provides for application for a negative clearance that Article 81(1) and/or Article 82 do not apply and for an exemption under Article 81(3). The notification does not confer any legality on provisions contrary to Article 81(3). This can be obtained only by a formal exemption decision by the European Commission. Notification does, however, provide protection from fines. Despite the number of block exemptions, the net of Article 81(1) is drawn so widely that the legal enforceability of large numbers of beneficial agreements remains uncertain throughout their lives.

Where a notified agreement infringes Article 81, the European Commission may impose cease and desist orders (see the section 'Enforcement and penalties' below) or require clauses to be deleted or impose other conditions as 'the price' of exemption or the issue of a comfort letter.

Under proposals for reform, the notification process will be abolished and national courts will be able to decide whether the conditions for application of Article 81(3) are met. National authorities and the European Commission will co-operate in applying Article 81.

Application for guidance or exemption of an agreement from Chapter I prohibition

The principle of exempting an agreement, including the position as regards temporary immunity from penalties, is the same as that for Article 81, except that application is made to the OFT. The OFT can impose conditions and obligations, subject to which the agreement will benefit from an exemption. In contrast to a decision, guidance provides no formal protection for the agreement against challenge in the courts. The OFT will refer suitable cases to a utility regulator with concurrent jurisdiction (for example the Rail Regulator; the Office of Water Services, OFWAT; or the Office of Telecommunications, OFTEL).

Notification for a decision or guidance is made to the OFT using Form N. The OFT will consult third parties in advance, then publicise a decision, but will generally do neither where guidance is sought. The OFT may withdraw the benefit of the vertical or land agreements exclusion or a block exemption in a particular case, if it allows anti-competitive behaviour.

The OFT has actively discouraged notifications and many of its decisions granting exemptions relate to horizontal agreements involving most or all members of an industry (for example, automated-teller-machine charges by banks or the standard terms of the Film Distributors' Association). It is likely that pre-notification in the United Kingdom will be abolished when the European Commission abolishes its pre-notification system.

Joint ventures and Article 81

The position of joint ventures under European competition law is complicated and it is worth giving their position a special mention. Joint ventures which are regarded as 'full function' are treated as mergers and fall outside Article 81. This type of joint venture, if dealt with under either the European Merger Regulation or national laws for the control of mergers, receives a rapid and clear decision from the competition authorities. However, Article 81 may apply to related restrictions. Mergers which are not full function would be dealt with under Article 81, in which case there is no clear cut decision, and approval may take more than a year. The full function test does, however, mean that most significant joint ventures with a European dimension are considered under the Merger Regulation.

Where a joint venture in the United Kingdom does not have a European dimension, it is more likely to fall within Chapter I than UK merger law. This is because UK merger law will not apply to most new business joint ventures, only to changes in control of existing businesses. In practice this has not caused major problems.

Article 82 and the United Kingdom's Chapter II prohibition

Prohibition of abuse of dominant position

Article 82 prohibits conduct by undertakings enjoying a 'dominant position' within the Common Market or a substantial part of it, which amounts to an abuse of that position in a way that affects trade between Member States. Article 82 affects only a small number of strong businesses, although there is now a tendency for the European Commission to apply Article 82 to businesses operating in markets where there are capacity constraints (for example, airlines and ferry companies) which are not necessarily strong in economic terms, but simply enjoy access to limited capacity. The Chapter II prohibition is essentially the same as that contained in Article 82, except that the abuse is prohibited if it may affect trade within the United Kingdom. The UK authorities may look at dominance in small local or regional markets within the United Kingdom as well as at dominance in the United Kingdom was a whole. In so far as possible, Chapter II cases will be interpreted in line with Article 82.

Dominant position

The ECJ has defined a dominant position as: 'A position of economic strength enjoyed by an undertaking which enables it to hinder the maintenance of effective competition on the relevant market by allowing it to behave to an appreciable extent independently of its competitors and customers and ultimately of consumers'.[14] Such an undertaking has a special responsibility not to allow its conduct to impair genuine undistorted competition in the Common Market. In the case of the Chapter II prohibition, the dominant position is within the United Kingdom as a whole or any part of it.

The test for determining dominance is made up of various elements including:

- identifying the relevant market in terms of products or services and in terms of geographical area; and
- ascertaining whether the position of the undertaking concerned is one of such power as to give freedom of action without significant concern for the reactions of competitors and customers.

Market definition

Product market

The test of dominance concerns the market power of an undertaking in relation to the market. Before it is possible to establish whether an undertaking has a dominant position and is abusing it, the market within which the undertaking operates must be delimited.

Market definition is an economic exercise. Products or services will form part of the same market if they are 'demand substitutable', that is, if they are considered directly interchangeable by the consumer or if a small increase in the price of one will result in an increase in the demand for the others (referred to as demand elasticity). Undertakings will also be considered to compete in the same market if, given a small change in production or supply by one undertaking, it would be economic for another to commence production or supply of a competing product or service (referred to as supply side substitutability).

Geographic market

When assessing the market power of an undertaking, it is necessary to define the geographical limits of the market in which it operates in order to identify potential competitors for the products or services in question. This is the market in which 'the objective conditions of competition applying to the products in question are the same for all traders'.[15]

The markets of easily transportable goods could be Europe or even the world. However, where there are legal, cultural or technical barriers, a market may be limited to one Member State, or even a part of a Member State.

The Common Market or a substantial part of it

An undertaking will be caught by Article 82 only if it holds a dominant position 'within the Common Market or a substantial part of it'. There is no doubt that an individual Member State such as the United Kingdom may form a substantial part of the Common Market.

In order to determine whether a limited market may be regarded as a substantial part of the Common Market, the pattern and volume of production and consumption as well as the habits and economic opportunities of vendors and purchasers must be considered. What at first sight might appear very localised markets have also been held to be substantial parts, certainly where they are intimately concerned with inter-state trade, for example, a single port or air route.[16]

The United Kingdom

The Competition Act prohibits abuse of a dominant position that 'may affect trade within the United Kingdom'. This includes any part of the United Kingdom (which covers England,

131

Wales, Scotland and subsidiary islands but not the Isle of Man or the Channel Islands, and Northern Ireland).[17] It follows that this prohibition can be applied to relatively local UK markets. If a dominant firm's abuse takes place within the United Kingdom but affects the UK's pattern of European exports, it may fall foul of both the Chapter II prohibition and Article 82. However, if there are local UK effects, but no European effects, the abuse will be a breach of the Chapter II prohibition but will not infringe Article 82. Conversely, where the abuse has effects or arises entirely outside the United Kingdom, it may infringe Article 82 but not the Chapter II prohibition.

Dominance and abuse

Dominance

The core element of the definition of dominance is the ability of the dominant undertaking to take business decisions without much concern for the reaction of its competitors or customers (see the section 'Dominant position' above).

The OFT has produced guidelines for the Chapter II prohibition which state that the essence of dominance is 'the power to behave independently of competitive pressures'. This is essentially an abbreviated version of the ECJ test, which must be followed by UK authorities and courts.

Identifying dominance

Dominance is the result of characteristics of the undertaking itself and of the market in which it operates. A market in which there are relatively few participants and where there are high barriers to entry, such as heavy start up costs or limited access to essential intellectual property rights, is more likely to have a dominant party than one with many participants and few barriers to entry.

Very large market shares in themselves are considered to show dominance. A 100 per cent share, as in statutory monopolies, clearly establishes dominance. In *Hoffman-La Roche*,[18] market shares of 75 per cent to 85 per cent over a three year period were considered so large as to be evidence of a dominant position. In *AKZO/ECS*,[19] the ECJ suggested that a 50 per cent market share would in itself show dominance. However, in establishing dominance, lower market shares will be important in conjunction with other factors such as the relationship with other market participants. A business which has worldwide size and strength or special technological resources is more likely to be dominant. A business that appears to have driven virtually every competitor from the market may easily be regarded as dominant.[20] The OFT's Chapter II guideline states that it is the development of market shares over time, rather than at a given point in time, that is important and that market share alone (for example, where there are very low barriers to entry into the market) is not enough to determine dominance.

Collective dominance

Article 82 and Chapter II both provide that a dominant position may be held by one or more undertakings. What may constitute 'shared' or 'joint' or 'collective dominance' is not yet clearly defined. Current case law under Article 82 suggests that there must be an economic link in the strict sense (for example, cross shareholdings or contractual arrangements) between the parties exercising collective dominance and common conduct on the market, not merely parallel behaviour. With respect to mergers, the Court of First Instance has indicated that there is no reason to exclude from the notion of economic links the relationship of inter-dependence existing between the parties to a tight oligopoly within which those parties are in a position to anticipate one another's behaviour in such a way as to maximise their joint prof-its.[21] In other words, mergers in certain oligopolistic markets which increase the risk of anti-competitive parallel behaviour can be found to result in the creation or strengthening of a collective dominant position.

Abuse

The mere existence of large firms with economic power is not enough to infringe either Article 82 or Chapter II. It is the abuse of such a position which is prohibited. The ECJ has stressed that the mere use of economic powers bestowed by a dominant position is not abuse.[22] There must be recourse to methods 'different from those which condition normal competition'.

Abuses may be split into two groups. The first is described as 'exploitative', that is, the dominant undertaking using market power to obtain a benefit not available to others. This might be raised prices or, in the case of a dominant purchaser, unduly reduced costs payable to suppliers. The second group is 'exclusionary', referring to abuses that tend to shut out new competition and weaken existing competitors without necessarily bringing an immediate gain to the dominant firm. These may be seen as an investment in achieving increased dominance, for example, charging extraordinarily low predatory prices in order to take over a competi-tor's customer base.

Negative clearance

It is possible formally to request the European Commission to confirm that there is no infringement of Article 82 or to seek an equivalent confirmation from the OFT regarding the Chapter II prohibition. These proceedings are very little used by dominant businesses and are likely to be abolished in reforms of European Commission procedure.

Enforcement of Articles 81 and 82

Enforcement and penalties

The administration of Articles 81 and 82 is covered by Regulation 17. In addition to provid-ing a system of notification (see the section 'Practices falling outside the Chapter I prohibi-tion' above), the regulation gives the European Commission powers to impose enforcement measures and penalties for breach of Articles 81 and 82, namely power to:

- make cease and desist orders and ancillary measures (including interim orders pending a final decision);
- impose periodic penalty payments; and
- impose fines of up to 10 per cent of worldwide group turnover in the most recent finan-cial year.

Recent fines imposed by the European Commission evidence its determination to come down hard on price fixing cartels. In November 2001, the European Commission imposed a fine of €855.22 million, of which the highest fine on an individual undertaking was €462 million. This is the highest in a series of severe financial penalties.[23] Financial institutions are not immune; in 2002 eight Austrian banks were fined a total of €124.4 million for participation in a price fixing cartel.

Investigations and process

The European Commission has power to send out written questionnaires under Article 11 of Regulation 17/62 and to make on the spot investigations under Article 14. The national authorities (for example, the OFT in the United Kingdom) are bound to assist them in these investigations and sections 61 to 64 of the Competition Act 1998 provide for this. The European Commission's powers will be strengthened by reforms which are due to come into force in 2004. Before taking a final enforcement decision, the European Commission must issue a statement of objections and afford the undertaking an opportunity to defend itself. Decisions may be appealed to the European Court of First Instance and ultimately, on points of law, to the European Court of Justice.

Third-party claims in UK courts

Articles 81 and 82 are directly effective in Member States, so that affected third parties have rights of action, whether or not in a contractual relationship with the undertaking or undertakings concerned. Remedies do exist, but their exact scope in the United Kingdom is unclear. Persons affected by the breach have a cause of action for breach of statutory duty. A party to an abusive agreement contrary to Article 81(1) can claim redress from the other party where that other party had significantly more negotiating power. It appears clear that, in a suitable case, the discretionary remedy of an injunction will be available on the same principles as in any other proceedings. In the leading case on private rights under Article 82, *Garden Cottage Foods v Milk Marketing Board*,[24] the majority in the House of Lords refused an interlocutory injunction on the basis that damages were available and provided an adequate remedy. The Enterprise Act 2002 clarifies that there is a right to damages and allows the Competition Appeal Tribunal (formerly the Appeals Tribunal of the Competition Commission) to award damages for breach of Article 81 or 82 or of the prohibitions in the Competition Act 1998.

Whistle-blowers

The European Commission will grant complete immunity from fines for a cartel participant who informs the European Commission of, and provides evidence as to, the existence of the cartel, unless the informer is the cartel's ringleader. If another cartel member has already qualified for full immunity, or if the European Commission has already commenced an investigation, a cartel member which co-operates fully with the investigation, will receive a reduction in the level of its fine.[25]

Enforcement of Chapter I and Chapter II prohibitions

Enforcement and penalties

Breaches of the Chapter I and Chapter II prohibitions are investigated and punished by the OFT. Where there has been a breach of the Chapter I prohibition, the OFT may:

- impose a fine of up to 10 per cent of group turnover in the United Kingdom for up to three years;
- direct termination of the agreement, and apply for a court order where this is not complied with; and
- impose interim measures.

Investigations and process

If the OFT has reasonable grounds for suspecting an infringement of either prohibition, it has far reaching powers of investigation including powers to demand information, explanation and to enter premises (including private houses and cars) without a warrant.

Procedures before the OFT are similar to those before the European Commission (see section on investigations and process). Up to a date to be fixed in 2003, appeal lies to the Appeals Tribunal of the Competition Commission (headed by a former judge in the European Court of First Instance). The role of the appeal body is to be enhanced with greater independence and additional functions pursuant to the Enterprise Act 2002. The new Competition Appeal Tribunal will take over all the functions and personnel of the Appeals Tribunal of the Competition Commission. On points of law there is a further right of appeal to the Court of Appeal and from there, with permission, to the House of Lords.

Whistle-blowers

The OFT has powers in respect of whistle-blowers which are very similar to those of the European Commission (see the section 'Whistle-blowers' above).[26]

Criminal sanctions

The competition provisions of the Enterprise Act 2002 are expected to come into force in June 2003. The Act introduces criminal sanctions for individuals who dishonestly participate in hardcore cartels. Hardcore cartels are agreements between parties at the same level of trade which, if operating as the parties intend, would do any of the following:

- fix prices;
- limit or prevent supply of a product or a service;
- limit or prevent production of a product;
- divide the supply of products or services to customers in the United Kingdom;
- divide the customers between suppliers; or
- rig bids.

The agreement in question must have been devised, implemented or intended to be implemented in the United Kingdom. The maximum penalty is five years' imprisonment and/or an unlimited fine. Investigative powers will include covert surveillance and interrogation.

The introduction of a criminal offence with such severe penalties signals the UK government's desire to tackle the issue of cartels and deal with it severely. Criminal sanctions supplement the existing civil sanctions of fines, voidness and private rights of action for breach of statutory duty.

Unreasonable restraint of trade

Restraint of trade

This common law doctrine may be applied by courts to deny enforcement of a contractual provision which is an unreasonable restraint of trade. Its most usual application is to non-compete clauses in employment and business sale agreements which are too widely drawn. It can, however, be applied to a wide range of other agreements.

Overview

Under the restraint of trade doctrine, a contract in unreasonable restraint of trade is unenforceable as being contrary to public policy. Despite the existence of a variety of statutory controls both under UK and EC law, the restraint of trade doctrine has retained an important place and has operated to some extent as a supplement to the statutory competition laws, particularly in areas where they are ineffective or inapplicable. Such areas include employment contracts, business sale agreements, and, in particular, contracts between parties with an unequal bargaining strength, for example petrol station 'solus' agreements between an oil company and a garage proprietor.

Definition

A contract is in restraint of trade if one party agrees with another party that he will restrict his future liberty to carry on trade with third parties (not parties to the contract) in whichever way he chooses.[27] In the case which established this test, Lord Denning stated that: 'Any contract which interferes with the free exercise of his trade or business, by restricting him in the work he may do for others, or the arrangements which he may make with others, is a contract in restraint of trade'.

Reasonableness

Once it is established that a restriction is in restraint of trade, whether it will be upheld or void will depend on the test for reasonableness.[28] For a restraint to be upheld three requirements must be satisfied:

- there must be an interest meriting protection;
- the contract must be reasonable as between the parties; and
- the contract must be consistent with the interest of the public, or reasonable in the public interest.

The courts have traditionally attached more importance to reasonableness as between the parties than to reasonableness in the public interest, in part because they will assume a public interest in upholding contracts freely entered into. Cases have therefore tended to review most carefully the details of the restriction to see that it does not go further than is reasonably necessary to protect the party relying on it: for example, a worldwide restriction on a former employee selling wine would not be reasonable to protect the interests of a wine merchant operating in the United Kingdom only.

136

Consequences

A contract in unreasonable restraint of trade is not unlawful. The parties are free to perform it if they wish to do so, but one party cannot enforce such an obligation against another. Such a contract will not provide adequate grounds for a conspiracy action, nor will it give rise to a claim for damages by a third party.

Merger control

EU merger control

Since the impact of laws concerned with merger control on leasing transactions is limited, this chapter does not look at EU merger control in great detail. One of the most common areas where merger control points can arise is where lessors deal with lessees that are joint venture businesses. It is worth noting that joint ventures that are approved as mergers under the European Merger Regulation have legal certainty denied to those considered under Article 81.

The Merger Regulation applies to takeovers and mergers, which includes full function joint ventures, that is, those operating as autonomous economic entities on a lasting basis.

Apart from any related restrictions, mergers are outside Articles 81 and 82. They are regulated by the European Commission or by national authorities, depending on the transaction in question. For the European Commission to have jurisdiction, the concentration must have a community dimension. A concentration will have a community dimension if the parties have a combined turnover of more than €5 billion, at least two of which must each have a turnover of more than €250 million within the EU countries, or, alternatively, a more complex test is satisfied. This alternative test applies to undertakings with a combined turnover of more than €2.5 billion (at least two of which have Community wide turnover of more than €100 million) and substantial businesses in each of three or more of the same Member States (more than €25m turnover for each of two parties and more than €100m in aggregate in each of three Member States). Even if either of these tests is satisfied, the European Commission does not have jurisdiction if all the parties generate two-thirds of their turnover in a single Member State.[29]

Mergers and full-function joint ventures that satisfy these tests must be pre-cleared and fines of up to 10 per cent of worldwide turnover may be imposed for failure to comply. Investigation takes one to six months and mergers which would create or strengthen a dominant position must be blocked unless commitments can be agreed which address that problem (for example, partial divestment).

Application

Where a leasing or other financing business is carried on by an industrial conglomerate, the use made of the leasing business may affect the ability of the conglomerate to make industrial mergers. In the case of General Electric (GE) and Honeywell's proposed merger in 2001, the European Commission banned the merger in part because of concerns that the aircraft leasing business of GE (which was not dominant in aircraft leasing) could be used to encourage potential aircraft purchasers to fit both GE engines and Honeywell avionics, in preference to competitors' products, so creating or strengthening a dominant position in relation to engines and/or avionics. The case is now under appeal.

UK merger control

Mergers are regulated in the United Kingdom by the merger provisions of the Fair Trading Act 1973, but the Enterprise Act 2002 (see above section on criminal sanctions) introduces a new merger system, which is expected to come into effect in June 2003. Both the present system and that envisaged by the Enterprise Act are outlined here. A UK merger will fall to be considered under the relevant merger provisions, and will generally fall outside the Chapter I prohibition. As with European merger law, the impact on leasing transactions is limited.

The present position

It is not essential to obtain prior clearance for a merger,[30] indeed only mergers which qualify for investigation by the Competition Commission[31] can be referred. It is common to approach the OFT to seek clearance from the Secretary of State for Trade and Industry where a reference to the Competition Commission is possible, that is, where the business being acquired has gross assets of over £70 million (referred to as 'the assets test') or the merger will increase the market share of the acquiring party to or above 25 per cent in respect of any description of goods or services in the United Kingdom or any substantial part of the United Kingdom (referred to as 'the market share test'). Special rules apply for mergers of water companies and newspaper businesses. UK merger control will not usually apply to a merger where the European Commission has jurisdiction, but in certain circumstances the UK authorities will be allowed jurisdiction.

A merger occurs where enterprises cease to be distinct. This occurs where enterprises come under common ownership and where enterprises come under common control and where, by agreement, one entity ceases to produce so that competition between itself and another entity ceases. Enterprises may come under common control because one entity ceases to produce so that competition between itself and another entity ceases because:

- a person who controls one enterprise acquires a controlling interest over another (for example, where a company becomes a subsidiary of another);
- that person acquires an ability to control the policy of another enterprise without acquiring a controlling interest (for example, a stake of more than 40 per cent in a quoted company); or
- that person acquires an ability materially to influence the policy of another person.

Material influence will be assumed if an entity has a 25 per cent holding, but may occur with holdings as low as 10 per cent to 15 per cent. Factors other than shareholding, including board representation and other links, will be taken into account in assessing material control.

If an entity moves from one of the levels of control set out above to another, this too will be a merger for the purposes of the legislation. The majority of mergers are cleared after initial investigation by the OFT. More difficult mergers are referred to the Competition Commission, which considers the public interest principally with regard to competition concerns. Some are blocked or cleared subject to conditions (for example, partial divestment or behavioural obligations). The process takes between about six weeks and six months. A merger may be referred to the Competition Commission before, during or up to four months after it has taken place, or, if later, after it came to the attention of the authorities.

The new system

Although mergers can continue to be carried out without it, prior clearance usually will continue to be sought by parties in cases that could be referred to the Competition Commission.

The test for the OFT to refer a merger to the Competition Commission and for the Competition Commission to block or impose conditions on a merger is changed to 'a substantial lessening of competition' in a market. The OFT will make a reference unless it decides that the market concerned is not 'of sufficient importance'. Nor will it make a reference if the merger is being dealt with under the European Merger Regulation.

The jurisdictional tests will remain unchanged, except for the assets test which is replaced by a turnover test where the turnover in the United Kingdom of the enterprise being taken over exceeds £70 million. The political element is being taken out of merger control (except for certain types of businesses, such as defence industries) and the Competition Commission will itself specify remedies. Other changes will streamline the process, but will not materially change the timetable.

Monopolies

Under the Fair Trading Act 1973, the Competition Commission can assess structural problems with markets and recommend measures to address public interest concerns. The Enterprise Act 2002 removes the political element in decision taking and gives the Competition Commission enhanced powers to intervene where there is an adverse effect on competition.

The present system

Types of monopoly situations

The FTA provides for regulation of monopolies in two forms: scale monopolies, in which a single business has a 25 per cent market share; and complex monopolies, in which a number of businesses (which together have over 25 per cent of an identifiable market) act in the same way, with or without an agreement between them. The FTA provides for the regulation of monopolies covering the United Kingdom as a whole or any part of the United Kingdom. Complex and scale monopolies may exist in the same market simultaneously.

In addition, the FTA applies to a no supply situation where, as a result of one or more agreements, goods or services of a particular description are not supplied at all, and to an export monopoly in relation to goods. Since the United Kingdom joined the EC, the provisions relating to export monopolies have not been used significantly, since they conflict with the jurisdiction of the European Commission under Articles 81 and 82. No supply situations are extremely rare.

Investigation by the Office of Fair Trading

Initial investigation is conducted by the OFT under enhanced powers given by the Competition Act 1998. Where the OFT investigates and finds competition concerns, the case may be referred for full investigation by the Competition Commission or disposed of by undertakings in lieu of a reference.

Reference to the Competition Commission

If the OFT cannot obtain a satisfactory solution or considers that a further investigation is necessary, then a reference will be made to the Competition Commission. The Secretary of State has concurrent power (alone or jointly with other ministers) to make monopoly references. Certain utility regulators also have concurrent jurisdiction.

All monopoly references must specify the description of the goods or services which the Competition Commission is to consider (commonly known as the 'reference market').

Competition Commission investigation and report

Following a monopoly reference, the task of the Competition Commission is to investigate and report within a given time (usually in the range of 6 to 12 months), which may be extended. The Competition Commission is asked to identify monopoly situations in the reference market, consider the public interest in relation to both the existence of the monopoly and the conduct of monopoly participants, and to make recommendations on remedies. The Competition Commission makes its report to the Secretary of State who has the final say on remedies; these are imposed by statutory instrument if not agreed. Divestment orders require an affirmative resolution of both Houses of Parliament. There are no provisions for fines.

The new system

Market investigation reference

The Enterprise Act 2002 introduces changes, the principal of which is the removal, except in certain sectors, of the political role and the introduction of very broad-based competition tests, both to found jurisdiction and as a basis for proposing remedies. These changes are expected to take effect in mid-2003. Procedure will remain much as at present,[32] except that the Competition Commission takes over the decision making role from the Secretary of State in most cases and takes the decision on remedies. Monopoly references will be replaced by 'market investigation references'. The OFT, or the relevant sectoral regulator, may make a reference to the Competition Commission if it has reasonable grounds to suspect that any feature or features of a market for goods and services (including conduct of market participants) prevents, restricts or distorts competition in that market in the United Kingdom or any part of the United Kingdom. The OFT may accept undertakings from the enterprises involved instead of making a market investigation reference.

Remedies

Once a market investigation reference has been made, the Competition Commission will publish a report of its findings within two years from the reference date. If it finds that there is an adverse effect on competition, it must then decide whether any action should be taken in order to remedy, mitigate or prevent the adverse effect or any resulting detrimental effect on customers. Detrimental effects on customers are matters such as higher prices, lower quality, less choice and less innovation. These must be weighed against any benefits provided to the customer by the particular features of the market.

The Competition Commission has the power to 'take such action... as it considers reasonable' to remedy the problem. It can impose a wide range of orders, for example prohibiting the making or performance of certain agreements, prohibiting the withholding of supply to certain parties, regulating prices and requiring disposal of part of a business or group of companies.[33] Alternatively, the Competition Commission may accept undertakings from the relevant parties. The decisions of the Competition Commission in the new regime are subject to a limited appeal to the Competition Appeal Tribunal, in the nature of judicial review of the lawfulness and fairness of the decision, not a rehearing.

PRACTICAL ISSUES FOR FINANCE LEASING

Agreements between lessors

Trade bodies

Article 81 and the Chapter I prohibition are primarily intended to prohibit cartels in which members of a single industry get together to fix prices or other terms of trade. It is now well known that such arrangements are illegal and if they exist at all are usually arranged secretly rather than through trade bodies as was common in the past.

Lessors have a number of organisations in which they discuss matters of common interest. These organisations play a valuable role in putting forward the views of the industry, in particular to governments and the European Commission on matters affecting the industry as a whole. They may also recommend standard contract terms, particularly for smaller transactions. As long as these are not mandatory and do not touch on prices or discriminate against other EU nationals and non-UK businesses, this type of recommendation should not normally infringe Article 81 or the Chapter I prohibition. The principal body, the Finance & Leasing Association (FLA) is particularly well informed on matters of European and UK competition law and would not wish to be a forum in which its members make agreements in breach of Article 81 or the Chapter I prohibition without the possibility of exemption. The FLA scrutinises its activities with this in mind.

Notwithstanding this, with the introduction of the Competition Act, the danger for national trade bodies has increased. Decisions by associations of undertakings can infringe Chapter I. An example of a decision capable of having this effect is a rule that required membership of a particular trade association in order to operate in a particular business,[34] or a standard form that provided for particular policy structures.[35]

Other agreements among industry participants

There may be agreements relating to particular types of industry initiatives involving only some participants. The European Commission or the OFT will review any restrictions that may be in breach of the Chapter I or Chapter II prohibitions, as well as any which fall foul of the restraint of trade doctrine. For example the European Commission and national authorities have considered and continue to review various aspects of the Visa International payment scheme.[36]

Big-ticket leases with two or more lessors

Sometimes particularly large transactions involve the bringing together of more than one lessor to provide the required tax capacity. Often, this is itself the result of a tender process to find the most suitable lessors and should not give rise to competition law problems provided that it is clear to the lessee that the lessors are tendering together, or the lessee asks them to combine. The detailed terms of the individual leases may vary, but it is the lessee rather than the lessors who will be concerned to keep documentation differences to a minimum so as to cut costs and keep the transaction manageable.

The Commission does not believe that Article 81 (and therefore the Chapter I prohibition) normally applies to agreements of common terms between lending banks in the case of syndicated loans. There is no reason to think that a different approach would be taken to syndicated leasing, unless a syndicate involving most of the major market participants imposed unusually harsh or discriminatory terms that could be shown to affect trade between Member States or trade within the United Kingdom. The OFT is likely to adopt the same approach as the Commission in relation to syndications.

Agreements for long-term co-operation falling short of a merger may be approved in the context of a competitive market, as for example, in the co-operation agreement between Banque Nationale de Paris and Dresdner Bank in 1996.[37]

One particular concern for managers of syndicated transactions is the formal nature of one of the parts of the two-part test for the new criminal offences introduced by the Enterprise Act 2002. A syndicated deal, by its nature, appears to meet the formal element of the test. It is important, therefore, that the syndication arrangements should be transparent to the lessee so that there is no risk that the arranging individuals could be accused of dishonesty (the other element of the criminal offence, which carries very heavy penalties). In relation to the criminal offence, deception (such as giving the impression that competitive terms are being offered when this is not the case) may be enough to support an allegation of dishonesty even if the transaction, individually, is not competitively significant from the point of view of the Chapter I prohibition. A criminal offence may also be committed if there is bid-rigging between rival tenderers to provide leasing services; if each rival tenderer is putting together syndicates and talking to the same potential syndicate members, particular care will be needed.

Leases
Application of the law

A plant, equipment or fixtures lease, like any other form of agreement, may fall within Article 81 or the Chapter I prohibition (unless the subject matter of the lease is land, in which case Chapter I will generally not apply). From time to time, borrowers in financial difficulties raise allegations that standard lending terms are in breach of Article 81 and/or 82,[38] but the English courts have been firm in rejecting such allegations. Terms are most likely to infringe competition law where they reflect agreements of all or most industry members or recommendations of a trade association of financiers (eg, lessors) to its members (see the section 'Trade bodies' above) or where two or more lessors are involved (see below).

Agreement as to terms

Where a lease has two or more lessors, those lessors are likely to proceed to a large extent on common terms and may sometimes agree that they will not change particular terms unilaterally, either in the lease or in agreements with suppliers of the equipment (including superior lessors in complex leasing transactions as well as manufacturers). If the lessors agree between themselves, even tacitly, to act in the same way when dealing with the lessee, a guarantor or a supplier, then there is a real possibility of breaching the Chapter I prohibitions and, where the agreement has European implications, Article 81. If such an agreement is not fully transparent to the lessee, there is a risk that responsible individuals could be guilty of one of the criminal offences introduced by the Enterprise Act 2002.

Restrictions on use of equipment

Tax-based leases may contain restrictions on the use of moveable equipment (particularly outside the United Kingdom) to ensure that eligibility for capital allowances is not jeopardised. Care should be taken that such provisions are not more restrictive than is justified by the tax legislation.

Resale price maintenance

Hire-purchase and conditional sale agreements (which are used in some equipment leasing structures, particularly those involving other jurisdictions) must not fix prices, either directly or indirectly. A hirer under a hire-purchase agreement or a purchaser under a conditional sale agreement cannot be bound to a minimum price for the sale of equipment or for its further hire-purchase, conditional sale or sublease, although it is not prohibited to make recommendations.

Ordinary leases may deal with the sale of equipment at the end of the lease, but this will usually be a sale by the lessor, even if the lessee acts as the agent, and therefore will not involve a resale price at all.

Abuse of a dominant position

Leasing is a competitive market and a dominant position is unlikely to exist even for specialised equipment, such as aircraft. A lessor which is dominant in a related market may possibly abuse his position by tying provisions in leases, or by offering lease finance only if its sister company's goods are acquired.

The restraint of trade doctrine

Normally this doctrine will not apply to a lease, because the lessee's rights are limited to those granted under the lease and there is no loss of a pre-existing freedom. If, however, the transaction started with a sale of equipment or novation of a supply contract and a lease-back as part of a single commercial transaction, a covenant which, for example, limited what the lessee could do with leased equipment would limit the prior freedom of the lessee and the doctrine could apply. In the case of *Amoco Australia v Rocca Bros Motor Engineering*[39], there had been a lease and lease-back of the site of a petrol filling station and the lease-back included a requirement that the petrol station operator (freeholder and sub-lessee) obtained all his petrol from the oil company lessee. Lord Cross said: 'It is not possible to regard the two leases as separate dispositions of property. The agreement... shows clearly that they were two parts of a single commercial transaction under which the respondent was to get a supply of petrol at an agreed rebate and the appellant a trade tie with security for its investment in the station. The statements to the contrary ... are simply untrue'.

There is no case involving a finance lease, but it is quite easy to see, in the light of this case, that a term in a sale and lease-back restricting the lessee from doing something which it could have done as the owner of the equipment (for example, choose the insurer of the equipment), could be subject to this doctrine if the restriction was unreasonable. It would be reasonable to restrict the choice of insurer to protect the lessor against the risk of inadequate insurance or the insolvency of the insurer, but not if the restriction was to ensure that insurance was placed only with an associated company of the lessor.

Agreements involving lessees

Projects and joint ventures

It is increasingly common for big-ticket leasing to be an important part of funding for projects and joint venture businesses. These businesses may be subject to control either under Article 81 (and therefore also under the Chapter I prohibition), as full-function joint ventures under the European Merger Regulation,[40] or as co-operative arrangements under Article 81 or the Chapter I prohibition.

European merger clearance may be obtained very quickly, but, where Article 81 or the Chapter I prohibition may apply, financing may need to be put in place before the competition authorities have expressed a firm view. For example, the leasing of European Night Services trains preceded approval of the operating joint venture by approximately two and a half years.

A joint venture formed to acquire an existing business may be subject to UK merger control, unless the EU Merger Regulation applies. UK procedures are relatively quick and, if clearance is sought, it should be given in less than two months unless the merger is referred to the Competition Commission, in which case a further three to eight months is added to the process.

In such a case it is important for lessors to address the possibility that the venture may not proceed in the form originally envisaged and to ensure that the lessee or its parents accept the associated risks. It has to be recognised that, even where a strong covenant accepts the financial risks of early termination, planning for use of tax capacity may be affected. The lessor will be concerned to know that any necessary formalities have been complied with.

Fortunately, it is usually possible to assess whether the venture itself will be allowed to proceed, even if details of its operation may have to be changed. The precise nature and financial effects of such changes are less easy to assess in advance. The European Commission is conscious of concerns that its competition decisions can harm beneficial development.

Supply agreements

If a firm with market power refuses to allow access to essential facilities, it may fall foul of the dominance provisions of Article 82 and/or the Chapter II prohibition. However, in practice this will have only limited application to leased equipment, as case law has established that the facility or equipment must be essential to the functioning of the market to the extent that it is impossible, or at least extremely difficult, for competitors to substitute or replicate. Examples of facilities capable of being essential in this way are a port[41] and oil and gas pipelines.[42] The OFT Guideline on Assessment of Individual Agreements and Conduct gives further examples of bus stations and utility distribution networks.

Lessees with a dominant position

There may be lessees with a dominant position under Article 82 and/or the Chapter II prohibition in the leasing finance market. This should rarely pose any problem in relation to the lease, but such businesses need to be aware that they are at greater than usual risk of regulatory intervention in their business activities.

Monopolies and market investigations

Industry practices

The monopoly provisions of the Fair Trading Act 1973 are well suited to review industry practices which fall outside the Competition Act 1998. Some financial sectors have been reviewed in this way, notably Credit Card Franchise Services (Cmnd 8034 (1980)) and Credit Card Services (Cm 718-1989), the latter report leading to a number of changes in practice. More recently, the review into banking practices in relation to small- and medium-sized businesses[43] has required a number of changes to banking practices.

Generally there is good warning of such inquiries and, if leading players respond to a dialogue with the OFT about their concerns, a reference to the Competition Commission may be averted. The revised test and decision taking introduced by the market investigation provisions of the Enterprise Act 2002 are expected to operate in a similar way.

Individual practices

When one market participant is notably stronger, or operates in a niche market where it has a 'corner', its practices will be reviewed under the Chapter II prohibition (and/or Article 82 where appropriate). This could be followed by a monopolies or market investigation capable of imposing structural changes.

Lessees

Business sectors, including motor manufacturing and trading, bus services, white and brown goods, photocopiers, beer, petrol, gas and film distribution, have all been the subject of detailed and repeated review by the Competition Commission. As a general rule such investigations are unlikely to affect directly existing leasing arrangements, but businesses which fear major changes flowing from a Competition Commission report may delay investment plans, just as they would do in response to any other major uncertainty. A Competition Commission review can be a catalyst for the restructuring of an industry in a way that might affect investment plans for the future and lead to changes in the scope and ownership of existing businesses.[44] Like other financiers, leasing companies are affected in their dealings with these businesses and may face unexpected risks.

Regulated industries

In relation to regulated businesses such as water, electricity, airports, gas, telecommunications, rail and broadcasting, other regulatory decisions under the licensing regime for the sector may affect these businesses more significantly than the competition laws described above. Many businesses in these sectors are subject to price control. The regulators (as well as the OFT) have the power to apply the Chapter I and Chapter II prohibitions to their respective sectors. Such intervention could affect business plans for which finance leased equipment was being acquired.

The water sector has special ring fencing rules to protect the availability of assets essential to the business of a water or sewerage undertaker, even if the business becomes insolvent. These rules could restrict the right of a lessor to repossess equipment and he could find himself effectively forced to deal with a new lessee who was not of his choice. Similar rules have been introduced into Railtrack's licence under the Railways Act 1993 and may affect its successor.

145

[1] Article 81(1) is directly applicable. Article 81(3) is applicable only by the European Commission, but new legislation will make it directly applicable in 2004.

[2] The fifteen Member States within the EU are Germany, France, Italy, Belgium, The Netherlands, Luxembourg, the United Kingdom, Ireland, Denmark, Greece, Spain, Portugal, Sweden, Austria and Finland. Norway, Iceland and Liechtenstein are members of the European Economic Area. Enlargement of the EU to include several eastern and southern European countries is currently underway (see Chapter 19).

[3] Void obligations have been severed and the remainder of the contract enforced in a number of English cases including *Chemidus & Wevin v TERI* [1978] 3 CMLR 514 (CA) and *Inntrepreneur Estates Limited v Mason* [1993] 2 CMLR 293 and *Inntrepreneur Estates Limited v Boyes* [1993] 47 EC 140, CA.

[4] Section 2(4) states that any provision in breach of Chapter I will mean that the agreement is void. See discussion of section 2(4) of the Competition Act 1998 in Livingston, *The Competition Act 1998: A Practical Guide* (Sweet & Maxwell, 2000).

[5] Case 48/69 *ICI v Commission* [1972] ECR 619, [1972] CMLR 557.

[6] Case 56/65 *Société Technique Minière v Maschinenbau Ulm GmbH* [1966] ECR 235, [1966] CMLR 357.

[7] However, when setting the level of fine, the OFT must have regard to any fine already imposed. Also, reforms in progress may mean that a single fine is assessed, but it is not yet clear that this would reduce the total exposure.

[8] Commission Regulation 2790/99. Some agreements between competitors will benefit from the exemption.

[9] Commission Regulation 2659/2000.

[10] Commission Regulation 2658/2000.

[11] Commission Notice 2001/C/368/07. This notice is updated by the Commission from time to time and reissued.

[12] However, the UK authorities are considering repealing the United Kingdom's vertical agreement exemption and relying on the parallel exemption from Article 81 only (see section above on Article 81(3) block exemptions).

[13] There are European Commission proposals to abolish the notification system. These are expected to come into effect in 2004.

[14] *Michelin v Commission* Case 322/81 [1983] ECR 3461, [1985] 1 CMLR 282.

[15] *United Brands v Commission*, Case 27/76 [1978] ECR 207, [1978] 1 CMLR 429.

[16] *British Midland/Air Lingus* OJ (1992) L 96/34, [1993] 4 CMLR 596; *Sealink/B&I* [1992] 5 CMLR 255.

[17] Livingston, *The Competition Act 1998: A Practical Guide,* page 181 paragraph 11.1.3.

[18] *Hoffmann-La Roche* [1979] 3 CMLR 211.

[19] *AKZO/ECS* OJ (1985) L374/1, upheld by the ECJ, Case C-62/86, [1991] ECR I-3359 [1993] 3 CMLR 215.

[20] *Tetra Pak II* OJ (1992) L 72/1, upheld by the CFI, Case T-83/71 [1994] ECR II – 755, and by the ECJ, Case C-333/94, Financial Times 26.11.96.

[21] Case T-102/1996 *Gencor Ltd v Commission of the European Communities,* ECR 1999 Page II-00753, at paragraph 273 ff.

[22] *Hoffmann-La Roche* [1979] 3 CMLR 211, at para 91. On dominance and abuse see also: *ICI and Commercial Solvents,* Cases 6-7/73, [1974] ECR 223, [1974] 1 CMLR 309; *Continental Com,* Case 6/72 [1973] ECR 215, [1973] CMLR 199; *United Brands,* Case 27/76 [1978] ECR 207, [1978] 1 CMLR 429; *Hugin,* Case 22/78 [1979] ECR 1869, [1979] 3 CMLR 345; *Hilti,* Case T-30/89 [1992] 4 CMLR and Case C53/92 [1994] 4 CMLR 614; *Tetra Pak I,* Case T-51/89 [1990] ECR II – 309, [1991] 4 CMLR 334; *AKZO/ECS,* Case C-62/86 [1991] ECR I-3359, [1993] 5 CMLR 215; BPB and *British Industries,* Case T-65/89 [1993] ECR II-389 and Case C-310/93 [1995] ECR I – 865.

[23] Vitamins – Commission Press Release IP/01/1625, 21 November 2001.

[24] *Garden Cottage Foods v Milk Marketing Board* ([1984] AC 130).

[25] Commission Notice on immunity from fines in cartel cases, 2002/C45/03.

[26] DGFT Guidance on the appropriate amount of a penalty, OFT 423.

[27] *Petrofina (Great Britain) Limited v Martin* [1996] Ch 146; [1996] All ER 126 CA per Diplock LJ; see also *Esso v Harper's Garage* [1968] AC 269, [1967] 2 WLR 871, [1962] 1 All ER 699.

[28] Expounded in *Nordenfeldt v Maxim Guns and Ammunition Co* [1894] AC 535.

[29] There are proposals for the Merger Regulation to be revised, which may take effect during 2004. In addition the EC Commission is issuing new and revised guidelines on their application of merger control.

[30] An exception to this is newspaper mergers which have special rules and criminal sanctions for breach.

[31] Formerly the Monopolies and Mergers Commission.

[32] Further change may be introduced by the OFT and the Competition Commission through their powers to make their own procedural rules.

[33] A full list of enforcement orders is set out as Schedule 8 to the Enterprise Act 2002.

[34] Decision of the DGFT No. CA98/1/2001 of 24.1.2001.

[35] Decision of the DGFT No. CA98/10/2002 of 1.2.2002.

[36] COMP/29.373; Commission Press Release IP/01/1198 of 10.8.2001

[37] Commission decision of 24 June 1996 IV/34.607.

[38] *Oakdale (Richmond) Ltd v National Westminster Bank plc, The Times* 20.8.1996.

[39] [1975] AC 561, [1975] 1 All ER 968 at 978G in All ER. See also *Alec Lobb (Garages) Ltd v Total Oil GB Ltd* [1985] 1 All ER 303, at 309B where, again, a lease and lease-back were considered as a single transaction and the doctrine applied, but the restraint was held to be reasonable.

[40] Generally, new joint ventures will not be UK mergers unless they involve the acquisition of an existing business.

[41] *Port of Rodby*, OJ [1994] L 55/22, [1994] 5 CMLR 457.

[42] For example, *Disma, XXIIIrd Report on Competition Policy* (1993), pp 141-143.

[43] *The Supply of banking services by clearing banks to small- and medium-sized enterprises within the UK*, CM 5319.

[44] This happened in the beer and gas industries.

Annex

Checklist

The competition checklist at the end of this Chapter includes a step-by-step approach to the

---

Exhibit 8.1

Competition checklist

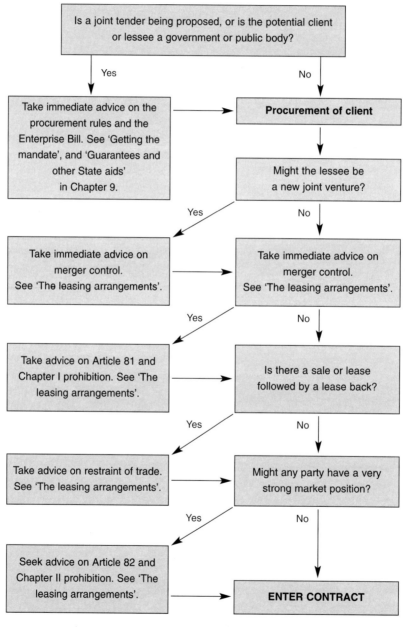

Source: Herbert Smith.

---

matters discussed in this Chapter and the following Chapter. An overview of the check list is displayed in Exhibit 8.1.

Financing leasing transactions: competition checklist

Getting the mandate

1. *(a) Is a collusive tendering arrangement in place or being proposed?*
   (b) Will there be more than one lessor?

The parties need to be aware of the criminal sanctions for certain cartels introduced by the Enterprise Act 2002 (expected to come into force in mid-2003). In particular, the Act provides for an offence of participating in 'bid-rigging arrangements', including collusive tendering. However, if the person requesting bids is informed of the arrangements at or before the time that a bid is made, the arrangements will not be 'bid-rigging arrangements' within the terms of the Enterprise Act 2002 and no offence will have been committed. Even if there is no competitive tendering which could be collusive, if there is to be more than one lessor then discussions with potential follow lessors need to be transparent to the potential lessee.

2. *(a) Is the potential client or lessee:*
   - *a government;*
   - *a public body (for example, a university, NHS trust, publicly-owned museum, theatre or concert hall);*
   - *funded by public funds (for example, a recipient of lottery fund money);*
   - *a utility including water or energy, a port, airport, rail transport or (in some EU States, although not in the United Kingdom) a public telecommunications supplier?*
   (b) If so, do the EU procurement rules apply to its acquisition of finance leasing services or related advisory services the value of which is above the relevant threshold for services?
   (c) Alternatively, is it acquiring equipment above the value of the relevant supplies threshold or obtaining works above the value of the relevant works threshold, which will become leased assets?
   (d) If so, has it advertised and sought tenders in accordance with the rules?

If the procurement rules apply and the lessee has not complied, take legal advice.

3. *Is the potential lessee regulated under special laws?*

If so, enquire whether there are any special rules relating to the assets it uses in its business.

The leasing arrangements

1. *Are there two or more lessors?*

If there are, take advice on the application of Article 81 and the Chapter I prohibition. If the competition provisions of the Enterprise Act 2002 are in force, special care must be taken not to breach the criminal offence provisions.

2. *Is the lessee a new joint venture?*

Find out whether it has any necessary merger control consents (in the case of a full-function joint venture) or is subject to regulation under Article 81 or the Chapter I prohibition (in the case of a co-operative joint venture).

Take advice in the light of the answers, bearing in mind that any consents will take a minimum of 6 weeks to acquire.

3. *Is there a sale (or assignment or novation) or a lease (or conditional sale or hire purchase) and lease-back?*

   If so, take advice on the restraint of trade doctrine.

4. *Is there a complicated chain of ownership, including conditional sale and/or hire-purchase arrangements?*

   Take advice on resale prices legislation under Article 81 and the Chapter I prohibition.

5. *Is the lessor using standard form documentation? If so, is it recommended by a trade or services supply association?*

   Check that the association has clearances or has received satisfactory advice on Article 81 and the Chapter I prohibition.

6. *Is the lessor adopting recommendations of a trade or services supply association in drawing up his terms?*

   Check that the association has clearances or has clearances or has received satisfactory advice on Article 81 and the Chapter I prohibition.

7. *Does any party have a very strong market position?*

   Take advice whether this affects the leasing transaction in any way with particular regard to Article 82, the Chapter II prohibition and the UK monopolies provisions under the FTA or market investigation provisions under the Enterprise Act 2002.

8. *Does the lessee need income from a particular source (for example, from running services between particular ports) in order to fulfil its obligations?*
   If so, is it reliant on particular contractual rights?

   Check whether that contract needs approval under Article 81, the Chapter I prohibition, or any special regulatory regime, and whether and when the consents will be available.

9. *Does the lessor take the benefit of equipment supply contracts or a construction contract?*

   Take advice on the application of Article 82 and the Chapter II prohibition where there is the possibility of dominance.

10. *Is there a tie into a particular maintenance contract?*

    Check whether this is justified in the light of competition law generally.

11. *Does the lease tie the lessee to a particular insurance arrangement or to a particular supplier of financial services?*

    Check whether this is justified in the light of competition law generally.

12. *See also the checklist on State aid at the end of Chapter 9.*

Note: Several of these questions and answers may apply to a single transaction.

Chapter 9

State aid and procurement

Dorothy Livingston

Introduction

The legal framework in Articles 87 to 89 of the Treaty of Rome for the regulation of State aid forms part of the competition law section of the treaty. While it is important to prevent anti-competitive State aid, a distinction has been made between distortive aid and aid that is valuable to the Community as a whole, for example because it improves the economy of a backward region or promotes a project of importance to economic integration. Examples of this include the various trans-European network projects that improve the communication infrastructure between Member States.

Article 87 identifies aid that is, or may be, compatible with the common market and imposes a general prohibition on other aid. Article 88 lays down a procedure for monitoring aid schemes and prior approval of major new aid by the European Commission. Unapproved State aid may, in certain circumstances, be recovered from the recipient.

The basic law

Impact on the leasing industry

Leasing is a common means of financing major capital projects. Such projects are often important to the economy of a Member State, or a region within it, and are natural beneficiaries of State aid in the form of grants and concessions. Furthermore, where lease financing involves a State-owned or supported business, the financing may depend upon guarantees from the State or from a body that may be regarded as an emanation of the State. In such cases, the lessor will be concerned that the financial position of the lessee or guarantor will not be undermined by irregularities in its receipt of State aid and that any guarantees will be enforceable even if given by the State or a State body.

Definition of State aid

Article 87(1) of the EC Treaty provides that: 'Save as otherwise provided in this Treaty, any aid granted by a Member State or through State resources in any form whatsoever which distorts or threatens to distort competition by favouring certain undertakings or the production of certain goods shall, in so far as it affects trade between Member States, be incompatible with the common market'.

The purpose of this legal framework is to police the actions of Member States that may use public funds, directly or indirectly, to enhance the competitive advantages of national industries and so distort competition between Member States.

The concept of State aid, as developed in the decisions of the Commission and the case law of the European Court of Justice (ECJ), is far wider than that of a direct subsidy. It includes not only positive benefits, but also any intervention which mitigates the charges or liabilities which are normally included in a company's budget and which therefore have the same effect as subsidies.

The wide definition of State aid covers a broad range of benefits given by States or bodies that may be regarded as an emanation of the State. These include:

- direct subsidies;
- low interest or interest free loans;
- capital injections;
- grants;
- the waiver of debts;
- preferential terms;
- the award of public contracts;
- reduction in social security charges borne by businesses;
- guarantees; and
- tax concessions.

In applying Article 87(1), no distinction is made as regards the receipt of aid between private sector businesses and those owned by the State. The ECJ has held that the provision of logistical and commercial assistance by a public undertaking to its subsidiaries, which are governed by private law and carry on an activity open to free competition, may also constitute State aid if the remuneration received in return is less than that which would have been demanded under normal market conditions.[1]

Payments which have commercial justification

In deciding whether the provision of public funds or other benefits constitutes State aid, the Commission has developed the so-called 'market economy investor principle'. State investment does not amount to aid where such an investment would have been made by a private shareholder with an anticipation of obtaining a satisfactory return on it. It is not sufficient to establish this principle that a very small number of private investors have made funds available in the same way as the State.[2]

Similarly, payments and guarantees made in the course of selling a business at a profit or otherwise disposing of an asset in a way that is advantageous to the State may not amount to aid. This is exemplified by a number of Commission decisions in the course of the privatisation of British Rail's businesses.[3]

Conditions for the application of State aid rules

Article 87(1) will not apply to a State aid unless it has certain characteristics.

152

- *Effect on competition.* Aid which does not distort or threaten competition by favouring certain undertakings or the production of certain goods will not fall within the State aid rules. The prohibition does not apply if all undertakings within a Member State benefit from a general aid designed to stimulate economic activity as a whole. On the other hand, where a State aid strengthens the position of one identifiable beneficiary compared to its competitors in the Community, competition must be regarded as distorted.
- *Effect on trade between Member States.* For an aid to fall within Article 87(1), it must have an effect on trade between Member States. This will usually be the case where there is a degree of cross-border trade and competition within the sector concerned.

Exemptions from prohibition on State aid

Automatic exemption

Article 87(2) provides that the following aid is always compatible with the common market:

- aid having a social character, granted to individual consumers, provided that such aid is granted without discrimination related to the origin of the products concerned;
- aid to make good the damage caused by natural disasters or exceptional occurrences; and
- aid granted to the economy of certain areas of the Federal Republic of Germany affected by the division of Germany.

Discretionary exemption

Article 87(3) provides that certain categories of aid may be compatible with the common market, subject to Commission approval. These categories include:

- regional aid to areas with abnormally low standards of living;
- aid to projects of common European interest;
- aid for the development of certain economic activities; and
- cultural aids.

Article 86(2): disapplication of the State aid rules

One situation in which State aid rules may not operate is where Article 86(2) of the EC Treaty applies. Article 86(2) provides that undertakings with a public service mission are subject to the rules in the Treaty 'insofar as the application of such rules does not obstruct the performance, in law or in fact, of the particular tasks assigned to them. The development of trade must not be affected to such an extent as would be contrary to the interests of the Community'.

Essentially, this means that where it can be established that a ban on State aid would obstruct the performance of an undertaking in its performance of its public service mission, such aid would be permitted. This exception has assumed increased importance in recent years.[4]

What can be done to clear the position in advance?

Article 88 of the EC Treaty establishes the framework within which Article 87 is enforced. Under Article 88(1) the European Commission, in co-operation with Member States, has a duty to keep under review all existing systems of aids operated throughout the Community. If the Commission decides that a particular measure has become incompatible with the common market, it must recommend to the Member State concerned those ways in which the relevant measure should be modified.

Article 88(3) requires Member States to notify the Commission of any plans to grant new aid or to make alterations to existing aid schemes of which it has already been notified. Any notification must be made before aid is actually granted. The Member State is prohibited from putting its proposal into effect until the Commission has decided upon the compatibility of the proposed aid measure with the common market.

Commission procedure

The Commission conducts an initial review of the planned aid. If the Commission comes to the conclusion that the notified aid is compatible with the Treaty, it must inform the Member State concerned and, as soon as the aid is granted, it becomes existing aid which should be kept under constant review under Article 88(1). On the other hand, if, at the end of the initial review, the Commission is in any way concerned that the aid may be incompatible with the common market, it must immediately institute the contentious procedure under Article 88(2) and thereby give interested parties an opportunity to comment.

The Commission will normally take a decision whether to open proceedings within about two months of the notification. Once its investigation is complete, it will adopt a decision declaring the relevant measure to be either compatible or incompatible with the common market. If the Commission institutes a full formal investigation of an aid scheme, any interested party may submit comments to the Commission.

Aid may be approved specifically, or a regional aid scheme may be approved. In the latter case, applications of the aid scheme in accordance with its terms are covered by the exemption, even if they have a significant effect on competition and on trade between Member States.[5]

In some cases the Commission will decide that a notified proposal is not aid for the purposes of Articles 87 and 88, such as where the payments are strictly what are required to fulfil a public service mission and Article 86(2) applies.

The risks when clearance is not obtained

Requirement for pre-clearance

The last sentence of Article 88(3) prohibits Member States from putting into effect proposed aid measures until the Commission has reached a final decision on their compatibility with the common market. If a Member State fails to comply, either by not notifying a measure to the Commission, or by illegally implementing it before the Commission has reached its final decision, that measure is illegal aid and its repayment may be ordered.

Suspension and repayment of illegal aid

Illegal aid must be suspended as soon as the Commission commences its investigation pursuant to Article 88(3) on the basis of illegality. However, Member States have no obligation to demand that the relevant aid is repaid unless the Commission has first established that the aid is incompatible with the common market on the basis of an investigation conducted under Article 88(2) of the EC Treaty.[6]

The Commission has adopted a communication[7] on the principles to apply in the recovery of illegal aid. Having given a Member State concerned notice to submit its views, the Commission reserves the right to require the Member State to recover all, or part, of the aid granted in breach of the Treaty. If a Member State is the addressee of a decision requiring illegal aid to be repaid, it has a duty to take all steps necessary to ensure that the relevant aid is repaid. Recovery must comply with national laws and interest must be charged from the time the aid was paid. Exceptions from the obligation to recover are limited.[8]

If a Member State does not comply with a Commission decision to recover illegal aid, the Commission and any other interested Member State have the right to bring an action before the ECJ. The case law of the ECJ has also confirmed that the last sentence of Article 88(3) has direct effect, conferring rights on private parties which national courts are bound to protect.[9]

The Commission has adopted a notice on co-operation in matters concerning State aid between national courts and the Commission. National courts are encouraged to contact the Commission for clarifications on the application of Article 88(3), to grant interim relief by ordering the freezing or returning of aid illegally paid, or to award damages to parties whose interests are harmed.[10]

Defences to claims for repayment

The Member State concerned and the recipients of illegal aid may seek to justify a refusal on their part to recover or repay aid on the basis that, at the time the aid was granted, they had a legitimate expectation that it was lawful. However, in order to rely on this defence, the recipient of the aid must have taken all reasonable steps to satisfy itself that the relevant aid was duly notified to the Commission. This is normally difficult to show,[11] however, there may be exceptional circumstances where repayment is inappropriate.

A late approval of a State aid cannot have retroactive effect or legalise the infringement after the event. The Commission's policy is generally not to require repayment of such aid, nevertheless, third parties may be able to take action before national courts seeking repayment. National courts may have discretion to refuse such claims, but the issue awaits a suitable case for a ruling by the ECJ.

Claims against the State

Independent of any obligation to recover aid, States may also be sued for damages in national courts on the basis of Community law by competitors that incur loss or damage as a result of unlawfully implemented aid. Further to the ECJ ruling in *Factortame*,[12] a Member State may be liable for damages if three conditions are met.

- The rule of Community law breached by the State must be intended to confer rights on individuals.
- The breach must be sufficiently serious.
- There must be a direct causal link between the breach and the damage.

How can State aid arise in a leasing transaction?

Aid to lessees

Dealing with a State

Lessee companies may have dealings with the State or State entity, such as a local authority or a State-owned commercial company. In some cases, a lessee may itself be a State-owned commercial company or public sector body.

When is the lessor concerned?

The interest for the lessor in examining that relationship will depend upon the nexus between the aid and the leasing transaction and the importance of the aid to the solvency of the lessee.

- If a single-purpose project company lessee is receiving land for less than its market value from a local authority to build a factory in which leased fixtures will be situated, the economics of the project may depend on the aid inherent in the acquisition cost of the land. The lessor will be concerned, as part of its credit assessment, to be satisfied that the aid has been approved and is not subject to repayment claims. As the fixtures will, in law, be part of the land, the lessee will be concerned that its rights could not be defeated by the transfer being ruled illegal and the land reverting to the local authority.
- If, on the other hand, a large multinational lessee is receiving a small element of State aid in relation to construction costs for building work in relation to a major project in which the leasing of moveable plant forms a small part of the financing, the lessee will be relaxed about the legality of the aid. It is neither directly relevant to the leased asset nor to the credit standing of the lessee.

State-owned lessee

Where the lessee is itself a State-owned business, there may be a more general concern to see that its finances do not depend on the past or present receipt of unauthorised aid. This is unlikely to be a problem in situations where a State-owned business is run commercially and makes profits. Where, however, the State is shoring up unprofitable businesses, this is a real concern. For example, the Italian State holding company EFIM[13] became insolvent when the Commission prohibited the Italian Government from giving it further aid. Many of its subsidiaries were either closed down or restructured. Those that were, or could be made, profitable were sold by EFIM's liquidators. Several national airlines that are not financially robust have received substantial aid, some of which may be liable to be recovered (see the Commission's recent action against Greece in relation to alleged unauthorised aid to Olympic Airways.[14]

State guarantees

Direct concerns for lessors

Banks and financial institutions, including finance lessors, may be recipients of State guarantees. In considering whether to accept a State guarantee or the guarantee of a State body or a State-owned business, a lessor will be directly concerned about the status of the guarantor and its guarantee.

Government financing guarantees often involve State aid and must be notified under Article 88(3) of the EC Treaty. The Commission has published a notice on the application of the State aid rules to aids in the form of guarantees.[15]

The first question to be considered is which party is aided? In most cases the beneficiary of the guarantee in economic terms is in reality the lessee, rather than the lessor. However, there may be some circumstances in which the lessor may also be seen to benefit from the guarantee and it is important to consider whether this might also be the case.[16] The lessee may have the benefit of lower financing costs than it could have obtained independently on the market, in which case the aid may be valued as the difference between the market rate and the financing charge actually paid by the lessee (including any guarantee fees paid to the guarantor). The Commission makes the same analysis and defines the aid content of a State guarantee as either:

- 'the difference between the market rate and the rate obtained thanks to the State guarantee after any premiums paid have been deducted'; or
- 'the difference between (a) the outstanding sum guaranteed, multiplied by the risk factor (the probability of default) and (b) any premium paid, ie (guaranteed sum x risk) – premium.'

The former is the standard form of calculation for individual guarantees and the latter for guarantee schemes. Any other objectively justifiable and generally accepted method may be used in the alternative if, for example, there are special features of the guarantee in question which make these methodologies less appropriate.

Furthermore, the Commission holds that the main issue with State guarantees is that they may have the effect of reducing the incentive on the lender to assess properly, and secure and minimise the risk arising from, the leasing transaction, and in particular to assess properly the lessee's creditworthiness. The Commission suggests that 'a percentage of at least 20 per cent not covered by a State guarantee will serve as an appropriate limit for inducing the lender to properly assess the creditworthiness of the borrower'. Therefore the Commission will in general examine critically any guarantees covering the entirety (or near entirety) of a financial transaction. It is more difficult if no financial institution would enter into the leasing transaction without a State guarantee, since the entire amount of the financing (that is, the value of the finance in addition to the value of the guarantee) could then be considered State aid.[17]

The principles expressed above require refinement in relation to transactions which are habitually guaranteed. For example, leasing transactions of subsidiary businesses are often guaranteed by the parent and the subsidiary may be incapable of raising finance without parental backing. If the parent is the State or a State-owned business, then the market economy investor principle discussed in the above section on commercially justifiable payments becomes relevant. If a parent company applying normal commercial principles would consider it in its economic interest to give a guarantee to support its subsidiary, then the State or a State-owned business would act commercially in giving a similar guarantee and such a guarantee should not be regarded as aid.

The European Commission's approach

Various types of guarantee are accepted as not constituting State aid, in addition to guarantees in respect of obligations of State-owned businesses which are given in circumstances where a private sector shareholder acting commercially would give the same guarantee.

157

Criteria in the notice

Individual guarantees which fulfil all of the criteria below do not constitute State aid.

- The lessee is not in financial difficulty.
- The lessee would in principle be able to obtain finance on market conditions from the financial markets without any intervention by the State.
- The guarantee is linked to a specific financial transaction or is for a fixed maximum amount, does not cover more than 80 per cent of the outstanding loan (or other financial obligation other than bonds and similar instruments) and is not open ended.
- The market price for the guarantee is paid, reflecting the amount and duration of the guarantee, the security given by the lessee, the lessee's financial position, the sector of activity involved and its prospects, the rates of default and other economic conditions.

Similar conditions are also set out in the Commission Notice regarding guarantee schemes.[18]

Privatisation

Procedures to be followed for privatisation of State-owned companies are set out in the Commission's 23rd Report on Competition:

- a competitive tender must be held that is open to all comers, transparent and not conditional on the performance of other acts such as the acquisition of assets other than those bid for or the continued operation of certain businesses;
- the company must be sold to the highest bidder; and
- bidders must be given enough time and information to carry out a proper valuation of the assets as the basis for their bid.

If the above conditions are observed it is assumed, without further examination, that no aid is involved. On the contrary, there is a presumption of aid (which must therefore be pre-notified under Article 88(3)) if the sale:

- is made by way of restricted methods or takes the form of a direct trade sale; or
- is preceded by a cancellation of public debts, by the conversion of debt into capital or recapitalisation; or
- is made in conditions which would not be acceptable between market economy investors, for example because the sale is at an undervalue.

Public works competitions

The principles applying to privatisations can readily be adapted to major public works concessions or service contracts in which State aid or guarantees may be given. The leading example of the application of this reasoning is the initial decision on State payments to the Channel Tunnel Rail Link project agreed at the time the concession was granted. Competition in cases where a body is entrusted with a service of general economic interest are dealt with in the Commission's 2002 'Non-Paper' (see note 4).

Guarantees that require State aid approval

Where a guarantee is regarded as aid, but can be justified, the Commission imposes conditions to minimise the amount of aid. The Commission normally clears State guarantees only if they are contractually linked to specific conditions, including that the guarantee may be honoured only after the guaranteed creditor has recovered what he can of the debt through the realisation of the debtor's assets, if necessary by the winding up of the company. Exceptions have been made for guarantees of bonds and other traded securities.

Enforcement of guarantees that have not been approved

There are a large number of guarantees that have been given by States, State bodies and State-owned businesses which have never been examined by the Commission. A large number of these may not be regarded as aid, applying the principles described above. Many others may constitute aid and there is a general concern that, even though the aid is to the primary debtor rather than to the financial institution entitled to claim on the guarantee, the courts may not be willing to enforce such unapproved guarantees.

The courts have not considered this issue definitively. However, there are good arguments that such guarantees should not be affected by the illegality in the State aid. The way in which a Member State will act to obtain repayment of aid is by exercising its rights to stand in the shoes of the creditor after payment on the guarantee. The State will then recover the aid from the debtor to the maximum extent possible. The State's claim would also include a charge for recovery of interest, or guarantee fee at a market rate, so as to place the transaction on a commercial footing.

When dealing with State-owned commercial companies, lessors should consider whether the guarantee would be given by a privately owned company in the same situation. The lessor and its legal advisers should also consider the appropriate evidence needed to establish that this is the case.

EU PUBLIC PROCUREMENT LAW

Policy and law

Policy background

Central and local government, together with other public sector bodies and utilities, are subject to EU procurement rules when placing valuable contracts with private sector firms. The procurement regime was completed as part of the EU's Single Market programme in the early 1990s. The regime reflects the procurement requirements of the Agreement on Government Procurement which forms part of the framework of the World Trade Organisation. The objective is to ensure that public and utility procurement is open to European-wide (and in some respects worldwide) competition. Suppliers in any European Union Member State should be given an equal opportunity to bid for, and win, public and utility contracts whether for works, goods or services.

Utilities procurement

Utility companies such as water and energy companies were excluded from the original procurement regime, whether public sector or private businesses. Reports in the context of the Single Market initiative concluded that utilities were heavily influenced by the State in their procurement practices, even if in the private sector. For example, for many years the

Department of Energy imposed a British content requirement on the UK offshore oil and gas industry, the most entrepreneurial of the business sectors treated as utilities by the procurement rules. Member State governments are thought to influence the procurement policy of utilities because they generally require government licences or concessions to carry out their business. Accordingly, a modified version of the rules was introduced for utilities.

Practical impact

Whenever a public sector body or utility awards a contract covered by the European Union procurement rules, it is under a statutory duty to comply with those rules. There are severe potential penalties where the rules are broken. Consideration as to whether the procurement rules apply must consequently be given at an early stage.

Where the rules do apply, the stringent procedural requirements must be built into the strategy and timing of the entire procurement process. In particular, there will usually be an obligation to advertise details of a proposed contract at the outset. Once the relevant contract or contracts have been advertised, great care must be taken to ensure that all applicants are given fair and equal treatment, and that the successful tenderer is selected in accordance with the rules.

Directives and regulations

The procurement rules are laid down in a series of European Community Directives.

- Works Directive 93/37, covering construction and civil engineering works contracts in the public sector.
- Supplies Directive 93/36, covering contracts for the purchase or hire of goods in the public sector.
- Services Directive 92/50, for services contracts in the public sector.
- Utilities Directive 93/38, for works, supplies or services contracts awarded by bodies (whether public or private) active in the utilities sectors of water, energy, transport and telecommunications.

The Directives have been implemented into UK law as regulations under a number of statutory instruments. Those regulations also implement two further Directives (89/665 and 92/13), which set out the remedies available to potential suppliers when the rules are violated. Full references for all the procurement legislation are set out in Annex I to this chapter.

The scope of the procurement rules

Who the rules apply to

The first three Directives listed above (the public sector Directives) apply to public sector entities (contracting authorities) which include the following:

- government departments;
- regional or local authorities; and
- bodies 'governed by public law'.

A body governed by public law means any organisation established to meet 'needs in the general interest', not having an industrial or commercial character and which is predominantly financed (by over 50 per cent), subjected to management supervision or appointed (over 50 per cent of the board), by the State or other public authorities.

The procurement rules therefore apply to a wide range of public or quasi-public bodies, including:

- central government (eg, DTI, Ministry of Defence);
- fire and police authorities;
- universities, and maintained schools and colleges;
- National Health Service authorities and trusts; and
- other non-departmental public bodies, such as the Health and Safety Executive and Urban Development Corporations.

Utilities

The public sector Directives do not apply to utilities operating in the water, energy, telecommunications and transport sectors. Such bodies, whether public authorities or undertakings, or private sector bodies enjoying 'special or exclusive rights', are subject to the similar, but generally more flexible, rules laid down in the Utilities Directive 93/38. Such bodies include:

- water, and water and sewerage companies (but not bodies that supply only sewerage services);
- electricity companies (including single power station generators that supply to the national grid);
- suppliers of gas or heat;
- railway companies;
- bus companies (although in the United Kingdom deregulation means that most bus companies are exempt from the rules);
- other transport businesses (automated systems, tramways, trolley buses and cable transport);
- provision of airport or port (inland or otherwise) facilities; and
- exploration and extraction of oil, gas, coal and other solid fuels by exploitation of a geographical area, subject to relaxation where authorisations are given in conditions of fair and objective competition.

Companies or public bodies in the utilities sector are subject to the rules if they supply to, or operate, fixed networks intended to provide a service to the public, or if they supply the relevant commodity or service. In the transport sector, the rules apply to operators of networks providing a service to the public. A 'network' may be either infrastructure or services.

Contracts covered by the procurement rules

The procurement rules apply whenever a public authority or utility awards a contract for construction, supplies or certain kinds of services provided the value of a contract exceeds the relevant threshold. The relevant threshold will depend on a number of factors, sometimes making it a complicated task to work out which should apply. The main thresholds applicable since 1 January 2002 are shown in Exhibit 9.1 and 9.2.

Exhibit 9.1

Public sector procurement thresholds

	Supplies	Services	Works
Central government departments, NHS trusts, health authorities etc[19]	£100,410 (SDR 130,000) (€162,293)	£100,410[20] (SDR 130,000) (€162,293)	£3,861,932[21] (SDR 5,000,000) (€6,242,028)
Other public sector authorities (eg, local authorities, universities, schools)	£154, 477 (SDR 200,000) (€249,681)	£154, 477[22] (SDR 200,000) (€249,681)	£3,861,932[23] (SDR 5,000,000) (€6,242,028)
In relation to indicative notices	£464, 024 (€750,000)	£464,024 (€750,000)	£3,861,932 (€6,242,028)

Note: SDR: Special Drawing Right.

Exhibit 9.2

Utilities sector procurement thresholds

	Supplies	Services	Works
Water, electricity, urban transport,[24] airport and port sectors	£308,955 (SDR 400,000) (€499,362)	£308,955[25] (SDR 400,000) (€499,362)	£3,861,932 (SDR 5,000,000) (€6,242,028)
Oil, gas, coal and railway sectors	£247,479 (€400,000)	£247,479 (€400,000)	£3,093,491 (€5,000,000)
Telecommunications (to the extent not exempt)	£371,219 (€600,000)	£371,219 (€600,000)	£3,093,491 (€5,000,000)
In relation to indicative notices	£464,024 (€750,000)	£464,024 (€750,000)	As per appropriate works threshold

Note: SDR: Special Drawing Right.

Which Directive applies?

Some projects involve a single contract for a combination of works, services and/or supplies. In such cases involving the public sector, it is generally necessary to look at the predominant purpose of the contract in order to determine which set of rules applies. The only exception to the 'predominant purpose' rule is where a single contract involves a mixture of supplies and services. Here it is the relative value of the two elements which determines whether the contract is subject to the Supplies Directive or the Services Directive.

In the case of utilities, all types of contract are dealt with in a single Directive.

Exclusions from the rules

The rules do not apply to contracts for the transfer of interests in land or to procurement for the supply of arms, munitions and war materials or to other contracts declared secret or subject to special security measures. There are also some very narrowly construed exceptions where it would be futile to put a contract out to tender, such as where, for technical reasons, only one supplier is capable of performing the contract.

The Services Directive and the services provisions of the Utilities Directive require the rules to be applied in full only to certain types of services. Many important categories are covered, including financial services, computer related (IT) services, accounting, management consultancy and architectural services. However, certain other categories are exempt from the main procedural requirements. These include legal, educational and health services. The legislation sets out a full list of the service categories which are covered and those excluded.

Contracts funded by public bodies

As an anti-avoidance provision, the public procurement rules are extended to cover certain contracts awarded by private sector firms where the contract is financed through public subsidies. Member States are required to ensure that public authorities comply or ensure compliance with the Directive where they subsidise directly by more than 50 per cent certain works and services contracts awarded by a private sector firm. This provision applies only to works and services contracts relating to civil engineering projects (roads, bridges, railways, etc) or the construction of hospitals, sports centres, school and university buildings or administrative buildings. A number of contracts in the United Kingdom funded with National Lottery awards are caught by this provision.

Concessions

The procurement rules lay down special provisions for public works concessions. These are defined as contracts under which all or part of the consideration consists of a right to exploit the subject matter of the contract. An example of a public works concession would be a contract to build a bridge for which all or part of the consideration involves giving the contractor the right to charge a toll on users of the completed bridge. These rules are much less restrictive than those for other works contracts. Services concessions fall outside the scope of the procurement rules.[26]

Private Finance Initiative/Public Private Partnerships contracts

The procurement rules often apply in the context of projects under the UK government's Private Finance Initiative (PFI) or Public Private Partnerships (PPP). For example, such projects involving the design, build, finance and operation (DBFO) of a hospital, or the construction of a highway, would be works and/or services contracts. Other PFI/PPP initiatives involve the leasing of goods, such as high value medical equipment. The contracts for purchase arranged by the potential lessee (for example, a NHS Trust) are usually supply contracts covered by the Supplies Directive, but the finance leasing element is a services contract.

Many PFI projects, such as the Channel Tunnel Rail Link, involve the award of concessions. This is because private operators are often given the incentive of being able to charge users for the service or construction which they provide in exchange for carrying out the works or services and bearing the risks of the transaction.

Competitive tendering

Advertising requirements

The Community-wide publicity of public procurement contracts over the relevant threshold is achieved by the publication of various kinds of notice in the Official Journal (OJ) of the European Communities. Generally these are referred to as a 'call for competition' and include:

- periodic indicative notices (PINs), giving advance notice of works contracts or of an authority's or utility's forthcoming requirements for different types of supplies or services;
- contract notices, giving details about an individual contract and inviting tenders (open procedure – see below) or inviting requests to tender (restricted and negotiated procedures – see below) or (utilities only) inviting requests to join a list of pre-qualified suppliers; and
- contract award notices, which must be sent to the OJ within 48 days of the award of any contract covered by the Directives.

Notices must be sent 'as rapidly as possible and by the most appropriate means' to the EC Office for Official Publications in Luxembourg, which ensures that they are published within 12 days on the Tenders Electronic Daily (TED) database. The notices should be set out as shown in the model notices annexed to the Directives.

Award procedures

In awarding contracts, public authorities and utilities must follow one of four types of procedure.

- Open procedure.
- Restricted procedure.
- Negotiated procedure.
- Public competition in a design contest.

Open procedure

Under an open procedure, all interested parties may submit tenders. A contract notice inviting tenders must be published in the OJ giving at least 52 days for submission of tenders (or 36 days if a periodic indicative notice has already been published) except where a utility invites tenders from suppliers on a pre-qualified list. The open procedure is most suitable where both the subject matter of the contract and the award criteria are fairly simple.

Restricted procedure

Where the restricted procedure is used, only those contractors invited by the authority may submit tenders. The notice published in the OJ invites requests to participate, allowing at least 37 days (or 15 days if the accelerated procedure is available) for interested parties to respond. Subsequently, the authority simultaneously invites selected candidates to submit tenders allowing at least 40 days (or 26 days if a PIN has already been published, or 10 days under the accelerated procedure) for them to do so. The number of candidates invited to tender should be 'sufficient to ensure genuine competition' and the contract notice may prescribe a minimum (at least five) and maximum (up to 20). Again, utilities may draw from a pre-qualified list without a specific notice.

Once tenders have been submitted, post-tender negotiations are generally not permitted. Clarification of tenders is permissible but needs to be done carefully in order to avoid any inference that it amounts to discriminatory post-tender negotiations.

Negotiated procedure

Under this more flexible procedure, an awarding authority consults contractors or suppliers chosen from those that have expressed interest and have the necessary qualifications. It negotiates the terms of the contract with one or more of them. The same time limits apply as for the restricted procedure.

Unlike the open and restricted procedures, the negotiated procedure is only permitted for public bodies in certain limited circumstances set out in Annex 3 to this chapter. Utilities may, however, use the negotiated process freely.

Where available to an awarding authority, the benefit of the negotiated procedure is that it enables exploratory discussions to take place to establish both what the suppliers are able to offer and, sometimes, precisely what contract specification would satisfy an authority's requirements. This may be a useful process, particularly where the subject matter is complicated and perhaps unfamiliar to the authority (for example, a large-scale IT development contract or an innovative PFI/PPP contract to design and build a major hospital and manage the building and ancillary services over a long period).

Design contest

In a design contest, providers of professional services, such as architects and landscapers, may be selected by public competition after publication of an OJ notice. This procedure was introduced by the Services Directive. It is in practice rather inflexible and lays down stringent requirements including the use of an independent jury that is unaware of the identity of individual designers.

Financial and technical qualifications

An awarding authority will usually wish to verify the suitability of tenderers or would-be tenderers in terms of legal, technical and financial factors before proceeding to award the contract to one or more of them. In restricted or negotiated procedures, it is usually only a selection of those candidates that establish suitability which are invited to submit tenders or to negotiate. Rules concerning this qualitative selection are set out in the Public Sector Directives. However, utilities are not restricted in this way.

The Directives describe the types of reference which applicants for public contracts may be required to furnish in order to prove their economic and financial standing and their relevant technical knowledge and ability. The published OJ notice must refer to the qualifications which applicants are required to establish.

Public authorities may only concern themselves with the nature of a contractor's experience and not how it was acquired. It would be unlawful discrimination for an authority to require, for example, that tenderers have carried out a certain number of similar contracts in the particular country or region where the advertised contract is to be carried out.

Disqualifying factors

A candidate may be disqualified on various grounds listed in the Directives, such as bankruptcy, criminal record, professional misconduct, non-payment of taxes, or social security or serious misrepresentation to the awarding authority. The authority may also require candidates to prove their enrolment in the trade or professional register of their home State (for example, a certificate from the Registrar of Companies in the United Kingdom). If the candidate can prove such registration, the authority cannot require an undertaking to hold an establishment permit in the State in which the contract is awarded.

Use of official lists of recognised suppliers

The Directives allow Member States to maintain official lists of recognised contractors or suppliers provided that they are based on the same legal, financial and technical criteria as those prescribed by the Directives for assessing suitability and do not discriminate against 'foreign' applicants. A contractor registered in an official list of one Member State shall be presumed by awarding authorities in any other State to satisfy certain of the Public Sector Directives' suitability criteria.

In addition, utilities may, following a call for competition, maintain their own lists of prequalified suppliers that may be invited to bid or called forward to negotiate.

Technical standards

In all award procedures, the use of discriminatory technical specifications is prohibited. The procurement rules require technical specifications to which authorities may refer in contract documents or published notices, to be defined by reference to European standards where they exist. There are several exceptions to this basic rule: the European standard need not be used, for example, if it would be incompatible with equipment already in use or would entail disproportionate cost or technical difficulty.

Technical specifications which favour or eliminate certain candidates may not be used unless indispensable for the subject of the contract. In particular, an indication that specifies trade marks, patents or origins is prohibited unless the subject matter cannot otherwise be precisely described, in which case such an indication must be accompanied by the words 'or equivalent'.

Non-EU bidders

The EU Directives give rights only to suppliers that are established in the European Union. However, a parallel set of rules has been agreed at an international level under the Agreement on Government Procurement (GPA), which was signed in April 1994 pursuant to the Uruguay Round of the General Agreement on Tariffs and Trade (GATT). The GPA, which came into force on 1 January 1996, is a plurilateral agreement that applies only to those parties which have signed it. The GPA signatories are: the European Union, the United States, Canada, Japan, Singapore, South Korea, Hong Kong, China, Israel, Switzerland, Norway, Iceland and Liechtenstein.

As a result of the GPA, central government bodies in the United Kingdom and elsewhere in the European Union must give due consideration to any bids received from potential suppliers based in other GPA signatory countries. The coverage of local government and public authorities which are not part of central government is more complex. The European Union has only granted access, under the GPA, to contracts awarded by these bodies to the extent that other GPA signatories agreed to open their own public sectors. Ultimately, the agreement's precise scope and effect can only be determined by reference to the entities, activities and derogations listed in the lengthy annexes for each signatory.

Award criteria

Having checked the financial and technical suitability of eligible candidates or tenderers, contracting authorities are required to award the contract to one of them on the basis of either the lowest price or the most economically advantageous tender. Most authorities and utilities are likely to opt for the latter since it allows the best value for money to be sought according to various criteria, for example: period for completion, running costs, profitability, and technical merit, as well as price, thus permitting a degree of subjective assessment.

The authority must make the criteria it intends to employ known to bidders in advance, for example, in the contract notice or invitation to tender or negotiate, where possible in descending order of importance. It may also specify that bids offering variations on the stated requirements will be considered.

The awarding authority may not reject any tender solely on the ground that it appears abnormally low in price without first asking for and considering the tenderer's explanations.

After the award

Within 48 days of awarding a contract, the authority or utility is required to send an award notice to the OJ giving brief details of the award. It should also keep a written record documenting each stage of the award procedure. The European Commission and Member State's treasury may ask to see a copy of this report.

The procurement rules require a public authority, within 15 days of a request, to inform an eliminated candidate of the reasons for his rejection. Where the bidder was rejected after reaching the negotiation or tendering stage, the debriefing should include the identity and relevant advantages of the successful bid. Private sector utilities are not subject to the latter obligation.

Risks of non-compliance
Penalties

A public authority or utility that breaches the procurement rules when awarding a relevant contract faces two main risks:

* being sued for damages and/or an injunction by an aggrieved contractor; and
* being the subject of a complaint to the European Commission, which can take action against the Member State (but not directly against any individual public body or utility).

Enforcement by national courts

The United Kingdom, like other Member States, has been required by the Remedies Directive 89/665 to put in place effective review procedures to deal with infringements of the procurement rules. The UK implementing Regulations therefore provide that breaches are actionable in the High Court in England, Wales and Northern Ireland, and in the Court of Session in Scotland.

An action may be brought by anyone who has an interest in obtaining a particular contract and who has been, or risks being, harmed by a breach of the procurement rules. The action must be brought promptly and in any event within three months from the date of the alleged infringement. Before commencing proceedings, the aggrieved party must inform the awarding body of its intention to do so.

The High Court has the power to:

- make an interim order (injunction) suspending the contract award procedure in question (for example, this occurred when Severn Trent Water challenged the award to United Utilities, without any call for competition, of a contract to manage another water company, Hyder[27]);
- order the setting aside of a decision taken by the awarding body as part of a procurement procedure or order the amendment of any document; and/or
- award damages to the complainant for any loss or damage suffered.

Where the contract in question has already been entered into, the only remedy available would be an award of damages. Contracts already concluded cannot be set aside by a national court, except, possibly, in cases where there has been insufficient time between announcement of the award and the contract for effective relief to be obtained.[28]

Damages would be likely to cover the costs of any abortive tender and may also compensate the aggrieved contractor for the loss of the profit which it stood to make if the contract had been awarded to it. The plaintiff would have to demonstrate a real chance of winning the contract in order for damages to be available.

Action by the European Commission

The European Commission may, particularly through complaints, become aware of infringements. If so, it has the power to call upon a Member State government to justify the procurement procedure in question and to rectify any infringement. If the problem cannot be resolved, the Commission may ultimately seek a declaration from the ECJ that the Member State is in breach of its Community obligations. In serious cases, the Commission may also apply for an interim order suspending the contract award procedure and possibly prohibiting performance of a contract which has already been entered into.

Reform of the public procurement regime

On 10 May 2000 the European Commission adopted a package of proposed amendments to simplify and modernise the public procurement Directives. The proposed legislative package has two objectives. The first is to simplify and clarify the existing Community Directives, and the second is to adapt them to modern administrative needs in an economic environment that is changing as a result of, among other things, the liberalisation of telecommunications.

In particular, the proposals involve the consolidation into one text of the Directives covering supplies, services and works procurement in the public sector. The new provisions are intended to be presented in a more user friendly and structured manner. The thresholds will also be simplified. A number of inflexible provisions are also to be relaxed in order to help achieve the objective of best value for money.

The amendments to the procurement regime were initially intended to be adopted and implemented by 2002, but now it is not clear when changes will be adopted, the earliest date being 2004.

Procurement and leasing transactions

Procurement of leasing services

Financial services are subject to the Services Directive for public bodies and to the Utilities Directive for utilities. There is, however, an exemption for financial services in the banking and investment services category in connection with 'the issue, sale, purchase or transfer of securities or other financial instruments and central bank services'.[29] Most of these services are described in the CPC[30] classification under heading 81. Financial leasing services have the separate sub-category 8112. Operational leases, however, are classified as supply contracts according to the nature of the goods supplied. Investment and banking services are classified separately and fall under different heads of classification 81. The securities exception therefore is not directly applicable to the procurement of either financial or operating leasing services in themselves, although the exception may apply to some other forms of financing for the same project.

Finance leases in general, and operating leases for equipment, should be procured by public bodies and utilities in accordance with the procurement rules. Major finance leasings are likely to have a value above the threshold for the application of the rules. If the rules are not followed, the selected lessor risks its prospective lessee being unable to proceed or, after the lease has been entered into, being exposed to a damages claim from a disappointed rival.

Risk of dispute

There has not been a great deal of litigation to date, and none in the finance lease sector. This is partly because a disappointed tenderer that hopes to do business in the future is unlikely to sue. Furthermore, the window of opportunity to sue is short (three months or less) and the amount available by way of damages is often uncertain. However, in other countries, for example, Germany and the Netherlands, litigation has become quite common. Recent successes by claimants in UK courts, in both getting a competition run (where a contract had been awarded without a competition) and recovering very substantial damages for loss of profit, make it likely that UK practice will become more litigious.

Advice on leasing

Advisory services, other than legal services, may also be caught by the full rigour of the rules as falling in the financial services category as financial consultancy services (81332) or insurance consultancy services (81402). Pure tax consultancy, like legal services, falls outside the compulsory advertising rules. Financial planning services (for example, for a project) are subject to the rules in the management consultancy services category (865), in particular sub-class 86502. Advice on both structuring a leasing transaction and insurance matters could be caught if the relevant value threshold is exceeded. Some advisory work will have a value

169

below the threshold. The large lead time to allow expressions of interest before awarding a contract requires careful planning by the prospective lessee or its parent company or companies to ensure that the timetable is not unnecessarily delayed.

Procurement of assets to be leased

If leasing is to be put in place after procurement of the relevant works or equipment, the lessor needs to be satisfied that the rules are being complied with, where applicable. If they are not, there is a chance that the acquisition could be blocked. Once the contract has been awarded, provided there has been reasonable opportunity for challenge beforehand, it depends very much on the profile of the lessee whether the lessor has any concerns. If the lessee can sustain any damages claim by a person who claims to have been affected by the failure to follow the rules, there should be little cause for concern for the lessor. If, however, the lessee is a single purpose company operating to a strict budget, this risk would be a cause for concern. Warranties on compliance may be sought and would be particularly important in a leasing programme for a portfolio of assets being acquired one by one during the early years of the lease.

Looking out for calls for competition

Like other potential service providers, finance lessors and advisers may find business opportunities advertised in the OJ. Even if lessors or advisers became aware of opportunities in other ways, where these are advertised there is a need to respond in the required time frame and with the required information.

Commission attitudes

As in the State aid area, the Commission increasingly looks to financiers to police compliance with Community rules. It expects major financial institutions to accept and work within the procurement rules, in so far as they apply to them as service providers, and to encourage compliance in relation to the acquisition of equipment, fixtures or construction work to be financed by finance leasing for clients that are bound by the procurement rules.

---

[1] Case C-39/89, *Syndicat Français de l'Express International v Le Poste,* judgment of 11.7.96, [1996] 3 CMLR 369, ECJ.

[2] Case *Compagnie Nationale Air France v EC Commission,* ECS, [1997] 1 CMLR 492, CFI.

[3] See CTRL Commission press release of 30 April 1996 where the Commission pronounced that in the light of the competition to establish the most economical way of getting the CTRL built, 'the price paid in terms of the support package, by the UK Government for the building of the CTRL is in no way a State aid as defined by the Treaty'. The treatment of government obligation in the context of the privatisation of the Roscos followed the Commission's standard approach on privatisation and can be described as following the notice on privatisation.

[4] Guidance is given in the 'Non-Paper' of 12 November 2002, published by DG Competition of the European Commission.

[5] *Salt Union v Commission,* ECJ, 22.10.96.

[6] *Re Boussac: France v Commission* (Case 30/81 [1990] ECR I-307).

[7] OJ (1995) C156/5.

[8] See *EC State Aid Law and Policy* by Quigley and Collins (Hart Publishing, 2003) at pp 302–04.

[9] *Lorenz v Germany,* Case 120/75 [1975] ECR 1471, *Capolongo v Maya,* Case 77/72 [1973] ECR 611.

[10] OJ (1995) C312/8. This approach has been recently upheld by the ECJ (Case C-39/89, *SFEI v La Poste,* judgment of 11.7.96, Financial Times 30.7.96).

[11] While the ECJ has accepted that the protection of legitimate expectations forms part of the legal order of the Community, this principle cannot be relied upon by aid beneficiaries to dispute the illegality of the aid: *Deutsche Milchkontor v Bundesamt für Ernührung und Forstwirlschaft* [1983] ECR 263. The Court referred to the mandatory nature of Article 88 and that a diligent businessman should normally be able to determine whether the procedure under Article 88 had been followed. The recipient cannot plead legitimate expectations purely on the basis of reliance on the Member State's obligation to observe Community procedures. Instead he should also verify whether in fact that obligation has been met.

[12] Factortame III and Brasserie du Pecheur [1996 1 CMLR 889].

[13] EFIM case: EC Commission v Italy C-349/88, ECR [1995] I-343.

[14] Aid C19/2002 – Olympic Airways – opening of procedure 2002 OJ (2002) C98/8

[15] OJ year 3 (2000) C71/07.

[16] The Commission Notice gives the example of a State guarantee being given ex post in respect of a transaction already entered into without the terms of the original transaction being adjusted or where one guaranteed loan is used to repay an unguaranteed loan to the same credit institution.

[17] For the particular concern where a State-owned business is underwritten by a general guarantee, for example the German Landesbanks, whose credit standing may change materially according to whether the State guarantee is taken into account, see *State Guarantees, Banks and EU prohibition of State Aid: Abetting Prohibited Aid?,* Dr J Frisinger and Dr A Behr, Recht der *International Wissenschaft,* September 1995, pages 705–792 and also *The German Landesbanken,* M Grunson and U Schneider, Columbia Business Carr Review, 1995, volume 2, page 337. The removal of these guarantees has now been negotiated with the Commission. See Commission Press Release IP/03/49 of 15 January 2003.

[18] Paragraph 4.3 of the Notice.

[19] Schedule 1 of the Public Supply Contracts Regulations 1995 lists central government bodies subject to the WTO Agreement on Public Procurement.

[20] With the exception of the services below which have a threshold of £123,740 (€200,000).

- Part B (residual) services.
- Research & development services (category 8).
- The following telecommunications services in category 5:
  - CPC 7524: television and radio broadcast services;
  - CPC 7525: interconnection services; and
  - CPC 7526: integrated telecommunications services.
- Subsidised services contracts under regulation 25 of the Public Services Contracts Regulations 1993.

[21] For subsidised works contracts under regulation 23 of the Public Works Contracts Regulations 1991, the threshold is £3,093,491 (€ 5,000,000).

[22] See note 2 above.

[23] See note 3 above.

[24] Contracting entities in the field of urban railway, tramway, trolleybus or bus services.

[25] With the exception of the services below which have a threshold of £247,479 (€ 400,000).

- Part B (residual) services.
- Research & development services (category 8).
- The following telecommunications services in category 5:
  - CPC 7524: television and radio broadcast services;
  - CPC 7525: interconnection services; and
  - CPC 7526: integrated telecommunications services.

[26] C-324/98 *Telaustria and Telefonadress v Telekon Austria* [2000] ECR 1-10745. However, general principles of non-discrimination and freedom to provide services apply to letting such concessions.

[27] *Severn Trent v Welsh Water, WPD and United Utilities,* High Court, October 2000.

[28] C-81/98 *Alcatel Austria and others v Federal Ministry of Science and Transport,* 28.10.99, [2001] Eu LR 136.

[29] The European Commission has recommended use of CPV codes instead of CPC, but the procurement Directives and regulations continue to refer to the CPC. The ECJ confirmed in case C-76/97 that the CPC provides the only binding guide to the services categories and these are therefore referred to here.

[30] There is some dispute as to the breadth of the exception turning on the meaning of 'securities or other financial instruments'. Some EU governments believe that the exception is limited to financial services related to government stocks (or the shares and quoted securities of the relevant utility), while other governments, including that of the United Kingdom, take a wider view. Some UK legislation (for example, the old Control of Borrowing legislation no longer in force) uses the term 'financial instrument' to include a simple loan agreement not involving any debenture stock or other separate 'instrument', but it is doubtful that the procurement exception was intended to go that far.

Annex 1

The Directives and UK implementation

Works Directive 93/37 (OJ L199/54 of 9.8.93)

Implemented in the United Kingdom by the Public Works Contracts Regulations 1991 (SI 1991. No 2680) (as amended), in force 21.12.91 amended 1993. This has since been amended by the Public Contracts (Works, Services and Supply) (Amendment) Regulations 2000.

Supplies Directive 93/36 (OJ L199/1 of 9.8.93)

Implemented in the United Kingdom by the Public Supply Contracts Regulations 1995 (SI 1995 No 201), in force 21.2.95. This has since been amended by the Public Contracts (Works, Services and Supply) (Amendment) Regulations 2000.

Services Directive 92/50 (OJ L209/1 of 24.7.92)

Implemented in the United Kingdom by the Public Services Contracts Regulations 1993 (SI 3228), in force 13.1.94. This has since been amended by the Public Contracts (Works, Services and Supply) (Amendment) Regulations 2000.

Remedies Directive 89/665 (OJ L395/33 of 30.12.89)

Implemented in United Kingdom as part of the Works, Services and Supply Regulations cited above.

Utilities Directive 93/38 (OJ L199/84 of 9.8.93)

Applicable since 1.7.94 to entities operating in the water, energy, transport and telecommunications sectors and implemented in the United Kingdom by the Utilities Contracts Regulations 1996 (SI 2911), in force 12.12.96. It replaced regulations in force from January 1993 which implemented an earlier version of the Utilities Directive, applicable only to works and supplies contracts. These have since been amended by the Utilities Contracts (Amendment) Regulations 2001.

Utilities Remedies Directive 92/13 (OJ L79/14 of 23.3.92)

Implemented in United Kingdom as part of the Utilities Regulations cited above.

Directive 97/52 (OJ L328/1 of 28.11.97)

Amending Directives 92/50, 93/36 and 93/37 above.

173

Directive 98/4

Amending Utilities Directive 93/38 above.

Directive 2001/78

Amending the Standard Forms to be used for the publication of public contract notices under Directives 92/50, 93/36, 93/37 and 93/38.

Annex 2

Valuation of contracts

Valuation

The procurement rules make it clear that a work, supply or service may not be undervalued or split solely in order to avoid those rules. When determining whether the relevant threshold is met, the value of the contract should usually correspond to the amount of consideration which the awarding body expects to give under the contract. In the case of a works concession, it is necessary to estimate the monetary value of the consideration which the authority would have given if the contractor had not been given the right to exploit the works.

If a supplies or services contract specifies option clauses, the awarding authority must presume that all the options will be exercised and so take the maximum possible value. Special valuation rules deal with long-term or indefinite contracts for services or the lease, rental or hire purchase of products; in effect, the projected value over a four-year period.

Specific rules are laid down to deal with mixed contracts that involve a combination of works, supplies and/or services. The value of a works contract includes the value of any services or supplies necessary for its execution. Likewise, the value of a services contract includes the value of any supplies necessary to carry out the services although, where those supplies are in fact worth more than the services, the whole contract is treated as a supplies contract.

Aggregation of contracts

A single purchasing requirement may not be split up with the intention of avoiding the procurement rules. If an awarding authority subdivides what is essentially a single contract into smaller units, the value of each part has to be added together to determine whether the relevant threshold is met.

It is also necessary to aggregate, over a one-year period, the value of regular or renewable contracts for services or supplies for which the purchaser has a recurrent need. This is an anti-avoidance provision to prevent authorities awarding low value contracts to a single supplier at regular intervals over a long period.

The aggregation rules are mitigated by an exception whereby the purchases of a so-called 'discrete operational unit' within a public authority do not have to be aggregated with those of other parts of the authority. For the exception to apply, that unit must be purchasing for its own requirements and take its procurement decisions independently from the authority as a whole.

Annex 3

Use of the negotiated procedure by public bodies

Without a call for competition

The specified grounds include the following:

- where no tenders, or no appropriate tenders, are received by the authority in response to an open or restricted procedure;
- when, for technical or artistic reasons, or for reasons connected with the protection of exclusive rights, the contract may only be carried out by a particular contractor;
- when, for reasons of extreme urgency brought about by events which were unforeseeable by and not attributable to the contracting authority, the time limits prescribed under the open and restricted procedures cannot be kept; and
- where works, supplies or services are additional to, or repeat, those provided under an earlier contract and the authority wishes to award them to the same supplier. This ground is subject to certain strict conditions. For example, additional works or services must have become necessary through unforeseen circumstances and not be worth more than 50 per cent of the value of the original contract.

Case law before the ECJ indicates that each of the above grounds is intended to be exceptional. As such, the grounds must be interpreted narrowly, with the onus of proof being on the authority seeking to rely on them.

With a call for competition

There are several other grounds on which a negotiated procedure may be used with the prior publication of a notice. The OJ notice calls for candidates to apply to be invited to negotiate and, providing there are a sufficient number of suitable applicants, the authority is required subsequently to invite at least three. The two most important of these grounds are listed below.

- When the nature of works or services, or the risks involved, do not permit prior overall pricing.
- When the nature of services being procured, particularly in the case of intellectual or financial services, is such that contract specifications cannot be established with sufficient precision to permit a (services) contract award using the open or restricted procedures.

Annex 4

Checklist

Guarantees and other State aid

1. *Is the guarantor the State, a government or local government body or a State-owned business?*

If so, the guarantee may be a State aid. Check whether the European Commission has given or been asked to give a State aid ruling. This would take several months, once central government accepted the need to apply for clearance, so should be early on the critical path.

Seek advice in the light of the actual situation.

2. *Is the lessee getting any government or local government grant, or subsidies, or any extra tax concessions which are important to its financial viability or directly relevant to the leasing?*

If so, ask about the State aid position and seek advice in the light of the answer.

Note: Several of these questions and answers may apply to a single transaction.

Chapter 10

Taxation

Philip Marwood[1]

Introduction

Tax incentives for lessors

Most jurisdictions provide tax incentives to companies that invest in equipment enabling them to defer or reduce their liabilities. However, such incentives are of real benefit only to those with taxable income. Companies with little or no taxable income are not, generally, directly helped by such incentives. In addition to its commercial merits, leasing can act as a convenient medium for transferring the benefit of tax incentives from a purchaser to a user of equipment and thus indirectly encouraging investment by companies that are not currently paying tax.

Lessors can save tax on their other income by claiming the tax allowances or credits and can transfer a large proportion of the benefits to the equipment user in the form of reduced rental.

Ownership for tax purposes

Tax incentives generally follow the ownership of the equipment. However, there is a significant division between the world's tax authorities in determining the tax ownership of an asset subject to a lease under which the lessee, and not the lessor, enjoys substantially all the risk and rewards of ownership of the leased asset.

Some authorities determine tax ownership on the basis of legal form and others on the basis of economic substance. Unless the generally accepted accounting treatment in the relevant jurisdiction is regarded as decisive on the point, specific legislation will usually be required to determine under what circumstances tax ownership is deemed to remain with the lessor, who has legal ownership, and when it is to be treated for tax purposes as having passed to the lessee. In the latter case, the lease will often be treated as a sale on deferred terms.

The countries which generally treat the lessee as the owner of lease equipment for tax purposes (thereby entitling the lessee to tax depreciation or credits) where the lessee has economic ownership of the asset include Germany, Japan, The Netherlands and the United States. Countries where the tax owner of the asset is normally determined by legal ownership include France and the United Kingdom. Hence in countries such as the United Kingdom the economic (as opposed to legal) ownership of the asset generally makes no difference to the entitlement to capital allowances (tax depreciation), though there may be an impact where purchase options exist.

Even where accounting policy is not decisive on the question of tax ownership, it may have an impact on other aspects of lessor and lessee taxation, for example, on the timing of rental recognition, and (particularly in the United Kingdom) in bringing into play restrictions on tax advantages.

The benefits for the tax owner are of two types: those which confer absolute tax savings, such as tax credits and investment allowances; and those which merely offer tax deferment, such as accelerated tax depreciation.

Accelerated tax depreciation enables tax to be deferred by creating tax deductions in the early periods of a lease contract which are greater than the capital element of the taxable rental income. In later periods, that element of the rental income will exceed the tax allowances. Such accelerated tax depreciation does not apply generally; some countries, for example, The Netherlands, use economic depreciation as the basis for tax purposes, thus limiting the tax benefit of leasing.

With an operating lease, the ownership of the asset for tax purposes will almost always rest with the lessor. Such leases, however, are usually unsuitable for tax-based leasing where, commercially, the lessor does not wish to assume obsolescence risks or to be involved in the active management of the leased equipment, or where the lessee requires the equipment for the greater part of its economic life.

A finance lease may be structured as either a single investor lease or as a leveraged lease. In a single investor lease structure, the lessor provides the whole of the funds for the purchase of the equipment from its own resources or from a general pool of borrowings and is therefore at risk for the entire cost of the equipment. In a leveraged lease, the lessor provides only a part of the funds from its own resources for the purchase of the equipment, borrowing the remainder from third parties on a non-recourse basis. The lending will typically be secured by a charge over the leased equipment and an assignment of rentals under the lease, but without recourse to other assets of the lessor. The lessor is therefore at risk for only a portion of the cost of the equipment and yet claims tax benefits based on the whole of the cost.

The extent of the tax benefits offered by leveraged leasing has led some fiscal authorities to seek to deny its benefits in certain cases. For example, a leveraged leasing market has never really developed in the United Kingdom as a result of tax difficulties.

Tax benefits for lessees

The rentals paid by a lessee must cover two broad elements of cost incurred by the lessor (as well as providing a profit):

- the financial carrying cost of the investment in a leased asset; and
- the depreciation of the asset's value as a result of the lessee's use.

A tax benefit may arise because of the different tax treatments of rentals as against tax depreciation and interest on funds borrowed to purchase equipment.

In most cases the benefit will be that mentioned in the opening paragraphs of this chapter, namely that the lessor, with taxable income to shelter, achieves relief in the form of tax depreciation, investment credit and finance expense which is faster than the recognition of rental income.

But in some other cases there may be a tax benefit in a lease with the opposite profile where the rentals are greater than the corresponding interest and tax depreciation. Tax is deferred if a greater deduction is available to the lessee which may not be offset by an equivalent acceleration of tax payable by the lessor because, for example:

- the lessor has unused losses or other reliefs;
- the rate of tax is different for industrial and commercial companies and for financial and leasing companies;
- leasing companies are taxed on the basis of the interest element of the rental (the finance method) rather than on the basis of the rental income and depreciation deductions (the operating method), whereas lessees deduct the full amount of rentals payable; or
- there is a tax holiday.

The method of recognising leasing income or expense in different territories or kinds of taxpayer can be a particular area of difficulty, or opportunity. Mismatching of different recognition profiles, which may be affected by the choice of accounting date, can have cash flow benefits.

Exhibit 10.1 demonstrates the tax impact of an operating lease, in particular the different recognition profile of rentals, interest and tax depreciation. The example below is highly simplified, but it does show key features of tax deferral. The lessor's tax depreciation, being given on a reducing balance basis, falls predominantly in the early part of the lease, as does its finance expense. However, the operating lease rentals arise uniformly over the lease term. The benefit is the deferral of tax, which is particularly valuable if under local tax law the losses on leasing can be offset against other income. The tax benefit of leasing is principally determined by the duration of the lease (the longer the better), the rate of accelerated tax depreciation/investment credit (the extent to which they exceed economic depreciation), and the rates of tax and interest (higher rates increase the value of deferring paying tax). The tax benefits in the example are enhanced because the anticipated residual is reflected in rentals, but not in tax depreciation given on cost (as is common in many jurisdictions).

Exhibit 10.1

Example of lessor's tax benefit from leasing

| | Tax deductions on purchase | | | Tax deferred by lessor through leasing | | |
Year	Tax depreciation (1) US$	Loan interest (2) US$	Total (3), (1)+(2) US$	Rentals (4) US$	Difference (5), (3)-(4) US$	Tax deferred (6) US$
1	300	61	361	200	161	64
2	210	51	261	200	61	24
3	147	40	187	200	(13)	(5)
4	103	29	132	200	(68)	(27)
5	40	19	59	200	(141)	(56)
Total	**800**	**200**	**1,000**	**1,000**	–	–

The example shows how the lessor might benefit in terms of tax. It makes the following assumptions:

- the cost of the equipment is US$1,000;
- tax depreciation is 30 per cent on a reducing balance basis based on cost;
- the lease term is five years, at which point residual value is US$200;
- annual rental of US$200, payable in arrears;
- the tax rate is 40 per cent; and
- the lessor's margin on finance expense is ignored.

Please note that the numbers are chosen purely for the purpose of this example and are highly simplified.

Attitude of the fiscal authorities

Because of the potentially significant opportunities for tax planning and saving offered by leasing, fiscal authorities have increasingly sought to restrict its scope and this trend continues. A somewhat extreme example is provided by the leasing rules introduced in Canada in the early 1990s that limit the amount of tax depreciation a Canadian lessor may claim to the amount of the notional principal portion of the lease payment. This has resulted in a change in the market place such that smaller players are no longer writing leasing business. The international leasing names did not leave the Canadian market, but instead continued to write leasing business that was less tax driven.

Revenue authorities are increasingly looking at developments in accounting treatment, the impact these have on tax depreciation rates and the timing of recognition of lease rental income. Statutory codes for accelerated tax depreciation have come under scrutiny.

Sometimes, as in Ireland, leasing activities may be ring-fenced in determining the lessor's tax position, so that non-leasing income may not be sheltered.

Also common are rules to limit or abolish tax benefits to lessors in a different country outside the lessor's tax jurisdiction, although in some cases exceptions have been made for such leases where the assets concerned are exports from the lessor country. These exceptions are generally in conflict with the World Trade Organisation, European Union or other non-discrimination principles.

Revenue authorities have also sought to eliminate excessive rental deductions for lessees by imposing various conditions on deductibility. A common example relates to luxury cars where there are often restrictions on depreciation allowances. More generally, if rentals have been accelerated, relief for them may be spread back over the term of the lease. However, the Eurowings case in 1999 found that a German law restricting trade tax deductions for rentals payable to non-German lessors was contrary to EU law in so far as it discriminated against lessors in other EU countries.

A number of countries have provisions that either restrict the availability of tax depreciation on assets that are sold and leased back (or sometimes on second-hand assets generally), or otherwise affect sale and leaseback transactions.

The continuing change in tax laws in different jurisdictions affecting leasing means that the focus of leasing business is always changing. However, following restrictions in the United Kingdom of the tax benefits on finance leasing during the 1980s and in particular in the two Finance Acts in 1997, there was strong growth in operating leasing. This example shows that leasing finance has many advantages other than the purely fiscal.

Individual country profiles

United States

Introduction

The US leasing industry has continued its pattern of constant growth despite numerous, and often inconsistent, changes in the US income tax laws. The demand for new and improved plant and equipment by start up companies, by companies with significant debt already on their books and by companies not wishing to bear the risk of obsolescence helped create an increasing pool of potential lessees. In addition, the federal tax benefits associated with asset ownership as well as potential residual economic value of the leased property made the lessor's position attractive.

Criteria for determining tax ownership

Pursuant to these procedures, the lessor must have the following indicia of economic ownership before the tax authorities will issue an advance ruling that the transaction is, in substance, a true lease for federal income tax purposes:

- the lessor's minimum at-risk investment in the property must be at least 20 per cent of the property's cost;
- the lessee must not have an option to purchase the property at a price less than its fair market value determined at the time the option is exercised;
- the lessee or any member of the lessee group cannot have an investment in the leased property (except with respect to so-called severable improvements) or any loans or guarantees;
- the lease term cannot exceed 80 per cent of the useful life of the property;
- at the end of the lease term, the property must have an estimated residual value equal to at least 20 per cent of its original cost;
- use of the property at the end of the lease term by a person other than the lessee must be commercially feasible; and
- the lessor must expect to receive a positive cash flow as well as an overall profit from the lease apart from the tax benefits.

While the criteria technically apply only where parties to a leasing transaction desire a tax authorities' private letter ruling, as a practical matter they serve as general guidelines against which true lease status is measured. Nevertheless, in leases where the parties agree not to strictly comply with all the tax authorities' standards, various US court interpretations may be relied upon in determining what constitutes a true lease. As a general rule, the courts apply a benefits and burdens of ownership test to determine if the lessor is the equipment's economic owner and tend to require that the lessor retain fewer ownership attributes for true lease status to be upheld than that required by the tax authorities. In particular, the courts consider the following facts to be particularly important:

- the form of the agreement is that of a lease;
- a business purpose (apart from tax benefits) exists for the lease; and

- the lessor retains some significant ownership attributes, such as some risk of loss and the possibility of some gain.

Tax incentives for leasing

The primary federal income tax advantage of asset ownership is depreciation. The 1986 Act replaced the accelerated cost recovery system enacted in 1981 with the so-called modified accelerated cost recovery system (MACRS). Most equipment placed in service after 31 December 1986 is depreciated over a three, five, seven or a ten year period. The asset's depreciation period depends upon its class life under the asset depreciation range system. Assets with no asset depreciation range class life are assigned to the seven-year class. The 200 per cent declining-balance method is used for these classes generally with a half-year convention, unless the taxpayer has a mid-quarter convention problem (discussed below).

Under the modified accelerated cost recovery system, shorter-life equipment such as computers remains in the five-year class, but benefits from the faster write-offs allowed by the 200 per cent declining-balance method as opposed to the 150 per cent method of the accelerated cost recovery system.

Most longer-life assets are in the seven-year or ten-year class. For example, commercial aircraft have an asset depreciation range mid-point life of 12 years and, therefore, are in the seven-year class.

While a half-year convention generally applies in both the year the equipment is placed in service and when it is disposed of, a special mid-quarter convention applies if more than 40 per cent of the owner's assets placed in service during the taxable year are placed in service during the last three months of the tax year. In this circumstance, all property placed in service during any quarter of a taxable year is treated as placed in service on the mid-point of such quarter. For example, assume that Corporation A, a calendar year taxpayer, places 30 per cent of its equipment in service in the first quarter of 2001, 25 per cent in the second quarter and 45 per cent in the fourth quarter. For modified accelerated cost recovery system purposes, it is treated as placing 30 per cent of the assets in service on 15 February, 25 per cent on 15 May, and 45 per cent on 15 November respectively. The result under the mid-quarter convention is usually less depreciation than that allowed under the half-year convention. Thus, a corporation which is approaching the 40 per cent limit needs to carefully monitor asset purchases.

Following the events in the United States on 11 September 2001, a special rule allows taxpayers to elect to compute depreciation on property placed in service in a tax year whose third or fourth quarter includes 11 September 2001 without regard to the mid-quarter convention. Taxpayers that make this election use the half-year convention for such tax year.

Under an economic stimulus package enacted in March 2002, taxpayers are entitled to take bonus depreciation for certain qualified property if its original use commences with the taxpayer after 10 September 2001 and before 11 September 2004. The bonus depreciation is equal to 30 per cent of the basis of the qualified property and is allowed for both regular tax and alternative tax purposes in the year in which the property is placed in service. The remaining 70 per cent of basis is depreciated under the regular rules. Qualified property includes MACRS property with a recovery period of 20 years or less, computer software (excluding computer software that is amortised as intangible property), water utility property and certain qualified leasehold improvement property.

Special Liberty Zone 30 per cent bonus depreciation is available for certain property placed in service after 10 September 2004 through 31 December 2006 if used in an area defined as the New York Liberty Zone (which includes the area in New York that was attacked and damaged on 11 September 2001). In addition, special Liberty Zone 30 per cent bonus depreciation is available for certain non-residential real property and residential real property placed in service in the New York Liberty Zone through to 2009.

Certain qualified leasehold improvement property placed in service through to 2006 in the New York Liberty Zone is treated as five-year property (instead of 39-year property) and depreciable under the straight-line method. For alternative minimum tax purposes (AMT, see explanation below), the recovery period for such qualified leasehold improvement property is nine years. Qualified leasehold improvement property is not also eligible for bonus depreciation.

Finally, an alternative depreciation system (ADS) must be used for foreign use property, property leased to a tax-exempt entity and tax-exempt bond financed property. The alternative system must also be used for earnings and profits and, with some modifications, for alternative minimum tax purposes. Under the alternative system, the recovery period is generally the property's asset depreciation range class life (for example, 12 years for commercial aircraft). If the property has no asset depreciation range class life, the recovery period is deemed to be 12 years. The straight-line method must be used, except for alternative minimum tax purposes, where the 150 per cent declining-balance method with a switch to straight-line is allowed for personal property. For property placed in service after 1998, alternative minimum tax depreciation will be calculated using the 150 per cent declining-balance method over the asset's MACRS life (for example, seven years for commercial aircraft). The bonus depreciation described above is not applicable to property that must be depreciated under ADS.

Alternative minimum tax

In order to help ensure that all US taxpayers that report a profit pay at least some tax, the 1986 act adopted a broad-based alternative minimum tax (AMT) applicable to individuals and corporations. The AMT calculation begins with regular taxable income; numerous adjustments and preference items then greatly expand the AMT income base and only certain credits may reduce any resulting AMT.

The AMT impacts many US lessors, primarily because of the different AMT depreciation rules. As noted previously, AMT depreciation for equipment is calculated using the 150 per cent declining-balance method over the asset's asset depreciation range class life (or, if none, 12 years) for assets placed in service prior to 1998 and over an asset's MACRS life for assets placed in service after 1998.

The AMT creates an incentive for those taxpayers that are potentially in an AMT situation to lease rather than purchase assets in order to reduce their depreciation amount and hence their AMT exposure.

The bonus depreciation discussed above is allowed for AMT purposes.

Value-added tax

The United States does not currently impose a value-added tax (VAT) or stamp duty tax on lease payments.

Current issues

Recent developments in the United States have focused much attention on tax strategies and tax avoidance. Under recent case law, courts have shown a greater willingness to disregard transactions designed primarily for tax advantages without substantial business purpose and economic substance. The tax authorities have indicated in many public pronouncements and notices that they will scrutinise tax-motivated transactions very closely, including those involving leasing. Certain corporate tax shelters, including certain tax-motivated leasing transactions, are subject to special disclosure and reporting requirements. In addition, structures and transactions that appear to allow non-US persons to avoid US tax are in particular disfavour with US lawmakers and authorities and may be heavily scrutinised.

The US courts and the tax authorities continue, however, to respect a properly structured lease as a valid business transaction for federal income tax purposes. However, in recent years US tax law changes have reduced the amount (and value) of the tax benefits that a lessor can pass through to a lessee in the form of reduced rents. Therefore, the cost advantage of leasing in the United States, while still significant, has declined as a result of these federal income tax changes. Nevertheless, for many companies currently unable to use the present tax benefits of property ownership or for those facing the prospect of a significant AMT liability, leasing continues to be an attractive financing vehicle.

The US tax climate for leasing transactions may be adversely affected if various proposals submitted by President Bush and various members of Congress are enacted into law. Many of these proposals (including long argued proposals that would replace the United State's current tax system with a flat tax) have not received serious consideration to date. However, the potential for additional US tax law and accounting changes must be considered.

Germany

Introduction

In 1978, investment by German leasing organisations stood at just 5 per cent of total economic investment, but by 2001 this had more than tripled to 16 per cent according to the German Finance & Leasing Association. As a financing instrument, leasing has become more and more important within the past two decades.

Criteria for determining tax ownership

Under German law, the economic owner of an asset is regarded as the owner for tax purposes. According to the tax law's definition of economic ownership, a person other than the holder of legal title under civil law may be treated as the economic owner of an asset when this person – *de facto* and under the normal expected development of facts – has the exclusive use of the asset for its normal useful life in such a way that the holder of legal title is excluded from using the asset.

This definition has been interpreted by the leading decision of the Supreme Fiscal Court on 26 January 1970 regarding financial lease agreements on movable assets.[2] The main points of this decision are shown below.

• The tax treatment of lease agreements will be determined by their economic features.
• Economic ownership is transferred when:

    – the usual useful working life of the equipment is considerably longer than the basic lease period and the customer has, on expiry of the basic period, the right (or option) to extend the lease period or to buy the equipment and, upon exercise of this option, the customer will be liable to pay an amount in the nature of an acceptance fee, which is considerably lower than the usual rental or purchase price calculated on expiry of the basic lease period;

– the usual working life and the basic lease term are approximately equal (in this case the existence of an option is not relevant); or

– the equipment is adapted according to the special requirements of the lessee and, on expiration of the lease term, can only economically and practically be used by the lessee (in this case the relationship between basic lease term and useful life is not relevant).

The tax regulations define a financial lease arrangement for tax purposes as follows: an agreement entered into for a fixed leasing period during which an ordinary cancellation is not possible, where rental payments during the fixed leasing period cover at least the acquisition or production cost plus additional cost, including the lessor's refinancing cost.[3] This financial lease is referred to as a full pay-out lease.

The tax regulation dealing with equipment leases states that the official depreciation rates must be used for determining the useful working life (tax-classified life) of the leased equipment. Additional criteria have been developed in order to determine to whom economic ownership is attributed. The tax regulations deal with typical clauses in financial lease agreements which may or may not include an option to purchase or to renew the lease, or which may deal with equipment which is acquired or produced for the special purpose of the lessee only. In general, a financial lease may only be qualified as a rental contract in cases where the fixed leasing period runs for at least 40 per cent, and does not exceed 90 per cent, of the useful life of the asset.

Where the lease agreements include options to purchase or to renew the lease, it is also regarded as decisive whether the option price for the purchase or rental payments for the additional lease period cover the remaining book value. This is computed according to the tax-classified lives and using the straight-line depreciation method or the lower fair-market value at the time the option is exercised.

Lease agreements regarding equipment acquired or produced for the special purposes of the lessee are nearly always treated as instalment sales which transfer the economic ownership to the lessee. However, there are a few cases where the tax authorities have actually accepted a special equipment lease.

An interpretational letter of the tax authorities deals with three categories of non-full-payout lease agreements which run over a non-cancellable lease period exceeding 40 per cent of, and less than 90 per cent of, the tax life of the equipment. According to the letter, the following clauses do not affect the economic ownership position of the lessor.

• The lessee is obliged to purchase the equipment at a pre-determined price upon request of the lessor if, at the end of the fixed lease period, the lease agreement is not renewed.

• If, at the end of the lease period, the asset is sold and the sale results in a loss, the lessee must reimburse the loss to the lessor. If the sale results in a gain, the contract provides for sharing the excess whereby the lessor is to receive at least 25 per cent of any cash surplus and the lessee is to receive the balance.

• The lessee may cancel the lease contract after a fixed lease period of at least 40 per cent of the tax life of the equipment. In this case the lessee must make a final payment to the lessor equivalent to the difference between the total cost to the lessor and the rental payments made during the term of the contract. This final payment is reduced by 90 per cent of the proceeds received by the lessor upon the sale of the leased equipment.

There are a variety of other types of non-full-pay-out leases that are not dealt with in any official regulations and these must be evaluated on a case-by-case basis.

Tax incentives for leasing

Under German tax law only the economic owner for tax purposes, as previously defined, is entitled to depreciate an asset and the assets must be depreciated over their expected economic life. Except for buildings, depreciation rates are not fixed by statute.

Exhibit 10.2

Tax-classified life for assets

	Years
Ships	20
Aircraft	12–21
Plant and equipment	7–15
Computers	3

Source: Depreciation – Table as of 1 January 2001, BStBl. 2000 IS.1532.

However the tax life of movable assets is classified in official depreciation tables. The general tax-classified life for assets is shown in Exhibit 10.2.

Commonly applied depreciation methods are the straight-line and the declining-balance methods. A taxpayer may change from the declining-balance to the straight-line method, but not vice versa. Rates under the declining-balance method for movable assets may not exceed twice the applicable straight-line rate, or 20 per cent, whichever is less. However, during 2002 the German tax administration intended to extend the tax classified life of specific assets.

Investment credits are, from time to time, provided under federal law for new acquisitions of fixed assets. At present, acquisitions of assets consisting of certain new movable equipment in certain industry sectors in the eastern states of Germany qualify for a 5 per cent cash subsidy. Leasing companies located in the eastern states are entitled to such credits.

Several other programmes for investment incentive grants are provided for under regional or structural programmes. In some cases, these programmes require that the respective assets be used on the investor's own premises. In addition, in such a situation a leasing company would be entitled to the grant if the applications refer to the lease finance of such assets.

Value-added tax

According to German VAT law, the leasing of movable assets (other than a means of transport) is subject to VAT only if the lessee's enterprise is located in Germany. Input VAT is refunded to the lessor.

The leasing of transportation equipment by a German lessor located in Germany is always subject to VAT. However, foreign entrepreneurs may apply for a special refund procedure pursuant to the European Union's 8th VAT Directive.

Leases of movable assets which qualify as rental contracts are subject to VAT at the regular rate, presently 16 per cent.

In cases where the lessor is deemed to be the owner of the asset for tax purposes, the VAT base is the arithmetic sum of all rentals payable. The VAT is payable upon delivery of the equipment.

If the lessee is deemed to be the owner for tax purposes, the lessor itself may claim, as input tax, the VAT charged to it in connection with the acquisition or production of the leased assets, as well as that levied on current operational expenses. VAT is levied in addition to the net rentals charged in each period. Although this VAT is paid by the lessee, it does not normally represent a cost since the VAT charged may be claimed as a tax credit when computing the lessee's VAT liability (except for businesses unable to claim full credit, such as banks, insurance companies or non-business lessees such as government agencies).

The input VAT charged to the lessee or to the lessor (depending on the attribution of economic ownership of the asset to either the lessee or the lessor) may be reclaimed.

Current issues

For German trade tax purposes, half the rentals payable by a lessee must be added to its income if the lessor is not obliged to pay trade tax. Since German lessors are subject to municipal trade tax, the addition has mostly to be applied to non-resident lessors.

However, the European Court of Justice decided that thus disallowing half of the rentals for trade tax purposes does not correspond with the treaty of the European Union, since the freedom to provide services would not be fulfilled in the case of non-resident EU-lessors.

Presently such trade tax disallowance is not applied, however the German tax authorities reserve the right to collect the corresponding trade tax in case a new legislative basis is embodied into the trade tax act.

The Netherlands

Introduction

The Netherlands has no specific requirements for leasing companies. Nevertheless, a lot of leasing companies are subsidiaries of banks or of major manufacturing companies. The major leasing companies are part of the NVL (Dutch Leasing Association) which was incorporated in 1972.

Both the markets for big-ticket leases and small-ticket leases are well developed.

Criteria for determining tax ownership

The Supreme Court of The Netherlands has decided that, under a lease agreement, the legal owner of the asset is the tax owner of the asset unless the economic interest in the asset has been transferred entirely to the other party. As a consequence, for tax purposes, a lease qualifies as an operating lease if the lessor has the legal title and has some of the economic interest in the asset. If all the economic interest in the asset is vested with the lessee, the lease is a finance lease.

To avoid discussions on whether the legal owner of the asset has sufficient economic interest in the asset to be considered as the tax owner, the tax authorities have issued a regulation that outlines safe harbour criteria for a lease to be considered as an operational lease where the lease agreement was concluded on or after 1 January 2000.

On the basis of the above mentioned regulation, lessors will, for Dutch income tax purposes, always be regarded as owners of a leased asset that has been made available by them under a lease contract if they:

- act as such;
- are the legal owner of the leased asset; and
- run a positive and/or negative residual value risk in respect of the leased asset.

The regulation stipulates that in order for sufficient residual value risk to be assumed by the lessor, the following conditions, amongst others, must be met:

- the fixed lease term cannot be longer than 85 per cent of the estimated useful life of the leased asset;

- the expected value of the leased asset at the end of the fixed lease term is at least 7.5 per cent of its historic cost price (although this percentage is subject to change if the lease term exceeds five years) and, furthermore, the exercise price of a purchase option and/or the present value of the lease payments in the case of an option to extend the lease is not below the expected value of the asset at the end of the lease;
- the residual value risk has not been hedged with the lessee or an affiliate of the lessee; and
- the lessee does not hold virtually the full beneficial interest in the leased asset by virtue of other agreements.

Lease agreements concluded before 1 January 2000 are eligible for the safe harbour criteria in force at that time. The main differences between the regulation outlined above and the pre-2000 criteria are that under the pre-2000 criteria:

- an exemption from the requirement that the lessor must have the legal title of the leased asset could be granted;
- the maximum fixed lease period was 90 per cent of the estimated useful lifetime of the leased asset; and
- the value of the leased asset at the end of the fixed lease period, the exercise price of an eventual purchase option and the present value of an eventual renewal option had to be equal to, or had to exceed 5 per cent of, the cost price for tax purposes of the leased asset.

Tax incentives for leasing
The tax owner of a fixed asset that reduces in value over time must depreciate the asset. The depreciation is based on the historic cost price, useful lifetime and residual value of the asset. Generally, fixed assets are depreciated according to the straight-line method, but in certain situations accelerated depreciation is allowed.

In the area of leasing, the major types of investment allowances are the investment deduction, the energy investment deduction and the environmental investment deduction. A financial risk reserve is available under certain restricted conditions.

Investment deductions against taxable income are allowed to taxpayers engaged in a trade or business in respect of investments in certain fixed assets, although investments in assets such as land, private cars, houses and goodwill are excluded.

Investment deductions do not affect the basis for tax depreciation of the particular asset. The investment deduction may have to be recaptured if an asset in respect of which the deduction has been claimed is disposed of within five years.

The investment deduction, which is a percentage of the investment amount, is based on a sliding scale which runs from 26.5 per cent down to zero per cent dependent on the total amount of investments in a particular tax year. The 26.5 per cent applies for total investments per annum of more than €1,900 (US$1,988) but not more than €31,000 (US$32,433) and will be zero for investments in excess of €270,000 (US$282,593). The investment deduction can only be claimed by the tax owner of the asset and is not applicable if the asset is put at the disposal of another taxpayer. Therefore, the lessor will not be eligible for an investment deduction if the lease is an operational lease. In a financial lease, the lessee will be eligible for the investment deduction.

The percentage of energy investment deduction is 55 per cent and can be applied to certain qualifying investments. The percentage of environmental investment deduction is 15 per cent, 30 per cent or 40 per cent. The maximum investment amount to which energy investment deduction can be applied is €99 (US$104) million per annum. The maximum amount for which environmental investment deduction can be claimed is essentially not capped, but in respect of investments in excess of €25 (US$26) million, environmental investment deduction is subject to EU approval. The energy and environment investment deductions can only be claimed by the tax owner of the asset and, contrary to the normal investment deduction, they can also be claimed if the asset is put at the disposal of another taxpayer. Therefore, the lessor in an operational lease can be eligible for energy or environmental investment deductions.

Assets qualifying for energy or environment investment deduction usually also qualify for a system of discretionary depreciation.

Value-added tax

The VAT treatment depends on the classification of the lease. If the lease is a finance lease, the lease agreement constitutes a supply of the leased asset. In this case, VAT is due at the start of the lease and on the basis of the discounted value of the lease payments. If the lease is an operating lease, the lease agreement constitutes a supply of services. The VAT is due during the lease period on the basis of each lease payment. The VAT lease regulation outlines the distinction between a financial lease and an operating lease.

Current issues

The Dutch government has recently taken the position that public law prohibits public entities such as provinces, municipalities and water authorities from entering into cross-border leasing transactions.

Tax reforms that entered into effect on 1 January 2001 and 1 January 2002 have affected certain leasing structures. Structures in place on the dates the reform became effective in many cases benefit from grandfathering clauses included in the tax reform acts. In respect of new transactions, it is still possible to realise tax benefits through alternative leasing structures.

Japan

Introduction

In comparison with the expansion witnessed in the 1980s, the leasing industry experienced nearly zero growth in terms of contract amounts in the 1990s due to the long lasting economic slump in Japan.

However, the utilisation of leasing has become widespread across all industries. There are several reasons why the leasing industry is well established among Japanese industries and why it expanded so rapidly. One of them is the capital outlay for plant and equipment required to be made by Japanese industry. Enterprises that could not finance such outlays, either in whole or in part, turned to leasing companies for help. Another reason is technological innovation, which results in machinery and equipment becoming obsolete in a shorter period.

Japanese leveraged lease transactions were introduced in the early 1980s and rapidly became widespread. Since 1998, however, due to a change of the depreciation method for cross-border finance lease assets, such cross-border leveraged lease transactions are no longer attractive and have largely ceased. Japanese leasing companies are currently looking for different forms of leasing to meet the demands of overseas lessees. Some leasing companies are turning to operating lease transactions as an alternative source of profits.

190

Criteria for determining tax ownership

Under Japanese tax laws, a lease means a finance lease. Operating leases are generally not covered. A non-cancellable lease, with lease charges that when aggregated are almost equal to the lessor's acquisition costs of the leased property and incidental costs (full pay-out type), is a finance lease. In this context, full means approximately 90 per cent or more. From the view of the tax treatment, finance leases are largely categorised as rental type and sales type leases.

Under a rental type lease transaction, as in an operating lease, a lessor maintains ownership of the lease asset and can claim depreciation for tax purposes. In return, a lessee recognises rentals paid as expenses of the period. A lease is treated as a rental lease when it does not satisfy any of the following conditions:

- it is agreed that, after the expiration of the term of the lease or before maturity, the leased property is to be transferred to the lessee for no (or nominal) consideration;
- the lessee is given an option to purchase the lease property for a price that is much lower than the market value after the expiration of the term of the lease or before maturity;
- a lease of machinery, plant or equipment is manufactured to meet a specific purpose designated by the lessee which, as a result, would make it too difficult for the asset to be used for any other purpose;
- the lease property is not identifiable; or
- a lease transaction, other than above, where the leasing period is shorter than 70 per cent of the statutory useful life of the property (or 60 per cent if the statutory useful life is ten years or more) or is longer than 120 per cent of the statutory useful life of the property, and the tax burden is considerably reduced.

A *sales type lease* (ie, a lease which is treated as a sales transaction for Japanese tax purposes) is a lease that does meet any one of the above conditions. For a sales type lease, the total lease charges, including the finance element, are recognised as sales proceeds upon delivery of the leased property. However, the instalment basis for recognition of profit from sales type leases may be permitted provided that the following conditions are satisfied:

- the sale proceeds are paid in a minimum of three instalments periodically;
- the period between the delivery date and the final instalment date is a minimum of two years;
- the payments up to the delivery date are a maximum of two-thirds of the total sale proceeds; and
- profits for the relevant period are calculated based on the instalment method and are recognised as such in the statutory accounts.

If profits are not recognised under this method in the statutory accounts and subsequently it is realised that the necessary conditions would have been satisfied, then previous accounting periods may be adjusted retrospectively.

The lessee is required to treat a sales type lease as a purchase of the asset and is able to claim depreciation for tax purposes instead of treating the lease payments as tax deductible expenses.

Tax incentives for leasing

A taxpayer entitled to tax depreciation may elect for a straight-line method or a declining-balance method for each class of fixed asset. The tax-deductible depreciation limit is based on

Exhibit 10.3

Examples of depreciation lives and rates

	Useful life (years)	Straight-line method (%)	Declining-balance method (%)
Personal computers (except servers)	4	25	43.8
Computers (other)	5	20	36.9
Aircraft (wide body)	10	10.0	20.6
Automobiles	6	16.6	31.9
Vessels (domestic use)	15	6.6	14.2
Buildings (office use)	50	2	n/a

Source: The Enforcement Regulations of the Statutory Useful Lives.

the statutory useful life prescribed by the Ministry of Finance. Exhibit 10.3 displays examples of statutory depreciation lives and rates.

Where the straight-line method is used for tangible fixed assets, the depreciation rates are applied to 90 per cent of costs (to take account of assumed 10 per cent residual value). In the case of the declining-balance method, the 10 per cent residual value is built into the rate of depreciation.

For lease contracts concluded on or after 1 October 1998 under which depreciable assets are leased to non-resident or foreign corporations, the annual tax depreciation limit for such leased assets (overseas leased property) will be calculated on a straight-line method over the leasing period. The following is the formula for the annual limit of the tax depreciation:

$$(A - B) \times C / D$$

where

A is the lessor's acquisition cost of the overseas leased property and incidental costs;
B is the estimated residual value at the end of the leasing period;
C is the number of months of the leasing period in the relevant accounting period; and
D is the number of months of the total leasing period.

Value-added tax

Japanese consumption tax is similar to value-added tax in EU countries. Under the consumption tax law, in addition to a normal sale and purchase, leases of assets within Japan, as well as the import of foreign goods, are charged with consumption tax at 5 per cent.

Export transactions, such as international transportation services, are exempt from consumption tax.

United Kingdom

Introduction

A number of major changes were made to the taxation of finance leasing in 1997. As a result of these, the timing benefits of finance leasing are significantly reduced and finance leases with lives of less than five years are generally now uneconomic. For operating leases and for longer-term finance leases, the UK leasing market continues to provide a reasonably flexible environment, both from tax and regulatory points of view. This is reflected in the high proportion of UK capital investment supplied by leasing and hire purchase.

There has been a healthy increase in operating leasing reflecting users' desire for asset risk and management to be shared with parties better able to undertake them. Tax depreciation on assets leased to non-UK lessees remains severely restricted. This has been a particular concern for UK leasing companies within the EU single market since they cannot compete with other EU lessors on equal terms outside their home country.

Criteria for determining tax ownership

There are three fundamental conditions that must be satisfied if a taxpayer is to receive capital allowances (the term used to describe depreciation for tax purposes).

- The taxpayer must incur capital expenditure on the provision of the leased asset.
- It must use the asset for the purposes of its trade (which can include leasing) or for other qualifying activities, such as property letting or non-trading leasing.
- The machinery or plant must belong to the taxpayer.

In general, in determining the last of these conditions, the United Kingdom gives no recognition for tax purposes to economic ownership; the legal owner is treated as the owner for tax purposes and is thus entitled to tax depreciation provided it satisfies the first two conditions above.

In relation to the first condition, UK case law confirms that expenditure financed by non-recourse borrowings may not be regarded as incurred by the lessor. Likewise, in the case of Barclays Mercantile Business Finance Ltd v Commissioners of Inland Revenue, the Inland Revenue is arguing that the lessor whose rental receipts are fully secured by a defeasance deposit may also not be held as satisfying the requirement (at the time of writing, this case is under appeal). Please refer to the section 'Current issues' below for further details.

Exceptions to the general principle are transactions, principally hire-purchase (HP) and conditional sale transactions, which satisfy the following two conditions (the HP conditions):

- ownership of the asset shall or may (for example, as a result of an option) pass to the lessee on conclusion of the contract; and
- the lessee incurs capital expenditure on the provision of the asset during the contract and effectively builds up some equity in the asset.

The latter condition is usually interpreted as meaning that the lease rentals not only cover the use of the asset but also purchase some financial interest in it, for example, by giving the right to a below market purchase option at the end of the contract.

The lessee/conditional purchaser under such a contract is treated as the owner for tax depreciation purposes from the outset and is deemed to acquire the asset for its full capital cost at the outset. The HP conditions are valuable since they can be used to achieve UK tax ownership on leases into the United Kingdom from overseas and in contract purchase arrangements.

Tax incentives for leasing

In the United Kingdom, tax depreciation allowances are given in the form of capital allowances worked out in accordance with detailed statutory rules. Subject to these, UK tax law generally permits a lessor, as legal owner, to claim capital allowances under financing or operating lease arrangements. Under an HP contract, however, the purchaser (lessee) and not the seller (lessor/funder) will normally be entitled to capital allowances.

Allowances incurred on the construction of industrial buildings and agricultural buildings will, under certain conditions, qualify for industrial buildings allowances and agricultural buildings allowances at a rate of 4 per cent on a straight-line basis.

Allowances for plant and machinery are given at a rate of 25 per cent per annum, on a reducing balance basis, unless the plant or machinery is a long-life asset in which case the rate is only 6 per cent. For expenditure on plant and machinery incurred by small- and medium-sized business (but not by lessors to such businesses) a first year allowance of 40 per cent is available. First year allowances of 100 per cent are available in certain circumstances, including:

- expenditure on or after 1 April 2001 on designated energy saving plant and machinery;
- capital expenditure incurred on or after 11 May 2001 on the renovation or conversion of empty or under-used space above shops and other commercial property to provide flats for rent (subject to detailed conditions); and
- expenditure incurred on or after 17 April 2002 on plant and machinery for gas refuelling stations.

Legislation gives some guidance as to what is and what is not plant. However, it is still not possible to produce a categorical list and specialist advice should be sought to ascertain the status of any particular item. The remainder of this section deals only with the rules for allowances on plant and machinery (equipment). The basic code for plant and machinery includes modifications for certain classes of asset, which include:

- ships;
- aircraft;
- transport containers;
- cars;
- computer software; and
- fixtures.

Leasing to non-UK lessees

There are severe restrictions on capital allowances for assets leased to non-residents. At most, 10 per cent per annum writing down allowances are available if, at any time in the qualifying period (generally ten years from the date when the equipment is brought into use by the person incurring the expenditure), the equipment is leased to a person who is not resident in the United Kingdom and does not use the equipment exclusively for earning profits subject to UK tax.

Capital allowances are given at 10 per cent per annum if certain conditions are met, in particular that the lease term is less than 13 years and the rentals payable are uniform and periodic. If these conditions are not met, no capital allowances are available at all.

These restrictions do not apply if the leasing is short-term as defined in the legislation or is so-called wet leasing of a ship, aircraft or transport container by a bona fide UK operator.

The Inland Revenue does not currently accept the view that under European law the restrictions do not apply for leases to EU lessees.

Special restrictions for finance lessors

With effect from 2 July 1997, where the expenditure concerned is incurred on equipment that is the subject of a finance (but not an operating) lease, the amount to be included in the pool in the year of acquisition is restricted by reference to the length of the lessor's accounting period then outstanding. For instance, if the expenditure is incurred three quarters of the way through the accounting period, the proportion of the expenditure eligible for inclusion in the pool is restricted to one quarter, with the balance being included in the following year. Where the lessor finances a purchase of equipment subject to a finance lease by means of a hire-purchase contract, this rule is varied so that the amount to which the proportional restriction is applied is limited to the capital element included in each hire-purchase installment paid by the lessor.

A shipping company may, providing an election is made, fall under the UK tonnage tax regime for the purposes of calculating its profits chargeable to corporation tax. Broadly, a notional profit is calculated in respect of each ship depending on its tonnage. Where a shipping company is taxed under this regime, there are restrictions on the capital allowances which finance lessors to it may claim. Generally, for defeased leasing and sale and leaseback arrangements, the lessor is not entitled to any capital allowances. For finance leases to tonnage tax companies, capital allowances are generally restricted so that up to £40 million of qualifying expenditure is eligible for 25 per cent allowances, £40 million to £80 million is eligible for only 10 per cent allowances, and any expenditure in excess of £80m is not permitted any capital allowances at all.

Fixtures

Special considerations apply where the leased equipment is to be affixed to land or buildings. Under English law, such equipment becomes part of the property to which it is affixed and so belongs to the freeholder of the property.

Where a person leases from an equipment lessor equipment which is to be affixed to land, there is specific legislation which permits the lessor and the lessee to make a joint election so that the equipment is treated as belonging to the equipment lessor for capital allowances purposes, subject to certain conditions. The most important of these conditions is that, in most circumstances, the equipment lessee should use the equipment for the purposes of a qualifying activity. (Thus, for example, allowances can be denied if the equipment lessee is a local authority.)

Similarly, if a tenant of leased premises installs equipment in those premises, he is deemed to own the equipment for capital allowances purposes provided he has incurred expenditure on it.

Because a fixture is legally part of the land to which it is fixed, rental income from a leased fixture is taxable on the lessor under somewhat different rules from those which apply for normal trading income. Consequently, depending on the precise legal terms of the arrangement, the lessee may be required to withhold income tax on the rentals if the lessor is non-UK resident and there may also be an impact on the manner in which excess capital allowances can be relieved. Specific advice should always be sought.

Value-added tax

Leasing and hire-purchase contracts are, in general, chargeable to VAT at the standard rate (currently 17.5 per cent). Only the general position is covered below and there may be exceptions or conditions for the treatment which are not set out here.

Hire-purchase, conditional sale and credit sale deals are all regarded as a supply of goods. Although the lessee pays for the equipment in instalments over the full term of the agreement, the lessor is obliged to account to Customs for the VAT on the full selling price of the goods at the commencement of the agreement.

Current issues

The commercial benefits of leasing are significant. For the lessor, an advantage of leasing over loan finance is a degree of credit security, in the event of default or insolvency, provided by the underlying asset.

From the lessee's point of view, there may be balance sheet advantages in the case of operating leases as the lease commitments are presently off balance sheet (although this may change in the medium term; see below). More importantly, there is a real ability to outsource risk which the asset user may not be well placed to manage. Furthermore, for all types of lease it will generally be easier than in the case of loans to match payment profiles to the expected income flow derived from investment in the asset and there is also greater flexibility on termination/upgrade arrangements than is possible for loan finance. The lessor must incur capital expenditure on the leased asset.

In order for a lessor (or other trader) to qualify for UK capital allowances, the lessor must incur capital expenditure on the provision of the leased asset. Case law confirms that expenditure financed by non-recourse borrowings may not be regarded as incurred by the lessor. Likewise, a recent case has held that the lessor whose rental receipts are fully secured by a defeasance deposit may also not be regarded as satisfying the requirement (although, at the time of writing, this case is under appeal). Non-recourse financing potentially has other difficulties apart from capital allowances and any financing structure with such characteristics requires specific advice. It is also doubtful whether a purchaser under a hire-purchase contract has incurred capital expenditure on an asset if the purchase option is exercisable at a price approximating to anticipated market value. Any such option needs careful review to identify which party is entitled to allowances; indeed it has sometimes been suggested that neither party may be entitled to allowances.

Possible corporation tax reform

The UK government published a consultation document in August 2002 which considered reforms to the UK corporation tax system. In the 9 April 2003 Budget it was announced that a further document would be issued in the summer of 2003, building on the responses and meetings held with representative groups and businesses on the 2002 document. Broadly, what is under discussion is whether companies should be taxed on the basis of the amounts recognised in their accounts (on a mark-to-market or realisation basis). Thus, in respect of fixed assets, they would obtain relief for commercial depreciation according to the amounts recognised in their accounts. It is acknowledged that the proposals would have significant implications for leased assets. The key issue is whether it would be preferable to maintain the existing capital-allowances system for some assets, particularly where the incentives provided by accelerated capital allowances are required, with mainly those assets currently outside the capital-allowances code being brought within the system of commercial depreciation. No final decision appears to have been taken on this point.

Barclays Mercantile Business Finance Ltd (BMBF) v Commissioner of Inland Revenue case

This case was an appeal by the taxpayer BMBF against a decision of Mr Justice Park in the High Court in July 2002 in relation to finance leasing. In that decision, Mr Justice Park held that because of the defeasance arrangements (under which the lessee's obligations were fully cash collateralised), BMBF had not incurred capital expenditure qualifying for capital allowances. Furthermore, Park J surprisingly held that the transaction was not a trading trans-action for BMBF. In a persuasively reasoned decision, the Court of Appeal unanimously overturned the decision of the High Court, finding for the taxpayer.

The decision will be welcomed by the asset finance industry, particularly because it dis-pels some of the uncertainty caused by Park J's judgement. The decision also clearly shows the importance of the quality of the evidence (especially the commercial and numerical aspects) and the professional standing and experience of witnesses in their relevant fields. Most importantly, however, this decision reflects commercial reality. The Court recognised the importance of the finance leasing industry and accepted the fact that tax, including the passing of capital allowances benefits to lessees, is an inevitable ingredient in the overall commercial arrangement of a finance lease. This recognition is a refreshing display of com-mercial acumen on the part of the judiciary. The House of Lords has agreed to hear an appeal from the Inland Revenue which is expected to take place later in 2003 or 2004.

Proposals announced in the UK Budget dated 9 April 2003 affecting leasing

From 1 April 2003, businesses will be able to claim 100 per cent first-year allowances in respect of expenditure incurred on qualifying technologies that can reduce water use and improve water quality. The Finance Bill issued on 16 April 2003 originally made no provi-sion for such first-year allowances to be available to lessors of such equipment. However, an amendment to the Bill to include lessors has since been tabled for inclusion during the Bill's progress towards Royal Assent.

From 1 December 2003, stamp duty will not be chargeable on transactions involving property other than land, shares and interest in partnerships. Accordingly, from that date, transactions involving lease and other receivables will be exempt from stamp duty.

The capital allowances anti-avoidance régime has been tightened.

- The first change concerns arrangements intended to accelerate the remaining capital allowances on assets by depressing the market value of qualifying assets on a sale. New anti-avoidance rules, which take effect on 27 November 2002, block these by denying a balancing allowance if the proceeds from a 'balancing event' (such as a sale) are less than they would otherwise have been as a result of a tax-avoidance scheme. The new rules apply to capital allowances for industrial buildings, mineral extraction, flat conversions, agricultural buildings and assured tenancies.
- Under current law there are three restrictions on the capital allowances that can be claimed by a finance lessor who leases a ship to a company within the Tonnage Tax regime. FA 2000 denies capital allowances where the lease is defeased or where there are sale and leaseback arrangements and restricts capital allowances where the ship costs more than £40 million.

Affecting all leases entered into on or after 19 December 2002, the three restrictions will also apply to operating leases unless either the lessor remains responsible for the operation of the ship throughout the duration of the lease, appointing the master and crew, or the lessor grants the lease on account of short-term over-capacity and the lease does not exceed three years.

- Small businesses are entitled to a 100 per cent first-year allowance in respect of capital expenditure incurred on software. This entitlement, however, is subject to section 46 CAA 2001, which denies a first-year allowance for expenditure 'on the provision of plant and machinery for leasing'. (Software is treated as plant and machinery for capital allowances purposes.) Presently, 'leasing' does not include other means of exploiting software (such as the grant of a right or license to use the software) and the Finance Bill will include provisions to ensure that it will do so in the future. The new rule will apply to expenditure incurred on or after 26 March 2003.

Foreign exchange considerations

The United Kingdom has detailed rules for the tax treatment of exchange gains and losses of financial instruments to eliminate interest and currency risk, and of debt instruments. The broad objective of the rules is to ensure that the tax consequences of these items are generally in line with their accounting treatments provided these are in accordance with normal UK accountancy practice.

The Finance Act 2002 has introduced a number of key changes to the foreign exchange gains and losses regime for tax purposes mainly applying for accounting periods beginning on or after 1 October 2002. Generally the foreign exchange rules are assimilated into the loan relationship and new derivatives regimes and are therefore more closely aligned to accounts based on generally accepted UK accounting practice. Accordingly, current specialist advice should be obtained in respect of foreign exchange related leasing transactions.

The foreign exchange rules may produce anomalies in certain cases, but the fact that companies are now allowed under certain circumstances to compute capital allowances in non-sterling currencies has reduced these. This is a complex area and specialist advice should be sought.

France

Introduction

Leasing in France is generally undertaken by the banking system, mainly because leasing with an option to buy falls within the scope of the banking regulations. Leasing is often viewed as a rather expensive method of financing which, nevertheless, offers practical advantages to the lessee.

The lessor is entitled to a special guarantee through his right of ownership. In addition, until now, the lessee was not required fully to disclose the corresponding liabilities on his balance sheet, even if there was a tendency to adopt such an economic approach for accounting consolidation purposes.

Criteria for determining tax ownership

No fundamental distinction is made between financial leases and operating leases or between full pay-out leases and other leases, and the legal owner is always treated as the owner for tax purposes. However, a fundamental distinction is made between the leasing of property without an option to buy granted to the lessee (*location simple*), and the leasing of property with an option to purchase given to the lessee, which is always treated as credit from the banking law viewpoint *(crédit-bail)*.

A true *crédit-bail* exists only if the following criteria are met:

- the lessor purchases the property with a view to subsequently leasing it;
- the lessor grants the lessee an option to purchase and the option price takes account of part or all of the rent previously paid; and
- the lessee uses the equipment for industrial or commercial purposes.

Registration as a financial institution *(établissement de crédit)* is compulsory in order to carry on *crédit-bail* and leasing transactions that include purchase options. Therefore, a company which enters into more than one *crédit-bail* transaction must have a banking licence. In order to obtain a banking licence, a company must be established in France, so if a company wants to enter into a *crédit-bail* transaction it must have a permanent establishment in France.

Crédit-bail exists only if the equipment has been purchased from a third party. If a manufacturer leases its own equipment, no *crédit-bail* arrangement can exist.

If the lessee does not have an option to purchase, but instead has an obligation to purchase the equipment, the operation will be considered as a *location-vente* with the risk of it not being possible to invoke the lessor's rights *vis-à-vis* other unpaid creditors in the case of bankruptcy. The lessee, not the lessor, may therefore be entitled to tax depreciation.

Tax incentives for leasing

Location simple and leasing with an option to purchase are treated in the same manner. Nevertheless, special rules apply to real estate leasing transactions.

The tax treatment is based on the accounting rules. Leasing operations are, in principle, not to be treated as sales.

The lessee is entitled to deduct the rent charged (except for company cars, where the basis for depreciation cannot exceed €18,300 (US$19,244) VAT included). A specific rent deduction limitation exists for real estate leasing *(crédit-bail)* contracts concluded as from 1 January 1996. This limitation means that a portion of rents corresponding to the depreciation of the land or of the building incurred by the lessor cannot be deducted depending on the location of the building.

The tax authorities retain the right to look through the *crédit-bail* agreement to determine whether or not the agreement is really a disguised sale. A typical example could be an exceedingly short leasing period, where the rent is abnormally high and the option price is abnormally low.

Rules exist that tend to place a business using leased property under *crédit-bail* (lease with an option to buy) in the same position as a business which purchases the property outright.

These rules essentially concern the treatment of the profit on an assignment of a *crédit-bail* contract as a capital gain for the assignor and the assignee of the contract. However, this no longer provides a specific advantage for the assignor, since all gains deriving from the leasing operations are subject to the full corporate tax rate for financial years from 1 January 1997.

From the assignee's point of view, the acquisition price of the contract is deemed to represent a fixed asset. A straight-line depreciation is allowed during the remaining useful life of the property, which may be different from the remaining duration of the contract.

The tax law provides two methods of depreciation: the straight-line method and the declining-balance method.

The declining-balance method is applicable to equipment used in manufacturing and processing; handling equipment; anti-pollution devices; equipment for the production of steam, heat and energy; safety installations; trucks; office equipment other than traditional typewriters; and scientific research equipment.

In order to benefit from the declining-balance method, qualifying assets must be new and have a normal useful life of at least three years. Buildings are normally excluded from this system, except for industrial buildings that have a normal expected useful life of less than 15 years.

Exhibit 10.4
Expected useful life guidelines

	Years
Ships	8–15
Aircraft	8–12
Plant and equipment	5–10
Machinery	7–10
Cars and other moving equipment	4–5
Computers	3–7
Fixtures	10–20

Source: Regulations of the Statutory Useful Lives.

As of 1 January 2001, the rate of declining-balance depreciation is obtained by multiplying the straight-line allowance by a coefficient of 1.25 (for an asset with a useful life of three or four years), 1.75 (if the useful life is five or six years) or 2.25 (if useful life is over six years).

The guidelines in Exhibit 10.4 can be used for the determination of the expected useful life.

It should be noted that the French tax authorities have indicated in an instruction dated 29 February 1988 that they will not disallow a period of depreciation adopted by companies if this period is 20 per cent greater or lower than the period normally used insofar as it may be justified for specific economic reasons.

If an asset is leased, the useful life of the equipment, rather than the duration of the lease, is taken into account in determining the depreciation period.

Nevertheless, according to the Finance Law for 2000, the financial establishments involved in *crédit-bail* could opt, from 1 January 2000, for a financial depreciation of their leased assets, that is, depreciation based on the duration of the lease and not on the useful life of the equipment.

Finally, gains or losses realised by a lessor on the sale of leased equipment which regularly undertakes leasing activities are always treated as ordinary income or loss, subject to corporate tax at the normal rate plus an additional surcharge (that is, a total of 33.33 per cent for the 2002 financial year and 33.33 per cent from 1 January 2003).

In the case of both *location simple* and *crédit-bail*:

• the lessor could ask for a lease cancellation payment; and
• from a corporate tax standpoint, the payment must be at arm's length and specific care must be taken with the VAT treatment of such indemnities.

Long-term capital gains can be taxed at a reduced rate, but this is now only applicable to the sale of shares. Sales of leased equipment are subject to the usual rate.

Value-added tax
When both the lessor and the lessee are established in France, the rent is subject to VAT. The VAT paid on the purchase or importing of equipment can be offset against VAT due on rent.

Excess VAT paid over the VAT on rent can be refunded by the government. The normal rate of 19.6 per cent usually applies to leasing transactions unless otherwise specified.

As a general rule, foreign companies leasing an asset located in France have to appoint a tax representative to execute on its behalf the administrative formalities and pay the VAT eventually due.

Current issues

Tax incentives for investment in French overseas territories

In addition to normal depreciation, a 100 per cent allowance is granted for investments made from 15 September 1997 until 31 December 2002 in depreciable assets used in the French overseas territories in industrial, agricultural, real estate, transport and new energy source sectors. Under a normal lease, the beneficiary of this allowance is the lessor, unless the lessee has an option to purchase, in which case he may use the allowance.

The allowance is deducted from the taxable results only, that is, it has no impact on the accounting results.

Investments in the sectors of hotels, tourism, fish, audio-visual production or distribution and transport may benefit from this system only upon prior approval from the government. Maintaining employment in the overseas territories is now a condition in order to obtain the prior approval. When investments do not exceed €1.52 (US$1.6) million, approval is generally always given. Investments in other sectors exceeding €0.76 (US$0.8) million may benefit from this system only upon prior approval from the government.

Tax authorities' approach

Over the past few years, the tax authorities have attacked a number of transactions involving French partnerships acting as lessors insofar as these tax transparent partnerships allowed the transfer of tax losses to investors. Litigation is still in progress for these past transactions, while a new law has cancelled the tax benefits for similar transactions with effect from 28 February 1998, unless a special ruling is obtained from the tax authorities.

Until now, the tax authorities have not challenged the principle of double-dip transactions realised in a cross-border context. Specific care must however be taken with respect to challenges regarding the structuring of these deals (that is, tax residency of the foreign company, defeasance etc).

Spain

Introduction

Leasing transactions have had great success in the Spanish market. This is due, amongst other things, to the favourable tax treatment given by the legislation to leasing transactions. As a consequence, this way of financing the acquisition of assets is preferred by the market to other forms of financing.

Criteria for determining tax ownership

Article 128 of the Spanish Company Income Tax (CIT) Law (Chapter XIII of Title VIII) regulates the special fiscal regime applicable to certain financial lease agreements. The following requirements should be met in order to apply the special fiscal regime:

- the contract must have the legal nature of a financial lease;
- it is generally understood that the lessor must be a financial entity subject to banking supervision from the Bank of Spain and duly authorised habitually to act as a lessor in financial leases in Spain;
- the assets leased under the contract must be used for a business or profession;
- the contract must necessarily include a purchase option;
- the contract must have a minimum duration of at least two years for movable assets, or ten years in the case of real estate or industrial premises;
- the lease payments must be disclosed in the written agreement, which must clearly itemise the cost of the asset and the financial charges; and
- the annual amounts of the lease payments that correspond to the recovery of the cost of the assets must be of a constant or increasing nature during the term of the contract.

The general tax regime in Article 11.3 of the CIT Law is applicable to lease arrangements, including a purchase option or a renewal agreement when no reasonable doubt exists that the lessee will exercise the purchase option, taking into account the economic circumstances of the transaction. Article 11.3 of the CIT Law is not applicable to contracts that fall under the scope of the special fiscal regime in Article 128 of the CIT Law.

The position of the lessee under Article 11.3 of the CIT Law is similar to the position of an actual owner of the assets. Thus, the lessee may depreciate the leased asset for tax purposes following ordinary CIT rules.

According to Article 11.3 of the CIT Law, it is deemed that there are no reasonable doubts that the lessee will exercise the purchase option (making the regime in Article 11.3 applicable) when the value of the option is lower than the amount that results from subtracting the maximum tax amortisation that would correspond to the leased asset during the term of the transaction from the acquisition cost or production cost of the asset.

The lessor is not required to be a financial entity subject to banking supervision in order to apply this regime.

The Spanish tax authorities have interpreted that it is not possible to waive application of Article 128 of the CIT Law. Therefore, a lease transaction that qualifies for application of the fiscal regime in Article 128 of the CIT Law must be treated in accordance with the provision of this Article, without it being possible to apply the general rules established in Article 11.3 of the CIT Law.

The CIT Law does not provide a specific definition of operating leases for tax purposes or a special tax regime for them. In general, the accounting treatment would be valid for fiscal purposes, although there may be certain exceptions (for example, limitation on the depreciation of the leased assets by the lessor).

Tax incentives for leasing
With some exceptions, tax provisions follow accounting principles. In the case of finance lease agreements, only the part of the lease payments corresponding to accrued interest would be considered as taxable income. The lessor may not depreciate the leased asset since such agreements are recorded as a sale of assets. Likewise, the lessor does not qualify for any tax benefits related to investments in fixed assets.

The position of the lessee under Article 11.3 of the CIT Law is similar to the position of an actual owner of the assets. Thus, the lessee may depreciate the leased asset for tax purposes following ordinary CIT rules. The difference between the amount to be paid to the lessor and the acquisition price of the asset will be considered as a deferred expense for CIT purposes to be recognised during the period of the lease.

Under CIT general rules, the depreciation of an asset would be tax deductible as long as it is effective and it has been recorded in the books.

According to the CIT Law, depreciation will be considered effective when:

- it is the result of applying a straight-line depreciation following official coefficients established in the CIT Regulations;
- it is the result of applying a constant percentage to the net value of the asset;
- it is the result of applying the decreasing balance method;
- it is in line with a plan formulated by the taxpayer and accepted by the Spanish tax authorities; or
- the taxpayer justifies the amount thereof.

Buildings, furniture and fittings cannot be depreciated by the second and third methods. Land cannot be depreciated.

In the case of financial lease agreements subject to Article 11.3 of the CIT Law, the lessee can claim a tax depreciation allowance on the leased asset for the same amount that corresponds to the leased asset under the methods described.

Any tangible or intangible fixed asset, excluding land, may qualify for depreciation for tax purposes.

The most common straight-line depreciation coefficients are the following:

- 2 per cent for buildings used for offices and services;
- 3 per cent for warehouses or industrial buildings;
- 16 per cent for cars;
- 10 per cent for furniture and other installations;
- 25 per cent for hardware; and
- 33 per cent for software.

In the case of a financial lease of ships, a special tax incentive that provides for an acceleration of the depreciation of the asset can be applied, subject to approval from the Spanish tax authorities.

In the case of financial lease contracts in which the lessor is a financial entity or bank, and provided that the special regime established in Article 128 of the CIT Law is applicable, the lessee can claim a depreciation allowance for the part of the lease payments corresponding to capital or cost repayment. This claim is limited to two times the depreciation of the asset calculated at the maximum annual straight-line depreciation coefficient applicable to the asset, without registering such tax expense in the profit and loss account. The excess over the above-mentioned limit would be deductible in the following years subject to the same limit. Since the asset would be depreciated for accounting purposes over its useful economic life, a tax deferral would be obtained.

In the case of operating lease agreements, lease payments recorded in the profit and loss account constitute taxable income. Since assets are kept in the lessor's balance, they should be depreciated for tax purposes subject to the maximum annual rates and useful life periods established in the CIT regulations. Likewise, lessors may qualify for any tax benefits of general application related to the acquisition of fixed assets. For the lessee, lease payments recorded in the profit and loss account would constitute tax deductible expenses. The lessee may not depreciate the leased asset.

Value-added tax
Lease transactions generally constitute a VAT taxable event. For VAT purposes, this taxable event is usually, but not always, considered a rendering of services rather than a supply of goods.

For Spanish VAT purposes, lease transactions must be examined in light of three different scenarios.

- The lessee does not commit itself to exercising the purchase option or the lease agreement does not include an option; the transaction would be considered a rendering of services and VAT would be levied periodically on the total amount of each lease payment at the general rate of 16 per cent.
- The lessee commits itself to exercising a purchase option and the lease agreement would be considered a supply of goods; VAT would be levied on the total cost of the asset leased, excluding interest; the applicable rate would depend on the nature of the assets leased; in general, the rate would be 16 per cent, but in some cases it would be the reduced rate of 7 per cent (applicable, for example, to medical equipment).
- The lessee does not commit itself to exercising the purchase option, but the option is exercised or the exercise is made before the termination of the agreement; the transaction would be a rendering of services until the purchase is exercised and a supply of goods thereafter; therefore, the exercise would imply the levying of VAT on the total amount owed by the lessee to the lessor, excluding interest, the applicable rate being the one corresponding to the nature of the goods leased.

Cross-border operations

The taxation of cross-border leasing operations is always complicated and specific advice should be sought whenever such operations are proposed. The following general points concerning the taxation of a lessor resident in one country leasing equipment in another country are made on the assumption that a double tax agreement exists between the two countries which substantially follows the Organisation for Economic Co-operation and Development (OECD) Model Tax Convention. This will usually be the case between industrialised countries although, wherever specific circumstances arise, the relevant treaty should be considered.

Rentals as royalties

Under the old OECD model convention still reflected in many tax treaties, equipment lease rentals fell in the first instance within the royalties article of the relevant treaty (see Article 12 (2) of the model convention, which refers to 'payments... for the use of... industrial, commercial or scientific equipment'), although some treaties dealt with leasing income only under the business profits article (see section below on business profit and the permanent establishment rules).

Where a royalties article follows the old OECD model, it usually, but not always, provides that the income from equipment leasing is taxable only in the country of residence, unless the lessor carries on business in the country of source through a permanent establishment there and the equipment on which the rentals are paid is effectively connected with that permanent establishment. In that case the business profits article of the double tax treaty becomes relevant (see below section on business profit and the permanent establishment rules).

For countries that retain in their treaties the right to tax royalties (generally at source), the measure of the income is usually the gross amount of that income. Whilst this may be acceptable for the royalties for which the article was designed (that is, income from intangibles such as copyrights, patents, trademarks and designs), income derived from equipment leasing is usually of a different nature. If rental income is taxed on a gross basis, it could easily result in excessive taxation; the depreciation, interest and other expenses of the lessor would be disregarded and the tax at source may not be fully creditable in the country of residence where the lessor is likely to be taxed on a net basis. It is for this reason that the modern OECD model convention makes no reference to equipment lease rentals in the royalties article, leaving this to be dealt with generally as business profits.

A number of countries do not apply withholding taxes to lease payments. For those that do, the rate will often be reduced where the lessor is resident in a country that has a double taxation agreement with the lessee's country of residence. Exhibit 10.5 shows the usual rates of withholding tax applied in the absence of a double taxation agreement and the usual treaty rates. Specific reference to the relevant treaty should always be made in appropriate circumstances.

Where the lessee's country regards the lessee as owner of the leased equipment and the rentals are apportioned between a capital and financial element, the above withholding tax approach will not apply. Instead, withholding tax will normally be levied on only the finance element as if it were interest. Different rules may also be applicable to rentals for equipment affixed to land.

The new, revised OECD Model Tax Convention excludes lease rentals from the royalties definition. If lease rentals are dealt with under business profits instead, there is no withholding or income tax liability if the enterprise has no permanent establishment in the host country. This is good news for foreign lessors. However, it will take some time for the new model to be adopted in practice as tax treaties are re-negotiated infrequently.

Exhibit 10.5

Rates of withholding tax

	Usual rate of withholding tax on lease rental (%)	Usual treaty rate of withholding tax (%)
Belgium	15	0
Canada	25	0–15
France	33.33	0–10
Germany	20	0
Japan	20	0–10
Netherlands	0	0
Spain	25	5–10
Switzerland	0	0
United Kingdom	0	0
United States	30	0

Business profit and the permanent establishment rules

As noted above, income from equipment leasing will, under the old OECD model treaty, usually be considered under the royalties article of a double tax treaty. However, where the income is attributable to a permanent establishment of the lessor in another country then, to the extent it is attributable, it will normally be taxable in the country of the permanent establishment. In such cases, the business profits article of the treaty or treaties will be relevant. It is not possible to give an exhaustive list of circumstances in which a permanent establishment may be created but there are two broad sets of circumstances to be considered.

Question 1: Could the presence of leased equipment create a permanent establishment of the lessor?
Some jurisdictions treat a lease as a taxable business presence under domestic law, although in most jurisdictions, if the lessor's involvement is limited to supplying the equipment (and perhaps installing it) there is unlikely to be a permanent establishment. However, to the extent that services provided by the lessor increase, there is an increased risk of creating a permanent establishment. In many countries, a permanent establishment will not be created if the lessor provides maintenance for the equipment, particularly if not undertaken by employees based in the territory of the lessee. If the lessor actually provides personnel to operate the equipment there may well be a permanent establishment, particularly if the personnel are based in the territory of the lessee. Therefore, where maintenance or operational services are to be provided, it should be by separate subsidiaries.

Question 2: Could business development create a permanent establishment of the lessor?
Once again, there are several possible approaches. A representative office, where involvement is limited to putting potential customers in contact with the head office and providing information, may not create a permanent establishment. An active marketing role, involving lease negotiation, may well create a permanent establishment even if contracts are concluded elsewhere. Of course, business development may occur in a third country that is neither that of the lessee nor that of the head office of the lessor and could potentially create a permanent establishment in that third country.

If a permanent establishment is created, the question then arises as to what part of the enterprise's profits should be attributable to it. If the permanent establishment has relatively limited functions it may be possible to regard it merely as providing ancillary services either to its head office (as lessor) or to the lessee and for it to be taxed on a mark-up basis; if not, it will be necessary to attribute to it part, or all, of the overall leasing income on leases for which it has a role or responsibility. Although a permanent establishment may expose a part of a lessor's profits to foreign taxation this is not necessarily disadvantageous. Any foreign tax paid is often creditable against tax due in the country of residence on those same profits. A permanent establishment may in fact be advantageous. For example, if gross rentals stand to be taxed at source, the taxation burden suffered by an enterprise may be reduced if those rentals were attributable to a permanent establishment which would be taxed on a net basis.

Exhibit 10.6 indicates whether a permanent establishment is typically likely to exist in specified circumstances and the likely measure of the attributable profits. But as noted above, specific advice must be sought for any particular cross-border lease.

Exhibit 10.6

Existence of permanent establishment (PE) and measure of profits

Activities in State S	*Does PE exist?*	*Attribution of profits*
Leased equipment operated, serviced, inspected and maintained by lessor's own personnel stationed	Yes, at least if these activities are carried out under the direction, responsibility and control of lessor.	Attribution of the full profit of leasing, deducting expenses of the head office.
Leased equipment operated, serviced, inspected and maintained by lessor by (a) the lessor's own personnel stationed permanently in State R; OR (b) independent enterprises hired.	No, if carried out under the direction and control by lessor. of lessee, otherwise variable.	If PE exists, profits might be attributed for the leasing as such or possibly only for operation, service, inspection, and maintenance.
Leased equipment operated, serviced, inspected and maintained wholly by lessee.	Generally not.	None.
Leased equipment (a) operated and serviced by lessee; OR (b) inspected and maintained by lessor.	Generally not, but variable if inspection and maintenance are not under the direction and control of lessee.	If PE exists, profits might be attributed to it only for inspection and maintenance.
Maintenance of an office in State S to be in contact with the market, conclude contracts, deliver the equipment, etc, but not participating in operation, servicing, inspection and maintenance of leased equipment.	Yes, according to the principles of Article 5 of the OECD Model Tax Convention on Income and Capital.	Attribution of profits only for the services actually performed by the office or for the whole profit of leasing equipment in State S, depending on involvement and responsibility of the office.

Note: State S = State of source; State R = State of residence; PE = permanent establishment.

Cross-border differences in taxation

The benefit of lease finance may be enhanced if there is a difference in leasing rules between the country of the lessor and country of the lessee. This arrangement has become known as double dipping. In some circumstances both the lessor and the lessee are treated as the owner of the equipment for tax purposes in their own country and are thus entitled to tax depreciation.

A double-dip lease can be more easily achieved if the lessee is in a country which distinguishes between economic and legal ownership and the lessor is in a country which generally makes no such distinction. Differences in the characterisation of entities may also have similar effects.

A double-dip lease of an asset is generally beneficial only where assets leased outside a country nonetheless qualify for accelerated tax depreciation allowances. This is less common then it was. Some countries – for example Australia, the United States and the United Kingdom – have passed special legislation providing that normal tax depreciation cannot be claimed, or must be claimed at reduced rates. Where there is a chain of leases, the UK Inland Revenue's current view is that the legislation that restricts tax depreciation on assets leased to non-UK lessees applies if any lessee in the chain is outside the UK tax net. Before 1999, they allowed non-UK intermediate lessees.

The UK grants tax depreciation for lessees under an HP contract (see above section on criteria for determining tax ownership). Lessors from certain other jurisdictions may also be able to claim allowances. For example, a number of leases have been structured so that both the German lessor and the UK lessee can claim allowances, the latter under the hire purchase provisions. (See also Chapter 7, Legal features of cross-border transactions.)

Conclusion: future developments

As noted in the introduction to this chapter, tax rules affecting leasing tend to be in a state of continuous development and therefore an attempt to forecast changes is likely to be unsuccessful. It is possible, however, to identify certain areas that may be of increasing importance.

Leasing of intangibles

There has been an increasing trend towards leasing intangible items such as trademarks or other intellectual property or rights. This can be an area of particular tax difficulty for a number of reasons. First, valuation of such items is more difficult and there is also a greater likelihood than with equipment that their value may increase above cost, resulting in capital gains which can give rise to tax difficulties. Secondly, the rules for giving tax depreciation on intangibles are often more complex than for equipment. However, the increasing awareness of companies of the value of their intangible assets means that this is likely to be an area of continued interest.

In addition, because of the restrictive nature of tax law on intangibles in certain countries, there may be scope for cross-border leasing. Thus the unrealised value of existing intangibles, such as household brands, could be unlocked by means of a sale and leaseback. The lessor would of course need to be located in a tax regime that allows the depreciation of intangible assets as a tax deduction and the lessee would need to be able to shelter any gain on disposal. The non-deductible capital cost of the brand would effectively be converted into a stream of revenue payments which would be deductible on an annual basis. Clearly, advice should be taken when contemplating such transactions with particular reference to the relevant double tax treaty to ensure that there is no withholding on the lease rentals (royalties). Since the values of even the most long-standing brands are potentially volatile, third-party leases of brands necessarily involve significant commercial issues, quite apart from tax issues and benefits.

Thin capitalisation

Multinational groups naturally have regard to tax relief for interest when arranging their finance. The factors affecting post-tax financing costs include the location of taxable profits as well as nominal tax rates.

There is an increasing move towards thin capitalisation restrictions in several countries, either codified or informal. This trend has been hastened by the revision in June 1995 of the OECD report on the subject entitled *Transfer Pricing and Multinational Enterprises (1979)*, which has tended to focus the attention of tax authorities. At present, the debt-to-equity ratio guidelines across the European Union vary significantly, ranging from parity, as frequently accepted by the UK Inland Revenue, to a more generous 9:1 ratio in Germany. In some territories there is an absence of regulations or guidance, resulting in uncertainty.

In view of the funding and capital requirements of their activities, this move is likely to have a major impact on multinational lessor groups. However, it is also important for lessees, since in some cases lease finance may reduce the risk of attack on thin capitalisation grounds.

In many countries, including the United Kingdom since the advent of Corporate Tax Self Assessment (CTSA), companies have to confirm when filing their tax computations that all transactions with related parties have been carried out on an arm's length basis. To support this, documentary evidence may have to be in place to show how the arm's length price was arrived at. Penalties may be charged if no such documentation is in place.

The single European market

The European Council's meeting in Lisbon in March 2000 set the European Union the goal 'to become the most competitive and dynamic knowledge based economy in the world'. The European Commission sees the reform of EU company tax as crucial for achieving this goal. However, the EC Treaty itself has very little to say about direct taxes and Member States today operate the same company tax systems as they did before the set up of the internal market. Member States themselves see tax not just as a method of raising revenue but as an important policy tool and a symbol of national sovereignty. As a result, the Commission's current approach is first to try to tackle tax issues which impede the functioning of the single market, such as withholding taxes on dividends and interest, and secondly, to deal with tax issues that constitute illegal State aid.

In the early 1990s, the Parent-Subsidiary Directive and the Merger Directive came into force along with the arbitration convention. The next substantial development was the proposal of a tax package which was originally intended to be agreed by the end of 2002. There are two proposed directives: one to remove distortions in the taxation of income from savings (the savings directive), and a second directive to abolish withholding tax on cross-border payments of interest and royalties between companies. The third element of the tax package is a code of conduct on business taxation designed to encourage Member States to abolish so-called harmful tax regimes.

The Commission hopes to build on these initiatives by focusing on further short-term measures such as improvements to the directives already in place and further work on transfer pricing and cross-border loss compensation, for example.

The Commission has produced a comprehensive study on the subject of company taxation in the internal market and also held a conference on the same subject. The outcome of the conference, which was attended by business representatives and academics, was that the Commission believes that there is broad support for a degree of company tax harmonisation, that is, a system whereby a company would file one tax return for its European operations on a common consolidated EU tax basis, with the taxable profit being apportioned between Member States on the basis of an allocation key which has yet to be determined. However, this idea has yet to meet with support from the Member States and the agreement to proceed with this seems a long way off. For the future, there is EU enlargement to consider with 10 potential entrants due to join the EU in May 2004. This will bring with it a variety of opportunities and possibilities, as well as a whole range of other issues to be considered.

In the meantime, it is the responsibility of the European Court of Justice (ECJ) to ensure that the tax systems of Member States are compatible with the EC Treaty. There are an increasing number of cases being referred to the ECJ from Member States' courts on questions of interpretation of the EC Treaty concerning the company tax systems of Member States. Cases have in the past generally been about frontier workers and the tax treatment of branches compared with subsidiaries. However, the trend now is for companies to question the fundamental basis of the tax systems. Tax payers are having remarkable successes and as a consequence Member States' tax laws are having to change.

For the time being it is clear that co-ordinated harmonisation of direct tax systems is some way off and opportunities for cross-border financing will therefore exist for the foreseeable future. Companies may also find that restrictive tax rules which hamper their access to particular markets in the European Union can be challenged in national courts on EU principles. Member States on the other hand can see a piecemeal convergence of their tax systems forced by market pressures and the ECJ.

With the completion of the single market on 1 January 1993 and the removal of fiscal frontier controls between Member States of the European Union, fundamental changes took place in the way VAT is charged and accounted for on goods moving between Member States, that is, based on the principle of taxing goods in the Member State of destination.

The rules introduced are complex, but are only intended to be transitional until a definitive system for the taxation of trade between Member States is introduced, that is, based on the principal of taxing goods and services (the category of supply into which leasing generally falls) in the Member State of origin. This system was due to be implemented on 1 January 1997 but required proposals to be agreed by 31 December 1995. This has not been possible and the transitional arrangements will continue to apply until a definitive system can be decided upon and entered into force.

On 10 July 1996, the European Commission released a document entitled *A common system of VAT – A programme for the single market* in which it stated that it would be premature at that stage to present proposals for legislation governing the transition to a new common system of VAT. Consequently, the document contained a work programme which the Commission intends to follow in the coming years for the purposes of presenting suitable proposals for shifting over to a new common system of VAT suited to the single market. Together with the work programme was included a timetable through to mid 1999 for putting forward proposals based on a step-by-step approach for progressing towards the common system.

However there is no longer a set date for the implementation of a common system. This is primarily due to the complexity of the required legislative amendments across all individual countries.

Furthermore leasing generally constitutes a supply of services and, as yet, there has been very little progress on harmonising VAT on services.

(See also Chapter 19, The European Union.)

Non-discrimination

One of the fundamental principles enshrined in the Treaty of Rome was the principle of non-discrimination. In recent years, there have been a number of cases heard by the ECJ which have sought to define the limits of this principle. It may be the case that certain legislation or practices adopted by EU countries in respect of leasing taxation contravene this principle. For example, UK legislation (with two exceptions, that is, short-term leasing and the leasing of ships, aircraft or transport containers for qualifying purposes) restricts writing down allowances to 10 per cent, or in some instances zero, where equipment is leased to foreign lessees. The rationale for this is that the UK Treasury either wants to reduce, or remove entirely, the effective subsidy given to a non-UK lessee in respect of equipment used in a trade whose profits are not subject to UK taxation. The view is widely held that such a rule contravenes the Treaty of Rome.

*Information in this chapter is current as of 30 April 2003.

---

[1] Philip Marwood would like to acknowledge the following for their contribution to this chapter: Philip J Wiesner, KPMG Washington; Helmut Rehm, KPMG Wiesbaden; Adriaan Aerts, KPMG Amsterdam; Hiroaki Sasaki, KPMG Tokyo; Guillaume de Brondeau, KPMG Paris; and Victor Mendoza Diaz Aguado, KPMG Madrid.

[2] See Bundesteuerblatt ('BStBl.') 1970 IIS.264.

[3] See Leasing-Circular as of 19 April 1971, BStBl. 1971 IS.264.

Chapter 11

Lease evaluation

David Maxwell

Introduction

This chapter is concerned with the evaluation of finance leases from the point of view of the lessee and the lessor. Leasing and lending money are, in substance, similar and hence the 'time value of money' principle is fundamental to lease evaluation techniques. As such, the evaluation of a lease is generally aimed at expressing its cost (to the lessee) or yield (to the lessor) in terms of a rate of interest so that a comparison can be made with alternative borrowing or lending opportunities. For a lessee an alternative approach that has merit is to compute and compare the net present values of alternative leases alongside other financing options.

In the case of tax-based leasing transactions, the effective cost to the lessee is by no means necessarily as great as the effective yield to the lessor by reason, in particular, of the way in which tax incentives for investment in equipment in various countries operate. Tax benefits are generally derived from leasing in situations where the tax position of a lessee does not enable it to obtain full tax relief on the tax allowances or credits to which it would be entitled on a purchase, and where a lessor has sufficient taxable capacity for this purpose.

Both the United Kingdom and United States have, in the past, been favourable environments for leasing. In the United Kingdom up to March 1984, a purchaser of equipment, whether user or lessor, was entitled to an immediate tax deduction for the full cost of the equipment, subject to compliance with various conditions. Many industrial companies exhausted their taxable profits through the use of these first year allowances and other deductions and were thus not able to take advantage of any further tax allowances. Meanwhile banks, financial institutions and some commercial enterprises such as retailers with relatively small capital expenditure requirements had tax liabilities that could be deferred by purchasing equipment (normally through leasing subsidiaries) for leasing to industrial and other users.

This deferral of tax payments constituted, in effect, an interest free loan from the UK Treasury, financing a material part of the lessor's investment. Most of the benefit of this cheap financing was then passed on to the lessee by way of reduced rentals, while some of the benefit was retained by the lessor as a reward for the use of its tax capacity. Such rentals thus produced a yield to the lessor over and above what could be obtained on a loan to the same customer, while the lessee gained low cost financing by virtue of the reduced rentals. Leasing therefore provides a means by which the benefit of tax incentives can be transferred from a lessor to a lessee and thus enables the lessee to obtain the benefit, in the form of cheaper finance, of those incentives which would not otherwise have been used.

212

Whilst the particularly beneficial 100 per cent first-year tax allowances have, except in some limited circumstances, ceased to exist in the United Kingdom, tax deferrals on a limited scale remain an important factor in the UK leasing market. The withdrawal of the investment tax credit and changes to the depreciation system have also reduced the potential tax benefits of leasing in the United States, but there remain numerous opportunities for lessors in the increasingly complex US tax environment.

In many countries, investment incentives give rise to tax benefits, either through tax deferment or tax savings, which a leasing facility can pass from a lessor with tax capacity to a tax-exhausted (or in some cases non-taxable) lessee.

The three most common forms of investment incentive found in tax-based leasing transactions are listed below.

- *Accelerated depreciation*. Ranging up to a 100 per cent allowance in the first year.
- *Investment tax credit (ITC)*. A deduction from tax, otherwise payable, of a percentage of the cost of (new) equipment acquired. Such as the 10 per cent ITC which used to be available in the United States.
- *Investment allowance*. An additional deduction from taxable income normally expressed as a percentage of equipment cost above the 100 per cent depreciation charge.

This first investment incentive gives rise to tax deferment, while the second and third represent tax savings (see the section 'Tax benefits for lessees' in Chapter 10). The second and third incentives are essentially the same if there is no recapture of the additional depreciation. With a 50 per cent rate of tax, a 10 per cent investment tax credit is equivalent to a 20 per cent investment allowance. Some countries encourage investment by having a combination of these forms of incentive.

Examples

This chapter is concerned with explaining the principles of lease evaluation rather than the detailed application in individual countries. For this reason, and to enable the principles to be illustrated as vividly as possible, the examples are based on a hypothetical tax regime, the main characteristics of which are that the whole of the cost of equipment may be deducted from taxable income in the year in which the expenditure is incurred (whether the purchaser uses the asset in its own business or for leasing) and the rate of corporation tax is 50 per cent.

As mentioned above, the 100 per cent first-year write off did in fact apply to much of the leasing business conducted in the United Kingdom until March 1984. Examples are also provided of the effect of the other main incentives listed above and of 25 per cent reducing balance allowances to illustrate the impact on leasing benefits of the changes enacted in the United Kingdom in 1984.

Lessee evaluation

The investment and financing decisions

In considering the acquisition of a capital asset, whether it is to be financed by outright purchase, leasing or in another manner, a user will first make an assessment of the return on the investment which such an asset may be expected to yield, having regard to the incremental gross earnings and overhead costs to which its exploitation may give rise. Such an assessment using discounted cash flow (DCF) or similar techniques will determine whether or not the equipment is to be acquired at all. Having determined to make the investment, the next step will be to consider the relative merits of the different methods of finance available.

Potential lessees will wish to have some measure of the cost of borrowing entailed in a finance lease. Assuming that the lease provides for a nominal secondary-period rental extending to the end of the effective working life of the asset, or alternatively a bargain purchase option, the finance lease may be regarded as a method of acquiring the exclusive right to the use of the asset on deferred payment terms.

There are two alternative approaches to evaluating the relative cost or benefit of a lease which provide answers to each of two different questions.

The equivalent interest rate (EIR) approach

Question: What is the rate of interest payable on a bank overdraft to finance the purchase of the asset that would leave one neither better nor worse off compared with the lease being considered?

The net present value (NPV) approach

Question: Given one's marginal cost of borrowed money (bank overdraft rate), what is the present value of the cost or benefit which one would experience by leasing rather than buying the asset?

A lease with the terms set out in Exhibit 11.1 is used in this chapter to illustrate these two approaches.

It should be noted that, besides the numerical evaluations set out below, there are likely to be other issues that need to be taken into account in deciding whether to lease or buy. For example:

- the lease may be off balance sheet;
- the lease may transfer residual value risk to the lessor;
- as a consequence of tax variation clauses, the lease may give rise to tax risks which a non-tax-paying lessee would not generally bear;
- the lease may give less flexibility in being able to modify or sell the asset;

Exhibit 11.1

Lease assumptions

Asset cost	US$1,000
Acquisition date	31 December 2003
Primary lease terms	Three annual rentals in arrears of US$360 each
Secondary lease terms	Indefinite period at a peppercorn
Lessee year-end	31 December
Tax payment date	31 December, one year after lessee year end
Tax rate	50%
Lessee's bank borrowing rate	5% per annum

- other services, such as maintenance, may be provided with the lease; and/or
- leasing may reduce administration costs such as those associated with the delivery and disposal of the asset.

The EIR approach

Non-tax-paying lessee

In the first case, it is assumed that the lessee is not in a tax paying position, either because of a surfeit of other allowances or tax losses or because, in principle, it is not subject to tax on the activity in question, for example as a government authority. The lessee sets down the incremental cash flows arising from a decision to lease rather than to buy, and then works out the discount rate that will give a total present value for all those receipts and payments equal to nil (see Exhibit 11.2). In other words, the present value of the rentals at that discount rate equals the cost of the asset. The incremental cash flows are all those cash flows that arise solely from the decision to lease rather than to buy. Thus they include the saving of the purchase price and the rental payments.

An alternative method of carrying out the calculations, which gives the same answer, is to determine the rate of interest which, when applied to the incremental cash flows, gives a final balance of zero, as shown by Exhibit 11.3.

Exhibit 11.2

Non tax-paying lessee: EIR

Date	Cost of asset saved (US$)	Rentals paid (US$)	Incremental cash flows (US$)	Discount factor (3.9% pa)	Present value (US$)
31 December 2003	1,000	–	1,000	1.000	1,000
31 December 2004	–	(360)	(360)	0.962	(346)
31 December 2005	–	(360)	(360)	0.926	(333)
31 December 2006	–	(360)	(360)	0.891	(321)
Total	1,000	(1,080)	(80)		0

Note: The discount factor can be readily found in a simple case by using a financial calculator.

Exhibit 11.3

Non-tax-paying lessee: alternative method of EIR calculation

Date	Incremental cash flows (US$)	Interest thereon (3.9% pa) (US$)	Cumulative cash flows plus interest thereon (US$)
31 December 2003	1,000	–	1,000
31 December 2004	(360)	40	680
31 December 2005	(360)	26	346
31 December 2006	(360)	14	–
Total	(80)	80	

What is the significance of the discount factor or EIR of 3.9 per cent per annum shown in Exhibits 11.2 and 11.3? It means that if the lessee could borrow money to buy the asset using a loan at an interest rate of 3.9 per cent per annum with repayment at US$360 per annum for three years, it would have no preference between buying, using this loan, or leasing on the stated terms. It is important to recognise that this is the only valid conclusion to be drawn from this calculation and, as will be seen later, it can be misleading to assume that one lease is preferable to another solely because it has a lower EIR.

Tax-paying lessee

If the same lease had been undertaken by a lessee in a tax-paying position, the incremental cash flows would have been as shown in Exhibit 11.4.

Exhibit 11.4

Tax-paying lessee: incremental cash flows

Date	Cost of asset saved (US$)	Tax thereon (50%) (US$)	Rentals paid (US$)	Tax thereon (50%) (US$)	Incremental cash flows (US$)
31 December 2003	1,000	–	–	–	1,000
31 December 2004	–	(500)	(360)	–	(860)
31 December 2005	–	–	(360)	180	(180)
31 December 2006	–	–	(360)	180	(180)
31 December 2007	–	–	–	180	180
Total	**1,000**	**(500)**	**(1,080)**	**540**	**(40)**

Exhibit 11.5

Tax-paying lessee: EIR

Date	Incremental cash flows (US$)	Interest thereon (7.5% pa) (US$)	Tax thereon (50 %) (US$)	Cumulative cash flows (US$)
31 December 2003	1,000	–	–	1,000
31 December 2004	(860)	76	–	216
31 December 2005	(180)	16	(38)	14
31 December 2006	(180)	1	(8)	(173)
31 December 2007	180	(13)	(1)	(7)
31 December 2008	–	–	7	–
Total	**(40)**	**80**	**(40)**	

Notes:

• Interest is calculated on the cumulative cash flow and is paid (or received) in arrears.

• Interest itself qualifies for tax relief, or is chargeable to tax, but the tax effect occurs one year after the payment of interest, for example the tax payable at the end of 2005 is 50 per cent of US$76 = US$38.

• In this example, interest on debit and credit balances has been credited at the same rate (see section on evaluation methods below).

• Interest in 2008 (7.5 per cent of US$7 = US$1) has been ignored.

Applying an interest rate of 7.5 per cent per annum to these cash flows gives a final balance of zero, as shown by Exhibit 11.5.

Exhibit 11.5 shows that if such a lessee were to borrow money at 7.5 per cent per annum to purchase the asset and were to apply the notional rentals together with tax relief on the asset cost less tax relief foregone on the rentals, in repayment of the loan, the loan would be exactly paid off with interest by the time all the incremental cash flows had worked their way through. In other words, at a borrowing rate of 7.5 per cent per annum a tax-paying lessee would have had no preference between buying the asset and taking this particular finance lease.

Leasing is thus less likely to have been an attractive proposition to the tax-paying lessee than to the non-tax-paying lessee in the example quoted. A tax-paying lessor in this example might have evaluated its yield at 7.5 per cent per annum by the converse of this calculation, whereas the non-tax-paying lessee perceives the EIR to be 3.9 per cent per annum. The difference in perception is real and represents the benefit contributed to the transaction by the tax authorities by way of deferral of the lessor's tax liability.

The NPV approach

Non-tax-paying lessee

The non-tax-paying lessee, with a bank borrowing rate of 5 per cent per annum, evaluates its position using the NPV approach in accordance with Exhibit 11.6.

The asset cost is greater than the present value of the rentals using the lessee's assumed bank borrowing rate of 5 per cent per annum and therefore leasing is an attractive proposition. Looked at in another way, this lessee could use its facility to borrow US$980 at 5 per cent per annum to provide a fund out of which it could pay the three annual rentals of US$360 as well as interest on the reducing overdraft. The lessee would then be US$20 better off than if it had bought the asset and thus borrowed US$1,000.

Tax-paying lessee

Because of the delay between the payment of interest and the cash benefit of tax relief thereon, the derivation of a net of tax discount rate from a pre-tax rate is not simply a matter of

Exhibit 11.6

Non-tax-paying lessee: NPV

	Date	Rental (US$)	Discount factor (5% pa)	Present value (at 31 December 2003) (US$)
	31 December 2004	360	0.952	343
	31 December 2005	360	0.907	326
	31 December 2006	360	0.864	311
Aggregate present value of rentals			980	
Present cost of asset				1,000
NPV = gain from leasing				20

deducting the standard rate of tax from the latter. Instead the following formula has to be used, which is itself an approximation satisfactory for small values of n:

$$r2 = r1 - \frac{r1 \times T}{[1 + (r1 \times T)]^n}$$

where:

$r1$ is the lessee's pre-tax borrowing rate from which the net rate is to be derived;

$r2$ is the net rate;

T is the rate of corporation tax; and

n is the delay in tax payment in years.

Thus, in this case, where the average tax delay is 18 months from the mid point of the year:

$$r2 = 0.05 - \frac{0.05 \times 0.50}{[1 + (0.05 \times 0.50)]^{1.5}}$$

$$= 0.05 - \frac{0.025}{1.038}$$

$$= 2.59 \text{ per cent per annum}$$

Exhibit 11.7 shows the calculation of the NPV to the lessee using this discount rate.

The NPV is negative which means that leasing on the terms offered costs more than purchasing using a source of funds costing 5 per cent per annum. In this case the lessee would have had to borrow US$1,013 at 5 per cent per annum to discharge the rentals taking into account the related tax effects. Clearly it would be better off borrowing US$1,000 to buy the asset.

Exhibit 11.7

Tax-paying lessee: NPV

Date	Incremental cash flows (Exhibit 11.4) (US$)	Discount factor (2.59% pa)	Present value (at 31 December 2003) (US$)
31 December 2003	1,000	1.000	1,000
31 December 2004	(860)	0.975	(838)
31 December 2005	(180)	0.950	(171)
31 December 2006	(180)	0.926	(166)
31 December 2007	180	0.903	162
Total	**(40)**		**(13)**

The approaches compared

Given two methods, the question is whether they both indicate the same preference in all cases, and if not, in a case of conflict which indication is correct.

The example examined so far has given rise to the same indications using both approaches: the tax-paying lessee should buy the asset whilst the non-tax-paying lessee should lease. This is not necessarily always the case, even under the generous hypothetical tax regime. The possibility of conflict is illustrated in the example in Exhibit 11.8 and it is suggested that the NPV approach is more useful for a lessee in case of conflict.

Should Company X purchase or lease and, if it should lease, which lease should it choose?

It is apparent to start with, from Exhibit 11.8, that Company X should lease rather than borrow, because both leases have an EIR less than the company's incremental borrowing rate and both leases show a positive NPV at that rate. However, Lease 1 has a lower EIR (3.9 per cent per annum) than Lease 2 (4.2 per cent per annum) and yet Lease 2 provides a higher NPV (US$28) than Lease 1 (US$20) each calculated at the lessee's incremental borrowing rate. The simplifying assumption has been made that the incremental borrowing rate for seven-year money is the same as for three-year money. Accepting this assumption and the non-tax-paying assumption, Company X should select Lease 2. This is because under Lease 1, the lease obligations are repaid faster and so, whilst it has a lower interest rate, this benefit is applied for a shorter period giving a lower overall benefit.

While the NPV approach is regarded as preferable to an evaluation based on EIR, the selection of an appropriate discount rate is not without difficulties. First, interest rates for debt with different maturities are likely to vary; secondly, the borrowing profile is not necessarily a simple reducing balance owing to the impact of tax cash flows; thirdly, there may be periods during a lease when the prospective lessee would have had a cash surplus rather than being overdrawn. In selecting the discount rate, it is necessary to give weight to these factors and this may, for example, involve applying different discount rates to a three-year and a seven-year lease respectively when comparing them.

Temporary non-tax-paying lessees

A lessee may be in such a position that it is not currently paying corporation tax on profits, perhaps because of the availability of past losses, yet foresees that before the expiry of a proposed lease it may become fully taxable.

Exhibit 11.8

EIR versus NPV

Example: Two proposals are quoted for leasing an asset, costing US$1,000 to Company X, which is unlikely to be paying tax for the foreseeable future.

	Lease 1	Lease 2
Primary term	3 years	7 years
Annual rentals in arrears	US$360	US$165
EIR to lessee (non-tax-paying)	3.9% pa	4.2% pa
Lessee's incremental borrowing rate	5% pa	5% pa
NPV of the lease to lessee	US$20	US$28

The evaluation of such a position is complex because it requires the taxable or tax-allowable cash inflows and outflows of the lessee to be accumulated gross during the initial non-tax-paying period and then charged to, or allowed for, tax in the year of changeover. The later in the lease that the changeover occurs, the less will be the effect on the evaluation and the more likely it will be that a lease alternative will still appear attractive. Such an evaluation, to be done properly, necessarily involves using a computer because it is not just the basic cash inflows and outflows which have to be accumulated in this way, but also the interest or discount itself which must be accumulated gross until the changeover point when all the past amounts become tax allowable.

The three-year lease assumptions set out in Exhibit 11.1 are used to illustrate the calculations involved. Exhibit 11.9 shows the EIR and NPV to the lessee, assuming that it changes over from being non taxable to fully taxable in each successive year. Exhibit 11.10 shows the detailed cash flow for changeover in 2004 by way of example.

A sophisticated computer program will permit a lessee to stipulate the available taxable profits in any given year so that the evaluation is not confined to a sudden or all or nothing changeover from non-tax-paying to tax-paying status.

Exhibit 11.9

Temporary non-tax-paying lessee

| | Lessee evaluation | |
| | EIR | NPV |
Year of change	(% pa)	US$ per US$1,000
Permanent tax-paying	7.5	(13)
2004	5.2	1
2005	4.3	7
2006	3.9	11
Permanent non-tax-paying	3.9	20

Exhibit 11.10

Lessee becoming tax paying in 2004

Date	Asset cost (US$)	Tax thereon (50%) (US$)	Rentals (US$)	Tax thereon (50%) (US$)	Incremental cash flows (US$)	Interest (5.2% pa) (US$)	Tax thereon (50%) (US$)	Cumulative cash flows (US$)
31 December 2003	1,000	–	–	–	1,000	–	–	1,000
31 December 2004	–	–	(360)	–	(360)	52	–	692
31 December 2005	–	(500)	(360)	180	(680)	36	(26)	22
31 December 2006	–	–	(360)	180	(180)	1	(18)	(175)
31 December 2007	–	–	–	180	180	(9)	(1)	(5)
31 December 2008	–	–	–	–	–	–	5	–
Total	**1,000**	**(500)**	**(1,080)**	**540**	**(40)**	**80**	**(40)**	

Residual values

A finance lease often provides for the lessee to enjoy the full benefit of the residual value of the asset at the end of the lease term. Depending on the tax rules, this may take the form of a purchase option for nominal consideration, a secondary lease term at a nominal rental, or a rebate of rentals effectively equivalent to the sale proceeds. In each case the lessee evaluation is unaffected because the right to enjoy the residual value is the same whether the lessee owns the asset or leases it.

Sometimes, however, the lessor may retain a significant interest in the residual value, such as 10 per cent of the sale proceeds, or be entitled to the whole residual interest. So, when comparing borrowing and leasing alternatives using either the EIR or NPV approaches, the lease alternative would have to include an additional cash outflow to reflect the effective cost of surrendering the agreed proportion of the lessee's estimate of the net sales proceeds.

Options

One also needs to consider the value of any options. For example, a lease might provide great flexibility for early termination although it appears expensive. Similarly, an apparently cheap lease may have expensive extension options or secondary period rentals that are more than nominal. Therefore, in comparing leases, the lessee should consider the entire cost for the period or periods for which it is likely to hold the asset and not just the specified primary period.

Sensitivity analysis

When comparing borrowing and leasing alternatives, potential lessees will generally recognise various uncertainties in the factors that affect the comparison. These may, for example, relate to the prospect of changes in marginal borrowing costs over the period affected by the lease, or doubts as to when the lessee may move into a tax-paying situation.

The correct approach to these uncertainties is to compute the NPV (or EIR if desired) of the lease under alternative assumptions about the matters in doubt. The results will indicate the sensitivity of the NPV or EIR to likely changes in the particular parameters and will enable the lessee to make a judgement about the most favourable financing option. The ability to carry out such sensitivity analyses in practical terms requires access to a computerised lease evaluation program that is specifically designed to allow for variations in the relevant parameters and to produce NPV and EIR as standard forms of output.

Extension of evaluation

The examples are based on annual rents where, in practice, monthly or quarterly interest and discount calculations are often used. However, it is essential to ensure that the difference between nominal and effective interest rates is clearly understood. These methods of evaluation can also be extended to incorporate other variables including: stage payments, uneven rentals, value added and other taxes, and different currencies. However, once again a comprehensive computer programme will normally be needed to arrive at the NPV or EIR.

Lessor evaluation

The basic approach: EIR

For lessors, the purchase of equipment for finance leasing has most of the characteristics of lending and evaluation is thus generally made in terms of effective interest rates. Sometimes the lessor retains more than a nominal interest in the residual value of the equipment at the end of the lease. However, if the present value of the estimated residual value, to the extent that this is not guaranteed to the lessor by the lessee or a third party such as the manufacturer, were significant, the lease would normally be classified as an operating lease rather than as a finance lease. Close to the border between finance lease classification and operating lease classification, the lease may still be considered by the lessor to be a form of finance (but with a higher profit margin to reflect the residual value risk) and evaluated accordingly. However, if the residual value risks are significant, the evaluation may then take on the characteristics of conventional investment appraisal that falls outside the scope of this book.

Finance lease evaluation from the standpoint of the lessor is essentially directed to computing interest rates implicit in lease proposals to help comparison with other lease proposals and lending opportunities. In considering the results of this comparison, lessors will take into account the cost of insuring or bearing the additional risks which they may assume by leasing as opposed to lending, for example public liability for any damage caused by the product which is the subject of the lease.

Because lessors evaluate their lease opportunities, both in absolute terms and for the purpose of comparing one with another, in terms of interest rates, lease evaluation appears to be a simple matter, given the availability of a computer to handle the mathematics. However, the variety of approaches and, in particular, the employment of gearing or leverage to increase the lessor's return makes the topic complex.

As discussed earlier, the financial benefit of leasing is frequently derived from the ability of the lessor to enjoy tax advantages that would not otherwise be available to the lessee because the lessor is tax paying whereas the lessee is not. This feature of leasing has given rise to the concept of tax capacity or tax shelter which has sometimes been regarded as an additional resource which the lessor contributes to the transaction and for which it is entitled to make a charge to the lessee as part of the rental calculation.

In some big-ticket transactions, an explicit charge is made to the lessee for the use of the lessor's tax capacity. This is done by crediting the cash flow with only a proportion, say 85 per cent, of the tax relief from the tax allowances or credits, while not correspondingly restricting the charge to the cash flow for tax on rental income. This basis is much less common than the straightforward approach, whereby the lessor simply looks for an interest rate on the funds employed at a rate which is higher than for a corresponding loan to compensate it for the additional risks to which it may be exposed through leasing and to reflect a share of the tax benefits dependent upon market forces. However, in some leveraged and other lease structures, where the funds employed by a lessor are in no way commensurate with the use of tax capacity or risks involved, a funds based, or at least a solely funds based, approach is inappropriate. In some cases, a return on capital approach may be more appropriate.

Risks

There are four main types of risk to which a lessor is subject.

Credit

The credit risk under a lease is no different in principle from that under a loan and leasing involves no special consideration on this score, except in leveraged leasing where the use of non-recourse finance limits the lessor's risk and enables it to gear up the tax benefits involved.

Interest rate variation

Generally there is no difference in principle between leasing and lending. It is not relevant to the evaluation of a lease that one of the marketing attractions of leasing is the fixed nature of the obligations, particularly in the case of small- or medium-ticket facilities. In some countries leasing of equipment has been one of relatively few sources of fixed-rate medium-term finance, due in part to the impact of tax benefits on a lessor's cash flows and in part to the reward for the use of tax capacity being available to compensate for the risk of adverse interest rate movements.

Who bears the interest rate risk is thus one of the lessor's choices, or marketing strategies and, having regard to the availability of interest rate swaps etc, is reasonably capable of being evaluated and built into the rental if the lessor wishes to offer fixed-rate terms and bear the risk of variation itself.

Tax variation

The tax risks of leasing do not arise in lending, since leasing generally involves accelerated tax reliefs, which reverse in later years, whereas income from lending is generally taxed as it arises. These risks described in Chapter 10 can be highly significant where the benefits of leasing derive substantially from tax factors.

Residual value/product

Leasing involves ownership of an asset by the lessor and therefore entails risks, such as the residual value risk and maintenance risks, which would not arise in the case of lending. (The risks concerned are considered in Chapter 16.) These are important risks, although for many of them insurance is available. The potential cost of these is a factor to be allowed for in assessing the comparative returns from leasing and lending if it is not separately built into the lease evaluation such as in the form of insurance costs.

The evaluation methods

In this section, the evaluation methods in common use are described and compared. For this purpose the assumptions set out in Exhibit 11.1 and used for the lessee evaluation example are again adopted.

Internal rate of return (IRR)

The calculation is identical to that for the tax-paying lessee shown in Exhibit 11.5, but with all the signs reversed. The lessor's view of the calculation is reproduced in Exhibit 11.11. The interest rate or internal rate of return (IRR) is 7.5 per cent per annum and often referred to as a yield in the case of a lessor.

A key point is that after two years during which the lessor has money invested in the lease, the lessor enjoys two years of cash surplus on which reinvestment income can be earned before the cash flow effects of the lease are concluded.

Exhibit 11.11

Internal rate of return (IRR)

Date	(Asset cost)/ rentals (US$)	IRR (7.5% pa) (US$)	Tax (50%) (US$)	Annual cash flows (US$)	Cumulative cash flows (US$)
31 December 2003	(1,000)	–	–	(1,000)	(1,000)
31 December 2004	360	(76)	500	784	(216)
31 December 2005	360	(16)	(142)	202	(14)
31 December 2006	360	(1)	(172)	187	173
31 December 2007	–	13	(179)	(166)	7
31 December 2008	–	–	(7)	(7)	–
Total	**80**	**(80)**	**0**	**0**	

The special feature of the IRR approach, and its ultimate weakness, is that this surplus cash is assumed to earn as high a return as the lease yield itself. Thus the more profitable the lease appears to be in terms of yield, the higher is the return which must be earned on the surplus cash to justify the calculation which produced the yield. This feature, the Achilles' heel of the IRR approach, becomes particularly dangerous when non-recourse borrowing is used to gear up the lease. The lessor's investment over time can be relatively low compared with the surplus cash, which the lease generates, and the IRR could result in a dangerously misleading appraisal of the lease yield by imposing an impracticable target for reinvestment return that in real life often relates to funds to be generated several years after the inception of the lease.

There is another technical problem with the IRR approach. If the cumulative cash flow repeatedly changes sign from negative to positive and back, there may be multiple solutions for the IRR, an additional solution for every change of sign. There is no basis upon which to determine that one such solution is more useful than another.

Dual rate of return

To overcome the problems of IRR, the dual rate approach was developed. The distinguishing feature of this method is that surplus cash is taken to earn a predetermined rate of interest that will typically be significantly lower than the yield expected from the lease. Having fixed this return, the computer is then left to calculate the yield that the stipulated lease terms will generate during the period when the lessor has a positive investment in the lease, or alternatively to calculate the rental which will generate a particular yield. The method derives its name from the fact that two different rates of interest are used in the calculation, but the dual rate itself refers to the lessor's yield during the investment period. The adoption of a fairly low fixed reinvestment rate ensures that the calculation of the lessor's return on investment (dual rate) is not dependent upon the ability to reinvest the cash surplus at the same rate. In this way it breaks the vicious circle of the IRR approach. The dual rate method also eliminates the problem of multiple solutions. The method, illustrated in Exhibit 11.12, uses the same assumptions as before but, in addition, assumes a return on surplus funds of 4 per cent per annum.

The dual rate of return is seen to be 7.1 per cent per annum, 0.4 per cent below the 7.5 per cent IRR. The difference between the dual rate and IRR methods is apparent from the

Exhibit 11.12

Dual rate of return (DRR)

Date	(Asset cost)/ rentals (US$)	Yield 7.1% pa Surplus 4% pa (US$)	Tax (50%) (US$)	Annual cash flows (US$)	Cumulative cash flows (US$)
31 December 2003	(1,000)			(1,000)	(1,000)
31 December 2004	360	(71)	500	789	(211)
31 December 2005	360	(15)	(145)	200	(11)
31 December 2006	360	(1)	(172)	187	176
31 December 2007	–	7	(179)	(173)	4
31 December 2008	–	–	(4)	(4)	–
Total	**80**	**(80)**	**0**	**0**	

much lower return assumed under the dual rate method in the period of cash surplus at the end of the lease. The lower the assumed rate of return, the lower will be the yield that the lease can bear whilst still breaking even. A differential of one percentage point between the IRR and dual rate methods may not appear great, but it is significant when related to a margin over cost of funds of perhaps 2 per cent per annum. The difference will be more significant in the case of leases financed by non-recourse loans.

Gross margin

The dual rate of return represents the maximum interest rate that the lessor could afford to pay on funds borrowed to finance the lease without incurring a loss (assuming a specified return on surplus cash).

If the lessor does in fact have a source of funds to finance the lease at a rate that is cheaper than the dual rate, it will enjoy a margin that may be regarded as a measure of its profit. The expression gross margin is used here to describe the excess of the dual rate over the lessor's assumed cost of funds.

In the example in Exhibit 11.12, if the lessor had a source of funds to finance its investment in the lease, repayable on the same profile as the reduction of the lease investment, at a funding cost of 5 per cent per annum, the lessor's gross margin would be 2.1 per cent per annum. Some lease evaluation programmes enable the gross margin, thus defined, to be calculated as an output and will accept as input a borrowing cost and return on surplus cash fluctuating over time to allow for expected or contracted future changes in interest rates.

Net of tax margin

The net of tax margin, also known as actuarial after tax margin or AATM, is the most commonly used measure of lessor profitability in the United Kingdom. This measure was approved by the High Court in London in 1990, in the case of Midland Montagu Leasing Limited v Tyne and Wear Passenger Transport Executive, as being appropriate in the circumstances of the case for computing variations to rentals resulting from tax changes.

It differs from the gross margin in treating the margin as a series of non-tax-deductible payments out of the lease; such payments are nevertheless calculated at a constant percentage rate on the lessor's net cash investment. It is as though the lease were the sole asset of a sub-

Exhibit 11.13

Net of tax margin

Date	(Asset cost)/ rentals (US$)	Interest payable 5% pa receivable 4% pa (US$)	Tax (50%) (US$)	Net of tax margin (US$)	Annual cash flows (US$)	Cumulative cash flows (US$)
31 December 2003	(1,000)	–	–	–	(1,000)	(1,000)
31 December 2004	360	(50)	500	(11)	799	(201)
31 December 2005	360	(10)	(155)	(2)	193	(8)
31 December 2006	360	(1)	(175)	–	184	176
31 December 2007	–	7	(179)	–	(172)	4
31 December 2008	–	–	(4)	–	(4)	–
Total	**80**	**(54)**	**(13)**	**(13)**	**0**	

sidiary, which distributed a dividend to its parent company at a constant percentage on its cash investment in the lease so as to leave a break-even position at the end. This approach is illustrated in Exhibit 11.13, which is based on the same assumptions as before with the additional assumption that the lessor's cost of funds throughout the lease is 5 per cent per annum.

The net of tax margin is 1.1 per cent per annum, which is not exactly 50 per cent of the gross margin of 2.1 per cent per annum, the difference being caused by the effect of the assumed delay in payment or receipt of tax.

Under this method, the net of tax margin is itself treated as a cash outflow, which has the effect of increasing the cash investment and hence the interest cost. This characteristic is sometimes referred to as profit take out since it treats the profit as being paid out by the leasing entity as it accrues. Some programs for calculating net of tax margin treat the margin as if it were retained within the lease and thus used to reduce borrowings or increase surplus cash generated by the lease. The net of tax margin in this case is likely to be significantly higher than with profit take-out and the profit take-out approach is considered to be a more appropriate and prudent measure of the lessor's margin. In particular, the profit will probably be treated as distributable for accounts purposes and may, in fact, be an actual cash outflow to the extent that it is used to pay overheads and dividends etc.

The net margin is computed only while the lessor has a positive investment in the lease. This is because a return on surplus cash has been predetermined and under the dual rate approach, of which this is a variant, it would be inappropriate to calculate an increased margin by assuming that the margin would also apply to reinvested surplus cash. Whilst not a common method, an acceptable variant on this is to calculate the net margin while the lessor has a positive investment in the lease but as a reduction in the return on surplus cash. Thus the lessor would earn a margin both when there is an investment in the lease and when there are surplus funds.

An important question is what measure of the cost of money should be used by the lessor in calculating its interest payable. The usual approach is to regard the entire investment as being financed using money borrowed at the lessor's incremental borrowing cost. This assumes that this can be done within the constraints imposed by the need to maintain appropriate capital ratios. It is possible to compute an average cost of capital for the lessor, including a proportion of equity, and to use this cost as the assumed interest rate. However, the usual incremental approach is satisfactory provided that the interest rate used or required margin reflects any additional charge which a lender might make having regard to the lessor's capital structure.

Net present value

A lessor may calculate the NPV of a lease proposal by discounting the incremental cash flows from the lease at its incremental borrowing rate, allowing for tax on the discount with the appropriate time delay. The NPV of the lease illustrated, using a 5 per cent per annum discount rate, is US$13 per US$1,000 of asset cost, calculated in exactly the same way as for a lessee (Exhibit 11.7).

The lessor may regard the NPV as the sum for which a lessor could sell the benefit of the lease to an investor which required a return on its funds equal to the discount rate used by the lessor, disregarding any tax effects resulting from the sale. The NPV is itself a net of tax amount.

A lessor is not likely to find the NPV approach nearly as useful as a lessee. The resource or commodity which a lessor is selling is predominantly money for a period of time and it is seeking to earn a margin from the use of the money related to time. The longer its money is invested in a given lease, the greater the absolute cash profit it will expect to earn. For example, a seven-year lease to produce the same net of tax margin to the lessor as the three-year lease illustrated in this chapter would result in an NPV of US$23 per US$1,000 of asset cost as against US$20 per US$1,000 of asset cost in the case of the three-year lease. Does this mean that the longer lease is more profitable? This would only necessarily be so on the assumption that the lessor had no confidence in its ability to redeploy the funds, which would be recovered more quickly from the three-year lease, in further business which yielded an equivalent net of tax margin. Provided that the lessor expects to be able to maintain its net margin in the future, the higher NPV portrayed by the longer lease does not present a useful signal. For this reason a lessor is predominantly concerned with interest rates, yields and margins.

Impact of accounting

So far, it has been assumed that the rentals are taxed either on a cash basis (that is, in the year in which the rental is received) or on an accruals basis (that is, in the period or periods to which the rental relates). A further complication has arisen in recent years in the United Kingdom in which, under certain circumstances, the rentals are taxed based on the higher of the rentals accrued and earnings recognised for accounting purposes. In these cases one needs a computer based evaluation system that can also generate the accounting figures.

Non-tax-paying lessor

In all the examples, it has been assumed that the lessor is tax paying. However, leasing can be advantageous in certain circumstances where the lessor is non tax paying (due, for example, to unused tax losses) and the lessee is tax paying, for example, if the lease generates significant tax charges for the lessor, but corresponding tax deductions for the lessee. The evaluation would follow the same principles as above, setting the tax rate to zero, or whatever is appropriate, in the lessor's evaluation and using the tax paying evaluation along the lines of Exhibit 11.5 or 11.7 for the lessee. However, instead of the lessor charging a profit margin for use of its tax capacity, it would charge a profit margin for use of its tax losses.

Leverage and gearing

The analysis of the rate of return from a lease to a lessor has so far been based on the assumption that the investment which the lessor has to service is the entire incremental borrowing to which the lease gives rise from time to time. But suppose that the lessor is able to borrow money at an attractive rate or on a non-recourse basis specifically to fund part of the investment in the lease; if it then computes the profitability by relating the profit to the balance of the investment not funded by such borrowing, the apparent return may be significantly improved.

Where the lessor remains liable for the repayment of the special loan which is funding the investment, there should be no difference in the approach to the evaluation. The lessor should earn a margin on all funds used, whatever the source, and any calculation of profit as a return on only part of the funds invested will generally give a deceptively attractive return for the use of the lessor's tax capacity and the risks assumed by it. Accordingly, the evaluation should be undertaken using a merged funds approach, that is, by relating the surplus to all funds used, be they special loans, overdraft or equity.

Some lessors do not consider it is necessary to use a merged funds approach in a leveraged lease where the lessor is not responsible to the lender for repayment of the non-recourse loans. How a lessor should evaluate a leveraged lease is beyond the scope of this book, but it is important that a lessor should be fully aware of the major pitfalls of relying wholly on a margin approach to the evaluation of many types of leveraged lease.

Assume, for example, that a non-recourse loan of 80 per cent of the equipment cost is available to the lessor (or equipment trust) at a rate of 5 per cent per annum repayable in three equal instalments. Exhibit 11.14 shows the cash flows involved and reveals that the lessor will earn 15 per cent per annum, a gross margin of 10 per cent after deducting its own cost of funds, again assumed to be 5 per cent per annum. The removal of 80 per cent of the credit risk is the only parameter to have changed. The same use of tax capacity now results in a margin 7.9 per cent higher than the 2.1 per cent arrived at on the merged funds basis set out in Exhibit 11.12. However, the earnings are down from US$87 (US$80 + US$7) to US$30 (see yields in Exhibits 11.12 and 11.14) solely because the investment upon which it is computed has been reduced by the borrowing; proportionately greater reliance is placed on the income from surplus funds. (The distortions are very much greater if the internal rate of return rather than the dual rate of return method is used.)

Exhibit 11.14

The leveraged lease evaluation pitfall

Date	(Asset cost)/ rentals (US$)	Loan/ (repayment) (US$)	Interest on loan (US$)	Yield 15% pa Surplus 4% pa (US$)	Tax (50%) (US$)	Annual cash flows (US$)	Cumulative cash flows (US$)
31 December 2003	(1,000)	800				(200)	(200)
31 December 2004	360	(267)	(40)	(30)	500	523	323
31 December 2005	360	(267)	(27)	13	(145)	(66)	257
31 December 2006	360	(266)	(13)	10	(173)	(82)	175
31 December 2007	–	–	–	7	(179)	(172)	3
31 December 2008	–	–	–	–	(3)	(3)	–
Total	**80**	**0**	**(80)**	**0**	**0**	**0**	

Structuring

The methods of lessor evaluation can be extended as for the lessee, to incorporate other variables and different rental payment frequencies (see above section on sensitivity analysis).

One of the most important skills required in arranging or packaging a lease is to identify the structure that can maximise the benefits under any given fiscal conditions. The features of a lease that can be altered to optimise the structure vary from country to country. The value of tax deferment is greater the higher the prevailing level of interest rates; the interest free nature of the deferral is then relatively more beneficial.

The most common ways of increasing the benefit of tax deferral in a leasing arrangement are:

- lengthening the lease;
- incorporating rentals payable in arrears rather than in advance;
- introducing stepped, balloon or other structured rentals;
- selecting the most favourable timing in the financial year to purchase the asset; and
- changing the method of tax depreciation during the lease term.

Investment incentive comparison

The evaluation techniques outlined in this chapter may be used to compare the values of various types of investment incentive. Exhibit 11.15 compares, for four different lengths of lease

Exhibit 11.15

Investment incentive comparison

		Rentals payable (US$) per US$1,000 of asset cost				
	Primary term (years)	*Case 1* *100% FYA*	*Case 2* *25% RBA*	*Case 3* *10% ITC* *25% RBA*	*Case 4* *10% ITC* *10% SL*	*Case 5* *10% SL*
No residual value						
	3	360	378	322	340	407
	5	223	239	200	211	253
	7	165	178	148	156	187
	10	122	132	109	115	138
10% residual value						
	3	335	360	298	315	382
	5	208	226	185	196	238
	7	153	168	137	145	176
	10	113	123	101	107	130
20% residual value						
	3	309	342	273	291	358
	5	192	213	170	181	222
	7	142	157	125	134	164
	10	105	115	93	99	121

term and three different residual value assumptions, the following incentives and tax depreciation rates:

- a 100 per cent first year allowance (FYA);
- a 25 per cent reducing balance allowance (RBA);
- a 10 per cent investment tax credit (ITC) (or 20 per cent investment allowance) and 25 per cent reducing balance allowance (RBA);
- a 10 per cent investment tax credit (ITC) and 10 per cent straight line allowance (SL); and
- a 10 per cent straight-line allowance (SL).

The common assumptions are:

- an asset cost US$1,000;
- an acquisition on last day of financial year;
- a full year's tax depreciation in year of acquisition;
- a full tax credit against taxable income in year of acquisition;
- equipment used by the lessee for 10 years;
- a peppercorn rental after primary term;
- a tax payable 12 months after the year-end;
- a 50 per cent tax rate;
- a borrowing cost of 5 per cent per annum;
- a reinvestment rate of 4 per cent per annum; and
- residual value retained by lessor.

For each case, the rentals payable annually in arrears are calculated to yield the lessor the same dual rate of return of 7.1 per cent per annum and gross margin of 2.1 per cent, per annum. In practice, a higher return would be expected for a longer lease period to compensate the lessor for the greater risks involved. With no investment incentive or a disincentive for short-term facilities (as in case 5), the gross margin is often more sensitive to different factors, such as anticipated interest rate fluctuations on funding of fixed-rate leases.

Conclusion

This chapter has summarised the key numerical calculations that are involved in the process of evaluating a lease. Some of these calculations are complex and will generally require the use of specialist leasing software. However, the concepts need to be understood if the results obtained from such software are to be interpreted correctly. In addition, non-numerical factors referred to in this chapter that could have an impact on the leasing decision should not be ignored.

Chapter 12

Lessor income accounting

Colin Dowsett

Introduction

The fundamental problem of lessor accounting is how to determine the allocation of income to accounting periods. As with the capitalisation of leases (see Chapter 13), it must first of all be noted that lessor accounting is an area of change and a number of the methods currently in use are likely to be threatened by future accounting standards. The principal methods are outlined in the first part of this chapter while other issues, such as the front loading of income and residual values, are considered in later sections.

Finance leases work in the following way: the amount outstanding decreases as the rental payments reduce the investment. A proportion of these rental payments represents a finance charge to the lessor. A method is therefore required to determine the proportion and hence the amount of the lessor's gross earnings; that is, the excess of payments due under the lease over the cost of the leased asset, to be allocated to each accounting period.

The various methods used are illustrated using an example for which the assumptions are set out below in Exhibit 12.1. The assumption of accelerated tax allowances helps to emphasise the differences between the methods described in this chapter.

The actuarial method before tax

The actuarial method before tax is the method required in the United States under Financial Accounting Standards Board Statement 13 (FAS 13) and also under International Accounting Standards Board Standard 17 (IAS 17) (although approximations to it are permitted).

Exhibit 12.1

Lessor accounting assumptions

Asset cost	US$10,000
Acquisition date	31 December 2003
Primary lease term	Five years
Rentals	20 quarterly in advance of US$540
Secondary lease	Indefinite period at a peppercorn
Lessor's year end	31 December
Tax payment date	31 December, 12 months later
Tax rate	50% throughout
Tax allowances	100% first-year allowance
Lessor's cost of funds	5% pa
Lessor's return on surplus finds	3% pa

The before tax calculation

Under this method, the gross earnings are allocated to accounting periods so as to produce a constant rate of return on the outstanding investment disregarding the tax cash flows. Thus the gross earnings are allocated as shown in Exhibit 12.2.

Exhibit 12.2 is constructed by calculating the appropriate periodic interest rate (0.8 per cent per quarter in this example) using a computer or sophisticated calculator. The earnings are then allocated to each period on the basis of the balance outstanding during that period. For example, US$9,460 x 0.82% = US$78. At the end of the year ending 31 December 2004, the lessor has incurred costs in purchasing the asset of US$10,000 and received rentals of US$2,700 of which US$290 is taken to represent his gross earnings; the balance of US$2,410 represents repayments of capital. Thus, the lease would be reflected in his financial statements as follows:

Investment in leased assets (US$10,000 - US$2,410)	US$7,590
Overdraft (US$10,000 - US$2,700)	US$7,300
Net assets (representing earnings before tax)	US$290

Exhibit 12.2

Lessor income recognition – actuarial method before tax

Quarter ending	Net investment at start of, and during, period (US$)	Gross earnings for period (US$)	Asset cost (US$)	Rentals (US$)	Net investment at end of period (US$)
31 December 2003	–	–	10,000	(540)	9,460
31 March 2004	9,460	78	–	(540)	8,998
30 June 2004	8,998	74	–	(540)	8,532
30 September 2004	8,532	71	–	(540)	8,063
31 December 2004	8,063	67	–	(540)	7,590
31 March 2005	7,590	62	–	(540)	7,112
30 June 2005	7,112	58	–	(540)	6,630
30 September 2005	6,630	55	–	(540)	6,145
31 December 2005	6,145	51	–	(540)	5,656
31 March 2006	5,656	46	–	(540)	5,162
30 June 2006	5,162	42	–	(540)	4,664
30 September 2006	4,664	39	–	(540)	4,163
31 December 2006	4,163	35	–	(540)	3,658
31 March 2007	3,658	30	–	(540)	3,148
30 June 2007	3,148	26	–	(540)	2,634
30 September 2007	2,634	22	–	(540)	2,116
31 December 2007	2,116	18	–	(540)	1,594
31 March 2008	1,594	13	–	(540)	1,067
30 June 2008	1,067	9	–	(540)	536
30 September 2008	536	4	–	(540)	–
Total		**800**	**(10,000)**	**(10,800)**	

As in the case of accounting by lessees described in Chapter 13, an acceptable approximation to the actuarial method before tax can, in some cases, be made by using the sum of the digits method to allocate the finance charge to accounting periods. However, the approximation becomes less accurate as the ratio of finance charges to capital increases (as illustrated in the section 'Alternative methods of apportioning finance charges' in Chapter 13).

The advantages of the actuarial method before tax include its relative simplicity and its broad symmetry to the accounting treatment adopted by a lessee which capitalises the lease. It also recognises that the lessor's main cost is that of providing finance and thus matches its gross earnings with its costs by recognising higher earnings in the early periods when there is a larger amount outstanding.

Tax implications

Where accelerated depreciation provides an opportunity for tax deferment, as in the case of the 100 per cent first-year write off illustrated here and in Chapter 11, the net of tax cash flows is uneven and a before-tax allocation method may not achieve an allocation of profits to accounting periods in proportion to the outstanding funds invested in a lease.

Exhibit 12.3 shows how the cost of the asset is deducted for tax and financial statement purposes for the lease assumptions set out in Exhibit 12.1 and illustrated in Exhibit 12.2.

Exhibit 12.4 sets out the taxable profits for the lease compared to the accounting profits, assuming no other transactions, or interest payments, arose in the period of the lease.

Exhibit 12.4 shows that over the full period of the lease the lessor is taxed at 50 per cent on the excess of the rental payments over the cost of the asset. However, if the financial statements reflected simply the tax recoverable or payable for the financial period, there would be a post-tax profit of US$5,000 reported in the year ending 31 December 2003 and post-tax losses in each of the five subsequent years.

Lessors generally recognise that the tax saved by allowances given for the cost of the asset simply represent a timing difference, rather than a permanent gift, by recognising a liability to deferred tax for the tax postponed. The liability is released as the cost of the asset is charged in the financial statements, thus equalising the tax charge. The amount of the liability at any point is equivalent to tax on the excess of the carrying amount of the investment

Exhibit 12.3

Tax and accounting depreciation

Financial year ending	Tax allowances (US$)	Financial statement amortisation (US$)
31 December 2003	(10,000)	–
31 December 2004	–	1,870
31 December 2005	–	1,934
31 December 2006	–	1,998
31 December 2007	–	2,064
31 December 2008	–	2,134
Total	**10,000**	**10,000**

Exhibit 12.4

Tax and accounting depreciation (taxable vs accounting profits)

Financial year ending	Capital allowances (US$)	Rental income (US$)	Taxable income/(loss) (US$)	Tax (recoverable)/ payable (US$)	Accounting profits before tax and interest (US$)
31 December 2003	(10,000)	–	(10,000)	(5,000)	–
31 December 2004	–	2,160	2,160	1,080	290
31 December 2005	–	2,160	2,160	1,080	227
31 December 2006	–	2,160	2,160	1,080	162
31 December 2007	–	2,160	2,160	1,080	95
31 December 2008	–	2,160	2,160	1,080	26
Total	**(10,000)**	**10,800**	**800**	**400**	**800**

Exhibit 12.5

Deferred tax

Year ending	Tax allowances (US$)	Accounts amortisation (US$)	Difference (US$)	Transfer (to)/from deferred tax (US$)
Profit and loss accounts				
31 December 2003	10,000	–	(10,000)	(5,000)
31 December 2004	–	1,870	1,870	935
31 December 2005	–	1,934	1,934	967
31 December 2006	–	1,998	1,998	999
31 December 2007	–	2,064	2,064	1,032
31 December 2008	–	2,134	2,134	1,067
Total	**10,000**	**10,000**	**0**	**0**

As at	Accounts carrying value of investment (US$)	Tax written down value (US$)	Difference (US$)	Deferred tax at 50% (US$)
Balance sheets				
31 December 2003	10,000	–	10,000	5,000
31 December 2004	8,130	–	8,130	4,065
31 December 2005	6,196	–	6,196	3,098
31 December 2006	4,198	–	4,198	2,099
31 December 2007	2,134	–	2,134	1,067
31 December 2008	–	–	–	–

Note: For the purposes of calculating deferred tax, the carrying value of the investment is shown before deducting rentals received for accounting periods after the balance sheet date.

Exhibit 12.6

Tax charge

Financial year ending	Accounting profit (US$)	Current tax (US$)	Deferred tax (US$)	Total tax charge (US$)	Tax charge as % of accounting profit
31 December 2003	–	(5,000)	5,000	–	–
31 December 2004	290	1,080	(935)	145	50
31 December 2005	227	1,080	(967)	113	50
31 December 2006	162	1,080	(999)	81	50
31 December 2007	95	1,080	(1,032)	43	50
31 December 2008	26	1,080	(1,067)	13	50
Total	**800**	**400**	**0**	**400**	**50**

over the cost of the asset which has yet to be allowed for tax purposes. In each accounting period, the liability will decrease by tax on the excess of amortisation charged in the accounts over any tax allowances arising in the period. Exhibit 12.5 shows these calculations on the same assumptions as set out in Exhibit 12.1.

The movement of deferred tax will be reported as part of the tax charge for the period. Exhibit 12.6 shows the resulting tax charges and compares them to the accounting profit. Thus by the technique of providing deferred tax, the tax charge may be adjusted to reflect the true tax effects of the transactions accounted for in each period, while the liability to tax which will arise in future as a result of transactions already undertaken is included in the balance sheet.

The topic of deferred tax is itself a complex area and one that has been subject to much debate both at the international level and in the United Kingdom.

The discussion above is based on the concept commonly used in the United Kingdom at present of deferred tax as a liability. In certain other countries, including the United States, deferred tax is viewed as a deferred benefit and accounted for using the deferral method. The differences between these two methods are of practical importance only when rates of tax change; but where deferred tax is viewed as a liability, arguments may be raised to the effect that there is no need to provide for the liability for the reasons explained below.

In the United Kingdom, until recently it was not necessary for all companies to provide in full for deferred tax. This was because an expanding investment in assets may result in a proportion of the deferred tax, in practice, never being paid or at least not within the foreseeable future.

There are further difficulties in any decision not to provide in full for deferred tax. The case for non-provision is based on a presumption of growth in new business in the foreseeable future which is usually taken to be three years and which is perhaps in conflict with other aspects of lessor income accounting which look to the life of the lease, often being five years or more.

Changes in legislation may also have a significant effect where the deferred tax has not been fully provided, as happened in the United Kingdom in 1984 when tax rates changed dramatically. Because of the effect of tax variation clauses, such a legislative change can also have a direct impact on pre-tax income. Indeed, if a lessor does not provide in full for deferred tax, the profit after tax recognised will exceed the income available from the leases on the books at the time. In other words, income is effectively being recognised from leasing business not yet written (possibly, from new lessees), notwithstanding the fact that the deferred tax benefit arising on new leases may well be passed onto current lessees by way of reduced rentals. However, the introduction of a new accounting standard for deferred tax in the United Kingdom has removed the option for partial provision and therefore all accounts should now be prepared on a consistent basis.

Exhibit 12.7

Lessor's cash flows

Date	(Asset cost)/ rentals (US$)	Taxation (US$)	Interest (payable)/ recoverable (US$)	Net of tax margin (US$)	Cumulative cash flows (US$)
31 December 2003	(10,000)				
	540				(9,460)
31 March 2004	540		(118)	(28)	(9,066)
30 June 2004	540		(113)	(26)	(8,665)
30 September 2004	540		(109)	(26)	(8,260)
31 December 2004	540	5,000	(104)	(25)	(2,849)
31 March 2005	540		(35)	(8)	(2,352)
30 June 2005	540		(29)	(7)	(1,848)
30 September 2005	540		(23)	(5)	(1,336)
31 December 2005	540	(858)	(16)	(4)	(1,674)
31 March 2006	540		(21)	(5)	(1,160)
30 June 2006	540		(15)	(3)	(638)
30 September 2006	540		(8)	(2)	(108)
31 December 2006	540	(1,029)	(1)		(598)
31 March 2007	540		(6)	(2)	(68)
30 June 2007	540		(1)		471
30 September 2007	540		4		1,015
31 December 2007	540	(1,059)	8		504
31 March 2008	540		4		1,048
30 June 2008	540		8		1,596
30 September 2008	540		12		2,148
31 December 2008		(1,082)	16		1,082
31 March 2009			8		1,090
30 June 2009			8		1,098
30 September 2009			8		1,106
31 December 2009		(1,098)	8		16
31 March 2010					16
30 June 2010					16
30 September 2010					16
31 December 2010		(16)			
Total	**(10,000)**	**(142)**	**(517)**	**(141)**	
	12,000				

Criticism of the actuarial method before tax

The actuarial method before tax does not take into account all the cash flows arising directly from the lease, in particular the benefits of tax deferment or tax credits.

Accordingly, although the actuarial method before tax does result in a greater amount of income being recognised earlier in the lease, it does not always adequately match the income to the lessor's outstanding cash investment or the costs (principally finance) arising from the lease.

The cash flows for the lease assumptions set out in Exhibit 12.1 are shown in Exhibit 12.7. Additionally, it has been assumed that the lessor pays dividends each quarter equal to the profit after interest and taxation, calculated in a manner which would typically be used in a commercial evaluation of the profitability of the lease (the net of tax margin method illustrated in Chapter 11). Using these cash flows the financial statements as presented under the actuarial method before tax are shown in Exhibit 12.8.

Exhibit 12.8

Lessor's financial statements (as at 31 December)

	2003 (US$)	2004 (US$)	2005 (US$)	2006 (US$)	2007 (US$)	2008 (US$)	2009 (US$)
Profit and loss accounts							
Gross earnings	–	290	227	162	95	26	–
Interest (payable)/ receivable	–	(444)	(104)	(45)	4	40	32
Profit/(loss) before tax	–	(154)	123	117	99	66	32
Taxation: current	(5,000)	858	1,029	1,059	1,082	1,098	16
deferred	5,000	(935)	(967)	(999)	(1,032)	(1,067)	–
	–	(77)	62	60	50	31	16
Profit/(loss) after tax	–	(77)	61	57	49	35	16
Distribution	–	(105)	(24)	(10)	(2)	–	–
Retained earnings/(loss) for period	–	(182)	37	47	47	35	16
Retained earnings at start of period	–	–	(182)	(145)	(98)	(51)	(16)
Retained earnings at end of period	–	(182)	(145)	(98)	(51)	(16)	–
Balance sheets							
Investment in finance leases	9,460	7,590	5,656	3,658	1,594	–	–
Cash surplus	–	–	–	–	504	1,082	16
	9,460	7,590	5,656	3,658	2,098	1,082	16
Deferred tax	5,000	4,065	3,098	2,099	1,067	–	–
Current tax	(5,000)	858	1,029	1,059	1,082	1,098	16
Cash deficit	9,460	2,849	1,674	598	–	–	–
Retained earnings/ (deficit)	–	(182)	(145)	(98)	(51)	(16)	–
	9,460	7,590	5,657	3,658	2,098	1,082	16

The limitations of the actuarial method before tax are clear from Exhibit 12.8. Although the lease is genuinely profitable to the lessor, a significant loss is reported for the first year of the lease. If the distribution policy is determined in accordance with the commercial evaluation of the lease there is a deficit on retained earnings throughout the period of the lease. For these reasons, many accountants believe that the actuarial method before tax is based on too narrow a view of the lessor's investment.

This difficulty is recognised in the United States where, as stated above, the actuarial method after tax is mandatory for most leases, particularly in the special circumstances of leveraged leases. These leases give rise to a complex pattern of cash flows and FAS 13 requires that profit under such leases shall be allocated in proportion to the net investment in the periods when the net investment is positive. For this purpose, the net investment is taken as the cumulative cash flow after taking account of the loan and loan repayments, including interest and tax effects. Interest on other funds employed and interest earned on cash surpluses is, however, excluded.

The investment period principle

The concept which has become accepted in the United Kingdom known as the investment period principle (IPP) seeks to overcome the objections to the actuarial method before tax and, in contrast to US practice, is applied to ordinary finance leases as well as to leveraged leases.

Under the actuarial method before tax, gross earnings are deemed to arise at a constant rate on the lessor's net investment which reflects only the cost of the asset, the rentals receivable and, to the extent it will be retained by the lessor, the residual value of the asset at the end of the lease. Methods based on the investment period principle are based on a much wider view of the lessor's net investment. The investment is therefore calculated inclusive of:

• the cost of the asset;
• the grants received in respect of the purchase of the asset;
• the rentals receivable;
• the taxation payments and reliefs;
• the residual value at the end of the lease (to the extent it will be retained by the lessor);
• the interest payment (to the extent not covered by profit take-out – see below);
• the interest received on cash surpluses; and
• the profit taken out of the lease (reflecting the notion that profit should not reduce the lessor's borrowing but should be applied in paying indirect costs and dividends).

The net total of the above items is referred to as the net cash investment in the lease, as distinct from the net investment in the lease, which is the basis of the allocation used in the actuarial method before tax.

The IPP owes its origins to techniques developed for lease evaluation from the standpoint of the lessor. Accordingly, many lessors believe that techniques based on the investment period principle closely reflect the commercial substance of the transactions undertaken.

Methods of applying the IPP are constantly evolving and differences arise in detailed application but two methods are particularly well known. These are the actuarial method after tax, and the investment period method. These are discussed below.

The actuarial method after tax

The actuarial method after tax is based on the evaluation technique described in Chapter 11 known as the net of tax margin. This allocates the lessor's net return on the lease after tax and interest in proportion to the net cash investment. Exhibit 12.7 sets out the cash flow calculations used in this method.

In the year ending 31 December 2004, for example, the total rentals of US$2,160 are regarded as being applied as follows:

	US$
Rentals*	2,160
Capital repaid	(1,506)
Gross earnings	654
Interest*	(444)
Profit before tax	210
Tax: current	858
deferred	(753)
	105
Net earnings*	105
Distribution	(105)
Retained earnings	–

Those items marked with an asterisk are derived from Exhibit 12.7 and 12.8 by adding the figures for the four quarters. It has been assumed that full provision for deferred tax is to be made at 50 per cent and thus the profit before tax can be found by multiplying the net earnings of US$105 by 100/50 (= US$210). The deferred tax credit and the capital repayments may then be found by subtraction. The lessor's balance sheet at 31 December 2004, would reflect the following:

	US$
Investment in finance leases (note 1)	7,954
Deferred tax (note 2)	4,247
Current tax	858
Cash overdrawn	2,849
	7,954

Note 1 The cost of the leased asset of US$10,000 has been reduced by all of the payment made at inception of US$540 and by the capital required in the year of US$1,506.

Note 2 The provision for deferred tax established at the time of acquisition of the asset (US$10,000 at 50% = US$5,000) has been reduced by the amount used in the year of US$753 (which is equivalent to 50 per cent of US$1,506).

Income from the lease is no longer recognised once the lease has generated surplus funds. The interest income, which arises in later periods, has already been anticipated in the calculation and, thus, is required to amortise the remaining investment in the lease rather than being dealt with in the profit and loss account. Thus the actuarial method after tax may be criticised as anticipating income that has yet to be earned. This is not merely a technical point: serious practical problems will arise where the interest on surplus funds is an important source of income and, for whatever reason, a fall in market rates of interest occurs or forecasts fail to be achieved. Such problems may be exacerbated in the case of longer leases and those where the rentals are structured to generate cash surpluses.

Investment period method

Another method of applying the investment period principle is that commonly known as the investment period method (IPM). Under this method, like the actuarial method after tax, earnings are allocated in proportion to the net cash investment. The most important difference between IPM and the actuarial method after tax is that under IPM the earnings which are allocated are only those which arise on the leasing transaction. Interest on surplus funds is not accounted for as part of the lease, but is recognised in the accounting periods in which it arises, thus overcoming the objection to the actuarial method after tax referred to above.

The calculation is set out in Exhibit 12.9. The figures for the net cash investment are obtained from Exhibit 12.7. The gross earnings are allocated in proportion to the cash investment, for example for the quarter ending 31 December 2004:

$$\text{US\$800} \times 8,260 = \frac{\text{US\$137}}{48,082}$$

Exhibit 12.9

Investment period method

Period ending	Net cash investment during period (US$)	Gross earnings for period (US$)	Gross earnings for year (US$)
31 March 2004	9,460	158	
30 June 2004	9,066	150	
30 September 2004	8,665	145	
31 December 2004	8,260	137	590
31 March 2005	2,849	47	
30 June 2005	2,352	39	
30 September 2005	1,848	31	
31 December 05	1,336	23	140
31 March 2006	1,674	27	
30 June 2006	1,160	19	
30 September 2006	638	11	
31 December 06	108	2	59
31 March 2007	598	10	
30 June 2007	68	1	11
Total	**48,082**	**800**	**800**

Using this analysis, the profit and loss account for the year ending 31 December 2004 may be drawn up as:

	US$
Rentals	2,160
Less capital repaid	(1,570)
Gross earnings	590
Interest paid	(444)
Profit before tax	146
Tax: current	858
deferred	(785)
	73
Net earnings	73
Distribution	105
Retained deficit*	(32)

* See table below

The gross earnings are taken from Exhibit 12.9; the rentals, interest paid and current taxation are found from Exhibit 12.7. The figures for capital repayments, deferred tax and net earnings may then be found by simple deduction.

The balance sheet figures at 31 December 2004 using IPM are set out below:

	US$
Investment in finance lease	7,890
Deferred tax	4,215
Current tax	858
Cash overdrawn	2,849
Retained earnings deficit*	(32)
	7,890

* This results from the assumption in the cash flow that the distribution from the lease would equal the actuarial profit after tax (US$105) rather than the IPM profit (US$73). In practice distribution would naturally be based on this amount.

Summary and comparison of methods

The profit before tax as reported under each of the three principal methods discussed is set out in Exhibit 12.10.

All three methods recognise more gross earnings in the earlier part of the lease term. The effect is least pronounced in the case of the actuarial method before tax. Indeed, the acceleration is insufficient to cover the lessor's cost of funds in the first year of the lease. The actuarial method after tax accelerates income to the greatest extent. This may not be appropriate on grounds of prudence, especially where there is uncertainty about the income that may be gen-

Exhibit 12.10

Profit before tax comparison

Financial Year ending	Actuarial method before tax (US$)	Actuarial method after tax (US$)	Investment period method (US$)
31 December 2004	(154)	210	146
31 December 2005	123	48	36
31 December 2006	117	20	14
31 December 2007	99	5	15
31 December 2008	66	–	40
31 December 2009	32	–	32
Total	**283**	**283**	**283**

erated from surplus funds later in the term of the lease. The investment period method, although similar in conceptual basis to the actuarial method after tax, seeks to avoid this criticism.

- The main advantages for lessors accounting by methods based on the investment period principle are that:
- the earnings are allocated in proportion to the lessor's principal cost which is the cost of finance; and
- since it is based upon techniques commonly used in lease evaluation, many lessors would agree that it closely accords with the economic realities of the leasing business.

The main disadvantages are that it may, in certain circumstances, accelerate the recognition of income to an extent some accountants would consider imprudent and that it is comparatively complex to calculate and difficult for the relatively unsophisticated reader of financial statements to understand. A further disadvantage is that, since the earnings are not allocated on the basis of the carrying amount of the investment in the lease in the balance sheet, it is more difficult to predict earnings from the information disclosed in the financial statements.

There is a great difference between the United States, where application of the investment period principle is not allowed under FAS 13, except in the case of leveraged leases, and the United Kingdom where, under Statement of Standard Accounting Practice (SSAP) 21, it is compulsory for all leases. IAS 17 only allows the actuarial before tax method and, as can be seen from the figures above, if this method is used universally there will be significant distortions particularly for deals in which the tax benefits are substantial.

Other problem areas

Not all leases are as straightforward as the example set out in Exhibit 12.1. In addition to the general principle of income allocations, common problems which can arise include the following:

- front loading of income;
- recognition of residual values; or
- accounting for permanent tax benefits.

These have all come under close scrutiny recently, particularly in the United Kingdom, following the collapse of some major leasing companies.

Front loading of income

There are two common reasons for lessors recognising part of the income from a leasing arrangement at the start of the agreement rather than allocating it all over the lease period as described in the earlier sections of this chapter. These are: either to match initial direct costs; or, the recognition of a sales or manufacturing profit in the case of a lessee that is also a manufacturer or dealer of the asset concerned.

Initial direct costs

It is generally accepted that initial direct costs incurred in obtaining new business may be deferred over the life of a lease. This is recognised in the United States by FAS I3, which requires initial direct costs to be deferred, and in the United Kingdom by SSAP 21, which permits initial direct costs to be deferred.

These initial direct costs may be deferred and spread over the lease period typically by being amortised on a profile that corresponds to that used for income recognition or more usually, and as is mandatory in the United States, the costs are written off immediately to the profit and loss account and an equal amount of income is recognised upfront to match the costs.

The problems arise in determining what costs should be deferred. FAS 13 defines the costs as: 'Those incidental direct costs incurred by the lessor in negotiating and consummating leasing transactions, eg commissions and legal fees'.

SSAP 21 also allows costs of credit investigations and costs of preparing and processing lease documents to be included. However, the recently introduced statement of recommended practice in the UK has moved the treatment of initial direct costs in line with US accounting.

Initial selling profit

When a manufacturer or dealer offers leases to its customers, it is generally accepted that a sales or manufacturing profit can be recognised. It is also generally accepted that this treatment is only appropriate where the lease is classified as a finance lease. These leases are often referred to as sales type leases.

In the United States, the selling profit, which can be recognised in this way, is the addition of the present value of the future rentals and the residual value less the asset cost. Under the UK standard, the selling profit is restricted to the excess of the fair value of the asset over its cost, that is, the selling profit the manufacturer or dealer would make under a normal sale. Similar to the US method, the selling profit should be further restricted to an amount that will enable the finance charges under the lease to be based on the rate which the lessor would normally expect to charge a lessee.

Recognition of residual values

A residual value that is guaranteed by the lessee or some other party is normally treated, for accounting purposes, in the same way as a rental. For finance leases, any unguaranteed residual value is, by definition, likely to be small otherwise the lease would normally be classified as an operating lease. The question therefore arises whether to:

- only recognise the unguaranteed residual amount when earned, recognising the uncertainty relating to the amount that will be realised; or
- include it in the calculation of the gross earnings to be allocated to accounting periods.

The first approach is more conservative but may give rise to unacceptably low profits in the early years of a lease since in the pricing of the lease the lessor may have taken the residual value into account. The question becomes more critical in a sales type lease where the recognition of an unguaranteed residual value can increase the initial selling profit.

There have been instances of a proportion of residual values, for example, its present value, being recognised at the inception of the lease. This is not generally considered acceptable unless the lease is a sales type lease and it is then subject to the same restrictions as any other initial selling profit.

Clearly any unguaranteed residual value recognised at the inception of the lease has to be determined in a prudent manner and should be regularly reviewed and revised downwards if necessary. It is not generally considered acceptable to revise an estimated residual value upwards to a level above that assumed at the inception.

An issue that arises is the treatment of any reduction in the expected residual value. The options are either to charge the full reduction to the profit and loss account as soon as such a reduction is anticipated, or to spread the reduction over the remaining life of the lease.

The second option would not be appropriate if this leaves an insufficient margin in future periods or even a loss. Therefore, in practice, the first option is likely to be the most appropriate.

Another issue relevant to residual values is the question of whether inflation should be anticipated in determining the figure for accounting purposes. Accounting standards, such as in the United Kingdom, attempt to prohibit the inclusion of inflation. The UK standard SSAP 12 requires residual values to be based on prices prevailing at the date of acquisition of the asset. However, in pricing an operating lease to be competitive, a lessor will use a figure for the residual value which is actually expected to be received, not some notional figure excluding inflation. If a different figure is then used for accounting, the accounts could misleadingly suggest that the lease is not as profitable as it is actually expected to be. Accordingly, in the United Kingdom, operating lessors generally take account of inflation and argue that they are complying with the SSAP 12 since the residual value is based on prices prevailing at the date of acquisition albeit adjusted for inflation.

Accounting for permanent tax benefits

The section on tax implications at the start of this chapter dealt with the case where the tax benefits derived from a lease represented a timing difference rather than a permanent benefit. However, there are examples of permanent benefits such as:

- the receipt of tax-free income, such as a tax-free grant or tax-free capital gain;
- a tax allowance or credit that exceeds its accounting cost; or
- tax timing differences combined with varying tax rates.

Exhibit 12.11

Impact of tax-free grants

	Actual transaction		Adjusted presentation	
	(US$)	(US$)	(US$)	(US$)
Rentals receivable		750		750
Asset cost	1,000		1,000	
Less: grant	(200)		(400)	
Net cost		800		600
(Loss)/profit before tax		(50)		150
Tax		125		125
Notional tax charge		–		(200)
Profit after tax		75		75

The first case used to be fairly common in the United Kingdom when tax-free regional development grants werc available and, more recently, various leases have been written involving tax-free capital gains. The last case arose in the United Kingdom following various tax changes in 1984. The example in Exhibit 12.11 illustrates the first case.

The actual transaction gives rise to a loss before tax but a profit after tax and some consider that such a presentation leads to difficulties in interpreting the accounts. In the United Kingdom, it has therefore become fairly common in circumstances where a permanent tax benefit arises to gross up the profit to arrive at the profit before tax in similar manner to the calculation of profit before tax under the actuarial method after tax (see above section on the actuarial method after tax). The profit before tax is determined by multiplying the net earnings of US$75 by 100/50 (= US$150). This gives rise to a notional tax charge of US$200 which is also added to the grant to increase it from US$200 to US$400. Hence, one is effectively presenting the accounts as if a taxable grant of US$400 had been received instead of a tax-tree grant of US$200.

Until recently, grossing was specifically allowed under UK Standard SSAP 21 in the case of tax free grants. Similar principles were applied by UK lessors to the other cases of permanent tax benefits. However, the UK Accounting Standards Board (on advice of the UK Urgent Issues Task Force) decided to prohibit grossing from mid 1997 and SSAP 21 was amended accordingly. There are two different methodologies now adopted for the treatment of permanent tax effects; the first is to spread them over the lease period so that the lease has a constant, although abnormal tax charge. The second is to recognise them in the initial period and then move to a normal tax charge thereafter. Clearly the latter of these two methods is less prudent, although if the permanent tax benefit is certain, it is not generally considered unreasonable to recognise it at this stage.

Conclusion

Lessor accounting is now moving towards pre-tax methods and, although this does imply uniformity of accounting, it poses risks as the applicability of this treatment for tax-based structures is questionable. When reviewing or considering the accounting for an individual entity it is important to bear these factors in mind.

Chapter 13

Accounting – the capitalisation issue

Colin Dowsett

Introduction

The main objective of financial statements is to provide a fair presentation of assets and liabilities, income and expense. What is fair presentation is not always an easy matter to determine; not only are standards of fairness constantly evolving, but even the question of presentation is different across the international spectrum. Despite some convergence of international accounting standards in recent years, the way in which financial statements are compiled still varies widely from country to country. Following the collapse of Enron in the United States, international accounting practices have become the focus of much serious debate.

In the United Kingdom, published financial statements are required to give a 'true and fair view'. Accounting principles in the United Kingdom have developed against a framework of understanding that the view is that of an investor or financier who requires regular, objective reporting of financial affairs because they are not closely involved in the business.

By contrast, in much of continental Europe (take Germany, for instance), the fundamental but unspoken presumption is that the financier (whether a family, proprietor or banker) has a closer knowledge of the business so that the preparation of financial accounts is less about giving an objective view or 'fair presentation' and more to do with compliance with legal and taxation requirements.

Significant differences remain in accounting principles from one country to another. Indeed, accounting for leased assets, which was a watershed topic in many countries in establishing the acceptability of accounting for the substance of a transaction rather than its legal form, remains at the heart of the debate over the accuracy and validity of financial statements.

There are, however, some signs that accounting standards are converging. In 1994 the United Kingdom, United States, Canadian and Australian standard setters jointly published a conceptual study that examined the concepts of assets and liabilities in financial accounting. Those same standard setters produced, in 1996, a joint discussion paper on accounting for leases, 'Accounting for leases: a new approach'. A further discussion paper on the implementation of the new approach was issued in 2000.

The International Accounting Standards Committee has also been publishing International Accounting Standards (IAS) since 1975 and has recently concluded a period of revision of those standards, principally to reduce the extent of optional accounting treatments. Listed companies throughout the European Union will be required to prepare accounts according to IAS from 2005, so many of the current accounting differences will be eliminated, although whether the standards will be consistently applied is clearly not guaranteed. The US securities market is also moving in the direction of acceptance of accounts under IAS.

Historical survey

The method of accounting for leases most widely adopted historically, and still adopted by lessees in a number of countries, is to treat the lease in accordance with its legal form, that is, as an agreement for the hire of an asset. Thus, the lessee's financial statements simply reflect an operating expense equal to the rentals payable over an accounting period. In the lessor's financial statements, the equipment is reflected as a fixed asset employed in its business and depreciated or amortised over the period during which it is expected to generate income. Credit is taken for rental income equal to the amount payable over an accounting period.

These accounting policies reflect the view that the asset belongs to the lessor and that the lessee has only limited rights to its use for a period of time. However, many accountants believe that a distinction should be drawn between finance and operating leases. The principle issue in lease accounting is whether the difference in economic substance between legally similar agreements should be reflected in financial statements. This may be stated as two fundamental questions.

Should the financial statements of lessees reflect their rights over assets and corresponding financial obligations in finance leases? Because of the inclusion as a liability of the capital value of the total financial obligation under the lease, and a corresponding amount representing the asset, this procedure is usually described as lease capitalisation.

Should the financial statements of lessors that enter into finance leases recognise that such transactions are, in substance, of a financing nature and thus reflect in the timing of profit recognition the higher amount of finance provided during the earlier periods of the lease?

Since these two questions are both essentially concerned with the issue of whether it is legitimate in preparing financial statements to consider the commercial substance of lease transactions, rather than their legal form, those accountants who favour capitalisation of assets and liabilities of finance leases in the accounts of lessees are also likely to support the recognition of profit in the accounts of lessors on a basis which reflects the financing nature of the transaction.

There is considerable divergence of views on the question of lease capitalisation. In some countries it is widely accepted that finance leases should be accounted for in the financial statements both of lessees and of lessors in accordance with their commercial substance; in other countries, the legal form is rigidly adhered to, although the number of such countries has reduced over recent years.

Exhibit 13.1 summarises the general position at December 2001 taken in a selection of countries.

Most English speaking countries have adopted the commercial substance approach, while many countries in the non-English speaking world prefer the legal form. However, as mentioned before, IAS will shortly require nearly all countries to follow this approach.

In general terms, the commercial substance countries are those with common law legal systems whilst the legal form countries tend to be those where the legal systems are more prescriptive. In the latter legal systems, the calculation of taxation liabilities is generally based directly upon the financial statements. In common law jurisdictions the tax calculation is

Exhibit 13.1

Lease accounting approaches in selected countries as of December 2001

| Commercial substance countries | | |
Lessor and lessee	Lessor only	Legal form countries
Australia	Austria	Denmark
Belgium	Germany	Finland
Canada	Luxembourg	France
Hong Kong		Italy
Ireland		
Japan		
New Zealand		
Norway		
The Netherlands		
Portugal		
Sweden		
Spain		
Switzerland		
United Kingdom		
United States		

based on prescribed rules, thereby allowing a distinction to be made between accounting and taxation transactions.

Arguments for and against capitalisation

Even though the debate may be moving on to the capitalisation of all leases, it is useful to understand the arguments for and against the capitalisation of finance leases. These are best appreciated by setting out the views of each side of the debate on the principal issues concerned.

What is the nature of the lessees' undertakings

Under a finance lease, a lessee undertakes to pay rentals to the lessor. Opponents of lease capitalisation liken this obligation to the commitment which arises under other long-term contracts. For example, it is generally agreed that contracts for the supply of materials should be accounted for by accruing only for amounts that become due under the contract. These would typically be amounts relating to materials received together with, perhaps, a penalty for failing to take an agreed minimum amount. Any amount relating to future periods might be disclosed by way of a footnote, but would not be recognised in the balance sheet. Similarly, expenditure under leases, it is argued, should be recognised in the accounts only as it accrues under the lease.

Opponents further suggest that, in some important legal respects, leasing obligations differ from other obligations generally recognised as liabilities, for example, in the amount outstanding on a loan. In the event of default on a loan, a creditor can usually sue for the full amount owing. In the event of default on a lease, the lessor can generally only sue for the loss he has been caused directly by the default. The lessor is also under an obligation to minimise his loss, for example, by seeking to negotiate a new lease with an alternative lessee.

248

Opponents of capitalisation suggest that these legal differences show that leasing obligations are different from other liabilities and should be excluded from financial statements.

Proponents of capitalisation, on the other hand, emphasise that under a finance lease, the lessee has incurred an obligation which he must repay out of future cash flow. Such obligations must be included in the balance sheet for the true level of financial commitments to be disclosed. They distinguish leases from such long-term contracts under which materials may be supplied by pointing out that under a finance lease, the lessor has typically fulfilled substantially all of its obligation in providing the asset for use by the lessee. It is argued that under other long-term contracts the supplier offers distinct goods and services throughout the period of the contract.

In the view of those who support capitalisation, the legal differences should not preclude recognition of the asset and the liability. This view is supported by the fact that financial statements are normally prepared on a going-concern basis, that is, the business is presumed to carry on without significant curtailment of its operations and be able to honour its debts as they fall due, except in the unusual circumstances where there are clear indications to the contrary. Hence, it should normally be presumed that the lessee will derive the benefit of the asset and honour his obligation on amounts falling due under finance leases.

Even if the legal arguments are relevant, proponents of capitalisation urge that they overemphasise differences between the position of a secured lender and that of a lessor. In many circumstances, in the event of a default, each will have rights to the asset whose acquisition was the object of the agreement between the lessor or lender and the defaulter, and each will have to seek legal redress for the balance of the amounts due.

Do lessees acquire assets under finance leases?

A fundamental characteristic of a lease is that legal title to the asset remains with the lessor, although rights to the use of the asset rest with the lessee. Opponents of capitalisation of finance leases consider that it is seriously misleading for financial statements to include assets to which the entity does not have legal title. They stress that legal title has important consequences; for example, the entity can pledge assets which it owns as security for borrowings or sell them whenever it is advantageous to do so.

Those who would capitalise assets held under finance leases point out that under such leases, in economic terms, a lessee is in a position similar to that in which he would be if he owned the asset outright. The lessee usually has the right to unrestricted use of the asset for all, or substantially all, of its useful life and it is the lessee that bears the risks of its failure to perform satisfactorily, or of its being unable to be put to profitable use. It is also the lessee that will usually benefit from any residual value and, conversely, assumes the risk of any fall in the market leading to an unexpectedly low residual value. It is therefore suggested that the asset should be reflected in the balance sheet of the lessee since its omission would understate the assets employed in the business.

Such treatment would not, in the opinion of those who support capitalisation, be precluded by the absence of legal title. The lessee has acquired economic ownership of the asset and this should be recognised in the financial statements, whatever view is taken of the legal ownership of the asset.

There are certain classes of lease under which title does at some point pass to the lessee, either upon the fulfilment of certain conditions, or by the lessee exercising a bargain purchase option. Some accountants, who believe that legal title to the asset is a fundamental issue, would favour capitalisation of these lease arrangements although they oppose capitalisation in all other cases.

The question of comparability

Proponents of lease capitalisation stress that the position of an enterprise which acquires the use of an asset by means of a finance lease may, in economic terms, be almost identical to that of another which acquires the asset by means of secured borrowings. As one of the principal uses of financial statements is to compare the performance of businesses, it is preferable for the transactions to be accounted for similarly in the two cases.

Those who are against the capitalisation of leases would not agree that this point is of sufficient force to overcome their objections.

Pragmatic arguments

Some of the arguments put forward against capitalisation of finance leases have been based on the possible economic consequences. Most companies' borrowings are constrained either under their constitution or, more commonly, by the existing quantum of borrowed money or by the terms on which they have borrowed money in the past. Typically, the restriction takes the form of a limit on the ratio of borrowings to shareholders' funds. Such clauses were in many cases drafted before lease finance became common and lease capitalisation generally accepted. In such circumstances, it may be unclear whether lease obligations should be included in borrowing. Opponents of capitalisation have argued that leasing obligations are more likely to have to be included in borrowings if they are required to be reflected in the accounts. Thus, if lessees were required to capitalise leases they might, for that reason alone, breach the restrictions.

However, experience seems to indicate that breaches of borrowing power will, in most cases, be occasioned by the act of entering into the finance leases rather than by adopting any particular method of accounting for them. Indeed, it could be argued that since finance leasing is in effect secured lending, it is important that the finance lease liabilities of an enterprise are considered alongside the other liabilities of the organisation.

A further pragmatic argument against the capitalisation of leases is that the calculations may be complex and impose an unacceptable burden, particularly on smaller, less sophisticated businesses. Those who favour the capitalisation of finance leases consider that the costs involved are more than outweighed by the benefits. They also stress that, where leases are relatively immaterial, an acceptable approximation may be achieved by using simplified methods.

Capitalisation of finance leases has also been opposed on other pragmatic grounds. For example, it may lead to tax incentives (which in many countries are given to the purchaser of business assets) being diverted from a lessor to a lessee that is unable to take advantage of them. Lessees may also be deterred from entering into finance leases due to the increase in their reported borrowing.

This problem remains unresolved. It is no coincidence that those countries opposed to the capitalisation of leases in financial statements are generally those where the taxation system is based upon financial statements rather than a separate body of principles.

Can the problem be resolved by footnotes?

Most accountants, on both sides of the debate, would concede that there is a great deal of force in their opponents' viewpoint and thus support the giving of supplementary information by way of footnotes.

Although it is tempting to suppose that this suggestion offers the possibility of a compromise solution, there are several reasons why many accountants consider it unsatisfactory. First, income statements and balance sheets invariably have a far greater impact on the reader of the annual report than information given by way of footnotes. Whilst this may be true of the less sophisticated user, even financial professionals may be misled by extracts from the financial statements which may be quoted in the press or statistical services, or simply may not have time to study the footnotes or carry out the calculations to adjust the main financial statements as appropriate.

Secondly, notes to financial statements are properly used to provide additional information which cannot easily be given in the body of the financial statements. For example, details of the nature of contingent liabilities and analyses of the figures contained in the financial statements. It is generally agreed that no amount of additional disclosure in the notes is an excuse for failing to reflect economic reality in the financial statements themselves. Proponents suggest that it is necessary to take a view on the correct treatment and apply it in the main financial statements, rather than provide the user of the financial statements with supplementary information. This is considered to be tantamount to a confession that is not possible to determine the correct treatment.

One argument put forward for the capitalisation of operating leases is that although detailed disclosure is given in the notes to the accounts, for certain industries the figures are of such a large quantum that their exclusion from primary financial statements leads to a material deficiency in those statements.

Which leases should be capitalised?

Those who favour the capitalisation of some leases are faced with the problem of identifying cases where capitalisation is appropriate. Various criteria were suggested in the debate leading to the issue of Financial Accounting Standards Board Statement 13 (FAS 13). In summary, these were:

- leases under which legal title passes to the lessee;
- leases which pass a material equity in the asset to the lessee;
- leases of property that are special purpose to the lessee;
- leases under which the lessee pays costs incidental to ownership;
- leases under which the lessee assumes an unconditional liability for rentals;
- leases where capital elements of lease payments approximate to the value of the asset concerned; and
- long-term leases.

FAS 13 and its international successors are thus based on the concept that leases which transfer substantially all the risks and rewards of ownership to the lessee should be capitalised.

The FAS 13 criteria

FAS 13 requires that a lease be treated as a finance lease if it meets any one of the following four criteria:
ownership is transferred to the lessee by the end of the lease term;

- the lease contains a bargain purchase option;
- the term of the lease (including bargain renewal periods) is at least as long as 75 per cent of the economic life of the leased asset; or
- the present value of the minimum lease payments is equal to, or greater than, 90 per cent of the fair value of the leased property less any investment tax credit retained by the lessor.

However, the third and fourth FAS 13 criteria are qualified by the statement that they do not apply to leases which begin in the last quarter of the estimated useful life of the asset. This caveat is intended to avoid what some consider an anomaly which might otherwise arise when an asset is let on a succession of leases. For example, if an asset with a life of 25 years was let on five successive identical leases, each for a term of five years, all of the first four leases would extend for less than 75 per cent of the remaining useful life of the asset and may thus be classed as operating leases. The last lease, however, would extend for all of the asset's remaining life and, but for the qualification to the lease term criterion, would have to be classed as a finance lease.

The FAS and IAS 17 approaches compared

The complex characteristics of a finance lease contained in FAS 13 may be contrasted with the simple definition given in International Accounting Standards Board Standard 17 (IAS 17) entitled Leases and the UK standard laid out in the Statement of Standard Accounting Practice 21 (SSAP 21) Accounting for leases and hire purchase contracts. Both these define a finance lease as 'a lease that transfers substantially all of the risks and rewards of ownership to the lessee'. This is amplified by giving examples of circumstances that would usually suggest, or create, a rebuttable presumption that a lease is a finance lease.

There is a significant difference between the two approaches. The principal advantage of the FAS 13 approach is that it minimises any ambiguity and, hence, maximises the probability that similar leases will be accounted for similarly. The approach of IAS 17 gives considerable scope for judgement and thus different views can be taken on identical leases. However, a consistent treatment should be adopted within any one set of financial statements and in financial statements for various years for any particular entity. Moreover, differing treatments are capable of reconciliation with IAS 17 only in those cases where the correct classification of a lease is indeterminate.

It may be that lessees (which may have a strong incentive to avoid capitalisation where possible as it increases reported borrowing levels and reduces reported return on capital employed) will interpret FAS 13 and IAS 17 as permitting non-capitalisation of leases which convey to the lessee substantial risks and rewards of ownership. Heavy reliance is placed on the responsible exercise of judgement in marginal cases.

In the United Kingdom, the requirement to use judgement rather than rely upon a rigid set of rules has been further emphasised by the issue of Financial Reporting Standard 5 (FRS 5), entitled Reporting the substance of transactions. This applies the principle of substance over form to all transactions and not just leases. It does not amend lease accounting standard SSAP 21, but it states that the general principles contained in FRS 5 will be relevant in determining the substance of leases.

The disadvantage of the approach adopted by FAS 13 is that lessees which are eager to avoid capitalisation tend to seek to negotiate leases which fall just outside the definition of a finance lease while still, as far as possible, retaining the benefits of finance leases. Thus a rigid definition tends to give rise to a great deal of ingenuity in drafting lease agreements that have many of the features of finance leases and yet need not (indeed cannot under FAS 13) be reflected as such in the financial statements.

Since the accounting concept underlying all the standards is that under a finance lease substantially all of the risks and rewards of ownership are transferred to the lessee, borderline cases are inevitable. Since every lease transfers to some extent the risks and rewards of ownership, the point at which 'substantially all' is arrived at is inevitably a position of some debate.

Accounting for the substance of a transaction is, virtually by definition, open to attack on the grounds that the ground rules are more subjective than a legal form approach. That may be true, but it is not in itself a convincing argument since no matter how tightly defined a legal structure may be, there always seems to be an opportunity for debate.

Accounting for leases: a new approach

This first international discussion paper issued, 'Accounting for leases: a new approach', issued in July 1996, identified a number of problems with current lease accounting, such as the somewhat subjective or arbitrary distinction which has to be made at some point between finance and operating leases (see above) and the fact that this lack of certainty has been exploited by the industry in devising ingenious off-balance-sheet structures. The paper proposes, as a solution, that no more distinction is to be made between finance and operating leases but, in return, all leases are to be capitalised in the accounts of lessees. This was followed by more detailed proposals as to the implementation of such an approach in the second discussion paper issued in April 2000.

Particular issues still taxing the standard setters include the question of what are the minimum lease payments, especially when a lease has a large number of options in place? For example if a lease has to be renewed on an annual basis, what should be capitalised, just one year's rentals or the rentals in respect of the whole period of expected use?

The question of contingent or variable rentals also needs to be considered since the minimum required rental may be small but the actual anticipated rental far higher. Again which figure should be capitalised?

These are just some of the many problems that still have to be dealt with before any final standard can be agreed. The reality is that it is unlikely that any hard and fast rules will be put in place; what is likely to happen is that judgement will be required in a variety of areas and a number of bright line tests are likely to evolve. Bright line tests may involve matters such as minimum lease rentals, or determining a guaranteed residual value. The result of this is most likely to be a move from a position of whether or not a lease should be capitalised to one in which significant judgement is required as to the value at which such capitalisation occurs.

It is clear that the debate will continue for some time and the results are by no means certain.

The mechanics of capitalisation

The objective of lease capitalisation is to reflect in the financial statements the full capital value of the obligations arising under the lease and a corresponding amount representing the asset. To give effect to this:

- the financial statements recognise as a liability the obligation which the lessee has entered into to pay the rentals which is stated at the present value of the minimum lease payments;
- rental payments are not simply regarded as an operating expense; instead, they are accounted for partly as a repayment of the finance and partly as a payment of a finance charge; and
- the asset is initially recorded at the same value as the obligation, that is, the present value of the minimum lease payments. Like any fixed asset, depreciation is provided over its useful life. In the case of a leased asset, however, the useful life may be limited by the period of the lease (which for this purpose would be taken as including any bargain renewal periods).

The accounting entries

A lease with the same assumed terms as in Chapter 11 is used to illustrate the calculations involved. The assumptions are set out in Exhibit 13.2.

In this example the cost of the asset is known, and hence the interest rate implicit in the lease can be calculated. This is the rate at which the lease payments plus any unguaranteed residual accruing to the lessor (in this case nil since the lessee can retain the asset indefinitely without significant payment) are discounted to the cost of the asset. In this case, the rate is 3.9 per cent per annum. The discounting of the lease payments is explained in Chapter 11 (see Exhibit 11.2) and reproduced in Exhibit 13.3.

The liability will be recorded at US$1,000. The total finance charge over the period of the lease is US$80 (that is, the difference between the total rentals payable and their present value). This is recognised over the period of the lease at the constant rate of 3.9 per cent per annum. The movement on the outstanding obligation over the period of the lease is shown in Exhibit 13.4.

The asset will be depreciated over its useful life of five years, since due to the availability of the secondary period, the lessee is assured of continued use of the asset for the full life. If a straight line method is used, annual depreciation of US$200 will be provided. The resulting effects on the lessee's financial statements are shown in Exhibit 13.5.

Exhibit 13.2

Lease assumptions

Asset cost	US$1,000
Acquisition date	31 December 2003
Primary lease terms	Three annual rentals in arrears of US$360 each
Secondary lease terms	Indefinite period at a peppercorn
Useful life of asset	Five years
Lessee year end	31 December 2004
Lessee's bank borrowing rate	5% per annum

Exhibit 13.3

Discounting rentals

Payment date	Rental payments (US$)	Discount factor (3.9% pa)	Present value (US$)
31 December 1998	360	0.962	346
31 December 1999	360	0.926	333
31 December 2000	360	0.891	321
Total	**1,080**		**1,000**
			(= asset cost)

Exhibit 13.4

Movements in outstanding obligation

	Year ending		
	31 December 2004 (US$)	31 December 2005 (US$)	31 December 2006 (US$)
Balance outstanding at beginning (and during) year	1,000	679	346
Finance charge (at 3.9% pa)	39	27	14
Payment	(360)	(360)	(360)
Balance outstanding at end of year	679	346	–

Exhibit 13.5

Effects on financial statements reflecting capitalisation

Balance sheets as at	Leased asset at net book value (US$)	Lease obligation (US$)	Effect on net assets (US$)
31 December 2003	1,000	(1,000)	–
31 December 2004	800	(679)	+121
31 December 2005	600	(346)	+254
31 December 2006	400	–	+400
31 December 2007	200	–	+200
31 December 2008	–	–	–

Profit and loss accounts year ending	Depreciation (US$)	Finance charge (US$)	Rental (US$)	Effect on Profit (US$)
31 December 2004	200	39	360	+121
31 December 2005	200	27	360	+133
31 December 2006	200	14	360	+146
31 December 2007	200	–	–	-200
31 December 2008	200	–	–	-200
Total	**1,000**	**80**	**1,080**	**–**

The total expenditure under the lease of US$1,080 is spread over the full period of the asset's life. The element of the payments that reflects the lessor's charge for financing the asset, however, is restricted to the period in which the lessee has outstanding rental obligations, that is, the first three years. During this period, the finance charge declines in proportion to the amount outstanding with the result that the charge to the profit and loss account is higher earlier in the lease and declines as the amount of financing obtained reduces. However, the depreciation, being spread over five years, has the effect of reducing the total charge against profits in each of the first three years of the lease, an effect which is reversed in the final two years.

Deferred taxation

In the United Kingdom, from the point of view of the lessee, the taxation of finance leases generally follows the accounting treatment. However, as discussed in the individual country profiles in Chapter 10, this may not be the case for all countries. Often the rentals accrued or paid in each accounting period are deducted from taxable profits and hence deductions from profit for finance charges and depreciation must be disallowed for tax purposes.

The timing differences relating to the lease (assuming a constant rate of tax of 50 per cent) would in these circumstances be calculated as shown in Exhibit 13.6.

Exhibit 13.7 shows how the figures would be presented in the financial statements. For clarity, it has been assumed that the company earns profits before depreciation and finance charges of US$1,000 in each year and that tax is payable in the year following that in which the profits arise.

Alternative methods of apportioning finance charges

The method of apportioning the finance charge illustrated in Exhibits 13.4 and 13.5 is known as the actuarial method. Although this method gives mathematically precise results, it suffers from the drawback that it is relatively difficult to calculate and, particularly where a large number of leases, each calling for many payments, is concerned, the process can become very tedious especially for those do not have access to sophisticated calculators or computers.

An alternative, simpler method is the sum of the digits method. Under this method, the finance charge relating to each accounting period is deemed to be a certain amount less than that relating to the immediately preceding period. The amount of the decrease between each period is the same as the amount allocated to the final period.

Thus, for a three-year lease, the proportion of the finance charge allocated to each year is:

Year	Digits	Fraction
1	3	3/6
2	2	2/6
3	1	1/6
Total	**6**	**1**

The method is known as the sum of the digits because the denominator of the fraction is found by summing the digits of the number of accounting periods (that is, $3 + 2 + 1 = 6$). (It is alternatively known as the Rule of 78, the 78 referring to the denominator used when the calcula-

Exhibit 13.6

Tax timing differences

Year ending	Expenditure charged in financial statements (US$)	Expenditure allowed for tax purposes (US$)	Timing differences originating/ (reversing) in year (US$)	Tax thereon (50%) (US$)
31 December 2004	239	360	121	61
31 December 2005	227	360	133	66
31 December 2006	214	360	146	73
31 December 2007	200	–	(200)	(100)
31 December 2008	200	–	(200)	(100)
Total	**1,200**	**1,080**	–	–

Exhibit 13.7

Financial statements reflecting deferred taxation

	31 December 2004 (US$)	31 December 2005 (US$)	31 December 2006 (US$)
Profit and loss accounts			
Profit before depreciation and finance charge	1,000	1,000	1,000
Depreciation	(200)	(200)	(200)
Finance charge	(39)	(27)	(14)
Profit before tax	761	773	786
Taxation: current tax charge			
(US$1,000 - US$360 @ 50%)	320	320	320
Deferred tax charge	61	66	73
	381	386	393
Profit after tax	380	387	393
Retained brought forward	–	380	767
Retained profit carried forward	380	767	1,160
Balance sheets			
Leased asset cost	1,000	1,000	1,000
Depreciation	(200)	(400)	(600)
	800	600	400
Obligation under finance lease	(679)	(346)	
Tax payable	(320)	(320)	(320)
Deferred taxation	(61)	(127)	(200)
Overdraft (representing cumulative rental and tax payments)	(360)	(1,040)	(1,720)
Other net assets	1,000	2,000	3,000
Net assets	380	767	1,160

tion is performed for the 12 monthly accounting periods comprising a year.) Thus, in our example where the total finance charge over the period of the lease is US$200, the finance charge recognised in each period would be calculated as shown in Exhibit 13.8, which also compares the result produced by the actuarial method (Exhibits 13.4 and 13.5).

In this example, the sum of the digits method produces results that correspond closely with the results of the actuarial method. However, this will not always be the case. It can only be assumed that the sum of the digits method will give a reasonable approximation to the actuarial method if the amount of the finance charge is small compared to the capital amount, that is, the lease term is relatively short and/or the rate of interest is low and payments are of a constant amount at fixed intervals. If this is not the case, then the sum of digits method can result in significantly distorted results.

For example, a lease that requires yearly payments in arrears of US$1,000 over an eight-year period with finance charges of 16 per cent per annum will give rise to a total finance charge of US$3,657 on a capital amount of US$4,343. The finance charge would be allocated under the actuarial and sum of the digits method, as shown in Exhibit 13.9.

A reasonable approximation is achieved only in the years around the middle of the lease term. The sum of the digits method significantly overstates expenditure in earlier years and understates it in later years.

Exhibit 13.8
Sum of the digits method

Year ending	Fraction	Finance charge (US$)	Actuarial method (US$)
31 December 2004	3/6	40	39
31 December 2005	2/6	27	27
31 December 2006	1/6	13	14
Total	1	80	80

Exhibit 13.9
Sum of the digits – eight-year lease

Year	Actuarial method (US$)	Sum of the digits method (US$)
1	695	813
2	646	711
3	590	609
4	524	308
5	448	406
6	359	305
7	257	203
8	138	102
Total	3,657	3,657

Another simplified method, known as the straight line method, is simply to apportion the finance charge evenly over the accounting period in question. The straight line method results in an allocation of finance charges quite different from that obtained under the actuarial method. In the case of the eight-year lease referred to above, it would allocate US$3,657/8, that is US$457, to each accounting period. It is, therefore, not a method which is widely applied. Nevertheless, it may be used in some cases where the finance charge in a lease is relatively insignificant to the financial statements in question.

Residual value treatments

The example is now modified to illustrate the treatments of residual value. Instead of an indefinite secondary period at a peppercorn rent, the lease is considered to terminate at the end of the third year, when the residual value of the asset as assessed at the outset (and which accrues to the benefit of the lessor) is estimated to be US$120.

Since the lessor retains a significant interest in the asset, classification of the lease is no longer clear cut. To clarify this, the present value of the payments due under the lease and the residual value must be compared. Using a sophisticated calculator or computer, the rate implicit in the lease is found to be 9.4 per cent per annum. This can be proved by performing the discounting calculations set out in Exhibit 13.10.

Since the present value of the lease payments (US$908) exceeds 90 per cent of the fair value of the asset (US$1,000), the lease will usually be classified as a finance lease. The obligation will initially be recorded at US$903, with a corresponding amount representing the asset.

The lessee's bank borrowing rate was assumed to be 5 per cent. Since this is less than the rate implicit in the lease, FAS 13 (but not IAS 17 or SSAP 21) would require the borrowing rate to be used both to determine the classification of the lease and for subsequent accounting. The discounting of rental payments is therefore as set out in Exhibit 13.11.

As US$980 clearly exceeds 90 per cent of the fair value of the asset, the lease again would be classified as a finance lease with an initial value of obligation and asset of US$980.

The lower the rate used to discount the lease payments, the more likely it is that the present value will exceed 90 per cent of the fair value and thus the lease will be classified as a finance lease. By prohibiting the use of an implicit rate higher than the borrowing rate, FAS 13 prevents a lessee avoiding capitalisation of a lease simply due to its unfavourable rate of interest.

Exhibit 13.10

Discounting calculation

	Date	Value (US$)	Factor (9.4% pa)	Present value (US$)
Rental payments	31 December 2004	360	0.914	329
	31 December 2005	360	0.836	301
	31 December 2006	360	0.767	<u>278</u>
Present value of rental				908
Residual value	31 December 2006	120	0.767	92
Cost of asset				1,000

Exhibit 13.11

FAS 13 present values

Date	Payment (US$)	Discount factor (5% pa)	Present value (US$)
31 December 2004	360	0.952	342
31 December 2005	360	0.907	327
31 December 2006	360	0.864	311
Total	**1,080**		**980**

Exhibit 13.12

Accounting entries reflecting residual values (year ending 31 December)

	Implicit rate 9.4% pa – IAS 17			Borrowing rate 5% pa – FAS 13		
	2004 (US$)	2005 (US$)	2006 (US$)	2004 (US$)	2005 (US$)	2006 (US$)
Movement on obligation						
Obligation outstanding at beginning of and during year	908	632	330	980	669	342
Finance charge (9.4%/5%)	84	58	30	49	33	18
Payment	(360)	(360)	(360)	(360)	(360)	(360)
Obligation outstanding at end of year	632	330	–	669	342	–
Leased asset						
Initial value	908	908	908	980	980	980
Accumulated depreciation brought forward	–	302	605	–	326	653
Depreciation charge for year	302	303	303	326	327	327
Accumulated depreciation carried forward	302	605	908	326	653	980
Net book value	606	303	–	654	327	–

Exhibit 13.13

Profit and loss account figures reflecting residual values

	Implicit rate 9.4% pa – IAS 17			Borrowing rate 5% pa – FAS 13		
Year ending	Finance charge (US$)	Depreciation (US$)	Total charge (US$)	Finance charge (US$)	Depreciation (US$)	Total charge (US$)
31 December 2004	84	302	386	49	326	375
31 December 2005	58	303	361	33	327	360
31 December 2006	30	303	333	18	327	345
Total	**172**	**908**	**1,080**	**100**	**980**	**1,200**

Conversely, where there are significant tax benefits such that the implicit rate is significantly less than the borrowing rate, the use of the borrowing rate can incorrectly result in a lease being classified as an operating lease. For example, using the example set out in Exhibit 13.2 for which there is no residual value, the lessor would not be assuming any asset risk, that is, the lease is clearly a finance lease. However, if the lessee's borrowing rate was 12 per cent per annum, present valuing the rentals (of US$360 annually in arrears) at this rate would give a figure of US$857, that is, 86 per cent of the fair value.

In the United Kingdom, the benefit of tax deferment and competition in the leasing industry have hitherto ensured that leasing rates are lower than lending rates so that the UK standard, for the above reason, precludes the use of a commercial lending rate as the discount factor.

The values to be reflected in the accounts for the above example are shown in Exhibits 13.12 and 13.13.

The use of the lower rate (the borrowing rate), because it reduces the amount of the lease payments regarded as being in respect of finance charges, increases the amount treated as being in respect of the cost of the asset. As finance charges are allocated, so as to be greater in the earlier periods of the lease whereas depreciation may be constant throughout, this tends to reduce the amount of front loading in the recognition of the total expense over the period of the lease.

As the depreciation life is reduced from five to three years in this example there is a marked increase in the expense over the primary lease term. If the depreciation period is the same as the lease term, capitalisation will always result in a greater charge against income earlier in the lease and a smaller charge later except when, unusually, the straight line method for allocating the finance charge is acceptable.

Variation clauses

The profitability of a lease to a lessor may be affected by changes in the costs relating to the lease, principally interest expense and taxation. Variation clauses for interest rates generally provide that the rentals will be adjusted in line with changes in a given base rate applied to the lessor's investment in a lease.

Lessees generally account for such leases as for any other lease and simply treat any difference between the rental actually payable for a period and that assumed in the initial calculations of the amounts relating to the lease as a variation in the finance charge for that period. This does not always give the theoretically correct result; that is, the finance charge remaining in proportion to the decreasing obligation. However, in all but the most extreme cases, the consequent distortion is minimal and the cost of eliminating it could hardly be justified, especially as interest rates are likely to change several times over the period of the lease.

Tax variations are generally more significant and less frequent, requiring a recalculation of the accounting figures.

Conclusion

The debate over whether leased assets and obligations should be capitalised in lessees' financial statements, and over international accounting standards in general, had been diminishing following the introduction of IAS 17 and its stipulation that assets leased under certain leases, that is, finance leases, should be included in the balance sheet of lessees. Although the two international discussion papers issued in 1996 and 2000 have sought to include all leases in the balance sheet of lessees, the issue is still far from resolved.

Although it now appears certain that a move towards the capitalisation of all leases will occur, there are still a large number of issues that need to be settled before the any new accounting standard in this area can be finalised. For this reason, the issuance and implementation of such a standard is still some way in the future. The issue therefore remains both relevant and very topical.

Chapter 14

Financing of leasing companies and related operational and security issues

Nicholas Sanderson

Introduction

In previous editions of *Leasing and Asset Finance*, the chapter on the financing of leasing companies was largely descriptive with limited analysis. However, developments since the last edition demand that this chapter start with the analysis, followed by a description of the market, regulatory and tax environment. The changes since 1997 are twofold: first, significant developments in the products offered by leasing companies to customers, particularly those relating to non-finance lease products; and second, the onward march of the capital markets and securitisation as a financing method. The two principal trends chronicled in this chapter are the business of a finance leasing company becoming disaggregated into separately identifiable risks borne by a number of companies, and the provision of equipment to customers being packaged so that customers bear less of the risks of ownership and use of the equipment. These trends already have, and will increasingly have, a profound effect on the nature and function of leasing companies themselves.

In this chapter, the initial analysis is of the nature of the lease contract in order to identify ways in which leasing risks are shared between lessors and customers. The second part of the analysis describes the ways in which leasing companies might operate and, in particular, trends in financing leasing companies that will lead, in due course, to leasing companies becoming disaggregated from their market as the different functions traditionally performed by them are performed by a number of distinct entities. The third part of this chapter deals with the practicalities of providing finance to a leasing company, including the requirements for the taking of security.

Nomenclature

For clarity, certain terms will be used with restricted meanings in the rest of this chapter. This is because, for example, a leasing company may be both a lessor to its customer and lessee from its funder.

Lessor is used to mean the provider of equipment to a customer. Lessors may themselves lease equipment from another party, but this chapter is about the way in which lessors finance the equipment they provide to their customers. So, the person providing finance to the lessor is always described as a 'funder', even though it may itself be a lessor.

Customer is used to mean the end user of the equipment. The customer may rent out the equipment, for instance a car rental company would be a customer, but the person hiring the vehicle would not be referred to as a customer. The customer will wish to use equipment for a business that, other than in the case of daily rental or short-term hire, does not involve supplying the equipment to another person on hire.

Funder is used to describe any person who provides a lessor with the ability to supply equipment to a customer. The funder may provide a loan of money to the lessor, or it may provide the equipment on lease for the lessor to sublease to the customer. The different ways in which a funder provides either money or equipment to a lessor are explored in greater detail later in this chapter.

Equipment in the context of this chapter is assumed to be any type of physical asset where possession and use can be transferred. One of the major trends over the past few years has been for intellectual or incorporeal, rather than physical, property to become more important as a means of production. Although the financing of intellectual property rights is outside the scope of this book, it must be recognised that, increasingly, much of the value of physical equipment is in the intellectual property that it contains. Computer systems are a classic example since the hardware is useless without the associated software. Another, more exotic, example is genetically modified sheep which combine the function of plant, in that they produce the raw material for the pharmaceutical industry and also embody in themselves significant intellectual property.

Lease is used In this chapter to mean an agreement whereby the lessee (probably a customer, although possibly a lessor) is enabled to enjoy the use of some equipment in exchange for a rent without acquiring or being entitled to acquire title to the equipment. One issue that needs to be noted, particularly in the context of leases of equipment that is then fixed to land, is that the lease needs to confer the right to possession or use of the equipment on the lessee as against the lessor. If the equipment becomes the property of the lessee, or of a third party who has not consented to the lessor providing the equipment to the lessee, then the lease ceases to be a contract of bailment and becomes, probably, some form of loan agreement.

A further necessary characteristic of a lease is that the lessee returns the lessor's equipment at the end of the lease. One example where this did not happen was a situation in which a pool of pallets was owned by a number of transport companies which, provided they received the same number of pallets back from their customers, were indifferent as to whether the pallets they received were their pallets or those belonging to another company. When the pool was found to contain fewer pallets than expected, the issue arose as to whether any company could look to any of the customers for their pallets. The answer was that they could not, since none of them expected to get their own pallets back and the agreements were not agreements for bailment.

The lease

As noted above, a lease is a form of bailment where the lessor provides an item of moveable equipment to a customer in exchange for a payment or series of payments, being rent. This part of the chapter explores the many variations on this simple theme since, as will become apparent later, the nature of the agreement between the lessor and the customer is key to the way in which a lessor can raise finance.

The lease will need to address a number of issues of which the following is a non-exhaustive list. It does, however, include most of the significant questions affecting the tax and accounting treatment of the transaction.

- How long is the lease to last? Will the term of the lease be for the whole of the economic life of the equipment or for a shorter period?

- At the end of the lease, is the equipment simply returned to the lessor or is it expected that the customer will either buy the equipment or arrange for it to be sold and enjoy the majority of the sales proceeds?
- How much rent is to be paid by the customer and, in particular, is the rent agreed to be paid sufficient for the lessor to recover the whole of its cost of providing the equipment? Alternatively, is the lessor relying upon the residual value of the equipment at the end of the lease in order to recoup part of its investment?
- Is the amount of rent payable variable and, if so, is the variation due to the use of the equipment, such as additional payments because the equipment has been used to a greater extent than anticipated (for example, excess mileage payments in the context of vehicle contract hire), or is the variation related to changes in the financial position of the lessor as a result, for instance, of changes in tax allowances or interest rates?
- Is the rent to be adjusted by reference to the performance of the equipment?
- Does the rent include payments other than for the use of the equipment, for example consumables, maintenance, or other services?
- Who is to take the risk of non-performance or non-availability of the equipment during the lease term and, allied to this question, who takes responsibility for insurance and/or maintenance of the equipment?
- Who has the right to modify the equipment and who is to pay for or benefit from those modifications?
- Is the provision of the equipment ancillary to some other arrangement between the lessor and customer? This might include, for example, either the use by the customer of the equipment to provide goods or services for the lessor (as in the case of some manufacturing equipment), or the provision of equipment to enable the lessor to sell products or provide services to the customer (as with the provision of a water dispenser or freezer cabinet by a seller of mineral water or ice cream manufacturer).

Typical classifications of leases

The typical classification of leases is between those leases where substantially all of the economic risk and benefit of ownership of the equipment is transferred from the lessor, to the lessee. This classification is used for accounting and, increasingly, for tax purposes.

Accounting standard setters have recognised, however, that the division of leases into only two categories, 'operating' and 'finance', or 'true' and 'capital', is inadequate and does not reflect the variety of risk and benefit sharing that lessors and customers have adopted, both for their own commercial purposes as well as to achieve a particular tax or accounting treatment. In a discussion paper issued in the autumn of 2000, they suggested a far more sophisticated treatment where individual risk and benefit components of a leasing transaction would be valued and reflected as a liability or an asset on the balance sheet of both lessor and customer. This approach, while logical, is potentially highly complex and was to be applied not only to equipment leases but also to real property lettings. Its introduction has therefore been delayed although reform of the current dichotomy between operating and finance leases is needed in order to reflect a more complex world than that existing when, for instance Statement of Standard Accounting Practice (SSAP) 21 was introduced in the United Kingdom in 1984.

This section summarises the terms of the more common types of agreement.

Finance or capital lease

This type of lease transfers substantially all of the economic benefit and risk of both owner-ship and use of the equipment to the customer, leaving the lessor with purely financial risks and benefits. The term of the lease will be for the anticipated economic life of the equipment and the customer will pay rent that will enable the lessor to recover the purchase price of the equipment together with its anticipated economic return. The term of the lease may, howev-er, be divided into two parts, the primary period during which the lessor recovers its invest-ment in the equipment and the secondary period which will extend for so long as the customer wishes to retain the equipment in economic use.

The customer will assume all risks of loss of, damage to, and performance by the equip-ment; and will obtain the appropriate insurance. The customer will indemnify the lessor against any claims arising in respect of the equipment and will agree to maintain the lessor's financial return from the transaction. The economic benefit of owning the equipment will be transferred to the lessee, either by the existence of a bargain purchase option by which the customer is entitled to acquire the equipment at the end of the term at a price significantly lower than its market value, or, in jurisdictions such as the United Kingdom where the tax treatment of a lease will be different if there is a bargain purchase option, by the customer having the right to sell the equipment on behalf of the lessor and to retain substantially all of the sales proceeds by way of a rebate of rental or sales commission.

The obligations of the customer in respect of the equipment are essentially those nor-mally owed by the grantor of security to a security holder rather than obligations owed to a person having an interest in the equipment, other than in the preservation of its value as secu-rity for a financial obligation. The lessor will only be concerned by a customer's wish to mod-ify the equipment to the extent that it affects its security value, rather than having a concern with its economic value.

Operating or true lease

The principal differences between an operating lease and a finance lease are that in the case of operating leases the risk of changes in the value of the equipment over the term of the lease is borne by the lessor and not the customer; and the lease is not for the entire-ty of the anticipated economic life of the equipment. At the end of the lease, the customer is obliged to return the equipment or to agree new terms for its continued use which are likely to reflect the current market value of the equipment and the availability and cost of substitute equipment. The lessor will make an estimate of the residual value of the equipment on expiry of the lease and will set the rent at a level where, assuming that the equipment is sold for the residual value, it will recover its investment in the equipment together with an economic return on its investment, including a premium for taking the residual value risk.

Operating leases have proved very popular in markets where there are opportunities for re-marketing more or less standardised types of equipment such as aircraft or motor vehicles. In addition, operating leasing has been a requirement for UK local authorities in order for them to avoid the cost of equipment being capitalised and the resulting trans-action being treated as a credit arrangement and, consequently subject to central govern-ment control.

Operating leasing has given rise to examples of significant shifts of real economic risks from customer to lessor, most notably in the case of motor vehicles and computer equipment where significant declines in prices have caused serious losses to operating lessors. These losses would have fallen on the customers but for their ability to return the equipment at the end of the fixed leasing term.

Hire purchase, lease purchase and conditional sale

The existence of an option for the customer to acquire title to the equipment at the end of the lease for a bargain price, a hire purchase or lease purchase, or for title to the equipment to pass upon payment of the last instalment of the purchase price, a conditional sale, are virtually indistinguishable economically and are treated as being the same as finance leases for accounting purposes.

A distinction must be drawn between circumstances where the purchase option or final purchase price payment is for a sum that is equal to the assumed market value of the equipment, or is a payment equal to market value at that time, and where the payment is set at a bargain rate so that there is no realistic possibility of the customer not paying it and acquiring the equipment, because upon payment he can then sell the equipment at market value and make a profit. It is possible to provide for any form of option from a simple pre-emption right for the customer to purchase at market value at the end of the lease to a bargain purchase, with any variant in between including a fixed price thought to reflect the anticipated residual value. It is possible to have an operating hire-purchase or lease-purchase agreement where the purchase option is high enough and reflects a significant proportion of the return to the lessor from the letting of the equipment.

Under UK tax law, the consequence of the existence of a purchase option is to deem the customer to be the owner of the equipment from the start of the lease if the rental payments under the lease are treated as including both capital and interest. If they only include interest, then the lessor of the equipment will remain the owner, which is the position under the general law.

Contract hire, service agreements and outsourcing

Increasingly, both commercial and governmental organisations are seeking to pay only for the use of equipment and to avoid all the risks of ownership. This trend started with motor vehicles, both cars and trucks, where the contract hire company provided a vehicle and maintained it throughout the term of the lease. These companies increasingly combined contract hire with fleet management where the lessor or an associate company provided a wide range of services from insurance, breakdown and recovery, maintenance and the initial procurement of the vehicles. They also financed the provision of the vehicle and took the residual value risk. The same approach was adopted in relation to computer installations where the customer had a concern about disputes between hardware and software suppliers and wished to have a bundled solution often including maintenance.

The next stage of development is the equipment service agreement where the customer only pays to the extent that the equipment is available for use in an agreed state of repair and cleanliness. This approach has been adopted notably by the train operating companies in the United Kingdom where, in procuring rolling stock, they have expected the manufacturer and financier jointly to provide an available train fleet fully maintained and cleaned each day with guarantees of performance throughout the term of the arrangement. The UK rolling stock market is suitable for this approach since the lease, which has a term matching that of the train operator's franchise agreement, is for a significantly shorter term than the economic life of the rolling stock.

The latest development has been that involving outsourcing of a part of the customer's business involving the use of equipment. Examples of this type of arrangement abound, from IT outsourcing by major government departments and local authorities to the transfer of non-core functions of the UK Ministry of Defence, for example, tank transportation and air-to-air refuelling of combat aircraft. A point is reached at which the service being provided extends beyond the provision of equipment and becomes the provision of a separate service in its own right for which equipment is required. At that stage the nature of the transaction ceases to be one of providing equipment under a lease since the equipment is never bailed to the customer but always used by the supplier of the service who, in turn, will need the use of the equipment and becomes the customer for the lessor.

Other funding methods

There are a number of methods for a customer to finance the use of equipment apart from those described above as a lease. The simplest method is by immediate purchase of the equipment by the customer with its own or borrowed funds. A variation is a credit sale involving the transfer of title to the equipment to the customer with the sale price left outstanding. In these cases the lessor may wish to secure its position by either retaining or acquiring title or a security interest in the equipment so as to put it in the same position economically as if it had ownership of, and had bailed, the equipment to the customer under a lease or a conditional sale. Even in this case, a customer can achieve the same economic effect as an equipment service agreement by entering into buy-back arrangements with a supplier or other party to insulate itself against changes in the value of the equipment, and outsourcing maintenance and cleaning so as to leave itself with ownership and the ability to use the equipment.

A customer may also hire equipment on a short-term and/or occasional basis as and when it needs such equipment. This is the way that contractors' plant or motor vehicles on daily rental or spot hire are provided. Ships and other assets are also hired for specific purposes, for example, ships on voyage charters or cranes hired for a specific construction project.

Exhibit 14.1 shows the usual division of risk and responsibility between the lessor (L) and the customer (C). Where both L and C appear then either lessor or customer could assume the risk without altering the nature of the transaction.

Exhibit 14.1

Usual division of risk and responsibility between the lessor and the customer

	Full payout	Residual value risk	Maintenance	Insurance	Title at end of lease
Finance	L	C	C	C	L
Operating	n/a	L	C	C	L
Lease/hire purchase, conditional sale	L	C	C	C	C
Contract hire	n/a	L	L/C	L/C	L
Out source	n/a	L	L	L	L

The lessor

Lessors are concerned to recover their investment in equipment together with a return from that investment and any income to be derived from the sale of ancillary services to the customer. The lessor has, at the same time, an interest in the preservation of the value of the equipment, either because the equipment forms the security for the customer's financial obligations or, in addition, because the lessor is taking the residual value risk and preservation of the equipment in a good state represents an opportunity for profit or the avoidance of loss on resale or reletting. The lessor needs to be confident that not only is the value of the equipment maintained, but that it can gain access to the equipment in the event of a default by the customer. Barriers to retaking possession of the equipment could arise either because the equipment is lost to the customer in some way, or because there is some other bar, whether physical or legal, on the lessor recovering possession of the equipment from the customer. Issues relating to security and title are considered later in the context of the ways finance is provided to the lessor by the funder.

The lessee

Historically, risks taken by the customer on the lessor were limited to the need to be sure that the lessor would be able to pay any rebate of rental resulting from a tax or interest rate adjustment or following the sale of the equipment under a sales agency. Customers were in a strong position generally because they had possession of the equipment and, certainly during the currency of the lease, were net debtors of the lessor. Customers could, however, find (as was the case with lessees from Atlantic Computers and some other computer lessors) that their rights to 'walk' or 'flex' were negated by the insolvency of the lessor. In those cases, the customer owed rent under a lease for a certain period, but the supplier and original lessor of the equipment had agreed that, at certain points in time, the customer could either terminate the lease without penalty, a 'walk' or upgrade and, in the context of the upgrade, hand back the existing equipment and the supplier would terminate the existing lease, a 'flex'. Following the insolvency of the supplier/original lessor, these rights became unenforceable by the lessee and it became a question of fact in each case as to whether the lessee remained liable to pay rent for the full terms of the lease.

The position with regard to credit risk has shifted further over the years as lessors provide more services to the customer and, given the number of lessors that have failed financially in the past 10 years, customers now pay far more attention to the creditworthiness of lessors. Leases, particularly those in equipment service agreements and outsourcing arrangements, purport to transfer risks from the customer to the lessor by providing that no payment is due if the equipment is not provided. However, customers need their trains, IT equipment, tank transporters and flight refuelling tankers and the fact that they may not have to pay for them is little comfort if they are unavailable or do not work. The risk for lessees is increased where lessors have external funding since funders are likely, as part of their security package, to take real security over the equipment that may rank ahead of the customer's contractual rights under the lease. In UK Private Finance Initiative (PFI) or Private Public Partnership (PPP) transactions customers, generally government departments or public bodies, have sought to secure their positions by having direct agreements with funders and lessors giving them rights to equipment on the failure of the lessor/project company.

Summary

The nature of leases has changed significantly over the past 10 years. In some cases, the provision of equipment is only part of the provision of a package of services, for instance in major outsourcing transactions. In other cases, transactions that would probably have been financing transactions 10 years ago are now structured so that the equipment is returned to the lessor and redelivered to the lessee on each and every day of the lease term.

These issues are important in deciding how lessors raise finance since no longer can they rely on a predetermined and certain cash flow from the lessee secured on the equipment. As the terms of leases have become more complex, so have funding methods for lessors.

Leasing companies

This section considers the functions discharged by leasing companies and the ways in which third parties are increasingly performing some of the roles leaving the leasing company as a co-ordinator of third-party suppliers.

The functions of a leasing company can be categorised as follows:

- origination;
- underwriting;
- financing;
- administration;
- enforcement;
- asset and residual value risk management; and
- provision of ancillary services.

In considering how leasing companies seek to outsource their various functions there will come a point at which it may be difficult to establish which function is essential to a leasing company. A company marketing and originating transactions may act like a broker, underwriting on the basis of the requirements of its funder. The funding may be provided by a special purpose company managed by the leasing company, but financed by the capital markets. The administration of transactions once established, and the enforcement of defaulted transactions, may be subcontracted to a specialist company. Asset management may be undertaken by the equipment manufacturer, the equipment supplier, a fleet manager or a specialist residual value insurer. Meanwhile, other services such as maintenance, software or consumables are often provided by companies other than the leasing company itself. This disaggregation of the functions of the traditional, and often bank-owned, finance company is the major development of the last few years and is set to continue.

Origination

Leasing companies have traditionally outsourced the origination of transactions, either in whole or in part, by using brokers or by making arrangements with suppliers of equipment. The ability to source business, particularly good quality business, is increasingly the key to the profitability of leasing companies. This is reflected in the large commissions paid to brokers and introducers and the heavy overheads borne by a traditional leasing company in branches, sales staff, and representatives. With larger-ticket transactions involving sophisticated or regulated lessees, lessors have found margins pared to the bone through competition and overcapacity in the market coupled with the heavy costs of bidding for transactions. The appropriate distribution method will vary depending on the market that the leasing company is addressing, varying from a quasi-investment-banking role to the receipt of proposals from a network of brokers or running a direct marketing operation. There is a continuum between the role of a leasing company in origination and marketing and that of a broker placing business with third party lessors. Some smaller leasing companies may broke larger deals or deals that are surplus to their handling capacity. At the larger end of the market, lessors will often syndicate deals for similar reasons.

An interesting development, particularly in consumer markets, is the stratification of a particular market depending upon the credit quality of the customer. This is perhaps most highly developed in the motor finance market where traditional motor finance companies look for prime credits, while a range of other companies service different grades of non-prime or sub-prime credits. A company that seeks to underwrite prime credits may also, and profitably, refer rejected proposals to companies specialising in non- or sub-prime lending, thus acting as both lessor and broker.

Underwriting

One of the core areas of expertise for leasing companies is deciding which potential lessees to accept and which to reject. Generally, within a single company, there has been little pricing according to credit risk; however, between companies, particularly in the context of prime and non-prime consumer finance, pricing for risk exists as a result of the differentiation of the type of business involved. Although lessors claim to price for risk, in reality, the choice is between accepting and rejecting the risk to fit the risk profile of the business.

While the underwriting function has been mechanised through credit scoring in smaller transactions, setting the credit criteria, establishing a factual basis for underwriting through credit checks and due diligence, and reviewing the credit risks against the structure and nature of the transaction are fundamental to the leasing business. Underwriting should not be about avoiding loss by rejecting all proposals, but about accepting a population of transactions that will have an acceptable overall loss rate given the pricing. Statistical analysis of rejected proposals is almost as important as an analysis of underwritten transactions. Ideally, a leasing company should experiment with underwriting criteria with small control groups of transactions to identify underwriting criteria that can be varied profitably.

With the development of capital markets based funding, leasing companies need to consider how their underwriting criteria will be viewed by rating agencies, particularly where their portfolio does not have a sufficient credit history to allow a proper evaluation of a particular performance. While funders have always had a concern with the business underwritten by a borrowing lessor, rating agencies will increasingly have views, based on the analysis of comparable portfolios, as to likely loss levels and the underwriting criteria acceptable for particular types of business.

Lessors may decide they cannot accurately predict the likely loss provision required in relation to their portfolios and will need to hedge this risk. There are a number of insurance and derivative products that can be used for this purpose. These range from relatively straightforward credit risk swaps, where the whole or part of the credit risk on a particular customer is transferred to a counterparty, to the provision of various types of credit risk insurance. These may range from a full credit risk policy on the portfolio, where the insurer takes the risk of customer default in exchange for premiums, to first loss or last loss policies where only a portion of the lessor's losses are met by the credit insurer. The advantage of credit insurance is that it provides both the lessor and the funder with external validation of the necessary loss provisioning, particularly for an unseasoned portfolio. The credit insurer is, in effect, making an assessment of the likely losses and setting its premium accordingly. The credit insurer will also wish to set the underwriting criteria for the lessor and will also need to have confidence in the ability of the lessor to administer the portfolio. A disadvantage of using credit insurers is that the policy, being one of insurance, is subject to an obligation of utmost good faith *(uberrimae fidei)* on the part of the lessor. The lessor must be extremely careful to make full disclosure of all material facts to credit insurers and ensure that, in administering its portfolios, it does nothing that could entitle a credit insurer to avoid paying, either in relation to a particular case or in relation to the portfolio as a whole.

Financing

Lessors need to put themselves into a position to provide equipment to their customers. Leasing companies have traditionally done this by using their own funds (equity) and borrowing money (debt) to enable them to purchase the equipment. Lessors do not, however, need to own equipment and in many cases do not do so, often leasing equipment from a funder so that the lease to the customer is a sublease. The lessor still provides the equipment and is the bailor of the equipment to its customer, even though it is not itself the owner of the equipment.

A lessor may procure a third-party owner or bailor to provide the equipment, for example, because it is acting as an agent of a special purpose company, or it may provide the equipment to a company that is not the end user of the equipment, for example, to a project company or an outsourcing company that wishes to use the equipment to provide services to the end user. Traditionally, lessors have also acted as undisclosed agents on behalf of funders, so that the lessee is unaware of the identity of the actual counterparty to the lease (the funder) and deals with the lessor as principal.

Lessors are concerned to minimise their cost of finance. Traditionally this has been achieved by the use of tax benefits, but this route is now much less prominent in the United Kingdom. The market is divided between those transactions, usually large ticket, where the financing cost is all important and the lessor is providing finance, and those transactions that are either insensitive to the cost of funding or where other factors predominate in dictating the overall cost to the customer of the right to use the equipment. Examples of such transactions include where non-prime consumer finance is concerned with percentage margins in the high teens or twenties, or where residual value assumptions have a dominant influence on the level of monthly rent payable by the customer. In the latter case, the correctness of such assumptions will determine the profitability or otherwise of the transaction for the lessor.

Administration and enforcement

Leasing companies traditionally maintained infrastructures to manage their portfolios. This involved accounting for payments, negotiating terminations, whether on expiry of a transaction or on default or voluntary termination prior to the end of the contract, and pursuing defaulters. In the larger-ticket market where rentals change with interest or tax rates, the administration of leasing portfolios involved continuing activity even in the absence of default or early termination.

The administration and monitoring of transactions provided the opportunity for leasing companies to establish a relationship with their customers and also to identify further opportunities for business. In the consumer- and small-ticket market, this process of identifying and generating new business opportunities from an existing client base is known as re-marketing and is a major source of profitable new business since introductory commissions do not, generally, need to be paid.

In many cases, the task of administration and enforcement is now outsourced, particularly where the funding for a portfolio is provided through the capital markets. Rating agencies and credit insurers are concerned that if an originator of a portfolio becomes insolvent that they have an alternative servicer available. A lessor may outsource a variety of functions, ranging from the employment of what is essentially a computer bureau running the appropriate software to administer the portfolio, to the complete delegation of the administration of its portfolio. However, the lessor needs to identify the risks of the failure of its servicer and have an appropriate backup in place. It also needs to identify the commercial opportunities that it may be losing or putting at risk by reason of the outsourcing; for example, the loss of opportunities to re-market or sell ancillary services or products. This is in addition to the regulatory concerns relating to data protection, consumer protection legislation and the possibility of a servicer damaging the lessor's reputation by its actions or omissions.

Many traditional leasing companies have excess administrative capacity and undertaking the servicing of other institutions' portfolios provides fee income without additional credit risk. It may also provide an opportunity for subsequent acquisition of the managed portfolio with which the servicer will have become familiar.

Asset and residual value management

Traditionally, lessors were providers of finance and asset management meant the economic disposal of repossessions. The growth of contract hire, operating leasing and other products where the residual value and other assets risks remain with the lessor, as opposed to the customer, has led to a need for lessors to undertake or outsource management of the assets provided to customers. In the United Kingdom, legislation to protect consumers enables consumers to hand assets back to lessors in certain circumstances when half the purchase price has been paid without bearing any further liability. This has forced lessors to consider asset values even where the purpose of the transaction is to provide finance and for the asset risk to be borne by the customer.

There have been a series of major failures by lessors to manage residual value risk over the past 10 years. These range from the computer industry where the progress of technology led to major declines in the price of hardware and a shortening of the replacement cycle, to recent declines in the price of motor vehicles in the United Kingdom causing losses to a wide range of lessors. In the latter case, losses ranged from companies providing contract hire where assumptions regarding residual values proved too optimistic to the losses suffered by consumer motor finance lenders that had vehicles returned to them in unexpectedly large numbers when the value fell below the minimum required to be paid by the consumer, as described in the previous paragraph. In other markets, such as those for aircraft, trains and ships, there have been and there remain significant uncertainties about residual values which are affected by economic and technical developments in ways that are difficult for a leasing company to predict.

Lessors can seek to mitigate their risks by transferring residual value risk to third parties. This has traditionally been the manufacturer or the supplier of the equipment that has used its willingness to assume residual value risk as a marketing tool. Captive finance companies in the computer, aircraft and automotive sectors have laid off asset risks with manufacturers. Customers increasingly want to see manufacturers forming part of consortia for the provision of equipment so as to underwrite life cycle costs and availability. This also gives manufacturers an incentive to build better quality assets in the knowledge that a requirement for maintenance will decrease their subsequent profits because of the demand for spares within the contract price. The inclusion of manufacturers as residual value underwriters is acceptable, but will increasingly give rise to difficulties for manufacturers in being allowed to recognise manufacturing profit if they retain risk in the asset over an extended period. The residual value risk also represents a significant incremental risk for manufacturers whose long-term interests traditionally have been in expanding the volume of sales, possibly at the expense of the price of existing equipment.

Clearly, residual value support from any third party, manufacturer or not, may destroy any possibility of the lessor assuming operating lease accounting treatment for the lease, although it may not impact the accounting treatment for the lessee.

A lessor can consider taking out residual value insurance if it cannot rely upon a manufacturer or supplier to assume residual value risk. The use of insurance to cover credit risks has been discussed above in relation to underwriting. Residual value risk insurance is quite common but requires the lessor to make a credit assessment of the residual value insurer on the assumption that there will be a significant call on the insurer because of a problem in the relevant market. The risk being underwritten is not simply that of the lessor's equipment, but probably that of similar equipment for other lessors. A collapse in that sector of the market could give rise to significant claims on the insurer. In addition, the lessor will need to ensure that the insurer cannot seek to avoid liability for material nondisclosure. The residual value insurer may have less incentive to help to manage the market for second hand equipment than a manufacturer of that equipment and, if the insurer is in financial difficulty, it may have an incentive to seek to avoid its liability under a residual value policy and have greater flexibility to do so than a manufacturer who is providing a buy-back guarantee rather than insurance.

Residual value risk management has become an integral part of lessors' businesses and many are taking steps to manage the risk actively. This involves pricing residual value risk correctly, which is not an easy task given the volatility of certain markets. As with underwriting credit risk, the skill is to ensure that sufficient risk, but not too much, is taken and, should the market for the equipment appear to be softening, that active steps are taken to manage the risk by seeking to extend leases or find innovative ways of re-marketing the equipment.

The converse of managing the residual value risk is arranging the procurement of equipment. For commodity items such as motor vehicles, the lessor is concerned both with the absolute level of the acquisition cost, since this will set the amount that needs to be financed, and with the difference between the acquisition cost and the residual value, since this establishes the amount that needs to be recovered from the customer during the term of the lease. Lessors, particularly those involved with taking residual value risk, are therefore becoming increasingly involved in the procurement process, whether by using their bulk buying power in the case of contract hire of vehicles, or forming joint ventures with manufacturers to bid for particular contracts, for example, in PFI and PPP transactions.

Provision of ancillary services

As noted above, lessors are increasingly providing additional services for their customers. The principal additional services related to the provision of finance and equipment are listed below.

- *Payment protection plans (PPP).* An insurance company agrees to make the payments due under the lease if the customer is ill or made redundant.
- *Gross asset protection (GAP).* An insurance company will meet the difference between the insurance value of the equipment (usually a motor vehicle) and the balance payable under the lease following a total loss by destruction or theft. The big-ticket equivalent of GAP insurance is the specification of a minimum agreed value for loss insurance of the equipment, the agreed value being sufficient to meet any termination sum due under the lease.
- *Warranty cover in respect of the equipment.* This can be sold equally well by the supplier since its existence reduces the risk of claims in respect of the quality of the equipment sold and provides another party against whom a claim can be made.
- *Maintenance.* This is increasingly important as part of the lessor's residual value management as well as part of fixing the cost of use of the equipment for the customer. The extent of the maintenance can be set at any level, from daily cleaning of a train or aircraft, to simply providing the annual service for a motor vehicle. In the case of complex equipment, for example, computer equipment or where maintenance is statutorily regulated and/or safety critical, it may be necessary for the manufacturer or some other authorised maintainer to carry out the maintenance. This may still be provided as part of a package with the lessor, either separately or as part of an overall procurement.
- *Breakdown and replacement equipment cover.* This cover is often combined with maintenance and the lessor's obligation to ensure that a minimum number of vehicles is available on a daily basis, as in the case of train service agreements.
- *Fleet management.* This combines a number of the above items including procurement and disposal of equipment, maintenance, breakdown and equipment replacement, together with insurance. Typically, fleet management is part of a package including contract hire or operating leasing, but the skills of lessors in arranging fleet management have resulted in the service being offered independently of the actual financing of the equipment. Fleet management may be the principal component of an outsourcing agreement and the lessor takes over the customer's existing fleet and replaces it with new equipment over time. Examples of this type of arrangement are the transactions between Virgin Trains and its train service providers where the latter, comprising the manufacturers of the new trains and a finance company, take over the existing rolling stock fleet and manage its availability until the new trains are ready to enter service.
- *Consumables and other services.* A typical example of this type of supply is tyres and other spares for vehicles, or items for sale in vending machines or items of office equipment. Virtually any service could be provided in conjunction with equipment, including crew to operate the equipment. At some point in this evolution, the principal supply made by the lessor ceases to be of the equipment and becomes a service that the lessee requires the equipment to perform.

Summary

Leasing companies, initially single entities providing principally finance to enable customers to procure and use equipment, are evolving into constellations of separate entities each providing part of the much more complex service demanded by customers. This evolution is being driven both by customers' demands and also by the need for lessors to generate greater profits than can be derived from simply providing finance. This need has, however, taken lessors into areas of business that they are not all well equipped to undertake, which has in turn led to their need to acquire additional skills, either organically or through joint ventures. The demands of customers, particularly in the bigger-ticket market, also require suppliers to provide finance as part of an overall package. The greater complexity both of the products offered by lessors, and of the lessors themselves, is reflected in a need on the part of funders to undertake a greater depth of analysis when providing finance to lessors. The rest of this chapter considers the implications for funders of the developments in the leasing market described above.

Funders

Funders may share some of the same characteristics as lessors, but will generally simply be concerned with earning a financial return. It is of course possible to have layers of lessors, sublessors, lessees and sublessees all taking the same or different risks in respect of particular equipment, but, for the purposes of this chapter, we will assume that there is one lessor and one or more funders whose interest is purely the earning of a financial return.

Types of funder

The original funders of leasing companies were banks that provided debt and took security over leasing companies' assets. When considering the terms of a financing transaction, we will consider the position of such a funder.

A variation on the bank funder is the head lessor that provides equipment generally on a finance lease, either purely as a method of financing or with the added benefit and cost advantage of providing tax benefits. These tax benefits can be either domestic or from a cross-border transaction.

The newest type of funding is from the capital markets which encompasses a composite arrangement comprising the actual funder, often a special purpose vehicle (SPV), the investment bank that arranges the issue of debt for the SPV to provide the finance and the rating agencies who, through their role as provider of ratings for the debt of the SPV, will dictate the financial and legal structure of the funding. There may be other parties involved including the provider of 'warehouse' funding to the lessor, to enable it to enter into transactions before refinancing them through the capital markets, and monoline insurers that provide financial guarantees to the holders of the SPV's debt in exchange for a premium. A more detailed description of a straightforward securitisation of lease receivables appears later in the chapter.

Funding from sources other than the capital markets may also appear in composite guise where, perhaps, one entity is able to obtain tax benefits from funding a transaction and can share those benefits with a lessor, but has no, or insufficient, appetite for the credit risk involved. In these cases, another party will need to be found to take the credit risk or the lessor itself may have to defease the transaction by providing acceptable security, generally in cash, to a third party. This third party is usually a bank which then guarantees the obligations to the funder.

Some funders are simply concerned to acquire assets for themselves and will purchase either individual transactions or blocks of transactions from lessors. These block discounters can enter into a wide variety of transactions with lessors but, in their purest form, will simply acquire transactions enabling the lessor to realise a profit immediately and to recycle its capital into the financing of new transactions. In this regard, block discounters are very similar to the capital markets in that they provide the ability for lessors to continue to finance new business.

The approach of funders

Funders' objectives are generally very straightforward: to obtain a financial return from the provision of finance and to recover the finance provided with a minimum risk of default. In the event of a default, they wish to hold the maximum security to ensure that recovery is made in full.

A funder generally looks both to the lessor as a corporate entity, having regard to its strength as a credit in its own right, and also to the security provided by the specific transactions that it is funding. The strength of the transactions is determined in two ways: first, if a funder has direct security, this security ensures that the funder is repaid in the event of the default by the lessor; and secondly, and more importantly, the funder will be concerned if the lessor is entering into risky transactions that may prejudice the lessor's financial health and, ultimately, its survival. A funder does not, or should not, lend purely on the basis that it will be able to recover its advance from the realisation of its security.

There are two ways in which the traditional approach to viewing the credit involved in a funding transaction is being modified. First, funders are being faced with lessors that either demand limited recourse funding or which have no intrinsic financial strength apart from the transactions to be funded. The provision of a borrower that simply holds transactions to be funded may be advantageous to the funder since it may be bankruptcy remote, that is, it will not be providing any security or taking on any obligations to parties other than the funder. Any credit support required for such an entity can be provided directly to the funder or via the borrowing lessor. The second way in which the approach outlined in the above paragraphs is changing is that transactions that form the security for the funder's lending are likely to be more complex and may depend for their value upon the actions of parties other than the lessor and the customer. For example, if equipment is let to a customer and the lessor or some other company is bound to provide maintenance or ancillary services as part of an overall agreement with the customer, then a funder will also need to be able to provide a continuation of those other services in the event of a lessor default in order to ensure that the customer continues to make payments under the lease.

Summary

Although there are an increased number of different types of funders in the market, they all have the same objectives: to lend, earn a return and be repaid. The next section discusses the requirements of the funder's security and the subsequent section the ways in which a funder may assess the level of finance to be provided and the effect that this may have on the position of a lessor.

Funding structures and security

Funders have a number of conflicting interests when considering the nature of the security they wish to take from lessors. Lessors will also have concerns to minimise the extent to which funders' requirements interfere or constrain their businesses and affect their relationships with their customers. The principal issues can be categorised as follows:

- security over the equipment;
- security over the obligations of the customer and other obligors;
- control over the cash flow from the customer;
- ability to administer the leases;
- control over, and ability to provide, any ancillary services required to fulfil the lessor's obligations under the lease; and
- an appropriate measure of corporate control over the lessor.

The security taken by funders needs to enable lessors to operate their businesses in circumstances where there is no default, but also be effective if there is a default and, in particular, where a lessor is subject to some form of insolvency procedure. The general subject of insolvency procedures in various jurisdictions is outside the scope of this chapter, however, this is of critical importance to funders and, so far as it affects customers, to both funders and lessors. Reforms being undertaken in the United Kingdom, which are proposed on an EU-wide basis, will tend to make the position of secured creditors and finance lessors less secure and privileged relative to other groups of creditors including, in particular, workers. A general proposition that can be advanced is that there should be as few legal entities (which are capable of being subject to insolvency procedures) between the funder and the customer as possible. Those that exist should, so far as possible, be bankruptcy remote by having no employees or liabilities other than the liability to the funder.

The rest of this section explores ways in which lessors can achieve that objective and also some of the issues that arise when funders requiring credit support from an entity other than a bankruptcy remote SPV obtain a guarantee from a third party, for instance the main trading entity of the lessor.

Security over equipment

A funder's purpose in taking security over equipment is threefold.

- To ensure that, should the lease terminate and the lessor become insolvent, it has a fixed charge over a valuable asset that can be realised to satisfy the lessor's indebtedness.
- To ensure that it is in a position to continue to supply the equipment to the customer in order to ensure that the customer continues to pay rent under the lease.
- Where part of its security comprises a buyback or other residual value guarantee from a third party, to ensure that it can meet the requirements of such arrangements, which will almost certainly require delivery of the equipment.

It can be argued that the best security over equipment is outright ownership. One of the reasons for the popularity of leasing is that it gives the lessor an unrivalled security position relative to a customer's other creditors and also against the customer itself disposing of the lessor's property. However, the advantage of ownership over a security interest is being whittled away by legislation as well as by the courts which are increasingly minded to enforce against a lessor the substance of the economic terms of the transaction with the customer, which, in the case of a finance lease is the provision of finance, rather than the strict legal rights and obligations of property ownership. In the same way that relief has historically been granted against forfeiture of a real property lease, the right of a customer to seek relief from forfeiture of an equipment lease has recently been upheld in the English courts in the case involving Michael Gerson Leasing Limited. Meanwhile, the increasing emphasis on the rescue culture in insolvency, rather than simply selling the assets as quickly as possible (for example, administration in the United Kingdom and Chapter 11 in the United States), will inevitably involve a further erosion of lessors' property rights.

The increasing use of operating leases and equipment service agreements may reduce the risk that the courts and legislature will override lessors' and funders' property rights to equipment since it will be less easy to re-categorise these transactions as though they were loans or pure financing arrangements, particularly where services are provided,.

The question of ownership may itself be in doubt, particularly if the asset leased becomes affixed to land so as to form part of that land. In these circumstances, the freehold owner of the land will be treated as owning the asset and should the customer only have a leasehold or other limited interest of which it is deprived in insolvency, then the rights of the lessor to the equipment will disappear with the rights of the customer. The same result can arise where there is a mortgagee of land to which the equipment becomes affixed and it enforces its security and sells the land, taking the affixed equipment with it. It is for these reasons, as well as to protect unfixed equipment from being removed and sold to pay rent, that a landlord's and mortgagee's waiver of its rights and acknowledgement of the lessor's ownership is customarily required. Such acknowledgement should also be in favour of a funder.

Ownership of equipment may expose funders to the risks of ownership, including the risk of incurring liability to third parties. Lessors will, in turn, be indemnified by their customers and can indemnify the funder against these risks. Insurance will also provide financial support for these indemnities but, in the context of a catastrophe giving rise to third-party liabilities, a funder owning equipment may end up facing claims on the basis of its deep pockets. In the United Kingdom, the railway accident at Great Heck near Selby involved multiple deaths, the destruction of an express passenger train and a freight train, and the closure of the east coast main line for some days. The accident was caused by a Land Rover that ended up on the line having driven off a road by a bridge over the railway. While the driver of the vehicle has been successfully prosecuted, nevertheless the claims arising from that accident of more than £100 million could, if not covered by insurance and if there had been any suggestion of defect in the vehicle, have been brought against the owner of the vehicle, possibly a leasing company.

If outright ownership of equipment is not available to a funder, then the next best thing is to ensure that the entity that has ownership of the equipment is not likely to become insolvent. This approach favours the use of an SPV as owner of equipment. The funder will still wish to have security over the equipment effective against the lessor, the customer and any person claiming through the customer, including creditors of the customer in the case of insolvency.

The method of taking security depends upon the asset over which security is to be taken, the jurisdiction that is relevant and the nature of the entity granting the security. Due to the bewildering variety of possibilities in different jurisdictions, this is a matter that requires advice in relation to each particular transaction. For instance, within the United Kingdom, fixed security over moveable equipment is not available in Scotland, where a limited floating charge has to be taken and is only available from a corporate borrower. Meanwhile, in England and Wales fixed security is available, but needs to be registered in the Companies Registry in the case of companies and where security is granted by an individual through a complicated process under the Bills of Sale Act 1882 in the High Court.

In the case of commercial aircraft and ships there is a separate registry in which mortgages are registered, although registration may also be required at the Companies Registry in these cases. The most effective security in the case of motor vehicles is non statutory, being registration with one of the two or three private organisations that record the existence of finance agreements against details of the vehicle. Other arrangements exist in other jurisdictions and it cannot be assumed that security once taken is effective. This is particularly the case with assets that can cross borders, for example, motor vehicles, ships and aircraft; and with consumer purchasers from a customer or third party that purchases without notice of the security and for full value.

Any security over equipment also needs to take into account the rights of customers either to acquire equipment under leases or hire-purchase agreements or to sell equipment through a sales agency and retain the bulk of the proceeds of the sale as a rebate of rental or sales commission in the case of a finance lease. In each case, these rights generally only arise where customers have paid the lessor all sums due under the lease. The risks in such circumstances are that customers pay a termination sum under the lease, but find that the equipment is charged to a funder by the lessor that is unable to deliver on its obligations to sell the equipment free of encumbrances. There will undoubtedly be a dispute as to the extent that the funder is bound by the obligations of the lessor under the lease and the extent to which the existence of these purely personal rights as between the lessor and customer can inhibit the property rights claimed by the funder by virtue of its security. A lessor granting security will seek to ensure that it retains the right, even under fixed security, to honour its obligations to customers and a funder should generally agree to this where the customer has made full payment under the lease.

Security over the obligations of the customer and other obligors

Ensuring that funders have access to the obligations of customers and other relevant obligors, in particular residual value guarantors and guarantors of the obligations of customers (obligors) is perhaps the most important aspect of the security to be taken from a lessor. This involves not only obtaining good legal security, but also ensuring that such security can be enforced practically. There is no point, from a funder's standpoint, in having perfected security over the obligations of a lessor borrower's obligors if you do not know who they are, cannot contact them and cannot require them to pay you rather than the liquidator of the lessor.

Under English law, the best security over the contractual rights of a lessor against an obligor is for the lessor to assign those rights to the funder absolutely, but with an obligation on the funder to reassign these once all debts have been paid. There are two types of assignment: legal and equitable. Legal assignment requires a written instrument to be executed by the assignor (that is, the lessor) and for notice to be given to the obligor notifying it that the lessor's rights have been transferred to the assignee (that is, the funder). Once notice has been given to the obligor, the funder can enforce the rights directly against the obligor; the lessor, unless authorised by the funder to act on the funder's behalf, has no right to enforce the assigned rights or to be paid by the customer. If, having received notice of the assignment, the customer pays the lessor, other than at the direction of the funder, then the obligor will have to pay the funder as well. In practice, many lessors object to giving notice to their customers that the financial obligations under their leases are now owed to a third party. In these cases, funders may be prepared to accept an equitable assignment, which, while effective against the lessor, carries the risk that a subsequent equitable or legal assignment, where notice is given to the obligors, will take priority over an assignment where no notice has been given. This risk is not merely theoretical as funders have found to their cost with lessors that have 'double funded' transactions. Those lessors that perfected their security by giving notice to obligors and asking the obligors to acknowledge that they had not received a prior notice of assignment protected themselves against these dishonest lessors; those that did not lost money.

Funders wish to take the benefit of the obligations of obligors under the leases and other instruments, but not assume the obligations of the lessor. In theory this is achievable under English law, but in practice a customer is likely to resist paying rent or other sums where it is not confident that the lessor's obligations will be met. Customers may well set up an equity or right of set off, whatever the terms of the lease may say. The ability of a customer to do this will be enhanced where a lessor has substantive obligations, such as the maintenance or cleaning of the asset or the provision of other services. In assessing the value of its security, funders need to be aware of these obligations and the likely effect that a failure by a lessor to perform them in the context of insolvency is likely to have on the willingness of the customer to make payment. The position is even clearer in the case of a buy-back guarantee or other arrangement for residual value support where the lessor is obliged to deliver the equipment in order to take advantage of the residual value guarantee. This requirement is one of the principal reasons funders need security over equipment.

Control of the cash flow

The rights of lessors against customers and other obligors result in payments that provide funds needed to repay the funder's advances to the lessor, whether by way of a loan or lease. Therefore, the funder needs to obtain and keep control of the cash flow emanating from obligors in order to ensure that it is repaid.

If the benefit of the leases has been assigned to the funder, then it is entitled to give notice to customers that all payments should be made direct to the funder, bypassing the lessor completely. The funder can then pass back to the lessor such funds as it needs, for instance in relation to value added or sales taxes for which the lessor is accountable on making supplies of the equipment to the customer under the lease.

However, given that the administration of the leases remains with the lessor, it may not be convenient to have payments made to the funder direct. One reason may be that the lessor has a number of funders and needs to run a combined administration system for its entire portfolio. It may prefer to collect rental under all the leases centrally and then to divide the funds received between the funders. This clearly gives each funder a collection risk on the lessor since, once payments have been made by customers to the lessor, the funds will form part of a mixed account and any fixed security over the proceeds of the leases will be lost.

Funders should therefore seek separation of the cash flow related to the leases over which it has security from the general cash flow of the lessor. This should be achieved by ensuring that payments from the funder's security flow into a separate bank account over which the funder exercises control. The element of control should not be theoretical since the intention is that the funder could continue to collect payments from customers even if the lessor became insolvent. To achieve this, the funder must show that it controls the funds generated from the leases. This area of the law concerning the circumstances in which a charge over book debts creates a fixed or a floating charge has been the subject of extensive litigation both in England and also in other common law jurisdictions. The basis of the decisions has been the extent of the control exercised by the chargor (the funder in the present case) over the proceeds of the book debts and whether the chargee (that is, the lessor) could use the funds as it wished. In the present case, funds received from customers and other obligors are required primarily to repay loans secured on particular leases or groups of leases, but if, for instance, the lessor were allowed to re-lend the funds and not to charge or assign the resulting new transactions, then that might call into question the fixed nature and extent of the funder's security over the receipts. There are separate practical issues discussed in the next section regarding the securing of the cash flows in the context of administering or taking over the administration of the leases.

Ability to administer the leases

Aside from the legal requirements for taking security, funders need to be able to take over the administration of leases in the event of lessor default. This could be a default by the lessor itself or where a third party servicer carries out the administration as a result of default by the servicer.

In the context of capital markets transactions, funders usually require a standby servicer to be appointed. Where the funder is itself a financial institution it may prefer to make contingency plans for the transfer of administration to its own facilities. To achieve this (and in the context of a capital markets transaction, to ensure that the standby servicer can take over smoothly) funders should ensure that data on the portfolio of leases is provided on a sufficiently frequent basis in a form that can be loaded onto its own systems or those of the standby servicer. This data is likely to be in the form of a data tape or electronic file with data in a form that is compatible with a standby system.

If the funder is intending to administer the leases itself, it should ensure that it has the necessary regulatory authorisations, for example, in the United Kingdom, the required licence under the Consumer Credit Act 1974 to act as a creditor in relation to leases to individuals; and anywhere in Europe, the required registration to handle personal data in respect of customers.

Linked with the need for regulatory approval may be the need to be able to access software used in the administration of the leases and, if the lessor itself uses an outside servicer, the right to take over the lessor's rights against that servicer. When checking this aspect of its security, funders should also carry out due diligence on the lessors' systems to ensure that their disaster recovery procedures and software escrow arrangements are adequate and will take effect for the benefit of the funder in relevant circumstances.

A separate area that funders need to consider relates to the ability to secure receipt of payments from customers. Very often, particularly in small-ticket and consumer transactions, payment of rents is made through an automated payment system either by way of standing orders or direct debits. The distinction is important for a funder to understand. A standing order is an instruction issued by a payer (the customer) to its bank to make a series of fixed payments to a payee (the lessor). The lessor cannot vary these payments, but the lessor can divert them without the payer's consent within the automated payment system. A direct debit, on the other hand is the grant of permission by the payer for the payee to take variable amounts from its bank account for particular purposes. Payees originate direct debits by the delivery of a magnetic tape containing instructions to their bank, which then uses the Bankers Automated Clearing System (BACS) to collect funds from the listed accounts. To operate the system it is necessary for a funder to have access and the ability to use the lessor's originator number and to produce the relevant tapes based on sums actually owed by the customers. Ensuring that the funder has the ability to operate the direct debit system on behalf of the lessor and to secure that payment flows into an account over which it has control is, in many cases, probably the most important part of the security that a funder should take. In order to be able to take advantage of such ability, funders also need to have access to lessors' accounting systems so that they know the amounts that need to be demanded.

Depending upon the nature of the leases, funders may also require the ability to sell equipment to residual value guarantors and to seek payment from other obligors. The legal issues involved in securing these rights were discussed in the previous sections, but funders also need to consider the practicalities of recovering vehicles, ensuring that return conditions are met on equipment and timely notices are served on suppliers, insurers and other residual value guarantors in order to comply with the requirements of the relevant arrangements. The same issues arise in the case of credit insurance policies where strict and full compliance with the terms of the policy is likely to be a requirement in order to receive the benefit.

Although these are all practical issues, a funder needs to consider them when making a loan or entering into a lease to provide finance to a lessor so that its security requirements are perfected at that time, rather than facing the practical problems of enforcement once a lessor has defaulted and the funder is facing insolvency practitioners whose main interest is in maximising recoveries for some other party.

Ability to provide ancillary services

The practice of bundling equipment and services supplied to a customer also creates risks for funders. In the context of major PFI and PPP transactions there will have been an analysis of the potential effects of a default by the lessor/project company and the public sector entity will probably have a direct agreement with the funder to ensure continued access to equipment. The public sector company will, consequently, compensate the funder for the use of the equipment; however, in less sophisticated transactions this may not be the case. In contract hire agreements, where the lessor provides maintenance, breakdown recovery and fleet management as a package, the customer may be unwilling to pay rent for vehicles under the lease if it is not receiving other parts of the package. The lessor may have made matters worse by charging a composite rent reflecting the provision of the services and equipment so as to conceal the economics of the transaction from the customer.

Funders need to consider any other services that customers may be expecting to receive in exchange for payments and make contingency plans if those services are not provided because of a lessor insolvency. Contingency plans may involve taking security over any contracts that the lessor has with the actual providers of the services, or entering into direct agreements with them. One key issue is whether the funder has taken security and can exercise control over all of the customer cash flows, including any separate payments made in respect of ancillary services.

If it is impractical to enter into contracts with standby providers of services then the funder may wish to ensure that it is able to access additional funds to employ substitute providers. This arrangement, similar to that motivating the holding of keyman insurance, is second best to having a fully worked out contingency plan, but is preferable to being wholly unprepared.

Exercising control over the lessor

The extent to which a funder should control a lessor is dependent upon the circumstances of each transaction. Where the funder has acquired transactions absolutely, as in the case of block discounting, and is itself carrying out the administration of the leases, control is likely to be irrelevant and inappropriate. Where the lessor is the obligor, is carrying out the administration of the portfolio, and is originating new transactions that the funder has agreed to finance, control becomes of great importance, particularly if the lessor has no great worth other than the leases being funded.

There are four principal types of control that can be imposed. The first is a covenant setting down the type of transactions that the funder will finance. This is appropriate only when the funder is providing a facility for new business. The second group comprises covenants in relation to the lease or portfolio of leases (see below). The third set of covenants relates to the operation of the security structure and, in particular, the control of cash flow and use of accounts. The fourth comprises covenants in relation to the lessor itself as a corporate entity, including general financial covenants, confirmation of corporate good standing and compliance with laws, including legal requirements for carrying on its business.

The first type of covenant regarding the type of business that the funder is prepared to finance is important in endeavouring to ensure that the credit character and quality of the funder's security does not deteriorate. Where the funder is providing finance against specific leases with particular customers, as would generally be the case with-bigger ticket transactions, then this type of covenant has no place. However, where funding is provided for a portfolio of smaller leases and the lessor is entitled to use the funding to enter into further transactions, then it is important to ensure that those additional transactions have defined characteristics. Covenants in this category would include the type of equipment, the nature of the obligors, the size of each transaction and the rate of interest to be charged. There may also be requirements in relation to documentation and notification of assignment to the funder.

The second type of covenant that requires consideration is sufficiency covenants. The funder's concern is to ensure that it will be repaid its financial exposure on an ongoing basis. The funder of a lessor will generally be dependent upon the performance of the leases to secure repayment. There are three types of sufficiency covenants: the first relates to the amount that the funder will advance in relation to a new lease; the second measures the worth of the portfolio of leases relative to the funder's exposure; and the third seeks information on the performance of the lease portfolio as an early warning of future problems.

As in the case of covenants relating to the types of lease that can be funded, where finance is provided for a single lease it is fairly easy to assess the credit risk being run by the funder. This is a credit risk on the customer and, provided the security taken over the lessor is effective, the funder should be able to look through the lessor to the underlying customer credit. Where, on the other hand, finance is provided in respect of a portfolio of leases, particularly where new business is being funded, assessing the ability of the lessor to make repayment may be more difficult and will require a relatively sophisticated statistical analysis of the behaviour of the portfolio. Vital to the ability of the funder to carry out such an analysis is the consistent composition of the lease portfolio. This is one of the reasons that the first type of covenant relating to the nature of the leases is required. There are several key issues that may need to be reflected in sufficiency covenants.

- Is the total future cash flow from the leases adequate to repay the funder's loan together with interest and also to fund the ongoing cost of collection and administration?
- Is the lessor intending to repay the funder from sources other than payments by customers, for instance from the sale of equipment at the end of leases or residual value guarantees?
- What assumptions should be made regarding losses due to default or shortfalls in residual value realisations and how much are insurers required to pay where there is insurance against default or residual value shortfall?
- Can customers acting within the terms of the leases diminish the anticipated cash flow by early termination without being required to pay an amount equal to the relevant proportion of the funder's exposure?
- What is the actual current performance of the portfolio?

Sufficiency covenants generally require a comparison to be made between the value of the leases and that of the funder's exposure. Many of these types of covenant rely on the accounting treatment to establish the realisable value of a lease. This approach has its drawbacks, described below in the section on the financial implications of funding structures, since a given cash flow arising from finance and operating leases will be treated differently for accounting purposes and the recognition of profit from each type of lease will be different. A safer measure is to consider either the present value of the future cash flow derived from leases that are not in default, discounted using a rate in excess of the funder's interest rate; or to look at the amount that could be realised assuming that all customers will default or terminate their leases either immediately or on an agreed, conservative, basis. If there is no credit insurance in place, then an assumption will need to be made regarding rates of default and recoverability. In the case of operating leases, even where there is no default, there is still a risk related to the residual value of the equipment; however, a funder providing finance against a residual value is already accepting that risk.

Covenants designed to provide constant monitoring of the performance of the portfolio need to be carefully crafted. Where new transactions are being added to the portfolio all the time, it is important that a measure is established that is some indicator of the future performance of the existing portfolio. This involves what is known as static pool analysis where the leases originated between certain dates, for instance, in a particular month or quarter, are treated as a separate pool and their performance monitored. The importance of this approach is that each pool will age and will give an indication of the way that succeeding pools will behave over time. An entire portfolio can be kept relatively new by increasing the volume of new business written. The performance of older transactions, and the likely future performance of the whole portfolio, may be masked where there is an increasing volume of new business written. The key parameters that should be included in such monitoring covenants are incremental default and early termination rates as a pool ages. These rates can then be applied to new business written to ascertain its likely future performance and, consequently, the ability of the portfolio as a whole to generate sufficient funds to repay the funder.

Funders will also wish to ensure that pools comprising leases written some time ago are representative of existing business being written, or to seek to ascertain whether current business is of better or worse credit quality, hence the covenants regarding the nature of new business referred to in the previous paragraph. As successive pools are established, their performance over time can be compared to earlier pools and a possible trend established as to whether the various parameters are moving significantly and, if so, in which direction, or whether the economic environment is changing.

Sufficiency covenants are used to trigger restrictions on the lessor at particular ratios of the value of the leases to the funder's exposure. The first restriction will be on the ability of the lessor to extract profit (a cashtrap); the second is likely to be a drawstop ending the funder's obligation to increase its exposure and requiring cash flow to be used to repay the funder. The final trigger will give rise to a default which will entitle the funder to appoint a receiver or otherwise to take over the administration of the leases.

Summary

A funder must, in each case, consider its security requirements. The taking of security is, however, no substitute for a proper assessment and acceptance of the credit risks inherent in a transaction.

Guarantees of lessees

One form of credit enhancement is the provision of guarantees of lessee obligations. While the point is usually ignored or overlooked in the context of smaller transactions, and also where the guarantor and the lessee are members of the same group, there is a potential legal trap for a guarantor of a lessee.

A guarantor that provides a guarantee at the request of the principal debtor, in this case the lessee, will be entitled, upon payment of the lessee's obligations under the guarantee, to take over the creditor's, in this case the lessor's, rights against the lessee. This is known as subrogation and applies also in the context of insurance, but not where a creditor has obtained a guarantee from a third party by way of credit enhancement without the consent, and not at the request, of the principal debtor. In the context of a loan transaction, the guarantor will pay the creditor and take over the creditor's rights under the loan against the debtor, including its security. In the context of a lease, however, the principal way in which a lessor will seek to recover its investment is by the sale of the equipment. Considerable complications will ensue unless the guarantee is specially drafted to take account of this and to give the guarantor rights to have the equipment sold and the proceeds applied in reduction of the lessee's debt prior to a claim being made under the guarantee. Simple guarantees of lessees' obligations under finance leases can leave a guarantor paying a termination sum, and the defaulting lessee entitled to a rebate of 99 per cent of the sales proceeds of the equipment.

Financial implications of funding structures

One of the key issues for both lessors and funders in deciding the method and extent of funding is the question of the lessor's gearing. Lessors have typically been very capital hungry enterprises and have also been subject to a tendency to financial instability. The reasons for these two tendencies lie in the nature of leasing and the accounting methods used.

As with other financial institutions, leasing companies incur costs on the establishment of new leases, which either form part of their overheads, where sales forces and branches are maintained, or are directly attributed to a particular lease, for example, dealer or broker commissions and legal costs. In big-ticket leases, origination costs are typically capitalised and in the case of early termination, customers are obliged to ensure that the lessor's after tax return on its investment (including costs) is maintained.

In the case of smaller-ticket transactions, broker costs have to be amortised from the net income of the transaction and, consequently, the lease will run at a loss, were it to terminate prematurely, for an initial period. However, the accounting treatment would not reflect this initial risk since the origination costs would probably be spread over the anticipated life of the transaction. There is a risk that if a significant proportion of the leases terminate sooner than anticipated, the lessor could, without suffering excessive defaults, still trade at a loss. Funders aware of this potential problem are cautious about the level of advance they make against new business and prefer to require the lessor to finance origination costs from their own funds.

Lessors typically account for a finance lease, a hire purchase, conditional sale, or credit sale transaction by spreading the finance charges/income element of rentals or instalments on the basis of maintaining an approximate constant rate of return on the investment in the lease. This is on the basis that the assumed residual value, in the case of an operating lease or contract hire transaction, will be realised. The result of this treatment is that as the lease or leases age, the proportion of the receipts representing income, as opposed to a return of capital, declines. With an ageing portfolio, the lessor will need to cut its costs to match the decline in income, otherwise it will tend to suffer declining profits. This result can also occur as a result of unexpected bad debts and a decline in new business.

The following is a simple illustration of the point. It assumes that the lessor writes a single finance lease on the first day in each of six years, each with a capital value of £10,000, an interest rate of 6.17 per cent per annum and a term of 60 months with no residual value. The assumed funding rate is 5.16 per cent and the table shows the net income arising in each of the 10 years that the leases run. As a comparison, Exhibit 14.2 illustrates how a portfolio of operating leases with similar characteristics would behave. They have an initial capital value of £10,000, but a residual value of £2,500. It is assumed that the accounting treatment of the operating lease will involve a straight-line depreciation of the capital value to the residual value over the term of the lease together with an amortisation of the associated funding on an annuity basis to a balloon payment equal to the residual value.

It can be seen from the table that with a constant level of new business, the income builds up in the case of both the finance and the operating leases to a plateau. However, in the case of the finance leases it is necessary not only to maintain but to increase new business in order to keep profits rising. Any decline in new business will have an immediate effect on earnings. In the case of operating leases, there is a rise in income when new business slows down and short-term earnings are depressed by expansion.

Where a funder relies on the accounting treatment of transactions in assessing the ability of a lessor to repay debt, it will need to bear in mind the different treatments of operating

Exhibit 14.2

Comparison of funding structure performance

Year	Leases in existence	Finance lease net income (£)	Operating lease net income (£)
1	1	89	(83)
2	2	162	(96)
3	3	218	(36)
4	4	253	101
5	5	266	320
6	5	266	320
7	4	177	403
8	3	104	416
9	2	48	356
10	1	13	218

and finance leases. An accounting based covenant will unduly restrict an operating lessor because new business will tend to reduce net assets. However, in the case of a finance lessor there is an imperative to write new business in order to maintain profitability. This has, in the past, encouraged lessors to relax credit criteria when markets become tight and, in the extreme, to commit fraud in order to try to avoid the downward spiral of stagnant or falling levels of new business leading to reductions in profit or losses and a consequent reduction in the ability to borrow to finance the new business needed to reverse the downward trend.

A funder's use of sufficiency covenants can also have a restrictive effect on the ability of a lessor to grow its business, particularly if one of the covenants is a restriction on the amount that a funder will advance against each new transaction, or the effect of the covenant is that the funder will not finance origination costs of transactions. In this case, until profit has been earned by the lessor from existing transactions, the lessor will need to provide equity to finance origination costs. In practice, subject to the exercise of caution, a funder should be able to advance funds against the interest only (or IO strip) being the future earnings represented by new business. This approach is reflected in the sufficiency covenants based on the present value of future cash flows, provided that the discount rate used is greater than that charged on funding.

There are three further related points that a funder must take into account.

- Changes in the tax treatment of the leases, which may result either in increased cost to the lessor or, where the tax treatment is beneficial, in an obligation to rebate or reduce rentals payable by the customer under tax adjusting finance leases.
- Changes in interest rates which may be reflected in rentals charged under variable rate leases, but will almost certainly affect the ability of the lessor to repay the funder, assuming that the leases are essentially fixed for interest rates.
- Where the lessor is taking a residual value risk on equipment that is not hedged by buy-backs or residual value guarantees, the funder needs to keep an eye on changes in the value of equipment, particularly where major shifts may take place in the second hand market as has been the case with motor vehicles and computers in the recent past which may impair the ability of a residual value guarantor to meet its commitments.

Typical financing structures

Introduction

This final section examines four structures typically used to finance leasing companies from the point of view of both lessors and funders. The structures are:

- lending to a full service lessor against a portfolio of leases with full security, but including variants where the funder has limited recourse;
- a structure involving the provision of equipment by the funder, either by headlease/sub-lease or by agency arrangements;
- block discounting and other refinancing arrangements; and
- a capital markets based structure involving an SPV and a lessor that is a co-ordinator of the provision of a package of services to a customer.

Secured loan transaction

Borrowing on a full recourse basis from a bank was traditionally the principal way in which lessors funded their businesses. A lessor would often start as a broker and then decide that it could make more money by leasing equipment itself. Even if its preferred method of financing was by way of block discounting, it would still need to have an initial bank facility to enable it to fund the creation of a block of business. Methods have moved full circle since this is precisely the methodology increasingly used to finance leasing businesses, with a combination of warehouse facilities coupled with securitisation.

A funder providing finance on this basis will often establish a debt-to-equity ratio measured by reference to the lessor's balance sheet. The combination of this covenant together with the method of accounting for finance leases described in the previous section led to the virtuous circles and vicious spirals typical of leasing companies. The virtuous circle comprised the increase in equity generated by increasing new business and often exaggerated by enhanced recognition of income on the inception of a new lease. Profits would also rise because leasing companies are highly geared operationally and as volumes rose, so the burden of overheads would fall. However, where either bad debt impacted on profitability or increases in new business were restricted by market conditions or lack of funding, the effect on profitability was immediate, as illustrated by Exhibit 14.3, based on the assumptions used in Exhibit 14.2. The additional assumptions are that the company starts with equity of £1,000 which is not invested; its overhead comprises £1 of servicing cost per lease per month, and £15 for origination and marketing costs per lease in the month of origination; and bad debts run at 1 per cent of instalments due in each year.

The point to note from the example is the rapid decline into loss once new business ceases to be written in Year 7. It should also be noted that profit increases year on year as new business and the portfolio increases, followed by a reduction between Years 4 and 5 as the portfolio stabilises. In addition, the debt-to-equity ratio increases to a peak of 17:1 and then declines. If the lessor wishes to maintain its upward trend in profit, it has to write an increasing annual volume of business, and the debt-to-equity ratio will then become excessive. If the debt-to-equity ratio is contained, the profit stabilises or falls.

Where the borrowing lessor is also the company that owns the infrastructure of the business – that is, staff, premises, IT – and enters into the commercial contracts, the funder will

Exhibit 14.3

Debt-to-equity ratios and profitability

Year	Equity at start of year (£)	Debt at start of year (£)	Total overhead for year (£)	Profit for year (£)	Debt: equity ratio
1	1,000	-10,000	-27	39	10
2	1,039	-18,196	-39	77	8
3	1,116	-24,495	-51	97	13
4	1,213	-28,799	-63	97	16
5	1,310	-31,005	-75	75	17
6	1,385	-31,005	-75	75	16
7	1,460	-21,005	-48	36	15
8	1,496	-12,809	-36	-2	9
9	1,494	-6,510	-24	-22	5
10	1,472	-2,206	-12	-22	2

have to consider, in addition to matters related to the lease portfolio, issues that arise whenever security is taken over a business. These issues include perfecting and registering security over real property, insurance and the impact of insolvency law on its ability to recover its debt and enforce its security and the relative priority of its claims to those of employees and trade creditors. In considering the levels of equity required, it is prudent for the funder to deduct from equity, as is done in calculating capital adequacy for banks, the equity tied up in operational assets which are not readily realisable.

Where a lessor needs or wishes to have a number of funders, a decision will need to be taken as to whether each funder will provide finance for a separate portfolio of leases over which it will have first priority security to the exclusion of other funders, or whether the funders will provide a syndicated facility where all will share rateably in the lessor's entire business. Where comprehensive security is being taken from a full service lessor, it will, in any event, be necessary for the funders to enter into an inter-creditor agreement and to appoint a security trustee so that, in the event of enforcement action being required, the trustee can take the lead in arranging for the effective administration of the leases. If the funders wish to take security over different parts of the lessor's business, then the alternatives are either to have a security trustee responsible for the division of realisations or, alternatively, each part of the business could be conducted in a separate company and security could be granted by each subsidiary to the relevant funder. This last approach marks a first step along the road that leads to a bankruptcy remote SPV no longer owned by the lessor.

The issues surrounding funders' security have been discussed at length in the previous section. Where funders are making a secured loan, they will need to have the full panoply of security discussed in the section on funding structures and security. In addition, a funder will have to consider the extent to which the lessor has hedged its interest rate exposures and ensure that appropriate hedging is put in place, either through the provision of fixed-rate funding or through derivatives. If derivatives are used, security will need to be taken over them and care will be needed to ensure that there is no automatic termination on default, since that would potentially result in an unhedged portfolio and a further liability arising for the lessor.

The issues that arise in the context of a secured loan arise in different guises with other funding structures. In some ways, secured loans are the least attractive method of funding for lessors since they generally involve no element of limitation on the recourse of the funder and require the provision of equity to support a particular level of debt. This inhibits business growth and can put an entire company at risk as a result of the non-performance of a lease portfolio or an unwillingness on the part of funders to continue funding. From a funder's point of view, the structure has the advantage that the lessor is committed to ensuring repayment of its loan, but it complicates any enforcement because of competing claims that may arise in an insolvency of a full service lessor. The alternative of having more limited security over specific leases may have its attractions.

Provision of equipment by a funder

Secured loans involve funders in the provision of money to lessors who then apply those funds in the acquisition of equipment which is let to customers. The second type of funding structure involves the funder owning equipment which it provides to the lessor so that the lessor can provide it to the customers. There are two principal variants on this type of transaction: the first is where the equipment is let by the funder to the lessor and the lessor sublets it to the customer; the second is where the lessor acts as the agent of the funder in letting the equipment to the customer on either a disclosed or non-disclosed agency basis. The headlease/sublease structure has been very popular but, when combined with sale and leaseback of the equipment by the lessor, it has proved to be capable of abuse by unscrupulous lessors seeking to raise finance from two funders against the same equipment and lease in what is known as double funding.

One reason for the popularity of the headlease/sublease structure is its flexibility and the ability to match or mismatch receipts and deductions in the lessor. There is a discussion in Chapter 15 of the tax implications of mismatched revenues and deductions, but such mismatches may be undertaken for commercial as well as tax reasons. There are three types of headleases.

- Finance leases are commonly used for the provision of pure finance by funders or for accessing tax benefits enjoyed by funders, but transferring the full economic benefit and burden of ownership of the equipment to lessors.
- Operating leases, where funders take residual value risk on the equipment, are common in the context of funding contract hire and daily rental companies, and are also appropriate where lessors are providing added value services to customers, but do not wish to take risks on changes in the value of the equipment.
- Hire purchase, lease purchase and conditional sale, where ownership of the equipment will vest in the lessor.

The three types of headlease are matched by equivalent subleases and although the usual position has matched types, that is, head finance lease and finance sub lease, there are opportunities for mismatching. So, where a funder either has no tax benefits to put into the lease, or those benefits are outside the United Kingdom, one way to fund equipment would be by way of hire purchase, since tax ownership in the equipment generally rests with the hirer (in this case the lessor) rather than the funder. The lessor is then in a position to provide the customer with the equipment under either a finance lease or an operating lease. The tax effect of having a head finance lease and an operating sublease are illustrated in Exhibit 15.2 in Chapter 15.

Consideration also needs to be given to the accounting implications of mismatches. A finance headlease may be entered into for a term that is shorter than the economic life of the equipment, because that is the longest period that the funder is willing to provide finance to the lessor. This will result in the lessor having to meet debt obligations equal to the capital value of the equipment over a shorter period than that in which the equipment is depreciated.

Where there is a headlease/sublease arrangement, funders needs to take as much, if not more, care over their security arrangements than in cases where they are making a secured loan. A crucial part of the security package should be an assignment of the benefit of the sub-lease so that the customer makes all payments under the sublease to the funder or to the lessor at the funder's direction. The giving of notice to the customer will prevent the lessor from being able to double fund the transaction.

In many cases, however, it is either commercially unacceptable or practically impossible to give notice to the customer, for example, because there are a large number of individual subleases. If a full legal assignment of the benefit of the subleases cannot be taken, then an equitable assignment should be taken which can be converted into a legal assignment by the giving of notice. The originals of the subleases should be secured physically and steps should be taken to ensure that the cash flow from the subleases is paid into a charged account and reconciliations are produced to account for all payments made by the customer. The funds in the charged account will then be divided on a periodic basis between those that are needed to pay the headlease rent and the balance which is remitted to the lessor.

The alternative to the headlease/sublease structure is for the lessor to acquire equipment and enter into a lease to the customer as agent, generally undisclosed, for the funder. This arrangement has the advantage that the lessor's insolvency is less likely to disrupt the flow of funds to the funder from the customer. The double funding risk is about the same and there are still issues regarding the security of the cash flow. There is, of course, no question of assigning the benefit of the lease to the funder, since the funder is the lessor under the lease in any event, albeit undisclosed. The disadvantage is that the funder does not have the bene-fit of the lessor's covenant under a headlease, although questions of the apportionment of risk are more flexible than this statement would suggest. The agency arrangement has consider-able advantages for the lessor as well since it removes the entire transaction from its balance sheet, except to the extent that it is providing quantifiable credit support.

As suggested in the previous paragraph, in this structure it is possible to vary the extent to which a funder takes credit risk on the customer and not on the lessor. This can be achieved by simply providing that payments under the headlease shall only be made to the extent that payments have been made under the sublease and that the lessor is not liable for the various covenants in the headlease to the extent that the same or similar obligations have been imposed on the sublessee and are being enforced. Where there is an agency arrangement and, *prima facie*, the lessor is not part of the chain of obligations, then the lessor can provide a guarantee of the obligations of the sublessee to the funder, taking into account the various considerations described above in the section on ancillary services.

The essence of the headlease/sublease or agency structure is its flexibility. The flexibili-ty has enabled it to be abused by unscrupulous lessors, but a funder who is careful can ensure ownership of the equipment and the establishment of an effective security structure.

Block discounting and other refinancing arrangements

The previous two sections have concentrated on funding arrangements that finance leasing transactions from inception. This section looks at ways in which a lessor can refinance transactions into which it has already entered. Block discounting does not describe a particular method of funding such as a loan, a headlease, a purchase of receivables or a purchase of transactions. Instead, it is the method by which a lessor enters into a number of transactions on its own account and then sells or refinances a block of transactions to, or with, a funder. There are four different methods of block discounting that will be considered.

- The sale of transactions in their entirety, including both the equipment and the lease.
- The sale of the lease receivables, but not the equipment.
- Sale and leaseback.
- Financing blocks by way of loan.

Sale of complete transactions

The most common way of block discounting is for a lessor to sell entire transactions to the funder. The technicalities of this apparently simple transaction are worth considering because they highlight important aspects of the leasing relationship. The lessor sells two assets to the funder: the ownership of the equipment and the benefit of the lease, in effect the rights against the customer. However, the lessor has undertaken obligations to the customer, at the least to provide the equipment during the term of the lease and, where the lease is a finance lease, obligations at the end of the lease either to sell the equipment to the customer under a bargain purchase option or to permit the lessor to sell the equipment as its agent and to pay the customer most of the net proceeds of sale by way of rebate of rental or sales commission. On sale, as a minimum, the lessor will require the funder to agree to perform the lessor's obligations under the lease and to indemnify the lessor against any claims arising from non-performance. Ideally, the lease should be novated, which involves the lessee entering into an agreement to release the lessor from its obligations in exchange for the funder assuming those obligations. It is possible, where it is anticipated that a lease will be sold by the lessor, to build in automatic novation provisions into the terms of the lease, so that the lessee is treated as agreeing to release the lessor upon service of a novation notice following sale of the equipment.

It is possible for the sale to be kept secret from the customer, but this will impair the security enjoyed by the funder. The effect of a sale without notice to the customer is substantially the same as that described in the previous section where a transaction is entered into initially by the agent of an undisclosed principal, the funder. The only difference is that the lessor will have undertaken obligations to the customer under the lease as principal but, commercially, contracting as the agent of an undisclosed principal generally leaves the agent with the obligations of the principal in relation to a third party.

The tax treatment of the sale of a complete transaction needs to be considered. The first question is whether the transaction is entered into by the lessor as a trading or a capital transaction. If the initial intention is to resell the equipment and the benefit of the lease, then it is arguable that the lessor should simply treat the transaction as part of its stock in trade. The effect of this would be that it was not entitled to claim capital allowances on the equipment, but that any rentals received would be treated as realisation of its stock.

If the only way in which the lessor is financed is by way of block discounting, and the sale took place shortly after the inception of the transaction, then this would probably be the proper way to account for and tax the transactions. If, however, sales of blocks of agreements only happens infrequently and the lessor holds the leases for an appreciable period, say, six months from inception, then the more likely treatment is as capital transactions.

The issue of companies treating transactions as stock in trade rather than capital transactions is likely to become important and contentious over the next few years. This is a particular issue for a number of companies who are undertaking PFI and PPP transactions with the public sector and are seeking to obtain tax relief by claiming that all expenditure on the provision or refurbishment of assets for use by the public sector is on trading stock, even where the result of such expenditure is the creation of an asset generating income for the company over the period of the concession.

If a lessor has entered into the transactions on capital account (the normal situation), there is a further tax issue related to the sale. This issue also arises where entire portfolios of leases are purchased, not as a method of funding an ongoing leasing trade, but as part of the disposal of the whole or part of a trade. The sale described above comprises both the equipment and also the benefit of the lease. Generally, the price for the sale is treated as attributed almost exclusively to the equipment, with only a nominal amount, if any, being attributed to the value of the lease. The result of this treatment is that the bulk of the price is treated as disposal proceeds for capital allowance purposes, so the lessor is treated as having bought equipment for its initial cost and resold it for the price realised for the transaction.

The correct analysis is, however, that the equipment should be valued at its open market value, and any difference, whether positive or negative, between that value and the price for the transaction in its entirety should be attributed to the lease and taxed either as a capital receipt or as accelerated income. In practice, the UK Inland Revenue does not seek to apply the strict position because of the administrative complications involved in valuing large amounts of equipment and the perception that the only loss to the revenue arises from possible timing differences. It is, however, a point that needs to be made to both a funder, which would only be entitled to claim capital allowances based on the market value of the equipment, and the lessor, which might be taxed on the excess as income or chargeable gains and be left with an excess of allowances in a pool of qualifying expenditure.

Sale of lease receivables

This technique involves the sale by a lessor of the benefit of the lease, but the retention of ownership of the equipment. The transaction is completed by an assignment of the benefit of the lease to the funder in the same way as described in connection with the funder taking security by way of assignment over the lease. However, the difference is that the lessor has no right to require a reassignment. As far as the funder is concerned, the technique has the advantage that the funder does not become the owner of the equipment and therefore does not have to establish an equipment leasing trade; it is simply concerned with the receipt of rentals. From the point of view of the lessor, it retains a greater involvement with the lessee because it retains ownership of the equipment and it is able to perform its obligations under the lease. The transaction is more like a funding rather than a disposal of part of its trade. The disadvantage from the point of view of the funder is that it does not control the equipment. Prudent funders will always take a charge over the equipment as part of their security to prevent lessors using the equipment as security elsewhere and to ensure that, in the event of an insolvency of a lessor, they are able to secure the continued provision of the equipment to the customer and, consequently, the continued payment of the rentals under the lease.

The sale of receivables has a number of interesting tax consequences that have motivated such transactions. First, it is arguable that a sale accelerates the receipt of income due under a lease or that it converts future income into a present capital sum. Whilst this is generally unattractive for a lessor, it has the advantage of enabling a lessor to manage the timing of taxable income for reasons discussed in Chapter 15.

The second consequence is that if the receipt arising from the sale of receivables is a capital sum, it may be offset by some or all of the cost of the equipment without resulting in any diminution in the capital allowances pool. This double deduction would be reversed and replaced by double taxation if the equipment was ever sold, but normally this is not contemplated by the lessor. The double deduction benefit of selling receivables is not, of course, available if the transactions are held as stock in trade rather than capital assets.

Thirdly, where withholding tax was applied to interest paid to funders other than banks, the sale of receivables at a discount, instead of the repayment of principal and interest out of the receipt of rentals, avoided withholding tax where the funder was not a bank. However, with the abolition of withholding tax on interest in the United Kingdom, this reason has disappeared.

From a funder's point of view, it is essential that it is carrying on a financial trade so that the purchase of receivables is treated as an application of circulating capital and is amortised against the receipt of the purchased rentals. The alternative treatment, as the purchase of a non-amortising but wasting capital asset matched by the receipt of wholly taxable pure income, is very unattractive since no deduction will be available to the funder against the receipts. A lessor will need to retain sufficient rentals from those sold to demonstrate that the equipment continues to be used in its own trade, and also retain any VAT for which it is accountable on the continuing supply of the equipment to the customer. The legal structure to achieve this involves the assignment of the entirety of the benefit of the lease to the funder. The funder then holds the excess of the rentals over what it requires to recover the purchase price and return for the benefit of the lessor.

Sale and leaseback

A sale and leaseback transaction will put the lessor and funder in the same position as had they entered into a headlease/sublease structure initially. The same issues regarding security for the funder and the ability to match or mismatch lease terms and cash flows exist, subject to certain restrictions related to taxation. However, there is one significant issue that needs to be considered in a sale and leaseback transaction: whether, in reality, it should be re-characterised as a secured lending transaction. The importance of this question is that there are registration formalities required where a company grants security and if they are not complied with, the security is unenforceable against the company or its liquidator.

Tax authorities have imposed certain restrictions on sale and leaseback transactions, mainly concerned with ensuring that receipts and rentals are taxable or deductible at commercial or market rates. The UK authorities introduced anti-avoidance legislation restricting the entitlement of a funder to capital allowances on a sale and leaseback amounts no greater than the 'notional tax written down value' of equipment acquired and leased back under a finance lease. The notional tax written down value is equal to the tax written down value on the assumption that all allowances to which the lessor would have been entitled in respect of the equipment have been claimed in full, ignoring the effect of pooling. The opportunities that this legislation have provided for the transfer of taxable income to funders with reliefs are described in Chapter 15 in relation to alternatives to purchasing leasing companies for tax reasons.

Financing blocks by way of loan

This section is included only for the sake of completeness in a description of methods of block discounting. The description of the provision of a secured loan in an earlier section did not describe the nature of the lending. One type of lending is by providing an overdraft facility, which is used by the lessor to finance the acquisition of equipment and origination costs. This would be coupled with a revolving term loan where each block financed by the overdraft is then refinanced with an advance intended to be amortised by the receipts from that particular group of leases. The funder may, in these circumstances, delay taking full security by way of assignment of the benefit of the leases and fixed charge over the equipment until they are refinanced.

Full recourse, buybacks and other commercial issues

All of the techniques described in this section are capable of being used on a full, partial or limited recourse basis. The sale of entire transactions and/or receivables is more naturally undertaken without recourse to the lessor. The tax treatment of a receivables sale with recourse might be different to one without; however, by requiring the lessor to guarantee the obligations of lessees by an option for the funder to put back transactions that do not perform or do not comply with the funder's requirements regarding underwriting or performance at the date of sale, any level of recourse to the lessor can be achieved. Likewise, as in the above discussion on headlease/sublease and secured loan structures, a sale and leaseback or loan secured on a block of leases can equally be with full, partial or limited recourse.

Lessors need to consider the extent to which they are prepared to cede contact with customers to funders by entering into financing transactions and, in particular, sales of entire transactions. From a funder's standpoint, the greater its contact with customers, the more secure its position is. Ideally, the funder should collect the rentals direct from the customers and account to the lessor for any surplus over the amount required to repay the financing.

Summary

The use of funding methods that enable existing transactions to be refinanced, particularly where lessors can employ more than one technique, greatly increases lessors' independence and flexibility. Independent lessors have always suffered from a lack of committed funding lines; in good times when funders are seeking opportunities to lend there is a feast, but when funders are restricting their exposure independent lessors are the first to suffer. However, the emergence of capital markets alternatives provide some welcome flexibility in the funding market.

Securitisation and the disaggregated lessor

Introduction

As mentioned in the introduction to this chapter, the major development of the past five years has been the growth in funding for leasing companies provided by the capital markets rather than by financial institutions. This development has proceeded together with a demand from customers for the provision by lessors of more than just finance for the acquisition of equipment. This section explores how lessors might evolve in order to take advantage of both of these developments. (For a detailed review of securitisation see Chapter 18.)

Customers' requirements

A customer may be a public body or a major corporate concerned to provide a service to its own customers or the public. The provision of the service involves the use of substantial items of equipment on a daily basis. The availability of such equipment is critical to the provision of the service and its non-availability or failure to function involves substantial financial and commercial penalties for the customer. The customer is not prepared to take risk on the equipment and it is likely that it will need to be replaced or substantially upgraded during the period of the contract. A typical customer's requirements, embodied in an equipment service agreement (ESA), can be summarised as follows:

- the equipment must be delivered on time and to specification;
- the lessor is responsible for ensuring that an agreed number of items of equipment are available to the customer's staff in agreed locations each day, clean and maintained to an agreed standard;
- the lessor is responsible for ensuring an agreed maintenance programme is carried out, but even if it is, that does not relieve the lessor of any of its responsibilities referred to above;
- if an item of equipment breaks down or fails to function to the agreed standard while in the possession of the customer's staff, the lessor is responsible for its recovery and in situ replacement (that is, not by making a further item available at the depot or base) within an agreed timescale; and
- it is recognised that the equipment will require replacement and/or a major upgrade during the term of the contract and the lessor is responsible for ensuring at periodic intervals the equipment is replaced or upgraded to a standard comparable with the best equipment then available in the market.

The customer will pay a composite charge for the above services which will be reduced on the basis of penalty points for failure to perform. This reduction is in addition to any liability that the customer suffers by reason of breach of the terms of the ESA. The customer requires transparency in the way in which the composite charge is calculated, benchmarking of all service providers on a regular basis and credit for any tax benefits or export subsidies introduced to the transaction by the manufacturer of the equipment. It should be noted that the customer does not require the provision of staff to operate the equipment.

The lessor's response

The lessor in this case has been a provider of finance by way of large-ticket finance leases and does not, itself, have any of the wider range of skills needed to support the ESA. It should be noted that a lessor could provide any of the skills and resources, but in the present case, for transparency, it is assumed that independent contractors provide them. Note also the comments below on recourse to lessors. There are several principal parties.

- *The funding SPV.* Λ special purpose company that is likely to be owned, ultimately, by a charitable trust. The SPV's purpose is to raise funds to pay for the purchase of the equipment. In order to do this, it needs to have access to the composite fee payable by the customer, security over the equipment and security, for the benefit of the providers of finance (the bondholders), over the lessor's rights under the ESA and the lessor's rights

297

against all other contractors. As funder and provider of the equipment to the lessor, the SPV may itself be a lessee under a cross-border lease-purchase agreement; its obligations under that agreement would be defeased with the funds it raises from its bondholders. The SPV will provide the equipment to the lessor under a lease-purchase agreement and will, therefore, not be treated as owning the equipment for UK tax purposes. A description of the securitisation arrangements undertaken by the SPV lies outside the scope of this chapter. However, it is important to note that the SPV needs to make full disclosure of the overall transaction to its bondholders and potential bondholders, including full financial information on the customer, since it is its credit standing that underpins the credit on the bonds.

- *The service provider.* Either a joint-owned company or a further SPV responsible for providing the maintenance, cleaning and other support services, including recovery and in situ replacement. The service provider enters into an agreement with the lessor for the provision of the services on a back-to-back basis with the lessor's obligations under the ESA. The service provider has contracts with the manufacturer, a facilities or fleet manager and a provider of the recovery services together with any other parties needed to fulfil its obligations.

- *The manufacturer.* It is assumed that there is a single main manufacturer or main contractor for the provision of the equipment. Apart from providing the equipment under a supply contract that contains provisions imposing penalties for late delivery and undertakings regarding quality and performance, the manufacturer has a contract with the service provider to provide support for the maintenance function and also has a contract with the lessor and/or the service provider to upgrade or replace the equipment. The manufacturer also provides a residual value guarantee to the lessor in respect of the equipment. This obligation might rest with a residual value guarantor or remain with the lessor, but for simplicity it is assumed that the manufacturer undertakes it.

- *The security trustee.* The entire structure is dependent upon the security trustee which may delegate some of is administrative functions to the lessor, but remains responsible to the service provider, the funding SPV, the lessor and, possibly, the customer, for holding all the rights related to the transaction.

Lessors' contractual rights
The lessor's principal obligation is to perform its obligations under an ESA. In order to do this, and to protect its position, a lessor will typically enter into the agreements below.

- A *lease-purchase agreement* with the funding SPV under which the lessor agrees to make a series of fixed rental payments in return for the hire of the equipment. The agreement contains a purchase option that will be at the same price as that at which the lessor is entitled to sell the equipment to the manufacturer pursuant to the manufacturer's residual value guarantee.

- A *services agreement* with the services provider for the provision of the maintenance, cleaning and other services needed to secure the availability of the equipment under the ESA, together with the recovery and *in situ* replacement services. The lessor will probably also require guarantees from the providers of the services to the service provider by way of direct obligations in respect of their services and a similar requirement is likely to be imposed by the customer.

- *A supply agreement* with the manufacturer to enable the lessor to pass on various warranties and undertakings to the customer and also to ensure that it has the necessary rights against the manufacturer in respect of the equipment.
- *A residual value guarantee* with the manufacturer under which the lessor can sell the equipment back to the manufacturer on its return by the customer.
- *A full security package* with the security trustee as security for its obligations under the various agreements to which it is party. This will comprise: an assignment of the benefit of the ESA including, in particular, the obligation on the customer to make payments; an assignment of the benefit of the supply agreement, services agreement, lease-purchase agreement and residual value guarantee together with any credit support provided in respect of any of them; a charge over a bank account into which all funds from whatever source are paid; and such other security as it agrees to offer.
- *An inter-creditor agreement* under which the various parties agree with the lessor and the security trustee the priority in which they will be entitled to be paid out of the composite charge under the ESA or from payments under other agreements. This agreement may also include direct agreements between the parties dealing with the contingency of the lessor becoming insolvent.

Other contractual issues

A transaction of the type described involves a large number of other elements, including interfaces with customers of the customer, particularly if the ultimate customer is a public body; the requirements of those advising the funding SPV, including the bond trustee and the security trustee for the bondholders, if different from the security trustee; the investment bank arranging the bond issue; possibly, a monoline insurer which would be the real provider of funding by the SPV and the party taking the credit risk on the transaction. The transaction does not contemplate a standby servicer or a standby lessor since it is anticipated that in the event of lessor insolvency, the receiver appointed by the security trustee would ensure that the lessor performed its obligations under the various contracts.

Recourse to lessors

The assumption in the scenario described above is that all parties have full recourse to the lessor. In practice, this is unlikely to be the case and the actual lessor will be a further special purpose company managed by the lessor. The effect of this is to keep the various liabilities away from the lessor's balance sheet and to ensure that the fulcrum on which all the various contractual relationships turn is itself bankruptcy remote, except for matters related to the particular transaction. The final contract would be a servicing agreement providing for the lessor to manage the project company.

Other types of transaction

While the example taken of a disaggregated lessor is in the context of a big-ticket project type of transaction, nevertheless many of the same issues arise in the context of other types of transaction, including smaller equipment lease transactions. For instance, a contract hire company could use a similar structure to provide a full service to its customer by using a funding SPV to take the credit risk on the customer and with responsibility for breakdown, recovery, maintenance and residual value risk on the vehicles being subcontracted to third parties with only the core competence of fleet management being retained by the company.

Conclusion

The aim of this chapter is to illustrate the many ways in which lessors can fund themselves to provide equipment to their customers. The possibilities are greater than ever before for lessors; they no longer need to be major financial institutions to access different sources of finance in order to support the provision of equipment. The advent of capital market funding and the increased complexity of many transactions has put a premium on the ability to arrange funding for transactions, rather than simply the possession of substantial financial resources. With greater flexibility has come greater complexity in terms of operational, administrative and security procedures and some of these issues have been highlighted in this chapter.

The market has changed significantly in the past five years. There is every prospect that the trends highlighted and discussed will continue and major financial institutions will become arrangers and providers of servicers as much as they are providers of finance.

Chapter 15

The purchase and sale of leasing companies

Nicholas Sanderson

Introduction

First of all, it should be noted that transactions involving the sale of equipment lessors are often unlike other apparently similar transactions involving the sale of commercial trading companies.

There are three main reasons a buyer might wish to acquire an existing leasing company. The first is to create a new leasing trade or expand an existing one for which the purchaser needs the infrastructure to generate and manage its new business. This type of acquisition is closest to the acquisition of a commercial trading company since the driving force is the ability of the acquired company to generate a future stream of profits.

The second type of acquisition is the acquisition of a portfolio of leasing assets by a buyer already in the business. In cases where an acquisition of a leasing company for its origination and management capabilities is undertaken, an acquisition of an existing lease portfolio is likely to be involved as well. However, the reverse is not always the case due to the fact that leasing companies, particularly those held within a larger financial group, may not, themselves, have any employees or fixed assets since these might belong to another company within the group.

A third type of transaction occurs where there is a difference between the tax treatment of the buyer and the seller so that the leasing company is more valuable to the buyer than to the seller. There is consequently a benefit for both parties from undertaking the transaction.

In the United Kingdom, the largest number of transactions related to the sale of leasing companies from the mid 1980s up to the time of writing were probably those in the third category. These transactions have been driven by the acceleration of tax allowances (as compared to depreciation) available to lessors. The timing difference can then be converted to an absolute benefit if its reversal can take place at a lower tax cost. The tax benefit from claiming allowances is enjoyed at, say, 30 per cent, while the tax cost, resulting from the reversal of timing differences is borne at, say, 15 per cent by the purchaser of the leasing company. The benefit to both parties (but not the tax authorities) is readily apparent. This type of benefit was enhanced in the mid 1980s by the change in the UK tax regime which progressively reduced allowances on plant and machinery in the first year of ownership of equipment from 100 per cent to 25 per cent over three years and, over the same period, reduced the rate of corporation tax from 52 per cent to 35 per cent.

Once the tax regime had largely stabilised, and following an initial rush of transactions in the mid and late 1980s, the next group of transactions of this third tax-driven type occurred in the early and mid-1990s involving banks, utilities and other financial companies that had losses, buying from similar entities with profitable leasing operations. In the late 1990s and up until 2000 there have been fewer loss making banks. Their place has been taken by a number of large corporates that have ongoing losses. The substantial advantages for lessors from these transactions has resulted in a number of major bank-owned leasing companies being sold to realise a tax benefit. The demise of this market has been predicted in each of the previous editions of this book, but opportunities to arbitrage the tax position of buyers and sellers continue to arise.

The purchase and sale of leasing companies, other than for tax reasons, is largely cyclical. As a boom market develops, financial institutions tend to enter the leasing market in search of higher margins than can be made from lending. They then dispose of these generally small operations, which they regards as non-core, during a downturn when some of the risks of leasing become apparent. There is, however, also a longer-term trend linked to developments in the leasing market described in the previous chapter on the financing of leasing companies. There is now only limited scope for leasing companies that simply provide finance for equipment without providing any additional services or taking any risks other than the financial risk on lessees. This trend has taken the majority of smaller, bank-owned and independent leasing companies out of the market by sale or closure. Larger bank-owned companies have the ability to lend relatively large sums; however, margins tend to shrink with the competition for a limited number of large transactions that still offer tax benefits. For this reason, larger bank-owned companies have had to enter the operating lease market and find ways of providing a wider range of services to their customers and take an increasing level of equipment and operating risk.

Companies that fund smaller-ticket and consumer transactions through the capital markets have also entered the market. These companies are simply origination and servicing (or managing) entities without any, or any significant, portfolio of owned assets.

Due to the changing nature of the leasing market, there will never be a shortage of transactions involving the buying, selling and financing of equipment leasing companies. The first area considered in this chapter is how the financial position of a leasing company is reflected in its accounts. This analysis is then viewed from the perspective of a prospective purchaser. The next section considers how a seller can maximise the benefit from selling a leasing operation. Finally, the documentation and completion of transactions is considered.

As in the previous chapter, in order to clarify matters certain terms are used in a particular way in this chapter. A 'company' refers to the leasing company targeted by a potential buyer. The person selling the company is the 'seller' and the purchaser is described as the 'buyer'. A lease is always the agreement between the company and a customer described as the lessee. A headlease refers to a lease to the company from a funder of equipment that is sublet under leases to lessees. A 'group' refers to the company (either the seller or the buyer as appropriate), its ultimate holding company and the subsidiaries of such ultimate holding company, save where group is defined for a particular purpose such as the companies required to prepare consolidated accounts, a group of companies registered as a group for the purposes of section 43 of the Value Added Tax Act 1994 or a group for some other purpose of UK tax legislation.

Three views of a leasing company

It is essential that all parties to the sale and purchase of a leasing company and those advising them have an understanding of the way in which a leasing company's accounts are constructed. A leasing company exists in at least three parallel areas: that reflected in its financial statements; in its tax computations; and in its worth to its owners and/or a potential buyer. It is rare (and probably coincidental) that these three views of a company coincide.

In some jurisdictions, the assets and liabilities of a leasing company shown in its financial statements are prepared in accordance with accounting conventions intended to reflect the economic, but not the legal position, of the company. For instance, the company's entitlement as finance lessor under a finance lease will be shown as an entitlement as a creditor in respect of receivables rather than as the owner of a fixed asset being an item of plant and machinery. If the lease were an operating lease, where there are virtually identical legal rights, the company would, however, be shown as owner of the item of plant and no account would be taken in the balance sheet of the obligations of the lessee under the lease.

However, in the United Kingdom a leasing company will be taxed on the basis of its legal entitlement rather than on the basis of its accounting profit. This approach is, however, increasingly being modified in tax legislation by the piecemeal application of accounting profit as the measure for taxation. In the United Kingdom, in certain instances the Inland Revenue takes the higher of the accounting profit and the legal entitlement to income in order to levy tax on it and gives credit when the position reverses. The important point to note is therefore that the accounting profit shown in the financial statements of a leasing company is unlikely to reflect its taxable income.

However, neither the accounting nor the taxation views of a leasing company give much indication as to what it might be worth to a buyer. Two examples from different types of companies illustrate the point. All finance leases and finance agreements, such as hire-purchase agreements, are shown in the balance sheet as an outstanding loan balance. This means taking the aggregate of outstanding payments due from the lessee and deducting that part which reflects income arising in subsequent periods. The resulting figure is included in the balance sheet as an asset. In either case, it does not reflect either the amount immediately payable by a lessee if the finance lease or finance agreement is terminated at the date of the accounts, nor is it likely to reflect, except coincidentally, the value to the company of the future cash flow to be derived from the lease. In the case of finance leases, a termination provision will probably result in a receipt from the lessee greater than the balance shown in the accounts. In the case of finance agreements, and certainly the case with regulated consumer agreements in the United Kingdom (Consumer Credit Act 1974), the minimum amount payable by a lessee will generally include two months' additional finance charges by way of penalty for early termination. A buyer will wish to value assets owned by a company and will not, generally, be satisfied with the amounts shown in the financial statements.

Leasing company accounts

Bearing in mind the analysis set out in the previous section, the accounts of leasing companies need to be examined in greater detail.

The balance sheet

As with all companies, a balance sheet provides a picture of the company at a particular date. It contains a statement of the future economic benefits to which the company is entitled (its assets) and of the future economic benefits that it is obliged to cede to other parties (its liabilities).

Subject to the qualifications set out in the previous section, Exhibit 15.1 illustrates a typical leasing company balance sheet. Also included is a calculation of the provision for deferred taxation.

Accounting treatment of leases

The company's business involves the ownership of equipment as capital assets which are let to lessees. Some of the equipment is let under operating leases and some under finance leases. The distinction between an operating lease and finance lease is discussed in greater detail in Chapters 11 and 16. Equipment let under an operating lease is simply shown as a fixed asset in the balance sheet, with no entry reflecting the benefit or liability by reason of the equipment being let. Where equipment is let under a finance lease there is no heading in the balance sheet for equipment. The reason for this is that finance leases are treated for accounting purposes as the financial rights under such leases and not the equipment let under them.

Exhibit 15.1

A typical leasing company balance sheet

Assets	US$	US$
Fixed assets		
Equipment let under operating leases		5,000,000
Total fixed assets		5,000,000
Current assets		
Investment in finance leases	25,000,000	
Less: advance rentals	(4,000,000)	21,000,000
Group relief receivable	150,000	
Cash	75,000	225,000
Total net current assets		21,225,000
Total assets		26,225,000
Liabilities		
Liability under headleases	9,000,000	
Loan from funder	12,000,000	
Accruals for interest and finance charges	350,000	
Payables	250,000	
Corporation tax	500,000	
VAT	210,000	
Provision for deferred taxation	2,100,000	24,410,000
Net assets		1,815,000
Shareholders' funds		
Revenue reserves		815,000
Ordinary shares		1,000,000
Total		1,815,000
Deferred tax computation		
Investment in finance leases	25,000,000	
Book value of equipment	5,000,000	
Less liability under headlease	(9,000,000)	
Tax written down value of equipment	(14,000,000)	
	7,000,000	
Deferred tax provision @ 30%	2,100,000	

Finance leases and advance rentals

Two figures appear in the balance sheet in respect of finance leases: one being the investment in finance leases; the other being the liability under headleases. It should be noted that where equipment is to be held under an operating headlease, it would not appear as a liability in the balance sheet, nor would the benefit of the operating lease under which such equipment might be let to a lessee. The equipment shown in the balance sheet must, therefore, either be owned outright by the company or held under a headlease or other finance agreement treated as a finance lease.

In the case of both the investment in finance leases and the liability under headleases, the figure represents the capital element of the finance lease concerned based on whatever accounting convention is used to spread the income and finance charges over the term of the leases. The method adopted for calculating the capital value shown in the balance sheet is to take the future rentals payable under the lease and to deduct an amount equal to income attributable to future accounting periods. Income is allocated to different accounting periods so as to maintain a constant rate of return on the capital balance outstanding in each period. This means that more income is allocated to earlier periods of a lease when a greater capital balance is outstanding. The method of making these allocations is discussed in greater detail in Chapters 11. The calculation normally takes into account tax benefits received by the company where such are relevant.

A balance sheet will sometimes show the gross amount of the receivables owed under the lease and then deduct that part attributable to unearned finance charges. This treatment does not, however, give any useful indication of the amount of the unearned finance charges that would be payable on an early termination of the lease, nor the period over which they are spread. The calculation of the balance payable under the headlease is carried out in an identical manner. The balance is amortised over the term of the lease with each rental comprising a mixture of capital and income.

On the assumption that income is recognised on an accruals (and not a cash) basis under the lease, the item shown as advance rentals will appear in the balance sheet. This represents rentals paid at the balance sheet date to the extent that, on an accruals basis, they had not been passed through the profit and loss account at that date. It is instructive to consider the implication of this statement for the balance sheet bearing in mind that what is said only applies to that part of the rentals that had not been accrued prior to the balance sheet date.

What has occurred prior to the balance sheet date is that:

- cash has been received;
- the loan to the funder may have been reduced or cash may have been retained;
- a liability to VAT has been incurred on the entirety of the rental;
- a liability is set up which is reduced as the rental is treated as accruing;
- no credit has been put through the profit and loss account as turnover/sales;
- no debit has been shown in the profit and loss account as 'cost of sales', which represents a combination of a credit to the investment in finance leases to amortise part of the capital invested and a debit to interest expense or finance charges under the headleases; and
- no corporation tax liability has been accrued to the extent that no profit has been recognised.

As noted below, the key point here is that although cash in respect of the rental has been received, it has not been recognised for either accounting or tax purposes.

Operating leases and residual value

As defined in Statement of Standard Accounting Practice (SSAP) 21, issued by the UK Accounting Standards Board, any lease that is not a finance lease is an operating lease. As explained in the introduction to this section, companies will recognise their ownership of equipment let under operating leases as fixed assets (assuming that they do not themselves rent the equipment under an operating lease, in which case they will not show it at all). Companies will charge depreciation on the equipment over its economic life and while not being required to mark it to market (that is, to value it each year at market value) they will need to consider whether the rates of depreciation are appropriate to amortise the value to that which can be realised on sale at the intended date of sale. For an operating lessor this means on expiry of the operating lease, unless it is realistically anticipated that the equipment will be re-let. The rentals arising under the lease are recognised by accrual over the period to which they relate. A profit or loss would then be struck between the rental received, on the one hand, and the aggregate of depreciation of the equipment and any funding costs, on the other.

One of the most important issues in valuing a company that undertakes operating leasing is the ability of the company to realise the amount anticipated on return of the equipment at the end of the operating lease, that is its residual value. A number of operating lessors, particularly in the information technology and automotive fields, have found themselves in difficulty through a failure to estimate likely residual values correctly. It should be noted that finance lessors could still have an exposure, although to a lesser extent, to residual value risk because guarantors of residual value may prove unable to meet their obligations in circumstances where the equipment values guaranteed have fallen sharply.

Deferred taxation

The question of deferred taxation comes as a balance sheet item rather than being related to tax since it is an accounting convention rather than an actual liability to pay a tax authority. There are four issues related to accounting for deferred taxation: first, conventional positive timing differences arising from differences in the amortisation of the net investment in finance leases or equipment for accounting purposes and the tax allowances available in respect of the ownership of such equipment; unusual negative timing differences giving rise to deferred tax assets where, for whatever reason, the balance of unrelieved expenditure and tax losses exceeds the unamortised investment in finance leases and the book cost of equipment; the effect of losses and reliefs from outside the company; and deferred taxation arising from differences between the method of recognising deductions in respect of rental payable under headleases for accounting and tax purposes.

The United Kingdom is, at present, unusual with regard to deferred taxation since the taxation of finance leases generally follows the legal form of the transaction, that is, ownership of equipment and receipt of rental rather than the accounting treatment which is as a loan. Until recently, provision for deferred taxation in the United Kingdom was permitted on the basis of liabilities that are reasonably foreseeable rather than on the basis of full provision for timing differences.

Deferred tax provision

As can been seen from the calculation at the foot of the balance sheet, the deferred tax provision depends upon three variables: the book value of the leases/equipment, the tax written down value (TWDV) of the equipment and the tax rate applied to the difference. The book value is the value of finance leases and equipment where the company is lessor, less the value of finance leases where the company is lessee. There is one factor that is missing. That is the possible availability to the company of losses or allowances in addition to the TWDV of the equipment. It will be a matter for discussion with auditors whether, under the current full provision method, external allowances can be taken into account. It is also worth noting that no reduction is made in the provision to reflect the fact that the liability to pay tax will only arise some time in the future.

Deferred tax assets
There is no obligation upon a company in the United Kingdom to claim tax allowances on equipment that it owns. As discussed below, allowances on equipment are pooled, which means that they remain latent until either claimed, offset by the sales proceeds of equipment or converted into allowances upon the company ceasing to trade. This means that where equipment is lost, stolen, sold for a low figure or where the company does not need to claim allowances, either because the lessees have stopped paying or it has losses available to it from elsewhere, the pool of allowances can continue without reduction.

Where a leasing company in the United Kingdom makes losses and writes off its investment in finance leases the result is not, generally, a loss for tax purposes. The effect will be to reduce the book value of its leases, probably below the TWDV of the equipment let. In addition, finance charges will either absorb such income as is received from rentals or will generate further losses. This scenario became all too common for UK leasing companies during the recession of the early 1990s and those companies that have not been liquidated (in which case the potential tax reliefs are lost) may have found themselves with allowances greater than their prospective tax liability.

Deferred tax assets are not generally shown on the face of the balance sheet since, in the absence of some plan for their use, they are difficult to realise for cash. However, they do have a significant value. The pricing of deferred tax assets is discussed in the context of the purchaser's approach to the pricing of a leasing company.

External reliefs
Reliefs, such as carried forward losses, were historically taken into account in setting the level of provision for deferred tax arising primarily from timing differences in obtaining tax relief on the ownership of equipment. In addition, reliefs can be both sold or purchased from outside the company. These reliefs will often arise from other members within the company's group. In the balance sheet there is an entry for a group relief receivable. This payment would be received from another member of the company's group for the surrender of tax allowances by way of group relief. The payment is tax free, but the surrender of allowances has the effect of making the company increase its deferred taxation provision. The result in balance sheet terms is neutral provided the amount paid for surrendered allowances is the same as the additional provision for deferred taxation by the company. In group terms, the transaction is neutral in accounting terms since the tax liability reduced by the surrendered allowances will, generally, be calculated at the same rate as the company's provision for deferred taxation. Nevertheless, where a discounted rate, or no payment, is made for the surrender of losses, the company will suffer a reduction in net assets. In economic terms, of course, the transfer of losses is highly beneficial and provides the mainspring for most tax-based leasing.

From what has been said in the previous section regarding deferred tax assets it is apparent that, where a full provision is required for deferred taxation, it is questionable whether external reliefs can be taken into account until actually used, thus saving tax allowances related to equipment which are counted in reducing the provision for deferred taxation. Ingenuity is applied in trying to value reliefs, for instance, in the case of group relief to be surrendered to a company, by obtaining an indemnity against taxation, which may be treated as an asset should the reliefs not be surrendered. In the context of the sale of a company, there is often an agreement for the company to receive group relief from within the seller's group or, following sale, the buyer's group. It is questionable whether, strictly, the company's deferred tax provision should be reduced in recognition of an agreement to surrender losses. However, the company's deferred tax position is effectively treated as an asset that can be set off against the provision for deferred taxation. The directors of the company would, however, need to make an assessment of the ability of the counterparty to perform its side of the bargain.

Deductibility and recognition of rent

Where, instead of owning equipment, a company leases it from another lessor, whether under an operating or finance headlease, a further discrepancy may arise between the treatment of rent received under leases and the deductibility of payments of rent under headleases. Where a leasing company is involved as an intermediate lessor with both headlease and lease being matching finance leases, there is unlikely to be any serious disparity since it will generally be possible to obtain a deduction for rentals paid that are matched with lease receipts as recognised for accounting purposes. Where, however, the lease is an operating lease and the company is taking a significant residual value risk on the equipment, then, under recently introduced anti-avoidance provisions, it may be difficult to be sure that a match will occur. See the section on tax issues below for a fuller discussion of the question of the recognition of income and the deductibility of rentals for tax purposes, including an example of the deferred tax effect of the current UK rules for the deduction of finance lease rentals.

Funding

Chapter 14 contains a detailed discussion of the ways in which leasing companies can be funded. This section deals only with those aspects that are relevant to a possible sale of the company.

Sources of funding

In the balance sheet, two sources of funding are shown: liabilities under headleases and loans from funders. There are several key issues in relation to funding.

• Is it intra group and thus capable of being altered by agreement with a friendly party?
• What are the terms of any loan finance? In particular, are the loans at fixed rates in the long term and/or in the short term (that is, up to 12 months). Is the loan repayable on demand or is it undocumented and thus only repayable on reasonable notice?
• In the case of both loan and headlease finance, what security or guarantees have been taken from the company and/or the seller for the finance; on sale, how would such security or guarantees be replaced?

308

- Would a sale result in the loan becoming repayable on demand and/or the headlease becoming terminable; what would the financial effects of such termination be?
- If the company wishes, or needs, to terminate the headlease, or repay the loan, what are the costs of so doing? In the case of the headlease, there may be significant costs associated with the unwinding of the funder's tax position.
- Are there any hedging instruments in existence that are economically or legally linked to any of the funding?

As noted in the discussion in Chapter 14, leasing companies are employing more complex structures to provide funding. This has two effects: first, much funding is kept off the balance sheet of the company and would not, therefore, be directly affected by a sale. However, to the extent that the sale of a company does require the consent of funders, it is probably more difficult to obtain since there are more participants in the more complex structures.

Hedging

Leases tend to be at fixed rates. It is only when dealing with larger-ticket transactions that provision is made for the rental to vary with changes in interest rates. That being so, a prudent lessor will ensure that its funding is matched with the interest and repayment profile of its lease portfolio. This can be done either through fixed-rate headleases and loans or through entry into interest rate swaps, caps or collars. The precise approach of different lessors will vary, but even more sophisticated lessors try to avoid taking risks with interest rate mismatches; that is normally left to professional treasury departments, whether internal or external.

One effect of substantially hedging a lease book is that, subject to performance by the lessees, profits can be locked in on entry into the leases and the net investment in finance leases will represent the realisable value of the leases when account is taken of the related hedging instruments. In the absence of hedging, a lease portfolio will behave like any other fixed-rate financial instrument such as a government stock. The capital value will rise when interest rates fall and fall when interest rates rise. The existence, or otherwise, of hedging is not generally apparent from the face of a balance sheet and is not shown in the balance sheet.

Miscellaneous

Prospective purchasers need to establish whether existing funding and any related hedging can be left intact or taken over. If either course is impossible then, in assessing the value of the company, they will need to take into account the cost of repaying existing facilities and the cost of replacement finance, including appropriate hedging.

Summary

In summary, the balance sheet of a leasing company needs to be interpreted with considerable care. It is prepared using accounting conventions governed by SSAPs and Financial Reporting Standards which result in figures that reflect the economic position of the company on the assumption that it continues as a going concern and on the basis of certain accounting conventions. The net realisable value of its assets may be higher or lower than the figures shown in the balance sheet and, because of the tax position, the company as a whole may be worth more than the net assets shown in its accounts. In addition, in valuing a company, consideration must be given to future contracted income that is not reflected in the balance sheet, for example, under operating leases or from future activities such as fleet management or lease broking. The ability of the company to generate new income streams must also be taken into account.

Tax issues

Many of the tax issues that affect leasing companies have been mentioned in the discussion of the balance sheet, particularly that part dealing with deferred taxation. It is, however, vital that anyone dealing with the purchase or sale of a leasing company, even with a transaction not primarily motivated by taxation, understands the tax position of the company. No apology is made, therefore, for returning to the principal tax issues in isolation. The comments in this section apply to the United Kingdom; the tax position in other countries needs to be considered in the light of the relevant local legislation.

Capital allowances

When considering a leasing company's entitlement to capital allowances, there are a series of propositions worth bearing in mind.

- Commercial depreciation of fixed assets does not give rise to an allowable deduction for tax purposes. Capital allowances are a substitute for depreciation.
- Capital allowances are only available to a person to whom the relevant equipment belongs for the purposes of tax legislation. A lessee under a lease purchase is treated for UK tax purposes as owning the equipment to the exclusion of the lessor or anyone else and is thus entitled to the capital allowances. It should be noted, however, that this only applies where the lease purchase is treated as a finance lease for accounting purposes. It is possible to have an operating-lease purchase agreement where the lessor retains the allowances because the option to purchase is not a bargain purchase option, but is at a realistic estimate of market value of the equipment at the relevant date.
- An equipment lessor may 'own' fixtures attached to land provided the relevant documents are signed by the owner of the land and the lessor and filed with the Inland Revenue, notwithstanding that the lessor has no possible right of ownership of the fixtures as a matter of law. Companies that make contributions to the capital expenditure of others on capital assets may be entitled to capital allowances. Those receiving such contributions will be denied a corresponding amount of relief. Apart from these exceptions, legal and beneficial ownership of equipment is required to obtain allowances.
- There may be limitations on the amount of expenditure that can qualify for allowances in particular circumstances, for instance: where fixtures are acquired; where the equipment has been purchased on a sale and leaseback; and, possibly, where an existing portfolio of let equipment is acquired.

Capital allowance rates

Capital allowances come in a variety of forms and at different rates. The main types are set out below.

- Plant and machinery not otherwise referred to below should qualify for allowances equal to 25 per cent per year on a reducing balance basis.
- Plant and machinery with a working life of more than 25 years will qualify for allowances equal to 6 per cent per year on a reducing balance basis. This limitation does not apply until at least 2010 to seagoing ships and assets used by railways and tramways.
- There are special rules for ships and aircraft, including tonnage tax which reduces allowances on UK registered ships.
- There are restrictions on allowances that can be claimed on cars costing more than £12,000. The allowances are at the lesser of 25 per cent of TWDV or £3,000, but any additional allowance is given on the sale of individual vehicles.
- Leases of equipment to those outside the United Kingdom can result in allowances for the lessor being restricted to 10 per cent per year on a reducing balance basis, or allowances being denied altogether if the lease does not fulfil certain requirements.

In this book we are concerned with equipment leasing companies which generally refers to companies leasing plant and machinery. Apart from fixtures treated as plant for capital allowance purposes, leasing companies can enter into leases that either intentionally or accidentally involve them in leasing buildings, land or structures. Some of these, particularly industrial buildings and structures, may qualify for capital allowances at the rate of 4 per cent per year on a straight line basis.

Pooling

Capital allowances are pooled in that, save in particular cases, different items of plant are treated as forming together a single entity on which allowances are claimed. Newly acquired plant is treated as joining the pool, sold plant as leaving the pool. Purchase consideration is added to the pool, disposal proceeds are deducted and capital allowances calculated on the balance. It is only when the company ceases to trade that the balance of the pool is allowed as a deduction.

Clearly, if equipment is habitually sold for less than its individually calculated TWDV, the balance of expenditure that is not amortised will accrue to the pool and be written off at the relevant rate. This is regarded as unfair since much modern equipment should be written off faster than is allowed by statute. For such equipment, a choice can be made for short life treatment. This means that if it is sold in the first three years of its life, it is treated as an individual item outside the pool and any difference between the sales proceeds and its individual TWDV is allowed as a deduction or taxed.

The analysis of the company's capital allowance position is clearly very important both to a seller and a buyer. The introduction of new legislation means that the task is becoming increasingly complicated.

Recognition of income and allowance of deductions

Where leases are accounted for as finance leases and rentals taxed as pure income rather than a mixture of income and return on capital, the recognition of income for tax purposes will, inevitably, differ from that reflected in the company's financial statements. A leasing company tries to accelerate the deductibility of rentals paid and to delay the recognition of rentals received. These efforts do not meet with wholehearted support from the Inland Revenue which is becoming increasingly keen to ensure that the recognition of income and allowability of deductions for tax purposes follow taxpayers' commercial accounting treatment.

Although some leasing companies were permitted to recognise the receipt of rental income on a cash basis (the income arose when received or, more practically, when invoiced and was not treated as accruing over time), this is no longer permitted since it enabled the payment of rental on the last day of an accounting period and the receipt of rental on the first day of a period without any accrual. Nowadays, some form of accrual is required.

Recognition of income

Where rentals payable under a lease are each of the same amount, each rental will be treated as accruing over the period to which it relates, either in advance or in arrears. Little difficulty arises for either the company or the Inland Revenue in these circumstances.

A company may, for commercial reasons, wish to alter this profile, either having more than one rental paid up front, a typical 3+33 pattern where three month's rental is paid in the first month and no rental is paid in month 35 or 36, or, alternatively, arranging for a terminal balloon payment to match, perhaps, the disposal value of the equipment. In these cases there is a question as to how the income is to be recognised. Is the upfront payment to be taxed in the period in which it is received or, effectively, attributed to the final periods by averaging the rent over the whole term of the lease? Is the balloon payment to be treated as accruing evenly over the whole term of the lease, or does it arise when payable?

Leasing companies have been aggressive in setting their rental profiles with stepped rentals and payments at the end of leases that are intended to arise in the form of capital not income. The UK and US tax authorities have moved to counter these tactics by introducing legislation designed to try to align the recognition of rental income for tax purposes with that for commercial accounting. Both sets of legislation are new and untried. From the point of view of the potential purchaser of a leasing company, the critical question is whether a reallocation of rental receipts will result in a change in the profile of anticipated tax liabilities

Deductibility of rentals

The evolution of the tax treatment for lessees of rentals paid under leases is the mirror image of that described above in relation to the recognition of lease income for lessors. Lessees, including leasing companies holding equipment under headleases, have been aggressive in trying to accelerate the deductibility of rentals, in many cases in order to obtain a faster rate of relief than would have been possible through the capital allowance system had they owned the equipment. In the leading case decided by the UK courts, an attempt was made to obtain full deductibility of the entire capital cost of equipment, in this case a new canal boat, in the first three years of a 25-year lease. This attempt was unsuccessful because the Inland Revenue argued, successfully, that deductibility should follow accounting treatment. The Inland Revenue's position is now somewhat anomalous for the deduction allowed where payments made under a finance lease are equal to the sum of the finance charges plus the amount claimed as depreciation in the lessee's commercial accounts in respect of the equipment. The curious results of this approach are illustrated in Exhibit 15.2.

In summary, it is vital that a prospective purchaser understands how income is recognised and whether there is likely to be any form of attack on such recognition by the tax authorities. The same care is required in assessing deductions for headlease rentals believed to be avail-

Exhibit 15.2

UK tax deduction on finance lease rentals

Year	Rent	Interest	Balance	Depreciation	Tax deduction	Tax deferral	Deferred tax provision
1	14,903	8,000	93,097	10,000	18,000	1,022	1,022
2	14,903	7,448	85,642	10,000	17,448	840	1,862
3	14,903	6,851	77,590	10,000	16,851	643	2,505
4	14,903	6,207	68,894	10,000	16,207	430	2,935
5	14,903	5,512	59,503	10,000	15,512	201	3,136
6	14,903	4,760	49,360	10,000	14,760	(47)	3,089
7	14,903	3,949	38,406	10,000	13,949	(315)	2,774
8	14,903	3,072	26,575	10,000	13,072	(604)	2,170
9	14,903	2,126	13,798	10,000	12,126	(916)	1,253
10	14,903	1,104	(1)	10,000	11,104	(1,254)	(1)

Notes:

• Cost of equipment, US$100,000.

• Interest rate, 8.00% per year payable annually in arrears.

• Depreciation for accounting purposes, straight line over 10 years.

• All amounts shown in US$.

able to the company. The risk of reallocation will tend to rest with a seller since the Inland Revenue will seek to accelerate the recognition of income and to delay the deductibility of rentals paid. The buyer may receive an unexpected bonus if these efforts are successful.

Continuance of trading

Where the purpose of selling a leasing company is to transfer the future taxable income or excess tax allowances to a new owner, a major concern is that the leasing trade of the company should be treated as continuing. On the cessation of trading, a company is treated as selling (and then re-acquiring) all of its let equipment at market value. Where the value of the equipment is greater than its TWDV, a deemed sale would result in an immediate tax charge. Where the reverse is the case, it would result in a loss that could, perhaps, not be used.

The conduct of a leasing trade comprises the letting of equipment and is essentially passive in nature. There is an argument that where a decision has been taken by the management of a leasing company not to enter into any more leases, or perhaps where a decision has been taken that at a future date the business will be sold, that the trading has ceased. However, the better view is that where a lease is entered into as part of a leasing trade, the trade continues while equipment continues to be let under that lease. An issue may arise as to whether the letting was originally part of a trade, or was let as an investment or non-trading activity, but, once it is established the company is trading, the activity constituting that trade, that is, the letting of equipment to lessees, does not cease until equipment ceases to be let.

Group issues

Leasing companies generally operate within groups of other companies, whether other leasing companies or banks, or within manufacturing or service companies. Apart from the commercial group relationships related to the intra-group pricing of goods and services (including finance), there are usually tax issues that need to be addressed, particularly from the point of view of a seller. The first question is to identify the various types of group that are relevant. 'Group relief' is the ability to transfer tax losses and allowances between members of the group. This is similar to the ability to complete a consolidated return for US purposes, but with detailed rules for determining when a company is, is not, or ceases to be, a member of a particular group for group relief purposes.

- Within the *chargeable gains* tax group assets can be moved within the group without triggering a loss or a gain, any gain or loss being realised only on a disposal to a non-group member by the member making the sale. The use of losses within a group in relation to gains arising on the sale of assets out of the group has recently been simplified, avoiding the need for actual transfers of assets.
- Within the *stamp duty* group assets can be transferred without stamp duty having to be paid. A formal application has to be made for this relief;
- A group for the purposes of section 343 of the Income and Corporation Taxes Act 1988 prevents a trade ceasing (with the consequences referred to in the section on the continuance of trading above), where a transfer of a business occurs between companies under common control; and
- A *VAT* group under which companies under common control can elect to be treated as a single taxable entity for the purposes of value added tax.

The second question is to determine which companies form part of which group and when the relevant group relationship ceases in the course of a sale; or, from the point of view of the buyer, when the company becomes a member of its group. Much legislation is involved with preventing what is known as the envelope trick, where an asset is sold (within a group) to a company with a view to the company being sold outside the group. If not prevented, the envelope trick is an obvious way of avoiding taxes on chargeable gains and stamp duty. Similar legislation is designed to prevent the establishment of artificial groups where the group relationship does not reflect the true economic interests of the parties or where there is an arrangement for the transfer of a member of a group to another group.

Trading issues

Except in cases where the sale of a leasing company is a transaction undertaken solely in order to achieve certain tax effects and the quality and management of the leasing trade is underwritten by the seller who is of undoubted financial standing, the buyer's main concern will be with the quality of the company's assets and trading performance. The first concern of a potential buyer will usually be the quality of the company's existing lease book. The bulk of the funds being expended on the acquisition of the company will generally be attributable to the existing lease book although, increasingly, with funding of leased assets being provided off balance sheet and with limited recourse to the lessor, funding may simply remain in place following an acquisition and the concern will be for the continued availability of such funding to a new owner of the company. Where the purchase is simply a method for the buyer to acquire additional assets, effectively a different method of structuring the purchase of a lease portfolio, no further question arises. In those instances, however, where the buyer is seeking to expand or establish a leasing business, the principal question will be the ability of the company's management to generate and manage new and profitable transactions given the circumstances that will exist following the purchase.

Quality of existing leases

There are two principal methods of assessing the quality of a leasing book: by reviewing the underwriting of individual leases or by considering the criteria used in underwriting of the portfolio as a whole and its historical performance. Reference should be made to Chapter 3 for a full discussion of issues relating to credit and the underwriting of leasing transactions. This chapter only deals with those aspects that are relevant to the assessment of an existing portfolio.

Underwriting each lease

Where the number of leases is limited and time and resources allow, the best method of assessing a portfolio is for the buyer to consider each transaction and assess whether it meets its own underwriting criteria. This assessment will include not only the credit quality of the lessee, but also the soundness of the documentation and the history of payment (or non payment). The buyer is, therefore, in a better position to assess the transaction than the original lessor. The buyer can decide from such review whether each lease is acceptable, acceptable with some support from the seller or unacceptable. The consequences of an existing transaction in a company's portfolio being unacceptable are that the buyer will either require it to be transferred by the company to another company in the seller's group, ask for some additional security, perhaps from the seller, or will arrange to pay for it on deferred terms dependent upon performance.

Assessing a portfolio as a whole

Where there is too large a number of leases to permit individual underwriting, a prospective buyer will have to decide how to satisfy itself on the quality of the portfolio as a whole. There are three main issues: initial underwriting of the leases; historical experience, particularly of default; and concentration of risk.

In carrying out this analysis it is essential to ensure that data on all the leases reflected in the company's accounts are included in the population to be examined. The completeness, accuracy and integrity of the data used will need to be underwritten by the seller in the sale and purchase documentation. A well run leasing company should, as part of its normal management information systems, be able to evaluate the returns on particular groups of business, particularly the levels of default. An examination of the portfolio is designed to validate those systems or, where no such systems exist, to provide the equivalent information on the basis of statistical sampling of the portfolio.

The key to a successful due diligence investigation is the segmentation of the portfolio into homogeneous populations capable of analysis. The most important method of segmentation, particularly with a large population, is static pool analysis where leases written at the same time or over a limited period, such as a month or quarter, are treated as a separate portfolio and the pattern of default or early termination is established. Examination of successive static pools will provide comparable information and also identify trends in the quality of underwriting and performance that cannot be obtained from an examination of the portfolio as a whole because of the effect of the pool being dynamic rather than static. Where the value of leases is unequal, a decision will be needed as to whether the sampling should be weight-ed towards higher value leases. If 'value' in this context means the capital value of lease bal-ances (as opposed to the original cost of equipment), this will bias the sampling towards more recent leases. Consequently, those transactions will have a greater effect on the future perfor-mance of the portfolio, but will understate default because they are newer and do not have a developed credit history. Over-emphasis on the value of individual leases would, however, be inappropriate since in most large portfolios the value of a large number of small transactions will tend to outweigh the relatively few larger deals. Any investigation needs to be able to identify the possibility of a failure of a significant part of the overall portfolio arising from a common cause, for example, by reason of defective documentation or technological obsoles-cence of a particular type of equipment.

Although examination of a large portfolio requires the application of statistical sampling techniques, the ability to audit sophisticated computer systems and to reconcile the numbers generated by such systems with the company's accounts, the proper identification of risk requires knowledge of the particular markets in which the company operates. Leasing involves the taking of risk and the purpose of examining a portfolio is to identify the risks inherent in the portfolio so that the buyer can assess the level of risk that it is accepting.

Management

The investigation of a company will also inevitably involve consideration of its management systems, personnel and trading prospects. The existing portfolio represents the result of the company's previous management and, if the management team is to be retained, it is this management that will determine the success of the acquisition. Management needs to be assessed in five main areas: honesty, financial performance, underwriting and origination of transactions, administration and other services.

Honesty

The question of the honesty of the management is the first on which a buyer needs to be sat-isfied. The pressures of running a leasing company have led more than one set of managers to act in a dishonest manner. Any due diligence examination of a leasing company must con-sider the possibility of systematic dishonesty by the management. This is most likely to arise in the form of suppression of levels of default, possible double funding of transactions (although this would be likely to emerge in the course of a purchase) or extraction of funds from the company by way either of a supply company inflating the prices paid by the com-pany for equipment, or the provision of services to the company by associated parties. Typical peculations in relation to enforcement, repossession and sale of returned or repossessed equipment are more often the perquisites of more junior management. If the senior manage-ment is honest, then the honesty of more junior members of the staff becomes a question of the senior management's competence. All financial institutions are subject to the possibility of fraud and the leasing industry is at greater risk than most, particularly with the involvement of suppliers and brokers in a market noted for its fierce competition.

Financial performance

Financial competence involves ensuring that information on the operation of the business is produced on a timely and accurate basis. It also involves the identification of financial risks such as mismatching and the correct pricing of the products offered to customers. The funding of the company must also be properly managed and the business conducted prudently, recognising the risks that do exist. A buyer is likely to take control of the financing of a company immediately after purchase and, consequently, the position in relation to funding will need to be established in the course of the purchase. The question of the completeness and accuracy of information provided to the buyer by management has been discussed in the previous section related to the quality of the lease portfolio, but it equally applies to financial information.

Underwriting and origination of transactions

The way in which transactions are generated and accepted is critical to the present and future prospects of the company. There are three separate questions: what criteria have been and are adopted for pricing and underwriting transactions; are those criteria applied properly in deciding whether to accept particular transactions; where have transactions come from in the past and where is it anticipated that future transactions will be originated?

Buyers will need to make their own assessment of the balance between risk, reward and volume that they are prepared to accept both in relation to existing and future business. The tendency mentioned in Chapter 14 is for the need to increase the volume of business written to drive down prices and increase the risks run by lessors. A buyer will need to satisfy itself that the company has the strong capacity to originate transactions that meet prudent pricing and underwriting criteria which is the essence of a successful leasing company. Any leasing company with a large portfolio that does not have a proportion of defaults is almost certainly mismanaging its business. It could have written more business at higher margins and would, by so doing, probably have maximised its profit. Underwriting that is too conservative is as commercially inept as underwriting that is too lax. In practice, underwriting which is too rigid tends to be corrected as competition for business intensifies. Underwriting which is too lax is corrected more obviously by bad debts and, more spectacularly, by corporate failure.

Administration

Apart from the usual issues regarding personnel and premises, administration involves the proper documentation and completion of transactions, dealing with lessees competently and vigorous enforcement in the event of default. While administration appears the poor relation of finance and underwriting, failure in this area can by itself destroy a company and its business. Defective documentation and non compliance with consumer protection legislation may result in entirely unenforceable leases. If the failure is systemic, rather than an isolated lapse, it can imperil the collectability of a significant part, or all, of the company's portfolio. Good administrative systems that document transactions will also reduce the ever present possibility of fraud by suppliers and lessees. A company's administration must also deal with the need to comply with various regulatory requirements. These include those required by the UK Consumer Credit Act, the UK Data Protection Act, various EU Directives on consumer protection and the requirements of industry associations. Currently, in the United Kingdom, the area of most concern in consumer protection relates to the definition of what constitute unfair terms under the Unfair Terms in Consumer Contracts Regulations 1999 which are being energetically enforced in relation to finance companies by the Office of Fair Trading. The regulations prevent the enforcement of terms that are unfair or which are not expressed in clear and comprehensible English.

Other services

The question of the sale of other services arises in three forms: first, is the company providing other value added services on an ongoing basis to the lessees, for example, fleet management in the automotive sector or maintenance inclusive leases in other areas such as information technology; secondly, are add-ons such as insurance, breakdown cover or third-party warranty and maintenance cover being sold to lessees at the time of inception of the lease; and thirdly, is there a possibility of re-marketing other services to the existing customer base?

A lessor is in a strong position to underwrite further transactions for existing lessees and to approach lessees whose payment records make them desirable customers. In order to make the best of the opportunities offered by the relationship with lessees, good administration is required, particularly with small-ticket portfolios. Direct selling means that commission does not need to be paid to brokers or suppliers. All of the opportunities for providing other services will enhance the profitability of a company and will reflect on the commercial competence of management.

A buyer's perspective

The beginning of this chapter identified three reasons why a buyer might wish to purchase a leasing company: expansion or establishment of a leasing trade, acquisition of a portfolio of assets, or tax arbitrage. These three motives are not mutually exclusive. A buyer seeking to expand its existing activities by acquisition will probably acquire an existing portfolio. The benefits of tax arbitrage may lead a seller to dispose of a company and enable a buyer to use its tax position to acquire high-quality leased assets at an advantageous price. This section will, before turning to the question of the pricing of the company, briefly consider alternatives to acquiring an existing company.

Establishing or expanding a leasing trade

For a company wishing to establish or expand a leasing trade, the alternatives are: to start a new business or area of business by recruiting appropriate staff and either using existing systems or creating new systems to service the business; or to acquire an existing operation. The advantages of establishing a new operation are that no premium has to be paid, except perhaps in order to hire appropriate management and staff; the risk profile can be managed and, once the business has been established, then acquisitions of portfolios can be undertaken with the benefit of home grown management to oversee and integrate such acquisitions. The disadvantages of this organic approach are that it will take time to establish a new business, and until the portfolio has grown to a sufficient size to provide income to support the overhead, the operation is likely to make losses. The risk of acquiring an existing business and management should not be underestimated. The difference between acquiring a trading company and a leasing operation is the speed with which disaster can strike if the acquisition is mismanaged. This is particularly true if the buyer provides extensive funding to management and encourages the expansion of the portfolio with insufficiently stringent controls or understanding of the risks being undertaken.

Acquisition of assets

A common factor between those buyers seeking to establish or expand a leasing trade and those principally motivated by tax considerations is that they will each end up acquiring a portfolio of leased assets. For some buyers, the acquisition of a portfolio of assets is the primary purpose of the proposed transaction. Such a buyer will regard the need for a company purchase as a means to an end, that is, the acquisition of the assets. A principal advantage of a company purchase is that it is unnecessary to transfer each lease to the buyer. Certainly this is a major concern with a portfolio comprising many individual small transactions where collection is operated by way of direct debit. It is unlikely that such leases will have any provision relating to a change of lessor control. With a portfolio comprising fewer larger transactions, it is more likely that the consent of the lessees will be required for a sale since the lessor will have a greater obligation to each of them by way of rebates or rentals on termination of the lease, rental adjustments for tax and/or interest changes and the lessee will be more concerned with the identity of the lessor in order to manage its banking relationships and limits.

The disadvantages of a company sale from the point of view of both the seller and the buyer are that there will need to be a sharing of risk in relation to the corporate entity and, in particular, in relation to its tax affairs. The buyer will wish to be compensated for not receiving allowances in respect of the entirety of the cost of the assets acquired and will also wish to ensure that any pre-sale liabilities remain or are indemnified by the seller. The sale of the company will limit the ability of the seller to manage any unforeseen tax liabilities and will require the seller to give undertakings and representations to the buyer regarding the company being sold.

The parties will need to evaluate the relative attractions of a portfolio sale versus a company purchase. In practice, the nature of the portfolio and the position of the seller, that is, whether the portfolio represents the entirety of its leasing business and whether it is easily transferred into a separate company, will dictate the method used.

Tax driven buyers

The primary purpose of a tax driven buyer will be to give value to tax reliefs that it is otherwise unable to use or to use quickly. Some tax driven buyers have not, however, had tax reliefs, but have had schemes for the avoidance of future tax liabilities of the company reflected in their balance sheets by the provision for deferred taxation. Until the late 1990s in the United Kingdom there has been no alternative for a tax driven buyer but to acquire a company. In the late 1990s the Inland Revenue introduced anti-avoidance legislation designed to stop companies with excess capital allowance pools selling them to tax paying lessors by way of the sale and leaseback of equipment. The result of this legislation was to open the way for tax paying companies with old but comparatively valuable equipment to enter into sale and leaseback transactions with lessors having reliefs and to transfer, in effect, taxable income from the seller/lessee to the buyer/lessor. These types of transaction which have not, at the time of writing, been countered by the Inland Revenue, represent a real alternative for a tax driven buyer to acquiring a company.

A buyer acquiring a company for tax reasons, and, to some extent, one that is purchasing primarily for commercial reasons, will have a concern regarding the anticipated profile of taxable profits or reliefs available from the company following purchase. Generally, it will expect to be indemnified against liabilities arising from events occurring prior to the completion of the purchase. Factors affecting the company's tax position were considered in the section on tax issues above. A buyer will, however, have some specific concerns arising from the fact of the sale and purchase.

Risk of a challenge from the tax authorities

The buyer will wish to know the likelihood of the tax authorities seeking to upset the tax affairs of the company as presented by the seller. This concern may arise from two sources. First, to what date has the tax authority agreed the company's tax affairs? Secondly, has the company undertaken any transactions that might be regarded as tax aggressive or risky? Where the primary motive for the transaction is to arbitrage the buyer's and the seller's tax positions, it should be assumed that the tax authorities will subject the tax affairs of the seller, the buyer and the company to more rigorous scrutiny than is usual and that concessions usually accorded to taxpayers may not be available.

If there appears to be a material risk of a challenge by the tax authorities, the buyer will wish to assess the likely long-term credit standing of the seller since a dispute with the tax authorities, particularly if it is not an isolated case and the issues affect a number of transactions or companies, may take many years to resolve. The seller will also be concerned with the credit standing of the buyer since there is legislation that enables certain tax liabilities of the company arising after the sale to be recovered from the seller or any member of the seller's group. It is customary for a buyer to indemnify a seller against such a liability.

Group relief and lessee recovery

In the UK, where a company has surrendered losses to the seller by way of group relief, the risk of a challenge may in fact rest with the seller, which has had the benefit of the reliefs, rather than directly with the company. If the seller (or a member of its group) paid the company for the transfer of losses, there may be a liability, either contractual or on general legal principles, that such payment must be returned by the company if the losses purportedly transferred do not materialise. Where the loss of reliefs is recoverable under the tax adjustment provisions in a lease, the seller will wish to ensure that it benefits from any such recovery from a lessee since it will have suffered the loss of reliefs. One of the most technical parts of the sale documentation is ensuring that a loss of allowances in the company results in the seller and members of the seller's group, the company and the lessee being placed in the same position as they would have been if there had been no sale without prejudicing the position of the buyer.

Pricing the company

The value of anything, including a leasing company, is what a buyer and a seller agree that it is worth. There are, however, some criteria by which the price of a leasing company is generally established. In principle, the price paid will be the value of the existing assets of the company less its liabilities (net assets) together with a figure, if any, representing the ability of the company to generate future business (goodwill). The net assets are not, however, valued in the same way as the figures shown in the balance sheet in Exhibit 15.1. The main adjusting factors reflect the time value of money, something not currently recognised in commercial accounting although an all pervading influence in the leasing industry, and the way in which any tax benefit arising from the transaction is to be shared between the buyer and the seller.

The discount rate used by the buyer and the sharing of the tax benefit coupled with any goodwill will determine the extent of the adjustments to the accounting balance sheet and the gain or loss shown by the seller for the purposes of its financial statements. The way in which a gain or loss is shown, whether above the line, as a pre-tax profit or loss, or on the tax line, is the subject of much discussion and is also capable of being varied by payments made between the buyer, the company and the seller or members of the seller's group in respect of group relief, funding costs, hedging or dividends.

Adjusting the value of the leases

As far as a buyer is concerned, the items shown in the balance sheet as investment in finance leases, equipment and liability under headleases should be replaced by a single figure representing the present value of the net future cash flows arising from the leases, having deducted rentals payable under headleases and discounted at the funding rate. The future cash flows will include any residual value expected to be realised for equipment let under operating leases which, the buyer will assume, is sold at the end of the current operating lease. From the buyer's point of view, the critical numbers are for future rentals and, in evaluating the leases, the buyer is assessing the likelihood that some of that future income flow will not materialise.

The principal reasons for the future cash flow not materialising are: a failure by the lessee to pay; the equipment not realising its assumed residual value; or adjustments being made to the rentals due under the leases by reason of changes in tax or interest rates. Where there is a significant risk of credit failure by lessees, the buyer will need to build in an assumed default rate or have the cash flow credit enhanced by the seller. The same degree of prudence will need to be shown where residual value risk on equipment is in issue. A prudent seller will not wish to give a guarantee of a lessee credit, or of residual value in respect of equipment, without a significant input into the continuing management of the portfolio. The sharing of risk and responsibility is a commercial matter for the parties but, generally, where the failure to recover an amount occurs by reason of facts existing at the date of sale, the seller will take responsibility under the sale and purchase documentation, unless the buyer has had a chance to undertake full due diligence.

A further major factor affecting the valuation of the future rentals is the need to match the interest profiles of the buyer's funding and the cash flow. If the buyer is able to take over within the company a swap or portfolio of swaps fixing the funding costs of the company at a particular level, then the only issue affecting funding is the margin over Libor at which the buyer will fund the company. There are certain risks other than lessee credit, residual value risk on equipment and the enforceability of documentation that may affect the future cash flow. These include changes in tax assumptions and early termination of the leases. Where a buyer is taking over a business as a going concern, those risks might reasonably be regarded as endemic to the leasing business. Where, on the other hand, the transaction is tax driven, the seller may need to indemnify the buyer and/or to hedge the exposure.

The value of tax reliefs or liabilities

The deferred taxation provision is a major figure in the balance sheet. The method of calculation is shown in the section on deferred taxation above. In assessing the price of the company, the purchaser should make two adjustments.

- The deferred tax calculation should be made on the basis of substituting for the net book value of the leases and equipment, the present value of the net future rentals as described in the previous section 'Adjusting the value of the leases'. This is because the difference between that figure and the gross rentals should be represented by amounts deductible for tax in future periods and specific provision will be made for tax on the rentals received in advance.

- The tax rate should be substituted by the value ascribed by the buyer to its tax reliefs. Where the transaction is not tax driven and the buyer is fully taxpaying, the figure will be the same as that used in calculating the existing provision.

The resulting figure should be substituted for the deferred tax provision in the balance sheet in calculating the price of the company. The value ascribed to the buyer's tax reliefs will reflect its profit from the transaction although, in practice, this may also emerge in an enhanced margin in the discount rate applied to the future rentals.

The price of the company

Exhibit 15.3 below shows the adjustments to the balance sheet appearing in Exhibit 15.1. On the basis of those adjustments the price comprises the aggregate of the shareholders' funds of US$3,412,000 plus the amount owed to the funder of US$12,000,000. This is on the assumption that the headlease remains in place and does not need to be terminated following sale.

Adjusting the balance sheet

Exhibit 15.3 illustrates the adjustments that would be made by the buyer to the balance sheet shown as Exhibit 15.1. No attempt has been made to be precise about these adjustments which are for illustrative purposes only.

Net investment in finance leases, equipment and liability under the headlease

To illustrate the point clearly, all of the above items have been removed from the adjusted balance sheet and replaced by a single item being the present value of net future rentals. The basis of this adjustment has been described above and, in practice, a buyer would split the single item into its component parts being the rentals contracted by the lessees, the liability to pay rentals under the headlease and the value ascribed to the equipment, that is, its residual value.

Loan from the funder

The figure that the buyer will actually wish to identify is the principal amount owed to the funder, including the accrual for interest up to the date of completion together with any break costs or payments to terminate or continue hedging. If the funder is a member of the seller's group, this figure may also be increased by the amount of any adjustments passed between the company and the seller's group prior to completion, such as dividends and group relief payments.

Corporation tax

The figure for corporation tax has been increased by the amount of tax payable on advance rentals. This figure, which represents tax on income that will accrue after completion in respect of rentals paid prior to completion, could have been added to the deferred tax provision. An issue that often arises between a buyer and a seller is how the corporation tax pro-

Exhibit 15.3

Typical price adjustments made to a leasing company balance sheet

Assets	Financial statements US$	US$	Price adjustment US$
Fixed assets			
Equipment let under operating leases		5,000,000	Nil
Total fixed assets		5,000,000	Nil
Current assets			
Investment in finance leases	25,000,000		
Less advance rentals	(4,000,000)	21,000,000	Nil
Present value of net future rentals			17,300,000
Group relief receivable	150,000		
Cash	75,000	225,000	225,000
Total net current assets		21,225,000	17,525,000
Total assets		**26,225,000**	**17,525,000**

Liabilities			
Liability under headleases	9,000,000		Nil
Loan from funder	12,000,000		12,000,000
Accruals for interest and finance charges	350,000		350,000
Payables	250,000		250,000
Corporation tax, including tax on			
advance rentals at buyer's tax rate	500,000		940,000
VAT	210,000		210,000
Provision for deferred taxation	2,100,000		363,000
Total liabilities		**24,410,000**	**14,113,000**
Net assets		**1,815,000**	**3,412,000**

Shareholders' funds			
Inland Revenue reserves		815,000	2,412,000
Ordinary shares		1,000,000	1,000,000
Total		**1,815,000**	**3,412,000**

Deferred tax computation			
Investment in finance leases	25,000,000		
Book value of equipment	5,000,000		
Less liability under headlease	(9,000,000)		
Present value of future rentals			17,300,000
Tax written down value of equipment	(14,000,000)		(14,000,000)
	7,000,000		3,300,000
Deferred tax provision @ 30%	2,100,000	@11%	363,000

vision should be taken into account in setting the price. The issues are:

- corporation tax that is due up to the date of completion will not be payable for some time and should, therefore, be discounted to reflect this delay in payment; and
- the tax on advance rentals should be calculated at a full corporation tax rate, not a reduced

323

rate to reflect the valuation of the buyer's losses. This argument arises, in particular, where there is no transparency as to the valuation of the buyer's losses. For instance, where it is reflected in an enhanced discount rate for the future rentals, the delay in payment of the tax on advance rentals will also be an issue as with current corporation tax.

Deferred tax

The calculation of the provision for deferred tax has been explained previously. The only differences reflect the substitution of the present value of future rentals arising from equipment, leases and headleases, the elimination of advance rentals (since tax is being provided on a current and not a deferred basis) and the substitution of the buyer's effective tax rate for the rate of corporation tax. The result is a reduction in the provision which represents the value to the buyer of its reliefs.

Overall effect of adjustments

The net effect of all these buyer's adjustments is to increase the net assets by US$1,597,000. The actions taken to amend the statutory balance sheet are discussed below in the context of the position of the seller.

Future plans

A number of issues related to the future management of the company will inevitably arise in the course of discussions related to the sale. The most important issue, but not of immediate concern to the buyer, is that the seller should be satisfied that the buyer's arrangements for paying tax are satisfactory. The seller will require an indemnity against any tax liabilities collectable from the seller by the tax authorities, but, irrespective of this protection, the seller should satisfy itself that the buyer is not itself, or on behalf of a third party, going to undertake a scheme to avoid tax that is likely to attract unwelcome attention from the tax authorities. From the buyer's point of view, it will need to address a number of issues related to the operation of the company after completion.

Management of the leases

Where the sale of the company is undertaken for tax reasons, or where the seller retains credit exposure to the lessees, the seller may wish to retain management of the leases. This may also suit the buyer if it does not have the ability to carry out the administration itself. The contents of the administration agreement are beyond the scope of this chapter, but it will need to provide for the administrator to:

- issue invoices to the lessee on behalf of the company;
- negotiate variations in rentals following changes in tax assumptions or early terminations of hiring;
- pursue unpaid rentals and enforce the terms of the leases, including the repossession of equipment (assuming that that is economically sensible);
- arrange for the payment of rentals into an account of the company; and
- arrange for the sale or re-letting of equipment returned at the end of operating leases in order to realise not less than the anticipated residual value.

The administrator is often remunerated by a combination of a fixed fee, a retention or share in any excess arising from the leases by way of secondary rentals or termination sums greater than a stated amount, or a retention of rentals collected by the administrator for a period prior to paying the funds over to the company. In addition, where the administrator is responsible for realising equipment coming off an operating lease, it is likely to receive an incentive by way of sales commission reflecting a high proportion of the excess over the anticipated residual value.

Post completion tax planning

A buyer acquiring a company for tax reasons will either wish to use its tax reliefs against the income of the company, or to use the company's tax reliefs against its own taxable profits. There are two principal methods of sheltering the company's income with a buyer's reliefs and essentially only one efficient way for a buyer to access excess reliefs in the company.

Accessing excess reliefs

Excess reliefs in a company comprising capital allowances in excess of the value of leases and equipment can be best accessed through a cessation of the company's trade which will result in a deemed disposal of its assets. In order to ensure that the reliefs are usable elsewhere in the buyer's group by way of group relief, a delay will need to occur following completion before the trade ceases since profits and losses can only be offset concurrently and, if the period from the buyer assuming ownership of the company to the cessation of trading is too short, insufficient profits of the buyer may fall into that period to absorb all of the reliefs generated. The method of terminating the company's trade will be by the sale of the leases and let equipment to a party not under common control with the company. If the sale were to a member of the buyer's group, then section 343 of the UK Income and Corporation Taxes Act 1988, described in the section 'Group issues' above, would prevent the trade being treated as ceasing. Care will be needed to ensure that the sale of the leases does not occur prematurely, and that the economic interest in the trade does not pass from the company to the seller. There would be a great temptation to arrange, prior to the sale of the company, that the leases are sold back to the seller or another member of the seller's group at a predetermined price subsequent to completion in order to generate the excess reliefs. This approach carries a number of avoidable tax risks and is not recommended. While an immediate cessation of the company's trade is the most efficient way to realise the reliefs, it is of course possible to continue the trade and claim the reliefs over time, generating a potentially continuing source of losses usable by the buyer's group by way of group relief.

Sheltering the company's income

There are usually two methods of using a buyer's reliefs in order to reduce the tax payable on the company's income. The first is by surrendering losses to the company by way of group relief, which requires the buyer to have losses available concurrently with the company's taxable income. The second method is by transferring the company's trade to the buyer and merging the company's trade into the buyer's trade. The second method requires the buyer's losses to have arisen in a trade into which the company's trade can reasonably be merged, for example, an existing leasing trade or a wider financial trade.

One risk is that the company does not become a member of the buyer's group because the economic interest in its trade remains with the seller's group. This is a risk arising from a similar factual matrix to that referred to in the previous section. The indicia of the trade not having been transferred would be: continued management by the seller; a guarantee of the lessees' credit by the seller; and the potential profit from conducting the trade being extracted from the company by way of the fee for management. The position would be exacerbated if the seller continued to finance the company after the buyer had purchased it.

A second risk is that on the transfer of the company's trade to the buyer, it is not accepted that it merges into the buyer's existing trade. This would not necessarily mean that no losses from the buyer's existing trade could be accessed, but they would need to be concurrent losses with the profits of the trade transferred by the company. In the context of a financial trade other than leasing, the losses would probably arise from provisions for bad and doubtful debts where there is likely to be a degree of flexibility as to when the provisions become specific and thus deductible for tax purposes.

The buyer may have some discretion to arrange for taxable income of the company or the trade to arise in the relevant accounting period to enable it to be sheltered by available losses. This may be achieved by selling the right to future income in order to accelerate the taxable receipt. This, and the writing of new business or the disposal of equipment, can provide the opportunity to ensure that taxable profits arise in an accounting period when they can be sheltered. There is, however, little that can be done where the losses in the buyer's existing trade have already crystallised and are being carried forward, but the trade transferred from the company does not merge with the buyer's trade.

Refinancing the company

Most leasing companies have substantial debts. It has been assumed in the balance sheet that all debt is owed to an individual funder, which may be the seller or associated with the seller. In addition, there are the liabilities under the headlease. On completion, it is likely that the seller will need to have the debt repaid. There are two issues: first, the refinancing of the company and secondly, the way in which interest rate exposures inherent in the company's lease portfolio are hedged. The method of refinancing will depend upon the tax and credit position of the buyer. Chapter 14 sets out a number of different possibilities including secured lending, headlease/sublease structures, the sale of the equipment and leases, and establishing an off-balance-sheet funding vehicle.

The income derived from the leases should match the profile of the company's borrowing. If the borrowing by the company prior to sale is intra group and interest free, then any hedge may be held at the level of the seller or the company will probably either be a party to swaps or the borrowing will be, at least to some extent, at a fixed rate or rates. The arrangements for refinancing the company will need to include the termination of any fixed-rate funding or its transfer to the buyer. This is on the assumption that the company is itself not a sufficiently strong counterparty to enter into swap transactions in its own right.

If there is any refinancing, care needs to be taken in the United Kingdom not to use the company's assets as security or otherwise to assist the purchase or funding of the purchase of the company's shares by the seller with any financial assistance originating from the company. If it is necessary to use the company's assets as security for borrowing or to secure part of the purchase consideration for its own shares, then, in the United Kingdom, it will be necessary to ensure that it can go through the procedures laid down in sections 155 and 156 of the Companies Act 1985, which require the company to have net assets and the directors supported by the auditors to make a declaration regarding the company's solvency.

A further complication may arise from the existence of headlease funding. The head lessor may be relying, in making its credit decision, upon the company remaining within the seller's group. There may be either, or both, a guarantee from the seller and a provision in the headlease providing for termination on a change of control of the company. The buyer and seller will need to decide how to approach this: either by accepting that the headleases will be terminated and including the price of so doing in their calculations of the price or by approaching the head lessor prior to sale to obtain confirmation that it is content to continue providing finance. If there is to be a transfer of the leasing trade by the company, the head lessor will need to be a party to the transaction since the headleases will need to be novated to the buyer by the company.

In summary, it is essential that the buyer has a plan as to how the company is to be managed following purchase. The requirements of this plan will need to be accommodated by arrangements with the seller and permitted (or at least not forbidden) by the purchase documentation. A further issue that a buyer will need to consider is the way in which the acquisition and subsequent transactions are to be accounted for. In particular, it is likely that the buyer will wish to show the profit above the line as an enhanced return on the leases, rather than below the line as an adjustment to the tax provision in the acquired company. This may require a fair value adjustment to the leases, particularly if there is to be a transfer of the leasing trade from the company to the buyer after completion.

The seller's perspective

This section considers the transaction from the perspective of sellers. Many aspects have already been discussed from the buyer's viewpoint and these are not revisited. There are, however, a number of issues that are of interest mainly to sellers. The likely motives for a sale are the mirror images of the reasons for buyers to purchase. As discussed in Chapter 14, continued profitability of a leasing company generally requires continuing new business. It is thus difficult to avoid losses in withdrawing from a leasing trade. Sellers contemplating stopping leasing, possibly following losses or a shift of focus in other sectors of their business, will probably incur smaller losses by selling their leasing business rather than allowing it to wind down. While the sale of leasing companies is not, in purely commercial terms, necessarily a sensible method of funding an ongoing leasing business, nevertheless, the need to finance ongoing leasing operations has certainly been a motive, in conjunction with tax benefits, for repeated sales by some lessor groups. One common motive has also been to prevent excessive credit exposures arising to single groups of lessees. The most common expressed motive is that of divesting non-core activities, often followed, a few years later, by a diversification into profitable and related areas.

This chapter is about the purchase and sale of a company. Leasing trades are not, however, always carried on within separate companies. If the seller's leasing trade is, for instance, conducted as an integral part of its financial or banking trade, or it wishes to sell only part of its leasing trade, it could simply sell the relevant equipment and leases in a relatively straightforward process, the mechanics and tax risks of which are described in Chapter 14 in relation to block discounting.

Such a transaction would, however, result in the receipt of taxable income equal to the sale price which, if it exceeded the TWDV of equipment owned by the seller, would be fully taxable. An alternative is to transfer the lease portfolio to a company owned by the seller and then to sell the company. Provided the transfer of the lease portfolio takes place with a company within the seller's group for the purposes of section 343 of the UK Income and Corporation Taxes Act 1988, the assets should be transferred at their TWDV with, consequently, no tax charge arising. If the transfer occurs sufficiently early, before there is any arrangement for the transferred company to leave the seller's group, no stamp duty should be payable. However, there are proposals to require payment of stamp duty on transfers of assets intra-group where the transferee subsequently leaves within two years of the transfer. In practice, the transfer tends to be decided upon at a stage when a purchaser has already been identified and, consequently, other means (such as a written offer and oral acceptance) have to be used to avoid the need to pay stamp duty on the transfer. A price also needs to be decided upon for the transfer. Normally, it would be preferable to make the transfer at the value shown in the books of the seller, however, this will necessitate adjustments to the resulting balance sheet of the company prior to sale. A buyer will, however, be concerned to ensure that the price paid is not less than market value so as to avoid the risk that a liquidator of the seller might try to set the transfer aside.

Changes to the balance sheet

Historically, sellers tended to make significant changes to the balance sheet in order to improve the tax efficiency of a sale. This included reducing the provision for deferred taxation to that shown in Exhibit 15.3 in order to increase the distributable reserves of the company, again as illustrated in Exhibit 15.3. A dividend was then declared prior to sale which reduced the reserves and increased the amount of loan owed to the funder/seller. The result was to reduce any chargeable gain suffered by the seller on the sale of the shares in the company.

The present position is, however, that there should be no chargeable gains on disposals of shares by a seller. There is a requirement to maintain a full deferred-tax provision and there is little incentive to pay a pre-sale dividend since the abolition of Advance Corporation Tax. Other than ensuring that all payments due to the seller have been made prior to completion, little adjustment is therefore required to the balance sheet as shown in Exhibit 15.1.

Alternatives to sale

As in the case of the buyer, the seller has possible alternatives to the sale of a company. If its intention is to withdraw from leasing, it could sell the portfolio rather than the company, although this might be a less tax efficient way of achieving a disposal. It could also seek to reduce its administrative costs by contracting out the management of the leasing business. A seller facing a tax liability as a result of a crystallisation of a deferred tax liability should consider other ways of mitigating its liability since it will need to pay a significant proportion of the anticipated tax liability to the buyer on the sale of a company. A seller seeking to raise funds from the disposal of its leasing operations could also consider refinancing the company with external, that is, non-group borrowings. Chapter 14 describes a number of methods of achieving this and, where limited recourse funding is coupled with external management of the leases, the seller will have reduced its practical and probably its economic and accounting exposure to leasing.

Summary

In summary, the seller needs to take considerable care in dealing with the sale of a leasing company since it is likely to be asked to underwrite the risks. In particular, any serious tax problem with the sale and the arrangements of the purchaser to shelter income are likely to result in problems for the seller and its group.

Documentation and execution of transactions

In earlier editions of this book, considerable detail was given as to the type of documentation expected on the sale of a leasing company. For the firms involved in these transactions, of which there are relatively few in the United Kingdom, the areas of difficulty tend not to be ones of documentation, but of identifying and apportioning risk between buyer and seller. This has become a greater issue since transactions are now taking place between parties of more equal bargaining strength. Documentation in a sale and purchase transaction, as with any commercial agreement, is designed to identify and apportion risk and reward between the parties in all the circumstances that the parties and those that advise them can contemplate. This section seeks to identify some of the main concerns and the ways in which they are typically dealt with in practice.

Buyer's concerns

There are a number of principal risks against which a buyer will wish to be protected.

Accounts

In most instances, a buyer is acquiring a company on the basis of some accounts including, in particular, a balance sheet drawn up, or to be drawn up at completion. The price payable is based on such accounts, although the calculation of the price will be in the form, more or less, of Exhibit 15.3. The fundamental warranty required by the buyer is that the balance sheet at completion does not omit any material liability and properly reflects the assets in accordance with appropriate accounting standards. If the accounts prove to be inaccurate, the question then arises as to the amount of the buyer's loss.

It is not uncommon for a buyer to stipulate that its loss, in the event of the accounts proving incorrect, should be compensated on a pound for pound basis for any diminution in the company's net assets. There are two issues customarily raised in objection to this. First, a change in the numbers appearing in the balance sheet for the net investment in finance leases and equipment let on operating leases will not affect the amount that the buyer would have paid for the company. The buyer will, in any event, wish to be compensated for any problems with the leases, as described below, so the measure of damage should not be the difference in the balance sheet numbers. Secondly, any loss of tax relief that could increase the provision for deferred tax in the balance sheet should, it is argued, be compensated at the buyer's effective tax rate (11 per cent in the example in Exhibit 15.3) not the full corporation tax rate of 30 per cent. The first argument is almost unanswerable, but the second will depend upon the respective negotiating strengths of the parties and the buyer's actual tax position.

Lease problems

The largest asset in the balance sheet will, almost certainly, be the rights of the company under leases. The warranties customarily given by a seller in relation to the leases and let

329

equipment cover not only the existence and enforceability of the leases, but the identification of risks with the equipment. However, the most important warranty is that a particular cash flow derived from the rentals payable under the leases is payable. This warranty will be qualified by statements that the rentals forming the cash flow may not be payable if the lease is terminated or if the rentals are adjusted in accordance with the terms of the leases for changes in tax or interest rates. Depending upon the terms of the transaction, the seller may also be asked to confirm that no lessee is in arrears nor is the seller aware that any lessee is insolvent. Where operating leases are concerned, more extensive warranties may be needed in relation to equipment since the sale proceeds of the equipment will form part of the cash flow forming the basis of the price paid by the buyer. A critical warranty relates to the enforceability of the leases. This could cover not only compliance with consumer protection legislation but also enforceability against public bodies where problems of the authorities' powers and ability to enter into leasing transactions have been encountered in the past.

Tax issues

The basic principle is that the seller is responsible for delivering the company to the buyer with a particular tax profile. This means, in the context of a leasing company, that the company's tax liability arising prior to completion has been fully provided for in the balance sheet or paid. It also means that the pool of capital allowances available at completion is no less than the buyer has assumed when calculating the price. A further concern is that income and deductions received or claimed by the company are as anticipated and will not be altered following tax authority scrutiny. The issues relating to compensating the buyer for loss are discussed above in the section on accounts.

Other issues

Other matters the seller will be asked to confirm to the buyer are the same as apply for any company purchase. Where the company has employees, premises, computer systems and trading arrangements, then these will be the subject of investigation by the buyer and information about them will be warranted by the seller. Generally, even where the company simply holds leases and equipment, the following warranties will be required:

- the corporate standing of the company and the accuracy of information regarding the company supplied;
- the compliance of the company with statutory obligations, including compliance with tax legislation and the enforceability of leases;
- confirmation that no liability will arise from ownership of real property, other than fixtures, or confirmation that no real property has ever been owned; and
- questions regarding employees and the systems that they operate.

Sellers' concerns

The seller is concerned with three main issues: first, to limit its liability under the warranties given to the buyer; secondly, to avoid a liability, particularly to tax authorities, arising from the activities of the buyer; and thirdly, to ensure that its loan to the company is repaid without any risk of recourse from the company, a liquidator of the company or its creditors.

Limitations on warranties customarily take three main forms: monetary limits so that the seller can never lose more than the price received for the company; obligations upon the buyer to make information available to the seller and to enable the seller to contest any dispute that could give rise to a claim, particularly in relation to taxation; and time limits on claims (typically, in the case of claims relating to the leases, a date after the expiry of the primary period of letting under the lease and, in relation to taxation, after the expiry of the right of the tax authorities to claim).

A buyer can cause a liability to arise for the seller principally by carrying out a provocative tax transaction. This could result in an investigation by the tax authorities with a view to countering the tax benefit derived by the seller and the buyer from the transaction. Furthermore, if the tax authorities are successful in attaching a liability to the company, and the buyer does not ensure that the company meets the liability, there are certain provisions of the tax legislation that might enable the tax authorities to collect the company's unpaid tax direct from the seller in certain circumstances. A failure by the company to pay tax that was found due would almost certainly lead to the company being put into liquidation. This could result in claims arising from the liquidator against the seller. If the scheme undertaken by the buyer results in a loss of tax, then the tax authorities will be keen to recover tax from the seller, which will have been the main beneficiary of the transaction.

The seller's principal concern is to ensure that its loan is repaid, or, if it has provided a guarantee, that the loan from a funder is repaid. Apart from the mechanics of completion designed to ensure that the loan is repaid, there are risks, even where the loan has been repaid, that a subsequent liquidator of the company might seek to set aside the repayment. This could arise in two main situations: if, when the loan is repaid the company is insolvent, the repayment might be set aside as a preference; and if the loan was repaid from funds advanced to the company in circumstances amounting to the company giving unlawful financial assistance in connection with the purchase of its own shares, then the source of repayment could be so tainted that the repayment might be set aside, particularly if the seller/funder was aware of the method of raising funds to secure the loan's repayment.

In addition to being repaid its loan, the seller will also wish to be released from any liabilities that it has in relation to the company, including, in particular: any guarantees given in respect of the company's borrowing or liabilities under headleases; the joint and several liability that goes with membership of a VAT group; and any obligations arising from hedging arrangements. The risks to the seller will be substantially reduced if the company is solvent at the time of sale. This is more likely to be the case now than in the past since the company will probably not have paid a pre-sale dividend or reduced a full provision for deferred taxation prior to the sale.

Description of typical documents

Share sale agreement
The principal document is the share sale agreement. This document contains the terms of the transaction and should provide for all the rights and protections of the parties. Typically, it contains the following main provisions:

- a provision for the sale and purchase of the shares in the company and for payment of the price;
- a clause dealing with the mechanics of completion, which are described in the next section;

- the warranties and representations by the seller which have been discussed above and upon which the buyer relies in acquiring the company (these statements are qualified by the disclosure letter to which reference is made below);
- lengthy provisions providing protections for the seller in the event of a claim arising under the warranties (again, these are described in the preceding section);
- undertakings and covenants by the seller, for instance, not to compete with the company after completion;
- undertakings and covenants by the purchaser, most critically in relation to the future conduct of the company in relation to tax, that it will not become non resident, will not pay a dividend that is abnormal so as to give rise to a possible liability on the seller, will honour obligations to lessees to the extent that these could impact on the seller and will change its name to something unrelated to the seller; and
- a separate part of the agreement that deals with taxation, including arrangements for the seller to deal with the preparation and submission of the company's tax computations in the period up to completion, to indemnify the purchaser for tax in any accounting period ended on or before completion, and a separate undertaking from the buyer not to carry out transactions that could give rise to a tax liability on the seller.

It should be noted that there is generally no explicit provision in the agreement for repayment of the company's indebtedness to the seller. The concern here is that such a provision might be construed as consideration for the shares and consequently subject to stamp duty at 0.50 per cent. However, this should not be a serious concern where the company is able to pay its debts as they arise.

There should also be provision, either in a specific clause of the share sale agreement or the tax covenant that forms part of it, for the pass back to the seller of the benefit of additional rental collected from lessees where this is designed to compensate for a loss of allowances that falls on a member of the seller's group through the operation of group relief. Alternatively, there would be an assignment of the right to recover such rental under the leases, although that is less common.

Disclosure letter

The disclosure letter qualifies the warranties given by the seller to the buyer in the share sale agreement. While it might be thought that the combination of warranty plus disclosure letter should contain the truth, so far as the seller is aware of it, this is not necessarily the case. The function of the warranties is to require the seller to disclose information and to apportion risks between the parties. The buyer will, therefore, resist accepting a disclosure letter that contains anything that might result in a claim under the warranties not being able to proceed. The extent to which a seller is able to disclose information and, critically, disclose the lease documentation will depend upon the relative negotiating strengths of the parties. In relation to the leases, the argument for the buyer is that the seller already has the risk of the leases not being enforceable and has, presumably, taken legal advice on them. All disclosure will do is to cause the buyer to have to pay its lawyers to review the leases again. If there are any problems with the leases then, one hopes, the buyer's lawyers will find it and the seller will be asked to indemnify the liability anyway, so little has been gained. In some cases where a seller believes that it should draw the buyer's attention to certain matters and disclose all matters of which it is aware but where the buyer is not prepared to accept these as disclosures that would limit the warranties, the parties resort to a two-part disclosure letter. The first part qualifies the warranties and limits the seller's liability; the second part is included for information purposes and to ensure that no claim can be made against the seller under relevant securities legislation that it misled the buyer.

Other documents

In addition to the two principal documents, the share sale agreement and disclosure letter described above, there are a number of other documents that often appear in connection with leasing company sales. These are referred to briefly below.

Administration agreement. If the seller or an associate is to continue to administer the portfolio on behalf of the company, then there will need to be a management or administration agreement dealing with the matters described in the section 'Management of the leases' above.

Guarantees. Either the buyer or the seller may be concerned at the credit standing of the other, in which case holding company or other guarantees will be sought. Alternatively, a guarantee may be provided by the seller, or a company in the seller's group, in relation to the liabilities of lessees whose credit standing is considered unacceptable by the buyer without such credit support. A discussion of some of the issues relating to guarantees of lessees is continued in Chapter 14.

Debt repayment documents. The method of securing the repayment of the loans by the seller or other funder of the company will need to be considered. Apart from documentation relating to actual repayment, it will be necessary to ensure that the debt from the company is actually repayable. A loan without documentation is generally repayable on reasonable notice, not immediately on demand. Voluntary early repayment can constitute a form of unlawful financial assistance by the company in connection with the purchase of its own shares.

'Bottom of the harbour' letter. This letter expresses the intention of the buyer to ensure that the company meets its debts and, in particular, its tax liabilities. It derives its name from the habit of Australian fraudsters after they had caused a company to become insolvent of placing the corporate records and documents in a bag, apocryphally weighting it with the company seal and slinging it into Sydney harbour. The bottom of the harbour letter expresses the buyer's intention to ensure that such an eventuality does not occur. If such a letter proved to be untrue, there could be the possibility of proceedings for fraud and, in any event, the seller would point out that it had taken every precaution to ensure that the transaction was a proper one. Currently, this type of letter is in less common use because of the requirement for the buyer to give more specific indemnities to the seller regarding its future stewardship of the company.

Ancillary documentation. The usual array of corporate documentation, including minutes, resignations, appointments and associated companies' registry forms, will be required.

Completion

While the completion of a purchase may seem relatively straightforward, with the parties signing the documentation and money being transferred in exchange for the executed share transfers, nevertheless there are a number of points that need to be considered.

Accounting period

One major issue that needs to be resolved is whether an accounting reference period of the company should end on completion. Administratively, it is convenient that it should so that the seller's accountants can take responsibility for the accounts and tax computations up to completion. If the accounting period is not closed then, generally, the buyer's accountants will need to deal with the entire period since they will be familiar with the buyer's tax planning. This can make the seller quite uncomfortable given the possible sensitivities of its arrangements with the company prior to sale. There can, theoretically, be an advantage in certain instances in not ending the accounting period, but these would need to be quite considerable in financial terms before leaving the period open would be outweighed by the administrative convenience of closing it.

Resignations

The directors and the secretary of the company will generally resign. It is the responsibility of the directors for the time being, not the directors at the relevant time, to sign off accounts. This means that the buyer's appointees will be required to approve the accounts for the period up to completion. The same principle applies to the auditor and, for this reason, auditors do not resign but agree not to offer themselves for reappointment at the general meeting of the company at which the accounts for the accounting period ended on completion are approved.

Minutes

It is essential that the decisions by the various corporate parties are properly minuted. If the reasons for taking the decisions are set out in a minute and read to the members of the board present, then such reasons will have greater credibility in, perhaps, persuading the tax authorities of the motivation of the parties in entering into the transactions. The reasons for actions contained in the minutes should be considered by those present. Minutes are not, in reality, legal documents requiring particular technical words and drafting but are records of the decisions of non-lawyers entering into a commercial transaction. The directors whose meeting is recorded in the minutes may be examined in the future as to their actions. The minutes will be used either to support or provide evidence against them.

Timing

Ideally a note should be taken of the completion meeting with the timing of various events. This may be important in showing at what point in the meeting the company ceased to be a member of the seller's group and became a member of the buyer's group. Where the assets of the company are being used to raise the funds to repay its borrowings it is particularly critical to show in which group it falls at which stage.

The documentation of any particular leasing company transaction will, of course, vary with the particular circumstances of such transaction. The points described above are generally relevant and designed to supplement the considerations that will arise in any company sale.

Conclusion

This chapter does not intend to provide a comprehensive guide to all aspects of buying or selling an equipment leasing company. Leasing companies come in too many different shapes and sizes for that, ranging from single purpose companies owning a single ship, aircraft or piece of infrastructure, to a company engaged in consumer finance or contract hire with thousands of individual contracts relating to individual items of equipment. It is clear, however, that transactions involving equipment leasing companies are set to continue. The announcements of the demise of transactions entered into for tax reasons have proved premature, at least so far.

Chapter 16

Operating leasing

Sam Geneen

Introduction

This is a particularly interesting point in the world's economic cycle. More attention is being paid to the accounts of major corporations, and their disclosures with regard to on- and off-balance-sheet assets and liabilities than at any other time. The collapse of companies such as Enron and the rapid decline in the fortunes of Worldcom, Vivendi, Xerox, Tyco and others begs the question of whether the accounts show a true and fair view and, if so, how the fortunes of these companies can have reversed so rapidly.

Some fear that it will only be a matter of time before regulators turn their attention to all forms of off-balance-sheet financing, including operating leasing. The accounting treatment of operating leasing has already been debated extensively in recent months and is moving up the agenda of national and international accounting standards boards. However, before worrying too much about the accounting treatment, the basics of operating leasing should be discussed.

Definitions

Under the accounting standards Statement of Standard Accounting Practice (SSAP) 21, issued by the UK Accounting Standards Board, and International Accounting Standard (IAS) 17, issued by the International Accounting Standards Board (IASB), an operating lease is defined as a lease other than a finance lease. According to SSAP 21, under a finance lease the lessee acquires substantially all the benefits of the use of an asset for the greater part of its useful economic life and takes on substantially all of the risks associated with ownership. In economic terms, it is similar to the purchase of an asset even though legal title to the asset remains with the lessor. The risks of ownership of an asset include unsatisfactory performance, obsolescence and idle capacity. The benefits include the right to the unencumbered use of the asset over most of its useful economic life.

It can therefore be assumed that an operating lease is an agreement whereby the lessee acquires the use of an asset for a period less than its useful economic life. In UK accounting terms, the 90 per cent rule tends to be used as the yardstick as to whether a lease is finance or operating. The calculation follows along the lines that if the minimum rentals due from the lessee discounted at the rate implicit in the lease (or a reasonable approximation if the actual rate is not known) total less than 90 per cent of the fair value of the asset, the transaction can be regarded as an operating lease and therefore need not be capitalised in the balance sheet.

When SSAP 21 was issued in 1984 it was regarded as revolutionary. Up until that time, leasing had been regarded as a form of off-balance-sheet finance. However, SSAP 21 introduced a distinction between finance and operating leasing. In the event, the accounting standard was open to some abuse and ten years later a different generation of accounting standard was introduced in the form of FRS 5.

FRS 5, is much wider than SSAP 21 and aims to ensure that substance over form prevails, that is, that the accounts reflect the commercial substance of a transaction and not merely its legal form. Although it applies to all transactions, it is primarily concerned with more complex situations where the substance may not be readily apparent. FRS 5 is largely a balance sheet standard. It does not deal extensively with issues of income and cost recognition.

History of operating leasing

Operating leasing is generally regarded as a new product, a financial instrument of the 21st century. It is assumed that UK lessors have been forced to pay more attention to operating leasing due to changes in tax legislation that restrict the allowances they can enjoy on finance leasing. All readers should be disabused of these views, be they lessor, lessee or tax inspector.

Operating leasing can be traced back to before 2000 BC since there is evidence that Sumerians used a form of operating leasing for agricultural implements and hand tools. (It is unlikely that capital allowances were in existence then.) There were detailed regulations first drawn up in Roman times that distinguished finance and operating leasing. The chartering of ships, another form of operating leasing, dates back to pre-medieval times and it was quite common for soldiers in the crusades to hire their suits of armour. Even the operating leasing of rolling stock dates back to the 1840s when the companies were known as wagon companies. Finally, operating leasing was not created by Americans and imported to the United Kingdom. The world's first registered leasing company, the Birmingham Wagon Company, was registered in 1855 and leased railway wagons to coal and other mineral proprietors for fixed terms of between five and eight years.

Size of the UK market

Statistics from the UK Finance & Leasing Association (FLA) displayed in Exhibit 16.1 give us some idea of the size of the market, although it should be noted that there are many oper-

Exhibit 16.1

Operating leasing statistics for the 12 months to 31 December 2002/2001 (£ million)

	2002	2001
New business	3,438	3,952
Source		
Direct business	2,350	2,858
Sales aid/vendor	1,088	1,094
Equipment type		
Commercial equipment	834	909
Cars	2,604	3,043

Source: FLA.

ating lessors that do not contribute to the FLA statistics base. The numbers detailed in Exhibit 16.1 might comfortably be doubled in order to give a more realistic picture of the UK operating leasing market.

Looking at these statistics, you must be wondering what all the fuss is about. However, once we consider the asset types as detailed in the following paragraph, which lend themselves to operating leasing, you can then understand the potential size of the market.

Operating lease assets

Beyond trains, planes and automobiles, the list of assets that can be subject to an operating lease is endless: rolling stock, materials handling equipment (forklifts), trucks, trailers, machine tools, print equipment, buses and coaches, construction equipment, and medical and IT equipment are just some of them. However, with all operating lease assets, there is one essential ingredient for operating leasing to work: the equipment must have a secondary value after the expiry of the primary lease term. The skill of the lessor in operating leasing is managing the residual value and optimising the return by forecasting the future value accurately based on sound techniques and/or risk sharing with third parties. Forecasting and securing residuals are covered later on in this chapter.

Types of operating leases in the market

The basic product

A lessor leases equipment for a fixed period, normally ranging from two to seven years, depending on the type of equipment. At the end of the primary period, the contract specifies that the lessee must return the equipment to the lessor in a condition commensurate with its use and age. In practice, lessors generally wish lessees to extend the lease for a further term at rates agreed between the parties. However, this is an arm's length negotiation, that is, the extension rentals must represent a fair market price, and there is no obligation on the lessee to extend the lease term beyond the initial period. The skill of operating lessors is in managing the asset to achieve maximum proceeds either through disposal, extension or re-leasing to a third party.

Typical assets that are financed in this way are IT equipment, aircraft, rolling stock and manufacturing equipment.

Contract hire

Contract hire is a widely used form of operating leasing and is mainly associated with car hire. The major difference between contract hire and basic operating leasing is that other services are included. The contract hire product is very much value added and continues to grow as demand for outsourcing gathers momentum in the United Kingdom. One advantage to lessors in contract hire arrangements is that the leasing company controls the maintenance and therefore ensures that when the asset is returned it is in the appropriate condition having been serviced to a high standard.

Whilst cars are recognised as the most common asset financed through contract hire, it is very common to see forklift trucks, commercial vehicles and even IT equipment subject to full maintenance agreements.

Supply and services

Supply and service arrangements are relatively new and very much a variation on the contract hire theme. They are used to finance assets that require further supplies, for example, vending machines, photocopiers, clinical analysers. The basic structure is that a lessee pays a fixed amount that includes the provision of these supplies and in many cases the lessor will work in conjunction with a manufacturer or supplier of the equipment. At the end of the term, the supplier may acquire the equipment from the lessor in order to control the used values and avoid a funder disposing of equipment at knock down prices.

Rentals

In leasing terms, the simple short-term rental is another form of operating lease. This can take the form of a short-term hire such as that used in the car rental business. Rental is also commonly used in the office equipment sector for small-ticket items such as personal computers, printers, office furniture and communications equipment. The supplier of the equipment may have a relationship with a third party lessor that rents the equipment to the end user. At the end of the period, suppliers normally have arrangements in place with a lessor such that any benefits from an extension or sales proceeds above an assumed residual value flow back to the dealer.

Wet lease

This refers to operating leases where the lessor may provide the manpower and services required to operate the equipment. It is a term commonly used in aviation where aircraft are leased to an airline together with a crew usually consisting of pilots, although sometimes cabin crew are also supplied under this arrangement. A typical example is the situation where one airline sublets an aircraft and suitable crews to another carrier.

The advantages of operating leasing

Although there are many different views on the advantages of operating leasing, the following are the most important and have withstood the test of time.

- The lessee spreads the cost over the useful life of the asset. Cash flow is therefore preserved and, if the asset is income producing, revenue and expenditure are recognised over a comparable timescale.
- The lessee acquires the use of the equipment over a period of time without the liability of disposing of the asset at the end of the lease period. Under an operating lease, the residual value risk and reward is assumed by the lessor which presumably has more expertise than the lessee in disposing of the equipment and in maximising the resale value. In addition, if contract hire is used, all costs in relation to the use of the equipment are known and there should therefore be no surprises to the operator of the equipment. The bottom line and principal attraction of operating leasing is that the lessee should benefit from a lower whole life cost.
- The operating lease is treated as off balance sheet and therefore may not be taken into account when calculating gearing ratios. However, it should be pointed out that the major-

ity of lenders apply a multiple to the annual operating leasing commitments included in the notes to the accounts in arriving at a company's debt level.

Other advantages, which also apply to finance leasing, include additional funding lines, 100 per cent financing of the equipment purchase, and fixed payments that help cash flow projections and protect against interest rate movements.

Forecasting residual values

Although operating leasing is not solely about residual values, a realistic residual value assumption certainly goes a long way towards making a deal profitable. Forecasting values of equipment in the future is not a precise science and, over the past two or three years, there have been significant losses in the car market despite the use of sophisticated forecasting techniques based on vast amounts of data. Presumably, no lessor predicted that car prices would reduce by such a large percentage over a relatively short period of time.

Cars are not the only area where future values have moved out of line with predicted cycles. In the US medical sector, a CT scanner cost US$1 million in 1995 and residual values were being taken at 20 per cent, or US$200,000. In 2000, a new CT scanner cost US$425,000, calling into question the forecasting techniques used in 1995.

One lesson to be learned from living in a low inflation economy is that assets can reduce in price, creating an extremely challenging business environment for operating lessors. High inflation is good for residual values.

Some rules on forecasting and securing residual values

Choosing the equipment/manufacturer

A quality supplier tends to denote a high quality product and therefore a high quality portfolio for the lessor. The equipment should be at the top of the range and the manufacturer should be financially stable. Residual values have a horrible habit of crashing if the manufacturer is no longer in business.

Responsive and resourceful management

It can take many years before residual value investments mature at the end of the initial or extended lease period. There are many instances when the management responsible for taking the decisions at inception are no longer around when the leases mature. People are the key to this sector and their importance should never be underestimated.

Active asset management

It is not enough to wait until the end of a lease before deciding how best to dispose of equipment. A proactive approach must be taken which will result in increased returns through upgrade options, early terminations, extension opportunities and, of course, being in a position to realise proceeds within a relatively short period of time after a lease expires.

Awareness of market influences

Market influences will have an impact on pricing and, most importantly, the level of residual value investment. This will vary according to whether the operation is in the small-, medium- or big-ticket sectors. Influences to be considered are: competition, regulation, buyer awareness, technology, environmental factors, availability of risk sharing (explained below) and legislation.

The use of statistical techniques
The advantages of using statistical techniques include the following:

- support for residual value forecasting;
- a continual programme of knowledge building;
- trends develop over time; and
- early warnings should become apparent.

The disadvantages include:

- reliable raw data is not always readily available;
- it is sometimes difficult to avoid a bias in the sampling techniques; and
- unforeseen circumstances cannot be taken account of.

Mitigating risk

Many practitioners believe that operating lessors should take residual risk themselves. Employing sound management techniques as described above will, over the medium term, result in an above average return on investment. However, there are occasions when a lessor can, or should, choose to share the risk or transfer it to a third party. The traditional methods used in the market to achieve this are listed below.

Manufacturer/supplier buybacks

The lessor swaps a residual value risk for a credit risk. Information technology and vehicle manufacturers have historically provided buybacks, but, with an increase in transparency and the emphasis on showing contingent liabilities on the balance sheet, this practice may reduce over time.

Residual value investments

The investor will buy out the residual value risk in an asset from a lessor by giving a net present value of the amount at risk to the lessor at the inception of a transaction rather than when the asset is returned at the end. The investor is therefore buying the risk from the funder and at the end of the lease the investor will enjoy the benefit of extension rentals and/or sales proceeds as a return on his investment. The lessor, meanwhile, has the certainty of a return from the residual value and no worries about subsequent disposal of the asset. One of the disadvantages of using such a technique is that the lessor can lose control of the customer and this can damage future business relationships. Normally, there is no relationship between an investor and operator, so a lessor's relationship with the operator (and future new business source) could be threatened if there is any tension between the operator and investor over renewal terms of the lease or any return conditions (perhaps too rigidly enforced). In addition, the returns required are calculated to match the level of risk and in some cases these can be regarded as high.

Residual value insurance

The residual value insurer tends to be used as a stop loss. The basic principles of insurance apply and if the risk is high, an insurer will look for a significant first loss to be taken by either the funder or another third party before a claim can be made. Residual value insurance can be complicated and the devil is generally in the detail. However, it is becoming more acceptable in the United Kingdom, the advantage being that funders maintain customer control at all times.

Operating lease pricing

Despite the rules and techniques described above, UK lessors are not as adept at operating lease pricing as they should be. This can be seen from the current rates available in the market where the basic rules of risk and reward are not being applied. The winner is without doubt the customer.

There are various different risks to be considered when pricing operating leases and these must be priced appropriately. In simple terms, the two risks to be considered are credit and residual risk. However, they must each be priced on a different basis.

The return on the credit risk element should vary according to the lessee profile and size of transaction. A local authority or National Health Service (NHS) Trust should not be priced on the same basis as a corporate risk. Residual risk pricing should mirror the different degree of risk: for example, a 30 per cent residual risk after five years on a commercial vehicle should not be viewed as comparable to a 30 per cent risk on a clinical analyser.

Another fundamental risk that now needs to be built in to the equation is third-party risk. We may see the operating lease product developing rapidly into a supply and services agreement, whereby a third party supplies the services. If the third party was, for financial or other reasons, unable to perform under the terms of the agreement, it is likely that the lessee would have the right to terminate. The lessor should certainly have recourse to the servicer, but if the servicer is unable to honour its obligations, or cannot provide an acceptable alternative service provider in the transaction, then the structure falls and the lessor will forgo its expected profits. It is vital that a lessor recognises and understands that its return is as dependent on the performance of other parties to the transaction as the content of the lessee's covenant.

The final comment on pricing is to be aware of the impact of the Basle Accord (see Chapter 4). This will in time focus lessor's minds on return on equity. It is already having an impact in the banking sector and it will only be a matter of time before the leasing community is similarly affected.

The future of operating leasing

From a lessor's point of view, operating leasing gives funders the opportunity to enhance their margins through adding value. Finance leasing has come under considerable margin pressure: it is now very much a traditional money-over-money instrument comparable to hire purchase or medium-term bank lending. Operating lessors have the opportunity to take additional risk and add value thereby enjoying higher returns than finance lessors.

Operating leasing demonstrates clear advantages, providing the lessee with lower whole life costs and off-balance-sheet financing whilst removing the risk of technological obsolescence from the end user. It also provides the lessor and/or supplier with much better customer control, thereby reducing the cost of future sales by maintaining contact and enjoying a constructive dialogue on the performance of the asset. Enhanced margin opportunities also arise from supply, maintenance, early termination, upgrades, residual values and extension rentals, but only if there is real commitment to the business.

Risks such as technology change, local and global economic conditions, and regulatory and political changes all need to be considered and managed. There are risk mitigation techniques in the form of residual value insurers and investors, and buybacks and strategic alliances that can be utilised properly to manage operating lease portfolios.

The future looks encouraging – the instrument has been in existence for two thousand years and no doubt it will continue to grow over the foreseeable future.

Chapter 17

Cross-border finance: concepts and issues

Philip Griffin

Introduction

Cross-border asset finance is a term capable of extremely wide application and is often used as a euphemism for any relatively complex asset financing involving more than one national jurisdiction.

However, leaving aside international debt, equity and quasi-equity transactions, cross-border asset finance typically involves some form of cross-border lease, that is, a lease transaction where the lessor is resident in one jurisdiction and the lessee is resident in another. It is this type of transaction that this chapter will examine. The objective of this chapter is to look at the cross-border lease market as it has developed over the past two decades, its segments, its ups and downs, and what might be expected of the market in the future. This chapter will focus on the supply side and the fundamental drivers that have led to the market emerging and continuing to flourish, notwithstanding the Cassandras who have predicted its demise with monotonous regularity.

One proviso should be made. Anyone who has had more than a cursory exposure to the cross-border leasing market will quickly have realised that it is a highly competitive and extremely secretive market. There is little information in the public domain that can confidently be regarded as reliable or accurate. Although various periodicals and conference organisers gallantly attempt to treat the market as if it were as transparent and commoditised as, say, the bond market, the fact is that market leaders would typically sacrifice non-essential body parts in preference to divulging information that might damage their competitive advantage. Paranoia reigns and misinformation is rife.

As a result, this chapter does not rely on statistics or published or official sources, but rather the observations and anecdotes of personal opinion in order to provide the reader with some insight as to why and how the market operates as a whole.

Two jurisdictions: what are the implications?

A lease is a transaction where an asset is 'owned' by one party while, pursuant to a lease contract, its exclusive use is provided to another. So what is so exciting about the lessor being in one jurisdiction and the lessee in another?

In itself, there is nothing particularly dazzling about this and indeed there are no doubt a multitude of transactions where residence of the parties is neither relevant to the deal, nor how the transaction is analysed, priced, structured, documented and booked. However, almost exclusively in the realm of big-ticket leasing, two fundamental factors capable of making cross-border leases a little more interesting are occurring: the involvement of international capital and investment flows, and cross-jurisdictional opportunities for arbitrage.

In the context of a cross-border lease, each of these factors can drive a transaction, but it is typically the arbitrage opportunities that motivate the adoption of a lease as the structure for implementing an international investment. Although investment decisions drive financing decisions rather than the other way around, additional benefits can be gained from using cross-border structures.

The term international capital flow requires no elaboration. But what is this mysterious arbitrage? It is the ability to take advantage of jurisdictional differences, particularly in the fields of accounting and taxation.

When a transaction is within a single jurisdiction, the accounting treatment for the lessor and lessee is governed by exactly the same standards. If a lease is a finance lease for the lessor, it will typically also be a finance lease for the lessee. Similarly, an operating lease will be treated as such in the books of both lessor and lessee. However, if the accounting standards applying to the lessor are different from those applying to the lessee, then it is possible that a leased asset might be an off-balance-sheet operating lease for the lessee, yet be an on-balance-sheet finance lease for the lessor. It should be noted that the international harmonisation of accounting standards means that opportunities for arbitrage between accounting jurisdictions are becoming rarer and will in the future infrequently comprise the motivating factor for a cross-border lease.

The arbitrage of taxation is, however, of continuing underlying importance. Within a single jurisdiction, equal and opposite positions are usually created in respect of taxation of the lessor and lessee; that is, if the lessor takes tax depreciation, the lessee does not. Rentals are fully tax deductible for the lessee while they are fully tax assessable for the lessor. The overall effect of this is that the lessor profile of tax deductions is accelerated when compared to that of the lessee. When the lessor takes this profile of deductions into account and analyses its return on a post-tax basis, the return is superior to that which would be generated by simple debt finance. Accordingly, on a cash basis, the lessor needs to charge the lessee less than would be the case under a loan, leading to a lower cost of funds for the lessee.

A limiting factor for the lease market in a purely domestic context is therefore the supply of lessees happy to accept a deferred profile of tax deductibility rather than arranging a loan, buying an asset and taking the accelerated tax deduction position themselves. This implies that the lessee must presently be unable to utilise the accelerated tax deductions associated with ownership. Within a single jurisdiction this limits the pool of potential lessees to those making losses and therefore not paying tax, or those that are tax exhausted or exempt from tax, for example, government organisations. The former group may often be financially weak companies (since they are loss making by definition) and not the type of client a lessor will fall over itself to engage. The availability of the second group as lessees is often restricted by domestic legislation preventing tax benefit transfer where non-taxpayers are involved, and/or strict policy limiting the ability of such bodies to raise finance from the market.

However, when the lessor's tax position is determined in accordance with a different set of rules from that of the lessee, this limitation on potential business can be removed. For taxation purposes, the lessor may be able to depreciate the asset in its own jurisdiction, while the lessee also takes tax depreciation in its separate jurisdiction. The rentals paid by the lessee might be fully deductible, but with only the interest component assessable in the hands of the lessor in its jurisdiction.

344

Accordingly, with the lessee and lessor in different jurisdictions, it may well be that the lessee has the benefit of the lower cash cost of a lease without sacrificing the tax benefits of ownership in its own jurisdiction. For example, a lessor in Country A may be required only to have legal title to an asset in order to be tax owner and depreciate the asset. The lessee in Country B may also be regarded as tax 'owner' if it is entitled to use of an asset under a lease with purchase option. Accordingly, the lessor grants a lease with a purchase option to the lessee with the result that the lessor gains a higher return (so making a more viable financing arrangement) and the lessee enjoys additional benefits from the cross-border structure without prejudice to its fiscal position in its own jurisdiction.

It is strongly arguable that the single biggest driver behind the emergence of the cross-border leasing market (aside from specific initiatives designed to promote exports) has been the desire of financiers and investors to achieve the superior post-tax returns associated with leasing. Therefore, there is a consequent need to develop a pool of financially strong clients that do not suffer adverse tax consequences as a result of leasing rather than purchasing an asset.

The main markets

Markets created as a result of government-endorsed export initiatives are dealt with separately below. This section looks at the supply-side markets that have emerged as a result of the workings of the invisible hand rather than official sponsorship. In these cases, lessors generally apply structures very similar to those made available in their domestic market, varying them where necessary to take account of international considerations. One example of this is the management of withholding taxes to ensure that lessors do not become taxable outside their own jurisdictions and to comply with any local legislation designed to limit or condition the circumstances in which a cross-border lease may be completed.

Over the past two decades significant lessor markets have existed at various times in Belgium, Canada, Denmark, France, Germany, Hong Kong, Ireland, Japan, The Netherlands, Norway, Sweden, the United Kingdom and the United States. This list is not necessarily exhaustive and lessors in countries such as Austria, Italy, South Africa, Spain and Switzerland have also done occasional deals.

What do all these countries have in common? There are three things: each has a well established leasing market; at the time the market existed the country was at a point in its economic cycle where high levels of business and investment income were being generated, and, at that time income was subjected to comparatively high levels of taxation.

Common features underlying the creation of a leasing market include: domestic leasing expertise; a system of taxation and regulation equipped to deal with leasing; the availability of investment; a profitable business environment; and high levels of taxation. It is interesting to note that there is a distinct correlation between countries with high levels of taxation and the incentive on the part of residents to reduce their tax burden legitimately by investing in complex cross-border leasing transactions.

Leasing markets can be divided into two sub-groups. First, there are those where the lessors are primarily institutional investors such as banks, finance houses and/or large public companies. This is the situation in countries such as Canada, France, Germany, South Africa, the United Kingdom and the United States. The investor base in the other countries has tended to be high-net-worth individuals or private companies. Of course there are also countries where both institutional and private investors participate in the market, notably Germany.

It is no coincidence that it is only those markets with a primarily institutional investor base that have maintained a relatively constant and reliable presence. This is because an institutional investor typically has other motivating factors beyond the reduction of its tax burden and will successfully argue that the reduction of tax is incidental to its commercial activities. These other factors include gaining international market share and diversifying portfolios (both in geographic and asset terms). Institutional investors are typically in the business of making finance available and leasing is just one product available to them. Institutional investors also tend, on the whole, to be more thoroughly and cautiously advised, and less aggressive in terms of the tax benefits derived. Institutional investors also collectively comprise an industry with political leverage and the ability to lobby hard for its preservation.

With private investor involvement, the predominant motivation tends to be the reduction of the burden of taxation. Transactions sometimes lack the commercially redeeming features of larger financings. With no industry lobby groups to defend their interests, these markets tend to be ephemeral, emerging when a particular structure becomes available or when economic conditions create a need for efficient tax planning or deferral methods. These markets disappear when the relevant revenue authorities either challenge the structure or change the law, or when an economic downturn reduces the supply of taxable profits in need of shelter. These markets tend to rely upon arrangers within a jurisdiction coming up with structures and marketing them to private investors.

Apart from the nature of the lessor base, the major points of distinction relate to the type of structure adopted and the sharing of tax risk. In these respects, the UK market stands alone in that most other jurisdictions accept the concept of leveraged leases. In the United Kingdom capital expenditure must be funded entirely from a lessor's own resources, that is, without specific external debt. The United Kingdom is also somewhat unique in that lessors generally, and steadfastly, refuse to take their own tax risk, either in terms of rate, timing or structural integrity.

It is worth speculating upon the reasons why the United Kingdom is distinct in these regards. In a leveraged lease, the lessor is typically a special purpose vehicle that raises, for example, 80 per cent of the capital cost of equipment by way of a loan or loans, with an investor or investors contributing the remainder of capital cost by way of equity. This has several advantages for the lease investor as, in most jurisdictions, a properly structured leveraged lease delivers to the investor the same quantum of tax benefits but in respect of a much smaller cash outlay. As the debt is typically limited-recourse, the lessor is only at risk for its equity stake, which is often bank secured in any case. Leveraged lease accounting also allows the lessor to calculate its return against its equity stake (rather than the whole asset cost) leading, on an internal rate of return (IRR) basis, to after tax returns that can be several multiples of market interest rates. The ability to book such higher notional returns, although not actually delivering any greater benefit to the lessor, is often considered attractive, particularly in the case of corporate investors.

In the case of private investor transactions, analysis is typically not so sophisticated, sometimes being little more than a present value comparison of the tax savings generated compared to the equity outlay. However, even in these markets, the principle of leverage is the same: enhanced returns on lower levels of exposure compared to alternative personal investments.

The reason the United Kingdom market has steered away from leverage is primarily because of the Ensign Tankers case (1992). This has led to a belief that, to the extent a lessor is not at risk because debt is non-recourse, it will not be regarded as having incurred that portion of the expenditure so leading to denial of writing down allowances. It is arguable that structures remain available whereby leverage can effectively be achieved. However, there does not seem to be any real pressure to adopt them given that the major lessors are financial institutions where results are mostly judged by volume of business written and where returns are measured as a margin above cost of funds in relation to the whole expenditure.

As regards UK lessors' reluctance to take their own tax risk, there has not been the commercial need for lessors to accept tax risk to attract cross-border business. However, the risk/benefit ratio for the transaction is totally different when compared to jurisdictions where lessors have greater tax risk appetite since the majority of benefits are passed to the lessee. Again, since the lessors are conservative financial institutions, the somewhat enhanced after-tax margin received is sufficient to motivate the writing of business without the need to chase extremely large returns. Experience shows that the number of lessees prepared to take tax risk has been more than sufficient to furnish acceptable levels of business.

As well as these major differences between the markets, each has its own idiosyncrasies, its likes and dislikes. For example, the Japanese market has always preferred to lease aircraft to national flag carrying airlines. The Nordic nations and Germany have been strong in shipping while institutional investors, particularly in the United States, have tended to work their way through asset types. Having started with aircraft in the early eighties, they then gradually broadened their portfolios into railway rolling stock and, more recently, infrastructure, high-tech equipment and shipping.

Cross-border leasing as a tool of policy

Although cross-border leasing tends to be high on the 'disliked list' for many revenue authorities, at various times and in various countries it has been seen by governments as a useful tool for enhancing the attractiveness of exports in support of domestic industry. It can also be seen to attract particular industries or skills to the host nation and sometimes fulfil more obscure policy objectives.

The most readily recognisable initiative of this nature has been the US foreign sales corporation (FSC) regime. This was initially intended to provide certain tax concessions to exporters, for example, the aircraft and rolling stock manufacturers at point of sale through commission FSCs, and to US companies providing use of export assets to non-residents by way of operating FSCs. However, the market quickly realised that the tax benefits available to FSCs could be structured into lease transactions involving exported assets, thus making the benefits available to the financial institutions and corporates that acted as lessors. As a result, benefits could be double dipped: once by the actual manufacturer in respect of first sale and secondly by the lessor on providing that asset for use by a non-US resident.

It is a matter for speculation how much of this benefit was actually reflected in lower sales prices at the factory and indeed whether the availability of concessional finance influenced the purchasing decisions of customers. In this respect it is interesting to note that far greater volumes of US leases have been closed on structures that do not involve use of an FSC compared to those that have.

Even supposing that the FSC regime was not a particularly efficient or effective way of supporting US exports, experience shows that purchasers of US manufactured equipment (particularly Boeing and McDonnell Douglas aircraft) took advantage of this break to the fullest extent possible. Although the effectiveness of the FSC regime in enhancing exports may be doubted, the authorities at the World Trade Organisation certainly felt that it provided an unfair advantage, having recently determined that the policy is unacceptable.

A more recent example of an initiative of this type is the recent acceptance of tax enhanced leasing by the Spanish government in the case of vessels manufactured in the European Union. This policy initiative requires the purchaser of a new vessel to be an operator of ships and to apply to the authorities for clearance to finance the vessel by way of a Spanish tax lease prior to the contract. Although the benefits are ostensibly available in respect of ships built at any EU yard, it will be interesting to see if anybody will bother to make an application in respect of vessels to be built outside Spain and, if they do, whether approval will be forthcoming.

Other jurisdictions, notably Germany and Sweden, have also in the past attempted to restrict cross-border leasing to transactions broadly in the national interest. This has been achieved by leasing being permitted only where there is requisite national content in the leased asset. In Germany the unofficial benchmark was 20 per cent German content. In other countries that have adopted this approach, the threshold for local content has often been higher, for example, 50 per cent. Similarly, a French lease will typically only be approved by the relevant ministry in the case of French manufactured assets, or assets that otherwise have a very substantial French content.

In efforts to attract investment, skills and industry to a host nation, governments have tended to take a slightly different tack, most notably and recently in the area of shipping. The tactic in these cases is to make leasing available, but only in the event that the lessee forms a satisfactory connection within the jurisdiction, effectively becoming resident through the establishment of an operating subsidiary or business within the host nation. The tonnage tax initiatives in the United Kingdom and the Netherlands are good examples of this. In each case, these initiatives allow a ship operator with substantial value-added activities within the jurisdiction to have their own income tax calculated, not by reference to conventional measures of profit, but by reference to the amount of tonnage being operated. The regimes have been designed to encourage or maintain within each nation the development of core and ancillary maritime industries. As a result, a shipping company that has the requisite level of operations in the host nation will be able to access the benefit of leasing without falling foul of rules against leasing to non-residents, but also without becoming subject to significant levels of tax on income derived as a result of those operations.

Mention was made above of the more obscure reasons that nations permit cross-border leasing. One example, which may be no more than apocryphal, is the case of Japan. During the most energetic period of Japanese leveraged leasing, the years 1985 through to 1991, an oft-cited reason for the government's relatively benign stance was that the massive purchases of US manufactured aircraft by Japanese lessors assisted in redressing the trade imbalance then existing between the United States and Japan. Although such a claim should be treated with a degree of scepticism, an alternative or additional explanation is that a trade policy objective was fulfilled by allowing large scale leasing to assist in the capture of market share by Japanese banks, especially in the aerospace field. At that time, Japanese banks were making aggressive forays into international financial markets.

How have the markets changed?

There have been numerous changes in the markets over the past few years. Apart from the waxing and waning of markets as economic conditions change, and shortages of willing lessors in the midst of a recession, the market has been forced constantly to adapt to changing regulatory environments.

Tax authorities are often concerned that cross-border leasing can allow the leakage of tax benefits outside national economies. Generally, but by no means in every jurisdiction, domestic leasing is largely viewed as acceptable since tax benefits are transferred within the same jurisdiction. The availability of accelerated depreciation was designed to encourage investment, with the benefit to the user transferred by way of reduced financing cost rather than through an end-user purchaser reducing its own tax burden through capital allowances. In the domestic context, it is robustly arguable that, if an accelerated depreciation regime is to be made available to encourage capital investment, it is in fact most efficient to place that depreciation in the hands of financiers (who are able to make use of it) rather than quarantining the benefit to end users who, quite often, are unable to take advantage of the deductions.

However, it is difficult to make that argument in the case of a cross-border lease. Accordingly, the changes that the industry has had to address are not only those directed at leasing in general, but also various measures specifically directed at overseas or cross-border leasing.

In relation to leasing in general, the trend has been to restrict the availability of accelerated depreciation (the main driver for leasing) to situations where the lessor is a true investor in equipment, that is, it is at risk in respect of the asset and the performance of the lessee. For example the United States 'true lease' rules attempt to ensure that the lessor has a true economic interest in the underlying asset. The general move away from defeased or money-go-round structures also reflects the concern of authorities that new capital is actually invested in lease structures. Generally, there has been a very strong trend towards a requirement that there is a real commercial purpose behind lease financing. A lack of new money invested and the absence of a true economic interest in asset values are widely regarded as the two primary indicators that a lease is entered into with the main purpose of reducing tax, rather than undertaking a true investment.

As regards measures aimed at overseas leasing, the United States provides some good examples. In the first instance, the Dole-Pickle legislation was introduced to restrict the degree to which depreciation could be accelerated by a US lessor where the end use of the asset did not contribute to the US revenue base. The response of the market was to develop the so called Pickle lease whereby a transaction was structured to still produce a benefit through substantially greater deferral of the tax-positive stage, both through the extension of the term and careful rent structuring. The benefits resulting were of course smaller, but still superior to a straight debt financing. Following that, the application of accelerator and replacement lease structures further enhanced benefits and overcame the negative impact of rules against highly structured rental profiles.

At the time the above changes were occurring, the market had available to it the FSC product and other structures were also developing, notably the like-kind exchange lease where basis or tax written down value could be refreshed on exchange of an old leased asset for a new leased asset. Next, non-depreciation based structures gained prevalence with the emergence of the lease-in, lease-out, or li-lo structure. In this case, tax deferral was achieved through accelerated deduction of rentals paid on the lease-in, and deferral of income on rentals received under the lease-out.

Finally, today, the main product is the lease to service contract, essentially a replacement lease structure with a service contract being substituted for the replacement lease term. This is effective as the depreciation profile is required to be spread over the term of any lease and any replacement lease. A service contract is not a lease, so it allows a shorter or more highly accelerated depreciation profile. The qualifying technological equipment (QTE) lease also remains a mainstay for some market sectors. The QTE lease has evolved because in the case of certain high-tech equipment, a more heavily accelerated depreciation regime is available without the restrictive rules regarding leases of other asset classes impacting upon the transaction.

Without doubt, the United States has been the most active cross-border leasing market and is where the greatest degree of ingenuity has been exhibited. Has this been because of an overwhelming demand from lessees and a desire of US lessors to service overseas customers? Almost certainly not. Rather, it has been driven by a booming US economy that led to high levels of taxable income and therefore tax capacity which in turn produced a supply side boom. At the same time, the lessee markets for US equipment leasing products were being rapidly developed. There has also been a definitive move away from aircraft and into rolling stock, infrastructure and high-tech equipment suitable for QTE leases (see Chapter 6). However, this has clearly been a supply-side initiative, with lessee markets (particularly amongst European rail authorities and providers of infrastructure) being developed primarily in order to satisfy the voracious appetite of US lessors for big deals.

Other contributing factors which led to the development of a huge US market are also worth comment. Firstly, the rule of law is extremely strong in the United States, particularly in the context of transactions being judged according to their legal and contractual form rather than their subjective underlying substance. In addition, the practice of grandfathering (where whole transactions have the protection of the law as at the date of a change in the law, irrespective of whether events under that transaction do not take place until after the date of a change in law) is particularly strong in the United States. Thus, when taking their own tax-risk US lessors are left effectively with the risk of tax rate and tax timing changes only. This allows a greater certainty of benefit to lessees. This is a much more palatable option for many potential lessees, especially when compared to, for example, a fully tax-indemnified UK lease where lessors do not enjoy the above certainties.

Secondly, the United States has a very strong after-tax culture. That is, taxation is regarded as a variable cost rather than a fixed overhead, with tax savings being regarded as just as valuable a contribution to a company's bottom line as any other form of income. There is a very clear recognition that after-tax earnings contribute to shareholder value and that pre-tax results are pretty meaningless.

Finally, the leveraged lease accounting rules allow excellent after-tax earnings to be generated, particularly in the early years of a transaction during the investment phase. This has been especially true of li-lo transactions and has been good news, particularly for the corporate sector of the lessor market. Transactions that produce extremely good after-tax results in the shorter term, with neutral earnings effect in the later years of the deal are always welcome in a business community where after-tax results based incentives can be a big driver. Also, since returns are analysed on a leveraged basis and are nominally very high, it would take quite a massive tax rate or tax timing change to produce a loss for a US lessor. Accordingly, the environment is right for a lessor to take these risks and open up transactions to tax-risk averse foreign lessees.

Again, the United Kingdom provides the most useful contrast. In the United Kingdom, the lessors are almost exclusively banks or the leasing arms of banks. These tend to be much more focused on building a sizeable book at a reasonable return without high levels of risk, or at least without risk arising from extraneous and uncontrollable things such as changes in legislation. There is also still a strong focus, particularly by analysts of banking stocks, on headline pre-tax results. Results-based remuneration tends still in many cases to use pre-tax rather than post-tax indicators as the yardstick of success, meaning there is less motivation to enter into tax effective transactions.

Although the prospect of truly retrospective changes in tax law are generally regarded as slight in the United Kingdom, grandfathering will not typically extend to events that occur after the date of a change, even if anticipated in a transaction before the date of the change. Given the relatively slim margins and nominal yields taken by UK lessors, it is not surprising that they are unwilling to take substantial tax risk. This means that the lessee benefit remains uncertain unless the transaction comes to an end without any intervening change in law having occurred (notwithstanding the fact that the transaction may have been entered into prior to the date of change in law). This has without doubt been a limiting factor in the development of the UK cross-border leasing market.

Additionally, the United Kingdom has also produced legislation specifically targeted at transactions where the end use of an asset does not, or will not, produce income within the UK revenue base. These rules deny capital allowances unless a lease to a non-UK end user meets quite strict tests regarding term, rental profile and the end user's rights to an economic interest in the asset. Even when those tests are satisfied, the rate of allowances available is reduced to 10 per cent per annum on a reducing basis, as opposed to 25 per cent.

This reduced rate of allowances, in combination with a much shorter term, materially reduces the economic benefit of a lease. The response of some market players was to devise structures that complied with offshore leasing rules and made up for the reduced drive of lower allowances by building very high residual values into the transactions; these residual-values would be realised without giving rise to a balancing charge on allowances previously taken, and/or in a way that generated a tax free capital gain in respect of that portion of the residual value which exceeded the original acquisition cost. These types of structure were stopped by the concerted attack on finance leasing contained in the two Finance Acts in 1997 and the 1998 Finance Act.

Notwithstanding the widespread legislative changes in the United Kingdom there has been renewed interest in leasing in recent years. This has largely been driven by the continually diminishing benefits available from the United States in the current very low interest rate environment and the fact that the UK lessor market is potentially a source of funding for lessees looking for a primary source of finance rather than simply a benefit. There is now also a greater willingness on the part of lessees to properly analyse the risks involved and their downside potential, rather than refusing point blank any tax risk whatsoever. Naturally, the focus is on transactions that comply in an acceptable way with offshore leasing rules, or which do not rely upon capital allowances to any degree for the development of benefit. In the United Kingdom a substantial volume of cross-border business is also starting to be written on true long-term operating leases where tax benefit is almost wholly incidental. In this case, the value added comes from the UK lessor providing finance and also assuming a level of residual value risk sufficient to provide the foreign customer with true off-balance-sheet funding.

Apart from Japan, other cross-border markets have tended to diminish over time, largely because the primary investor base was comprised mainly of private citizens. Such opportunities have been steadily eroded by revenue authorities requiring leasing transactions to expose investors to levels of real asset and credit risk which, realistically, are not appetising to non-industry participants whose principal interest is in the reduction of personal taxation. The corporate and bank markets in most other countries have similarly become less active, with good corporate citizens, particularly in Germany and Sweden, limiting their participation to transactions that assist national manufacturing and exports.

There have, however, been some notable exceptions. For example, the German market for ship leases makes use of private equity and substantial volumes of business have been, and continue to be, done notwithstanding the fact that true exposures to the shipping market are involved to some degree. In addition, the private investor market in the Netherlands has in recent years been tapped for ship leases due to certain taxation incentives that can be factored in to make an attractive transaction.

The case of Japan is an interesting one. In the mid to late 1980s and even stretching into the early 1990s, Japanese lease investors (although invariably represented by the leasing arms of Japanese banks and securities houses) were almost exclusively private investors. An investment in a lease of aircraft to a flag carrying airline was simply one of the products vigorously offered to the client base by securities salesmen and bank advisers. Although the true workings of the underlying investor market were quite opaque to outsiders, there is a sneaking suspicion that a large number of these investors did not undertake a particularly sophisticated analysis, focusing simply upon net tax savings produced in the first few years of the transaction.

It was mentioned earlier that, for one reason or another, the Japanese authorities had a relatively benign stance in relation to the market and it was only during the latter part of the boom that rules started to be imposed restricting allowances to transactions where there was true risk. This ensured that the benefit of real business generation was retained for the Japanese banks and disallowed transactions where a party was entitled to claim depreciation allowances in another country. As various arrangers and advisors designed new products to help sustain the market, the Japanese economic bubble burst. This led to a shortage of investors at the same time that serious doubts started to emerge in relation to the financial wellbeing of worldwide aviation.

A new Japanese market has now emerged for Japanese operating leases. It is tempting to suggest that this is no more than a dusting off of a structure that was under development prior to the demise of the Japanese bubble economy. It is also tempting to suggest that the major reason the product has been dusted off is that investors in the first wave of Japanese leverage leasing are now (if not unprofitable and so self-sheltering for tax purposes) starting to see large tax bills emerging as their earlier investments mature, so stimulating demand for new tax shelter products.

Conclusion: what lies ahead?

Leaving aside the special treatment for which the cross-border market is so frequently singled out, what the future holds for the leasing market is an interesting question.

For so long as policy provides accelerated depreciation in an effort to encourage investment, there will be continuing efforts to transfer the benefit of these allowances to financiers that can make effective and efficient use of them rather than restricting availability to lessees who cannot. As discussed above, the use of depreciation allowances in such a way ought not to be seen as objectionable since it is simply a market making best use of incentives essentially for the purpose for which they are provided, that is, to support capital investment.

The issue for cross-border leasing is that the transfer of tax benefits outside a national economy is seen as a net leakage without any benefit to the host nation. It is tempting to observe that, putting purely national interests aside, this nonetheless will encourage investment on a global basis, and what is good for the global economy is good for its constituent parts. An interesting issue in Europe is how long nations will continue to be entitled to discriminate against residents of other EU member nations through legislation that treats a lease to a fellow national quite differently from a lease to a fellow European.

As discussed earlier, the tax benefit transfer by way of leasing has actively been promoted as a means of furthering policy aims, particularly in the case of US FSC leasing, the new Spanish ship leasing regime and various countries permitting leasing, but only if it is demonstrably in the national interest.

Nations are increasingly using leasing as a tool of policy, not by encouraging cross-border leasing in itself, but by making leasing available to those it is able to attract to its shores. The Dutch and UK tonnage tax regimes are good examples of this. Particularly in the case of the United Kingdom, provided a shipping company is willing to make the requisite level of investment in its UK operations and meet cadet training requirements, leasing is specifically available without the lessee developing an exposure to substantial UK taxation.

For so long as national differences in tax treatment remain, there will be those who seek to arbitrage the differences and they will continue to be successful. Generally, we have seen the benefits available from leasing steadily decline along with generally declining tax rates, interest rates and the tightening of regulation. Even so, leasing continues to flourish. So long as lease structuring can produce some benefit – at least enough to compensate for the additional time and cost involved in a lease – there will continue to be a cross-border leasing market.

Chapter 18

The securitisation of European lease receivables

Bruce Gaitskell

Introduction

Securitisation is still a relatively new phenomenon in Europe; the first transaction involving a UK mortgage portfolio was in 1987, with the first UK lease transaction in 1993. Securitisation spread across other European jurisdictions during the 1990s; however, penetration into the leasing sector has been more limited than with other financial assets such as mortgages or credit cards. For example, 1993 and 1994 saw the first securitisations of equipment lease receivables by Leyland DAF Finance, Anglo Leasing and Sabre. In 2001 and 2002 there has been further activity with, amongst other things, the securitisation of receivables by the rolling stock leasing company Angel Train Contracts and Eurotunnel. This contrasts with the United States where securitisation has been an ever growing capital market funding technique since the mid 1960s. Over one third of non-public sector debt in the US capital markets is securitised.

What is securitisation?

Securitisation is hard to define in a single sentence or paragraph and is perhaps better defined by its features.

- The creation and separation of a relatively homogeneous pool of assets into a ring-fenced special purpose company (SPC) or trust.
- The provision of third-party credit enhancements to protect against risks in the portfolio (such as credit, liquidity, asset casualty etc).
- The structuring of an asset-backed security whose interest and principal payments are supported by the underlying cash flows.
- Documentation to create a comprehensive legal and administrative structure that protects investors.
- The acquisition of a credit rating(s).
- Underwriting and distribution to capital market investors.

There are examples where not all these features are present, in particular privately placed securitisation transactions that may not have a credit rating and may be distributed on a best endeavours basis rather than being underwritten, and unfunded synthetic securitisations (see below).

Securitisations often allow around 90 per cent of the portfolio value to be financed by the issue of AAA notes. Clearly a portfolio on its own would not justify such a high rating. It is the careful structuring and the provision of various credit enhancements, typically from highly rated counterparts, that allows such efficiency. Many transactions also feature mezzanine notes rated at the lower end of investment grade that lift the total percentage externally financed to between 96 per cent and 98 per cent. The balance is typically retained by the originator in the form of unrated subordinate notes.

Structuring

It is perhaps already becoming clear that such highly structured transactions take time and money to achieve, therefore a leasing company needs to achieve significant benefits from securitisation to justify the endeavour.

There are a number of different ways in which a portfolio might be securitised. The first factor to influence the choice of transaction type is the size of the transaction.

Size of transaction

The upfront costs of undertaking a securitisation transaction are semi-fixed. In particular, legal costs will be about the same whether one securitises £50 million of assets or £500 million, whilst underwriting of a public bond transaction will be subject to a minimum based on a transaction of around £150 million or €250 million. This transaction size represents around the minimum for an efficient public transaction, whilst double that figure is perhaps the optimum balance between minimising costs per unit of asset securitised and achieving the best pricing on the rated securities in the market. Smaller portfolios are most likely to be securitised through a multi-seller commercial-paper-funded conduit (CP conduit) described in the section on CP conduit securitisation below.

Tax

The second factor will be whether the leases are tax based (that is, whether the lessor receives a tax benefit, typically through some form of depreciation allowance on the underlying leased asset). If this is the case, the lessor will not wish to transfer ownership of the lease to a special purpose company (SPC) outside the group. In the case of a corporate entity, this will require a double SPC structure: the first SPC will be a group company that holds the asset on behalf of both the original lessor and the securitisation investors (sometimes described as a receivables trust); the second SPC will issue asset-backed debt securities and use the proceeds of the securitisation to make a secured loan to the first SPC. This is illustrated in Exhibit 18.1.

In the case of regulated institutions, there is a choice between issuing credit-linked notes or entering into a synthetic securitisation transaction. If a credit-linked note is issued, a bank lessor issues securities in its own name but the payments of interest and principal due to investors are linked to the performance of the securitised portfolio. As in a conventional securitisation, the originator retains some element of first loss or subordinate debt to support the investment grade senior and mezzanine notes, but the underlying portfolio will not be transferred into a separate SPC since it is merely a reference portfolio. Regulators generally accept that the issuer has passed the risks of the portfolio through to investors since losses in excess of the first loss element retained are borne by the investors and not the originator. From the investors' perspective, there is an additional credit consideration over and above those normally of concern to investors in securitised transactions. The investor is taking a counterparty risk on the issuer and for this reason only high investment grade institutions can in practice

Exhibit 18.1

Secured loan securitisation structure (simplified)

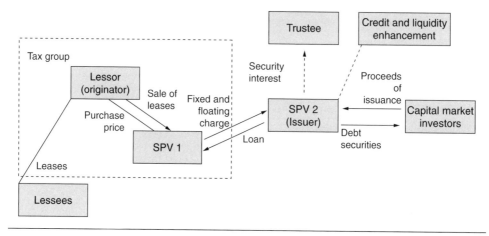

Notes:

- The lessor sells a pool of leases to SPV 1, a ring-fenced subsidiary of the lessor. The lessor and SPV 1 are tax grouped so no tax issues arise on the sale. The lessor enters into an administration agreement with SPV 1.

- SPV 1 borrows sufficient from SPV 2 to meet the purchase price and grants a fixed and floating charge over the assets and the administration agreement.

- SPV 2 gives first-ranking security over the loan agreement and all other contracts to a trustee acting for all the secured creditors (including capital-market investors).

- SPV 2 issues debt securities and uses the proceeds to make a loan to SPV 1 and pay for the cost of the securitisation transaction.

issue credit-linked notes. The senior notes cannot be rated higher than the issuer's own rating and this will most often be AA rather than AAA. The lower rating of the senior notes and the additional counterparty risk taken by investors usually means credit-linked notes will be priced at a premium to a conventional term securitisation transaction.

Synthetic structures

Synthetic securitisation has developed as a technique only over the past few years. Unlike other types or forms of securitisation, the majority of the transaction is not funded (that is, no securities are issued to the market), but rather the party that wishes to securitise the asset enters into a credit default swap with a highly rated counterpart (generally, but not always, an AAA-rated entity). Such credit default swaps are generally available only on a super-senior basis which means that the swap provider will only cover a percentage of the portfolio, which is slightly less than could be conventionally financed through the issue of AAA securitised notes. This proportion is insufficient for the lessor to achieve any capital relief and so they will usually issue a series of funded securitised notes to the market rated AAA through to low investment grade (typically BBB+ or, if market conditions allow, even to sub-investment grade levels), thereby leaving a first loss amount with the lessor which is in the range one to four per cent.

By way of example, the credit default swap might cover 85 to 88 per cent of the portfolio value with the series of funded notes covering a further seven to nine per cent of the portfolio value. Any losses on the portfolio will first be covered by the lessor's retained amount, then the funded notes in their order of priority (lowest rated notes bearing losses before higher rated notes) and then, and only then, by the credit default swap provider.

Other considerations

The third and most important factor that determines the transaction type and structure is the objective which a leasing company seeks to achieve. These objectives tend to be different for regulated financial institutions than for corporate entities. As most large lease portfolios in Europe are held by banks or their subsidiaries we will address them first.

Banks are trapped between an ever increasing pressure to improve return on shareholders' equity and the requirement to hold a certain amount of regulatory capital in respect of balance sheet assets. Securitisation gives a bank (or indeed other regulated institution) the opportunity to reduce the amount of regulatory capital which needs to be held in respect of an asset whilst increasing the return on capital (and therefore shareholders' equity) that is achieved in respect of the asset. This is perhaps best illustrated by way of an example.

Bank A has a portfolio of, say, £500 million medium term leases which it funds at Libor flat. The leases yield an average return of 125 basis points (bp) over Libor and the cost of administering the portfolio is 25bp. The capital requirement for holding this portfolio will be £40 million (eight per cent x £500 million) and the return on capital employed will be one per cent (125bp - 25bp) x 100/8 = 12.5 per cent.

The lease portfolio is securitised such that the bank retains a first loss position of three per cent of the portfolio and the all-in cost of funds (the margin paid to investors and the amortised upfront expenses of the transaction) total Libor + 40bp. The bank charges the SPC 25bp to administer the assets.

Although the bank lessor has securitised the portfolio, it will still have a capital requirement since it is still exposed to a limited risk of loss. This capital requirement will be equal to the retained first loss position, in this case three per cent x £500 million = £15 million. The net return on the assets has now reduced to 60bp (being the Libor + 125bp average return on the portfolio less the funding cost (Libor + 40bp) and the administration charge (25bp)).

The post-securitised return on capital is therefore 0.60 per cent x 100/3 = 20 per cent; nearly double the previous return. One should note that the profit to the bank post-securitisation is less than previously, so securitisation is only worthwhile if the bank can reinvest the freed-up capital in creating further income producing assets.

A secondary motivation for a regulated institution might be to reduce exposure to a particular sector or asset type since, post-securitisation, the maximum credit loss that the institution can experience is the first-loss retained amount.

Unlike regulated institutions, corporate lessors have a diverse range of reasons for considering the securitisation of lease portfolios. For a corporate, the equivalent of a capital requirement are gearing covenants imposed through its bank funding arrangements. A growing lessor may reach a point where it either needs to raise new capital or reduce the capital it has committed to existing assets. Through securitisation, gearing, that is, an entity's debt-to-equity ratio can be increased from the typical 10 times permitted in banking agreements to 25 times or even 50 times. Such high gearing is achieved by issuing mezzanine notes at the BBB+ level through to as low as BB. Lower rated notes carry a much higher coupon than high investment grade senior notes so a corporate that does not wish to gear excessively may decide to issue senior notes only (typically giving a gearing of around 10 times) or to issue higher rated mezzanine notes (perhaps single A) which will carry a lower coupon but still allow gearing of around 15 times.

Many gearing covenants capture all assets and all debt shown on the accounting balance sheet. This is not an issue for regulated institutions since regulators look at the regulatory balance sheet rather than the accounting one. International accounting standards have made it difficult for corporates to remove assets from the balance sheet and if this were the case it would be necessary for a corporate to renegotiate the definition of which assets and what debt were taken into account in determining the gearing ratio for the purposes of complying with banking agreements. In the United Kingdom it is sometimes possible for a corporate to get linked presentation where the securitised assets and related capital market debt are excluded from the main balance sheet but shown in a pro forma consolidated balance sheet appearing as Note 1 to the Report & Accounts.

A further and often stronger motivation for corporate lessors is the opportunity to obtain funding from a new and more diverse group of investors. A public rated securitisation is likely to be placed widely across Europe, whereas bank funding may be only obtainable from a small group of domestic banks.

Securitisation funding is in place throughout the life of the assets that have been securitised and this may be considerably longer than the terms available from the banking market. This would typically be the case for an unrated lessor with a lease portfolio of industrial or transport equipment. Securitisations can therefore improve asset liability management by providing matched funding.

Small-ticket lessors

Lessors in the auto or small-ticket sector would have the opposite situation where the average remaining life of a portfolio was quite short, perhaps only 12 to 18 months. Securitisation

Exhibit 18.2

Dealing with short life assets

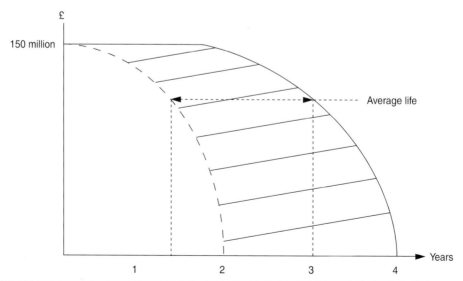

investors typically like average lives of around three to five years and, although the margin paid to investors increases with duration, the effect of amortising the upfront costs of a securitisation over a longer term tend to mean that the all-in cost of funds is lowest for a three to five year average life transaction. A lessor with short-life leases therefore has the opportunity to structure a transaction where, for some period of time, new assets can be substituted to replace maturing assets. Typically this period will be two or three years and, for example, in the case of auto leases more new assets will be substituted in total than the amount of assets initially securitised. Securitisations with a substitution option effectively pre-fund future business. This is illustrated in Exhibit 18.2.

The diagram shows an original amount of leases securitised of £150 million with an average life of 16 months and a final maturity of 24 months. The shaded area shows the effect of substitution with a new average life of three years and a final maturity at year four. The amount of leases financed in total exceeds £350 million.

Substitution

Substitution is an option rather than an obligation, so if future business levels are below that required the transaction amortises more quickly. More importantly new assets can only be substituted if the existing, securitised portfolio is performing within certain pre-agreed parameters; in particular, that arrears or write-offs in the previous three or six months have not exceed the agreed limits. The parameters are agreed between the issuer and the rating agency at the outset of the transaction. The more aggressively geared the transaction is, the tighter the parameters will be and so a lessor needs to balance the desire to gear up with ensuring that funds will continue to be available for new business even if asset performance deteriorates. The lessor therefore needs to optimise between these two conflicting objectives and this is illustrated in Exhibit 18.3 below.

Exhibit 18.3

Optimising gearing

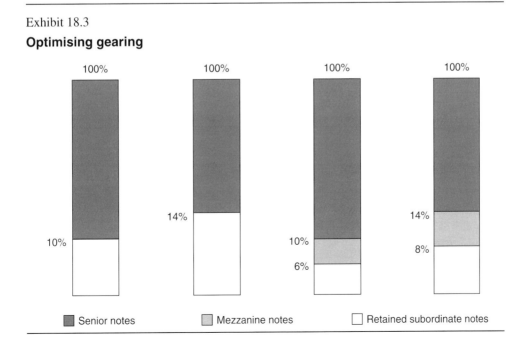

Exhibit 18.3 is a presentation taken from an actual case in which the finance director was keen to securitise in order to increase gearing and reduce dependence on a small group of bank funders. He was concerned, however, that if business conditions worsened he could find himself without the ability to substitute new business into the securitisation. The first and third bars show what was achievable using fairly tight substitution criteria. The third bar is a multi-tranche option where both senior and mezzanine notes would be issued to the market whereas the first is a senior tranche only. The client was happy with 10 times gearing but the first option (senior notes only) still had the tight substitution criteria. The answer was the fourth bar: two public tranches of notes (senior and mezzanine) with relaxed substitution criteria (losses and arrears at four times current levels). This option still allowed gearing of 12 times, well in excess of the 5 times allowed by the client's bankers.

Funding cost

Finally, but by no means least, the all-in cost of funds for a corporate may be cheaper through securitisation than through other more traditional forms of finance, particularly when comparing funding costs over comparable terms. An all-in cost of around Libor + 35bp to 50bp would not be unusual for a three- to five-year average life transaction. If a corporate were to use CP conduit securitisation the cost may be lower still (see next section).

Even if the securitisation funding cost is lower than traditional funding, it is unlikely that a prudent treasury will want to abandon its relationship banks. Rather, it has the opportunity to demonstrate that it has other means of funding, including the ability to refinance bank debt if some banks wish to discontinue funding. The lower cost of securitisation funding also adds benefit if the banks are looking for higher margins than are thought to be justified by the risk.

CP conduit securitisation

CP conduits are securitisation programmes established by individual banks that allow many sellers to securitise their assets through a single capital market vehicle. The quantum of assets securitised through CP conduits exceeds that financed through term transactions (both public and private). Unlike term securitisation, assets are financed through the issue and continuous re-issuance of securitised commercial paper.

CP conduits are designed to fund relatively short-term assets (trade receivables, loans to retail and small- and medium-sized enterprises, motor leases and other interest-bearing assets) and are used both by the sponsoring bank and its various clients to securitise suitable financial assets.

The bank establishes the programme, including its legal documentation and corporate structure, and provides 100 per cent liquidity to the programme (which is syndicated to a group of banks as the programme breaches the US$500-million mark or so) as well as providing a programme-wide credit enhancement (PWCE). A simplified CP conduit structure can be represented in diagram form shown in Exhibit 18.4.

Each seller provides its own credit enhancement by discounting the receivable into the conduit (that is, selling it for an initial 95 to 98 per cent of its face value) such that is capable of achieving a rating of around A/A-, the equivalent of a short-term rating of A1-P1.

The sponsoring bank (on its own or with other suitably rated banks) provides PWCE for two reasons: first, most programmes are issued at A1+/P1; and secondly, each seller needs

Exhibit 18.4

Typical conduit structure

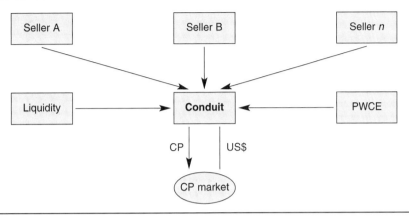

protection from the performance of other sellers (since they have no veto over who the bank allows to use the programme) such that if an individual portfolio does not perform to the extent that the relevant seller's enhancement is exhausted, then it is the bank's PWCE that is used to cover losses and not the enhancement provided by other sellers.

Investors buy CP through a dealer panel, one of which is usually the sponsoring bank. While CP (predominantly US$ denominated) is in theory issued for five to 364 days, in practice it is mainly issued for 30 days. The average life of the receivables in the conduit will be much longer – perhaps 18 to 30 months – so although in practice issuing new CP refinances each tranche of maturing CP, there is no assurance that the programme can always sell CP. The rating agencies require that 100 per cent of asset value of the programme is covered by a liquidity facility provided by one or more banks that are each rated as high as the programme rating. In the event that CP cannot be rolled over (that is, refinanced by the issue of new CP) then the liquidity facility is drawn and the liquidity facility provider is treated as if he were a CP holder.

Programmes are continuous and revolving allowing sellers to continue to sell new assets and replace maturing assets so long as they continue to meet eligibility requirements and the performance of previously sold assets is satisfactory.

Advantages of CP conduit securitisation to the seller

The bank meets all the initial costs of establishing the conduit and recoups these costs over time from many different sellers. The initial costs of each user are much lower than a stand-alone transaction and, by blending a large and diverse portfolio of assets, the level of credit enhancement for each seller is less than that which would be required for a term transaction. The credit enhancement level required is further reduced by the bank providing a second layer of credit enhancement (the PWCE). (The final short-term rating of A1+ on the securitised CP is the equivalent of AA- long term rating – less than that of most term securitisations.) The lower the credit rating to be achieved, the less credit enhancement is required.

The programme is continuous and revolving and this allows sellers to increase or decrease the quantum of assets financed through the conduit to fit their requirements.

The all-in cost of funds for a conduit used is around Libor + 30bp which compares well with the Libor + 40bp to 50bp if the seller were to undertake its own term securitisation transaction. Conduits can accommodate quite small portfolios from individual sellers. The actual minimum will be set by the sponsoring bank and is likely to be in the region of US$50 million. Once a seller becomes established, incremental sales of as little as US$10 million to US$20 million are possible. Established sellers may also be permitted to originate assets directly into the conduit, bypassing their own balance sheet completely.

The combination of the bank shouldering some of the credit and all of the liquidity risk of individual portfolios and the lower rating level of the CP (compared with senior notes of the term transactions) is particularly advantageous for operating lease portfolios in that it is often possible to retain the asset on the lessor's balance sheet and merely assign the leases as security to the CP conduit.

Disadvantages of using conduits over term deals

The conduit is pre-structured and documented so a user has no ability to make any changes to either. A term transaction would be customised to meet exactly the needs of the single originator/seller.

Unlike a term transaction, the funding cost is not fixed for the life of the asset. The cost of the CP may vary with market conditions and the perceived credit strength or otherwise of the sponsoring bank. More importantly, there are circumstances where no CP can be issued and the bank provided liquidity has to be drawn. Such an event can increase the all-in funding cost above Libor + 50bp.

The US$ CP market is much bigger and deeper than other currencies, so most of the CP will be issued in US$ rather than in euros or sterling. The conduit will therefore need to enter into swaps to eliminate currency risk and the cost of such swaps is another variable that can add to the cost.

The ability to sell further assets to replace maturing assets is subject to amortisation triggers based on the credit and liquidity performance of assets previously sold. There is a danger that a seller may become overly dependent on this form of finance and be in a difficult position if they are unable to sell-in new receivables. A prudent treasurer will therefore wish to maintain a balance between conduit and traditional finance, even if the latter is more expensive.

The rating of a CP conduit is directly linked to the short-term rating of the bank or banks that are providing the liquidity. The biggest single risk for a user of a conduit is that the liquidity bank is downgraded, leading to a combination of more expensive CP pricing and difficulty in fully funding the programme in the CP markets. Sellers should therefore select a programme where the sponsoring bank has a very strong long-term rating (AA/Aa2 or better).

Finally, individual sellers get no profile in the capital market when using a CP conduit whereas in the term market there is an opportunity to develop a profile and build a relationship with investors.

Attractions of operating a CP conduit for a bank sponsor

Introducing clients to conduit securitisation can be a win-win situation for client and bank in that the client gets lower cost funding whilst the bank gets a higher return on capital from the client's conduit business than from providing balance sheet lending.

The programme has 100 per cent liquidity support, but this is provided on a committed 364-day facility which currently is capital free to the providing bank whilst it remains undrawn.

The PWCE provided by the bank is typically 1.5 to 2 per cent and this will count as a direct deduction from the bank's capital. This compares well with the eight per cent capital requirement for lending to corporates. The majority of the income a bank derives from operating a CP conduit is fee rather than margin income and the former has no capital requirement associated with it.

Credit ratings

With the exception of some private placements, securitisation transactions are rated by two or, occasionally, all three major international credit rating agencies. The main agencies are Standard & Poor's, Moody's and Fitch; all have a broadly similar and yet subtly different approach to rating securitisation transactions. Ratings are a feature of securitisation transactions because of their complexity. It would be both difficult and inefficient for each potential investor in a transaction to have to read every page of legal documentation and to conduct individual due diligence. Investors therefore tend instead to rely heavily on the ratings assigned to the various classes of public debt issued. The major investors do however discuss the structure in detail with the lead manager to understand how various difficult issues have been dealt with. Co-investing with the leading players in the securitisation investment community comforts other investors.

The major part of rating any securitisation transaction is the construction of a cash flow model. The rating agencies will make certain assumptions about arrears and credit defaults of the subject portfolio. The assumptions will be more severe at high investment grade and less so as the rating sought on a particular class of notes is reduced.

The agencies will examine historic defaults in the originator's portfolio, historic performance of the asset class in the relevant jurisdiction and other factors to come up with the arrears and credit loss assumptions. The portfolio will be divided up, typically in loan-to-value (LTV) bands with higher arrears and credit losses assumed where the borrower or lessee has little equity at risk. In the case of operating leases, the agencies will make severe assumptions about declines in residual values over and above the lessor's own assumptions about the residual value.

From the cash flow model it is possible to work out, at each rating level, what percentage of the portfolio can be supported by the underlying cash flows assuming the levels of arrears and default set by the agencies. For AAA-rated senior notes this will typically be 88 to 92 per cent of the portfolio value whereas at the BBB+ level it might be 94 to 97 per cent. Taking a specific example, it may be that the rating agency model suggests that it is possible to rate 90 per cent of the portfolio value at AAA and 96 per cent at BBB+. The securitisation of £100 million of assets would therefore allow £90 million of AAA notes to be issued and a further £6 million of BBB+ mezzanine notes (being £96 million minus £90 million). The originator would therefore keep £4 million, usually in the form of unrated subordinate notes.

The agencies will want to understand the credit underwriting process and arrears management procedures of the lessor. They will also be concerned to ensure that the electronic data about the assets is accurate. To give comfort on both these points the lessor's auditors will be required to perform an asset audit, usually on a sample basis giving a 99 per cent level of confidence (this contrasts with normal statutory audit requirements of 95 per cent confi-

dence). On a portfolio of 5,000 leases the sample size would be in the order of 850 random-
ly selected leases. The agencies will also make a one or two day visit to the proposed administrator (usually the original lessor) to discuss origination, arrears and systems issues. If the
administrator is not judged to be investment grade then the rating agencies will assume that
the administrator fails during the life of the transaction and will therefore require a standby
administrator to be put in place that is contractually obliged to assume the administrator's
duties. In many cases, the lessor will be a bank subsidiary and the parent will contract to be
the standby administrator.

The agencies will also review all the legal documentation and seek legal opinions from
the lawyers acting for the SPC on any areas of legal uncertainty. They will also want the documentation used to create the individual leases to be examined to ensure that they achieve the
intended purpose.

Additional rating issues

Over and above the general approach and requirements for all forms of securitisation, the rating agencies have a number of additional requirements and concerns relating to leases.

A major concern is owner liability. If a leased item of equipment causes damage, for
example the death of a user or a third party, the lessor is potentially liable for damages. Rating
agencies will either require that the ownership of the asset has not been transferred to the
securitisation SPC or that adequate insurance is in place to protect investors from such risk.

Many leases, particularly UK operating leases on motor vehicles, include services such
as maintenance and/or replacement. These leases are difficult to unbundle and the rating
agencies will usually require substantial reserve accounts to cover these potential liabilities
or for the liabilities to be laid off to an investment grade third party at a fixed price.

It is increasingly common for finance and synthetic leases (for example, personal contract purchase arrangements for cars) to feature a compulsory or optional balloon payment
which is a substantial multiple of the monthly lease payment. The rating agencies assume that
a lessee may have more difficulty making this large final payment than finding the regular
monthly lease payments and therefore attribute a much higher level of arrears and defaults on
these final payments.

As previously mentioned, rating agencies have a much less optimistic view of residual
values than the leasing industry. This often makes the securitisation of operating leases less
attractive than finance lease securitisation. This potential difficulty can be overcome in one
of two ways. Residual value insurance could be purchased from an investment grade counterpart; or, the residual value element of the lease could be retained by the lessor and only the
contractual receivables sold through for securitisation.

Conclusion

The final question to be addressed has already been raised: why has the penetration of securitisation financing been less than for many other financial assets? The main part of the
answer lies in the rating agencies' negative view of residuals and the tendency of leases to
contain a bundle of other services over and above the hire of an asset.

The other major factor is that banks, in seeking to release regulatory capital through securitisation, have a wide range of assets on their balance sheets from which to choose and oper-

ate in a number of different legal jurisdictions. It is natural for a bank to choose to securitise assets that are relatively easy and straightforward to deal with in jurisdictions where the legal and taxation systems best facilitate asset transfer and securitisation. Leases, particularly complex operating leases, are not the easiest asset to securitise and banks therefore tend to concentrate their securitisation on other asset types.

A corporate lessor has less choice and therefore needs to weigh the balance of securitisation benefits with cost and complexity of execution in deciding whether securitisation offers an attractive funding option.

Chapter 19

The European Union

Chris Boobyer

Introduction

Although the foundation of the European Union dates back to 1955, confusion and ambiguity remains over why and how it was constructed, what it actually is today and where it is heading as a political and economic entity. At the most basic level, national states that wish to be members of the European Union have to be physically located in Europe (however defined), have established liberal democratic political systems and functioning market economies. To some observers that is where the similarities stop. This chapter attempts to address some of these issues in a concise form: it is not intended to be an in depth structural or economic analysis of the European Union or its member states. However, it may unfold and explain some of the perhaps confusing characteristics of the European Union and why it is sometimes much more difficult than might be imagined to start writing business within the European Union, especially when the idea is assessed or originated from outside of the region.

This chapter will examine the European Union's relatively brief history, its current organisational structure and governance framework, the challenges it has yet to face as it attempts further expansion and the impact of the single currency that was launched on 1 January 2002. There are agreed proposals to enlarge the European Union from its current 15 member states in 2002 by an additional 13 countries. Accession negotiations were successfully concluded with 10 of them at the European Council meeting in Copenhagen in December 2002. These countries are expected to sign accession treaties in Athens in June 2003 and their formal membership in the European Union will begin in 2004. Many of the proposed member countries already have established asset finance industries and some are already larger than existing members. What opportunity does that present for business expansion for the incoming and existing member states: an enlarged market place to exploit or even greater competitive pressures?

Before trying to explain what the European Union is, perhaps it might be helpful to first explain what the European Union is not. For example, it is not the European equivalent of the United States of America in the sense of the United States of Europe, and there is not yet a European Constitution. Neither is the European Union a single state or country; the European Union currently consists of 15 individual member states each with its own elected government. There is not a single European electorate; EU member governments are elected on a national basis and largely on an agenda of national issues. There is not a single EU army or defence force, nor is there a single EU police force or civil aviation authority. There is no single EU language or EU identity. Individual national languages remain very strong, although English is becoming the accepted European language of business. Individual national (and some fiercely independent regional) identities remain: few EU citizens would consider themselves to be European ahead of their national identities.

There is no single political or economic definition of what Europe is. Not all European countries are part of the European Union: of those that are members, not all of them participate in the common European currency, the euro.

In January 2002, former President of France Valery Giscard d'Estaing was appointed head of a 105-member convention to consider and present a report on the future of Europe. He presented a draft European Constitution on 28 October 2002 with a proposal that it be debated and agreed by June 2003. The draft broadly focuses on seven areas intended to further strengthen the supranational status of the European Union and lead its citizens to regard themselves not as members of their national states, which is the case at present by a substantial majority, but as European citizens first and foremost. A further draft Constitution reflecting the initial work of member states is expected early in 2003. To convey the groundbreaking nature and breakneck speed of this work compared to the slow origins and history of the European Union to date, this chapter provides a short review of the European Union before illustrating and explaining what opportunities it may hold for the asset finance industry.

History and development of the European Union

In 1948, Europe experienced a number of different strains and tensions, and nation states were recovering from the second world war. France had by then been invaded by Germany during conflicts three times in less than a hundred years (1870, 1914 and 1939). The new plan was to prevent war from occurring by stripping from individual nation states the resources and ability to make weapons, primarily in the form of coal and steel. To this end, a proposal was advanced in 1951 by the then French foreign minister Robert Schuman to put the French and German coal and steel industries under common control. In 1952, the European Coal and Steel Community (ECSC) was brought into life among six European nations: Belgium, France, Germany, Italy, Luxembourg and The Netherlands.

Almost from the start of the ECSC, further integration amongst other European states was firmly on the agenda, although no expansion beyond the original six occurred until 1973. In 1957 the principal Treaty of Rome was signed, which established the European Economic Community (EEC). This effectively tightened the focus of the ECSC onto greater economic co-operation and mutual development through the creation of a customs union which abolished all quotas and tariffs among the six members and set a common external tariff as protection against external trade and competition.

A second Treaty of Rome established the European Atomic Energy Community (Euratom), which sought to develop collaboration and co-operation in the advancement of nuclear technology. Both Treaties became operable in 1958 and the three organisations, ECSC, EEC and Euratom, survived independently until 1965 when the Brussels (Merger) Treaty brought all three into a single entity. With effect from 1967 they became the European Communities (EC), with a common Council and Commission. The Treaty on the European Union signed in Maastricht in Holland in 1992 brought the European Union into being and founded the three pillars on which EU policy and governance is based: the European Communities, the Common Foreign and Security Policy, and Justice and Home Affairs. The Treaty also set the timetable and programme for the development of economic and monetary union that led to the preparation for the circulation of the common euro currency in January 2002 together with other earlier economic controls by the European Central Bank.

In 1961 seven other European states which were not part of the EC – Austria, Denmark, Norway, Portugal, Sweden, Switzerland and the United Kingdom – formed the European Free Trade Association also in an attempt to create a free trade area but without a common external tariff which was thought harmful to their trading relationships with the rest of the world. It was unable to negotiate any suitable free trade relationship with the EEC and subsequently floundered. This failure to establish a competitive trading organisation to the EEC further strengthened the EEC's position as the principal economic entity/trading bloc in Europe.

Initial steps to expand the EEC started in 1961 with applications from Denmark, Ireland and the United Kingdom. France vetoed the UK application in 1963 on the basis of its initial disinterest in the ECSC and concerns over its close economic and political relationship with the United States. Membership discussions were again started in 1967 and in 1969 Norway also applied for membership. The four applications were approved in 1972 after President Pompidou became the President of France in 1969. Denmark, Ireland and the United Kingdom joined the European Community in 1973 after national referendums; however, the Norwegians voted against Community membership in 1972.

Further integration occurred with applications from Greece in 1975 (joined in 1981); Portugal and Spain in 1977 (both joined in 1986); Turkey in 1987 (application suspended[1]); Austria in 1989 (joined in 1995); Cyprus and Malta in 1990 (agreed in Copenhagen in 2002); Sweden in 1991 (joined in 1995); Finland in 1992 (joined in 1995); Switzerland in 1992 (application suspended following a national referendum); Hungary and Poland in 1994; Romania, Slovakia, Latvia, Estonia, Lithuania and Bulgaria in 1995 (all except Bulgaria and Romania agreed in Copenhagen in 2002); and Czech Republic and Slovenia in 1997 (agreed in Copenhagen in 2002). A list of current EU members and their dates of entry is shown in Exhibit 19.1.

The process of joining the European Union is painstaking and slow. There have been three distinct phases of increased membership: in 1973, 1981/86 and 1995. The completion of accession negotiations for ten applicant states at the European Council meeting in Copenhagen means that the first new members will join the European Union in 2004 following membership negotiations that started in 1998. Of necessity, this will remain a moving target but there is no doubt that the European Union will expand from its current 15 member states to 25 with a potential total of 28. The question is why and how.

The European Union has often been described as a political project, but there is a continual high level of debate amongst existing member states about the attractiveness of further

Exhibit 19.1

EU member countries and dates of entry

Date	Countries
1957	Belgium, France, West Germany, Italy, Luxembourg, Netherlands
1973	Denmark, Ireland, United Kingdom
1981	Greece
1986	Portugal, Spain
1995	Austria, Finland, Sweden

integration. The process of increasing membership is generally referred to as widening the European Union. There is an equal and opposite debate that rages with the same intensity about the deepening of the European Union representing the increasing power and control over the domestic affairs of the member states – agreed through various treaties – of the EU central institutions such as the Commission, the Parliament and European Court of Justice.

It is important to realise in describing the growth of the European Union that apart from some changes to the formation and powers of the European Parliament, the institutional structure of the European Union remains very close to the original model designed to govern just six members of the ECSC in 1952. The current EU bureaucracies cope with the increasingly complex affairs of the current 15 members, but many feel that fundamental institutional reform is vital if further widening and deepening is to be sustained. It is arguments about these issues that are likely to raise the tension in and temperature of the debate about further increases in the size and scale of the European Union. It is a political project without a formal plan but with an ideal to form an integrated Europe. Robert Schuman started with a plan in sharp focus that has become blurred, but also very successful in many of the original objectives. It is the responsibility of the current custodians, politicians and bureaucrats, to be equally insightful and disciplined.

Structure of the European Union

As an economic unit of around 370 million citizens, the European Union is a major world trading bloc. Its geographic area is less than half that of the United States, but its 2001 GDP represented around 95 per cent of US GDP at US$9,700 billion; its growth rate was 1.6 per cent compared to the United States at 1.2 per cent in that year. The European Union is a collection of 15 individual member states, last enlarged in 1995, and has an agreed programme of enlargement to include 10 of a potential additional 13 new member states starting in 2004. There is an argument that the European Union cannot afford further integration. Its bureaucratic structure is already severely strained and is unlikely to cope with further demands on it. In one sense it is equally unaffordable in pure economic terms: the integration of the former East Germany cost US$100 billion between 1990 and 2000, which is almost equivalent to the European Union's budget for one year, and it materially damaged economic growth in Germany and more broadly within the European Union. Ten of the prospective new member states are former communist economies whose economic demands in terms of integration simply could not be met if on the same scale. However, in another sense, integration is vital to the continued success of the European Union as a political project of stability and for the inclusion of all European countries as members to develop further and encourage economic growth.

Generally, the purpose of the European Union is to develop and promote co-operation between the governments of member states for the common good of the European Union and the shared pursuit and achievement of objectives that might not be secured through unilateral action. The other key purpose is to achieve economic and political advantages through the same co-operation. For this to happen, individual nation states have to pool sovereignty, that is, their rights to govern within their own borders without question or external interference, and to defend themselves against aggressors. The principle of European state sovereignty goes back to the Treaties of Westphalia in 1648 which defined the concept of the nation state as part of the settlement of the Thirty Years War in Europe at that time. Sovereignty is a very delicate subject, particularly in relation to the increasing power and reach of EU bureaucracy. Many member state governments play down the impact of the EU voice and power in their domestic affairs, but on entry into the European Union each member state accepts the principle of *acquis communautaire*, which is an agreement to accept and endorse the vast body of existing EU laws and Treaties on entry. Each new member country adopts the acquis communautaire by enacting new domestic legislation that gives EU law full force and effect within member states. In theory, any member could repeal the enabling legislation, thereby preserving its right of sovereignty, although in practice this is unlikely. Whilst the European Union has enjoyed expanded membership no member has ever left.

How the European Union is governed

One has to look at the relationships between the member states and the central institutions. The process of government by member states and governance by EU institutions is a delicate balance. Yet it is this balance that facilitates cross-border trade, the free movement of capital, goods, people and services, the common standards of production, and a single view on global economic relationships and on trade policy at the EU level. It also enables individual members to have single views on a wide range of domestic issues that can be the cause of bitter disputes between member states from time to time, for example, fishing quotas or meat imports.

The initial governance process of the ECSC, the EEC and initially the European Union was largely biased toward intergovernmental agreement. Unanimity on all material decisions was required and individual nation states could exercise a veto on proposals that did not favour their individual position (for example, France vetoed UK membership throughout the 1960s). However, the overarching concept and ideology of the founding entities, and one that is certainly still current within the European Union, is a degree of cross-border governance with a reduced level of individual member interests being able to stop or delay whatever might be described as progress or further development of EU policies or objectives. This concept of supranational governance is key to the debate about deepening the European Union. The European Union has now changed to become more of a supranational body than an intergovernmental organisation. Given the broad range of policy responsibilities it promotes and develops, one might argue that its only chance of success is by moving closer to a supranational model. The fact that both supranational and intergovernmental governance processes operate side by side and in concert with each other makes the European Union a unique political and economic phenomenon.

The hierarchy of EU governance

The president of the European Council

The hierarchy of EU governance is organised as follows. The most senior body is the European Council which is comprised of the heads of government and foreign ministers of member states. Leadership of the Council, in the form of the European President, is rotated around the heads of government every six months. The European Council has the responsibility to consider and decide the future of the European Union in regard to shape, agenda and timetable. As noted earlier the Copenhagen European Council in December 2002 has most recently illustrated that agenda with its agreement for 10 new member states to join the European Union starting in 2004.

The Council of Ministers

The next most senior body is the Council of Ministers, which is the generic term given to a forum comprised of the relevant ministers from member governments necessary to address whichever topic is under discussion. These two councils are the main decision-making bodies and are the legislature and executive of the European Union. They have the power to make decisions that can affect all member states and citizens of the European Union, but are not directly elected to these positions. They are, however, indirectly elected as members of individual member states' governments which have themselves been the subject of a democratic election process. Their decisions are on the basis of intergovernmental agreement, although qualified majority voting procedures have been introduced for issues concerning Pillar 1, the Communities pillar introduced in the Treaty of the European Union in 1992. Decisions under any of the other two pillars, Common Foreign and Security and Justice and Home Affairs, are decided on a strictly intergovernmental basis with each member retaining the right of veto. Both Councils have the responsibility to resolve inter-member disputes and to ensure the smooth running of the permanent bureaucracy and institutions of the European Union.

The European Commission

The agenda of the European Council and Council of Ministers are prepared and presented by the European Commission, which is headed by a president appointed by the European Council for a five-year term. Including the president, there are currently twenty Commissioners who are appointed by their member states but have a duty to concern themselves only with matters and outcomes that benefit all of the community; they are not expected to be partisan in any way. Individually they have responsibility for all of the various policies of the European Union (a list by policy responsibility and nationality is shown in Annex 2 at the end of this chapter). The Commission has no power of decision and can only recommend acceptance or rejection of proposals to the Councils; however, it can be argued that the Commission controls the agenda of the European Union, thereby indirectly wielding material influence. It has the responsibility to provide all administration services to the European Union and to enforce and protect all EU treaties. There are 24 individual director generals who have responsibility for specific policy areas and the Commission has a permanent staff of around 30,000 organised along functional and policy lines.

The European Parliament

The European Parliament consists of 626 Members of the European Parliament (MEPs) who have been directly elected since 1979. MEPs are elected by their own nation state every five years and the number of each country's MEPs is determined by its total population. There is no common system for electing MEPs across Europe and each country utilises its own electoral system. Therefore, it may not be surprising that local elections for MEPs tend to reflect local member state issues rather than pan-European concerns. There are also no pan-European political parties and no single party has an overall majority. Therefore, votes within the European Parliament depend on coalitions; there are broad groupings of political parties throughout Europe and MEPs naturally form coalitions but also tend to reflect the local political flavour of their national party. In common with global trends in political elections, voter interest and turnout is poor throughout the European Union and recently has been materially less than the turnout in national elections.

371

The European Parliament's powers are limited to comments and joint decision making with the European Council on Pillar 1 Community[2] issues and sanctions over the Commission. It therefore has a broad agenda to follow but to exercise any form of control or to make decisions it has to achieve a majority of its membership in voting, that is, 314 out of 626, not just a majority of votes cast on any issue. Coalitions, and therefore compromise, loom large in many decisions reached by the European Parliament.

One of its key roles lies in its ability to dismiss and sanction the appointment of the members and President of the European Commission. However, to achieve this it has to secure not only the normal majority of half of its membership but also two thirds of the votes cast in support of the proposal.

Clearly, this measure is only to be used in the most extreme circumstances; it was invoked in January 1999 against the Commission headed by President Jacques Santer over concerns with the 1996 EU budget. The vote on censure of the Commission was narrowly defeated, although it led to a report on their conduct in managing the budget that culminated in the resignation of the entire Commission in March of that year. The new Commission headed by President Romani Prodi was appointed in the following September.

The European Court of Justice

The final EU institution to explain is the European Court of Justice (ECJ).[3] It is situated in Luxembourg and is a good example of the cross-border nature of European governance. Its heritage stems from the ECSC, where it was one of four institutions, although it was largely recast in its current form by the Treaty of Rome. It has evolved from being viewed as an international law-maker (whose decisions could be followed or ignored as with all international law by sovereign states) to become an integral part of the European law system with far reaching powers and supremacy in all matters affecting the European Union in relation to Pillar 1 European Communities issues. It has no jurisdiction over the other two pillars of Common Foreign and Security Policy and Justice and Home Affairs since these remain the preserve of member states' governments.

There are in fact two European Courts: the ECJ, which is the senior body, and the lower Court of First Instance. This was formed to relieve some of the pressure on the ECJ and deals with minor infringements or lower priority disputes. Its judgments are considered final on issues of fact but can be appealed to the ECJ on points of law.

The ECJ is currently comprised of 15 judges, one representing each member state. Each judge sits for a fixed six-year term that can be extended. Members of a current team of nine advocates-general, one from each of the five largest states and four rotated amongst other members, are individually assigned to cases and research and review the relevant case law to assist the judges. It is rare for all fifteen judges to hear the same case; normally they sit in teams of three, five or, when a full court hearing is necessary, a minimum number of nine is required. The ECJ is responsible for cases where individual EU institutions refer other institutions or member states to the Court, or where member states refer EU institutions or, on occasion, other members to the Court. The latter is relatively unusual but does happen. The preferred route for any inter-member disputes is for the Commission to refer the defaulting member state to the ECJ rather than bilateral action amongst states.

ECJ decisions are binding across all EU members and individual decisions do not need to be enacted separately by local legislative systems to be operative. This causes some concern amongst anti-Europeans on the basis that legal sovereignty has been passed to the

European Union. This remains a moot point and the subject of intense debate amongst the different factions. The ECJ has no ultimate power of penalty other than fines on any member state that chooses to ignore its judgments, for example, there is no power of expulsion from the European Union.

This should not be interpreted to mean that the relationship between local legislatures and the ECJ is wholly combative. There is a close working relationship between national lawmakers and the ECJ on issues affecting all of the EU community. The ECJ receives many referrals for advice on the interpretation of local laws in a broader EU context. Its powers and presence have certainly increased since its inception, yet it relies heavily on local enforcement of its judgments. There is no common legal system in the European Union and each member state operates its own legislature for all domestic issues. There are certainly laws within the Communities pillar that are applied across the European Union and, like many of the principal institutions, the prospect of further enlargement is going to introduce a severe strain on the burgeoning EU legal system.

European monetary union

There is now a single physical currency operating within, but not throughout, the European Union. The euro was first introduced as a virtual currency in January 1999, and notes and coins were introduced into 12 participating euro countries[4] in January 2002. Questions addressed in this section include how and why this happened, what the principal political and economic drivers were and why some EU members are not participating. Individual currencies were seen as one of the biggest obstacles to open and free trade within the European Union. Now that a single currency has been introduced, has it materially affected the trading patterns between EU members? The answer is probably not, but, in terms of business costs and exchange rate risk, it has been a very positive development since cross-border capital flows by international/transnational businesses are now much more easily achieved. This will in turn affect manufacturing and foreign direct investment decisions, have a beneficial effect on international capital movements and perhaps an unintended consequence will be the opening up – and therefore increased competition – within the continental European capital and commercial markets.

Support for a single, centrally managed economic area and currency was borne from the suspicion that the creation of a single European market envisioned by the 1985 Single European Act would continue to be frustrated as long as individual member states operated individual economies and separate currencies. There is an additional view that a strong and widely used European currency within a harmonised and efficient economic bloc provides effective competition to the global strength of the US dollar. Generally, the 1992 Treaty on European Union was the next logical step from the 1985 Single European Act, and it is the foundation for the increasing pace of integration and ever closer relationship and centralisation of political and economic powers within the European Union.

The concept of a single, centrally managed EU economic area and currency was formally considered for the first time in a study commissioned by the European Council in 1988. Its feasibility was endorsed as part of the 1992 Treaty on the European Union and the timetable for the introduction of Economic and Monetary Union (EMU), including a single currency, was established. Planned in three phases, the timetable envisaged an initial closer working arrangement between EU members' central bankers, followed by the management of the individual economies within tougher and tighter disciplines of the existing Exchange Rate Mechanism. This was effectively a cap and collar on member states' relative exchange rates that required close economic management by member states' central bankers.

The final stage started in 1997 and led to the introduction of the euro currency in 1999 that involved member states committing to managing their respective economies within strict convergence criteria. This required member states to achieve strict macro-economic measures relating to long-term interest rates, price stability, public sector debt and government budget deficit funding. Its purpose was to have all potential EMU countries operating within reasonably close parameters, otherwise the body responsible for a single economic policy (ultimately the European Central Bank) would not be able to set or co-ordinate economic policy over the complete eurozone. Whether this is ever going to be achievable given the enormous diversity of the member economies in the simplest measures of their maturity, resilience and growth rates is, unfortunately, outside the scope of this chapter.

Denmark and the United Kingdom negotiated an opt-out from EMU in the 1992 Treaty on European Union. They reiterated their opposition to it in 1998 when the European Union decided which member states had achieved the convergence criteria and could now proceed to the final stage of EMU, that is, the formation of the euro currency zone. Although two of the 13 member countries pursuing EMU strategies – Greece and Sweden – were judged not to have met the convergence criteria, the remaining 11 countries prepared for the introduction of a virtual euro currency in January 1999 and a physical currency in notes and coins in January 2002.

The principal affects in January 1999 were the dual pricing of all goods and services in local currencies and in euros, and exchange rates between the 11 countries became fixed. Greece achieved the convergence standards in 2001 and joined the eurozone in time to participate in the launch of the physical euro currency in January 2002. Denmark, the United Kingdom and Sweden have remained outside the eurozone.

The European Central Bank

The European Central Bank (ECB) was formed in 1998 and operates from Frankfurt in Germany. Its key role is to manage monetary policy over the whole area of the 12 member states that fall within its responsibility and to manage the relative value of the euro against other world currencies. Its key objective is to maintain price stability, that is inflation, through monetarist policy and interest rate mechanisms although it has no fiscal responsibilities. Existing central banks within the eurozone countries became members of the European System of Central Banks, effectively local branches of the ECB concerned with monitoring and analysing local issues and their impact on the broader responsibilities of the ECB.

The ECB is modelled on the former German central bank, the Bundesbank, which was famously independent from successive national governments by design. The ECB enjoys independence from formal EU governance fora but does have to provide annual reports to the Council of Economic and Finance Ministers and the European Parliament. Representatives of the European Council and the Commission are entitled to attend the ECB Governing Council, which is its principal decision-making forum, although they do not have a vote. Therefore, there can be no overt political influence or pressure applied to ECB decisions on price stability and exchange rate management.

However, one of the weaknesses it faces in regard to price stability is its lack of any fiscal controls over member states whose independent action, if sufficiently large or co-ordinated, could have an impact on inflationary tendencies throughout the European Union. Eurozone countries have very little autonomy in regard to national budgeting; all monetary policy is the preserve of the ECB and strict criteria are applied to government funding. Governments can, however, finance growth and increased public spending through a combination of tax raising measures, government borrowing (subject to limits) or through issuing securities.

These two mechanisms remain under national government control and some commentators argue that the ECB's responsibility should include all economic measures and controls, including fiscal policies. Others complain that the ECB already has a material democratic deficit; its policies affect many parts of the European Union yet its President and members of the Executive Board are appointed by the European Council and are not subject to any democratic election or voting process by citizens affected by their decisions.[5]

Denmark and the United Kingdom opted out of the plans for EMU due to their concerns for the efficiency of one centrally-driven monetarist economic policy governing such a geographically large and, more importantly, economically diverse region. Monetarist policy uses interest rates as its principal economic lever to maintain price stability.

The ECB's adherence to this policy in an effort to achieve its objective is likely to have a material, and different, impact on the diverse economic cycles being experienced in different parts of the region. This will be particularly acute when its policies come under pressure. For example, if one part of the eurozone is struggling with a recessionary or stagnating economic environment, the appropriate monetarist measure would be to lower interest rates gradually or quickly depending on the severity of the problem. This will reduce the cost of borrowing, thereby stimulating consumer and commercial confidence and demand that will help the economy recover its former vigour.

However, if in another part of the eurozone, the local economy is buoyant and witnessing inflationary tendencies, then the worst control measure would be to reduce interest rates, and the reverse is likely to be the most appropriate action. Therefore, even an elementary example illustrates the apparent weakness of central economic management across such a diverse economic environment. Of course, the EMU convergence criteria were designed to make sure that the economies of member countries were not too diverse and could be managed within a reasonable band of growth and recessionary cycles. Critics argue that the pilot period was very short compared to normal economic cycles and did not effectively answer how EMU would avoid a similar economic crisis to that which saw countries forced to exit the Exchange Rate Mechanism (ERM), one of the early convergence measures used for EMU. This may have helped shape the subsequent diverse opinions on the benefits of EMU.

The United Kingdom's position

As noted earlier, one of the major economies within the European Union has not joined the ERM for a number of reasons. As part of its concerns with the issues noted above, the UK government is worried about the asymmetric levels of house ownership between the United Kingdom and continental Europe. The United Kingdom has a much higher proportion of personal home ownership, and consequently a much larger exposure to long-term debt through the mortgage market. Therefore, any fluctuations in interest rates, particularly increases, will have a proportionately bigger impact on the relative wealth of UK citizens compared to continental European citizens, who have a bigger propensity to lease or rent property and therefore a lower exposure to movements in debt interest rates.

Bearing in mind that individual member states are governed by nationally elected governments, it becomes a lot easier to understand that even on a very basic political analysis there is a major political disincentive to allow a remote and independent central bank to have complete responsibility to manage a wide and diverse economic region. Although 12 member states have taken, and appear comfortable with, that decision, six months after winning the 1997 general election the UK government established what it describes as five economic tests to help it determine whether entry to EMU is attractive and viable before committing to a referendum for the electorate. These are listed below.

- *Convergence.* GDP growth rates together with interest rates, trade balances and employment levels need to be in synchronisation with the rest of Europe for a period, otherwise the problems identified above with one rate for a huge region could reduce economic growth.
- *Flexibility.* Is there enough flexibility to deal with any problems that might emerge? The recent US economic control and response issues have highlighted a major difference in attitudes between the United Kingdom and Europe. The United Kingdom, to an extent, mirrored the US Federal Reserve's actions on interest rates. The ECB, in the emerging economic slowdown of late 2001 and early 2002, was initially much less sympathetic. This has prompted debate in the United Kingdom about the wisdom of having a central bank for such diverse regions, particularly where the levels of growth and relationships with the US are so different.
- *Investment.* Will the United Kingdom in the eurozone be more attractive to foreign investors than outside it? There are many examples of UK – and foreign-owned – manufacturers making opposing arguments on this point.
- *The City.* What effect will there be on the UK financial services industry? Is it viable to have an independent market to the Frankfurt financial centre?
- *Employment.* Would EMU improve GDP and therefore stimulate job growth in the United Kingdom?

Cynical views of the five tests are that they are so broad that they can be used either to support or detract from EMU, and therefore the decision to recommend UK entry to the electorate will be made on political not economic grounds. The UK Chancellor of the Exchequer is committed to review the economic tests by June 2003 to enable a decision on whether a referendum should be held on membership of EMU and, if a recommendation is made and there is a positive referendum, this could mean UK entry by 2006.

Europe's political experiment

A broader question affecting the further acceptance of the euro and its future stability is the fact that it remains part of the European political experiment. There is no other currency that is not underpinned by a common taxation system. Tax harmonisation within the European Union is often on the agenda and a much sought after goal by some European policy makers. Individual interests of member states have so far successfully derailed any progress towards it. Personal, corporate and service-related taxes have differing thresholds, rates and scope in many parts of the European Union. This allows member states some room for flexibility in their local fiscal affairs away from the direct control of the ECB where its jurisdiction applies, and this situation is unlikely to be readily relinquished.

Consider, also, the impact of further EU political integration. The recently accepted 10 new member states will at some point be expected to achieve economic convergence as part of their membership commitment. Given their respective starting points and the existing gap in their economic capability and potential demands on their new partners, will the ECB be able to manage their economic integration, exercising effective economic policy control on a materially larger and even more economically diverse region than it currently does?

Questions such as this will continue to challenge and promote debate amongst the EU economic and political leadership for many years to come. In the meantime, the European Union continues to function and is beginning to occupy an increasingly important role on the global economic stage in representing a population of nearly 400 million and growing.

Leasing and asset finance opportunities

There is no doubt that the European leasing landscape has changed dramatically over the past decade. The Leaseurope contribution from Marc Baert in the next chapter vividly illustrates the changes he has seen in his stewardship over the past twenty years. The pace and pressures of European integration can be expected to present even more change and even greater challenges. Leaseurope's new business has doubled in the past decade at a time when its membership has consolidated through acquisition and merger activity. Exhibit 19.2 shows the size of the potential prize by considering the size of EU member states in waiting compared to existing EU members.

In some instances, these states in waiting already outrank established EU members, and therefore their potential for growth with access to a developing pan-European free market is enormous. The investment demand for all of their domestic economies as they start to increase and harmonise their economic pace and activity within the EU club will provide new business opportunities and competition within the asset finance market.

The global leasing and asset finance market must become acutely aware of the development opportunities, particularly as the more developed domestic economies are becoming over-crowded and potentially stagnant in regard to new development opportunities. It can reasonably be expected that the new EU member countries have everything to gain and little to lose from the accelerated pace of integration within the global asset finance market. The level of competition in developed markets is likely to be to their advantage as lessors and financiers seek out new markets. As we have seen, the existing EU area has seen tremendous growth over the past decade. The opportunities presented by further political and economic integration should present an even more exciting and undoubtedly challenging outlook.

Membership of or affiliation with Leaseurope is a key part of trying to fathom the depths and intricacies of the broad potential of European leasing and asset finance growth. As with any new market, knowledge and understanding is crucial to success. However, whilst there are many lessors that have already made a solid start in developing their pan-European operations, I firmly believe that no-one has properly joined up the dots to operate a fully integrated pan-European asset finance operation. By this I mean a single operating system, front and back office, one-touch customer record and data entry capability throughout its European sites, and the ability to have single billing for customers with multi-site European operations.

The opportunity is certainly there, although the cost and necessary efficiencies, and certainly the scale, may remain absent, and will remain so until such time as there is fiscal har-

Exhibit 19.2

Comparison of EU member and potential-member countries with asset finance activity (€ billions)

EU member countries	Plant and machinery	IT equipment	Ships/ aircraft/ rolling stock	Road transport/ vehicles	Cars	World ranking* 2001
Germany	4.0	5.5	1.5	3.0	19.0	3
United Kingdom	7.1	6.7	2.1	4.7	10.0	4
France	7.7	2.9	–	6.1	4.4	5
Italy	10.2	1.4	0.3	3.3	3.7	6
Spain	3.1	0.2	0.6	2.4	1.3	8
Sweden	0.5	1.0	0.5	0.3	2.8	10
Netherlands	0.8	1.2	0.2	0.9	0.3	15
Austria	0.3	0.2	0.3	0.5	1.5	14
Belgium	0.7	0.8	0.03	0.5	0.7	17
Portugal	1.1	0.1	0.03	0.5	0.7	16
Denmark	0.4	0.5	0.1	0.6	0.5	20
Ireland	0.3	0.2	0.04	0.3	1.0	26
Finland	0.1	0.3	–	0.1	0.2	31
Greece	–	–	–		–	36
Luxembourg	–	–	–		–	45

Potential member countries	Plant and machinery	IT equipment	Ships/ aircraft/ rolling stock	Road transport/ vehicles	Cars	World ranking 2001
Czech Republic	0.5	0.07	0.01	0.8	1.3	22
Poland	0.5	0.1	0.08	0.9	0.05	18
Hungary	0.2	0.04	–	0.4	1.1	27
Turkey	0.5	0.1	–	0.03	0.06	23
Slovakia	0.1	0.01	–	0.2	0.4	40
Estonia	0.1	0.01	0.02	0.05	0.2	46
Slovenia	–	–	–		–	44
Bulgaria	–	–	–		–	Outside top 50
Cyprus	–	–	–		–	–
Latvia	–	–	–		–	–
Lithuania	–	–	–		–	–
Malta	0.1	0.02	–	0.1	0.1	–
Romania	–	–	–		–	–

* World Leasing Yearbook 2002 ranking.

Source: Leaseurope data, www.leaseurope.org.

monisation to match an integrated monetary system for all EU members. This remains some way off, so in the meantime the leasing and asset finance industry will continue with the European patchwork approach, solving lessees' needs and making money on a sub-optimal basis until such time as EU policy and individual member country's interests coincide. It is likely to be a long wait.

Conclusion

This chapter sets out the recent history and developments of the European Union and examines its structure and potential opportunities for new business development. There is no doubt that the principal aims of the EU founding fathers have been achieved, that is, peace and increasing political and economic integration. There is also no doubt that the political and economic engine of Europe is getting into a higher gear and looking to expand and develop new markets consolidating its many achievements so far. The European Union remains a political and increasingly economic experiment on the basis that there is no set timetable or framework. Its success to date has been the result of a few visionaries and a committed bureaucracy rather than any determined or cohesive effort from its members in aggregate. An external or indeed an internal observer might be forgiven for thinking that, at times, there is more effort invested by member states in trying to prevent progress than promoting it.

There is a strong element of reverse thrust on occasion and, on one level, the many options for the future are tangled and ensnared by individual member's conflicting interests. Further political and economic integration might suit some countries very well; others might feel resentment and concern over increasing the power of a remote, and by strict definition an undemocratic, body that can directly affect national affairs and, therefore, local and personal political aspirations.

European citizens appear equally divided and confused. Euro barometer polls between 1992 and 1998 show that only:

- 4 to 5 per cent of those polled saw themselves as having a European identity first;
- between 38 and 44 per cent considered their national identity as relevant; and
- a declining percentage (48 per cent in 1992 compared to 41 per cent in 1998) felt that their second identity was European.

There is a long way to go to achieve the many forms of harmonisation within the European Union, and citizen's personal feelings seem to indicate there is a massive hill to be climbed in regard to an overall feeling of European identity. However, there appears to be a direct correlation between the greater the distance from the European Union and one's identity with it. In Asia and some parts of the United States, for example, there is a general view of people being Europeans rather than necessarily being British, French or German.

This is indicative of the confusion and ambiguity that prompted this chapter. There is no escape from some of the confusion over what is going to happen next or what the plans for further integration will be, or even any firm indication of a timetable; it will simply happen when it happens. There has been too much at stake during the formative years of the European Union to rush its development. There has never been a clear definition of what or where Europe starts and ends. Following the dramatic events that heralded the end of the Cold War, which has presented the opportunity to further consolidate democracy, and introduce 'open market' economic models, why would you rush to define the boundaries of the EU? If firm boundaries had been established in the mid-1980s, for example, a number of states who will sign accession treaties in June 2003 may not have been eligible for membership. The rewards of the continued expansion of the EU, such as the spread of democratic political systems and free market economies, are probably worth waiting for and will be delivered in due process.

The current work on the proposed European Constitution, led by Valery Giscard d'Estaing, is expected to reach some sort of conclusion by June 2003. No doubt it will add another bold colour to the palette of opinions on and controversies over the EU's direction and purpose. The European Constitution is intended to further shape and inform the political project and its authors already claim that it will be as important to the future of Europe as the work of the founding fathers was to the future of the United States. There is an equal chance that the success or failure of the European Constitution will depend on a variety of opinions from supporters and detractors; two certainties are that any agreement to change is unlikely to be reached quickly and any defeat of the proposals will not be the end of the story. Europe has much unfinished business; lasting peace in every part of Europe has not yet been achieved, existing and new economic challenges remain unsolved and the possibility of an efficiently designed method of governance with a single representative voice throughout the European Union is as far distant today as it was in 1952. With work on these matters comes many opportunities and my fervent hope is that asset finance will play its traditional role in helping economies to modernise and reduce the pressure on the high cost of vital manufacturing and service sector investments. In short, to continue doing what it has done for the developing economies of the soon to be member states (but what seems to have been forgotten by the mature western European economies).

For further, more detailed study on the history of the European Union and the challenges it faces, see the following two textbooks: G Thompson, *Governing the European Economy,* (Sage 2001); and S Bromley, *Governing the European Union* (Sage 2001).

---

[1] The European Council of Ministers was formally advised to reject the application for membership from Turkey in 1989. The European Commission suspended Turkey's application, but in 1999 it was granted candidate status and advised that membership discussions could start at some future point although a number of material concerns remained over its application.

[2] The majority of issues facing the European Union on a day-to-day basis (such as the broad range of social and welfare policies, competition irregularities, common standards of production, labelling and material content, economic issues and, of increasing concern, environmental issues, waste disposal and recycling) fall under the Communities Pillar.

[3] The European Central Bank is discussed in the section below on European Monetary Union.

[4] Participating euro countries in January 2002 were: Austria, Belgium, Finland, France, Germany, Greece, Ireland, Italy, Luxembourg, The Netherlands, Portugal and Spain.

The three non-participating countries are Denmark, Sweden and the United Kingdom. Each government is under pressure to hold a referendum on whether to adopt the euro. The United Kingdom must decide whether to hold a referendum by June 2003; Sweden is expected to hold a referendum in September 2003; Denmark has announced a possible referendum after 2004 or 2005.

[5] The same argument can be applied to many of the EU governance bodies, with the exception of the European Parliament, so such criticism should not be over estimated in this context. This summary view of the European Union does not provide an adequate platform to argue the merits of such criticisms, whether for or against, but it is illustrative of the broader framework and challenges under which the European Union operates. One way in which this manifests itself is in the extraordinarily low turn-out rates (generally less than 25 per cent) for European elections.

Annex 1

EU institution offices, addresses and telephone numbers

European Parliament	Rue Wiertz/Wiertzstraat
	B-1047 Brussels
	Belgium
	Tel: (32-2) 284 21 11
	Plateau du Kirchberg
	BP 1601
	L-2929 Luxembourg
	Tel: (352) 43 00-1
	Allée du Printemps
	BP 1024/F
	F-67070 Strasbourg Cedex
	France
	Tel: (33) 3 88 17 40 01
	www.europarl.eu.int
European Commission	Rue de la Loi/Wetstraat 200
	B-1049 Brussels
	Belgium
	Tel: (32-2) 299 11 11
	http://europa.eu.int
Court of Justice	Palais de la Cour de Justice
	Boulevard Konrad Adenauer
	Kirchberg
	L-2925 Luxembourg
	Tel: (352) 43031
	www.curia.eu.int
Court of Auditors	12 rue Alcide De Gasperi
	L-1615 Luxembourg
	Tel: (352) 43981
	www.eca.eu.int
European Central Bank	Postfach 16 03 19
	D-60066 Frankfurt am Main
	Germany
	Tel: (49) 69 1344 0
	www.ecb.int

Annex 2

EU Commissioners and their responsibilities (2002)

Commissioner	*Responsibility*
Romano Prodi	President
Neil Kinnock	Vice-President, Administrative Reform
Loyola de Palacio	Vice-president, Relations with the European Parliament Transport & Energy
Michel Barnier	Regional Policy
Frits Bolkestein	Internal Market Taxation and Customs Union
Phillippe Busquin	Research
David Byrne	Health & Consumer Protection
Anna Diamantopoulou	Employment & Social Affairs
Franz Fischler	Agriculture, Rural Development & Fisheries
Pascal Lamy	Trade
Erkki Liikanen	Enterprise & Information Society
Pedro Solbes Mira	Economic & Monetary Affairs
Mario Monti	Competition
Poul Nielson	Development & Humanitarian Aid
Chris Patten	External Relations
Viviane Reding	Education & Culture
Michaele Schreyer	Budget
Günter Verheugen	Enlargement
Antonio Vitorino	Justice & Home Affairs
Margot Wallström	Environment

Annex 3

The 15 EU member states, 10 accession/transition states and remaining applicants

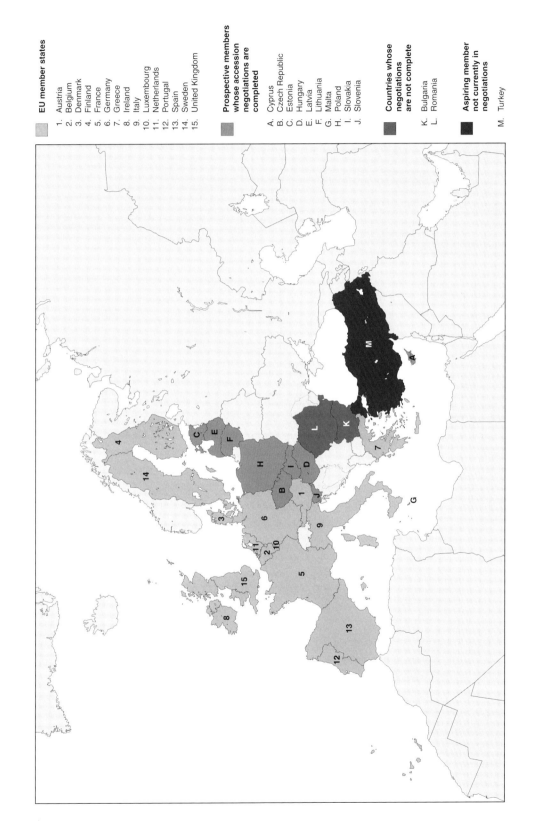

EU member states

1. Austria
2. Belgium
3. Denmark
4. Finland
5. France
6. Germany
7. Greece
8. Ireland
9. Italy
10. Luxembourg
11. Netherlands
12. Portugal
13. Spain
14. Sweden
15. United Kingdom

Prospective members whose accession negotiations are completed

A. Cyprus
B. Czech Republic
C. Estonia
D. Hungary
E. Latvia
F. Lithuania
G. Malta
H. Poland
I. Slovakia
J. Slovenia

Countries whose negotiations are not complete

K. Bulgaria
L. Romania

Aspiring member not currently in negotiations

M. Turkey

Chapter 20

International perspectives

PART 1: THE AUSTRALIAN LEASING INDUSTRY

Ron Hardaker

Lease market structure

Market background

Leasing has long been available in Australia and has become a widely used form of equipment finance. Its use was pioneered by member finance companies of the Australian Finance Conference (AFC), the national finance industry association, in the late 1950s and early 1960s and since that time most financial institutions have moved to include leasing in their product range.

Lease finance rose strongly through the 1960s, 1970s and into the 1980s as acceptance of the ideas behind leasing broke down earlier attitudes against this non-equity form of financing. In addition, from the mid 1970s onwards a more neutral tax system allowed leasing to compete more equally with other equipment financing techniques. The proportion of new private capital expenditure financed by leasing peaked at around 30 per cent in 1989 and 1990 due to the then mix of investment incentives, capital allowances, interest and tax rates. It subsequently eased to below 20 per cent due to changes in the above and some state tax distortions and has now settled at around 25 per cent in the absence of any major tax driver or major distortion. Lease and non-lease equipment finance together regularly account for 45 to 50 per cent of equipment capital expenditure.

In the early years most leases were motor vehicle related and even today around 50 per cent of lease volumes involve motor cars, trucks, vans, motor buses and coaches. Big-ticket items such as aircraft, ships and heavy earth-moving vehicles comprise another sizeable section of the leasing market. From the late 1980s, operating leases developed in importance, particularly for motor vehicles, computers and office machinery, and today account for around 20 per cent of the equipment finance market.

Leasing is generally offered as part of a range of financing products. This allows its particular merits in relation to other finance techniques to be weighed and tailored to a customer's particular needs and financial position. Applicants can usually choose between a number of sources, including financiers or lessors with whom they have an existing relationship, those offering leasing at point of sale and those operating independently in the market. Sophisticated transaction packagers, as well as lease brokers, also play a role in promoting the leasing product.

Generally, leases are written for most capital equipment items, provided they are used for commercial purposes, and for periods ranging between two and five years; implicit rates are competitive and are usually fixed for the period of the lease. Provided that the commercial use test is met, lessees can claim the full amount of the lease rentals as a tax deduction. The lessor, as owner, claims the depreciation and usually any investment incentives. Either the lessee or the lessor, as appropriate, could have claimed the latter, as in the case of the investment allowance. In this way, leasing is one of the few tax benefit transfer mechanisms recognised by the tax system.

There can be no option during the lease contract to purchase the leased goods at the end of the term, otherwise the transaction is a credit sale with rentals that are no longer deductible. However, the lessee may re-lease the goods at the end or make an offer for them. Lessees account for finance leases on their balance sheet, disclosing notional depreciation and interest as expenditure. No balance sheet disclosure is required for operating leases, with full rental payments deducted as expenses and future contracted rentals footnoted.

For the past decade or more, the national taxation system has been relatively neutral in relation to the various equipment financing options. Each product alternative is able to compete on the basis of its appropriateness and flexibility in relation to a particular investment need. However, in September 1999, the federal government adopted several recommendations included in its commissioned *Review of Business Taxation* (*the Ralph Review*), one of which was to introduce a Simplified Tax System (STS) for small businesses. This allows small businesses access to accelerated depreciation which is denied to the lessor of the same equipment to the same customer.

Aside from this distortion, a range of other policy changes also came into effect. The principal one was a drop in the company tax rate from 36 per cent to 30 per cent from 1 July 2001. As the policy package overall had to be revenue neutral, some A$2.8 billion (US$1.6 billion) of the A$3.5 billion (US$2.0 billion) annual cost to revenue of the drop in tax rate was recouped by the removal of the acceleration within the earlier broad-banded safe harbour depreciation schedules, with rates for investment from September 1999 to be based on the asset's effective life. The government has yet to decide on another of the review's recommendations to treat non-routine leases as sales and loans for tax purposes. As with the STS measure, the Australian Equipment Lessors Association (AELA) continues to make industry representations in the policy formulation process.

Current market activity

Total equipment finance has continued its strong growth, reaching A$25 billion (US$14 billion) in calender year 2002, surpassing previous peaks. Equipment finance markets have continued to be highly competitive with fine margins. Fortunately, this growth is being matched with low levels of delinquency and losses.

In the past year, finance leases worth some A$7 billion (US$3.9 billion) have been written, compared to A$3.3 billion (US$2 billion) of operating leases and A$14.7 billion (US$8.2 billion) of non-lease equipment finance (that is, hire purchases and chattel mortgages). These figures (see Exhibit 20.1) reflect a swing away from finance leases towards non-lease equipment finance products due to GST timing disadvantages for some lessees and some remaining state tax distortions for leases.

Against a backdrop of broader demand in particular market segments, finance leases should continue to recover from the introduction of the GST distortion and fill a significant market need for plain vanilla leasing. The specialised market position of operating leases will

385

Exhibit 20.1

Australian lease market share (A$ million)

New business 2002	Finance lease	Operating lease	Total lease	Non-lease commercial finance	Total equipment finance
Non-bank	5,047	2,915	7,962	8,039	16,001
Bank	1,953	335	2,288	6,711	8,999
Total	**7,000**	**3,250**	**10,250**	**14,750**	**25,000**

Sources: Australian Bureau of Statistics and AELA estimates.

continue to grow, particularly in sectors with reasonably deep second-hand markets, for example, vehicles, mobile manufacturing plant and computers/office machines. Non-lease equipment finance products should also continue to be promoted.

Leasing in all of its forms is a proven equipment financing technique, both in times of economic recovery and recession. It will continue to play an important role in supporting and developing the economy's productive base.

The main providers of lease finance in Australia are non-banks (such as finance companies and general financiers) and banks. In the calender year 2002, their volumes of new leases were A$4.7 billion (US$2.6 billion) and A$1.9 billion (US$1.1 billion) respectively.

Lease industry representation

Finance companies pioneered leasing in Australia in the 1950s and continue to provide the majority of new lease and other specified equipment finance. With lease finance accounting for over 30 per cent of financiers' lending operations, their national industry association, the AFC, had for many years fulfilled the role of lessor industry association in terms of legislative and tax representations. However, in the latter part of 1986, a series of meetings of participants in the wider lease market led to the establishment of the AELA.

The AELA's objectives are to promote the strength and vitality of the lease and equipment finance market and the association's council meets as frequently as necessary to deal with various lease-related matters on which industry action is deemed appropriate. The council is comprised of representatives from the major institutional groupings: financiers, banks, merchant banks, packagers and vendor-lessors. To date, AELA membership has reached in excess of 90 financiers and associated participants in the market and in aggregate these members account for over 90 per cent of lease business in Australia. Although using the nationwide resources of the AFC, the AELA has been established and structured as an independent association.

Advantages and disadvantages of leasing

When investors in plant and equipment consider how best to finance the acquisition or utilisation of their intended investment, they usually compare the before- and after-tax cash flows of the various alternatives, whether finance or operating leases, hire purchase or chattel mortgage. As discussed separately, the leasing product has a tax benefit transfer capacity which may make it preferred, however this will depend on the prevailing inflation, interest, tax and depreciation rates and the investor's tax, cash flow and credit position. Also relevant to the financing decision will be the availability or otherwise of government incentives. There is no simple answer to the comparison as each needs to be assessed on its particular merits and circumstances.

The regulatory framework

Aside from taxation, the main regulatory impact on leasing in Australia is in relation to generally applicable legislative provisions, lease accounting and common law or similar contractual requirements.

Prudential regulation or licensing

There are no separate leasing company licensing or prudential tests as such. If a lessor is a bank or other prudentially regulated financial institution, it needs to meet those specific criteria. If it is simply a company not prudentially regulated, it just needs to meet its corporations law requirements, including those for fundraising. There is nothing in these specific to leasing or lessors.

Security interests

Across the range of equipment finance products, from rentals to chattel mortgages, financiers have different security interests, registration requirements and ways of realising their investment. For leases and hire-purchase contracts, the lessor/financier is the equipment owner and in a range of default situations can take possession of the item and sell it. Under the lease, the lessor is typically entitled to the full amount of the rentals outstanding less a discount for receiving those rentals earlier than contracted. By comparison, enforcement of the hire-purchase agreement will involve a rebate of the interest/terms charges. Under either scenario, the calculations must not be able to be characterised as a penalty at law. One difference is that the hirer must receive the benefit of any surplus after the sale of the asset and settlement of the account; the lessee on the other hand may not receive such benefit. However, in the current low inflation environment, surpluses are rare.

For chattel mortgages, in general law the respective parties' rights will be determined by the terms of the contract. Generally those terms will allow the mortgagee (financier) to take possession of the secured asset, sell it and proceed against the mortgagor (borrower) for amounts that remain outstanding under the contract, including any personal covenants or guarantees.

The principle of seize or sue, which requires the financier to make an election between being satisfied through the taking of possession or leaving the asset with the defaulting customer and suing for the full amount, is not part of Australian debt recovery jurisprudence. This enables much better credit risk assessment, to the benefit of equipment finance availability and pricing.

Over recent years, considerable progress has been made on a national link-up of state- and territory-based encumbrance registers (albeit only for motor vehicles and, in particular jurisdictions, some other registerable goods and boats). At this point, a national personal property security regime has yet to pass preliminary cost/benefit analysis.

Financier/lender liability

A major part of the AELA lobbying framework deals with lender liability issues. These can include environmental penalties and the impact of remediation statutes, forfeiture and product defect liability. When such laws have been introduced in recent years they have generally included passive financier exemptions, which have assisted members.

However, these liability regimes can arise out of obscure statutes (for example, occupational health and safety, damage by aircraft, alcohol or broadcasting licensing) and a regular review of the regulatory framework, especially when insurance conditions change, is required. Also, the more financiers are actually involved in the maintenance or operation of the equipment, the less effective can be the relevant exemptions.

Commercial unconscionability, privacy and money laundering

There has been recent deliberation of extending some consumer-type disclosure requirements to small business and farmer lessees. This has been strongly resisted by AELA as counterproductive to the better interest of these new 'consumers', not because of the requirements themselves, but because of the operational rigidities that they can imply. The commencement of commercial unconscionability provisions in the Trade Practices Act from 1 July 1998 therefore caused some concern. The operation of these provisions is closely monitored, however, and they have yet to prove a compliance issue.

Late in 2001, National Privacy Principles were enacted to apply to the private sector. These affect the collection, handling and storage of personal information about individuals and affect equipment financier processes in relation to individuals as lessees/borrowers, guarantors, directors, brokers and other introducers. The AELA provided detailed compliance assistance to members and minimal disruption has been reported to date. More recently, the national money laundering provisions have been tightened for anti-terrorist purposes. A potential exists for equipment financiers and their equipment to be inadvertently caught by these restrictions. The AELA will keep these changes under review.

Contractual regulation and the common law

In relation to contractual regulation (unlike hire purchase, personal loans, mortgages, etc) specific statute coverage of lease finance is limited to consumer leases or deemed credit sale agreements. This coverage is hedged with monetary limits and business use and corporate nature of lessee tests.

Other than this limited coverage arising from consumer credit statutes, the lease contract is governed by common law principles (for example, correspondence with description, quiet enjoyment and fitness for purpose) and by the Trade Practices Act 1974 (for goods under A$40,000 (US$22,400) which provides for common law remedies plus conditions as to merchantable quality, and some liability where the lessor is 'linked' to the supplier through a regular, commercial relationship).

Consumer reforms have generally avoided commercial areas such as leasing, thereby allowing flexibility in contractual arrangements within common law and the Trade Practices Act framework of protections. However, as a complex framework of state and federal laws operates with varying tests and exemptions, it is advisable to explore carefully the legal requirements for contracts before contemplating any involvement.

In addition, and as with other areas of the law, the impact of judgments in cases coming before the courts in relation to contract terms and practices needs to be closely monitored. Decisions of the High Court of Australia in the case of *O'Dea v Allstates Leasing System* (1983), of the New South Wales Supreme Court in the case of *Citicorp Australia v Hendry* (1984) and of the High Court of Australia in the case of Austin v UDC (1984) have placed restrictions on the amounts recoverable from lessees by lessors where the lessees default in their rental repayments and the lessors are forced to repossess the leased goods. During 1988 an appeal of a particular case *(Esanda v Plessnig)* was handed down in favour of the lessor. More recently the *BWAC v Riga* (1992) decision also served to clarify the present state of the law on this matter.

Lease accounting

In July 1986, the Australian Accounting Standards Review Board (ASRB) approved in release ASRB 1008 an accounting bodies' standard of April 1984 that requires lessees to capitalise finance leases. The Australian approach outlined in Australian Accounting Standard (AAS) 17 issued by ASRB uses the US quantitative criteria given in Financial Accounting Standards Board (FASB) 13 as a guideline only, hinging the definitions of a finance lease and an operating lease on the notion of effective transfer from lessor to lessee of substantially all of the risks and benefits incidental to the ownership of the leased property.

In August 1997 Exposure Draft (ED) 82 was released for comment. It subsequently changed AAS17 and ASRB 1008 to bring them into line with International Accounting Standard (IAS) 17 by requiring greater disclosures by lessors. For non-leveraged transactions, these generally did not seem to present a problem for Australian lessors.

More recently, a series of discussion papers has been released under the auspices of the International Accounting Standards Board (IASB) which, by adopting an approach based on the asset/liability concept, would have the effect of putting all material leases (operating, finance and rentals) on the lessee's balance sheet. The AELA continues to liaise with other national and regional leasing bodies and with lessee representative groups to ensure that the practical consequences of this major change in accounting concept (and its partial application only to leases) are fully understood. Should the new approach proceed, a concerted effort will be required to educate analysts, investors and others used to historically-based balance-sheet ratios.

Commonwealth taxation

By far the major statute affecting leasing in Australia is the Commonwealth (national) Income Tax Assessment Act 1936. In summary this act provides for a business lessee to claim tax deductions for the full amount of the lease rentals. This contrasts with other forms of commercial finance (for example, a hire purchase or chattel mortgage) wherein deductions for depreciation and interest charges are claimable. The act provides for the lessor, as owner, to claim the depreciation for the goods leased as an offset against rental income received.

The balance between leasing and other financing methods (from the lessee's point of view) therefore lies in the respective cash repayment streams and the relative write-off period between interest/depreciation on the one hand and lease rentals on the other, as reflected in the lessee's after-tax cash flows.

389

Prior to 1975, investment incentives were directed at items that were owned and used in particular economic sectors (for example, primary industry and manufacturing) and therefore in the case of leased equipment, where ownership was vested in the finance sector, these did not apply. This represented a major distortion against leasing. Since then however, with minor exceptions, leased goods have attracted the incentives and the basic tax treatment of leasing has not significantly changed. What has changed, however, are the underlying rates of depreciation (safe harbour with 100 per cent acceleration, with 20 per cent acceleration, with some broad-band acceleration, with no acceleration; or longer safe harbour rates to reflect Tax Commissioner's assessment of economic life, also self assessment); company tax (from 49 per cent to 30 per cent); investment incentive (40 per cent, 20 per cent and 18 per cent investment allowance); interest (20 per cent to 6 per cent); and inflation (18 per cent to 2 per cent). It is the mix of these which affects the equipment financing decision. Please refer to Exhibit 20.2 for some current Australian depreciation rates.

Investment disincentives can also be seen to apply neutrally. The 21 August 1979 federal budget introduced a depreciation limit for luxury motor vehicles costing initially over A$18,000 (US$10,080). This limit has been indexed each year and for the fiscal year beginning 1 July 2002 is A$57,009 (US$31,925). Since the index number for a number of years up until recently had been negative, the AELA successfully lobbied to hold the limit at this level rather than reduce it. Because several arrangements were in operation to minimise the effect of the limit, the 1996 federal budget introduced a measure to convert for tax purposes such leases into notional sales and loans and the market seems now to have adjusted to this.

The impact of all of these depreciation and investment (dis)incentive changes on leasing has to be understood, first, in terms of their effect on the underlying economics of asset acquisition and utilisation and, secondly, on how they operate, or are perceived to operate, between the different financing alternatives. Because leasing is effectively after tax (that is, lease pricing models incorporate the various changes into the amount of the lease rental), such policy changes have an immediate and obvious result. Other financing alternatives, such as hire pur-

Exhibit 20.2

Australian depreciation rates

	(%) current effective life safe harbour rates Australian depreciation schedules	
	Prime cost	*Diminishing value*
Aircraft/general	12.5	18.75
Container ships	6.25	9.375
Computer systems	25	37.5
Earthmoving equipment	15	22.5
Lathes/computer	10	15
Locomotives	5	7.5
Motor cars*	12.5	18.75
Trucks/heavy Haulage	20	30
Telephone systems/PABX	5	7.5

* Depreciation limit applies.

Source: Australian Taxation Office.

chase or chattel mortgage, can seem to remain unchanged because the after-tax impact is in the customer's books. This was most recently obvious in September 1999 when the investment effect of the company tax rate drop and the removal of accelerated depreciation was immediately obvious in lease quotes. It took longer for investors to assess the overall impact of the policy change on financing an acquisition via non-lease financing alternatives.

The Tax Act also has a number of other sections that affect leasing. For example, the 1979 budget introduced an amendment to ensure that profits made by the lessee on the resale of a vehicle in the event of a purchase for the residual value would be taxable where before they may not have been. The September 1999 changes also removed the long-standing 13-month rule which had allowed up to 13-months' worth of deductions to be claimed in the relevant tax year. This was in order to facilitate the revenue neutrality requirement of the reduction in the company tax rate.

In addition, the Income Tax Assessment Act 1936 has given discretionary powers to the Tax Commissioner to oversee leasing practices. The broad thrust of this oversight has been to ensure that leases were not disguised purchase or conditional sale arrangements; if they are, then they will take on the nature of a capital transaction for the lessee. It should be noted in passing that because title passes with the last payment within the contract, hire purchase has been ruled (Income Tax Ruling (IT) 196) by the tax office to be capital in nature, that is, the hirer claims depreciation and interest rather than the amount of the repayments. It is for this reason that, for tax purposes, leases in Australia cannot include an option to purchase.

Over the years, tax office guidelines on leasing have developed and they find focus in a number of rulings and are implicit in the operation of the lease market. Care should be taken however in their interpretation as often the guidelines have changed without particular parts of the rulings being updated. IT 28, for example, was originally issued in 1960. Among other things it includes a schedule of acceptable residual values (refer to accompanying extract below), which need to be read in conjunction with the 1962 tax office advice which allows the special circumstances of particular cases to be considered by lessors when formulating their own scale of residual values. These should, however, bear reasonable comparison with the schedule and not be commercially unrealistic or purely nominal. Reference should also be made to any other relevant rulings or statements, for example, IT 213 sets lower acceptable residuals for livestock taking into account their particular circumstances.

The guideline included in IT 28 that a lessee could not indemnify a lessor for any loss on sale was also overtaken by a subsequent tax office statement withdrawing their objection to such a condition in recognition that it was necessary to discourage abuse of the equipment in the possession of lessees.

The rather fragmented nature of these guidelines has been a factor over the years in the tax office or the government announcing reviews with a view to a more comprehensive and explicit regime. The AELA has regularly been a participant in this process. Following the government's 1988 review of tax benefit transfer, the AELA commissioned the Bureau of Industry Economics to study the issue. Their report, *Tax Losses and Tax Benefit Transfer* found, among other things, that leasing was an important means of overcoming the distortions associated with tax-loss carry forward. In September 1990, the tax office announced a review of the various rulings over the years and asked the AELA to prepare a draft omnibus ruling for the consideration of a working group comprising the tax office, industry and professional bodies.

Subsequently, in June 1995, the government announced a joint treasury/tax office review of leasing arrangements. The objective of this review was to replace the current leasing framework (based on tax office public and private rulings and advices and on passing regu-latory references) with a comprehensive legislative framework which did not: 'place unwar-ranted road blocks in front of legitimate separations of economic from legal ownership (including in relation to private sector participation in infrastructure provision) while also preventing unwarranted tax benefit transfers.' The AELA made preliminary input to the review. It has, however, been overtaken by the policy formulation flowing from the 1999 *Review of Business Taxation Report* which recommended that leases, other than routine leas-es, be treated as sales and loans for tax purposes.

Such treatment has been the traditional official response to curbing real and/or perceived leasing abuses (for example, tax-exempt sector leasing) over the years. Provided that the response is properly measured to the particular abuse (for example, as with the luxury vehi-cle depreciation limit), the AELA can understand these actions and the industry role is to ensure that the vast bulk of legitimate equipment leases are unaffected.

The criteria put forward in the latest review however (that is, a routine lease of equipment costing A\$500,000 (US\$280,000) or less can be written only for a term of 90 per cent of its effective life; for equipment costing up to A\$1 million (US\$560,000), a maximum five-year lease term applies, while that costing up to A\$5 million (US\$2.8 million) and over A\$5 mil-lion can only have a maximum term of three years and one year respectively), remain unduly restrictive. The AELA is therefore in current discussions with officials to develop more pur-posive criteria which, in the industry's view, should not affect ordinary commercial leases.

The issue of tax benefit transfer

Paradoxically, the long history and high utilisation of leasing in Australia has often led to a misunderstanding of its attributes. The 1985 government white paper on tax reform, for example, tended to characterise leasing as merely a form of tax shelter.

This view raised the issue of tax benefit transfer and the extent to which the policy frame-work will allow financial product innovation as against restricting financing forms to only those that have become standardised.

In this regard, leasing captures and crystallises taxation deductions and incentives avail-able within the system and within government policy, focusing their effect on the area where it will have the most impact: reduced cash flow to the lessee.

When government and other inquiries urge action to develop sunrise industries or to smooth the restructuring of other sectors or industries, it is ironic that the financing technique best suited to achieving both these objects (that is, leasing), is inappropriately and disparag-ingly described as a tax shelter.

A business that is just starting out, or one that is in the process of restructuring, is unlike-ly to be generating current year taxable income. In these circumstances tax deductions for depreciation or investment incentives do not achieve their desired policy effect, but instead simply add to carry-forward losses. Through leasing, a lessor can claim these deductions against his taxable income, crystallise the benefit and pass on that benefit to the lessee in the form of the tangible incentive of reduced cash repayments.

Unfortunately, the aggregation of such deductions in the books of a relatively few lessors can be misunderstood and can result in the contemplation of restrictions.

Such a view, by focusing on only one side of the transaction, can ignore the essential symmetry of taxation systems, that is, if through a tax benefit transfer the lessor's taxable income is reduced, such reduction in a competitive market flows on to lower rentals which

Exhibit 20.3

Extract of Income Tax Ruling IT 28 (originally issued 6 July 1960 and recently updated as TD 93/142)

Minimum residual values – percentage of cost
  Plant and machinery
  Classified according to income tax effective life

Term of lease (years)	5	6.67	10	13.3	20
lst year	60	63.75	67.5	68.5	70
2nd year	45	52.5	60.0	62.5	65
3rd year	30	41.25	52.5	55.0	60
4th year	14	30.0	45.0	50.0	55
5th year	nil	18.75	37.5	45.0	50

Note: This ruling formed part of lease tax guidelines. Noting the difficulty of prospective variation, Ruling IT 174 of 16 January 1981 indicated as follows:

'In relation to plant other than motor vehicles, it is felt that in the vast majority of cases, the present guidelines are adequate. It is appreciated that, due to inflation, the market value of plant upon the termination of lease may be in excess of the residual value calculated four years or more earlier in accordance with the guidelines. But equally, it may be much less which is what is presently being claimed in respect of, for example, much computer-oriented equipment. Consideration has been given to the view that the residual value should represent a bona fide estimate of the market value of the plant on the termination of the lease but this approach would immediately raise the problem as to how the Taxation Office would estimate market value in several years' time or check such an estimate, particularly in relation to specialised plant. Reliance upon expert opinion (and in most cases the lessees would be such experts) could put our administration of this area in a much worse position than adherence to the guidelines would. It is confirmed, therefore, that the current guidelines should continue to be applied in considering leasing transactions.'

Source: Income Tax Ruling (IT) 28.

represent a reduced tax deduction. This issue was brought into focus during 1988 in the context of the government's consideration of a ruling (IT 2512) on Financing Unit Trusts. On 20 December 1988, the government announced the result of its review as follows:

> *This review has confirmed the need to act against tax effective financing. Tax effective financing relies upon the ability to transfer, or share, tax benefits. The government considers that the broad scheme of the tax law requires that tax losses be carried forward by the taxpayer who in substance incurs them and that, in general, such losses should not be available for transfer to other parties, including financiers. An exception, long accepted by revenue authorities, has been in respect of genuine leasing transactions for plant and equipment but the government believes that other forms of tax benefit transfer should not be accepted.*

The AELA welcomed the decision in relation to leasing. With its tax benefit transfer capacity, leasing is an essential financing tool for a dynamic and competitive economy. If from time to time a new application or financial product development tests the legislative or taxation framework, this should be seen as a healthy and necessary sign of an innovative financial system.

As can be seen from this, a major role of the AELA is to put the case for ensuring that particular legislative responses do not unduly impair leasing's tax benefit transfer capacity to the detriment o. the economy's production, investment and employment. This was especially the case in the need to respond to the 1999 *Review of Business Taxation* (Ralph Committee) proposal of treating all leases as sales and loans for tax purposes. While this might solve the complexities and lack of a cohesive and explicit tax regime for leasing, it would also remove its tax benefit transfer capacity; AELA continues to argue strongly against such proposals.

In terms of indirect taxes on leasing transactions at the Commonwealth level, up until 30 June 2000, a system of Wholesale Sales Taxes on particular items of equipment operated with a range of tax rates and exemptions. From 1 July 2000, a uniform 10 per cent GST applies. From a financier's perspective, a key element of the GST regime is the fact that financial supplies (for example, chattel mortgages) are exempt, which means that the lender is input taxed (that is, unable to claim back the GST components of its input costs), resulting in the customer paying unspecified higher interest or fees which cannot be claimed back. Leases on the other hand are taxable supplies, which means that business lessees claim the GST component of their rentals as a reduction of their GST liability. Hire-purchase contracts can be a mix of taxable and financial supplies, depending on whether or not the interest element is documented. A range of other nuances, especially in the transitional period when many existing leases were to attract GST, but loans and hire purchases would not, saw a switch away from leases. The market is now settling down on the basis of the actual rather than the perceived GST incidence.

The introduction of the new GST system was a testing time for all businesses, especially financiers. Policy changes to better implement the tax from members' viewpoint have been pressed by the AELA, with operational and compliance costs minimised. The AELA was also successful in gaining amendments which provided operating lessors of vehicles with notional input tax credits for the GST liability on rentals received after 1 July 2000.

Stamp and financial institutions duties

The second level of the taxation context of leasing in Australia relates to stamp and financial institutions duties. These are forms of taxation at the state government level. From the early 1970s, each state government introduced these tax levies in the range of 1.5 per cent to two per cent of rentals (variously defined). The primary liability for these duties was on the lessor, but they were generally passed on to the lessee, the impact being to increase the cost of lease finance. Since lease quotes can be given with or without stamp duty, it is important to be clear as to what rental quotes include when shopping around for finance (if a lessee) or attempting to match the market (if a lessor).

Initially, as similar duties applied to many other forms of finance, the competitive disadvantage in the commercial area was largely limited. The introduction from 1982 onwards of a broad-based financial institutions duty (FID) in most states was, however, accompanied by the abolition of duty on hire purchase (then a consumer product). With the introduction of a national personal credit regulatory regime, however, hire purchase was soon to become a burgeoning commercial finance technique.

Unfortunately for leasing, none of these states at the time chose to rationalise the 1.5 to two per cent hiring arrangement/rental business duty applicable to lease finance. As a result leasing attracted both the old stamp duties and the new FID – an anomaly that clearly disadvantaged leasing over competing non-double taxed financing methods. For the last 15 years, therefore, the AELA has successfully lobbied the respective State governments to amend their legislation to remove the distortions and to include greater uniformity.

While a range of differences for equipment finance at the state tax level continues, the position is much improved and much less distorting, enabling greater efficiencies for financiers operating nationally that want to offer standard contracts with common compliance and support systems. The AELA continues to press for this objective.

Conclusion: lease issues in the 1990s

Like the economy, the Australian lease and equipment finance market began recovering in the 1990s from the worst recession for more than 40 years. With only slight variation, economic growth has been consistently strong over the decade. Equipment investment and demand for equipment finance has likewise been strong. Against this backdrop, the lease product issues over that period have largely been focused on removing or preventing tax or other regulatory distortions to the financing decision. While there were many potential such distortions, few were substantive.

Building on the progress of the previous 15 years, the 1990s saw the maintenance of tax benefit transfer finance leases, the growth and profitable development of operating leases and the increasing use of leasing-type structuring techniques in traditionally more staid non-lease equipment finance products. This latter development included flexible repayment alternatives, balloon payments, and service and break options. Product distortions have been gradually reduced, lender liability and other security issues along the product spectrum have been settled, and particular risks and delivery mechanisms have been disaggregated and more transparently rebuilt and priced. The various tax and other regulatory changes over the period forced regular demand and supply swings between equipment finance techniques, leading to a financier culture used to offering a range of products and a customer base increasingly asking for different product features.

All this has been in the context of ongoing consolidation of financial and banking groups, re-engineering and rationalisation, strengthened competition for available business and a reduced quantum of tax shift to be priced.

Lease issues up until 2010

At the AELA's industry lobbying level, the challenge is further to reduce the remaining regulatory distortions (and prevent or minimise future distortions), to maintain leasing's tax benefit transfer capacity and ensure reasonable and credible passive financier exclusions and security protections.

To do this it needs to ensure that the lease product is not perceived as some actual or potential tax or security abuse. Given the valuable economic role leasing plays, this should not be too difficult.

A harder challenge is at the market level. As financial groups get larger and more extensive, their cost of funds becomes lower, but they also come under an increased pressure of managing a larger bureaucracy and delivering customer service. As the scale of financial groups increases, how do these groups control the compliance costs of a range of different products for a similar customer solution in the emerging Basle capital adequacy world? Will the larger groups price for particular product/security risk, or price on the customer's wider group relationship, or simply on volume? How will competition from niche and new players, cherry picking on the basis of some equipment knowledge/service or short-term loss leader edge, be met? How will management ensure that the front desk is actually pricing or delivering in terms of the latest tax or other regulatory compliance requirements for the particular finance product, item of equipment financed or category of customer?

Moreover, will the larger institutional administrator's preference for the compliance simplicity of an homogenous debt product for equipment finance coincide with borrower/lessee's CFO indifference, once all material financings are on-balance sheet?

Only in time will these questions be answered. There is reason to be confident however that the current spread of lease and other equipment finance products will each bring their particular strengths to satisfying the equipment investing customer's particular credit, risk or flexibility needs. In Australia, the industry has always managed to position the lease product to best meet that demand and this is expected to continue.

PART 2: JAPAN'S LEASING INDUSTRY

Katsuhiko Otaki

Market structure

Scale of the leasing market

The total leasing volume in the fiscal year 2001 marked ¥7.7 trillion (US$ 64.4 billion). That is more than ¥1 trillion less than the peak of ¥8.8 trillion reached in the fiscal year 1991 (see Exhibit 20.4).

The volume of capital investment financed by leases (the purchase price of leased assets) in the fiscal year 2001 was ¥6.9 trillion. Meanwhile, leasing's share of total private capital investment was 9.24 per cent. After this share reached 9 per cent in the fiscal year 1995 and increased to 9.33 per cent in the fiscal year 1996, it has stayed between 8 per cent and 9 per cent from the fiscal year 1997 to the fiscal year 2001.[1]

Leasing volumes by equipment type, size of lessee and type of business

Leasing volumes by equipment type

Since almost all moveables, software, and some buildings are leased, equipment types involved in leasing vary widely in Japan. Of particular note is the fact that about 35 per cent of all leased assets in Japan are computers, which is higher than in other countries.

The top five types of leased equipment in the fiscal year 2001 were computers (33.2 per cent), commercial and service equipment (14.4 per cent), industrial equipment (13.3 per cent), office equipment (8.5 per cent), and automobiles (7.2 per cent).

In Japan, automobile leases represent only a small share, in contrast to many other countries. It is estimated that the leasing volume of automobiles would be almost three times as large as those presented in Exhibit 20.5 if we were to include the volume of the member companies of the Japan Automotive Lease Association (JALA). However, even with that volume included, the share of automobile leases in the whole market is still small. Significant growth in the automobile lease market is expected in the future.

Exhibit 20.4

Changes in leasing volume, leasing capital investment and lease market share[2]

Fiscal year	Leasing volume (¥ billion) A	Change from previous year (%)	Leasing capital investment (¥ billion) B	Change from previous year (%)	Private capital investment (¥ billion) C	Change from previous year (%)	Lease market share (%) (B/C)
1990	8,415.2	19.1	6,542.0	13.7	91,319.3	14.0	7.16
1991	8,801.6	4.6	6,884.3	5.2	93,986.1	2.9	7.32
1992	7,774.2	(11.7)	6,281.3	(8.8)	85,811.9	(8.7)	7.32
1993	7,182.5	(7.6)	5,978.0	(4.8)	75,533.2	(12.0)	7.91
1994	7,349.7	2.3	6,163.1	3.1	71,147.0	(5.8)	8.66
1995	7,621.4	3.7	6,580.4	6.8	72,756.0	2.3	9.04
1996	8,286.7	8.7	7,223.8	9.8	77,413.3	6.4	9.33
1997	7,930.4	(4.3)	7,018.0	(2.8)	83,570.8	8.0	8.40
1998	7,144.5	(9.9)	6,315.0	(10.0)	77,796.8	(6.9)	8.12
1999	7,402.4	3.6	6,586.2	4.3	75,232.4	(3.3)	8.75
2000	7,945.7	7.3	6,992.2	6.2	79,788.3	6.1	8.76
2001	7,733.7	(2.7)	6,914.8	(1.1)	74,874.6	(6.2)	9.24

Note: Fiscal year begins on 1 April and ends on 31 March. Private capital investment volumes as published by the cabinet office. Data for 2001 are estimated.

Exhibit 20.5

Leasing volume by equipment type

	Leasing volume (¥ billion) 1998	1999	2000	2001	Component ratio (%) 1998	1999	2000	2001	Yearly change (%) 1998	1999	2000	2001
Information systems	3,142	3,227	3,162	3,075	44.0	43.6	39.8	39.8	93.4	102.7	98.0	97.2
Computers	2,714	2,759	2,685	2,567	38.0	37.3	33.8	33.2	93.3	101.6	97.3	95.6
Telecommunications	428	468	477	508	6.0	6.3	6.0	6.6	93.9	109.4	101.9	106.6
Office equipment	576	596	633	661	8.1	8.1	8.0	8.5	83.3	103.5	106.2	104.4
Industrial equipment	865	982	1,031	1,027	12.1	13.3	13.0	13.3	80.8	113.5	105.0	99.6
Factory equipment	170	186	227	183	2.4	2.5	2.9	2.4	80.5	109.0	122.2	80.9
Construction equipment	155	196	217	161	2.2	2.6	2.7	2.1	100.7	126.1	111.0	74.2
Transport equipment	472	479	586	627	6.6	6.5	7.4	8.1	83.3	101.4	122.2	107.0
Automobiles	383	412	514	554	5.4	5.6	6.5	7.2	87.1	107.6	124.8	107.7
Medical equipment	274	286	328	330	3.8	3.9	4.1	4.3	102.6	104.2	114.8	100.6
Commercial and service equipment	1,037	1,025	1,195	1,112	14.5	13.8	15.0	14.4	89.5	98.9	116.6	93.0
Commercial equipment	651	629	713	631	9.1	8.5	9.0	8.2	93.0	96.7	113.2	88.6
Others	451	426	565	557	6.3	5.8	7.1	7.2	101.9	94.3	132.8	98.5
Total	**7,144**	**7,402**	**7,946**	**7,734**	**100.0**	**100.0**	**100.0**	**100.0**	**90.1**	**103.6**	**107.3**	**97.3**

Leasing volume by size of lessee

Leasing allows companies to make capital investments without using large sums at the outset. This is one reason why leases are widely used by small- and medium-sized enterprises (SMEs) that lack funds for equipment procurement. This is the same in all major lease markets, including Japan.

However, in the latter part of the 1990s, capital investment by smaller businesses decreased amidst the deteriorating economic situation. Meanwhile, larger companies gradually showed a higher degree of lease usage in order to reduce cost, rationalise operations and improve their balance sheets. The result was a higher percentage of larger lessees among the total leasing volume. The percentage of large companies exceeded SMEs for the first time in the fiscal year 1998. This situation has not changed since and in 2001 the respective use of leasing was 47.7 per cent for large companies and 45.1 per cent for SMEs (see Exhibit 20.6).

Leasing volume by lessee type

In the fiscal year 2001, in terms of leasing volume by type of lessee, the non-manufacturing sector marked a much higher ratio (65.9 per cent) compared with the manufacturing sector (26.4 per cent) (see Exhibit 20.7). This is supported by noting that the leasing volume of computers is the biggest while equipment leases (factory equipment and machine tools) for the manufacturing sector lag the former in volume.

Regarding lessee industry type, machinery maintains the highest share percentage (10.7 per cent), followed by retail (9.7 per cent), wholesale (8.5 per cent), financing and insurance (6.1 per cent), construction and real estate (5.8 per cent), and transport and communication (5.1 per cent). At 29.9 per cent, other services consist of a variety of service industries including medical (4.1 per cent), entertainment and information services.

Principal players in the market: lessors

Industrial groups

The Japanese leasing industry was born in the 1960s when city banks, major trading firms and large manufacturers successively established their respective leasing companies. Various other industries followed this move by establishing their own leasing companies in the 1970s, taking note of the prospect for potential growth in the leasing industry.

Classifying lessors according to the industry of their parent companies, Exhibit 20.8 shows that more than half are affiliated with financial institutions (149 companies, representing 50.2 per cent), followed by independents and others (65 companies, representing 21.9 per cent), manufacturers (51 companies, representing 17.2 per cent), and trading firms (32 companies, representing 10.8 per cent).

While more than half of the lessors originate from financial institutions, their leasing volume is just ¥3.6 trillion, or 46.7 per cent of the total of the entire leasing market. The leasing volume of companies originating from manufacturers is ¥2.2 trillion (28.9 per cent), which is comparatively large considering their 17.2 per cent share among the total number of companies. Additionally, the average leasing volume per company of ¥43.7 billion is higher than that of companies from other groups. Meanwhile, the leasing volume of companies in the independents and others group is ¥939.3 billion (12.2 per cent), which is small for the group's 21.9 per cent share among the companies. The average leasing volume per company is lower than for companies in other groups at ¥14.5 billion.

Exhibit 20.6

Leasing volume by lessee size

	Leasing volume (¥ billion)				Component ratio (%)				Yearly change (%)			
	1998	1999	2000	2001	1998	1999	2000	2001	1998	1999	2000	2001
Large companies (capital with ¥100 million or more)	3,512	3,656	3,777	3,690	49.2	49.4	47.5	47.7	94.7	104.1	103.3	97.7
SMEs (with capital of less than ¥100 million and individual firms)	3,313	3,388	3,674	3,490	46.4	45.8	46.2	45.1	85.0	102.3	108.5	95.0
Public sector and others	319	359	494	553	4.5	4.8	6.2	7.1	97.7	112.3	137.7	111.9
Total	**7,144**	**7,402**	**7,946**	**7,734**	**100.0**	**100.0**	**100.0**	**100.0**	**90.1**	**103.6**	**107.3**	**97.3**

Exhibit 20.7

Leasing volume by lessee business type

	Leasing volume (¥ billion)				Component ratio (%)				Yearly change (%)			
	1998	1999	2000	2001	1998	1999	2000	2001	1998	1999	2000	2001
Primary sector	54	55	60	59	0.8	0.7	0.8	0.8	84.0	102.3	109.3	99.0
Manufacturing sector	1,985	2,000	2,078	2,041	27.8	27.0	26.1	26.4	84.8	100.8	103.9	98.3
Iron & steel	106	111	105	115	1.5	1.5	1.3	1.5	87.0	104.2	95.2	109.5
Machinery	710	757	843	825	9.9	10.2	10.6	10.7	83.1	106.5	111.4	97.8
Chemical	146	162	147	137	2.0	2.2	1.9	1.8	82.9	111.2	90.5	93.0
Textile	65	60	48	39	0.9	0.8	0.6	0.5	82.1	91.5	79.8	82.5
Foods	327	330	304	296	4.6	4.5	3.8	3.8	90.9	101.1	92.0	97.6
Others	631	581	631	629	8.8	7.8	7.9	8.1	84.3	92.0	108.6	99.7
Non-manufacturing sector	4,717	4,942	5,244	5,095	66.0	66.8	66.0	65.9	91.9	104.8	106.1	97.2
Electricity & gas	59	51	55	71	0.8	0.7	0.7	0.9	88.1	87.6	107.5	128.1
Wholesale	762	803	708	656	10.7	10.8	8.9	8.5	94.2	105.4	88.1	92.7
Retail	697	751	868	750	9.8	10.1	10.9	9.7	88.5	107.7	115.7	86.4
Financing & insurance	563	574	572	469	7.9	7.8	7.2	6.1	106.9	101.9	99.7	81.9
Transport & communication	320	315	314	393	4.5	4.3	4.0	5.1	83.6	98.3	99.7	125.2
Construction & real estate	384	398	447	445	5.4	5.4	5.6	5.8	86.9	103.6	112.2	99.7
Other services	1,933	2,050	2,280	2,312	27.1	27.7	28.7	29.9	91.3	106.1	111.2	101.4
Medical	276	278	314	321	3.9	3.8	3.9	4.1	105.3	100.8	112.7	102.3
Others	388	405	564	538	5.4	5.5	7.1	7.0	98.2	104.3	139.2	95.3
Total	**7,144**	**7,402**	**7,946**	**7,734**	**100.0**	**100.0**	**100.0**	**100.0**	**90.1**	**103.6**	**107.3**	**97.3**

Exhibit 20.8

Lessors by industrial group

Industrial groups	Number of companies	Component ratio (%)	Leasing volume (¥ billion)	Component ratio (%)	Average volume per company
Financial institutions	149	50.2	3,599.8	46.7	24.2
Manufacturers	51	17.2	2,227.4	28.9	43.7
Trading firms	32	10.8	945.7	12.3	29.6
Independents and others	65	21.9	939.3	12.2	14.5
Total	**297**	**100.0**	**7,712.2**	**100.0**	**26.0**

Notes:

1. Among the financial institutions are banks, life insurance companies, the Norinchukin Bank,[3] Shinkin Bank,[4] and credit associations.

2. The number of lessors is 297, excluding 7 casualty insurance companies from the 304 member companies of Japan Leasing Association, as of 1 April 2002.

3. Leasing volumes are based on fiscal year 2000 performance. Note that 23 of 297 companies did not trade or report during this period.

Note that 2 and 3 apply to Exhibits 20.9, 20.10 and 20.11.

Size of capital

When lessors are classified by the size of their capital, it can be seen that the greatest number possess capital of between ¥100 million to ¥200 million (53 companies, representing 17.8 per cent of the total number of companies), closely followed by those with between ¥50 million to ¥100 million (48 companies, representing 16.2 per cent), and ¥200 million to 500 million (47 companies, representing 15.8 per cent). There are many lessors with relatively small amounts of capital in Japan; Exhibit 20.9 shows 118 companies (39.7 per cent) with capital of less than ¥100 million. Although 38 companies are capitalised with more than ¥3 billion (12.8 per cent), less than half of them provide leasing as their main business.

The leasing volume produced by companies with capital of more than ¥3 billion is ¥5.0 trillion, representing 64.4 per cent of the total market, and the average leasing volume per company is ¥130.7 billion. Meanwhile, the leasing volume of companies with capital of less than ¥100 million is ¥511.5 billion (6.6 per cent), and the average volume is merely ¥4.3 billion.

Number of employees

In terms of the number of employees, companies with 10 to 29 employees represent the largest category of lessors (83 companies, representing 27.9 per cent), followed by those with 30 to 49 (49 companies, representing 16.5 per cent), and those with less than 10 (46 companies, representing 15.5 per cent). The number of companies with less than 50 employees is as many as 178 (59.9 per cent), while there are only 28 companies with more than 500 employees (9.4 per cent). When classifying them by number of employees rather than by size of capital, we can clearly see that there are more small lessors.

The volume of leases written by companies with more than 500 employees is ¥4.1 trillion (52.5 per cent) which is more than half of the total volume of the market and the aver-

Exhibit 20.9

Lessors by size of capital

Capital (¥)	Number of companies	Component ratio (%)	Leasing volume (¥ billion)	Component ratio (%)	Average volume per company
Less than 30 million	35	11.8	92.0	1.2	2.6
30 million to 50 million	35	11.8	143.7	1.9	4.1
50 million to 100 million	48	16.2	275.8	3.6	5.7
100 million to 200 million	53	17.8	466.2	6.0	8.8
200 million to 500 million	47	15.8	317.7	4.1	6.8
500 million to 1 billion	19	6.4	695.3	9.0	36.6
1 billion to 3 billion	22	7.4	754.2	9.8	34.3
More than 3 billion	38	12.8	4,967.3	64.4	130.7
Total	**297**	**100.0**	**7,712.2**	**100.0**	**26.0**

Exhibit 20.10

Lessors by number of employees

Number of employees	Number of companies	Component ratio (%)	Leasing volume (¥ billion)	Component ratio (%)	Average volume per company
Less than 10	46	15.5	68.2	0.9	1.5
10 to 29	83	27.9	355.5	4.6	4.3
30 to 49	49	16.5	424.5	5.5	8.7
50 to 99	37	12.5	531.8	6.9	14.4
100 to 199	23	7.7	590.8	7.7	25.7
200 to 499	31	10.4	1,689.6	21.9	54.5
More than 500	28	9.4	4,051.8	52.5	144.7
Total	**297**	**100.0**	**7,712.2**	**100.0**	**26.0**

age leasing volume per company is ¥144.7 billion. Meanwhile, the leasing volume of the companies with less than 50 employees is ¥848.2 billion (11.0 per cent), and their average volume is only ¥4.8 billion (see Exhibit 20.10).

Amount of leased assets

In terms of the amount of leased assets, lessors with less than ¥5 billion in assets represent the largest number of companies (84 companies, representing 28.3 per cent of the 297 active leasing companies, followed by companies with ¥5 billion to ¥10 billion of leased assets (57 companies, representing 19.2 per cent), and companies with ¥10 to ¥20 billion of leased assets (55 companies, representing 18.5 per cent). The number of companies with less than ¥20 billion in assets reaches 196 (66.0 per cent) while only 29 companies have more than ¥100 billion in assets (9.8 per cent).

The leasing volume for companies with more than ¥100 billion in assets is ¥5.7 trillion,

Exhibit 20.11

Lessors by balance-sheet value of leased assets

Amount of leased assets on balance sheet	Number of companies	Component ratio (%)	Leasing volume (¥ billion)	Component ratio (%)	Average volume per company
Less than 5 billion	84	28.3	109.4	1.4	1.3
5 to 10 billion	57	19.2	189.6	2.5	3.3
10 to 20 billion	55	18.5	370.5	4.8	6.7
20 to 30 billion	23	7.7	227.7	3.0	9.9
30 to 50 billion	29	9.8	517.3	6.7	17.8
50 to 100 billion	20	6.7	596.9	7.7	29.8
More than 100 billion	29	9.8	5,700.8	73.9	196.6
Total	**297**	**100.0**	**7,712.2**	**100.0**	**26.0**

accounting for 73.9 per cent of the total, and the average leasing volume per company is ¥196.6 billion. Meanwhile, the volume for companies with less than ¥2 billion in assets is ¥669.5 billion (8.70 per cent), with an average of only ¥3.4 billion (see Exhibit 20.11).

Economy

The 1990s were the lost decade for the Japanese Economy. After the bursting of the bubble economy at the beginning of the decade, the economy deflated and both companies and individuals lost vitality. The Japanese government produced a series of economic stimuli. The Bank of Japan cut its official discount rate to a record low of 0.5 per cent in September 1995, continuing to ease monetary policy by adopting a zero per cent interest-rate policy in February 1999.

Thanks to these fiscal and monetary policies, the Japanese economy showed signs of recovery on three separate occasions throughout the 1990s. Unfortunately, these recoveries did not prove robust enough to sustain a continued economic recovery. The Japanese economy also faced a number of troubling incidents with unfavourable impacts. Among these was the sharp appreciation of the yen in the early 1990s, an increase of the consumption tax, the currency and financial crises in other Asian countries, and the collapse of major financial institutions in the latter half of the decade.

The unemployment rate continued to rise in the wake of a series of bankruptcies and extensive corporate restructuring amidst the severe economic situation. The rate was stable around four per cent between 1999 and 2000, but went beyond five per cent in 2001. Poor corporate earnings and the deterioration of the job market seriously affected personal income and consumer confidence and therefore consumption remained stagnant despite declining prices. The deflation and slowdown in consumption badly damaged the retail market, which resulted in the collapse of several large retailers.

Capital investment was mostly restrained throughout the 1990s, except for the period between the second half of the fiscal year 1999 and the first half of the fiscal year 2000 when an increase was boosted by IT-related investment.

In the latter half of the decade, a downward-spiralling bad debt situation among financial institutions surfaced. A series of bank collapses and life insurance and securities company failures followed. Simultaneously, financial system reforms accelerated the liberalisation and internationalisation of the financial system causing mergers, acquisitions, and a regrouping of financial institutions. The situation remains unsettled.

The aftermath of the bursting of the bubble has not yet fully played out. The Japanese economy has been struggling within a vicious cycle of deflationary asset values and prices, increasing bad debts caused by successive bankruptcies of business enterprises, a persistently high unemployment rate and stagnant consumption. Companies are trying to weather in the severe economic conditions by radically revising their management styles and corporate policies, promoting mergers and acquisitions, consolidating business sectors or management units and aggressively promoting alliances with other companies.

Lease market

Changes in the market

The volume of leases written reached ¥1 trillion in the fiscal year 1978, only fifteen years after the establishment of the first leasing company in 1963. The industry experienced an average annual growth of 30.2 per cent throughout the 1970s and maintained two-digit growth (17.3 per cent) during the 1980s when the Japanese economy was in a period of stable growth.

By the end of the 1980s, leasing had grown more popular as a new type of financing for industry due to its convenience, and had come into widespread use. Throughout this period of leasing growth, volumes kept growing at a faster rate than both that of economic growth and private capital investment, pushing up the share of leasing in private sector capital investment in relation to other types of financing. However, this increase in the number of companies using lease financing and the share of leasing in private sector capital investment made the demand for leases quite sensitive to fluctuations in capital investment and industry. This influence became more evident in the 1990s when almost 90 per cent of all companies in Japan used leasing to finance their capital investments. Exhibits 20.12 to 20.14 illustrate the changes in the size of the entire lease market as well as the composition of the leased assets and the lessees.

The circumstances surrounding the leasing industry changed significantly in the 1990s. Leasing volume declined for the first time in the fiscal year 1992 due to Japan's long-term economic slump and has been in a state of flux thereafter. The average growth rate of leasing volume in this past decade was a disappointing 0.9 per cent.

Comparing the fiscal year 1991 to the fiscal year 2000, there was a sharp decline in the share of total leasing equipment comprised of industrial and factory equipment, which lowered the share of the manufacturing sector as lessees by 10 per cent. As noted previously, the share of SMEs as lessees fell, reflecting the decline in capital investment among them, while the share of large enterprises grew. As for the type of leased assets, the share of computers declined in the fiscal year 2000. This was due to a sharp decline in price together with the implementation of a new tax treatment for computers (100 per cent depreciation allowed at the time of acquisition), which did not apply to leased computers. Consequently, these events negatively affected the demand for computer leasing in the fiscal years 1999 and 2000. It is noteworthy that during this period, automobiles and commercial and service equipment gained in share. Deregulation of automobile leasing was one of the factors that explains this growth.

The composition of equipment type and lessee will continue to change, reflecting economic conditions, changes in the regulatory framework for leasing, and diversification of user needs.

Exhibit 20.12

Leasing volume by equipment type

	1991	2000
Information systems	41.1	39.8
Computers	35.7	33.8
Telecommunications	5.4	6.0
Office equipment	8.8	8.0
Industrial equipment	16.5	13.0
Factory equipment	5.4	2.9
Construction equipment	1.7	2.7
Transport equipment	5.8	7.4
Automobile	4.3	6.5
Medical equipment	2.8	4.1
Commercial and service equipment	12.7	15.0
Commercial equipment	7.0	9.0
Others	5.3	7.1
Total	**100.0**	**100.0**

Exhibit 20.13

Leasing volume by lessee size

	1991	2000
Large companies (more than ¥100 million in capital)	45.9	47.5
SMEs (less than ¥100 million in capital and/or individual)	49.9	46.2
Public sector and others	4.3	6.2
Total	**100.0**	**100.0**

Exhibit 20.14

Leasing volume by lessee type

	1991	2000
Primary sector	1.0	0.8
Manufacturing sector	36.0	26.1
Non-manufacturing sector	57.3	66.0
Others	5.8	7.1
Total	**100.0**	**100.0**

Lease transactions

Most lease transactions in Japan are classified as finance leases. Though many changes and incidents have taken place over leasing's forty-year history in Japan, finance leases continue to be the main type of lease transaction provided by leasing companies.

However, among airlines at home and abroad, the mid 1980s saw the rising popularity of Japanese leveraged leases which offer tax benefits to lessors (the investors) which are passed on to lessees in the form of cheaper rental fees. Even so, the leveraged lease is merely a variation of the finance lease. Following a tax reform, leveraged lease transactions have become practically impossible since the fiscal year 1998 in cases where foreign corporations are the intended lessees.

In Japan, automobile leasing is accomplished by maintenance leases that include not only the leasing of the asset, but also maintenance, repair and other services associated with the asset's use. This type of lease accounts for about 60 per cent of all automotive leases. Thanks to a well-developed secondary market for automobiles, it is relatively easy to establish the residual value of leased cars at the end of the lease term. Thus there are many leases that are not fully paid out, exposing lessors to residual risk. Such leases are classified as operating leases.

Consequently, most domestic lease transactions in Japan are finance leases with the exception of some operating leases for automobiles. Operating leases have not become popular in Japan principally because of the non-existence of secondary markets for most equipment. Moreover, there has been no business demand for operating leases. In other words, companies received enough benefits from finance leases, denying incentives for lessors to provide operating leases and any reason for lessees to choose them. However, Japanese lessors do actively participate in operating leasing for international assets such as aircraft and shipping for which global residual value markets exist.

Leasing companies

The number of member companies in the Japan Leasing Association continued to increase through the mid 1990s, as shown in Exhibit 20.15. This resulted in severe competition among leasing companies and a decline in their profitability. High profitability of financial business supplemented the low profitability of leasing business during the period of growth until the 1980s. After the bubble economy burst, financial assets turned into bad debts and many leasing companies had to shift their energies for debt disposal. Furthermore, leasing volume decreased as a result of the decline in capital investment and the continued acute competition. These factors put the management of leasing companies in an increasingly difficult position.

Several finance companies that originally specialised in real estate finance and actively promoted financing businesses, as well as some large leasing companies, collapsed in the latter half of the 1990s. Moreover, many companies expedited the restructuring of the operations of their affiliated companies from the end of that decade and started to withdraw from leas-

Exhibit 20.15
Number of member companies of the Japan Leasing Association

	1971	1975	1980	1985	1990	1995	1998	1999	2000	2001	2002
No of companies	19	43	155	237	329	368	370	360	340	328	315
Change		24	112	82	92	39	2	(10)	(20)	(12)	13)

Note: As of March 2002.

ing business that offered lower profitability while requiring a vast amount of assets and liabilities. The merger of parent companies sometimes brought about the subsequent merger and integration of their associated or subsidiary leasing companies.

Following this trend in the industry, the Japan Leasing Association has experienced a significant drop in its membership from 370 member companies in March 1998 to 315 in March 2002. This trend is likely continue for some time.

Regulatory framework

Regulations for the leasing business and leasing companies

There is no specific law governing leasing and anyone can enter the leasing business and establish a leasing company. The government ministry overseeing the leasing industry is the Ministry of Economy, Trade and Industry. The ministry's primary activities, however, are more focused on supporting the industry from a political stance than in supervising it, given the absence of any particular laws regulating the industry.

In Japan, leasing has basically developed in an unregulated and free environment. Attention should be paid to the following cases, however, where regulations are applied to a particular aspect of the leasing business.

Automotive leases

The law requires registration of automobiles and permission for transportation businesses. Likewise, permission from the Ministry of Land, Infrastructure and Transportation is required for engagement in the automotive leasing business.

It used to be difficult to develop automotive leasing on any meaningful scale. Leasing companies had to follow numerous documentary procedures to satisfy regulatory requirements and the restrictive nature of some of the provisions in leasing contracts. This situation improved in the latter half of the 1990s when these regulations were either lifted or significantly relaxed. The automotive lease market rapidly expanded thereafter.

Leases provided by bank affiliated companies

Bank affiliated companies used to be allowed to provide only finance leases according to the Banking Act . Since April 2002, they have been allowed to provide leases other than finance leases as long as income from finance leases is no less than half of the total income generated from leasing business.

Leasing contracts with consumers

The Consumer Contract Act which came into force in April 2001 is applied to every type of contract, including leasing contracts, between a company and an individual (with the exception of labour contracts).

Under this act, lessors are required to supply all the pertinent information on the contents of the contract to the lessee before entering into an agreement. In the event that a lessor's misstatement leads to a misunderstanding by the lessee of material issues in the contract, the lessee has the right to cancel the contract at any time.

Any disclaimer of a lessor's warranty liability is inoperative. Typically, however, a contract between a lessor and a supplier of the assets to be leased stipulates that the supplier is responsible for warranty liability for the leased asset. Under such an arrangement, disclaimer of a lessor's warranty liability is valid.

Environmental regulations on the disposal of leased assets

In Japan, the Waste Disposal Act 1971 was revised in 1997 and laws promoting the recycling of consumer electric appliances have been enacted in order to cope with environmental issues.

Leased assets are returned to the leasing company as the legal owner at the end of the lease term. When disposing of the asset, the lessor is required to comply with the Waste Disposal Act. According to this law, a leasing company has to issue a manifest of the assets which certifies that the resultant waste will become the responsibility of a business legally authorised to transport and dispose of industrial waste. When disposing of leased equipment that must be recycled, a leasing company is then required to request the manufacturer or vendor of that equipment to dispose of it for a fee. The fee is currently ¥5000 (US$40) for four types of electric appliances (air-conditioners, television sets, refrigerators and washing machines) which are included under the Recycling of Home Electric Appliances Act of April 2001. For other equipment, the fee is dependent on the amount necessary to cover the expenses and the profit for the company that performs the disposal; it will depend upon the quantity, size and weight of the equipment. The manufacturer or vendor has no right to refuse such a request under the new legislation.

Legal position of lease contracts

A leasing company may enter into any lease transaction that it desires based on the principle of freedom of contract, so long as the lease contract does not violate the doctrine of good faith or public order and decency. Furthermore, a leasing company may enter into any contract provided that it does not come into conflict with any enforceable provisions of the Japanese Civil Code.

The Civil Code provides for thirteen types of contract. There are two groups of views on the legal character of the finance lease contract: one considers it basically a rental transaction; the other considers it a financial transaction.

A finance lease contract is, in its economic substance, a financial transaction. The lessor aims to recover almost all the value of the leased asset from payments made by the lessee. It also stipulates that a lessor does not take on warranty liability, assume the risk of loss or have the obligation to repair and maintain the leased asset.

Despite the above statement, a leasing contract should not be regarded as a financial transaction or an instalment sale, as both would ultimately neglect its character as a rental transaction and the intention of the parties concerned. The Japan Leasing Association views a lease contract as a rental agreement, because: first, the intention of the parties to a lease contract is a rental transaction, neither a sale or a financing; secondly, the owner of the leased asset is the lessor, which expects to enjoy a profit on the sale of the leased asset at the end of the lease term; and thirdly, rent is paid for the use of the asset. Therefore, lease contracts should be characterised as a new type of contract, basically rental, which also contains the nature of a financial and service contract.

Tax treatment of lease transactions

Under the tax reform of the fiscal year 1998, rules concerning the tax treatment of lease transactions were altered. The changes were specified in the Enforcement Order of the Corporation Tax Law and in the Basic Circular on Corporation Tax Law, in detail. The Enforcement Order and Circular provide that certain kinds of finance leases should be treated as sales or financial transactions for tax purposes.

Under the order and the circular, a lease contract is a rental contract, provided that, first, cancellation before maturity is prohibited, and, secondly, the lessor recovers almost all of the acquisition cost and ancillary expenses throughout the lease term (that is, more than 90 per cent in principle). A lessee can deduct the entire sum of rental payments as an expense for the year it is paid, except for leases treated as sales, and leases:

- that allow automatic transfer of title of the leased asset;
- that contain a bargain purchase option;
- of a specialised nature such that only the lessee can use the asset (for example, land, building, fixtures and equipment for special purposes);
- of assets unidentifiable when mingled with assets owned by a lessee;
- with a lease term shorter than 70 per cent of the useful life of the asset (60 per cent when the useful life is less than 10 years) or longer than 120 per cent;
- the renewal of which at nominal rents (that is, less than one twelfth of the original rent) is obvious;
- in which a financial institution undertakes the debt with funds of the lessee;
- which aim to incur losses in the first half of the lease term and have a detrimental effect on taxation, even if the lease term is appropriate (from 60 per cent to 120 per cent of the useful life of the asset);
- that are treated as financial transactions; and
- that are sale and leaseback transactions which have financing purposes.

Accounting standards for leases

Japan's Lease Accounting Standards were set in June 1993. On 1 April 1994 they became applicable to companies that are under the jurisdiction of the Security Exchange Act 1948 (such as companies listed on national stock exchanges).

The standards prescribe that finance lease transactions be treated as sales in principle and that operating lease transactions be treated as rental (or true lease) transactions. Notably, finance leases are classified into ownership transfer and non-ownership transfer transactions: the former are required to be treated as sales and capitalised on the lessee's balance sheet, while the latter are allowed to be treated as rental transactions and capitalisation on the lessee's balance sheet is not required.

Ownership transfer leases are:

- leases with an automatic title transfer clause;
- leases with a bargain purchase option; or
- leases where the asset was custom made for the lessee.

Non-ownership transfer leases are those that meet either of the following two criteria:

- the present value of the total lease rentals is approximately 90 per cent or more of estimated acquisition cost of the leased asset; or
- the non-cancellable lease term is approximately 75 per cent or more of the useful economic life of the leased asset.

A lessee has to make a footnote disclosure of the amount equivalent to the acquisition cost of the leased asset and the amount equivalent to the total of future lease payments when the non-ownership transfer finance lease is treated as a rental transaction.

Prospects for leasing

Leasing volume and lease market share

Although the scale of the Japanese lease market shrank in the 1990s, leasing penetration stayed around 8 per cent. This amount is lower than that of the US and major European countries, although a different formula is used for calculation in Japan (see above section on the scale of the leasing market).

A lease is an effective equipment procurement instrument and 90 per cent of the companies in Japan are taking advantage of it. While computer users normally prefer leasing to purchasing, most other kinds of equipment are still purchased rather than leased.

This implies that there is a large potential demand for leasing in the future if leasing companies can create sufficient demand for leasing amongst their target audience. Companies will prefer leasing if leasing companies are successful in providing highly value-added leases and this could raise Japanese leasing penetration to the level of major European countries in the relatively near future.

Such a forecast will come true only if no major changes are made to the existing tax treatment and accounting standards related to leases. As discussed below, changes in the lease accounting standard would bring a drastic contraction of the lease market in addition to a slowdown in the growth of the leasing industry,

The form of lease transactions

Most lease transactions in Japan are finance leases. Companies can enjoy various benefits by using finance leases (such as funding, treatment of rentals as deductions for tax purposes, easier cost control, rationalised office procedures, disposal of leased assets by the lessor and off-balance-sheet treatment of assets etc).

As stated earlier, operating leases are not widely used for domestic leasing due to the non-existence of secondary markets (except for automobiles) and the establishment and acceptance of the benefits of finance leases, as noted above. Although there are leasing companies which provide operating leases for personal computers, industrial equipment, machine tools, construction equipment and transportation equipment (including automobiles and aircraft), their volume is estimated to be small.

Rapid growth of operating leases cannot be expected in Japan unless strong demand arises from corporations and leasing companies actively work toward it. From 1999 to 2001, some companies shifted ownership of their manufacturing facilities to leases by utilising sale and leaseback (operating lease) transactions in order to improve their balance sheet structure.

Though this transaction is an operating lease, it would still be too early to speculate from this phenomenon that the popularity of operating leases will expand.

Value-added leases: differentiation and new services

Since most Japanese leasing companies, rather than specialising in particular types of equipment, undertake lease transactions for various types of assets for lessees in a wide range of industries, they can differentiate themselves from their competitors only by rental amounts. Lessees tend to choose among lessors primarily by the rents charged. Even though finance leases provide various benefits to lessees, too much focus on rents causes keen competition with banks and among leasing companies, and this may be counterproductive to raising the status of the leasing industry.

Therefore, the key to the future prosperity of the Japanese leasing industry is for each lessor to provide new and unique services to meet the individual needs of lessees. In other words, lessors should provide value-added leases. Operating leases in which a leasing company bears the residual risk of the leased asset are an example of this. However, many hurdles to providing true operating leases still remain.

It is possible to provide highly value-added leases in the form of a finance lease by offering:

- comprehensive services, ranging from model selection to disposal of the asset;
- fine-tuned service by focusing on target lessees and/or on a particular type of equipment; and
- services over the internet.

This was the recommendation made by a special panel organised by the Japan Leasing Association to explore the vision of the leasing industry in the early part of the 21st century. Large leasing companies have already inaugurated the development of internet services. The development of value-added lease transactions, whether finance leases or not, is beginning to shape the Japanese leasing industry. However, lessees' future demands on lessors and lease benefits can be expected to become more diversified and complex.

Conclusion: five key issues for the next five years

The major issues faced by the Japanese leasing industry over the next five years are most likely to be the following:

- countermeasures to possible changes in lease accounting standards;
- response to environmental issues;
- establishment of a legal characterisation of lease contracts;
- response to regulations of new lease types; and
- strengthening the management bases of leasing companies.

Possible changes in lease accounting standards

Finding countermeasures to possible changes in lease accounting standards is the most important issue faced by the Japanese leasing industry. While FAS 13 and IAS 17 require lessee recognition of assets and liabilities related to the transaction of a finance lease (or capital lease), Japan allows lessees in almost all finance lease transactions to make them off balance sheet, except for leases where title to the assets will be transferred to the lessee.

In the process of reviewing the accounting for the impairment of fixed assets, Japan's Business Accounting Council, the advisory body for the Finance Service Agency (formerly the Ministry of Finance), expressed the opinion that existing lease accounting standards that allow off-balance-sheet treatment of assets and liabilities under finance leases should be revised. Furthermore, the newly established Accounting Standard Board Japan (ASBJ) set the following agenda: first, that the off-balance-sheet treatment of finance leases should be revised (a short-term objective); and secondly, a comprehensive revision of the lease accounting standards, including capitalisation of assets and liabilities under operating leases (a medium- to long-term objective). They launched the former project in May 2002.

The International Accounting Standards Board (IASB) is on course to revise IAS 17 in order to require the capitalisation of assets and liabilities from all types of leases, including operating leases, on the lessee's side. The ASBJ was one step behind the IASB review when it started discussion on the capitalisation of assets and liabilities under finance lease on lessee's balance sheet in August 2002.

On-balance-sheet treatment of leases would deprive lessees of the inherent benefits of easy cost control and rationalised office procedures, to say nothing of the accounting benefits. Revision of the lease accounting standards would greatly diminish corporate interest in using leases and seriously affect the business of leasing companies. In Japan, corporate income tax is calculated from accounting income, with minor adjustments. Exactly how to adjust the gap between the depreciation expense of capitalised assets (accounting) and rentals deducted for tax purposes would be a difficult question. Moreover, changes in the accounting standards might influence tax treatment of leases themselves and the possible loss of tax benefits under the current system could ultimately develop into a crisis for the leasing industry.

The leasing industry is coping proactively with this issue to alleviate the negative impact of this impending change.

Response to environmental issues

Leasing companies, as owners of the assets, have a legal obligation to dispose of them appropriately at the end of the lease term in accordance with the regulations. Meanwhile, for companies that deal with vast amounts of assets, this strict disposal procedure, with the preparation of manifests and promotion of recycling, increases office procedures and costs. Furthermore, it is expected that regulations on environmental issues will be further enforced with targets for reducing, reusing, and recycling the disposed assets. Business procedures and the costs of disposing of leased assets will further increase and this may influence the future management of the leasing business.

While the leasing industry should initially formulate its own creative approach in order to promote the efficient disposal of leased assets in accordance with the relevant law, co-operation and understanding of the manufacturer, supplier and lessees is indispensable. In other words, the leasing industry should not try to address these environmental issues by itself. It should work together with related and specialist industries as necessary in order to cope with these new environmental issues and standards.

Establishment of a legal characterisation of lease contracts

In Japan, the legal characterisation of finance lease contracts has yet to be established due to various views established in precedents and theories. The reality is, however, that in the process of a lessee bankruptcy, finance lease contracts are considered financing in substance and thus often have to go through enforced reduction of claims on lease receivable and extension of the lease term. Lessors are treated quite unfairly due to the lack of an established legal characterisation.

With this background, we have grave concerns that the view adopted in lease accounting standards such as Statement of Financial Accounting Standards (SFAS) 13 or IAS 17, stating that a finance lease is in its substance a financing, would influence the legal concept of Japanese finance lease contracts.

The leasing industry ought to establish a dialogue and express its opinions so that the legal characterisation of lease contracts will be established based on the view that leases belong to a new category of contract, that is, one that is primarily a rental and has aspects of finance and service.

Response to regulations on new lease types

As referred to above, in order for the leasing industry to continue growing steadily, each leasing company ought to take an initiative in developing and providing new kinds of leases, or highly value-added leases. They can be leases for specific kinds of assets, leases for specific lessees, transactions over the internet, or operating leases.

However, these new kinds of leases will probably encounter the hurdles of regulation and new restrictions imposed on the transactions, similar to those placed on automobiles, software and leveraged leases. The Japan Leasing Association is not aware of any regulation that would have a very serious impact on the leasing industry. However, the leasing industry should be well prepared for any indication of potentially unfavourable regulatory actions and should take swift action to counter any such move.

Strengthening the fundamental structure of leasing companies

The fundamental structure of leasing companies must be solid in order to actively develop leasing business. The components of a solid structure for a leasing company are:

- business competence (competitiveness, quality of service, expertise and excellent human resources);
- administration (collection and management of customer information, credit control, management and disposal of leased assets, office management and revenue management); and
- funding.

Funding is crucial for the management of a leasing company since the leasing business requires a vast amount of funds. Leasing companies used to rely mostly on loans from banks for such funds, but the situation changed in the mid 1990s with financial deregulation and the completion of related legal systems. As a result, capital markets funding (such as securitisation of lease receivables, the issue of commercial paper and the issue of corporate bonds) have gradually increased.

While some companies raise more than half of their funds from the capital markets, the leasing industry as a whole mainly relies on bank loans. It is an important task for all leasing companies to improve their financial structure and operational performance in order to enable them to raise increasing amounts of funds at competitive rates from the capital markets. This will provide the financial stability and strengthen the management base of the company.

PART 3: THE EUROPEAN LEASING INDUSTRY

Marc Baert

Market structure

Twenty years ago, leasing was a flamboyant and slightly conspicuous product. The famous 'double dip' expression conjured up glamorous images of international finance. However, although cross-border leasing was widely discussed, it was rarely completed. The market was dominated by well-known bank-owned lessors. Captive leasing companies were seen as children playing on the elementary school playground, active but not troublesome. The Declaration of Seville had once and for all closed the accountancy debate and Basle was just a sleepy Swiss town on the Rhine. The pre-programmed IBM typewriters were the most advanced communication tool and rumours about the existence of a fax machine started to circulate. The 'iron curtain' was too clearly separating the eastern part of Europe for many years to come.

The European Commission wrote a white paper on the internal market on the principle of a level playing field and on the introduction of the euro. Asset financiers reacted in a very supportive way and many of them did not wait for regulations or harmonisation measures to spread their web across Europe.

In 2001, the total volume of new leasing business in Europe amounted to €200 billion and the depreciated value of assets exceeded €400 billion, still far behind comparative US figures. Put simply, this means that the total leasing volume has doubled in ten years, during which time the total number of market players has fallen to 1,200. It is estimated that 20 per cent of all investment is acquired through leasing, the automotive sector representing 50 per cent of the moveable asset volume.

Leasing is now becoming less of a tax driven product and more focused on the operating capability and future value of assets; these are the real issues today. Lessors have discussed profit margins for years and have sometimes complained. They are now discovering a wide variety of ancillary products that can create additional value to lessees and additional profits for lessors. It has been found that, for once, adding value delivers profits.

Many traditional leading lessors have disappeared, or at least their names, in the latest frenzy of mergers and acquisitions which became a global phenomenon and has shrunk the leasing fraternity. It is too early to predict the long-term impact of this trend. However, a vast network controlled by some 15 leasing groups is active in nearly every European country and influences a substantial market share. These groups can offer increasingly pan-European clients financial and other services wherever the lessee or the leased asset may be. It is estimated that approximately 25 per cent of the European leasing portfolio is directly or indirectly foreign-owned, including EU member states' leasing companies and non-EU companies.

413

Regulatory framework

The legal and accountancy debate is still an aria performed in the local opera house. Looking at the enormous impact of the recent accountancy and capital adequacy debates, it is clear that the real strategic decisions are taken in Brussels (in the form of EU regulations) far away from the member state capitals.

Other issues under review include:

- the draft Directive on insurance intermediation (whereby the leasing industry succeeded in introducing an amendment exempting member states from the burden of additional supervisory regulations for categories of insurance intermediaries that have this activity as an ancillary);
- the draft Directive on environmental liability (whereby legal ownership of a given real estate can be seen as a possible ground for liability in case of environmental damage; Leaseurope has been advocating that lessors are not actually operating the equipment or the industrial building under consideration); and
- the review of the Directive on consumer credit (1987) (whereby leasing operations could be assimilated to credit, consumers would no longer be seen as the traditional physical person carrying out his professional activities, and consumer protection measures would apply to traditional leasing customers).

Of particular note is the EU draft Directive on electronic and electrical equipment waste, the so-called WEEE directive. Leaseurope, the UK Finance & Leasing Association (FLA) and the German association Bundesverband Deutscher Leasing-Unternehmen (BDL), in particular, lobbied their members of the European Parliament (MEPs) and Rapporteur MEP Karl-Heinz Florenz to push for the adoption of Amendment 18 concerning the definition of 'producer' where under certain circumstances a lessor-importer cannot be viewed in the same way as the producer. The main idea was, and still is, that lessors, as financiers, should never be viewed as producers. Work still needs to be done concerning the notion of distributor. The industry managed to have lessors-importers excluded from the concept of distributor, but not all lessors are excluded.

Lease accounting has been under discussion for some years at an international level. New proposals could revolutionise lease accounting by moving away from the so-called economic approach widely used to adopt an asset and liability approach. The new approach would significantly increase costs and raise new implementation problems for lessees and lessors. Leaseurope is of the opinion that leasing should not be penalised by the introduction of a new accounting rule when compared with other funding alternatives. One should mention that the European Commission adopted a draft regulation that would require all EU companies listed on a regulated market, including banks and insurance companies, to prepare their consolidated accounts in accordance with international accounting standards by 2005. This may be in advance of international agreement on a truly international standard and may cause some consternation amongst asset financiers operating throughout the European Union.

Leaseurope reacted promptly on the consultative papers from the European Union and the Basle Committee on Banking Supervision to reform the solvency capital ratio framework. Regarding capital requirements, no studies have been conducted so far on leasing credit risk. Leaseurope is therefore currently defining a framework to estimate the total capital requirement for leasing portfolios. Since regulators have based their work on empirical results only, our study should be of considerable use. Indeed, according to the current proposal there is no recognition of marketable physical collateral security such as cars, airplanes, trucks, ships and industrial machinery, etc.

The use of such collateral security, whereby title to the asset belongs to the lessor, is specific to the leasing industry by the very nature of the product. This specific focus on assets reduces risks incurred by leasing businesses, particularly in the event of default. Leaseurope's study to establish the total capital requirement for leasing portfolios should go some way towards defining a benchmark for an adequate weighting ratio for the capital requirements of leasing businesses. In contrast with wholesale commercial loans (for which financial market prices and financial and rating agency data can be readily obtained), fewer data sources are available for the leasing industry.

Leaseurope has also decided to conduct a study taking into account leasing specifics with the support of European leasing companies. The first step is to show that unexpected losses are rather low in our industry. The objective is to have a comprehensive research report on the issue of leasing credit risk in the leasing business at European level. A working group composed of people active in the small- and medium-sized enterprise (SME) end of the leasing business has been set up, representing at least seven European countries. Participants are providing data about lease contracts and will focus on additional arguments to be submitted at a latter date.

Preliminary documents have already been drafted and results confirm that the capital adequacy ratio is too high for the leasing industry in view of its risks. Our empirical results are based on credit risk models (Creditrisk+ and Bootstrap technique) which are used worldwide. Although leasing has its own specific characteristics, results point to the same conclusions as those of Dietsch and Petey (published in the *Journal of Banking and Finance*)[5] for SME loans portfolios. Their results demonstrate that the capital required by the Basle proposal is far too high in relation to the underlying risks. Leaseurope's conclusions are available on their website www.leaseurope.org.

Eastern Europe started as a 'springtime' market with wild growth in every sense of the word. This is rarely the right approach to basic and solid growth, and there is no exception here. However, Leaseurope's statistical overview indicates that in several central European countries, leasing is becoming a well-known product in a stable and consolidated market. Leasing has played a major and supportive role in many developing economies and there is no reason why it should not perform the same function in these new emerging European markets.

Lessors have fortunately retained the fast disappearing skill of making sound decisions based not just on corporate covenants, but on the potential and ability of a business to succeed. Their decisions are usually more widely based than on simple credit risks. That has been its route to growth in the past and is likely to be its saviour (and a saviour for others) in the future. It is a great pity that a sometimes hostile environment has been created by some of the EU-based regulatory and fiscal authorities.

Leaseurope, which was once seen critically as a wining and dining club, has changed into an efficient lobby organisation with excellent connections. Sometimes it can be difficult to interpret member organisations real demands and it can be even more difficult to get everyone facing in the same direction.

Conclusion: what the future holds

Leasing groups active in Europe may take a leading role in the continued development of the

415

asset finance industry and in Leaseurope itself. The concept of shareholder value has refo-cused a lot of people's minds back to the immediate and important daily tasks. However, it is too easy to underestimate the importance of a long-term strategic approach. The challenge for the leasing industry is to build on past experiences and to encourage the active contribution of the younger members of the community. Many lessors and advisors have contributed a great deal to lessees' businesses, to national economies and their own organisations. Many have also had immense enjoyment from their business and their leasing association roles in whatever capacity they serve. The foundation for further developments and evolution of our asset finance industry is the duty of today's participants; the responsibility to carry it further belongs to the next important generation.

For further information visit www.leaseurope.org.

PART 4: THE UK VIEW

Martin Hall

Introduction

In the tenth anniversary year of the UK Finance & Leasing Association (FLA) it may be appropriate to look back at the past decade to assess what has happened to the asset-finance market. It is also an opportunity to look forward.

The players

Since mergers and acquisitions are a constant theme in the United Kingdom, the most strik-ing development is the rate of change in terms of market participants. So is the entry of over-seas players, with businesses from the United States, other European countries and Asia all playing prominent roles.

The asset-finance subsidiaries of the major UK banks play the biggest role, but even here there is change. Lombard is still a big name in the market, but now it belongs to the Royal Bank of Scotland following its acquisition of the National Westminster Bank. Meanwhile, some of the former building societies have converted into banks and have entered the asset-finance market.

Bank-owned asset-finance companies do not have the market to themselves by any means. Finance houses, which are not regulated in the United Kingdom as banks, play a sig-nificant role. GE Capital is the best known and there are a number of others. Finance arms of manufacturers (known as captives in industry parlance) are also big players in IT, vehicle, construction equipment and other types of leasing. In fact, IT illustrates the pace of change well, where the fast development of that industry's hardware and software is reflected in the number and variety of finance providers.

A recent report by the Competition Commission, the UK's competition watchdog, on banking services to small- and medium-sized enterprises (SMEs), gave the industry a clean bill of health on competition. With the fierce competition that exists among a large number of players that was no surprise, although it was good to see it formally acknowledged.

416

The products

The range of products has changed too. As late as 1996, the FLA was only collecting data on leasing, without any attempt to distinguish between finance and operating leases. Yet operating leasing grew by 71.6 per cent per cent from 1997 to 2001. This reflects a more general trend in the UK economy and elsewhere. Companies (and increasingly public services) wish to outsource risks that are not core to their activities. Operating leasing outsources financial risk. Since it is increasingly delivered with services (for example, fleet management, IT services, hospital laundry etc), other risks can also be bundled with the product and managed appropriately by specialist suppliers.

Finance leasing is still a big market: £6.9 billion (US$11.1 billion) in 2001. However, that is only about half what it was in 1996. A move to operating leasing is probably one reason. Another is certainly the impact of the tax system. If ever a case study is needed in how a badly designed tax can damage a business, the changes in the mid 1990s to the UK tax treatment of finance leasing, introduced by successive governments, can provide it. Yet lessors' once acute nostalgia for tax-based leasing in the United Kingdom has pretty well disappeared. The industry recognises that finance leasing has a commercial role, and cannot and should not live off the tax advantages it once enjoyed. We need a tax environment that is level, fair and facilitates the growth of our industry and our customers; that is a quite different approach. (This issue is separately addressed in Chapter 2.)

The rise of operating leasing demonstrates the industry's ability to adapt, and yet there is still room for innovation. Venture asset finance or venture leasing is a case in point. This form of asset-backed financing complements venture capital for companies in their early stage of development. It flourishes in those parts of the United States where venture capital flourishes in appropriate market conditions. It takes place in the United Kingdom only on a tiny scale; and even then only with mainly US-based players. Perhaps others will consider it in the years to come if the market for early stage ventures improves. UK venture capital is currently going through a lull in the wake of the dotcom boom and bust. Once growth resumes, it may well seek to innovate as its sister industry in the United States has done. Venture asset finance, which shares risks on more palatable terms for early stage ventures than additional venture equity capital, could meet that need. The UK government kick-started venture capital in the 1990s with tax incentives. Venture asset finance may need similar treatment.

The market

In business terms, the 1990s were very much 'a game of two halves' as football commentators used to say. The first half was a time of spectacular growth, reaching 58 per cent in 1996. The United Kingdom was coming out of recession in the early part of the period, which no doubt played a material role in such aggressive growth rates. Academic research on the industry is scarce, an omission which the FLA is beginning to repair. So it is only possible to speculate on the other reasons for growth. Outsourcing must have contributed. Companies in the 1990s continued the trend that took off in the previous decade. They sought to strip out non-core activities in various ways. Where asset ownership and management are not integral to the business, companies increasingly sought to outsource them (and associated services, especially in vehicles and IT). However, growth in the second half of the decade was much flatter and the total market for asset finance has hardly changed up to 2001. It is tempting, but probably wrong, to think of the market as mature. Nor has the industry run out of steam. Fresh markets need to be conquered while existing ones are maintained. The industry itself will determine its own future. The following are some suggestions for possible growth.

Opportunities

Successive UK governments in the past decade have adopted fresh approaches to providing public services, with a growing role for the private sector. The private sector contributes both management expertise and finance under what was known as the Private Finance Initiative and has now become Public Private Partnerships (PPP). Asset finance has played a role, notably in a multi-hundred million pound transaction to provide new rolling stock for the London Underground; but other forms of finance have been even more active. Project finance has been particularly prominent in the UK market, across all of the PPP sectors. There are signs that the asset-finance industry is addressing this market much more actively. The National Health Service and local government are potentially big markets, and there are many others. Asset finance is a feature in at least one of the bids for the new air tanker project for the Royal Air Force, the biggest PPP project the armed forces have ever conducted.

The UK tax system currently makes it difficult, although not impossible, to do cross-border business. The FLA is working with the UK Inland Revenue to address this issue and find a solution to achieve a more level playing field with continental European colleagues. UK-based providers are already active in other markets, particularly in the European Union. There is nothing like a single market in asset finance in the European Union, but the borders will start to come down and UK businesses will play a big role in achieving that.

There are still product markets where purchase is much more common than using asset finance. Machine tools are a topical example and this is an industry in which UK manufacturing has traditionally under invested. Asset finance can help the manufacturing sector manage such assets much more efficiently.

The market in operating leasing, coupled more and more with service provision, looks set to grow. There is just one caveat, which brings us to the subject of regulation of the industry.

The challenge of regulation (and the opportunity)

There are two big regulatory challenges facing the industry: the implementation of International accounting standards and new Basle proposals on capital adequacy (Basle II). The first would impact directly on operating leasing because, in common with many other parts of the world, under UK accounting standards operating leasing is off balance sheet. Standard setters have been working for the past six or seven years on a radical change in lease accounting. In effect, their general approach would dissolve the distinction between finance and operating leasing. Every lease would appear on the balance sheets of both lessor and lessee. Although an apparently attractive move towards greater transparency, this in fact raises many practical obstacles. It could be possible to produce accounts that are less transparent under the asset/liability approach than at present. The FLA has an open and constructive relationship with the UK Accounting Standards Board, which reports to the International Accounting Standards Board on this project. The FLA will continue to communicate forcefully the industry's views on the accounting issues and their assessment of their commercial impact.

The second big regulatory challenge concerns banking supervision, which is addressed in greater detail in Chapter 4 of this book. The new regime remains under discussion with implementation forecast by the supervisors in late 2006. This is the latest in a series of dead-lines, with each being later than its predecessor. Basle II, as it is informally known, will impact on all asset-finance providers. Bank-owned providers will be directly regulated, so it is very important to get the regime right. The industry has made some progress in making the argument to the regulators that asset finance is low risk, given the security taken in individual assets and the record of credit loss in the industry. It is increasingly recognised in the United Kingdom that Basle II is also an issue for non-banks, both for finance houses and captives. In so far as the banking players have to provide more or less capital for their asset-finance activities, competition amongst the various banks and asset-finance companies is bound to be affected.

Regulation has begun to pose a challenge in Europe, especially on the environmental front. This has already started with directives on vehicles and IT, and there is more to come. What is needed is a regime that gives responsibility for disposal to those with disposal expertise. The Directive on Electrical and Electronic Waste, in particular, has recently completed its passage through the European Union's legislative procedure. Under the directive, responsibility for the disposal of assets at the end of their economic life is shared among manufacturers and others. Although the details of how this will work will be set out in national legislation introduced once the directive becomes law, it is already clearly a major change in the sectors affected. The FLA, with the help of European colleagues was successful in clarifying the role of finance providers in the Directive. However, there remains much work to be done to get a rational result in the national legislation. The European Commission is also currently consulting on environmental liability more generally. Similar issues apply here.

Asset finance is not heavily regulated in the United Kingdom at a national level. The Consumer Credit Act 1974 (CCA) provides consumer protection not only for individual consumers, but also sole traders, unincorporated businesses and partnerships for transactions currently below £25,000. It is at present under review and the industry hopes that a more rational system will result. For example, there is little distinction between what the CCA describes as consumers (for example, big legal and accountancy partnerships get the same protection as a couple in partnership running a corner shop).

Other than this, asset finance is self regulated. The FLA has a Business Code[6] that sets out ethical business standards1. Members must adhere to the code as a condition of membership. Increasingly, it is seen as a marketing tool rather than a cost. Local authorities, for example, often need to know that they are dealing with an ethical finance provider.

Therefore, on the whole, regulation of the UK asset-finance market is fairly benign. Certainly, the rise of operating leasing has not been impeded by the kinds of legal constraints common, at least until recently, in some other European countries. For example, both Portugal and Italy have in the past put legislative restrictions on banks doing operating leasing, although Italian law has been recently relaxed. The eventual shape and outcome of Basle II is likely to be significant. Lease accounting also will be crucial for the future of operating leasing.

Future moves

When it comes to examining the future challenges, it is worth looking at the SME and corporate sectors separately, for they differ in important ways.

There has been a debate in the United Kingdom about appropriate financing for SMEs at least since the last recession in the early 1990s. Their traditional dependence on debt, usually in overdraft form (or for micro-enterprises and others, possibly even credit cards) looked to many to be an inappropriate way of financing investment. This argument gave asset financiers a real opportunity, which they enthusiastically took.

The Centre for Business Research at Cambridge University surveys SME finance every two years. At its peak, the market share of asset finance was around 27 per cent. However, this slipped sharply in the 2000 survey. This accords with the FLA's own data; the flat market recorded was against the backdrop of a growing economy. Furthermore, the proportion of business done with SMEs slipped five percentage points from 1999 to 2000 in the FLA's Annual Business Survey. The FLA will be closely examining the 2002 and subsequent Cambridge Surveys, to see if 2000 was the beginning of a trend or simply a blip.

The Competition Commission Inquiry mentioned earlier has effectively turned the banks and the traditional products they offer to SMEs into a regulated industry. This might give further impetus to give asset financiers an opportunity to grow materially their business in this sector. Asset finance is SMEs' second most used facility behind debt. Some asset financiers would like to see asset finance first, but that's a big ambition. The current capital allowance system has a bias against leasing by SMEs in favour of purchasing assets; that needs serious attention by government.

At present, an SME considering investment can only access the special encouragement given to it to invest through a 40 per cent capital allowance. This will take effect from the start of its financial year irrespective of when the investment happened (an accruals-based allowance), if it purchases the asset itself using its own cash resources or from a bank loan. However, if the same SME wishes to acquire the same asset through leasing, it will only be entitled to receive the benefit from the lessor of the equivalent of a 25 per cent time-apportioned capital allowance. The argument in defence of this unequal treatment is that the higher capital allowance available directly to the SME is balanced by the lower rate of corporation tax payable by companies in that sector. In direct comparison, the lower capital allowance and the different time-apportioned treatment for a lessor is accordingly reflected in the higher rate of corporation tax paid by larger companies and banks. (SME dependence on asset finance is examined in Chapter 2.)

It remains the strong view of the FLA that a government fiscal initiative, focused on a key part of the UK economy, suffers from a fundamental flaw that is affecting investment decisions and the underlying performance of the UK economy and its competitiveness. The issues in the large corporate world are different. Equity is a major source of finance for UK corporates and recent global events have set the scene for the exciting and dynamic times. The dot com boom and bust happened in the United Kingdom as elsewhere. Big established companies have also seen catastrophic falls in their share prices, though some have begun to recover. In contrast, the bond market is flourishing. Asset finance is a well known product to FTSE corporates. So whilst there are opportunities for asset finance, they arise in a sophisticated capital market with strong competition. The lease accounting debate is also very important here; finance directors have to scrutinise the impact of financing on balance sheets carefully.

In both SME and corporate markets, the prospects for the economy remain an important factor. The United Kingdom has been growing continuously for a very long time, by the standards of the past 40 years. Recession has threatened several times, but not arrived. A continued, gentle upswing looks to be the most likely scenario currently.

The current government has put a big emphasis on improving the quality of public services. Public expenditure as a share of GDP is creeping upwards. That entails considerable capital investment. The trend looks set to continue at least until the next general election in 2005 or 2006, barring an economic crisis. For this reason, the asset-finance industry is right to look to public services as a growth opportunity.

Tax, however, remains a concern. The structure common in big ticket deals produced a perception in government, among politicians, the tax authorities and other civil servants, that leasing was purely tax driven. This perception has always been a caricature and it is now almost without substance. However, perceptions built up over a long period can only be dismantled over a long time too. As every UK budget approaches there is a feeling, thankfully falsified by events in recent years, that industry trepidation is in order. The industry hopes this will diminish in the near term. The leasing industry and government both need to ensure that the legitimate role of asset finance in the UK economy is recognised.

Existing players look set to continue the restructuring of the industry. Deals are often rumoured and some will undoubtedly be done. If the UK economy does continue to grow in the medium term, it will also continue to be attractive to inward investors, in asset finance as in other industries.

The debate on whether the United Kingdom should join the Eurozone is highly important. It is not only politically controversial. Views differ sharply on its commercial and economic impact. The asset-finance industry is awaiting a decision on entry before investing in preparations on any major scale. Given the national nature of asset-finance markets in Europe and the UK restrictions on cross-border leasing mentioned earlier, the Euro looks unlikely to have a big impact in the near term, whether the United Kingdom joins or not. However, the medium-term prospects look less clear; for example, will the Euro give a fillip to cross-border trade in asset finance in the Eurozone and prompt a review of the current restrictions by the UK Inland Revenue?

The internet has been a global phenomenon in recent years. It arrived for individual consumers in the United Kingdom around 1995 and started to take off as a business system in 1998 and 1999. In 2000 the stock market went mad and what was dot com quickly became dot gone. Even so, asset financiers remained level headed; only a few were seduced and only a small amount was lost. Initially seen as a distribution channel, the internet's uses are widening. Web auctions are increasingly common; online contact with customers is growing and some businesses intend to make it their main line of communication; and web broking has started in a small way. As in the US and UK consumer markets, it is probably best suited to small-ticket items. But the technology is young and business analysis of it is even younger. So precise forecasts must be made with caution. It seems certain that it will change the way asset finance does business, particularly in the small and medium sectors, but it is unlikely to have a major impact at the big-ticket end.

Tips for asset-finance providers

- Pay close attention to regulatory risk and opportunities. The costs can be considerable. Any new regulatory regime offers chances to compete. It is a mistake to simply focus on the minuses.
- The public sector in the United Kingdom looks like a good business opportunity in the near term.
- More creativity is needed in financing the UK venture asset-finance sector and a broader approach incorporating the bundling of services as well as the asset being financed.

- When it comes to tax, the way ahead seems to be constructive engagement seeking fair treatment rather than avoidance bolt-holes.
- Europe poses challenges, but the single market may come, at last, and the United Kingdom should be active there.

Prospects for prosperity?

On the whole leasing has had a good decade in the United Kingdom, though the last five years could have been better. The future holds a series of challenges, some fundamental, but there are a lot of opportunities too.

PART 5: THE US MARKET

Michael Fleming

Market structure

The US equipment leasing and finance business has continued to grow consistently for five decades. While the growth rate has flattened in recent years, it remains a dynamic business. While the industry shows steady growth and profitability, it is quite fragmented and elements of the industry are changing constantly. The following summary provides an overview of the industry and discussion of trends in 2002. However, a keen student can remain informed of the latest trends and analysis by visiting the Equipment Leasing Association of America (ELA) websites detailed at the end of this paper. The following overview is taken from current resources available on those sites.

The leasing industry continues to finance approximately 30 per cent of all business equipment and this penetration rate has remained virtually unchanged over the past ten years. Dominant reasons for choosing leasing over other finance options continue to be: cash flow management; convenience and flexibility; efficient use of tax incentives for investing in capital equipment; financial statement management; and protection against technological obsolescence. Leasing has now become a traditional option for managing the acquisition of equipment and the risks that go with it.

Strategic questions faced by equipment leasing companies as they plan how they will do business in the future include: what is the value they offer and how do they differentiate themselves and their product from others? Increasingly, industry executives are repositioning their companies to provide a variety of asset-based financing options or are changing how they do business and how they interact with customers.

In 2002, the US equipment leasing and finance business is coming out of a mild economic recession that saw a drop in volume from US$247 billion in 2001 to US$242 billion in 2002. The forecast for 2002 is for slight growth to US$244 billion in new business volume. In addition, equipment leasing and finance companies experienced a slight decline in profits in 2001, but that is expected to improve in 2002 for several strategic and structural reasons.

There are two dramatic problems for the US equipment finance and leasing marketplace today. The first, and most immediate, is the absence of demand for new equipment. With the exception of healthcare, all sectors remain flat. In the case of airlines, there is an actual crash in demand and credit quality. Most lessors see an upturn in economic demand as more important to their success than any other factor. The second issue is financial accounting. The standards and the culture are changing. Off-balance-sheet treatment and structures make many customers nervous. Consolidation will change structures and the cost of, and access to, capital. The decline of accounting treatment as an incentive to lease is creating uncertainty for future products and customer decision making.

For the most part, companies that had focused primarily on growth in recent years are now turning their focus on quality of business, risk management, productivity and profits. In addition, as the industry continues to consolidate and access to capital tightens, margins are improving somewhat. Most companies use return on equity (ROE) as a measure of profitability and most rates have been between 14 per cent to 16 per cent. Banks typically measure profits based on assets with return on assets (ROA) of slightly over 1 per cent.

As a group, independent companies, both public and private, face the greatest economic and financial stress amongst equipment leasing and finance companies. Compared to banks and captive companies, their ability to grow and be profitable has been seriously hurt by the lack of capital. While independent companies are the most entrepreneurial, the banks and captives enjoy funding, institutional and customer relationship advantages. Independents reported the highest rate of new business while banks reported the lowest rate in the most recent studies. However, the number of independent companies is decreasing rapidly through consolidation and exiting the business.

Independent companies are not regulated. They are subject to a wide range of commercial and tax law, but there is no regulation that might dampen the culture for providing leasing and other services to customers that might not fit a bank's profile.

However, although captive companies show very low growth rates, they dominate in terms of profitability in their pre-tax margins. Captive lessors operate with a clear advantage over independents and banks through their point-of-sale origination base, their ability to subsidise finance costs with product sales, their proprietary knowledge of residual values and their ability to profitably resell the asset at the end of the lease.

The good news for independents is that they have the opportunity to become the lessors of choice for businesses with higher credit risks or the need for transaction and service structures not considered by banks and many captive companies. However, exploiting this opportunity takes the right strategy and access to capital.

Banks have a unique opportunity to leverage their existing client trust to compete effectively in leasing. Many businesses view themselves as having a relationship with their bank and are willing, to some degree, to trust them with their financial lives. Banks have the opportunity to leverage this trust, their existing client relationships and their stable access to funding to gain an even larger share of the leasing market.

However, banks face two main challenges: one regulatory, the other cultural. Banks may need to be even more diligent than independents and captives concerning risk management. Bank regulations dictate the amount and types of exposure a bank leasing company can maintain. For this reason, and because of their unique relationship with customers, banks are often seen as choosing only the best customers with the best credit, leaving non-bank competitors to scramble for what they turn down. Many banks also operate with cultural barriers to leasing success. Banks primarily think of themselves as lending institutions and, for some, leasing does not fit within that definition.

The US marketplace remains very fragmented even after dramatic consolidation. Just 25 out of the hundreds of competing companies represent nearly 80 per cent of the business. However, it would be unusual for a company to dominate a market either by equipment type, geography or industry type. Among these 25 companies are the largest banks and captives, plus financial services companies such as GE Commercial Equipment Finance and CIT. In addition, several non-US banks such as the Royal Bank of Scotland are growing aggressively. The latter has the advantage of access to capital and no mature portfolio. As the market is so huge, even the largest equipment leasing and finance companies find that their market share can barely reach double digits. For example, GE may be at 14–15 per cent even though it is by far the largest player in the market. The market is characterised by many competitors offering a range of products. Smaller companies compete by being very specialised, either by industry, equipment type or a small geographical area. Even large companies tend to specialise and build organisational structures that facilitate specialisation.

Most leasing business is done on a direct basis. However, as transaction sizes become smaller (under US$250,000), the majority of the business is originated by vendors (including captives). Statistics available from the ELA websites give detailed breakdowns of this range.

Companies tend to follow either product-focused or customer-focused marketing strategies. The large-ticket business is one of the purely product-oriented transactional segments left. For more and more companies, the strategy is becoming more customer focused.

The shift is from a traditional marketing approach that emphasises the product to an approach that emphasises the customer. The difference between these two approaches is summarised below:

The traditional product-focused is comprised of:

- a knowledge of the product;
- a transactional focus;
- the notion that volume is key to reducing product cost;
- a focus on cost/revenue per product;
- the notion to sell to anyone who buys;
- a tendency towards commoditisation; and
- the notion that growth that requires product innovation and market knowledge.

The new customer-focused is comprised of:

- a knowledge of the customer;
- the notion that customer share is key to reducing cost; acquire customers consistent with position;
- a focus on cost/revenue per customer;
- the notion that some customers are better than others;
- a tendency to mass customisation;
- marketing costs that go down because focus is on retention;
- marketing that is solutions oriented; and

- the notion that growth requires both a knowledge of the customer and delivering value to the customer.

The maturity and commoditisation of the leasing product is driving most companies towards a more customer-focused strategy. This is because the elements of customisation provide more opportunity for adding value and providing more perceived risk management/service for the customer. Companies are stressing effective execution, with the best companies winning the competition wars.

Access to capital and cost of capital remain critical to every company. How companies address these differs widely and continues to change. Some general points can be made.

- The sources of capital are fewer due to consolidation of traditional sources and decreased interest in funding asset-based financing companies that offer longer term financing.
- Rated companies can get capital.
- Banks have the easiest access to capital for several reasons; however, they need to compete for capital with other divisions in the institution that may provide better opportunities or less perceived risk.
- Risk exposure caps put limits on growth.
- Banks are more active in syndication as buyers and sellers to balance their portfolio.
- Captive companies can usually access capital because of the status of their parents' ratings; however, captive's parent companies are not used to the kind of leverage that a financing subsidiary requires. Captives do have to use techniques such as securitisation to get sales treatment and avoid consolidation to the parent's balance sheet.
- Independents have the greatest challenge in getting funding because few are rated; however, companies that have been in existence for a long time and have relationships with several funding sources can still access capital.
- The use of securitisation remains very important with as much as US$30 billion securitised annually through various forms; however, minimum size of pools limits the number of companies that can access the securitisation vehicles. The transferor has to retain some risk.
- Quality is a ubiquitous term (it can refer to credit quality, quality documentation, quality presentations, quality information on underlying companies and assets and quality of leasing company administration and operations).
- Slow to moderate growth strategies with conservative accounting practices are favoured.
- Sources of capital must understand the company's business.

Conclusion: industry challenges

Economic challenges and declining volume

Investment growth in business equipment appears likely to remain flat to slow in the near term. Several sectors including construction and healthcare will do better than others through 2003.

Access to funding

Funding will continue to be an issue, as securitisation volume declines, banks pull back and credit requirements become stricter.

Continuing consolidation

Economic and funding issues will encourage further industry consolidation, hitting indepen-dents particular.y hard regarding access to funds and scalability.

Use of technology

The internet's promise as an effective sales channel has so far failed to materialise, but it is making larger inroads into the total customer relations system. In addition, technology holds the answer to improving productivity and integrating all phases of an enterprise's operation.

Changes in accounting standards and regulations

The US Financial Accounting Standards Board (FASB), is poised to change accounting stan-dards and interpretations that influence the way leasing companies operate and the way in which lease products are structured. Leasing companies and others use special purpose enti-ties (SPEs) for a wide number of purposes related to managing risks. However, new inter-pretations issued by the FASB is forcing these SPEs to be consolidated in many cases. This may affect the use of securitisation in funding and the structure of products such as synthet-ic leases that use SPEs. This is an ongoing effort that should be reviewed constantly.

In addition, the FASB is developing new standards related to accounting for guarantees. Guarantees are also important in structuring lease transactions and the accompanying risks. The US Treasury continues to scrutinise structured transactions that may be characterised by the treasury as abusive. There is always a risk that regulations or audits can go too far and attack traditional lease products.

Branding equipment leasing and finance

The equipment finance companies and their products are susceptible to brand image and rep-utation more than ever as the industry matures. Branding can differentiate and create confi-dence and this is something that is clearly important in a fragmented and matured market place. When a business or product is considered complex, brand confidence is key.

Equipment leasing and finance is an ever-changing business in the United States. To understand the business, observers must learn the fundamentals and understand the trends of the changes. Those wanting further information on the ELA and on the current situation in the US industry can access the following resources designed to provide current information, analysis and profiles.

- The Equipment Leasing Association of America (http://www.elaonline.com/).
- The Equipment Leasing and Finance Foundation (www.leasefoundation.org).
- The Asset Management Central (www.assetmanagementcentral.com).

---

[1] In Japan, buildings are included in the volume of private capital investment in the denominator when calculating lease market share. Financing of buildings is usually not included in the numerator since that is done by means other than leasing due to tax reasons. Consequently, the shares calculated below are less than actual shares. Even after taking this factor into account, however, these share figures for Japan are lower than those for the US and Europe. Transactions that are classified as sales or financing for tax and accounting purposes are excluded from the leasing statistics of the Japan Leasing Association shown in the table below and from all other statistics shown in this article.

[2] The Japan Leasing Association prepared Exhibits 20.4 through 20.15.

[3] Norinchukin Bank is the central banking organisation for agricultural, fishery and forestry co-operatives. These co-operatives are also the shareholders of the bank.

[4] Shinkin banks are small regional co-operative banks basically specialising in finance to small member enterprises and individual members.

[5] M Dietsch and J Petey, 2002, 'The credit risk in SME loans portfolios: Modelling issues, prices and capital requirements', *Journal of Banking Finance*, 26, pp 303–322.

[6] The FLA Code of Practice can be accessed on line at www.fla.org.uk.

Appendix A

International and national leasing associations

International associations

Asian Leasing Association (Asialease)
World Trade Centre
13 Floor, Jl Jenderal Sudirman Kav 29-31
Jakarta 12920
Indonesia
Tel: 62 21 521 1491
www.asialease.or.id

Federacion Latino Americana de Leasing (Felalease)
Rua Libero Badaro 377 – 19 andar-conjunto 1910, 01009 – 906 Sao Paulo – SP
Brazil
Tel: 55 11 3104 4846
www.felalease.net

European Federation of Equipment Leasing Company Associations (Leaseurope)
267 Avenue de Tervuren
1150 Brussels
Belgium
Tel: 32 2 778 05 60
www.leaseurope.org

European Car and Truck Rental Association (ECATRA)
Avenue de Tervuren 402
1150 Brussels
Belgium
Tel: 32 2 761 66 14
Email: DO@intermar.be
www.ecatra.com

Leasing Confederation of the Commonwealth of Independent States (CIS Leasing)
2-nd Shchemilovskiy per 4/5
103474 Moscow
Russia
Tel: 7 095 978 52 51, 55-16
Email: vgnit@com2com.ru

European Computer Leasing & Trading Association (ECLAT)
1285 Stratford Road
Hall Green
Birmingham
West Midlands
B28 9AJ
United Kingdom
Tel: 0121 778 5327
www.atchou.com/eclat.html

African Leasing Association (Afrolease)
C/o Leasafric Ghana Limited
No 7 Main Street Tesana
PO Box CT2430, Canonments
Accra-Ghana
Tel: 233 21 228323
Email: info@afrolease.org
www.afrolease.org

National associations

Argentina
Asociacion de Leasing de Argentina
Tte.Gral. Peron 1833 4th suite H
C1040AAA Buenos Aires
Republica Argentina
Tel: 5411 4974 2293
Email: asocleasing-argentina@arnet.com.ar

Australia
Australian Equipment Lessors Association (AELA)
GPO Box 1595
Sydney
Australia 2001
Tel: 61 2 9231 5479
Email: aela@afc.asn.au

Austria
Association of Austrian Leasing Companies
Seidlgasse 21
8 Stock, Tür 24
A1030 Vienna
Austria
Tel: 43 1 714 29 40
Email: voel@leasingverband.at
www.leasing-verband.at

Bangladesh
Bangladesh Leasing & Finance Companies Association
Hadi Mansion (7F)
2 Dilkusha C/A
GPO Box No. 3160
Dhaka-1000
Bangladesh
Tel: 880 2 9560111
Email: planning@idlc.com

Belgium
Association Belge des Enterprises de Leasing
C/o Fortis Lease
Gentsesteenweg 1440 Chausée de Gand
1082 Brussels (Sint-Agatha-Berchem)
Belgium
Tel: 32 2 506 03 82
Email: lease@kbclease.be

Brazil
Associacáo Brasileira das Empresas de Leasing
Rua Líbero Badaró
377-19o andar – conjunto 1901
CEP 01074-900
São Paulo
SP-Brazil
Tel: 011 3104 4846
www.leasingobal.com.br

Canada
Canadian Finance Leasing Association
15 Toronto Street, Suite 301
Toronto
Ontario
M5C 2E3
Canada
Tel: 1 416 860 1133
www.cfla.acfl.ca

Chile
Chilean Leasing Company Association (ACHEL)
Bandera 206, Piso 5
Santiago
Chile
Tel: 56 2 3655950

Colombia

Colombian Leasing Association (Fedeleasing)
Cra 7 No 71-21 Of.705 Torre A
Santa Fe de Bogota
Colombia
Tel: 571 622 7350
www.fedeleasing.org.co

Cyprus

Finance Houses Association of Cyprus –
Bank of Cyprus
2 Evrou Str.
2003 Strovolos
Nicosia
Cyprus
Tel: 357 2247 4602
Email: info@finance.bankofcyprus.com

Czech Republic

Association of Leasing Companies of the Czech Republic
Strelnicna 8/1680
8 Kobylisy
CZ-182 00 Prague
Czech Republic
Tel: 420 2 688 5675
http://infos.eunet.cz/leasoc

Denmark

Association of Danish Finance Houses
HJ Holst Vej 5C, 2
2605 Broendby
Denmark
Tel: 45 36 72 55 80
Email: management@adfh.dk
www.adfh.dk

Estonia

Estonian Leasing Association
Maleva 2
11711 Tallinn
Estonia
Tel: 372 66 19 474
Email: liising@uninet.ee
www.uninet.ee/~liising

Finland
Finnish Finance Houses Association
C/o Finnish Bankers Association
Museokatu 8A
PO Box 1009
SF – 00101 Helsinki
Finland
Tel: 358 9 405 6120
Email: reima.letto@fba.fi
www.rahoitusyhtiot.fi

France
Association Française des Societes Financieres
24 avenue de la Grande Armée
F-75854 Paris Cedex 17
France
Tel: 33 1 53 81 51 51
Email: asf-france@wanadoo.fr
www.asf-france.com

Germany
Bundesverband Deutscher Leasing-Unternehemen eV
Kommandantenstr 80
10117 Berlin
Germany
Tel: 49 30 20 63 37 0
http://bdl-leasing-verband.de

Interessenverband Deutscher Leasing – Unternehmen eV
Bahnstrasse 42-46
61381 Friedrichsdorf
Germany
Tel: 49 6172 7 70 36
Email: leasingverband@t-online.de

Greece
Association of Greek Leasing Companies
C/o EGNATIA Leasing SA
189 Syngrou Avenue
Nea Smirni 17121
Athens
Greece
Tel: 30 210 9396 380
      30 210 9396 381
Email: leasing@egnatiabank.gr

Hong Kong
Hong Kong Equipment Leasing Association
17/F Prince's Building
10 Charter Road
Central
Hong Kong
Tel: 852 2957 7560
Email: info@hkela.org.hk
www.hkela.org.hk

Hungary
Hungarian Leasing Association
Postfach 1056
1245 Budapest
Hungary
Tel: 00-361-4370-175
Email: nyerges.hla@matavnet.hu

Indonesia
Asosiasi Leasing Indonesia
Wisma Nugra Santana,
7th Floor, Suite 707
Jl Jenderal Sudirman Kav 7-8
Jakarta 10220
Indonesia
Tel: 62 21 570 0133
www.ali.or.id

Ireland
Irish Finance Houses Association
ICB House
Newstead
Clonskeagh Road
Dublin 14
Ireland
Tel: 353 1 26 00 388
Email: seamus.otighearnaigh@icb.ie
www.ifha.ie

Israel
The Israel Equipment Lessors Association
3 Daniel Frisch Street
Tel Aviv 64731
Israel
Tel: +972 3 693 5615

Italy

Associazione Italiana Leasing
Piazzi di Priscilla 4
00199 Roma
Italy
Tel: 39 6 86 22 53 1
www.assileas.it

Japan

Japan Leasing Association
Secom Sonpo Building 2-6-2
Hirakawa-cho
Chiyoda-ku
Tokyo 102-0093
Japan
Tel: 81 3 3234 1501
www.leasing.or.jp

Korea

Korea Non-bank Financing Association (KNFA)
LeeMa Building 11F KNFA
PO Box 110–140
146-1, Susong-Dong
Chongro-Ku
Korea
Tel: 822 3788 0700
www.knfa.or.kr

Luxembourg

Association Luxembourgeoise de Leasing
Eurolease – Factor SA
14 rue Aldringen
L 2951 Luxembourg
Tel: 352 4799 5270
Email: dire@eurolease-factor.lu

Malaysia

Equipment Leasing Association of Malaysia
No. 5.2, Jalan 3/116D
Kuchai Entrepreneurs Park
Jalan Kuchai Lama
58200 Kuala Lumpar
Malaysia
Tel: 782 1920

Mexico
Asociacion Mexicana de Arrendadoras Financieras AC (AMAF)
Paseo de la Reforma 369
Torre 2 Piso 2
Col. Cuauhtemoc
CP 06500,
Mexico, DF
Tel: 52 5 533 0847
www.amaf.com.mx

Morocco
Association Professionnelle des Societes de Financement (APSF)
95 Boulevard Abdelmoumen
MA Casablanca
Morocco
Tel: 212 22 48 56 53
Email: apsf@casanet.net.ma

The Netherlands
Nederlandse Vereniging van Leasemaatschappijen (NVL)
Maliesingel 20
PO Box 354
NL-3500 AJ Utrecht
The Netherlands
Tel: 31 30 232 08 01
Email: info@nvl-lease.nl
www.nvl-lease.nl

Nigeria
Equipment Leasing Association of Nigeria (ELAN)
Plot 294, Gbagada Expressway
Gbagada, Phase II
Gbagada
Lagos
Nigeria
Tel: 234 01 7740473

Norway
Finansieringsselskapenes Förening
Postboks 2330 Solli
N-0201 Oslo
Norway
Tel: 47 23 28 44 80
Email: firmapost@finfo.no

Pakistan

Leasing Association of Pakistan
LRBT Building
First Floor, 37-C
Sunset Lane Four, Phase-II Ext
Defence Housing Authority
Karachi-75500
Pakistan
Tel: 92 21 5888378
Email: lap@super.net.pk

Panama

Asociacion Emphresas Arrendadoras
C/o Leasing de Panama, SA
Edificio Banco de Boston
(Pizo 12)
Via Espana No 122
Panama, Republic of Panama
Tel: 507 263 7677

Peru

Asociacion Peruana de Empresas de Leasing
Av.Nicolas De Rivera 540
Lima 27
Peru

Philippines

Philippine Finance Association Inc (PFA)
Unit 1715, Cityland, 10 Tower 2
HV dela Costa cor Valero St
Salcedo Village
Makati City
1200 Philippines
Tel: 819-3356/814-0948
Email: pfasect@pasicific.net.ph

Poland

Konferencja Przedsiebiorstw Leasingowych W Polsce
Filtrowa 71A apt 3
PL-02-055
Warsaw
Poland
Tel: 48 22 825 19 43
Email: kplzp@it.com.pl
www.leasepol.com.pl

Portugal

Associacao Portugesa de Empresas de Leasing (Apelease)
Edificio Aviz
Avenida Fontes Pereira de Melo, nº 35-6ºB
1050-118 Lisbon
Portugal
Tel: 351 1 3110440
Email: apelease@mail.telepac.pt

Russia

Russian Association of Leasing Companies
Staraya Ploshad
10/4 Moscow
Russia
Tel: 7 095 2060105
www.rosleasing.ru

Slovakia

Association of Leasing Compagnies of Slovak Republic
Cintorinska 21
SK 811 08 Bratislava
Tel: 421 2 529 631 72
Email: asocleas@isternet.sk
www.lizing.sk

Slovenia

Slovenian Leasing Association
KBM Leasing doo
Ulica Vita Kraigherja 5, 2000 Maribor
Slovenia
Tel: 386 61 520 14 50
Email: izajec@nkbm.si

Spain

Asociacion Española de Leasing
Plaza de Santa Maria Soledad Torres Acosta,
2-1a planta, 28004 – Madrid
Spain
Tel: 91 426 07 78
Email: ael@asociacionleasing.com

Sri Lanka

Leasing Association of Sri Lanka
100/1, Sri Jayewardenepura Mawatha
Rajagiriya
Sri Lanka
Tel: 865602

437

Sweden
Associations of Swedish Finance Houses (AFINA)
Box 14034
S-104 40 Stockholm
Sweden
Tel: 46 8 660 68 90

Switzerland
Schweizerischer Leasingverband
Ramistrasse 5
PO Box
8024 Zürich
Switzerland
Tel: 41 4 250 49 90
Email: Mhess@hswlaw.ch

Taiwan
Taipei Leasing Association
Room 904, 9th Floor
Fl No. 65
Sec 3 Nanking E Road
Taipei
Taiwan
Republic of China
Tel: 886 2 2504 3492
Email: tpeleas@ms54.hinet.net

Thailand
Thailand Leasing Association
19th Floor, Sathorn City Tower
175 South Sathorn Road
Tungmahamek
Sathorn
Bangkok 10120
Thailand
Tel: 662 679 6161

Turkey
Finansal Kiralama Dernegi (Fider)
Nispetiye cad Levent Is Mrk.No:6 K:2
80600 1 Levent/Istanbul
Turkey
Tel: 90 212 284 53 10
Email: fider@fider.org.tr
www.fider.org.tr

United Kingdom
Finance & Leasing Association
2 Floor, Imperial House
15-19 Kingsway
London WC2B 6UN
United Kingdom
Tel: 020 7836 6511
Email: info@fla.org.uk
www.fla.org.uk

United States
Equipment Leasing Association
4301 N.Fairfax Drive
Suite 550
Arlington
Virginia 22203
United States
Tel: 1 703 527 8655
www.elaonline.com

International Accounting Standard IAS 17

Leases

This Standard is effective for financial statements covering periods beginning on or after 1 January 1999.

In April 2000, paragraphs 1, 19, 24, 45 and 48 were amended, and paragraph 48A inserted by IAS 40 Investment Property. IAS 40 is effective for annual financial statements covering periods beginning on or after 1 January 2001.

In January 2001, paragraphs 1, 24 and 48A were amended by IAS 41 Agriculture. IAS 41 is effective for annual financial statements covering periods beginning on or after 1 January 2003.

The following SIC Interpretations relate to IAS 17:

- SIC-15 Operating Leases – Incentives.
- SIC-27 Evaluating the Substance of Transactions in the Legal Form of a Lease.

Introduction

This Standard (IAS 17 (revised)) replaces IAS 17 Accounting for Leases ('the original IAS 17'). IAS 17 (revised) is effective for accounting periods beginning on or after 1 January 1999.

This Standard sets out improvements over the original IAS 17 it replaces based on a review conducted in the context of the limited revision that identified changes considered essential to complete a core set of standards acceptable for cross-border funding and stock exchange listing. The IASC Board has agreed to undertake a more fundamental reform in the area of lease accounting standards.

The major changes from the original IAS 17 are as follows:

1. The original IAS 17 defined a lease as an arrangement whereby the lessor conveys the right to use an asset in return for rent payable by a lessee. IAS 17 (revised) modifies the definition by substituting the term 'rent' with 'a payment or series of payments'.

2. In stipulating that the classification of leases should be based on the extent to which risks and rewards incident to ownership of a leased asset lie with the lessor or lessee, justified by the application of the principle of substance over form, the original IAS 17 provided examples of situations as indicators that a lease is a finance lease. IAS 17 (revised) has added additional classification indicators to further facilitate the classification process.

3. The original IAS 17 used the term 'useful life' in the examples referred in the above for purposes of comparison to the lease term in the classification process. IAS 17 (revised) uses the term 'economic life', taking into account that an asset might be used by one or more users.

4. The original IAS 17 required the disclosure of contingent rents but was silent as to whether contingent rents should be included or excluded in the computation of minimum

lease payments. IAS 17 (revised) requires that contingent rents be excluded from minimum lease payments.

5. The original IAS 17 was silent on the accounting treatment of initial direct costs incurred by a lessee in negotiating and securing leasing arrangements. IAS 17 provides guidance by requiring costs that are directly attributable to activities performed by a lessee for securing a finance lease, to be included in the amount of the leased asset.

6. The original IAS 17 provided a free choice of method in the allocation of finance income by a lessor, namely the recognition of income basing on a pattern reflecting a constant periodic rate of return based on either:

   (a) the lessor's net investment outstanding in respect of the finance lease; or
   (b) the lessor's net cash investment outstanding in respect of the finance lease.

   IAS 17 (revised) requires that the recognition of finance income should be based reflecting a constant periodic rate of return basing on one method, namely the lessor's net investment outstanding in respect of the finance lease.

7. IAS 17 (revised) draws reference to the International Accounting Standard dealing with impairment of assets in providing guidance on the need to assess the possibility of an impairment of assets. The original IAS 17 did not address the matter.

8. IAS 17 (revised) mandates enhanced disclosures by both lessees and lessors for operating and finance leases through black letter lettering in comparison to the disclosure items required under the original IAS 17.

   New disclosures required by IAS 17 (revised) include:

   (a) the total of minimum lease payments reconciled to the present values of lease liabilities in three periodic bands: not later than one year; later than one year and not later than five years; and later than five years (required of a lessee);
   (b) the total gross investment in the lease reconciled to the present value of minimum lease payments receivable in three periodic bands: not later than one year; later than one year and not later than five years; and later than five years (required of a lessor);
   (c) the related finance charges in (a) and (b) above;
   (d) the future minimum sublease payments expected to be received under non-cancellable subleases at balance sheet date;
   (e) the accumulated allowance for uncollectible minimum lease payments receivable; and
   (f) contingent rents recognised in income by lessors.

9. The original IAS 17 included Appendices 1-3 which represented examples of situations in which a lease would normally be classified as a finance lease. The appendices have been omitted in IAS 17 (revised) in the light of the additional indicators included therein to further clarify the lease classification process.

10. It is noted that the provisions relating to the sale and leaseback transactions, in particular, the requirements involving a leaseback that is an operating lease, contain rules that prescribe a wide range of circumstances, based on relative amounts of fair value, carrying amount and selling price. IAS 17 (revised) includes an Appendix as further guidance in interpreting the requirements.

Contents

International Accounting Standard IAS 17

Leases

International Accounting Standard 17 Leases (IAS 17) is set out in paragraphs 1–60 and Appendix A. All the paragraphs have equal authority but retain the IASC format of the Standard when it was adopted by the IASB. IAS 17 should be read in the context of its objective, the Preface to International Financial Reporting Standards and the Framework for the Preparation and Presentation of Financial Statements. These provide a basis for selecting and applying accounting policies in the absence of explicit guidance.

Objective

The objective of this Standard is to prescribe, for lessees and lessors, the appropriate accounting policies and disclosure to apply in relation to finance and operating leases.

Scope

1. This Standard should be applied in accounting for all leases other than:

   (a) lease agreements to explore for or use minerals, oil, natural gas and similar non-regenerative resources; and

   (b) licensing agreements for such items as motion picture films, video recordings, plays, manuscripts, patents and copyrights.

   However, this Standard should not be applied to the measurement by:

   (a) lessees of investment property held under finance leases (see IAS 40 Investment Property);

   (b) lessors of investment property leased out under operating leases (see IAS 40 Investment Property);

   (c) lessees of biological assets held under finance leases (see IAS 41 Agriculture); or

   (d) lessors of biological assets leased out under operating leases (see IAS 41 Agriculture).

2. This Standard applies to agreements that transfer the right to use assets even though substantial services by the lessor may be called for in connection with the operation or maintenance of such assets. On the other hand, this Standard does not apply to agreements that are contracts for services that do not transfer the right to use assets from one contracting party to the other.

Definitions

3. The following terms are used in this Standard with the meanings specified:

   A *lease* is an agreement whereby the lessor conveys to the lessee in return for a payment or series of payments the right to use an asset for an agreed period of time.

   A *finance lease* is a lease that transfers substantially all the risks and rewards incident to ownership of an asset. Title may or may not eventually be transferred.

443

An *operating lease* is a lease other than a finance lease.

A *non-cancellable lease* is a lease that is cancellable only:

(a) upon the occurrence of some remote contingency;
(b) with the permission of the lessor;
(c) if the lessee enters into a new lease for the same or an equivalent asset with the same lessor; or
(d) upon payment by the lessee of an additional amount such that, at inception, continuation of the lease is reasonably certain.

The *inception of the lease* is the earlier of the date of the lease agreement or of a commitment by the parties to the principal provisions of the lease.

The *lease term* is the non-cancellable period for which the lessee has contracted to lease the asset together with any further terms for which the lessee has the option to continue to lease the asset, with or without further payment, which option at the inception of the lease it is reasonably certain that the lessee will exercise.

Minimum lease payments are the payments over the lease term that the lessee is, or can be required, to make excluding contingent rent, costs for services and taxes to be paid by and reimbursed to the lessor, together with:

(a) in the case of the lessee, any amounts guaranteed by the lessee or by a party related to the lessee; or
(b) in the case of the lessor, any residual value guaranteed to the lessor by either:
  (i)   the lessee;
  (ii) a party related to the lessee; or
  (iii) an independent third party financially capable of meeting this guarantee.

However, if the lessee has an option to purchase the asset at a price which is expected to be sufficiently lower than the fair value at the date the option becomes exercisable that, at the inception of the lease, is reasonably certain to be exercised, the minimum lease payments comprise the minimum payments payable over the lease term and the payment required to exercise this purchase option.

Fair value is the amount for which an asset could be exchanged or a liability settled, between knowledgeable, willing parties in an arm's length transaction.

Economic life is either:

(a) the period over which an asset is expected to be economically usable by one or more users; or
(b) the number of production or similar units expected to be obtained from the asset by one or more users.

Useful life is the estimated remaining period, from the beginning of the lease term, without limitation by the lease term, over which the economic benefits embodied in the asset are expected to be consumed by the enterprise.

Guaranteed residual value is:

(a) in the case of the lessee, that part of the residual value which is guaranteed by the lessee or by a party related to the lessee (the amount of the guarantee being the maximum amount that could, in any event, become payable); and

(b) in the case of the lessor, that part of the residual value which is guaranteed by the lessee or by a third party unrelated to the lessor who is financially capable of discharging the obligations under the guarantee.

Unguaranteed residual value is that portion of the residual value of the leased asset, the realisation of which by the lessor is not assured or is guaranteed solely by a party related to the lessor.

Gross investment in the lease is the aggregate of the minimum lease payments under a finance lease from the standpoint of the lessor and any unguaranteed residual value accruing to the lessor.

Unearned finance income is the difference between:

(a) the aggregate of the minimum lease payments under a finance lease from the standpoint of the lessor and any unguaranteed residual value accruing to the lessor; and

(b) the present value of (a) above, at the interest rate implicit in the lease.

Net investment in the lease is the gross investment in the lease less unearned finance income.

The *interest rate implicit in the lease* is the discount rate that, at the inception of the lease, causes the aggregate present value of (a) the minimum lease payments and (b) the unguaranteed residual value to be equal to the fair value of the leased asset.

The *lessee's incremental borrowing rate of interest* is the rate of interest the lessee would have to pay on a similar lease or, if that is not determinable, the rate that, at the inception of the lease, the lessee would incur to borrow over a similar term, and with a similar security, the funds necessary to purchase the asset.

Contingent rent is that portion of the lease payments that is not fixed in amount but is based on a factor other than just the passage of time (eg, percentage of sales, amount of usage, price indices, market rates of interest).

4. The definition of a lease includes contracts for the hire of an asset which contain a provision giving the hirer an option to acquire title to the asset upon the fulfilment of agreed conditions. These contracts are sometimes known as hire purchase contracts.

Classification of leases

5. The classification of leases adopted in this Standard is based on the extent to which risks and rewards incident to ownership of a leased asset lie with the lessor or the lessee. Risks include the possibilities of losses from idle capacity or technological obsolescence and of variations in return due to changing economic conditions. Rewards may be represented by the expectation of profitable operation over the asset's economic life and of gain from appreciation in value or realisation of a residual value.

6. A lease is classified as a finance lease if it transfers substantially all the risks and rewards incident to ownership. A lease is classified as an operating lease if it does not transfer substantially all the risks and rewards incident to ownership.

7. Since the transaction between a lessor and a lessee is based on a lease agreement common to both parties, it is appropriate to use consistent definitions. The application of these definitions to the differing circumstances of the two parties may sometimes result in the same lease being classified differently by lessor and lessee.

8. Whether a lease is a finance lease or an operating lease depends on the substance of the transaction rather than the form of the contract.[1] Examples of situations which would normally lead to a lease being classified as a finance lease are:

   (a) the lease transfers ownership of the asset to the lessee by the end of the lease term;
   (b) the lessee has the option to purchase the asset at a price which is expected to be sufficiently lower than the fair value at the date the option becomes exercisable such that, at the inception of the lease, it is reasonably certain that the option will be exercised;
   (c) the lease term is for the major part of the economic life of the asset even if title is not transferred;
   (d) at the inception of the lease the present value of the minimum lease payments amounts to at least substantially all of the fair value of the leased asset; and
   (e) the leased assets are of a specialised nature such that only the lessee can use them without major modifications being made.

9. Indicators of situations which individually or in combination could also lead to a lease being classified as a finance lease are:

   (a) if the lessee can cancel the lease, the lessor's losses associated with the cancellation are borne by the lessee;
   (b) gains or losses from the fluctuation in the fair value of the residual fall to the lessee (for example in the form of a rent rebate equalling most of the sales proceeds at the end of the lease); and
   (c) the lessee has the ability to continue the lease for a secondary period at a rent which is substantially lower than market rent.

10. Lease classification is made at the inception of the lease. If at any time the lessee and the lessor agree to change the provisions of the lease, other than by renewing the lease, in a manner that would have resulted in a different classification of the lease under the criteria in paragraphs 5 to 9 had the changed terms been in effect at the inception of the lease, the revised agreement is considered as a new agreement over its term. Changes in estimates (for example, changes in estimates of the economic life or of the residual value of

the leased property) or changes in circumstances (for example, default by the lessee), however, do not give rise to a new classification of a lease for accounting purposes.

11. Leases of land and buildings are classified as operating or finance leases in the same way as leases of other assets. However, a characteristic of land is that it normally has an indefinite economic life and, if title is not expected to pass to the lessee by the end of the lease term, the lessee does not receive substantially all of the risks and rewards incident to ownership. A premium paid for such a leasehold represents pre-paid lease payments which are amortised over the lease term in accordance with the pattern of benefits provided.

Leases in the financial statements of lessees

Finance leases

12. Lessees should recognise finance leases as assets and liabilities in their balance sheets at amounts equal at the inception of the lease to the fair value of the leased property or, if lower, at the present value of the minimum lease payments. In calculating the present value of the minimum lease payments the discount factor is the interest rate implicit in the lease, if this is practicable to determine; if not, the lessee's incremental borrowing rate should be used.

13. Transactions and other events are accounted for and presented in accordance with their substance and financial reality and not merely with legal form. While the legal form of a lease agreement is that the lessee may acquire no legal title to the leased asset, in the case of finance leases the substance and financial reality are that the lessee acquires the economic benefits of the use of the leased asset for the major part of its economic life in return for entering into an obligation to pay for that right an amount approximating to the fair value of the asset and the related finance charge.

14. If such lease transactions are not reflected in the lessee's balance sheet, the economic resources and the level of obligations of an enterprise are understated, thereby distorting financial ratios. It is therefore appropriate that a finance lease be recognised in the lessee's balance sheet both as an asset and as an obligation to pay future lease payments. At the inception of the lease, the asset and the liability for the future lease payments are recognised in the balance sheet at the same amounts.

15. It is not appropriate for the liabilities for leased assets to be presented in the financial statements as a deduction from the leased assets. If for the presentation of liabilities on the face of the balance sheet a distinction is made between current and non-current liabilities, the same distinction is made for lease liabilities.

16. Initial direct costs are often incurred in connection with specific leasing activities, as in negotiating and securing leasing arrangements. The costs identified as directly attributable to activities performed by the lessee for a finance lease, are included as part of the amount recognised as an asset under the lease.

17. Lease payments should be apportioned between the finance charge and the reduction of the outstanding liability. The finance charge should be allocated to periods during the lease term so as to produce a constant periodic rate of interest on the remaining balance of the liability for each period.

18. In practice, in allocating the finance charge to periods during the lease term, some form of approximation may be used to simplify the calculation.

19. A finance lease gives rise to a depreciation expense for depreciable assets as well as a finance expense for each accounting period. The depreciation policy for depreciable

leased assets should be consistent with that for depreciable assets which are owned, and the depreciation recognised should be calculated on the basis set out in IAS 16 Property, Plant and Equipment and IAS 38 Intangible Assets. If there is no reasonable certainty that the lessee will obtain ownership by the end of the lease term, the asset should be fully depreciated over the shorter of the lease term or its useful life.

20. The depreciable amount of a leased asset is allocated to each accounting period during the period of expected use on a systematic basis consistent with the depreciation policy the lessee adopts for depreciable assets that are owned. If there is reasonable certainty that the lessee will obtain ownership by the end of the lease term, the period of expected use is the useful life of the asset; otherwise the asset is depreciated over the shorter of the lease term or its useful life.

21. The sum of the depreciation expense for the asset and the finance expense for the period is rarely the same as the lease payments payable for the period, and it is, therefore, inappropriate simply to recognise the lease payments payable as an expense in the income statement. Accordingly, the asset and the related liability are unlikely to be equal in amount after the inception of the lease.

22. To determine whether a leased asset has become impaired, that is when the expected future economic benefits from that asset are lower than its carrying amount, an enterprise applies the International Accounting Standard dealing with impairment of assets, that sets out the requirements for how an enterprise should perform the review of the carrying amount of its assets, how it should determine the recoverable amount of an asset and when it should recognise, or reverse, an impairment loss.

23. Lessees should, in addition to the requirements of IAS 32 Financial Instruments: Disclosure and Presentation make the following disclosures for finance leases:

(a) for each class of asset, the net carrying amount at the balance sheet date;

(b) a reconciliation between the total of minimum lease payments at the balance sheet date, and their present value. In addition, an enterprise should disclose the total of minimum lease payments at the balance sheet date, and their present value, for each of the following periods:
(i) not later than one year;
(ii) later than one year and not later than five years;
(iii) later than five years;

(c) contingent rents recognised in income for the period;

(d) the total of future minimum sublease payments expected to be received under non-cancellable subleases at the balance sheet date; and

(e) a general description of the lessee's significant leasing arrangements including, but not limited to, the following:
(i) the basis on which contingent rent payments are determined;
(ii) the existence and terms of renewal or purchase options and escalation clauses; and
(iii) restrictions imposed by lease arrangements, such as those concerning dividends, additional debt, and further leasing.

24. In addition, the requirements on disclosure under IAS 16 Property, Plant and Equipment, IAS 36 Impairment of Assets, IAS 38 Intangible Assets, IAS 40 Investment Property and

IAS 41 Agriculture, apply to the amounts of leased assets under finance leases that are accounted for by the lessee as acquisitions of assets.

Operating leases

25. Lease payments under an operating lease should be recognised as an expense in the income statement on a straight line basis over the lease term unless another systematic basis is more representative of the time pattern of the user's benefit.[2]

26. For operating leases, lease payments (excluding costs for services such as insurance and maintenance) are recognised as an expense in the income statement on a straight line basis unless another systematic basis is representative of the time pattern of the user's benefit, even if the payments are not on that basis.

27. Lessees should, in addition to the requirements of IAS 32 Financial Instruments: Disclosure and Presentation make the following disclosures for operating leases:

    (a) the total of future minimum lease payments under non-cancellable operating leases for each of the following periods:
        (i)   not later than one year;
        (ii) later than one year and not later than five years;
        (iii) later than five years;
    (b) the total of future minimum sublease payments expected to be received under non-cancellable subleases at the balance sheet date;
    (c) lease and sublease payments recognised in income for the period, with separate amounts for minimum lease payments, contingent rents, and sublease payments;
    (d) a general description of the lessee's significant leasing arrangements including, but not limited to, the following:
        (i)   the basis on which contingent rent payments are determined;
        (ii) the existence and terms of renewal or purchase options and escalation clauses; and
        (iii) restrictions imposed by lease arrangements, such as those concerning dividends, additional debt, and further leasing.

Leases in the financial statements of lessors

Finance leases

28. Lessors should recognise assets held under a finance lease in their balance sheets and present them as a receivable at an amount equal to the net investment in the lease.

29. Under a finance lease substantially all the risks and rewards incident to legal ownership are transferred by the lessor, and thus the lease payment receivable is treated by the lessor as repayment of principal and finance income to reimburse and reward the lessor for its investment and services.

30. The recognition of finance income should be based on a pattern reflecting a constant periodic rate of return on the lessor's net investment outstanding in respect of the finance lease.

31. A lessor aims to allocate finance income over the lease term on a systematic and rational basis. This income allocation is based on a pattern reflecting a constant periodic return on the lessor's net investment outstanding in respect of the finance lease. Lease payments relat-

ing to the accounting period, excluding costs for services, are applied against the gross investment in the lease to reduce both the principal and the unearned finance income.

32. Estimated unguaranteed residual values used in computing the lessor's gross investment in a lease are reviewed regularly. If there has been a reduction in the estimated unguaranteed residual value, the income allocation over the lease term is revised and any reduction in respect of amounts already accrued is recognised immediately.

33. Initial direct costs, such as commissions and legal fees, are often incurred by lessors in negotiating and arranging a lease. For finance leases, these initial direct costs are incurred to produce finance income and are either recognised immediately in income or allocated against this income over the lease term. The latter may be achieved by recognising as an expense the cost as incurred and recognising as income in the same period a portion of the unearned finance income equal to the initial direct costs.

34. Manufacturer or dealer lessors should recognise selling profit or loss in income for the period, in accordance with the policy followed by the enterprise for outright sales. If artificially low rates of interest are quoted, selling profit should be restricted to that which would apply if a commercial rate of interest were charged. Initial direct costs should be recognised as an expense in the income statement at the inception of the lease.

35. Manufacturers or dealers often offer to customers the choice of either buying or leasing an asset. A finance lease of an asset by a manufacturer or dealer lessor gives rise to two types of income:

    (a) the profit or loss equivalent to the profit or loss resulting from an outright sale of the asset being leased, at normal selling prices, reflecting any applicable volume or trade discounts; and
    (b) the finance income over the lease term.

36. The sales revenue recorded at the commencement of a finance lease term by a manufacturer or dealer lessor is the fair value of the asset, or, if lower, the present value of the minimum lease payments accruing to the lessor, computed at a commercial rate of interest. The cost of sale recognised at the commencement of the lease term is the cost, or carrying amount if different, of the leased property less the present value of the unguaranteed residual value. The difference between the sales revenue and the cost of sale is the selling profit, which is recognised in accordance with the policy followed by the enterprise for sales.

37. Manufacturer or dealer lessors sometimes quote artificially low rates of interest in order to attract customers. The use of such a rate would result in an excessive portion of the total income from the transaction being recognised at the time of sale. If artificially low rates of interest are quoted, selling profit would be restricted to that which would apply if a commercial rate of interest were charged.

38. Initial direct costs are recognised as an expense at the commencement of the lease term because they are mainly related to earning the manufacturer's or dealer's selling profit.

39. Lessors should, in addition to the requirements in IAS 32 Financial Instruments: Disclosure and Presentation make the following disclosures for finance leases:

    (a) a reconciliation between the total gross investment in the lease at the balance sheet date, and the present value of minimum lease payments receivable at the balance sheet date. In addition, an enterprise should disclose the total gross investment in the lease and the present value of minimum lease payments receivable at the balance sheet date, for each of the following periods:

   (i)   not later than one year;

   (ii) later than one year and not later than five years;

   (iii) later than five years;

  (b) unearned finance income;

  (c) the unguaranteed residual values accruing to the benefit of the lessor;

  (d) the accumulated allowance for uncollectible minimum lease payments receivable;

  (e) contingent rents recognised in income; and

  (f) a general description of the lessor's significant leasing arrangements.

40. As an indicator of growth it is often useful to also disclose the gross investment less unearned income in new business added during the accounting period, after deducting the relevant amounts for cancelled leases.

Operating leases

41. Lessors should present assets subject to operating leases in their balance sheets according to the nature of the asset.

42. Lease income from operating leases should be recognised in income on a straight line basis over the lease term, unless another systematic basis is more representative of the time pattern in which use benefit derived from the leased asset is diminished.[3]

43. Costs, including depreciation, incurred in earning the lease income are recognised as an expense. Lease income (excluding receipts for services provided such as insurance and maintenance) is recognised in income on a straight line basis over the lease term even if the receipts are not on such a basis, unless another systematic basis is more representative of the time pattern in which use benefit derived from the leased asset is diminished.

44. Initial direct costs incurred specifically to earn revenues from an operating lease are either deferred and allocated to income over the lease term in proportion to the recognition of rent income, or are recognised as an expense in the income statement in the period in which they are incurred.

45. The depreciation of depreciable leased assets should be on a basis consistent with the lessor's normal depreciation policy for similar assets, and the depreciation charge should be calculated on the basis set out in IAS 16 Property, Plant and Equipment and IAS 38 Intangible Assets.

46. To determine whether a leased asset has become impaired, that is when the expected future economic benefits from that asset are lower than its carrying amount, an enterprise applies the International Accounting Standard dealing with impairment of assets that sets out the requirements for how an enterprise should perform the review of the carrying amount of its assets, how it should determine the recoverable amount of an asset and when it should recognise, or reverse, an impairment loss.

47. A manufacturer or dealer lessor does not recognise any selling profit on entering into an operating lease because it is not the equivalent of a sale.

48. Lessors should, in addition to the requirements of IAS 32 Financial Instruments: Disclosure and Presentation make the following disclosures for operating leases:

(a) the future minimum lease payments under non-cancellable operating leases in the aggregate and for each of the following periods:
  (i)   not later than one year;
  (ii) later than one year and not later than five years;
  (iii) later than five years;
(b) total contingent rents recognised in income; and
(c) a general description of the lessor's significant leasing arrangements.

48A. In addition, the requirements on disclosure under IAS 16 Property, Plant and Equipment, IAS 36 Impairment of Assets, IAS 38 Intangible Assets, IAS 40 Investment Property and IAS 41 Agriculture, apply to assets leased out under operating leases.

Sale and leaseback transactions

49. A sale and leaseback transaction involves the sale of an asset by the vendor and the leasing of the same asset back to the vendor. The lease payment and the sale price are usually interdependent as they are negotiated as a package. The accounting treatment of a sale and leaseback transaction depends upon the type of lease involved.

50. If a sale and leaseback transaction results in a finance lease, any excess of sales proceeds over the carrying amount should not be immediately recognised as income in the financial statements of a seller-lessee. Instead, it should be deferred and amortised over the lease term.

51. If the leaseback is a finance lease, the transaction is a means whereby the lessor provides finance to the lessee, with the asset as security. For this reason it is not appropriate to regard an excess of sales proceeds over the carrying amount as income. Such excess, is deferred and amortised over the lease term.

52. If a sale and leaseback transaction results in an operating lease, and it is clear that the transaction is established at fair value, any profit or loss should be recognised immediately. If the sale price is below fair value, any profit or loss should be recognised immediately except that, if the loss is compensated by future lease payments at below market price, it should be deferred and amortised in proportion to the lease payments over the period for which the asset is expected to be used. If the sale price is above fair value, the excess over fair value should be deferred and amortised over the period for which the asset is expected to be used.

53. If the leaseback is an operating lease, and the lease payments and the sale price are established at fair value, there has in effect been a normal sale transaction and any profit or loss is recognised immediately.

54. For operating leases, if the fair value at the time of a sale and leaseback transaction is less than the carrying amount of the asset, a loss equal to the amount of the difference between the carrying amount and fair value should be recognised immediately.

55. For finance leases, no such adjustment is necessary unless there has been an impairment in value, in which case the carrying amount is reduced to recoverable amount in accordance with the International Accounting Standard dealing with impairment of assets.

56. Disclosure requirements for lessees and lessors apply equally to sale and leaseback transactions. The required description of the significant leasing arrangements leads to disclosure of unique or unusual provisions of the agreement or terms of the sale and leaseback transactions.

57. Sale and leaseback transactions may meet the separate disclosure criteria in IAS 8 Net Profit or Loss for the Period, Fundamental Errors and Changes in Accounting Policies, paragraph 16.

Transitional provisions

58. Retrospective application of this Standard is encouraged but not required. If the Standard is not applied retrospectively, the balance of any pre-existing finance lease is deemed to have been properly determined by the lessor and should be accounted for thereafter in accordance with the provisions of this Standard.

Effective date

59. This International Accounting Standard becomes operative for financial statements covering periods beginning on or after 1 January 1999. If an enterprise applies this Standard for financial statements covering periods beginning before 1 January 1999, the enterprise should disclose the fact that it has applied this Standard instead of IAS 17 Accounting for Leases approved in 1982.

60. This Standard supersedes IAS 17 Accounting for Leases, approved in 1982.

---

[1] See also SIC-27 Evaluating the Substance of Transactions in the Legal Form of a Lease.

[2] See also SIC-15 Operating Leases – Incentives.

[3] See also SIC-15 Operating Leases – Incentives.

Appendix A

Sale and leaseback transactions that result in operating leases

The appendix is illustrative only and does not form part of the Standard. The purpose of the appendix is to illustrate the application of the Standard to assist in clarifying its meaning.

A sale and leaseback transaction that results in an operating lease may give rise to profit or a loss, the determination and treatment of which depends on the leased asset's carrying amount, fair value and selling price. The table on the following page shows the requirements of the Standard in various circumstances.

Sale price established at fair value (paragraph 52)	*Carrying amount equal to fair value*	*Carrying amount less than fair value*	*Carrying amount above fair value*
Profit	No profit	Recognise profit immediately	Not applicable
Loss	No loss	Not applicable	Recognise loss immediately
Sale price below fair value (paragraph 52)			
Profit	No profit	Recognise profit immediately	No profit (Note 1)
Loss not compensated by future lease payments at below market price	Recognise loss immediately	Recognise loss immediately	(Note 1)
Loss compensated by future lease payments at below market price	Defer and amortise loss	Defer and amortise loss	(Note 1)
Sale price above fair value (paragraph 52)			
Profit	Defer and amortise profit	Defer and amortise profit	Defer and amortise profit (Note 2)
Loss	No loss	No loss	(Note 1)

Note 1: These parts of the table represent circumstances that would have been dealt with under paragraph 54 of the Standard. Paragraph 54 requires the carrying amount of an asset to be written down to fair value where it is subject to a sale and leaseback.

Note 2: The profit would be the difference between fair value and sale price as the carrying amount would have been written down to fair value in accordance with paragraph 54.

Appendix C

Unidroit convention on international financial leasing

(Ottawa, 28 May 1988)

THE STATES PARTIES TO THIS CONVENTION,

RECOGNISING the importance of removing certain legal impediments to the international financial leasing of equipment, while maintaining a fair balance of interests between the different parties to the transaction,

AWARE of the need to make international financial leasing more available,

CONSCIOUS of the fact that the rules of law governing the traditional contract of hire need to be adapted to the distinctive triangular relationship created by the financial leasing transaction,

RECOGNISING therefore the desirability of formulating certain uniform rules relating primarily to the civil and commercial law aspects of international financial leasing,

HAVE AGREED as follows:

Chapter I – Sphere of application and general provisions

Article 1

1. This Convention governs a financial leasing transaction as described in paragraph 2 in which one party (the lessor):

   (a) on the specifications of another party (the lessee), enters into an agreement (the supply agreement) with a third party (the supplier) under which the lessor acquires plant, capital goods or other equipment (the equipment) on terms approved by the lessee so far as they concern its interests; and

   (b) enters into an agreement (the leasing agreement) with the lessee, granting to the lessee the right to use the equipment in return for the payment of rentals.

2. The financial leasing transaction referred to in the previous paragraph is a transaction which includes the following characteristics:

(a) the lessee specifies the equipment and selects the supplier without relying primarily on the skill and judgment of the lessor;

(b) the equipment is acquired by the lessor in connection with a leasing agreement which, to the knowledge of the supplier, either has been made or is to be made between the lessor and the lessee; and

(c) the rentals payable under the leasing agreement are calculated so as to take into account in particular the amortisation of the whole or a substantial part of the cost of the equipment.

3. This Convention applies whether or not the lessee has or subsequently acquires the option to buy the equipment or to hold it on lease for a further period, and whether or not for a nominal price or rental.

4. This Convention applies to financial leasing transactions in relation to all equipment save that which is to be used primarily for the lessee's personal, family or household purposes.

Article 2

In the case of one or more sub-leasing transactions involving the same equipment, this Convention applies to each transaction which is a financial leasing transaction and is otherwise subject to this Convention as if the person from whom the first lessor (as defined in paragraph 1 of the previous article) acquired the equipment were the supplier and as if the agreement under which the equipment was so acquired were the supply agreement.

Article 3

1. This Convention applies when the lessor and the lessee have their places of business in different States and:

(a) those States and the State in which the supplier has its place of business are Contracting States; or

(b) both the supply agreement and the leasing agreement are governed by the law of a Contracting State.

2. A reference in this Convention to a party's place of business shall, if it has more than one place of business, mean the place of business which has the closest relationship to the relevant agreement and its performance, having regard to the circumstances known to or contemplated by the parties at any time before or at the conclusion of that agreement.

Article 4

1. The provisions of this Convention shall not cease to apply merely because the equipment has become a fixture to or incorporated in land.

2. Any question whether or not the equipment has become a fixture to or incorporated in land, and if so the effect on the rights *inter se* of the lessor and a person having real rights in the land, shall be determined by the law of the State where the land is situated.

Article 5

1. The application of this Convention may be excluded only if each of the parties to the supply agreement and each of the parties to the leasing agreement agree to exclude it.

2. Where the application of this Convention has not been excluded in accordance with the previous paragraph, the parties may, in their relations with each other, derogate from or vary the effect of any of its provisions except as stated in Articles 8(3) and 13(3)(b) and (4).

Article 6

1. In the interpretation of this Convention, regard is to be had to its object and purpose as set forth in the preamble, to its international character and to the need to promote uniformity in its application and the observance of good faith in international trade.

2. Questions concerning matters governed by this Convention which are not expressly settled in it are to be settled in conformity with the general principles on which it is based or, in the absence of such principles, in conformity with the law applicable by virtue of the rules of private international law.

Chapter II – Rights and duties of the parties

Article 7

1. (a) The lessor's real rights in the equipment shall be valid against the lessee's trustee in bankruptcy and creditors, including creditors who have obtained an attachment or execution.

   (b) For the purposes of this paragraph 'trustee in bankruptcy' includes a liquidator, administrator or other person appointed to administer the lessee's estate for the benefit of the general body of creditors.

2. Where by the applicable law the lessor's real rights in the equipment are valid against a person referred to in the previous paragraph only on compliance with rules as to public notice, those rights shall be valid against that person only if there has been compliance with such rules.

3. For the purposes of the previous paragraph the applicable law is the law of the State which, at the time when a person referred to in paragraph 1 becomes entitled to invoke the rules referred to in the previous paragraph, is:

   (a) in the case of a registered ship, the State in which it is registered in the name of the owner (for the purposes of this sub-paragraph a bareboat charterer is deemed not to be the owner);

   (b) in the case of an aircraft which is registered pursuant to the Convention on International Civil Aviation done at Chicago on 7 December 1944, the State in which it is so registered;

   (c) in the case of other equipment of a kind normally moved from one State to another, including an aircraft engine, the State in which the lessee has its principal place of business;

   (d) in the case of all other equipment, the State in which the equipment is situated.

4. Paragraph 2 shall not affect the provisions of any other treaty under which the lessor's real rights in the equipment are required to be recognised.

5. This article shall not affect the priority of any creditor having:

   (a) a consensual or non-consensual lien or security interest in the equipment arising otherwise than by virtue of an attachment or execution, or
   (b) any right of arrest, detention or disposition conferred specifically in relation to ships or aircraft under the law applicable by virtue of the rules of private international law.

Article 8

1. (a) Except as otherwise provided by this Convention or stated in the leasing agreement, the lessor shall not incur any liability to the lessee in respect of the equipment save to the extent that the lessee has suffered loss as the result of its reliance on the lessor's skill and judgment and of the lessor's intervention in the selection of the supplier or the specifications of the equipment.
   (b) The lessor shall not, in its capacity of lessor, be liable to third parties for death, personal injury or damage to property caused by the equipment.
   (c) The above provisions of this paragraph shall not govern any liability of the lessor in any other capacity, for example as owner.

2. The lessor warrants that the lessee's quiet possession will not be disturbed by a person who has a superior title or right, or who claims a superior title or right and acts under the authority of a court, where such title, right or claim is not derived from an act or omission of the lessee.

3. The parties may not derogate from or vary the effect of the provisions of the previous paragraph in so far as the superior title, right or claim is derived from an intentional or grossly negligent act or omission of the lessor.

4. The provisions of paragraphs 2 and 3 shall not affect any broader warranty of quiet possession by the lessor which is mandatory under the law applicable by virtue of the rules of private international law.

Article 9

1. The lessee shall take proper care of the equipment, use it in a reasonable manner and keep it in the condition in which it was delivered, subject to fair wear and tear and to any modification of the equipment agreed by the parties.

2. When the leasing agreement comes to an end the lessee, unless exercising a right to buy the equipment or to hold the equipment on lease for a further period, shall return the equipment to the lessor in the condition specified in the previous paragraph.

Article 10

1. The duties of the supplier under the supply agreement shall also be owed to the lessee as if it were a party to that agreement and as if the equipment were to be supplied directly to the lessee. However, the supplier shall not be liable to both the lessor and the lessee in respect of the same damage.

2. Nothing in this article shall entitle the lessee to terminate or rescind the supply agreement without the consent of the lessor.

Article 11

The lessee's rights derived from the supply agreement under this Convention shall not be affected by a variation of any term of the supply agreement previously approved by the lessee unless it consented to that variation.

Article 12

1. Where the equipment is not delivered or is delivered late or fails to conform to the supply agreement:

    (a) the lessee has the right as against the lessor to reject the equipment or to terminate the leasing agreement; and
    (b) the lessor has the right to remedy its failure to tender equipment in conformity with the supply agreement, as if the lessee had agreed to buy the equipment from the lessor under the same terms as those of the supply agreement.

2. A right conferred by the previous paragraph shall be exercisable in the same manner and shall be lost in the same circumstances as if the lessee had agreed to buy the equipment from the lessor under the same terms as those of the supply agreement.
3. The lessee shall be entitled to withhold rentals payable under the leasing agreement until the lessor has remedied its failure to tender equipment in conformity with the supply agreement or the lessee has lost the right to reject the equipment.
4. Where the lessee has exercised a right to terminate the leasing agreement, the lessee shall be entitled to recover any rentals and other sums paid in advance, less a reasonable sum for any benefit the lessee has derived from the equipment.
5. The lessee shall have no other claim against the lessor for non-delivery, delay in delivery or delivery of non-conforming equipment except to the extent to which this results from the act or omission of the lessor.
6. Nothing in this article shall affect the lessee's rights against the supplier under Article 10.

Article 13

1. In the event of default by the lessee, the lessor may recover accrued unpaid rentals, together with interest and damages.
2. Where the lessee's default is substantial, then subject to paragraph 5 the lessor may also require accelerated payment of the value of the future rentals, where the leasing agreement so provides, or may terminate the leasing agreement and after such termination:

    (a) recover possession of the equipment; and
    (b) recover such damages as will place the lessor in the position in which it would have been had the lessee performed the leasing agreement in accordance with its terms.

3. (a) The leasing agreement may provide for the manner in which the damages recoverable under paragraph 2 (b) are to be computed.

(b) Such provision shall be enforceable between the parties unless it would result in damages substantially in excess of those provided for under paragraph 2 (b). The parties may not derogate from or vary the effect of the provisions of the present sub-paragraph.

4. Where the lessor has terminated the leasing agreement, it shall not be entitled to enforce a term of that agreement providing for acceleration of payment of future rentals, but the value of such rentals may be taken into account in computing damages under paragraphs 2(b) and 3. The parties may not derogate from or vary the effect of the provisions of the present paragraph.

5. The lessor shall not be entitled to exercise its right of acceleration or its right of termination under paragraph 2 unless it has by notice given the lessee a reasonable opportunity of remedying the default so far as the same may be remedied.

6. The lessor shall not be entitled to recover damages to the extent that it has failed to take all reasonable steps to mitigate its loss.

Article 14

1. The lessor may transfer or otherwise deal with all or any of its rights in the equipment or under the leasing agreement. Such a transfer shall not relieve the lessor of any of its duties under the leasing agreement or alter either the nature of the leasing agreement or its legal treatment as provided in this Convention.

2. The lessee may transfer the right to the use of the equipment or any other rights under the leasing agreement only with the consent of the lessor and subject to the rights of third parties.

Chapter III – Final provisions

Article 15

1. This Convention is open for signature at the concluding meeting of the Diplomatic Conference for the Adoption of the Draft Unidroit Conventions on International Factoring and International Financial Leasing and will remain open for signature by all States at Ottawa until 31 December 1990.

2. This Convention is subject to ratification, acceptance or approval by States which have signed it.

3. This Convention is open for accession by all States which are not signatory States as from the date it is open for signature.

4. Ratification, acceptance, approval or accession is effected by the deposit of a formal instrument to that effect with the depositary.

Article 16

1. This Convention enters into force on the first day of the month following the expiration of six months after the date of deposit of the third instrument of ratification, acceptance, approval or accession.

2. For each State that ratifies, accepts, approves, or accedes to this Convention after the deposit of the third instrument of ratification, acceptance, approval or accession, this

Convention enters into force in respect of that State on the first day of the month following the expiration of six months after the date of the deposit of its instrument of ratification, acceptance, approval or accession.

Article 17

This Convention does not prevail over any treaty which has already been or may be entered into; in particular it shall not affect any liability imposed on any person by existing or future treaties.

Article 18

1. If a Contracting State has two or more territorial units in which different systems of law are applicable in relation to the matters dealt with in this Convention, it may, at the time of signature, ratification, acceptance, approval or accession, declare that this Convention is to extend to all its territorial units or only to one or more of them, and may substitute its declaration by another declaration at any time.
2. These declarations are to be notified to the depositary and are to state expressly the territorial units to which the Convention extends.
3. If, by virtue of a declaration under this article, this Convention extends to one or more but not all of the territorial units of a Contracting State, and if the place of business of a party is located in that State, this place of business, for the purposes of this Convention, is considered not to be in a Contracting State, unless it is in a territorial unit to which the Convention extends.
4. If a Contracting State makes no declaration under paragraph 1, the Convention is to extend to all territorial units of that State.

Article 19

1. Two or more Contracting States which have the same or closely related legal rules on matters governed by this Convention may at any time declare that the Convention is not to apply where the supplier, the lessor and the lessee have their places of business in those States. Such declarations may be made jointly or by reciprocal unilateral declarations.
2. A Contracting State which has the same or closely related legal rules on matters governed by this Convention as one or more non-Contracting States may at any time declare that the Convention is not to apply where the supplier, the lessor and the lessee have their places of business in those States.
3. If a State which is the object of a declaration under the previous paragraph subsequently becomes a Contracting State, the declaration made will, as from the date on which the Convention enters into force in respect of the new Contracting State, have the effect of a declaration made under paragraph 1, provided that the new Contracting State joins in such declaration or makes a reciprocal unilateral declaration.

Article 20

A Contracting State may declare at the time of signature, ratification, acceptance, approval or accession that it will substitute its domestic law for Article 8(3) if its domestic law does not permit the lessor to exclude its liability for its default or negligence.

Article 21

1. Declarations made under this Convention at the time of signature are subject to confirmation upon ratification, acceptance or approval.
2. Declarations and confirmations of declarations are to be in writing and to be formally notified to the depositary.
3. A declaration takes effect simultaneously with the entry into force of this Convention in respect of the State concerned. However, a declaration of which the depositary receives formal notification after such entry into force takes effect on the first day of the month following the expiration of six months after the date of its receipt by the depositary. Reciprocal unilateral declarations under Article 19 take effect on the first day of the month following the expiration of six months after the receipt of the latest declaration by the depositary.
4. Any State which makes a declaration under this Convention may withdraw it at any time by a formal notification in writing addressed to the depositary. Such withdrawal is to take effect on the first day of the month following the expiration of six months after the date of the receipt of the notification by the depositary.
5. A withdrawal of a declaration made under Article 19 renders inoperative in relation to the withdrawing State, as from the date on which the withdrawal takes effect, any joint or reciprocal unilateral declaration made by another State under that article.

Article 22

No reservations are permitted except those expressly authorised in this Convention.

Article 23

This Convention applies to a financial leasing transaction when the leasing agreement and the supply agreement are both concluded on or after the date on which the Convention enters into force in respect of the Contracting States referred to in Article 3(1)(a), or of the Contracting State or States referred to in paragraph 1 (b) of that article.

Article 24

1. This Convention may be denounced by any Contracting State at any time after the date on which it enters into force for that State.
2. Denunciation is effected by the deposit of an instrument to that effect with the depositary.
3. A denunciation takes effect on the first day of the month following the expiration of six months after the deposit of the instrument of denunciation with the depositary. Where a longer period for the denunciation to take effect is specified in the instrument of denunciation it takes effect upon the expiration of such longer period after its deposit with the depositary.

Article 25

1. This Convention shall be deposited with the Government of Canada.
2. The Government of Canada shall:

  (a) inform all States which have signed or acceded to this Convention and the President of the International Institute for the Unification of Private Law (Unidroit) of:

      (i) each new signature or deposit of an instrument of ratification, acceptance, approval or accession, together with the date thereof;

      (ii) each declaration made under Articles 18, 19 and 20;

      (iii) the withdrawal of any declaration made under Article 21 (4);

      (iv) the date of entry into force of this Convention;

      (v) the deposit of an instrument of denunciation of this Convention together with the date of its deposit and the date on which it takes effect;

  (b) transmit certified true copies of this Convention to all signatory States, to all States acceding to the Convention and to the President of the International Institute for the Unification of Private Law (Unidroit).

IN WITNESS WHEREOF the undersigned plenipotentiaries, being duly authorised by their respective Governments, have signed this Convention.

DONE at Ottawa, this twenty-eighth day of May, one thousand nine hundred and eighty-eight, in a single original, of which the English and French texts are equally authentic.

Parties to the Ottawa convention

Country	*Date of ratification or accession*
France	23.4.91
Italy	29.11.93
Nigeria	25.10.94
Panama	26.3.97
Hungary	7.5.96

Glossary

Accelerated Cost Recovery System (ACRS)

The system of tax depreciation in general use in the United States prior to 1988.

Accelerated depreciation

A rate of depreciation higher than the normal rate, generally for tax purposes.

Accrual method

An accounting term that describes a method of keeping accounts whereby expenses incurred and income earned for a given fiscal year are shown in the books even though they may not have actually been paid or received in that period.

Actuarial rate of return

The rate at which profit can be withdrawn from the lease over the period in which there is a positive net cash investment in the lease.

Alternative Minimum Tax (AMT)

A US tax system designed to ensure that a minimum amount of income tax is paid by corporate and non-corporate taxpayers. The AMT rate is currently 20 per cent for corporates and 26-28 per cent for individuals

Amortisation

The retirement of debt through repayment.

Asset Depreciation Range (ADR)

Refers to a depreciation method which permits shorter or longer asset lives to be used in computing tax depreciation.

Back-to-back lease

Leased equipment which is leased to an intermediate lessor and then sub-leased to the actual user.

Balloon payment

Rentals are paid over the term of the lease with a larger rental, known as a 'balloon payment', paid at the end of the lease period. This results in lower periodic rentals than under a fully amortised lease and can aid cash flow for the lessee.

Bargain purchase option

A provision allowing the lessee, at his option, to purchase the leased asset for a price that is sufficiently lower than the expected fair market value (at the date such option becomes exercisable). The exercise of the this option appears, at the inception of the lease, to be reasonably assured.

Bargain renewal option

A provision allowing the lessee, at his option, to renew the lease for a rental sufficiently lower than the expected fair rental for the property (at the date the option becomes exercisable). The exercise of this option appears, at the inception of the lease, to be reasonably assured.

Big ticket lease

A lease in which the asset's capital cost is very large, generally in excess of £20 million/US$20 million.

Blind pool

A specific type of lease financing in the United States, whereby funds are raised from individual investors by a leasing intermediary acting as a 'general partner', with no predetermined particular asset. The instrument offers investors advantages of diversification and time flowing from the latitude allowed to the general partner.

Broker

A company or person arranging the sale or lease of equipment for a fee.

Burdensome buyout

A provision in a lease allowing the lessee to purchase the leased equipment at a predetermined value, in excess of termination value or at a value to be determined in some fashion when the buyout is exercised, in the event that payments under the tax or general indemnity clauses are deemed by the lessee to be unduly burdensome.

Call option

An option to purchase an asset at a set price at some particular time in the future.

Capital allowances

The amount of depreciation allowed by the UK Inland Revenue to be offset against taxable profits.

Capital lease

For financial purposes, a lease in the United States is generally classified and accounted for by a lessee as a capital lease if it meets any of the following criteria:

- the lease transfers ownership to the lessee at the end of the lease term;
- the lease contains an option to purchase the property at a bargain price;

- the lease term is equal to 75 per cent or more of the estimated economic life of the property; or
- the present value of minimum lease rental payments at the inception of the lease is equal to 90 per cent or more of the fair market value of the leased property.

Casualty value

See 'Insured value'. Also used to mean the stipulated loss value payable on a total loss of the equipment.

Certificate of acceptance

A document whereby the lessee acknowledges that the equipment to be leased has been delivered and is acceptable.

Conditional sale

A transaction for the purchase of an asset under which legal title is passed on fulfilment of the final condition in which the user may, for tax purposes, be treated as the owner of the equipment at the outset of the transaction.

Consortium lease

A lease in which a number of lessors participate. The usual reason for this is that the cost or the potential risk is too high to be borne by one lessor.

Contingent rentals

Rentals in which the amounts are dependent upon some factors other than passage of time.

Contract hire

UK expression for an operating lease, usually for vehicles or handling equipment. Lessors carry the residual value risk, and the fixed rentals may include a maintenance charge.

Cross-border leasing

Facility where the lessor and lessee are in different countries and/or subject to different legal systems.

Currency swap

Technique of trading currency exchange risks with a counterparty (or a bank acting as intermediary between two counterparties).

Defeasance

The prepayment of financial obligations, usually through a third party, in circumstances where the third party assumes the responsibility to discharge such financial obligations (economic defeasance) and, if the lessor has no recourse to the original obligor, legal defeasance.

Deficit Reduction Tax Act   The Deficit Reduction Tax Act of 1984 reduced the tax benefits for property used by tax-exempt entities defined as governmental agencies, tax-exempt organisations and certain foreign persons. Generally, personal property leased to tax-exempt entities is ineligible for ITC and depreciation benefits are limited to straight-line deductions over a recovery period equal to the longer of 125 per cent of the lease term or the ADR mid point life.

Direct financing lease   Under US accounting rules, a lease is classified as a direct financing lease if there is no 'manufacturer's or dealer's profit or loss' to the lessor and if it meets criterion definitions for a capital lease (see above). The extra requirements that the collectability of the minimum lease payments is reasonably assured and that no uncertainties surround the amount of unreimbursable costs to be incurred by the lessor must also be met.

Discounted cash flow (DCF)   A technique for assessing the present value of future income and payments which takes account of the time value of money.

Double-dipping   The structuring of leases to take advantage of tax benefits on capital investment in more than one country (see 'Cross-border').

Dry lease   Refers to the lease of an asset (usually aircraft) only; crew and back-up are not included in the lease package.

Dual rate of return   An internal rate of return measure. An arbitrary reinvestment rate is applied to periods in which cash surpluses arise under the lease. The appropriate pre-tax borrowing rate at which the lease breaks even is then determined by iterative procedures.

Economic life of leased property   The estimated remaining period during which the property is expected to be economically usable by one or more users, with normal repairs and maintenance, for the purpose for which it was intended at the inception of the lease.

Economic Recovery Tax Act (ERTA)   An Act, in 1981 in the United States, which introduced the 'safe harbour lease'.

Enhanced Equipment Trust Certificates (EETC)
An advanced ETC structure (see below) where investors receive ETC's which are rated paper or have other credit enhancements to increase an investor's confidence of being repaid.

Equipment Trust Certificate (ETC)
A financing structure whereby an issuing vehicle acquires title to an asset from the manufacturer by contract assignment from the lessee, raises the equipment cost from investors by issuing ETC's and amortises the ETC debt from rentals paid by the lessee.

Equity participants
Investors in a lease seeking the tax benefits resulting from ownership as distinct from the debt participants.

Estimated residual value of leased property
The estimated fair value of the property at the end of the lease term.

European Enhanced Equipment Trust Certificates (EEETC)
Like EETC's discussed above only with modifications to satisfy English law and practices in the Eurobond market.

Evergreen renewal option
A US Tax Act proposal to help leases of equipment with high residual values (like aircraft) to be both attractive and remain within the true lease guidelines. Each 'renewal' was an alternative to purchasing at fair market value.

FASB
Financial Accounting Standards Board.

Finance lease
A financing arrangement whereby a user can acquire use of an asset for most of its useful life. Rentals are net to the lessor, and the user is responsible for maintenance, taxes and insurance. Rent payments over the life of the lease are sufficient to enable the lessor to recover the cost of the equipment plus a return on its investment. A finance lease is distinguished, for accounting purposes, from an operating lease.

Financial Accounting Standard (FAS) 13
Statement of Financial Accounting Standards No. 13, 'Accounting for Leases', November 1976, which sets forth financial accounting standards on accounting for leases.

First lien
The first security interest against an asset.

Fixed price purchase option
A purchase option where the price a lessee would have to pay to become the equipment owner on lease

termination is established at the start of the lease, and may be nominal.

Floating rental rate A rental which is subject to upward or downward adjustments during the lease term, by reference to floating interest rates (such as Libor).

Floating to drawdown In the United Kingdom, when leases have been negotiated some time before the primary period begins, the rate may be fixed according to a formula which allows for changes in funding cost occurring before the drawdown. Thereafter, rates remain fixed for the life of the lease.

Forward sale Selling equipment for a fixed price with delivery at an agreed future date.

Full payout lease See 'Finance lease'.

Grantor trust A trust used as the owner trust in a US leveraged lease transaction, usually with only one equity participant. The Internal Revenue Code refers to such a trust as a grantor trust.

Grossing up The requirement to increase payments under leases subject to the deduction of tax at source so that the net amount received by the payee is equal to the amount expressed to be payable.

Groupement d'lnteret Economique (GIE) A French corporate entity which is a grouping of mutual economic interests, transparent for tax purposes.

Hell-or-high-water clause A clause in a lease which reiterates the unconditional obligation of the lessee to pay rent for the entire term of the lease, regardless of any event affecting the equipment or any change in the circumstances of the lessee.

Hire purchase agreement English terminology for a lease with a purchase option.

Indemnity A provision whereby a lessee or another person holds the lessor or another person blameless against any cost or loss arising by reason of the occurrence of certain events or circumstances, such as the non-achievement of the desired tax treatment of the transaction.

Indenture trust An agreement between the owner trustee and the inden-

469

ture trustee whereby the owner trustee mortgages the equipment and assigns the lease and rental payments under the lease as security for amounts due to the lenders. The same as a security agreement or mortgage.

Indenture trustee

In a US leveraged lease, the indenture trustee holds the security interest in the leased equipment for the benefit of the lenders. In the event of a default, the indenture trustee exercises the rights of a mortgagee. The indenture trustee is also responsible for receiving rent payments from the lessee and using such funds to pay the amounts due to the lenders with the balance being paid to the owner trustee.

Initial direct costs

The direct costs incurred by a lessor in negotiating and consummating a lease, such as commissions and legal fees.

Institutional investors

Investors such as banks, insurance companies, trusts, pension funds, foundations and educational, charitable and religious institutions.

Insured value

The agreed value of equipment for insurance purposes at various times during the term of the lease.

Interest rate implicit in a lease

The discount rate which, when applied to minimum lease payments, causes the aggregate present value of such lease payments to equal the cost of the leased property at the inception of the lease.

Interest rate swap

The technique of trading interest risks with a counterparty (or a bank acting as intermediary between two counterparties).

Interim rent

The rental accruing from delivery, acceptance and/or funding until the start of the basic lease term. This is often used when equipment deliveries take place over a period of time.

Internal rate of return

Investment appraisal method which establishes the discount rate which would be necessary to make present and future costs and returns balance out, using discounted cash-flow techniques.

International Accounting Standard (IAS) 17

An international accounting standard on treatment of leases, first published by the International

Accounting Standards Committee in 1982 and reformatted in 1994. The standard is not binding on individual lease transactions but is expected to serve as a model for mandatory rules adopted by national organisations in the future.

Investment period method

A lessor accounting method ,finding favour in the United Kingdom, which apportions profit earned on a lease to those periods where the lessor has an after tax net cash investment in the lease.

Investment tax credit (ITC)

Note: the Tax Reform Act 1986 generally repealed the 10 per cent ITC for equipment placed in service after 31 December 1985.

JALCO

A Japanese operating lease (JOL) containing a purchase option.

Japanese leveraged lease (JLL)

A technique, introduced in 1985, which is used for the cross-border financing of large commercial aircrafts and other equipment. In a Japanese leveraged lease a pool of investors provides equity for the lease while non-recourse debt is provided by financial institutions. This structure became economically unattractive after the Japanese corporation tax law change in 1998.

Japanese operating lease (JOL)

An operating lease that satisfies the requirements of the 1998 Japanese corporation tax reform.

Lease

A contract between a lessor and lessee for the hire of a specific asset. The ownership of the asset is retained by the lessor but the right to the use of the asset is given to the lessee for an agreed period of time in return for a series of rentals paid by the lessee to the lessor.

Lease line

A lease line of credit similar to a bank line of credit which allows a lessee to add equipment, as needed, under the same basic terms and conditions without negotiating a new lease contract.

Lease rate

The equivalent simple annual interest rate implicit in minimum lease rentals. Not the same as the interest rate implicit in a lease.

Lease term

The fixed term of the lease. Includes, for accounting

purposes, all periods covered by fixed rate renewal options which for economic reasons appear likely to be exercised at the inception of the lease.

Lease underwriting

An agreement whereby a packager firmly commits to enter into a lease on certain terms and assumes the risk of arranging any financing.

Lessee

The user of the equipment being leased.

Lessee's incremental borrowing rate

The interest rate which the lessee, at the inception of the lease, would have incurred to borrow over a similar term the funds necessary to purchase the leased assets. In a leveraged lease the rate on the bonds is normally used.

Lessor

The owner of the equipment which is being leased to a lessee or user.

Level payments

Equal payments over the term of the lease.

Leverage

An amount borrowed. In a leveraged lease, the debt portion of the funds used to purchase the asset represent leverage to the equity holder.

Leveraged lease

A lease in which at least three parties are involved: a lessee, a lessor and a long-term creditor. The financing provided by the creditor is substantial relative to the overall size of the transaction and generally without recourse to the lessor.

Lien

The right to keep another person's property until a debt owed in respect of it is paid.

Limited partnership

Constituting a general partner and numerous limited partners, this instrument is frequently used to enable individuals to invest collectively in lease transactions. The general partner, usually a leasing company, will manage the investment which is put up by the individual or limited partners.

Limited use property

Plant or equipment which would not have any identifiable market value because of its specialised purpose for the lessee. Ineligible for depreciation benefits in some jurisdictions.

Loan certificates	Debt certificates or bonds issued to lenders.
Loan participant	A lender or a holder of debt in a leveraged lease evidenced by loan certificates or bonds issued by the owner trustee.
Master lease	A lease line of credit which allows a lessee to add equipment under the same basic terms and conditions without negotiating a new lease contract.
Minimum lease payments	All payments the lessee is obligated to make or can be required to make in connection with leased property, including residual value guaranteed to the lessor and bargain renewal rents or purchase options, but excluding guarantees of lessor's debt (seldom encountered) and executory costs such as insurance, maintenance and taxes.
Net lease	In a net lease, the rentals are payable net to the lessor. All costs in connection with the use of the equipment are to be paid by the lessee and are not a part of the rental. For example, taxes, insurance and maintenance are paid directly by the lessee. Most capital leases and finance leases are net leases.
Net present value	The discounted value of a future rental stream, allowing for the time value of money. Also, an investment appraisal method which starts by choosing an appropriate discount rate to apply to future payments and income, and compares this with the present cost for each alternative.
Non-recourse finance	Debt funding where the creditor's rights, either expressly or in practice, do not extend to all of the borrower's assets; or those assets comprise only the relevant equipment.
Novation	The substitution of one party for another in a contract. Where the lessee has already placed an order for the equipment when the leasing facility is agreed, the lessor may acquire title by having the existing contractual arrangement cancelled and replaced by new arrangements between the lessor and the supplier. The lessee is thereby released from the obligation to pay the supplier.
Open-ended lease	A lease which contains a provision for the extension

of the lease on predetermined terms after the end of the fixed period.

Operating lease

For financial accounting purposes, a lease which does not meet the criteria of a capital lease or finance lease. Also used generally to describe a short-term lease whereby a user can acquire use of an asset for a part of the useful life of the asset. The lessor may provide services in connection with the lease, such as maintenance, insurance and payment of personal property taxes.

Option finance

A financing structure which allows an equipment user either to return the equipment at a certain date or dates without penalty or to continue leasing it for the remainder of its useful life.

Owner trustee

The entity acting as trustee for the owner/equity participants in a transaction.

Packager

A leasing company, investment banker or broker which arranges big ticket leases.

Participation agreement

An agreement between the owner trustee, the lenders, the equity participants and the lessee which spells out the obligations of the parties and procedures for closing a transaction typically found in leveraged leases.

Peppercorn rental

The nominal rental paid during the secondary period of a lease.

Pickle-Dole Bill

US legislation restricting cross-border leasing in the United States, which became the Deficit Reduction Tax Act 1984.

Present value

The current equivalent value of cash available immediately for a future payment or a stream of payments to be received at various times in the future. The present value will vary with the discount (interest) factor applied to the future payments.

Primary period

The period, in a finance lease, during which the lessor expects to recover the full capital cost of the asset, its money and other costs, and its profit.

Purchase option

An option to purchase leased property at the end of the lease term.

Put	An option one person has to sell an asset to another person at a set price at some established point in time in the future. In lease agreements, a lessor sometimes negotiates an option to sell leased equipment to the lessee or to some third party at an established price at the end of the lease term.
Qualified Technological Equipment (QTE)	Equipment as defined by s 186(i)(2) of US Internal Revenue Code 1986. Often a double-dip or cross-border lease transaction where the US lessor claims depreciation in the US and the end user of the qualifying equipment claims depreciation in its (separate) jurisdiction.
Rear-end loading	The practice of constructing a rental schedule where the larger payments are made towards the end of the lease.
Reinvestment rate	The interest rate a lessor earns on lease cash surpluses during the period following the investment period of a lease.
Related parties	For US financial accounting, related party transactions are those where one of the parties has the ability to influence the actions and policies of the other. Examples include a parent and its subsidiaries; subsidiaries of a common parent; or a firm and its principal owners, management or affiliates. Under the Internal Revenue Code, family membership or 50 per cent ownership are general tests for related parties.
Renewal option	An option to renew the lease at the end of the initial lease term.
Rental rebate	A refund of rentals to a lessee, commonly found in UK finance leases where it is used to pass back the residual to a lessee by reference to the proceeds of the sale of the leased asset at the end of a lease.
Residual, or residual value	The value of equipment at the conclusion of the lease term.
Residual sharing	An agreement between the lessor and another party providing for a division of the residual value between them.

Residual value certificate (RVC)

A certificate which gives the investor rights to a stated portion of the residual sales proceeds of the asset at lease termination.

Residual value insurance

A policy that insures a specific value on a specific piece of equipment, at some specified period in time (usually not less than two years). If the equipment at the end of the stipulated period was sold for a lower price than that stipulated on the policy, then the insurer would pay the difference. Also known as asset value insurance or equipment value insurance.

Return on investment

The yield. Interest rate earned by the lessor in a lease which is measured by the rate at which excess cash flows permit recovery of investment. Also the rate at which the cash flows not needed for debt service or payment of taxes amortise the investment of the equity participant.

Safe harbour provisions

The provisions in the US Economic Recovery Tax Act (1981) defining the basic criteria under which a financing transaction could meet the definition of a lease for tax purposes. The rules represented a considerable liberalisation of former IRS guidelines on true leases, and allowed pure tax benefit transfers. (As noted below, these were effectively repealed by TEFRA.)

Sale-leaseback

A transaction which involves the sale of the property by the owner, and a lease of the property back to the seller.

Salvage value

The minimum value for a depreciable asset. After sufficient depreciation is taken, so that cost, less accumulated depreciation, equals salvage value, no more depreciation may be taken. This is not the same as residual value.

Secondary period

The, frequently optional, period in a finance lease which follows the full payout of the lessor's investment plus profit.

Security agreement

In a leveraged lease, an agreement between the owner and the lender whereby the owner assigns title to the equipment, the lease and rental payments under the lease to the lender as security for amounts due to the lender. The functional equivalent of an indenture trust.

Short-term lease	Generally refers to an operating lease.
Single investor lease	A lease structure that only involves a lessor and a lessee. The lessor provides, from its own funds, all the capital necessary to purchase an asset.
Sinking fund	A reserve or a sinking fund established or set aside for the purpose of payment due at a later date. (Generally applicable only in leveraged leases.)
Sinking fund rate	The rate of interest allocated to a sinking fund set aside for a future payment.
Special purpose company (SPC)	A company usually formed for a specific purpose in a domestic or cross-border lease or financing arrangement
SSAP 21	The UK Accounting Standard, 'Accounting for leases and hire-purchase transactions', issued by the Accounting Standards Committee 1984, amended 1997. Under the standard, finance leases should be capitalised by the lessee. It also has detailed provisions for lessor accounting.
Stepped rentals	Rental payments which vary from one another in a structured lease. Usually done for specific cash-flow and/or tax reasons.
Stipulated loss value	The sum payable on an early termination of a lease.
Straight-line method	An accounting method for depreciating assets which spreads the depreciation equally over the estimated useful life of the asset.
Strip debt	Debt in connection with a leveraged lease, arranged in tiers with different maturities and amortisation to improve the lessor's cash flow and reduce the lessee's costs.
Strip exposure	The degree of unsecured exposure between the total level of security held, either based solely on the value of the leased/financed asset and/or any additional security, and the potential difference between maximum liability whether contingent or real.
Sub-lease	A transaction in which leased property is re-leased by the

original lessee to a third party, and where the lease agreement between the two original parties remains in effect.

Sum of the digits method

An accounting method for depreciating assets which provides for the largest depreciation to be taken at the beginning of the asset's life, and the smallest depreciation to be taken in the later years.

Synthetic lease

Generally, a US lease facility that achieves off-balance-sheet treatment of the leased asset for the lessee but allows the lessee to access depreciation and interest deductions as though the asset had been acquired through a loan i.e. a lease for accounting purposes and a loan for tax purposes

Tax benefit transfers (TBT)

A TBT lease, made possible in the United States by the 1981 Tax Act (ERTA), was severely limited by the 1982 Act (TEFRA). The transaction is set up so that the lessee is also the lender under a leveraged lease arrangement and all payments except an initial sum paid by the lessor (the tax benefit buyer) cancel each other out. That is, one company effectively pays another a fee for the tax benefits associated with capital investment.

Tax Equity and Fiscal Responsibility Act (TEFRA)

A 1982 US Tax Act that put limitations on safe harbour leasing moving towards repeal, and slightly liberalised conventional leasing.

Tax indemnity clause

A clause in a tax-based lease providing for increases in rentals in the event of legislation that adversely affects the lessor's ability to claim tax benefits on the equipment.

Tax variation clause

A clause in a lease which allows the lessor to vary the rentals if either the rate of tax or the tax system changes.

Tax written down value

The value of an asset after deducting the total depreciation allowances claimed from the cost of the asset.

True lease

A true lease in the United States is a transaction which qualifies as a lease under the Internal Revenue Code so the lessee can claim rental payments as tax deductions and the lessor can claim tax benefits of ownership as depreciation.

Unguaranteed residual value   The portion of residual value 'at risk' for a lessor in his yield computation, that is, for which there is no party obligated to pay.

Useful life   The period of time during which an asset will have economic value and be usable. Useful life of an asset is sometimes called the economic life of the asset.

Walkaway lease   A lease permitting the lessee to walk away or terminate the lease at agreed times on notice without cost.

Wet lease   The leasing of an asset (usually aircraft) with crew and other back-up.

Withholding tax   This may be payable on the rentals received from cross-border leases, depending on the double taxation arrangements between the countries involved.

Writing down allowance   A depreciation allowance where each year's allowance is based on a percentage of the written-down value at the end of the previous year.

Yield   The interest rate earned by the lessor or equity participant in a lease, which is measured by the rate at which the excess cash flows permit recovery of investment. Also the rate at which the cash flows needed for debt service or payment of taxes amortise the investment of the equity participants.